MW00989951

The Qur'ān and the Bible

THE QUR'ĀN
AND THE BIBLE

Text and Commentary

Gabriel Said Reynolds

Qur'ān Translation by Ali Quli Qarai

Yale

UNIVERSITY
PRESS

New Haven and London

Yale University Press books may be purchased in quantity for educational,
business, or promotional use. For information, please e-mail sales.press@
yale.edu (U.S. office) or sales@yaleup.co.uk (U.K. office).

Set in Times New Roman type by Newgen.
Printed in the United States of America.

Library of Congress Control Number: 2017952016
ISBN 978-0-300-18132-6 (hardcover : alk. paper)

A catalogue record for this book is available from the British Library.

This paper meets the requirements of ANSI/NISO Z39.48-1992 (Permanence of Paper).

10 9 8 7 6 5 4 3 2 1

To my family

So if you are in doubt about what We have sent down to you, ask those who read the Book [revealed] before you.

—Qur'ān 10:94

CONTENTS

Acknowledgments

Many of the insights of this work are due to long and fruitful conversations I had during the course of 2015 and 2016 with Joseph Witztum. Professor Witztum spent many hours with me addressing problems in earlier drafts and discussing the issues raised by this work, as well as the history of scholarship on those issues. His generous spirit and expertise on Qurʾānic matters left a profound impression on me. I hasten to add that I am solely responsible for any errors that remain in this work.

I would like to thank Mr. Ali Quli Qarai, who generously accepted having his translation of the Qurʾān included in this volume and who provided a new, revised version of his translation for that purpose. At times in my commentary I contrast my own interpretation of the text with that of Mr. Qarai. On the whole, however, I find his work to be excellent, for which reason I was eager to have his translation (out of the dozens of available English translations) included with this volume. I encourage interested readers to purchase and use the Arabic-English edition of Qarai's translation to accompany the present volume, an edition I myself use for my research.

This work is truly the fruit of a collective effort. While I am ultimately responsible for its contents I would not have been able to see this work through without the assistance of a number of people. I am especially indebted to the graduate students at the University of Notre Dame who offered insights on the Biblical subtext of the Qurʾān and who did remarkable work in editing the text at various stages: Rufino Dango, Matthew Kuiper, Breanna Nickel, Andrew O'Connor, and Mourad Takawi. Andrew O'Connor in particular discussed with me various passages in this work in great detail in my office at Notre Dame. I am also very grateful to the friends and colleagues who read drafts of various sections of this work and offered insights, including Anne-Sylvie Boisliveau, David Lincicum, Abdelmasih Saadi, Mehdy Shaddel, Joseph Witztum, and Holger Zellentin. I also owe a special debt of gratitude to my friend Mehdi Azaiez, with whom I have discussed the ideas in this work at great length.

I find it important also to mention here the scholars whose work I have benefited from in developing the commentary in the present work. To a great extent there is very little of my own original thought in this work, and very much from the insights of scholars with whom I am proud to associate myself. These include, among others, Mohammad-Ali Amir-Moezzi, Mehdi Azaiez, Rachid Benzine, Anne-Sylvie Boisliveau, Michel Cuypers, Guillaume Dye, Emran El-Badawi, Sidney Griffith, Manfred Kropp, Christoph Luxenberg, Paul Neuenkirchen, Angelika Neuwirth, Michael Pregill, Samir Khalil Samir, Mehdy Shaddel, Stephen Shoemaker, Nicolai Sinai, Devin Stewart, Mun'im Sirry, Joseph Witztum, Hamza Zafer, and Holger Zellentin.

It is important to add here as well that I have benefited substantially from my work with the International Qur'ānic Studies Association, or IQSA. In my service to IQSA I have come to know a wide range of scholars of the Qur'ān from around the world, and I have had the occasion to hear a wide range of lectures during the association's annual and international meetings. This experience has significantly shaped the way I think about the Qur'ān and advanced my understanding of the Qur'ān's origins.

I would also like to thank my colleagues in the Theology Department at the University of Notre Dame who have supported me and helped me to see the Qur'ān in the broader perspective of the Late Antique Near East. I am especially grateful for the support and mentorship of John Cavadini. This work is dedicated to my parents, my stepparents, and my wife and children, who are a constant source of support, inspiration, and joy.

Abbreviations and Conventions

ABBREVIATIONS OF LANGUAGES

Am.	Aramaic
Ar.	Arabic
Gk.	Greek
Hb.	Hebrew
Syr.	Syriac

ABBREVIATION FOR "QUR'ĀN"

Q

ABBREVIATIONS OF BIBLICAL BOOKS

Gen	Genesis	1Ch	1 Chronicles	Jer	Jeremiah
Exo	Exodus	2Ch	2 Chronicles	Lam	Lamentations
Lev	Leviticus	Ezr	Ezra	Eze	Ezekiel
Num	Numbers	Neh	Nehemiah	Dan	Daniel
Deu	Deuteronomy	Est	Esther	Hos	Hosea
Jos	Joshua	Job	Job	Joe	Joel
Jdg	Judges	Psa	Psalm	Amo	Amos
Rut	Ruth	Pro	Proverbs	Oba	Obadiah
1Sa	1 Samuel	Ecc	Ecclesiastes	Jon	Jonah
2Sa	2 Samuel	Sol	Song of	Mic	Micah
1Ki	1 Kings		Solomon	Nah	Nahum
2Ki	2 Kings	Isa	Isaiah	Hab	Habakkuk

Zep	Zephaniah	Rom	Romans	Phm	Philemon
Hag	Haggai	1Co	1 Corinthians	Heb	Hebrews
Zec	Zechariah	2Co	2 Corinthians	Jam	James
Tob	Tobit	Gal	Galatians	1Pe	1 Peter
Mal	Malachi	Eph	Ephesians	2Pe	2 Peter
Wis	Wisdom	Phi	Philippians	1Jo	1 John
Sir	Sirach	Col	Colossians	2Jo	2 John
Mat	Matthew	1Th	1 Thessalonians	3Jo	3 John
Mar	Mark	2Th	2 Thessalonians	Jud	Jude
Luk	Luke	1Ti	1 Timothy	Rev	Revelation
Joh	John	2Ti	2 Timothy		
Act	Acts	Tit	Titus		

Rabbinic Texts are abbreviated according to the
SBL Handbook of Style, 2nd ed. (2014), pp. 130–33.

ABBREVIATIONS OF SOURCES

BEQ   H. Speyer, *Die biblischen Erzählungen im Qoran* (Gräfen-
               hainichen: Schulze, 1931; reprint, Hildesheim: Olms, 1961)

b.   Babylonian Talmud

BSOAS   *Bulletin of the School of Oriental and African Studies*

CSCO   *Corpus Scriptorum Christianorum Orientalium*

EI2   *The Encyclopaedia of Islam,* 2nd ed. (Leiden: Brill,
               1954–present)

EQ   *The Encyclopaedia of the Qurʾān,* ed. J. McAuliffe (Leiden:
               Brill, 2001–2006)

FV   A. Jeffery, *The Foreign Vocabulary of the Qurʾān* (Baroda:
               Oriental Institute, 1938; reprint, Leiden: Brill, 2007)

GdQ1, 2, 3   (1) T. Nöldeke, *Geschichte des Qorāns* (Göttingen: Verlag der
               Dieterichschen Buchhandlung, 1860); (2) T. Nöldeke, *Über den
               Ursprung des Qorāns,* 2nd rev. ed., and including F. Schwally,
               Die Sammlung des Qorāns, ed. and revised by F. Schwally
               (Leipzig: T. Weicher, 1909, 1919); (3) 2nd ed. including G.
               Bergsträsser and O. Pretzl, *Die Geschichte des Koran-texts*
               (Leipzig: T. Weicher, 1938; reprint, 3 vols. in 1, Hildesheim:
               Olms, 1970). Trans. *History of the Qurʾān,* ed. and trans. Wolf-
               gang H. Behn (Leiden: Brill, 2013)

JAOS	*Journal of the American Oriental Society*
JNES	*Journal of Near Eastern Studies*
JQS	*Journal of Qur'anic Studies*
JSAI	*Jerusalem Studies in Arabic and Islam*
JSS	*Journal of Semitic Studies*
KU	J. Horovitz, *Koranische Untersuchungen* (Berlin: de Gruyter, 1926)
m.	Mishnah
MIDEO	*Mélanges de l'Institut dominicain d'études orientales du Caire*
MW	*The Muslim* (or, in earlier volumes, *Moslem*) *World*
OC	*Oriens Christianus* (serial)
PL	*Patrologia Latina*
PO	*Patrologia Orientalis*
PS	*Patrologia Syriaca*
QBS	G. S. Reynolds, *The Qur'ān and Its Biblical Subtext* (London: Routledge, 2010)
QC	Angelika Neuwirth, Nicolai Sinai, and Michael Marx, eds., *The Qur'ān in Context: Historical and Literary Investigations into the Qur'ānic Milieu* (Leiden: Brill, 2009)
QHC	*The Qur'ān in Its Historical Context,* ed. G. S. Reynolds (London: Routledge, 2008)
QHC2	*New Perspectives on the Qur'ān: The Qur'ān in Its Historical Context 2,* ed. G. S. Reynolds (London: Routledge, 2011)
QS	J. Wansbrough, *Quranic Studies: Sources and Methods of Scriptural Interpretation* (Oxford: Oxford University Press, 1977; reprint, Amherst, NY: Prometheus, 2004)
QSC	*Qur'ān Seminar Commentary*
SI	*Studia Islamica*
TS	R. Payne Smith, *Thesaurus Syriacus,* vol. 1 (Oxford: E Typographeo Clarendoniano, 1879), and vol. 2 (Oxford: E Typographeo Clarendoniano, 1901)
ZDMG	*Zeitschrift der deutschen morgenländischen Gesellschaft*

CONVENTIONS

Italicized text in the translation designates use of the second-person singular in the Arabic original.

Citations from *Tafsīr al-Jalālayn* and al-Wāḥidī are always from the published English translation:

Tafsīr al-Jalālayn. Trans. F. Hamza. Louisville, KY: Fons Vitae, 2008.

al-Wāḥidī, Abū l-Ḥasan. *Al-Wāḥidī's Asbāb al-Nuzūl*. Trans. M. Guezzou. Louisville, KY: Fons Vitae, 2008.

I do not give the bibliographic reference for each citation from these two works but simply refer to the Sura and verse from which the citation is taken. Those two works do not transliterate fully Arabic names or terminology, and I have kept their usage when citing from them. The translator of *Tafsīr al-Jalālayn* has used British spelling conventions, which I have also kept; so, too, for citations from the New Jerusalem Bible. The translator of al-Wāḥidī's work chose to keep honorific declarations, such as that which appears after the mention of Muhammad's name ("Allah bless him and give him peace"); these I have removed for the sake of conciseness. In the course of my commentary I frequently refer to primary or secondary sources with abbreviated references. The full references (along with dates of composition for primary works) can be found in the bibliography. In this work I use the English forms of words that have been Anglicized (e.g., Sura, hadith). When quoting other works in my commentary, I have kept their conventions, and so the reader will find that words in quotations are transliterated differently, or that different spellings are used.

Dates in the work are given first according to the Islamic *hijrī* calendar, and then according to the standard Gregorian calendar. Finally, to credit colleagues who have offered me insights on particular passages I add a parenthetical reference (cr.).

PRINCIPAL BIBLICAL AND POST-BIBLICAL CHARACTERS IN THE QUR'ĀN

For Qur'ānic references, please see the Index to the Qur'ān.

Aaron—Brother of Moses, called on by God to help Moses in his prophetic mission and his confrontation with Pharaoh.

Abraham—Father of Isaac and Ishmael, monotheist by natural observation. Confronts his idolatrous people and is persecuted, builds a house of God with Ishmael.

Adam—First human, described as a "vicegerent" (*khalīfa*). Disobeys God by eating from, or approaching, the forbidden tree in paradise.

Alexander the Great—Named "the possessor of two horns" (Dhū l-Qarnayn) in the Qur'ān. Travels to the ends of the earth.

David—Described like Adam as a "vicegerent" (*khalīfa*), noted in the Qur'ān for his praise of God and knowledge. Kills Goliath.

Elijah—Briefly mentioned in the Qur'ān for his rejection of the worship of Baal.

Haman—Appears as an assistant to Pharaoh in Egypt, commanded to build a tower to heaven.

Iblis—The devil as cosmic adversary of God. The Qur'ān names the devil instead Satan when he appears as the tempter of humans.

Isaac—Son of Abraham whose miraculous birth is announced on several occasions. Perhaps the son of Abraham who was to be sacrificed before he is redeemed.

Ishmael—Builds a house of God with his father Abraham. Described as "true to his promise."

Jacob—Father of Joseph (and other sons) who has prophetic knowledge of Joseph's fate.

Jesus—Son of Mary and named *al-masīḥ* ("Christ"). Distinguished by his miraculous birth, the miracles which he accomplishes (even in childhood), and his ascension to heaven after his life.

Job—Mentioned briefly in the Qur'ān for his prayer. Commanded to reprimand his wife.

John—Son of Zechariah, born in his parents' old age. Given judgment while still a child, said to confirm the word of God.

Jonah—A prophet who is said to have "gone off angry" and ends up in the belly of a fish, for which reason he is named "man of the fish" (*dhū l-nūn*)

Joseph—Son of Jacob who is enslaved and taken to Egypt where he is first imprisoned. Later becomes a powerful figure and receives his family.

Lot—Revered as a prophet in the Qur'ān and closely connected to Abraham. Condemns his people for their deviant ways.

Mary—Mother of Jesus, praised in the Qur'ān for her purity and faithfulness.

Moses—Prophet who confronts Pharaoh, speaks directly with God, and receives a divine revelation (*al-tawrāt*).

Pharaoh/Fir'awn—Name (not title) of the Egyptian ruler in the time of Moses who considers himself a god but meets his demise.

Queen of Sheba—A pagan queen who visits Solomon and comes to believe in God.

Sarah—Named "wife of Abraham" in the Qur'ān, remembered for her incredulous reaction to the annunciation of a son (Isaac) in her old age.

Saul—Referred to as Ṭālūt, a king before David who leads Israel to war.

Solomon—Remembered for his knowledge and his miraculous authority over natural and supernatural beings, converts the Queen of Sheba to belief in God.

Sons of Adam—While their names are not given the Qur'ān alludes to Cain's killing of Abel.

Zechariah—Father of John, receives an angelic annunciation of his son's birth after imploring God.

THE QUR'ĀN AND THE BIBLE

INTRODUCTION

Today Christians know the Bible as a work in two parts, the Old and New Testaments, and they may find it obvious that both belong in their scripture. For some in the early church, however, the inclusion of the Old Testament was not obvious. Marcion (d. ca. AD 160) made the case that the God of the Old Testament was a demiurge, a tribal deity not to be identified with the heavenly father of the New Testament. Accordingly, he argued that only the New Testament (and in fact, not all of the New Testament) should be considered scripture. The majority opinion of the early church, however, was different, namely that the Hebrew Scriptures are indeed the word of God. They were ultimately included in the Christian Bible.

Early Islam was faced with a similar choice in regard to the Jewish and Christian Bible. Muslims, in theory, could have considered the Bible authoritative scripture. There are some signs that the author of the Qur'ān attributed such authority to the Bible. In one place the divine voice of the Qur'ān commands its Prophet to confer with those "who read the Book" in times of doubt (Q 10:94).[1] In another place this voice commands that the "People of the Gospel" judge according to what God has revealed in it (Q 5:47). However, in other passages (e.g., Q 2:42, 59, 79; 3:71, 187; 4:46; 5:13; 7:162), the Qur'ān suggests that the Jews (especially) and the Christians (also) have misread scripture, have hidden passages, or have pretended that things which they themselves have fabricated are scripture.[2] In part inspired by such passages, the early Islamic community decided that the Bible was not authentic but rather falsified (*muḥarraf*) scripture. That community could have, conceivably, made a different decision, recognizing the authority of one kind or another of the Bible as scripture, as the early Christians did with the Hebrew Bible (and as Mormons, or Latter-Day Saints, would later do with the Bible, or as Baha'is would do with the Bible and the Qur'ān).

1

The decision to relegate the Bible to a status of inauthenticity had significant implications for the ways in which traditional Muslims and academic scholars alike would approach the Qur'ān. It is true that Muslim commentators not infrequently turn to Biblical traditions, and occasionally the Bible itself,[3] in their efforts to understand the Qur'ān. Most Muslim commentators, however, did not have a copy of the Bible open on the desk next to them as they studied the Qur'ān. The same could be said for most Western academic scholars. Although things have begun to change, for much of the second half of the twentieth century, students pursuing Qur'ānic studies were trained in Islamic languages and literature but not in the Bible and Biblical literature. Their formation was comparable to that of a student of the New Testament who is never introduced to the languages, literature, and culture of second temple Judaism and the Mediterranean Roman world.

In the present work Bible and Qur'ān are brought together.[4] This work is meant to make a contribution to our understanding of the Qur'ān by bringing to light its conversation with Biblical literature. The terms "conversation" and "Biblical literature" are key to understanding the methodology behind this work. By "conversation" I mean the way that the Qur'ān alludes to, and develops, earlier traditions. By "Biblical literature" I mean not simply the canonical Bible but also those post-Biblical (but pre-Qur'ānic) Jewish and Christian writings which became part of the repertoire of sacred history among Jews and Christians and, eventually, for the author of the Qur'ān.

My conviction, a conviction which has only increased during my work on this book, is that the Qur'ān is an original work in literary and religious terms, but also a work which depends heavily on its audience's knowledge of the Bible and the traditions which developed out of the Bible. The present work accordingly seeks to promote an appreciation for the meaning of the Qur'ān by providing both relevant Biblical traditions and some commentary on the nature of the Qur'ān's references to them.[5]

According to Faruq Sherif, approximately one-fourth of the Qur'ān's verses are concerned with narratives of prophets or other figures from Jewish and Christian tradition.[6] Yet the Qur'ān's relationship to Biblical material goes well beyond narrative.[7] Its vision of creation and eschatology (the beginning and end of things), its cosmology, its use of parables, and its discussion of legal matters are all intimately connected to Biblical tradition. Even the Qur'ān's concept of Muḥammad's prophethood (i.e., the idea that God would send an angel to one man and task him with communicating the angel's messages to his people) is Biblical.[8]

Readers of the work will also notice that the Qur'ān tends not to quote the Bible verbatim. Indeed, it may be argued that the Qur'ān contains no direct citations of the Bible whatsoever. The closest thing to a citation in the Qur'ān is perhaps 21:105 ("We wrote in the Psalms, after the Remembrance: 'My righteous servants shall inherit the earth'"), but in fact this verse merely resembles certain elements of Psalm 37.[9] The Qur'ān (7:40) refers to the Biblical maxim of the "eye of the needle," but it does so in a unique manner. Similar observations might be made about the way the Qur'ān refers to a "mustard seed" (Q 21:47; 31:16), "uncircumcised hearts" (Q 2:88; 4:155), or the "twinkling of an eye" (16:77).[10] In each case a Biblical turn of phrase is cited, but to a different effect. Perhaps the closest thing to a quotation in the Qur'ān is 5:32 ("That is why We decreed for the Children of Israel that whoever kills a soul . . ."), but then this is a quotation of the Jewish text known as the Mishnah, and not of the Bible.[11] All of this suggests that the Qur'ān emerged in a context where Biblical expressions permeated the oral culture; they were "in the air."

In other words, the absence of direct quotations of Jewish and Christian texts in the Qur'ān reflects the path these texts took to reach the Qur'ān's author.[12] As Sidney Griffith has argued, neither the Bible nor other Jewish and Christian texts were available in Arabic at the time of the Qur'ān's origins.[13] The author of the Qur'ān would have heard only descriptions or paraphrases of such texts rendered into Arabic orally, most likely from some form of the Semitic language known as Aramaic. Yet the Qur'ān's author also played an active role in developing Biblical material. The Qur'ān has not simply borrowed material from Jews or Christians.[14] Instead, it has consciously reshaped Biblical material to advance its own religious claims.[15]

My argument that the Qur'ān is so closely, or organically, related to the Bible represents a departure from traditional ideas that the background of the Qur'ān is largely pagan (and partially Jewish). In terms of method, however, the present work is rather unoriginal. As mentioned earlier, classical Muslim exegetes, beginning already with the earliest commentators, such as Muqātil b. Sulaymān (d. 150/767), often provide Biblical traditions in their attempts to render the Qur'ānic text more intelligible. Eventually such traditions would come to be known as Isrā'īliyyāt and would be maligned by some tradition-minded scholars as unreliable (because they did not come through trusted chains of traditions leading to the Prophet or his companions).[16] By then, however, many of the hadith which such tradition-minded scholars would cite instead to explain Qur'ānic material were themselves infused with material from the Bible or post-Biblical Jewish and Christian literature.

Much recent scholarship on the Qur'ān, such as the recently published Harper-Collins *Study Qur'ān* (edited by S. H. Nasr and others), sets the Qur'ān's relationship with the Bible aside. The *Study Qur'an,* which is the fruit of extensive research and collaboration, provides readers with summaries of Islamic commentaries and various essays. It does not provide an analysis of the Qur'ān's relationship to Biblical literature.[17]

The present work, by contrast, focuses less on medieval commentaries and more on the religious traditions of the Qur'ān's own context, the period known as Late Antiquity.[18] Thus, one might say that this volume is meant to be at once a reference work and an argument about the importance of a "contextual" reading of the Qur'ān.[19]

METHOD

My concern to read the Qur'ān independent of medieval traditions leads me to avoid a "chronological" approach to the text, that is, an approach which assumes that certain passages can be assigned to certain moments of Muḥammad's life. That the Qur'ān should be read according to a chronology of his life is often assumed. Some scholars have gone so far as to rearrange the Qur'ān's chapters, or Suras, according to an imagined chronological order, dividing them between those supposedly proclaimed in Mecca ("Meccan Suras") during the first part of Muḥammad's career and those supposedly proclaimed in Medina ("Medinan Suras").[20]

I have already made the case against reading the Qur'ān chronologically,[21] and my skepticism of chronological readings of the Qur'ān has only increased through the work that accompanied the current project. While writing this book, I was reminded time and again how many Biblically flavored passages there are in so-called Meccan Suras (e.g., Q 7, 19, 26, 28, 46, 71), although Mecca should have been a thoroughly pagan city (according to the Prophet's biography). Such passages must have been proclaimed to, or written for, a Biblically minded audience—including Jews and Christians—and not an audience of idolatrous pagans. Accordingly, in this work I do away with the labels of "Meccan" and "Medinan."[22] This is hardly a radical decision. After all, no Sura in the Qur'ān describes itself with either term. These are external categories of medieval Islamic tradition, not Qur'ānic categories.[23]

The question of a "chronological" reading of the Qur'ān is in part a larger problem of whether the medieval stories known as "Occasions of Revelation," which are meant to provide the historical context of Qur'ānic passages, in fact do so.[24] It is my conviction that they do not, that these traditions are later efforts to provide a narrative context for Qur'ānic material.[25] It is true that such traditions often seem to explain the Qur'ānic text in a logical way. For example, an Occasion of Revelation tradition makes 96:1 ("Read in the name of your Lord who created") the first words spoken to Muḥammad (who at the time was meditating in a cave outside of Mecca) by the angel Gabriel. Another Occasion of Revelation tradition for a passage later in that same Sura, Qur'ān 96:9–10 ("Tell me, he who forbids * a servant when he prays"), relates how Muḥammad's antagonist Abū Jahl later sought to prevent him from praying.[26] If such traditions seem to "fit" the Qur'ānic passage with which they are associated, this is because they were written to do precisely that. They were written to weave a Qur'ānic passage into the fabric of Muḥammad's life.

Yet our goal in the current work is to look at what the Qur'ān tells us, and not what later storytellers relate about the Qur'ān. Elsewhere I have referred to this approach as "Qur'ānist"—a label which is meant to reflect a respect for the text of the Qur'ān, free of later categories created by the interpretive tradition.[27] The avoidance of a chronological reading of the text opens up interesting possibilities in thinking about the authorship of the Qur'ān. If we are no longer restricted to thinking about the Qur'ān as a transcript of Muḥammad's proclamations between AD 610 and 632, then we might consider the possibility that it includes multiple sources and a complicated history of redaction and editing.

My reasons for not labeling passages in this work according to chronological periods of the medieval biography of the Prophet are similar to those for not relying on so-called pre-Islamic, or "Jāhilī," poetry to explain Qur'ānic verses. Nöldeke already realized (for him this was a progression in his thinking) that so-called pre-Islamic poetry which includes Qur'ānic vocabulary or turns of phrase is better thought of as post-Qur'ānic Islamic poetry.[28] Indeed, the most important point about Jāhilī poetry is that all of it is preserved from a much later period. Yet there are other problems as well with the case for its authenticity, many of them noted by Ṭāhā Ḥusayn in his work (controversial in Egypt at the time of its publication) *Fī l-shiʿr al-jāhilī* (On Pre-Islamic Poetry).[29] For example, although the most famous Jāhilī poets are said to come from different tribes (e.g., Imruʾ al-Qays from Kinda, Ṭarafa from Rabīʿa, Labīd from Qays), no evidence of particular Arabic dialects is found in their works.[30]

We might turn to Umayya b. Abī al-Ṣalt as a case study of the problem of Jāhilī poetry, inasmuch as his work includes a significant number of parallels to the Qur'ān and accordingly has attracted significant interest from scholars of the Qur'ān.[31] Umayya by tradition was one of the *ḥunafāʾ*, the pure pre-Islamic monotheists of Arabia (he is thought to have died between 2/624 and 8/630, without embracing Islam). His poetry is first reportedly preserved in the works of Muḥammad b. Ḥabīb, who died in 244/859.[32] Those works, however, are not extant, and the earliest extant quotations of Umayya come from the *K. al-Bad' wa-l-ta'rīkh* of al-Maqdisī (d. late fourth/tenth century). Nöldeke argues that some of the religious poetry which later Islamic tradition attributes to Umayya, after careful scrutiny, might be thought of as genuine.[33] However, he inclines to the view that passages in the poems of Umayya which have Qur'ānic language are better thought of as later compositions, themselves influenced by the Qur'ān and only attributed to Umayya.[34] Since Nöldeke's qualified assessment, a number of scholars have weighed in on the usefulness of Umayya's poetry for our knowledge of the Qur'ān. The majority of scholars have followed the opinion of Tor Andrae, according to which the religious poetry of Umayya is not a trustworthy guide to the meaning of Qur'ānic vocabulary.[35] In my opinion the same can be said generally for the Qur'ānic material in all Jāhilī poetry.[36] Arguments about the meaning of Qur'ānic vocabulary which are constructed on the basis of Jāhilī poetry are necessarily unstable.

In the present work, then, I investigate the Qur'ān's relationship with those traditions—above all, Biblical traditions—that can be reliably dated to the pre-Islamic period. Such an investigation will lead, hopefully, to a better appreciation of the originality of the Qur'ān itself.

From a traditional dogmatic perspective the Qur'ān is original because it has no relationship with earlier traditions. Here we will see that the Qur'ān's originality lies in the nature of that relationship, not in its absence. To appreciate this point, however, it is necessary to appreciate the Qur'ān in its own historical context, which necessarily involves the setting aside of certain medieval traditions.[37]

While the present work will help advance our appreciation for the Qur'ān's originality, there is much that it does not do. As a rule, I do not investigate the etymology of individual Qur'ānic words or turns of phrase.[38] And while I do include cross-references throughout the work so that the reader will be able to compare parallel Qur'ānic passages, I do not investigate in detail the internal relationship of those passages, what Joseph Witztum (following Claus Schedl), has called the Qur'ānic "Synoptic problem."[39] The present work is thus limited in scope.

STRUCTURE AND SCOPE

There are two elements to the present work: the (revised) Qur'ān translation of Ali Quli Qarai and my commentary, including discussion of Qur'ānic passages with Biblical material or allusions, and excerpts of Jewish and Christian texts which help illuminate the sense of those passages.[40] As the goal of this work is to illuminate the relationship of the Qur'ān and the Bible, I generally refrain from commenting on elements of the Qur'ān with no connection to Biblical tradition. On certain occasions, though, such as regarding the "mysterious letters" in Q 2:1, I break this rule and add some brief notes on the Qur'ān itself for the sake of readers unfamiliar with the Islamic scripture.

I consider Qarai's to be among the best of those translations which seek to render the Qur'ān according to traditional Islamic understanding.[41] Not infrequently my commentary suggests alternative interpretations of the Qur'ānic text inasmuch as it is informed by a different understanding. I am solely responsible for the commentary in this work.

I have modified Qarai's translation, which renders Arabic *Allāh* as "Allah," so that *Allāh* is rendered as "God." The Qur'ān has a very particular doctrine of God.[42] It does not define God in an abstract way common to all creeds, and it means to say things about *its* God vis-à-vis other gods or ideas of God (accordingly I occasionally use "Allah" in my commentary; e.g., on Q 17:40). Still, to avoid the impression that the God of Islam is foreign or substantially different from other conceptions of God I found it better to use "God."

Unlike other works which compare the Qur'ān and the Bible, this work proceeds according to the order of the Qur'ān and not that of the Bible. Scholars interested in presenting the Qur'ān and the Bible together have tended to shape their works according to a Biblical order, so as to bring together into one place the material scattered throughout the Qur'ān on a certain character or theme.[43] This has a certain advantage, although it should be noted that the Bible, too, includes material on the same character or theme in different places (indeed, scholars have tended to neglect, for example, the material in the Psalms, the prophets, and the New Testament that develops narratives known from the Pentateuch). In any case the order of the present work, which follows the Qur'ān from *al-Fātiḥa* (Sura 1) to *al-Nās* (Sura 114), also has a certain advantage. It allows readers interested in a particular passage of the Qur'ān to find a discussion of that precise passage (or at least a reference to a parallel passage with such a discussion). It also allows one to appreciate the form and structure of the Qur'ān.

The commentary is not meant to be comprehensive. I focus above all on relationships between the Qur'ān and Biblical traditions, and even then I often do not discuss Qur'ānic passages which have a Biblical flavor but which are general enough that there is no reason to think that the Qur'ān is expressly responding to anything in particular in Biblical tradition. For example, in the Qur'ān we occasionally find the declaration that to God "belongs whatever is in the heavens and whatever is on the earth" (e.g., 2:255, 284; 3:109, 129; 4:126, 131) or some variation thereof (e.g. 3:29: "He knows whatever there is in the heavens and whatever there is in the earth"). This declaration is close to expressions we find in the Psalms.[44] However, the language of this declaration is so general that there is no reason to think that the Qur'ān is particularly in conversation with the Bible.[45]

Many passages in the shorter, more rhythmic Suras of the Qur'ān also have much in common with the Psalms, and yet I avoid making simple comparisons; instead, I quote the Psalms only where doing so adds to our appreciation of the Qur'ānic passage (to this end, for example, I quote Psalm 136 to help explain the presence of a refrain in Q 55).[46] The point of the commentary, in other words, is not simply to compare Qur'an and Bible (although there is some of that) but especially to provide Biblical material (and as much commentary as necessary) when such material can help us better to understand the Qur'ān.

When I do add Biblical or other citations to help the reader understand a Qur'ānic passage, I present (by necessity) only those citations which I believe are closest to the Qur'ānic passage at hand. Thus, for example, in discussing the Qur'ānic material on the "golden" calf (e.g., commentary on Q 20:83–98), I include citations from Exodus and 1 Kings but not from Deuteronomy 9. When it comes to material from extra-Biblical sources—for example, from the writings of the Syriac fathers—I offer short, select excerpts. In other words, this work hardly provides an exhaustive compendium of the Qur'ān's Biblical subtext.[47] Hopefully, however, it provides enough material to make the Qur'ān's relationship to that subtext clearer.

In addition to a discussion of the Qur'ān's relationship to its Biblical context, readers will occasionally find in the commentary some discussion of the Islamic interpretations of the passage at hand. The goal of this discussion is to contrast the reading of the Qur'ān through the lens of medieval tradition and the reading of the Qur'ān in its Late Antique Near Eastern context. To represent that medieval tradition, I have relied on two standard works of Sunni exegesis: the *Asbāb nuzūl al-Qur'ān* of 'Alī b. Aḥmad al-Wāḥidī (d. 468/1076) and the *Tafsīr al-Jalālayn* of Jalāl al-Dīn al-Maḥallī (d. 864/1459) and Jalāl al-Dīn al-Suyūṭī (d. 911/1505).[48] Both works are available in English translation, which will allow interested readers to investigate these sources. These commentaries do not represent the fullness of the Islamic exegetical tradition, but then such is not the goal of the present work, as is certainly clear by now.[49]

In this work Biblical citations are cited according to the New Jerusalem Bible (although I have edited the text to change the divine name YHWH to "Lord"), except when noted. The Babylonian Talmud is quoted according to the English translation of Soncino Press. The other texts cited are all included in the bibli-

ography at the end of the work. There I have included the approximate date for
the composition of those cited works. I have done my best to include only works
which can be dated before the Qur'ān, but there are many texts for which the
dating is questionable, or texts which contain some older material that was later
redacted (in the Islamic period), such as the *Pirke de-Rabbi Elieser,* the Targum of Pseudo-Jonathan, and *Exodus Rabbah.* I have generally avoided these
works entirely, although several times I have occasion to discuss the *Pirke de-
Rabbi Elieser* (*ad* Q 5:27–32; 10:90–92; 37:148). In this category is the *Targum
Sheni* of Esther, which has telling similarities with the Solomon material of the
Qur'ān.[50]

EARLIER SCHOLARSHIP ON THE QUR'ĀN AND THE BIBLE

The reader will notice that many different Jewish and Christian sources are
compared to different Qur'ānic passages in this work. These various comparisons show that the Qur'ān is not so much borrowing from any particular work,
but rather emerging from a religious culture in which these traditions were discussed and elaborated. As with other Late Antique Near Eastern religious texts,
the Qur'ān absorbed various traditions which were circulating in this dynamic
environment. That the Qur'ān reflects the diversity of religious traditions in this
context is not a surprise. The Qur'ān is the first book in the history of Arabic literature. There was no preexisting canon of Arabic works to which the Qur'ān's
author could turn. Accordingly he benefited from a variety of different linguistic
and literary traditions which were transmitted orally in the Late Antique Near
East.

In analyzing the Qur'ān's complicated relationship with earlier traditions I
was highly reliant on earlier scholarship.[51] The following brief discussion will
give the reader an idea of the principal scholarly works which have shaped my
thinking on the Qur'ān. For more precise information on my sources, see "A
Note on Sources" at the end of this work.

A number of works include explorations of the Qur'ān's Biblical subtext, and
I relied on them in thinking through particular Qur'ānic passages. These include
two German works: *Was hat Mohammed aus dem Judenthume aufgenommen* of
Abraham Geiger and especially Heinrich Speyer's *Die biblischen Erzählungen
im Qoran.* I also worked closely with *A Commentary on the Qur'ān* of Richard
Bell, the rich Corpus Coranicum website, and Arthur Droge's excellent annotated translation of the Qur'ān.[52]

Mehdi Azaiez's work on the Qur'ān's counterdiscourse has helped me appreciate the literary qualities of Qur'ānic language.[53] Azaiez shows how the

Qur'ān actively shapes its rhetoric in a way that contributes to the effectiveness of its polemic and apologetics. Of great importance generally to my work are the insights of Emran El-Badawi on the Qur'ān's relationship to the Syriac Gospels.[54] Scholars interested in an abstract theological or literary comparison of the Qur'ān and the Bible often look to the Greek Gospels, but El-Badawi's research illustrates that for those concerned with the historical context of the Qur'ān, it is the Syriac Gospels which matter most. In regard to the Syriac tradition Holger Zellentin demonstrates in his work *The Qur'ān's Legal Culture* that even in its nonnarrative, legal aspects, the Qur'ān is in conversation with its historical context, a context in which not only the Bible but also post-Biblical works including the Syriac *Didascalia Apostolorum* were central.[55] Indeed, Zellentin indicates certain elements of the *Didascalia* which suggest that this text has a special relationship with the Qur'ān.

Christoph Luxenberg's much-criticized book *Die Syro-aramäische Lesart des Koran* in many ways inspired the remarkable series of studies in the past fifteen years on the Qur'ān's relationship to the texts in the Christian Semitic language of Syriac.[56] Of these I am indebted especially to the excellent works of Sidney Griffith,[57] Adam Silverstein,[58] Tommaso Tesei (whose work I rely on especially for Qur'ān 18),[59] and Kevin van Bladel (whose work helped me appreciate further the Qur'ān's cosmology).[60]

I must emphasize above all how much I have benefited from the Princeton PhD dissertation of Joseph Witztum, "The Syriac Milieu of the Qur'an."[61] In the past Western scholars have, almost instinctively, sought to explain material in the Qur'ān related to the Hebrew Bible/Old Testament through Jewish sources, and this because they made certain assumptions based on the biography of the Prophet (the *sīra*) and the various anecdotes therein on Muḥammad's encounter with the Jews in Medina. Witztum shows that their instincts were wrong. In regard to Abraham and Ishmael, Cain and Abel, Joseph, and other protagonists, he shows how closely the Qur'ān follows the particular details of Biblical narratives as they had been shaped in Syriac literature. The reader will note that (particularly in the commentary on Q 12) I rely heavily on the results of his research.

Certain research on the Qur'ān points to a Palestinian background to elements of the Qur'ān. Already Arthur Jeffery, in his *Foreign Vocabulary* of the Qur'ān, pointed out that the particular shape of Qur'ānic terms is often closer to Christian Palestinian Aramaic than to Syriac.[62] More recently, Stephen Shoemaker and Guillaume Dye have shown that the Qur'ānic material on Mary, particularly in Qur'ān 19 (named after her), is connected with the Kathisma church on the road between Bethlehem and Jerusalem, a church which seems to have been the site of devotions surrounding the birth of Christ and a miracle involving a spring of water and a palm tree. These miracles are associated with the "flight to Egypt" (of the holy family) in most early texts, but in Sura 19 of the Qurʾān they are indeed associated with Christ's birth.[63]

Other elements of Qurʾānic vocabulary, and in particular Christian vocabulary (notably *ḥawāriyyūn,* "apostles or disciples"; *injīl,* "Gospel"; and *māʾida,* the table which Jesus calls down from heaven in Q 5:112–15) seem to originate from Ethiopic (Geʿez). In addition, certain insights into Qurʾānic vocabulary are gained from various pre-Islamic Arabian dialects (both South Arabian and North Arabian). For example, the work of Christian Robin and others on these inscriptions has shed light on the reason the Qurʾān uses the name "the Compassionate" (Ar. *al-raḥmān*) for God, the particular form of the Qurʾānic expression for "Holy Spirit" (Ar. *rūḥ al-qudus*), and the reason the Qurʾān uses the term *miḥrāb* for buildings when in later Islamic Arabic the term refers to a prayer niche in mosques.

As a rule I do not comment extensively in this work on questions of the Qurʾān's structure or coherence. Still, I have come to recognize that the Qurʾān's concern for its internal organization often exerts a shaping influence on the way it discusses Biblical (or other) topics. In this regard I am particularly grateful for the work of Michael Cuypers on the Qurʾān's "Semitic rhetoric."[64] Cuypers makes the case that the Qurʾān, like the Bible, reflects a sophisticated process of editing marked by concentric structures common to other Semitic literary works. He also shows—and this element of his work has received less attention—that the Qurʾān is best understood when read in conversation with Biblical literature (or, what he calls the Qurʾān's "contexte interscripturaire"). I have also benefited from the considerable work of Angelika Neuwirth on the internal structure of the Qurʾān's shorter Suras.[65]

Finally, another area of recent scholarship on the Qurʾān which has influenced my understanding are those works on the self-referentiality, or metatextuality or the Qurʾānic corpus, and in particular *The Qurʾān's Self-Image* of Daniel Madigan and *Le Coran par lui-même* of Anne-Sylvie Boisliveau.[66] Both scholars point out the Qurʾān's remarkable and pervasive tendency to refer to the revelation given to its Prophet, references often taken by the tradition to refer to the canonical text of the Qurʾān itself. Both scholars argue convincingly that these references are instead generally to unwritten revelation, the heavenly scripture. Boisliveau argues that the Qurʾān's concern with defending its heavenly origin reveals something of the sectarian context in which it emerged.

CONCLUSIONS

The present work also has its own arguments to make regarding the nature of the Qur'ānic text, and I would like to highlight five of them. First, readers will note that the Qur'ān has a special relationship with Christian tradition, and in particular the writings of the Syriac Christian fathers. While there are certainly cases in which the Qur'ān develops themes or traditions known only from Jewish texts (e.g., the case of the term *ḥiṭṭa* in 2:58 or *rā'inā* in Q 2:104, or the Qur'ān's response to a tradition known from the Mishnah in Q 5:32), in the majority of cases, and even for material or characters drawn ultimately from the Hebrew Bible/Old Testament, the Qur'ān is in conversation with Christian sources. This is evident with the Qur'ān's account of God's commanding the angels to bow before Adam, and the devil's refusal to do so, a tradition prominent in Christian tradition (where Adam—before the Fall—is a prototype of Christ) and largely avoided in Jewish tradition. It is also seen in the accounts of the Companions of the Cave or Dhū l-Qarnayn ("The Two-Horned Man") in Qur'ān 18 (related to the Christian legends of the Sleepers of Ephesus and Alexander, respectively).

A close reading of other Qur'ānic accounts which involve characters or themes known both to Judaism and to Christianity usually shows that it is the Christian version of the account with which the Qur'ān has engaged. This is seen in the way the Qur'ān makes Abel (Q 5:28) into a willing and passive sacrifice,[67] in the appearance of a wolf (or wolves) in the Qur'ān's Joseph account (Q 12:13),[68] or in the way the Qur'ān describes the Israelites as "killers of the prophets" (Q 2:91; 3:21, 112, 181, 183).[69] The Qur'ān alludes to the Christian metaphor of Christ as a shepherd who protects his sheep by giving the Companions of the Cave a dog (Q 18:18–22).[70] The idea that the prophets or the righteous would be threatened with stoning (Q 11:91; 18:20; 19:46; 26:116; 36:18; 44:20) does not match the Hebrew Bible/Old Testament, but it does match the New Testament.[71]

Another sign of the Qur'ān's particular relationship with Christian tradition is its fashion of using turns of phrase found in the New Testament, although it often applies them in new ways. The Qur'ān (as already mentioned) refers to (7:40) the New Testament maxim of the "eye of the needle" and speaks on two occasions of a "mustard seed" (21:47; 31:16).[72] It also speaks of walking "humbly on the earth" (25:63), of heaven as a "tillage" (42:20), of "tasting" death (3:185; 21:35; 29:57; 44:56) and it transforms the Gospel tale of the foolish virgins (57:12–15).[73]

Second, the Qur'ān is much more than a simple transcript of one man's proclamations or his conversation with opponents; that is, it would be simplistic to reduce to the Qur'ān to "what was really said." The Qur'ān is shaped throughout by the concern of its author(s) with crafting polemical and apologetical messages, even when that involves putting words in its opponents' mouths. This is seen perhaps most clearly in the way it exaggerates the religious doctrines of its opponents, for example, by declaring that the Jews say "Ezra is the son of God" (Q 9:30) or that the Jews and Christians worship their clergy (Q 9:31). This insight might be applied more generally to the way the Qur'ān reports the things which all of its opponents say or, to use the expression of Mehdi Azaiez, to the Qur'ān's "counterdiscourse."[74] This applies not only to the opponents of the prophets of the past, or to the unbelievers damned in hell in an eschatological future, but also to the opponents of the Qur'ān's own Prophet. Their statements cannot be taken as a recording of what was really said, any more than the reports of the things they do cannot be taken as clear a clear reflection of what they really did.[75]

Third, the Qur'ān's concerns about theology and prophetology shape the way in which it presents Jewish and Christian material. For example, in the Christian story of the Sleepers of Ephesus the ultimate goal of the author is to argue through that the body will be resurrected. This too is found in the Qur'ānic account of the Companions of the Cave (Q 18:21), but this account is framed by verses which warn against those who say that God "has taken a son" (Q 18:4) and declare that there is "no guardian besides Him" (Q 18:26). Similarly in the parable of "two gardens" (Q 18:32–44), a parable close to the parable of the rich fool in Luke 12, the righteous companion is made to say, "I do not ascribe any partner to my Lord." In both cases an originally Christian account has been transformed by the Qur'ān's theological focus, namely that to be righteous one must say the right things about God, one must recognize and affirm that He has no rival or partner. It is also telling that in the Qur'ān, Hebrew Bible/Old Testament characters become intensely concerned about proper theology. Whereas Noah in the Old Testament says nothing at all (until after the flood), and in the New Testament he is simply a preacher of righteousness (2Pe 2:5), in the Qur'ān he becomes a preacher of theological righteousness, declaring to his people that there is no god but Allah (Q 7:59; 11:26; 23:23; 71:3). Similarly Abraham hardly preaches in Genesis but in later Jewish and Christian tradition (e.g., the *Apocalypse of Abraham*), and in the Qur'ān, he becomes an advocate of monotheism. All of this also reflects the way in which the Qur'ān's author makes earlier prophetic figures into prototypes of its own prophet. Similarly, the way in which those figures often demand that their people "obey God *and* the messenger" (n.b. Q 26, where Noah, Hud, Ṣāliḥ, Lot, and Shuʿayb demand that their people obey them; Jesus does the same in 3:50 and 43:63)—something which Biblical prophets are not in the habit of saying—reflects the demand of the Qur'ān's own prophet that his people obey him (e.g., 3:32, 132; 4:13–14, 42, 59, 69, 80; n.b. 4:80: "Whoever obeys the Apostle certainly obeys God"). Thus the Qur'ān's particular theological and prophetological concerns explain some of its departures from Biblical tradition.

Fourth, my research for the present work has taught me to appreciate the Arabic language of the Qur'ān. The "Syriac turn" in Qur'ānic studies has been an auspicious development in the way it encourages scholars to appreciate the Qur'ān's historical context in the Late Antique Near East. Nevertheless, it should not be missed that the Qur'ān repeatedly insists that it is a scripture in Arabic.[76] There is no reason to assume that the Arabic of the Qur'ān is the fully developed Classical Arabic of medieval grammarians.[77] This, however, does not make the Qur'ān any less Arabic. Indeed, at the very heart of the Qur'ānic message is the idea that in earlier times God had revealed himself in other languages to other peoples. Now (finally!) God has spoken in Arabic: "This is a confirming book, in the Arabic tongue" (Q 46:12).

Fifth, this work raises the question of how much the author of the Qur'ān knew of the Bible itself. This question, like many others, is difficult to answer when one considers the way in which literary and polemical concerns shape the Qur'ān's expressions.[78] Thus we are faced with an interesting dilemma when considering passages in the Qur'ān which depart from the Biblical tradition, such as (to give only a few of many possible examples) the naming of Abraham's father Āzar, not Terah as in the Bible (Q 6:74), the idea that the Jews called Ezra the "Son of God" (9:30), the suggestion that both Isaac and Jacob are sons of Abraham (6:84; 11:71; 19:49; 21:72; 29:17), the presence of Haman in Egypt instead of in Persia as in the book of Esther (Q 28:6, 8, 38; 29:39–40; 40:23, 36–37), the presentation of Mary the mother of Jesus as the sister of Aaron (hence Moses) and daughter of 'Imrān/Amram (see Q 3:35–36; 19:28; 66:12), or the suggestion that Pharaoh's wife (not his daughter) adopted Moses (Q 28:9) and that the Pharaoh who raised Moses is the same Pharaoh whom Moses later confronted (Q 26:18).[79] In some cases one can perceive that the Qur'ān has departed from the Biblical account in order to develop a certain symbolism. In other cases, however, the Qur'ān seems simply to be following a legendary adaptation of a Biblical account (this seems to be the case with the case of Haman, who presumably ends up in Egypt because of a detail in the ancient Aḥīqar legend); in still other cases there seems to have been some confusion (as with the case of Āzar, a name which seems to come from the name of Abraham's servant Eliezer who appears in the Targums, Peshitta, and Septuagint of Gen 15:2; likely too in the case of Mary).[80] Perhaps the best thing that can be said in this regard is that the Qur'ān seems to know the Bible as it was read and transmitted orally by Jews and Christians in Late Antiquity, with the diversity of interpretations that had developed by that time and which informed their reading of the scripture.

A FINAL REFLECTION

I consider the authorship of the Qur'ān to be an open question. From a traditional Islamic religious perspective the author of the Qur'ān is simply God (although we should not underestimate the diversity of Muslim approaches, both classical and contemporary, to the process of the revelation of the Qur'ān). From a traditional Orientalist perspective the author of the Qur'ān is simply Muḥammad, and indeed most early Orientalists explain particular turns of phrase in the Qur'ān in light of the ups and downs of his prophetic career that they read about in medieval biographies. This position is an adapted form of the traditional doctrine of "serial" revelation, to use an expression of John Wansbrough.[81] Beginning with Wansbrough, however, some scholars began to see that the idea of serial revelation is a way of explaining how the Qur'ān could have one author despite the diversity of material therein.

Indeed, it seems to me that there is simply no compelling academic reason (theological reasons are of course another story) to refuse categorically the possibility that the Qur'ān has multiple authors and/or editors.[82] Indeed, this possibility is one way of explaining why the Qur'ān includes material as diverse as Qur'an 5 (*al-Mā'ida*), Qur'ān 53 (*al-Najm*), and Qur'ān 55 (*al-Raḥmān*). In light of this possibility readers will find me referring in the present work neither to what God says nor to what Muḥammad says but simply to what the "Qur'ān" says. I grant that this is a way of avoiding the question of authorship, but given the present uncertain state of research I feel that there is no better solution.

Finally I would add that, despite all of the nontraditional ideas presented in this brief introduction, my hope is that the present work will be useful (and, perhaps, interesting) to a wide range of readers, including pious Muslims. As Fred Donner has explained in a lucid reflection,[83] what is at stake in academic research on the Qur'ān is not whether or not the Qur'ān is revealed—a question which surpasses the domain of the historian—but instead how it can be best understood.

Ultimately, if the present book makes any argument, it is that the Qur'ān itself, by referring regularly to Jewish and Christian traditions, demands that its audience know those traditions. The Qur'ān, in other words, has an intimate relationship with the Bible. We should thus learn to appreciate the Qur'ān not only as the scripture of Islam but also as a central work in the history of Biblical literature.

NOTES

1. "So if you are in doubt about what We have sent down to you, ask those who read the Book [revealed] before you. The truth has certainly come to you from your Lord; so do not be among the skeptics." Note also that Qur'ān 16:43 and 21:7 both end with the divine counsel: "Ask the People of the Reminder if you do not know."

2. On this see, among many works on the topic, G. S. Reynolds, "On the Qur'ānic Accusation of Scriptural Falsification (*taḥrīf*) and Christian Anti-Jewish Polemic," 1–14; G. Nickel, *Narratives of Tampering in the Earliest Commentaries on the Qur'ān* (Leiden: Brill, 2011).

3. These include early medieval scholars such as al-Yaʿqūbī (d. 292/897) and al-Masʿūdī (d. 345/956), and Ismāʿīlī scholars including Abū Ḥātim al-Rāzī (d. 322/934), along with later scholars including al-Ṭūfī (d. 716/1316) and al-Biqāʿī (d. 885/1480). For al-Ṭūfī's commentary on the Bible see L. Dejmiri, *Muslim Exegesis of the Bible in Medieval Cairo.* For al-Biqāʿī's treatise on the legitimacy of citing the Bible in certain contexts see W. Saleh, *In Defense of the Bible.* See also, and more recently, J. Witztum, "Ibn Isḥāq and the Pentateuch in Arabic," where Witztum argues, on the basis of citations from Abū Jaʿfar al-Ṭabarī, that Ibn Isḥāq had access to an Arabic translation of the Peshitta in the second/eighth century; and R. Vollandt, *Arabic Versions of the Pentateuch* (Leiden: Brill, 2015), esp. chap. 3.

4. An English translation (Bakhtiar) of the Qur'ān has now been published in one volume with the Bible: *Three Testaments.* This work, however, is principally an effort at religious dialogue and does not include a critical examination of the historical relationship of Bible and Qur'ān.

5. For some time scholars of the Qur'ān have sought to wash their hands of the sins of earlier generations of Orientalists by declaring, as a sort of prolegomenon to their research, that they believe the Qur'ān is an original work and not marked by "borrowing" from the Bible or other Jewish and Christian texts. Such declarations already mark, for example, contributions to the collected work: W. M. Brinner and S. D. Ricks, eds., *Studies in Islamic and Judaic Traditions* (Atlanta: Scholars Press, 1986), and they are even more common today. This is still an important point to emphasize, even if it is no less important to insist that the Qur'ān is nevertheless intimately related to Biblical literature.

6. "1453 or about one fourth of the total number [of Qur'ānic verses] consists of narratives concerning the prophets, sages and other historical or legendary celebrities of ancient times." F. Sherif, *Guide to the Contents of the Qur'an,* 46.

7. In my earlier work *The Qur'ān and Its Biblical Subtext* I focus principally on narrative material and ask whether the Qur'ān's close conversation with Biblical tradition can be found with other forms of Qur'ānic material (see *QBS,* 24). The present work is in some ways a response to that question.

8. On this, note the comments of Devin Stewart: "While scholars have long recognized the important connections between the Quran and the Bible, they have not sufficiently stressed the point that Muhammad's prophecy was formulated in Biblical terms, instead showing that elements were borrowed from Judaism and Christianity or com-

paring Quranic material with Biblical accounts." "Understanding the Koran in English," 40.

9. Notably Psa 37:9 and 28–29.

10. For the "eye of the needle" see Mat 19:23–24; Mar 10:25; Luk 18:25. For "mustard seed" see Mat 13:31–32; Mar 4:30–32; Luk 13:18–19. For "uncircumcised hearts" see Deu 10:6; 30:6; Jer 4:4, 9:24–25; Act 7:51–53; Rom: 2:28–29; Phi 3:3; Col 2:11. For "twinkling of the eye" see 1Co 15:51–52.

11. M. Sanhedrin 4:5.

12. On this point see H. Hirschfeld, *New Researches into the Composition and Exegesis of the Qoran,* 104.

13. S. Griffith, *The Bible in Arabic,* esp. 41–51.

14. This much is implied by the question which serves as the title of Abraham Geiger's 1833 work: *Was hat Mohammed aus dem Judenthume aufgenommen* ("What has Muḥammad taken from Judaism?").

15. On this point see my article "On the Presentation of Christianity in the Qurʾān," 42–54. Note also the approach of Morris Seale in his reflection on the Qurʾān as commentary on the Bible: "How the Qurʾan Interprets the Bible," 51–66. For an interesting and measured consideration of whether the Qurʾān could have any direct dependence on one particular Biblical book, see D. Brady, "The Book of Revelation and the Qurʾan," 216–25.

16. This development might take place in the fourth/tenth century with Masʿūdī (d. 345/956). See R. Tottoli, "Origin and Use of the Term Isrāʾīliyyāt in Muslim Literature."

17. The *Study Qurʾan* is a pious work. The introduction ends with a prayer and the editors openly declare their decision not to use sources which "do not accept the Qurʾān as revelation." *Study Quran,* "General Introduction," xliv.

18. On the importance of transcending an understanding of the Qurʾān which is shaped by medieval *tafsīr,* see D. Marshall, *God, Muhammad and the Unbelievers,* esp. 8–12. I do not, however, follow Marshall's reliance on the traditional chronology of the Qurʾān or his assumption that the *sīra* is basically authentic (see pp. 15–17).

19. It is important to note the argument of some scholars that the Qurʾān, despite the abundance of Biblical material therein, is nevertheless best understood in the light of Arab paganism. Particularly interesting arguments to this effect have been made by Jacqueline Chabbi in her *Le seigneur des tribus* and her more recent *Les trois piliers de l'Islam,* as well as by Aziz al-Azmeh in his monumental work *Emergence of Islam in Late Antiquity.* Both scholars still appreciate the significant role of Biblical material in the Qurʾān, something also emphasized by Chabbi in *Le Coran décrypté.* For her part Angelika Neuwirth argues that certain concepts discussed in the Qurʾān, especially that of "time," reflect the world of pagan Arab poetry: "Der Koran ist also ebensosehr eine Neulektüre der Poesie, wie er eine Neulektüre biblischer Traditionen ist." *Der Koran als Text der Spätantike,* 107. The classical studies of Arab paganism and the Qurʾān include L. Krehl, *Über die Religion der vorislamischen Araber;* J. Wellhausen, *Reste arabischen Heidentums;* H. Lammens, *Le culte des bétyles et les processions religieuses chez les Arabes préislamiques;* C. Brockelmann, "Allah und die Götzen:

Der Ursprung des vorislamischen Monotheismus"; G. Ryckmans, *Les religions arabes préislamiques;* and T. Fahd, *La divination arabe.*

20. This has been tried most recently by Sami Aldeeb Abu Sahlieh in bilingual French-Arabic and Arabic-alone editions: *Le Coran: texte arabe et traduction française* and *Al-Qur'ān al-karīm bi-l-tasalsul al-ta'rīkhī* (Ochettaz, Switzerland: Aldeeb, 2015).

21. I lay out my arguments against dependence on a chronological reading of the Qur'ān in "Le problème de la chronologie du Coran." See also the excellent article of E. Stefanidis: "Qur'an Made Linear." Here I would add that the problem of a chronological reading of the Qur'ān wedded to the traditional *sīra* is evident in Bell's *Commentary on the Qur'ān.* Bell frequently makes observations in that work meant to link a particular verse or passage with a particular moment in the *sīra.* Yet because so many different perspectives are found within the same Sura, this leads him to imagine that individual passages (or verses) from many different periods have been joined together, or indeed that certain passages meant to be replaced by new passages (written on the back of the same material) were ultimately included in the text. One is left with a picture of total incoherence. Thus, for example, with Sura 5, he comments that verses 51–53, come from "a more advance stage of the breach between Muhammad and previous monotheists," although verse "52 argues for a date still before Uhud" (Bell, *Commentary,* 1:160); verse 55 "cannot be very late" (1:162); verses 64–65 "would probably be in the time shortly before or shortly after Uhud" (1:162); verse 67–69 and 70–71 are early, being "scraps on the back of which vv. 64–65 were written"; verses 82–85 "perhaps date from Muhammad's disappointment with the Jews in his first years in Medinah" (1:166); verses 87–88 "seem to be early Medinan" (1:166); verse 95 "after the conquest of Meccah" (1:169); verse 97 "fairly early; about the time of the change of the *qiblah*" (1:169), and so on.

22. I might add here that another problem with labeling Suras as "Meccan" or Medinan" (although this is not the fundamental problem) is that very often *asbāb al-nuzūl* anecdotes deal with only certain portions of Suras. For example, the story of Muḥammad's being wrapped up in a blanket (connected to the opening of Q 74) effectively puts Qur'ān 74:1–7 in between Qur'ān 96:1–5 and 96:6–19. Can Qur'ān 96, then, properly be thought of as an "earlier" Sura than Qur'ān 74? Most Muslim scholars answer yes. They tend to date the Suras according to the Occasion of Revelation story of its opening verses. But this is not always the case. Most Muslim scholars conclude that the first ten verses of Qur'ān 29 ("The Spider") refer to the battles against pagans that Muḥammad led during the Medinan period of his life. However, the Occasion of Revelation stories for the greater part of the Sura (vv. 11–69) involve Muḥammad's Meccan period, and the Sura as a whole was generally labeled "Meccan."

23. For a counterargument see N. Sinai, "Qur'an as Process"; and more recently Sinai, "Inner-Qur'anic Chronology." Sinai convincingly argues that there are different sorts of literary material in the Qur'ān. However, whether this material should be classified into only two categories ("Meccan" and "Medinan") and whether such categories should be assigned to elements of the medieval biography of the Prophet remain open questions. On the question of developing an inner-Qur'ānic chronology see also J. Witztum, "Variant Traditions, Relative Chronology, and the Study of Intra Quranic

Parallels." The notion of Medinan insertions in Meccan Suras is important for scholars who seek to redeem the chronological model for reading the Qur'ān from a simplistic classification of Suras into Meccan and Medinan. On this see especially T. Nagel, *Medinensische Einschübe in mekkanischen Suren.*

24. For an effort to identify certain characteristics of "Meccan" and "Medinan" material in the Qur'ān without reference to the tradition, see N. Sinai, "Unknown Known."

25. On this see A. Rippin, "The Function of *'Asbāb Al-Nuzūl'* in Qur'ānic Exegesis."

26. To offer a more detailed example, Qur'ān 3:153 begins, "When you were fleeing without paying any attention to anyone, while the Apostle was calling you from your rear" and is explained with a story about the Battle of Uḥud, that Muhammad was urging those fleeing at Uḥud to turn around and fight, calling out: "Come to me servants of God, this way, servants of God" (*Tafsīr Jalālayn,* ad loc.). The very next verse (Q 3:154) begins: "Then He sent down to you safety after grief—a drowsiness that came over a group of you." *Tafsīr Jalālayn* explains: "They would become dizzy (*yamīdūna*) under their shields and their swords would fall from their hands; and a party whose own souls distressed them, that is, they caused them grief, so that their only wish was their deliverance, regardless of the Prophet and his Companions, and they were unable to fall asleep: these were the hypocrites" (ad loc.). Now one might recognize that the story, with the strange detail about dizziness, was written to explain verse 154 and in particular a word in that verse (*nuʿās,* "drowsiness"). The same, I would submit, should be recognized for the previous verse. The bit of Muḥammad's calling out to his fleeing followers at Uḥud may seem more natural for a story about a battle than the "dizziness" bit and therefore, perhaps, more historical. However, if one were to write a story based on Q 3:153, this is precisely what that story would look like. In other words, what we have are two stories, both written to explain turns of phrase in the Qur'ān. The point is not, in other words, that sensational or fantastic episodes are to be doubted from a sort of modernist skepticism about miracles. The point is that all stories, sober or sensational, are to be doubted from an appreciation of the exegetical nature of the *sīra.*

27. See the introduction to *QSC.*

28. *History of the Qur'ān,* 14ff.; cf. *QBS,* 30–33. Despite this, Josef Horovitz (*KU*) makes extensive use of pre-Islamic poetry in his analysis of Qur'ānic vocabulary.

29. Ṭāhā Ḥusayn, *Fī l-shiʿr al-jāhilī* (Cairo: Dār al-Kutub, 1926); a revised version (with Ḥusayn's responses to criticism of the book) was published as *Fī l-adab al-jāhilī* (Cairo: Maṭbaʿat al-Iʿtimād, 1927). On these two books see Y. Ayalon, "Ṭāhā Ḥusayn's *Fī al-Shiʿr al-Jāhilī* and Its Sequel," *Die Welt des Islams* 49 (2009): 98–121.

30. A creative method to defend the authenticity of Jāhilī poetry was developed by James Monroe in a 1972 article entitled "Oral Composition in Pre-Islamic Poetry," *Journal of Arabic Literature* 3 (1972): 1–53. Monroe applies the ideas developed by Milman Parry (d. 1935) and his student Albert Lord (d. 1991), who attempted to identify oral formulas in the Homeric corpus (Parry also studied the live performances of Serbian singers). Monroe's method was later followed by M. J. Zwettler: *The Oral Traditions of Classical Arabic Poetry* (Columbus: Ohio State University Press, 1978), esp. 98–172. Both argue that there are signs of orality in the Jāhilī poetic corpus which redound

to the authentic preservation of pre-Islamic oral performances of these poems. However, the conclusions of Monroe and Zwettler were effectively challenged by Gregor Schoeler, who, citing examples from classical Islamic Arabic poetry, shows that poems with formulaic qualities (i.e., formulas which are repeated throughout the text) can be the product of careful written composition. See G. Schoeler, "Oral Poetry Theory and Arabic Literature."

31. On Umayya see C. Huart, "Une nouvelle source du Qoran." Louis Cheikho believed that Umayya was a Christian. See his *al-Naṣrāniyya wa-adabuhā bayna ʿarab al-Jāhiliyya* (Beirut: Dār al-Mashriq, 1912–23); French trans.: *Le christianisme et la littérature chrétienne en Arabie avant l'Islam* (Beirut: Imprimerie Catholique, 1923); and more recently T. Seidensticker, "The Authenticity of the Poems Ascribed to Umayya Ibn Abī al-Ṣalt," in *Tradition and Modernity in Arabic Language and Literature,* ed. J. R. Smart (London: Curzon, 1996), 87–101.

32. For the poems attributed to Umayya see I. Frank-Kamenetzky, "Untersuchungen über das Verhältnis der dem Umajja b. Abi ṣ Ṣalt zugeschriebenen Gedichte zum Qorān" (PhD diss., Königsberg, 1911), recently translated by D. R. Ross and available online. The standard collection is that of Frank-Kamenetzky's teacher F. Schulthess, *Umajja ibn Abī ṣ Ṣalt: Die unter seinem Namen überlieferten Gedichtfragmente gesammelt und übersetzt* (Leipzig: Hinrichs, 1911).

33. See T. Nöldeke, "Umaija b. AbiṣṢalt," *Zeitschrift für Assyriologie* 27 (1913): 159–72, esp. 163.

34. For a number of the terms and turns of phrase in Umayya's poetry which reflect Qurʾānic usage, see Nöldeke, "Umaija b. AbiṣṢalt," 164–65.

35. Andrae compares the way Muslim scholars attributed Qurʾānic ideas to Umayya with the way they attributed exegetical opinions to Ibn ʿAbbās. He concludes: "Les poésies d'*Umayya* sont à rejeter de la discussion de l'origine de la théologie coranique." *Les origines de l'Islam et le Christianisme,* 63. See also J. W. Hirschberg, "Der Sündenfall in der altarabischen Poesie," *Rocznik Orjentalistyczny* 9 (1933): 22–36; T. O'Shaughnessy, *Development of the Meaning of Spirit in the Koran,* esp. 19–20, 41, 49; R. Blachère, *Histoire de la littérature arabe* (Paris: Adrien-Maisonneuve, 1964), 2:305–6. See also M. Valoro, review of Bahjat ʿAbd al-Ghafūr al-Ḥadīthī, *Umayyah ibn Abī ṣ-Ṣalt, ḥayātuhu wa-shiʿruhu,* in *Oriente Moderno* 57 (1977): 176–83. For more optimistic views of the authenticity of Umayya's poetry see N. Sinai, "Religious Poetry from the Quranic Milieu." Cf. T. Bauer, "Relevance of Early Arabic Poetry for Qurʾānic Studies Including Observations on *Kull* and on Q 22:27, 26:225, and 52:21," *QC,* 699–732; and A. Neuwirth, *Der Koran als Text der Spätantike,* 51–53.

36. For a recent consideration of the problem more generally, see the work K. Dmitriev, "An Early Christian Arabic Account of the Creation of the World," *QC,* 349–87, and in particular the bibliographic references therein. Dmitriev studies the works attributed to the Christian poet ʿAdī b. Zayd al-ʿIbādī (d. ca. 600) and takes an optimistic view toward their authenticity (although ʿAdī's poetry was first recorded by Hishām b. al-Kalbī, d. ca. 206/821). While Dmitriev's detailed analysis of one particular poem attributed to ʿAdī b. Zayd is excellent, his arguments regarding authenticity are putative. More convincing is F.-C. Muth, who concludes that early Arabic poetry is not a

reliable source for our understanding of the Qur'ān. See his "Reflections on the Relationship of Early Arabic Poetry and the Qur'ān."

37. Here it is worth repeating a quotation of John Burton, in a review of W. M. Watt's problematic *Companion to the Qur'ān:* "The complacency of Orientalists vis-à-vis the Islamic traditions on the Qur'ān has prevented not merely the solution but the very identification of the central Qur'ān problem." J. Burton, review of W. M. Watt, *Companion to the Qur'an, BSOAS* 32 (1969): 387–89, 388, quoted by A. Droge, *The Qur'ān: A New Annotated Translation,* xxx.

38. For etymologies of Qur'ānic words the best source is still A. Jeffery, *The Foreign Vocabulary of the Qur'ān* (Baroda: Oriental Institute, 1938; Leiden: Brill, 2007). Of use as well is Zammit, *Comparative Lexical Study of Qur'ānic Arabic;* and A. A. Ambros and S. Procházka, *Concise Dictionary of Koranic Arabic.* Of particular use for Qur'ānic turns of phrase is still the opening section of *History of the Qur'ān* (1–46 of the English translation).

39. On this see J. Witztum: "Variant Traditions," 1ff. The original expression comes from C. Schedl, *Muhammad und Jesus,* 416. Witztum's article represents the best introduction to this question, although one might note also the contributions of A. Neuwirth, including *Zur Komposition der mekkanischen Suren;* "Form and Structure of the Qur'ān," *EQ,* 2:245–66; *Der Koran als Text der Spätantike.* Neuwirth's approach (like that of R. Bell) is always closely linked to chronology. Neuwirth's approach to inner-Qur'ānic relationships might be contrasted to that in the works of (among others) F. van der Velden, "Kotexte im Konvergenzstrang"; G. Dye, "Lieux saints communs, partagés ou confisqués"; C. Segovia, *Quranic Noah and the Making of the Islamic Prophet;* and now especially the work of K.-F. Pohlmann, *Die Entstehung des Korans.* Pohlmann's work might be read together with the critical responses to it by J. Witztum: "Variant Traditions" (see 2, 4, 12–13, 21, 25).

40. The translation of Qarai included in the present volume is a slightly revised version of the second edition of his *English Arabic Qur'ān* (Elmhurst, NY: Tahrike Tarsile Qur'an, 2011). Mr. Qarai wrote the following in personal communication to me: "The translation enclosed in two parts is a recently revised all-English version of the phrase-by-phrase text published earlier with the Arabic" (November 8, 2011).

41. At times his notes reflect a particular interest in Shi'ite traditions. Like all recent translators of the Qur'ān, Qarai (even though he occasionally mentions variants) works on the basis of the standard version of the Qur'ān first published in 1924 in Cairo, and revised later in 1924 and again in 1936 (the so-called King Fārūq Qur'ān), based on the Ḥafṣ (d. 180/796) 'an 'Āṣim (d. 127/745) reading (today the standard Arabic version is *Al-Qur'ān al-karīm, Muṣḥaf al-Madīna al-nabawiyya* [Madīna: Mujammaʿ al-Malik Fahd li-Ṭibāʿat al-Muṣḥaf al-Sharīf, 1994–95]). It will be auspicious when translators are less reliant on the work of the Egyptian committee for religious education which commissioned that text (for more on this see G. S. Reynolds, "Introduction," *QHC,* 2–8). Notably recent scholarship on ancient Qur'ān manuscripts has uncovered new readings, not attested in the traditional literature on *qirā'āt.* These include readings in the inferior text of palimpsests, especially that of Ṣanʿā' (DAM 02-27.1) which are certainly more ancient than the later, standardized text. B. Sadeghi has explained

the variants on the inferior text of the Sanʿāʾ manuscript by suggesting that they are the work of an unknown companion whose text was replaced by the text of ʿUthmān. Without his layer of interpretation imposed, however, all we have is a more ancient text with variant readings. See B. Sadeghi and U. Bergmann, "The Codex of a Companion of the Prophet and the Qurʾān of the Prophet," *Arabica* 57 (2010): 343–436; B. Sadeghi and M. Goudarzi, "Sanʿāʾ 1 and the Origins of the Qurʾān." See more recently the excellent (and more balanced) study of the manuscript: A. Hilali, *The Sanaa Palimpsest.* Prof. Hilali analyzes both the work of Sadeghi and the detailed work on the same manuscript by E. Puin in German.

42. The Qurʾān's specific doctrine of God is evident in the particular names it gives Him, as well as in the names it does not give Him. It is meaningful, for example, that the Qurʾān calls God "king" but not "father." On this see further G. Anawati, "Le nom supreme de Dieu (*ism Allāh al-Aʿẓam*)," in *Atti del terzo congress di studi Arabi e Islamici, Ravello 1–6 settembre 1966* (Naples: Istituto Universitario Orientale, 1967), 7–58; D. Gimaret, *Les noms divins en Islam: Exégèse lexicographique et théologique* (Paris: Éditions du Cerf, 1988); A. Rippin, "God," in *The Blackwell Companion to the Qurʾan,* ed. A. Rippin (Oxford: Blackwell, 2006), 223–33.

43. Here I am borrowing the term of Jay Crook, a scholar writing explicitly from an Islamic perspective: "The scattered form of the stories in the Quran clearly shows that the context could have been supplied by any reasonably interested Arab of that period; otherwise, their inclusion in their Qurʾānic form would have been pointless." *The Bible: An Islamic Perspective: Introduction to the New Testament* (Chicago: Kazi Publications 2005), 2.

44. E.g., Psa 89:11; 115:15; 121:2; 124:8; 134:3; cf. also 1Ch 29:11. This point is made by Richard Bell: *Commentary,* 1:53.

45. More attention to general Qurʾānic phrases with a Biblical flavor is found in Speyer, *BEQ* (note in particular the list at 442–61) and in the online database of the Corpus Coranicum project (http://www.corpuscoranicum.de/kontexte/). To give another example: the opening (vv. 1–4) of Qurʾān 13 is a passage filled with references to signs in nature which point toward the existence of a powerful God. For this passage I have commentary on verse 2, as its reference to the sky being raised "without any pillars" is better understood in light of a cosmology shared by the Bible according to which heaven is a dome stretched out above the earth. I do not add commentary to the other verses in this passage, even though Biblical parallels for them could be found (e.g., the references to mountains, streams, and fruit in Q 13:3 might be compared with Psalm 104:10), because they are general enough that there is no reason to think the Qurʾān is in conversation with the Bible. Likewise when the Qurʾān describes God's sending rain (e.g., Q 16:10) I do not simply insert a similar passage on rain from the Bible (e.g., Deu 11:14; Psa 104:13–14; Mat 5:45).

46. Those interested generally in the parallels between the Psalms and the shorter Suras of the Qurʾān will find numerous references in A. Neuwirth, *Der Koran: Band 1 Frühmekkanische Suren.* Neuwirth, for example, points out therein (353) that Q 73:11 is similar to Psalm 37:10–11 and (256) that Q 87:1 is similar to Psalm 9:2 and 148:5.

47. For that the most important work is still H. Speyer, *Die biblischen Erzählungen im Qoran (BEQ)*.

48. In each case I have cited these works according to the English translations produced by Fons Vitae: *Tafsīr al-Jalālayn*, trans. F. Hamza; and *Al-Wāḥidī's Asbāb al-Nuzūl*, trans. M. Guezzou. I have also compared these translations to the Arabic editions (see bibliography).

49. Those interested in such an approach might consult the notes in Muhammad Asad's *Message of the Qur'ān* or the recent *Study Quran*. For excerpts from, and discussion of, a wide range of Islamic exegetical works on one Qur'ānic theme, see F. Hamza and S. Rizvi, eds., *An Anthology of Qur'ānic Commentaries* (London: Institute for Ismaili Studies, 2008).

50. Estimations of the date of this text (and, consequently, the direction of influence) vary widely, but following Jacob Lassner, I assume that it largely precedes the Qur'ān. See J. Lassner, *Demonizing the Queen of Sheba,* 132.

51. In this regard I benefited in particular from the work of directing, along with Mehdi Azaiez, the Qur'ān Seminar and subsequently editing, with Mehdi Azaiez, Tommaso Tesei, and Hamza Zafer, the commentary produced by the seminar (*Qur'ān Seminar Commentary*).

52. A. Droge, *The Qur'ān: A New Annotated Translation*.

53. M. Azaiez, *Le contre-discours coranique*.

54. E. El-Badawi, *Qur'ān and the Aramaic Gospel Traditions*.

55. Holger Zellentin, *Qur'ān's Legal Culture*. Zellentin is also particularly interested in the possibility that Jewish Christianity, as reflected in the *Clementine Homilies* and (through refutations) in the *Didascalia* was influential in the Qur'ān's milieu. From my perspective this possibility is interesting but often unnecessary, as the Qur'ān's legal and doctrinal positions can be seen as original developments which emerged in the course of the nascent community's competition with orthodox Judaism and Christianity.

56. C. Luxenberg, *Die syro-aramäische Lesart des Koran*.

57. S. Griffith, "Syriacisms in the Arabic Qur'ān"; "Christian Lore and the Arabic Qur'ān."

58. A. Silverstein, "Hāmān's Transition from the Jāhiliyya to Islam"; "Qur'ānic Pharaoh."

59. T. Tesei, "Notion of Barzakh and the Question of the Intermediate State of the Dead in the Qur'an"; "Some Cosmological Notions from Late Antiquity in Q 18:60–65."

60. K. van Bladel, "Heavenly Cords, and Prophetic Authority in the Quran and Its Late Antique Context"; "*Alexander Legend* in the Qur'ān 18:83–102."

61. J. Witztum, *The Syriac Milieu of the Qur'an*. In addition to his dissertation I have benefited from a number of Witztum's articles, including "Foundations of the House" and "Joseph among the Ishmaelites."

62. Jeffery relied in large part on the Christian Palestinian Aramaic dictionary of Friedrich Schulthess: *Lexicon Syropalaestinum*.

63. S. Shoemaker, "Christmas in the Qur'an"; id., *Death of a Prophet*. G. Dye: "Lieux saints communs, partagés ou confisqués." These texts might be read together with P. Crone, "Jewish Christianity and the Qur'ān (Part Two)," esp. 15–19. Crone contrasts

the Qur'ān's insistence that Mary suffered birth pains (19:23) with the common position of the Chalcedonian tradition (to which the Kathisma church in Jerusalem belonged) that Mary did not suffer during her labor.

64. M. Cuypers, "Une analyse rhétorique du début et de la fin du Coran"; *Le festin,* English trans.: *The Banquet; L'apocalypse du Coran; La composition du Coran,* English trans.: *The Composition of the Qur'an.*

65. In particular *Studien zur Komposition der mekkanischen Suren* and *Der Koran: Band 1 Frühmekkanische Suren.* Neuwirth notably makes the case (against the position of Bell and Watt by which even some shorter Suras are composite texts made up of originally discrete pericopes) that at least the so-called Meccan Suras are unified units of text. She also develops a theory by which middle Meccan Suras are composed in an intentional tripartite structure: hymnal or poetical material; prophetic or narrative material; and hymnal, didactic, or polemical material. On this see *Studien zur Komposition der mekkanischen Suren,* 175–78. See also the helpful synopsis of N. Sinai, *Fortschreibung und Auslegung,* 61ff. However, the coherence she finds in Meccan Suras could also be explained through a process of redaction by which the text was reworked in different stages.

66. D. Madigan, *Qur'an's Self-Image;* A.-S. Boisliveau, *Le Coran par lui-même.*

67. On this see Witztum, *Syriac Milieu,* 111–53.

68. Ibid., 201–5.

69. See G. S. Reynolds, "On the Qur'an and the Theme of Jews as 'Killers of the Prophets.'"

70. On this see M. Tardieu, "Les Septs Dormants."

71. Mat 23:37; Luk 13:34; Act 5:26, 7:55–59, 14:5.

72. Mat 13:31–32; Mar 4:30–32; Luk 13:18–19.

73. Walking "humbly on the earth": Mat 5:4. Heaven as a "tillage": Mat 13:23; Mar 13:20; 2Co 9:10; Gal 6:8. "Tasting" death: Mat 16:28; Joh 8:52. Parable of the foolish virgins: Mat 25:1–13. One might add here that the Qur'ān seems to have a particular interest as well in preaching to the Christians. In the Qur'ān the Jews are a people whom God has already punished for their unbelief; they have been cursed (Q 2:88; 4:46; 5:13, 60, 64; 17:60) and their hearts have been made hard (5:13). The position of the Christians in the Qur'ān seems to be fundamentally different. The Qur'ān does not seem to report any punishment given to them other than internal discord (Q 5:14). Meanwhile, the Qur'ān admonishes them directly, imploring them to remember the words of Jesus, asking them not to go to excess in their religion (Q 4:171). Indeed, it uses Jesus to preach to them (Q 3:50–51; 5:72). The Christians are a people whose fate is yet to be determined (something suggested by Q 5:118). Particularly instructive in this regard is the contrast between Q 5:13, where the Jews are said to have broken their covenant, to be cursed, to have hard hearts, and to have perverted words from their meanings, and the very next verse, which speaks of the Christians in noticeably milder language.

74. Reflecting on this term, Azaiez comments, "Le contre-discours serait donc l'intégration du discours de l'adversaire et plus précisément un contre-discours rapporté." M. Azaiez, *Le contre-discours coranique,* 53.

75. For this reason it is an unreliable method to use particular turns of phrase in the Qurʾān as a starting point for a quest to find some sect or heretical group (often imagined to have found refuge in the Arabian desert) which influenced Muḥammad's religious ideas. On this see further S. Griffith, "*Al-Naṣārā* in the Qurʾan"; G. S. Reynolds, "On the Presentation of Christianity in the Qurʾān." For examples of this method see Abū Mūsā al-Ḥarīrī, *Nabī al-raḥma* (Beirut: Diyār ʿAql, 1990); id., *al-Qass wa-nabī* (Beirut: n.p. 1979), French trans.: J. Azzi, *Le prêtre et le prophète,* trans. M. S. Garnier (Paris: Maisonneuve et Larose, 2001); F. de Blois, "*Naṣrānī* and *Ḥanīf:* Studies on the Religious Vocabulary of Christianity and Islam," *BSOAS* 65 (2002): 1–30; id., "Elchasai - Manes - Muhammad: Manichäismus und Islam in religionshistorischen Vergleichs," *Der Islam* 81 (2004) 31–48; É. Gallez, *Le messie et son prophète: Aux origines de l'Islam* (Versailles: Éditions de Paris, 2005); J. Gnilka, *Die Nazarener und der Koran, eine Spurensuche* (Freiburg: Herder, 2007); A. Yousef, *Le moine de Mahomet: L'entourage judéo-chrétien à La Mecque au VIème siècle* (Monaco: Rocher, 2008).
76. Q 12:2; 13:37; 16:103; 20:113; 26:195; 39:28; 41:3; 42:7; 43:3; 46:12.
77. On this see J. Wansbrough, *Quranic Studies,* 102–3; K. Vollers, *Volksprache und Schriftsprache im alten Arabien* (Strassburg: Trübner, 1906); T. Nöldeke, *Neue Beiträge zur semitischen Sprachwissenschaft,* 1–5.
78. On the Qurʾān's creative rhetorical expression see D. Stewart, "Poetic License in the Qurʾān"; S. Griffith, "*Al-Naṣārā* in the Qurʾan"; Reynolds, "On the Presentation of Christianity in the Qurʾān."
79. In Exodus it is only when the Pharaoh who sought Moses' life on account of his murder of an Egyptian dies, and a new Pharaoh ascends to the throne, that Moses returns to Egypt from Midian (Exo 4:19).
80. See A. Silverstein, "Haman's Transition from the Jahiliyya to Islam."
81. On the origins of this idea see Wansbrough, *Qurʾānic Studies,* 37–38.
82. It is true that the Qurʾān regularly (but not always) refers to a prophet (*nabī*) or messenger (*rasūl*) and is framed as revelations to him. However, many of the prophetic books of the Old Testament are framed as revelations to one figure, although their composite nature has long been recognized. On this see further the aforementioned work of Pohlmann, *Die Entstehung des Korans.*
83. F. Donner, "Historian, the Believer, and the Qurʾān."

QUR'ĀN TEXTS
AND COMMENTARY

1. *AL-FĀTIḤA*, THE OPENING

---

¹In the Name of God, the All-beneficent, the All-merciful.

²All praise belongs to God, Lord of all the worlds,

³the All-beneficent, the All-merciful,

⁴Master of the Day of Retribution.

⁵You [alone] do we worship,

and to You [alone] do we turn for help.

⁶Guide us on the straight path,

⁷the path of those whom You have blessed

—such as have not incurred Your wrath, nor are astray.

1:1–7 The first chapter, or Sura, of the Qur'ān is given the simple title "The Opening Sura" *al-sūra al-fātiḥa* (usually shortened to *al-Fātiḥa*). Verses 2–4 of *al-Fātiḥa* declare God's praises in the third person, whereas verses 5–7 have the believer address God in the second person in a prayer for guidance. The Sura has some similarities to the Our Father (although according to Islamic tradition this Sura, like the rest of the Qur'ān, is the word of God):

⁹. . . Our Father in heaven, may your name be held holy,

¹⁰your kingdom come, your will be done, on earth as in heaven.

¹¹Give us today our daily bread.

¹²And forgive us our debts, as we have forgiven those who are in debt to us.

¹³And do not put us to the test, but save us from the Evil One. (Mat 6:9b–13; cf. Luk 11:2b–4)

The placement of this short chapter at the beginning of the Qur'ān, despite the general progression of the Qur'ān's Suras from longer to shorter, suggests that *al-Fātiḥa* is meant to be prayed before reading or reciting the scripture.

Nöldeke et al. (*History of the Qur'ān,* 93n163/V) suggest that verse 6 here corresponds to Psalm 27:11 ("Lord, teach me your way, lead me on the path of integrity because of my enemies"). Cuypers notes (*La composition du Coran,* 176–78) that Sura 1, which acts as an introduction to the Qur'ān, reflects Psalm 1, which acts as an introduction to the psalter. He emphasizes in particular the parallel between Q 1:7 and Psalm 1:6: "For the Lord watches over the path of the upright, but the path of the wicked is doomed" (see also Psa 27:11).

Following the common understanding, Qarai renders the expression (v. 2) *rabb al-'ālamīn* as "Lord of all the worlds." However, this expression seems to mean simply "Lord of all people" (cf. the use of *'ālamīn* in 2:47, 122, 251; 3:33, 42, 96, 108; 5:20, passim; on this see Paret, *Kommentar,* 12; cr. Joseph Witztum).

On the term in v. 4 that Qarai renders "Retribution" (Ar. *dīn*), see commentary on 83:11 (with further references).

Tafsīr al-Jalālayn reports (following a common tradition) that those who have incurred God's wrath (v. 7) are the Jews, and those who are astray (v. 7) are the Christians.

2. *AL-BAQARA*, THE HEIFER

In the Name of God, the All-beneficent, the All-merciful.
¹*Alif, Lām, Mīm.*

2:1 This Sura, along with twenty-eight others, begins with a series of Arabic letters that are not well understood (for which reason they are occasionally referred to as "mysterious" letters).

---

²This is the Book, there is no doubt in it, a guidance to the God-wary, ³who believe in the Unseen, maintain the prayer, and spend out of what We have provided for them; ⁴and who believe in what has been sent down to *you* and what was sent down before *you,* and are certain of the Hereafter. ⁵Those follow their Lord's guidance and it is they who are the felicitous.

⁶As for the faithless, it is the same to them whether *you* warn them or do not warn them, they will not have faith. ⁷God has set a seal on their hearts and their hearing, and there is a blindfold on their sight, and there is a great punishment for them.

2:7 On the "sealing" of hearts, see commentary on 7:101 (with further references). Regarding God's preventing of people from hearing and seeing, one might compare Isaiah 6:9: "Go, and say to this people, 'Listen and listen, but never understand! Look and look, but never perceive!'" (cf. Jer 5:21; Mat 13:14; Mar 4:11; Luk 8:10; 2Pe 1:9). See also Q 2:17–18, which has God himself take away light from the unbelievers, and 2:171; 6:39; 41:17.

---

[8]Among the people are those who say, 'We have faith in God and the Last Day,' but they have no faith. [9]They seek to deceive God and those who have faith, yet they deceive no one but themselves, but they are not aware. [10]There is a sickness in their hearts; then God increased their sickness, and there is a painful punishment for them because of the lies they used to tell.

[11]When they are told, 'Do not cause corruption on the earth,' they say, 'We are only reformers!' [12]Behold! They are themselves the agents of corruption, but they are not aware.

[13]And when they are told, 'Believe like the people who have believed,' they say, 'Shall we believe like the fools who have believed?' Behold! They are themselves the fools, but they do not know.

[14]When they meet the faithful, they say, 'We believe,' but when they are alone with their devils, they say, 'We are with you; we were only deriding [them].' [15]It is God who derides them, and leaves them bewildered in their rebellion.

2:15 On God's deriding of the unbelievers, one might compare Psalm 2:4: "He who is enthroned in the heavens laughs, the Lord makes a mockery of them."

---

[16]They are the ones who bought error for guidance, so their trade did not profit them, nor were they guided.

[17]Their parable is that of one who lighted a torch, and when it had lit up all around him, God took away their light, and left them

sightless in a manifold darkness. [18]Deaf, dumb, and blind, they will not come back.

[19]Or that of a rainstorm from the sky, wherein is darkness, thunder, and lightning: they put their fingers in their ears due to the thunderclaps, apprehensive of death; and God besieges the faithless. [20]The lightning almost snatches away their sight: whenever it shines for them, they walk in it, and when the darkness falls upon them they stand. Had God willed, He would have taken away their hearing and sight. Indeed, God has power over all things.

[21]O mankind! Worship your Lord, who created you and those who were before you, so that you may be Godwary. [22]—He who made the earth a place of repose for you, and the sky a canopy, and He sends down water from the sky and with it brings forth crops for your sustenance. So do not set up equals to God, while you know.

[23]And if you are in doubt concerning what We have sent down to Our servant, then bring a *sūrah* like it, and invoke your helpers besides God, if you are truthful. [24]But if you do not—and you will not—then beware the Fire whose fuel will be humans and stones, prepared for the faithless. [25]And *give* good news to those who have faith and do righteous deeds, that for them shall be gardens with streams running in them: whenever they are provided with their fruit for nourishment, they will say, 'This is what we were provided before,' and they were given something resembling it. There will be chaste mates for them, and they will remain therein [forever].

2:25 Here and elsewhere the Qur'ān presents heaven as a garden. Some scholars describe this presentation as a reflection of the desires of desert-dwelling Arabs, who dreamed of well-watered, fruit-filled oases (along with "chaste mates"). However, the Qur'ānic presentation of paradise more likely emerges from an idea that the souls of the blessed will return to the same garden in which God once placed Adam, the Garden of Eden (on this see, e.g., 9:72, 13:23, 16:31, 18:31). The Qur'ān follows a cosmology by which the Garden of Eden exists on the top of a "cosmic mountain" the summit of which is in the heavenly realm (note how, in 2:36 and 7:24, Adam, Eve, and Satan are told to get "down" from the garden). This cosmology is already found, for example, in Ephrem's *Hymns on Paradise:*

> With the eye of my mind / I gazed upon paradise;
>> the summit of every mountain / is lower than its summit,
> the crest of the Flood / reached only its foothills;
>> these it kissed with reverence / before turning back,
> to rise above and subdue the peak / of every hill and mountain.
>> The foothills of Paradise it kisses / while every summit it buffets. (1:4)

Qarai's translation relates that rivers run "in" the gardens of paradise, although the Arabic relates that they "run below" (Ar. *taḥt*) them (see, e.g., 3:15, 136, 195, 198; 4:13, 57, 122; 5:12, 85; passim). This particular description of rivers is not limited to paradise but is applied on three occasions (2:266; 6:6; 43:51) to earthly gardens. On this see D. Waines, "Agriculture and Vegetation," *EQ* 1:41 (cr. Joseph Witztum).

The Qur'ān also mentions the presence of "purified companions" (our translation has "chaste mates") in the garden (cf. 3:15). Muslim commentators explain that their purity consists in an absence of bodily impurities. *Tafsīr al-Jalālayn* reports, "And there for them shall be spouses, or houris and others, purified, from menstruation and impurities." Hilali-Khan translate here, "and they shall have therein pure wives, (having no menses, stools, urine, etc.)."

———————————

²⁶Indeed, God is not ashamed to draw a parable whether it is that of a gnat or something above it. As for those who have faith, they know it is the truth from their Lord; and as for the faithless, they say, 'What did God mean by this parable?' Thereby He leads many astray, and thereby He guides many; and He leads no one astray thereby except the transgressors ²⁷—those who break the covenant made with God after having pledged it solemnly, and sever what God has commanded to be joined, and cause corruption on the earth—it is they who are the losers.

[28]How can you be unfaithful to God, [seeing that] you were lifeless and He gave you life, then He will make you die, and then bring you to life, and then you will be brought back to Him?

[29]It is He who created for you all that is in the earth, then He turned to the heaven and fashioned it into seven heavens, and He has knowledge of all things.

2:29 On the seven heavens in the Qur'ān see commentary on 67:3 (with further references).

---

[30]When your Lord said to the angels, 'I am indeed going to set a viceroy on the earth,' they said, 'Will You set in it someone who will cause corruption in it and shed blood, while we celebrate Your praise and proclaim Your sanctity?' He said, 'Indeed, I know what you do not know.'

2:30 In this verse God announces the creation of a "viceroy" (Ar. *khalīfa;* see 6:165; 7:69; 10:14) or "representative," something that seems to reflect the Biblical idea of man's creation "in the image of God" (Gen 1:26). The Qur'ān's report that the angels were opposed to the creation of Adam emerges ultimately from speculation on Psalm 8:4–5:

> [4]What are human beings that you spare a thought for them, or the child of Adam that you care for him?
> [5]Yet you have made him little less than a god, you have crowned him with glory and beauty. (Psa 8:4–5; cf. Job 7:17; Psa 144:3–4; Heb 2:6–9)

Certain Jewish interpreters read Psalm 8:4–5 as the angels' response to God's creation of man and developed traditions accordingly. Q 2:30, which gives the angels foreknowledge of the trouble humans will cause on earth, may reflect in particular a tradition in the Babylonian Talmud in which the angels learn of, and object to, the future misdeeds of humans:

> When the Holy One, blessed be He, wished to create man, He [first] created a company of ministering angels and said to them: Is it your desire that we

make a man in our image? They answered: Sovereign of the Universe, what will be his deeds? Such and such will be his deeds, He replied. Thereupon they exclaimed: Sovereign of the Universe, What are human beings that you spare a thought for them, or the child of Adam that you care for him? Thereupon He stretched out His little finger among them and consumed them with fire. The same thing happened with a second company. The third company said to Him: Sovereign of the Universe, what did it avail the former [angels] that they spoke to Thee [as they did]? the whole world is Thine, and whatsoever that Thou wishest to do therein, do it." (b. Sanhedrin, 38b; cf. also Psa 14:2–4, with its condemnation of humanity)

Many Muslim commentators, careful to avoid any ideas that would compromise God's transcendence (or superiority to man), often prefer to interpret *khalīfa* not as "viceroy" but as "successor." They are thereby left to explain exactly whom Adam succeeded. *Tafsīr al-Jalālayn* reports a well-known tradition by which Adam was made to be the successor to the *jinn,* beings who had been created by God to inhabit the earth before humans. According to this narrative, the *jinn* "caused corruption" and "shed blood" while on earth (for which reason God sent angels to fight against them). *Tafsīr al-Jalālayn* thus paraphrases the angels' words in 2:30:

> "They said, 'What, will You appoint therein one who will do corruption therein, through disobedience, and shed blood, spilling it through killing, just as the progeny of the *jinn* did, for they used to inhabit it, but when they became corrupted God sent down the angels against them and they were driven away to islands and into the mountains."

---

³¹And He taught Adam the Names, all of them; then presented them to the angels and said, 'Tell me the names of these, if you are truthful.'

³²They said, 'Immaculate are You! We have no knowledge except what You have taught us. Indeed, You are the All-knowing, the All-wise.'

³³He said, 'O Adam, inform them of their names,' and when he had informed them of their names, He said, 'Did I not tell you that I know the Unseen of the heavens and the earth, and that I know whatever you disclose and whatever you conceal?'

2:31–33 The Qur'ān presents things here differently from the account of Genesis 2:19, by which Adam himself names the animals:

> So from the soil the Lord God fashioned all the wild animals and all the birds of heaven. These he brought to the man to see what he would call them; each one was to bear the name the man would give it.

The point of the naming of things in this Qur'ānic passage (the Qur'ān does not say whether this concerns only the names of the animals) is to illustrate God's knowledge. God chooses to give this knowledge to Adam (Q 2:31), who then shows off his knowledge to the angels (Q 2:33)—thereby proving the superiority of man to the angels (already suggested by 2:30).

---

³⁴And when We said to the angels, 'Prostrate before Adam,' they prostrated, but not Iblis: he refused and acted arrogantly, and he was one of the faithless.

2:34 This verse follows the illustration (vv. 31–33) of Adam's privileged knowledge of names, and thus the superiority of humanity to the angels. The bowing of the angels is the logical fulfillment of God's description of man as His viceroy (v. 30). The tradition of the bowing of the angels before Adam is prominent in early Syriac Christian texts, notably *Cave of Treasures,* which make Adam a prototype of Christ. It is curious that the angels, who complained about the creation of man (v. 30), now (except for the devil, "Iblīs") agree to worship him. For more on this tradition see commentary on 7:11–12 (with further references).

---

³⁵We said, 'O Adam, dwell with your mate in paradise, and eat thereof freely whencesoever you wish, but do not approach this tree, lest you should be among the wrongdoers.'

2:35 Here (cf. 7:19) the Qur'ān has God tell Adam and "his mate" not to *approach* the tree, whereas in Genesis (2:17; cf. 3:3, which includes the command not to touch the tree) God tells Adam not to *eat of* the tree (specifically described as the "tree of the knowledge of good and evil"). Genesis also refers to a second tree, the tree of life (2:9; 3:22, 24). The Qur'ān refers to only one tree, apparently (see 20:120: "tree of immortality") the tree of life. With these matters the Qur'ān reflects Syriac Christian exegesis of Genesis (on this see commentary on 7:19–22). Witztum, *Syriac Milieu*, 81–88, who refers to earlier literature, including Speyer (*BEQ*, 71), suggests that the Qur'ān's position may be a response to those Biblical verses (see Pro 3:18; Wis 17:11) that seem to connect the themes of life and wisdom or knowledge.

---

³⁶Then Satan caused them to stumble from it, and he dislodged them from what [state] they were in; and We said, 'Get down, being enemies of one another! On the earth shall be your abode and sustenance for a time.'

2:36 In Genesis (3:1) only a snake appears in the garden. The association of this snake with Satan is made in the New Testament (see Rom 16:20; Rev 12:9) and accordingly is taken for granted by most Christian authors (most Jewish authors, in contrast, consider the snake to be nothing but a snake). The Qur'ān takes the Christian idea further by getting rid of the snake entirely and having only Satan in the garden.

Satan's eagerness to "dislodge" Adam and Eve follows from verse 34. There Iblīs (when referring to the devil as a rebellious angel the Qur'ān always names him Iblīs; when referring to him as a tempter of humans, it always names him Satan) becomes an unbeliever when he refuses to prostrate before Adam. The connection between the story of the prostration and Satan's plot against Adam and Eve is already found in Christian texts such as *The Life of Adam and Eve*, according to which the devil blamed Adam for his fall and desired revenge:

> Satan also wept loudly and said to Adam. "All my arrogance and sorrow came to pass because of you; for, because of you I went forth from my dwelling; and because of you I was alienated from the throne of the cherubs who, having spread out a shelter, used to enclose me; because of you my feet have trodden the earth."
>
> Adam replied and said to him, "What are our sins against you, that you did all this to us?"
>
> Satan replied and said, "You did nothing to me, but I came to this measure because of you, on the day on which you were created, for I went forth on that day. When God breathed his spirit into you, you received the likeness of his image. Thereupon, Michael came and made you bow down before God. God

said to Michael, 'Behold I have made Adam in the likeness of my image.' Then Michael summoned all the angels and God said to them, 'Come, bow down to god whom I made.' Michael bowed first. He called me and said. 'You too, bow down to Adam.' I said, 'Go away, Michael! I shall not bow down to him who is posterior to me, for I am former'" (*The Life of Adam and Eve,* Armenian version, 12.1–14.3).

On the temptation of Adam and Eve see commentary on 7:19–22 (with further references).

The Qurʾān has God send Adam, Eve, and Satan (the command "Get down!" is second-person plural) *down* from the Garden because it conceives of paradise, in line with Jewish and Syriac Christian tradition, on the top of a cosmic mountain (see commentary on 2:25 and 2:38).

---

³⁷Then Adam received certain words from his Lord, and He turned to him clemently. Indeed, He is the All-clement, the All-merciful.

2:37 The Qurʾān here suggests that God forgave Adam for his sin or transgression. Hilali-Khan translate the phrase "He turned to him clemently" as "And his Lord pardoned him." This would seem to mark a departure from the Bible, as Genesis does not mention God's forgiveness of Adam (although God's mercy may be suggested by his sewing of garments for Adam and Eve in Gen 3:21). However, in certain Syriac Christian texts—including *Cave of Treasures*—God addresses Adam with words of comfort before Adam leaves the garden (cf. the Qurʾānic phrase "Adam received certain words from his Lord").

God spoke to Adam, comforted him, and said: "Do not grieve Adam, because I will restore your inheritance to you. Look at how I have loved you. I cursed the land because of you, but I have preserved you from the curse." (*Cave of Treasures* [Oc.], 5:2–4).

---

³⁸We said, 'Get down from it, all together! Yet, should any guidance come to you from Me, those who follow My guidance shall have no fear, nor shall they grieve.

2:38 The Qur'ān follows a cosmology common in Late Antiquity, especially among Syriac Christians, by which the Garden of Eden lies on top of a cosmic mountain, and therefore here has God tell Adam, Eve, and Satan "Get *down* from it" (see commentary on 2:25). This verse might be compared with the poetic lines of the Syriac Christian author Jacob of Serugh (d. 521), who has Satan drag Adam down to earth in his *Homily on the Departure of Adam from Paradise:*

> When the deceiver attempted to knock down the house of Adam, / he himself
> fell from the celestial station.
> His fall cast him into the deep. / Once among the watchful,
> He seized Adam and, / fell with him who had been weakened. (vv. 135–40)

The Qur'ān here also has God comfort Adam with a mention of divine guidance (cf. 7:25, where God informs Adam of the resurrection; see commentary on 7:23–25).

---

³⁹But those who are faithless and deny Our signs, they shall be the inmates of the Fire and they shall remain in it [forever]. ⁴⁰O Children of Israel, remember My blessing which I bestowed upon you, and fulfill My covenant that I may fulfill your covenant, and be in awe of Me [alone].

2:40 The Qur'ān shifts here from a third-person description of the fall of Adam (and the devil) to a discourse in which God speaks directly to the "Children of Israel." It is not always clear if the Qur'ān means this passage to be God's words addressed to the Israelites in the past or words addressed to the Jews living at the time of Muḥammad.

That the Qur'ān has God command the Israelites to "remember" (v. 40) may follow from the manner in which God, in the Pentateuch, asks the Israelites to remember God's favors to them, above all in rescuing them from the grip of Pharaoh (and the waters of the sea) in Egypt and in inviting them to form a special covenant with him on Mt. Sinai (cf. the end of v. 40):

> Remember the Lord your God; he was the one who gave you the strength
> to act effectively like this, thus keeping then, as today, the covenant which

he swore to your ancestors. (Deu 8:18; cf. Exo 13:3; Deu 5:15b; Deu 7:18; 15:15; 16:12; 24:18)

---

⁴¹And believe in that which I have sent down confirming that which is with you, and do not be the first ones to deny it, and do not sell My signs for a paltry gain, and be wary of Me [alone].

⁴²Do not mix the truth with falsehood, nor conceal the truth while you know.

2:42 The suggestion that the Jews conceal the truth is a prominent theme of the Qur'ān's anti-Jewish polemic. In this regard the Qur'ān is not far from the arguments of the Syriac Christian fathers who claim that the Jews have failed to recognize the meaning of their scriptures. See further commentary on 4:46 (with further references).

---

⁴³And maintain the prayer, and give the *zakāt,* and bow along with those who bow [in prayer].

⁴⁴Will you bid others to piety and forget yourselves, while you recite the Book? Do you not exercise your reason?

2:44 Wāḥidī comments on this verse: "This was revealed about the Jews of Medina. . . . They used to enjoin people to follow Islam while abstaining themselves from doing so." In fact, this verse is reminiscent of the polemic against the Jewish Pharisees in Matthew 23:1–4:

¹Then addressing the crowds and his disciples Jesus said,
²'The scribes and the Pharisees occupy the chair of Moses.
³You must therefore do and observe what they tell you; but do not be guided by what they do, since they do not practise what they preach.
⁴They tie up heavy burdens and lay them on people's shoulders, but will they lift a finger to move them? Not they! (cf. Luk 11:46; Rom 2:18–21)

⁴⁵And take recourse in patience and prayer, and it is indeed
hard except for the humble ⁴⁶—those who are certain they will
encounter their Lord and that they will return to Him.

⁴⁷O Children of Israel, remember My blessing which I bestowed
upon you, and that I gave you an advantage over all the nations.

2:47–74 *overview* Verse 47 seems to reflect the prominent Biblical doctrine
(as seen, for example, in Exo 4:22; 19:5–6; Deu 7; 10:15; 2Sa 7:23–24; Isa
43:20–21) according to which Israel was the one nation with whom God had a
special relationship. See commentary on 2:122–23.

The passage that follows (vv. 48–74, with certain interludes) refers to anecdotes connected principally with the wanderings of the Israelites in the desert.
However, the Qur'ān does not simply report these anecdotes as they are found
in Exodus or Numbers. Instead it weaves these references into a larger argument
about the infidelity of the Jews. In this way its approach is like that of Psalm 106,
in which the Psalmist recalls the infidelity of his own people:

> ⁹At his rebuke the Sea of Reeds dried up, he let them pass through the deep
> as though it were desert,
> ¹⁰so he saved them from their opponents' clutches, rescued them from the
> clutches of their enemies.
> ¹¹The waters enveloped their enemies, not one of whom was left.
> ¹²Then they believed what he had said, and sang his praises.
> ¹³But they soon forgot his achievements, they did not even wait for his
> plans;
> . . .
> ¹⁹At Horeb they made a calf, bowed low before cast metal;
> ²⁰they exchanged their glory for the image of a grass-eating bull.
> ²¹They forgot the God who was saving them, who had done great deeds in
> Egypt . . . (Psa 106:9–13; 19–21; cf. Exo 32:1–6, 23; Num 14:20–23; Psa
> 95:8–11; Jer 31:31–32)

One might also compare this passage to the speech of Stephen before the
Sanhedrin in Acts of the Apostles, in which Stephen reprimands the Israelites
for the manner in which they have been unfaithful to the God who did so much
for them (Act 7:39–42; cf. 1Co 10:1–11).

[48]Beware of the day when no soul will compensate for another, neither any intercession shall be accepted from it, nor any ransom shall be received from it, nor will they be helped.

2:47–48 In regard to v. 47 *Tafsīr al-Jalālayn* specifies that God preferred the Israelites over other nations "of their time." To this end Hilali-Khan add to their translation: "(of your time period, in the past)."

These two verses (cf. the parallel passage 2:122–23) are a refrain with a two-part message: God chose Israel among all nations (cf. 2:122; 7:140; 44:32; 45:16), but this election will not save them on the Day of Judgment. The message is similar to that of Paul in Romans 3:1–6.

[49][Recall] when We delivered you from Pharaoh's clan who inflicted a terrible torment on you, and slaughtered your sons and spared your women, and in that there was a great test from your Lord.

2:49 Cf. 7:127, 141; 14:6; 28:4; 40:25:

[15]The king of Egypt then spoke to the Hebrew midwives, one of whom was called Shiphrah, and the other Puah.
[16]'When you attend Hebrew women in childbirth,' he said, 'look at the two stones. If it is a boy, kill him; if a girl, let her live.' (Exo 1:15–16)

[50]And when We parted the sea with you, and We delivered you and drowned Pharaoh's clan as you looked on.

2:50 On the drowning of Pharaoh and his army see commentary on 54:41–42 (with further references).

⁵¹And when We made an appointment with Moses for forty nights, you took up the Calf [for worship] in his absence, and you were wrongdoers.

2:51 On the golden calf episode in the Qurʾān, see commentary on 20:83–98 (with further references).

⁵²Then We excused you after that so that you might give thanks.

2:52 Cf. 4:153; 7:155:

¹¹Moses tried to pacify the Lord his God. 'Lord,' he said, 'why should your anger blaze at your people, whom you have brought out of Egypt by your great power and mighty hand?

. . .

¹⁴The Lord then relented over the disaster which he had intended to inflict on his people. (Exo 32:11, 14)

⁵³And when We gave Moses the Book and the Criterion so that you might be guided.

2:53 "The Book" is a translation of *al-kitāb*. This term indeed means "book" in modern standard Arabic, but in its Qurʾānic context it means "divine revelation" ("written" in heaven but not necessarily a book on earth). Here it seems to be a reference to the revelation of the "covenant" to Moses on Mt. Sinai (see Exo 34:1–28; cf. Exo 24:12, 18; 31:18; Deu 9:9–11; 10:3–5).

The word Qarai translates as "criterion" here is *furqān*. Most commentators generally understand this term according to the normal Arabic sense of the root *f.r.q.*: "difference" or "distinction." *Tafsīr al-Jalālayn* explains *furqān* as "the one that discriminates (*faraqa*) between truth and falsehood and between what is licit and illicit, so that you might be guided, by it away from error." Yet *furqān* (like *qurʾān*) reflects the morphology of Syro-Aramaic, in which language the root *f* (or *p*).*r.q.* relates to "salvation." As Arthur Jeffery points out (*FV,* 227), following Geiger (*Judaism and Islam,* 40–41), *furqān* is particularly close to the Aramaic *purqānā* (used by the Targums for Psalm 3:8, meaning "salvation"). It is equally possible that the term derives from Syriac or from Christian Palestinian Aramaic. In 8:29 and 8:41 the Qurʾān indeed seems to use *furqān* with the meaning of "salvation." Here (and in Q 2:185; 3:4; 21:48; 25:1), however, *furqān* seems to have the meaning of "revelation." Thus "Book" and *furqān* seem to be two euphemistic references to revelation, much like "the Book and the Wisdom" (Q 2:129, 151, 231; 3:48, 81, 164; 4:54; passim).

---

⁵⁴And [recall] when Moses said to his people, 'O my people! You have indeed wronged yourselves by taking up the Calf [for worship]. Now turn penitently to your Maker, and slay [the guilty among] your folks. That will be better for you with your Maker.' Then He turned to you clemently. Indeed, He is the All-clement, the All-merciful.

2:54 Understood literally the Qurʾān here has God command the Israelites to kill themselves. *Tafsīr al-Jalālayn* relates that God sent down a dark cloud that kept the Israelites from discerning the innocent from the guilty. They proceeded to slaughter one another until seventy thousand were dead. Our translator, however, adds in brackets "the guilty among" to suggest that God was commanding the righteous to kill the unrighteous. If his understanding is correct, the Qurʾān may be developing Exodus 32:26–27:

> ²⁶Moses then stood at the gate of the camp and shouted, 'Who is for the Lord? To me!' And all the Levites rallied round him.
> ²⁷He said to them, 'the Lord, God of Israel, says this, "Buckle on your sword, each of you, and go up and down the camp from gate to gate, every man of you slaughtering brother, friend and neighbour."

However, the Arabic word (*anfusakum*) translated here "your folk" can also mean "your souls," and the Qurʾān could be using this expression metaphorically to speak of repentance (this interpretation is suggested by 4:66). This metaphorical usage might reflect a number of New Testament passages (e.g., Mat 10:39; 16:24–26; Mar 8:34–37; Luk 9:23–25; 14:26b; 17:33; Joh 12:25; Eph 4:22–24). Asad, for example, understands the "killing" to be metaphorical and translates, "mortify yourselves."

On the golden calf episode in the Qur'ān see commentary on 20:83–98 (with further references).

---

⁵⁵And when you said, 'O Moses, we will not believe you until we see God visibly,' a thunderbolt seized you as you looked on. ⁵⁶Then We raised you up after your death so that you might give thanks.

2:55–56 The report that the Israelites sought to see God (v. 55) is also found in 4:153. It may be related to Exodus 19:21, where God tells Moses, "Go down and warn the people not to break through to look at the Lord, or many of them will perish" (Exo 19:21). As Speyer (*BEQ*, 289) mentions here, the midrashic work *Exodus Rabbah* (29:3; 41:3) declares explicitly that the Israelites demanded to see God.

Here the Qur'ān relates that the Israelites were struck by a *ṣā'iqa* (Qarai renders this as "thunderbolt"—cf. 2:19, "thunderclaps"; 4:153; and the verb *ṣa'iqa* at 39:68) for the impudence of their demand and then raised up (v. 56) for doing so. This is connected to a tradition found in the Babylonian Talmud on the effect of the divine word on the Israelites (one might also compare the fire, lightning, and thunder in the theophany accounts of Exo 19:16–18; 24:17):

> R. Joshua b. Levi also said: At every word which went forth from the mouth of the Holy One, blessed be He, the souls of Israel departed, for it is said, My soul went forth when he spake. But since their souls departed at the first word, how could they receive the second word?—He brought down the dew with which He will resurrect the dead and revived them. (b. Shabbat 88b)

In Exodus 33:18 Moses asks to see God (and is allowed only to see him from behind); this is alluded to in 7:143. The Qur'ān also alludes to the impious demand of Pharaoh to see God (28:38). Q 7:155, without much explanation, has the Israelites struck instead by a *rajfa* (according to Qarai, an "earthquake").

---

[57]We shaded you with clouds, and sent down to you manna and quails [saying]: 'Eat of the good things We have provided for you.' And they did not wrong Us, but they used to wrong [only] themselves.

2:57 The Qur'ān here alludes to manna and quails (on which see commentary on 7:160, with further references). The reference to quails appears both in Exodus 16 and Numbers 11, and is alluded to in Psalm 78 (cr. Holger Zellentin):

[23]Even so he gave orders to the skies above, he opened the sluice-gates of heaven;
[24]he rained down manna to feed them, he gave them the wheat of heaven;
[25]mere mortals ate the bread of the Mighty, he sent them as much food as they could want.
[26]He roused an east wind in the heavens, despatched a south wind by his strength;
[27]he rained down meat on them like dust, birds thick as sand on the seashore,
[28]tumbling into the middle of his camp, all around his dwelling-place.
[29]They ate as much food as they wanted, he satisfied all their cravings;
[30]but their cravings were still upon them, the food was still in their mouths,
[31]when the wrath of God attacked them, slaughtering their strongest men, laying low the flower of Israel. (Psa 78:23–31)

---

[58]And when We said, 'Enter this town, and eat thereof freely whencesoever you wish, and enter while prostrating at the gate, and say, "Relieve [us of the burden of our sins]," so that We may forgive your iniquities and soon We will enhance the virtuous.' [59]But the wrongdoers changed the saying with other than what they were told. So We sent down on those who were wrongdoers a plague from the sky because of the transgressions they used to commit.

2:58–59 This passage is parallel to 7:161–62. The "town" (*qarya*) of verse 58 may be Jerusalem, notwithstanding the context of this passage, namely the Exodus of the Israelites (cf. 5:21–26). In the Bible the Israelites enter Jerusalem only in Judges 1 (and then to destroy it). However, the Qur'ān seems to reflect here the prophetic announcement of Moses in Exodus 15 (when the Israelites are still at the beginning of their exodus) of the foundation of Jerusalem: "You will bring them in and plant them on the mountain which is your heritage, the place which you, the Lord, have made your dwelling, the sanctuary, the Lord, prepared by your own hands" (Exo 15:17).

The reference to eating (cf. the similar phrase addressed to Adam in 2:35), meanwhile, reflects the prophecies in Deu 12:7 and 12:20: "And that is where you must eat in the presence of the Lord your God, rejoicing over your labours, you and your households, because the Lord your God has blessed you" (Deu 12:7; cf. Deu 12:20; Isa 25:6; Luk 14:15; Rev 19:7–9).

The latter part of this verse connects the command to "enter prostrating at the gate" (cf. 4:154; 7:161) with the command to say *ḥiṭṭa,* a word that has long confused commentators (Qarai adds a phrase in his attempt to render this word: "Relieve [us of the burden of our sins]"). *Ḥiṭṭa* corresponds with the Hebrew word that means "wheat," and in Deuteronomy 8:8 the promised land is called "a land of wheat." Yet the Qur'ān does not seem to be interested in wheat here. Speyer (*BEQ,* 337) explains this term with a reference to Numbers 14:40, where the Israelites, referring to the land, declare that they have sinned (Hb. *ḥāṭā'nū;* compare also the Syriac: *ḥṭīn*): "Early next morning they set out for the heights of the hill country saying, 'Look, we will set out for the place about which the Lord said that *we have sinned*'" (Num 14:40).

The command to enter the gate prostrating in verse 58 might be related to Jeremiah 7:2: "Stand at the gate of the Temple of the Lord and there proclaim this message. Say, 'Listen to the word of the Lord, all you of Judah who come in by these gates to worship [lit. "prostrate to"] the Lord'" (Jer 7:2).

The "plague from the sky" (v. 59) appears to be a reference to one of the punishments meted out to the Israelites during their wanderings in the desert, perhaps that referred to in Numbers 11:33. One might also compare (see *BEQ,* 338) this phrase with Romans 1:18: "The retribution of God from heaven is being revealed against the ungodliness and injustice of human beings who in their injustice hold back the truth."

---

⁶⁰And when Moses prayed for water for his people, We said, 'Strike the rock with your staff.' Thereat twelve fountains gushed

forth from it; every tribe came to know its drinking-place. 'Eat and drink of God's provision, and do not act wickedly on the earth, causing corruption.'

2:60 The Qur'ān here integrates the story of Moses striking a rock at Massah and Meribah (Exo 17:1–7; cf. Num 20:1–22; Deu 33:8; Psa 95:8) with a detail in Exodus 15 where the Israelites (a people divided into twelve tribes) find twelve springs at Elim. The connection with Elim seems to be confirmed by the way the Qur'ān also commands the Israelites to eat in this verse, as the Israelites also found seventy palm trees (from which one might eat dates) there:

> [5]The Lord then said to Moses, 'Go on ahead of the people, taking some of the elders of Israel with you; in your hand take the staff with which you struck the River, and go.
> [6]I shall be waiting for you there on the rock (at Horeb). Strike the rock, and water will come out for the people to drink.' This was what Moses did, with the elders of Israel looking on. (Exo 17:5–6; cf. Num 20:11)
> So they came to Elim where there were twelve springs and seventy palm trees; and there they pitched camp beside the water. (Exo 15:27)

---

[61]And when you said, 'O Moses, 'We will not put up with one kind of food. So invoke your Lord for us, so that He may bring forth for us of that which the earth grows—its greens and cucumbers, its garlic, lentils, and onions.' He said, 'Do you seek to replace what is superior with that which is inferior? Go down to any town and you will indeed get what you ask for!' So they were struck with abasement and poverty, and they earned God's wrath. That, because they would deny the signs of God and kill the prophets unjustly. That, because they would disobey and commit transgressions.

2:61 The opening passage of this verse relates to a recurring theme in the Biblical accounts of the Israelites' exodus, namely their declarations of regret for having been taken out of Egypt (as in Num 11:4–6; also Exo 16:3; Num 21:5), where they ate well. Qarai's translation has God declare in response, "Go down to any town." The word translated as "town" (*miṣr*) is more likely a reference to Egypt (thus the passage would mean "Go back to Egypt and you will get what's coming to you!"). Elsewhere (Q 12:21, 99; 43:51) the Qur'ān uses *miṣr* for Egypt.

The Qur'ān also alludes here to the punishment which God inflicted on the Israelites for the way they complained about their food (see Num 11:33). The anti-Jewish perspective of this verse, including the description of the Israelites as a people who "kill the prophets," is connected to New Testament passages such as Matthew 23:34–38 (cf. Luk 13:34–35) and Acts 7:52 (see Paret, *Kommentar*, 20; Horovitz, *KU*, 40). See also commentary on 3:181–82 (with further references).

---

⁶²Indeed, the faithful, the Jews, the Christians and the Sabaeans—those who have faith in God and the Last Day and act righteously—they shall have their reward near their Lord, and they will have no fear, nor will they grieve.

2:62 This verse is largely parallel to 5:69. The identity of the Sabaeans is a matter of debate to classical Muslim interpreters and academic scholars alike; the most common hypothesis is that the term refers to the Mandaeans (known by the misnomer: "Christians of St. John") of southern Iraq. Bell (*Commentary*, 1:12), comments that this term "has baffled all investigators."

Many Muslim interpreters argue that the promise of salvation to Jews and Christians here applies only to those who lived before Muḥammad. Hilali-Khan explain in a footnote to this verse: "After the coming of Prophet Muḥammad on the earth, no other religion except Islam, will be accepted from anyone."

---

⁶³And when We took a pledge from you, and raised the Mount above you, [declaring], 'Hold on with power to what We have given you and remember that which is in it so that you may be Godwary.'

2:63 The Qur'ān here returns to the story of the Israelites. The Mount is Mt. Sinai, where God gave the Law to Israel. The idea of "raising the Mount" above Israel—which may be difficult to picture—reflects an interpretation of Exodus 19:17 (cf. Deu 4:10) preserved in the Babylonian Talmud (cf. 4:154; 7:171):

And they stood under mount: R. Abdimi b. Ḥama b. Ḥasa said: This teaches that the Holy One, blessed be He, overturned the mountain upon them like an [inverted] cask. (b. Shabbat, 88a; cf. Avodah Zarah, 2b)

---

[64]Again you turned away after that; and were it not for God's grace on you and His mercy, you would have surely been among the losers.

[65]And certainly you know those of you who violated the Sabbath, whereupon We said to them, 'Be you spurned apes.' [66]So We made it an exemplary punishment for the present and the succeeding [generations], and an advice to the Godwary.

2:65 On the curse of the People of the Sabbath, see commentary on 7:163–66 (with further references).

---

[67]And when Moses said to his people, 'God commands you to slaughter a cow,' they said, 'Are you mocking us?' He said, 'I seek God's protection lest I should be one of the ignorant!'

[68]They said, 'Invoke your Lord for us, that He may clarify for us what she may be.' He said, 'He says, She is a cow, neither old nor young, of a middle age. Now do what you are commanded.'

[69]They said, 'Invoke your Lord for us, that He may clarify for us what her colour may be.' He said, 'He says, She is a cow that is yellow, of a bright hue, pleasing to the onlookers.'

⁷⁰They said, 'Invoke your Lord for us, that He may clarify for us what she may be. Indeed, all cows are much alike to us, and if God wishes we will surely be guided.'

⁷¹He said, 'He says, She is a cow not broken to till the earth or water the tillage, sound and without blemish.' They said, 'Now have you come up with the truth!' And they slaughtered it, though they were about not to do it.

2:67–71 The Qur'ān (vv. 67, 71) here has the Israelites resist the command (cf. Num 19:1–3) to slay a cow, whereas they eagerly performed the unholy rite of worshipping another cow: the golden calf. The Qur'ān's emphasis on the Israelites' uncertainty about exactly what sort of cow is called for reflects debates in Mishnah *Parah* over the age of the cow, its purity, and its precise color (in v. 69 the Qur'ān uses a word, *ṣafrā'*, that today is understood to mean "yellow," but its original sense might be closer to "red"; the Hb. word in Numbers means lit. "blood-colored"):

> R. Eliezer ruled: The heifer must be no more than one year old and the red cow no more than two years old. But the Sages ruled: The heifer may be even two years old and the red cow even three or four years old. R. Meir ruled: Even five years old. One that is older is valid, but they did not wait with it so long since it might in the meantime grow some black hairs and [thus] become invalid. (m. Parah, 1:1; cf. Parah 2:5)

While the notion of slaughtering a cow which has not been put to work reflects Numbers 19:1–3, the following passage (Q 2:72–73; see commentary on those verses) reflects Deuteronomy 21 (on this juxtaposition, see Hirschfeld, *New Researches,* 108; Bell, *Commentary* 1:13).

---

⁷²And when you killed a soul, and accused one another about it—and God was to expose what you were concealing—⁷³We said, 'Strike him with a piece of it:' thus does God revive the dead, and He shows you His signs so that you may exercise your reason.

2:72–3 This passage—in which the Israelites are commanded to strike a murder victim with a piece of a slaughtered cow (the "it" of v. 73 is feminine in Arabic, as is the Arabic word for cow) is related to Deuteronomy 21:1–8, which instructs the Israelites to kill a cow as part of a ritual to deal with an unsolved murder. Most scholars argue that in verses 67–73 the Qur'ān joins two different rituals involving two different cows (the red cow of Num 1–3 for vv. 67–71 and the cow of Deu 21 for vv. 72–73). The reason for this joining may be that while Deuteronomy 21 describes a ritual involving the corpse of a murder victim found in the open country, Numbers 19 explains that the water with the ashes of the red cow should be used to purify those who touch a corpse (v. 11)—and specifically mentions those who touch the corpse of a murder victim found in the open country (v. 16).

Yet there is something more in the Qur'ān's account here, namely the idea that touching the victim will bring him to life, presumably so that he can accuse his murderer. This idea seems to be related to a report in the Infancy Gospel of Thomas by which Jesus raised one of his dead friends in order to exonerate himself from the accusation of murder:

> And again, after many days, Jesus was playing with other children on a certain roof of an upstairs room. And one of the children fell and died. The other children, seeing this, went to their homes. And they left Jesus alone. The parents of the dead child came and accused Jesus saying, "You knocked down our child." But Jesus said, "I did not knock him down." And while they were raging and shouting, Jesus came down from the roof and stood beside the body and cried out in a loud voice saying, "Zeno, Zeno—for this was his name—rise and say if I knocked you down." And he rose and said, "No, Lord." (*Infancy Gospel of Thomas*, 8:1–3)

This report signals the power of Jesus over life and death, while the Qur'ān uses the case of a cow's bringing the victim to life to signal how God has the power to "revive the dead."

Tafsīr al-Jalālayn provides here an account of a murdered man, explaining: "When he was struck with its [i.e., the cow's] tongue or its tail, he came back to life and said, 'So-and-so killed me,' and after pointing out two of his cousins, he died; the two [killers] were denied the inheritance and were later killed."

———————

⁷⁴Then your hearts hardened after that; so they are like stones, or even harder. For there are indeed some stones from which streams gush forth, and there are some of them that split and

water issues from them, and there are some that fall for the fear of God. And God is not oblivious of what you do.

[75]Are you then eager that they should believe you, though a part of them would hear the word of God and then they would distort it after they had understood it, and they knew [what they were doing]?

[76]When they meet the faithful, they say, 'We believe,' and when they are alone with one another, they say, 'Do you recount to them what God has revealed to you, so that they may argue with you therewith before your Lord? Do you not exercise your reason?'

[77]Do they not know that God knows whatever they hide and whatever they disclose?

[78]And among them are the illiterate who know nothing of the Book except hearsay, and they only make conjectures.

[79]So woe to them who write the Book with their hands and then say, 'This is from God,' that they may sell it for a paltry gain. So woe to them for what their hands have written, and woe to them for what they earn!

2:78–79 The word that our translation renders in verse 78 as "illiterate"—*ummiyyūn* (sing. *ummī;* cf. 3:20; 3:75; 7:157–58; 62:2)—in fact refers to those who do not know the word of God (cf. 3:20). The Qurʾān refers to Muḥammad as an *ummī* prophet (Q 7:157–58) because he came from a people to whom God had not yet sent down revelation ("the Book"); in 29:47–48 the Qurʾān, as Holger Zellentin points out (*The Qurʾānʾs Legal Culture,* 158n2), denies that Muḥammad wrote down the scripture, but this of course is not the same as affirming that he was illiterate. Thus the Qurʾān is not referring here to those who cannot read or write (which would make it rather difficult for them to "write the Book with their hands"; v. 79) but to those who do not know divine revelation. It seems to be accusing certain Jews (the larger context of this Sura involves the Israelites and their sins) of not knowing the word of God and therefore being *ummī*. This polemic is close to that of several New Testament passages (Mat 15:7–9; Mar 7:1–9; Luk 11:39–42).

On verse 79 al-Wahidi relates, "This was revealed about those who had changed the description of the Prophet and altered his traits. Al-Kalbi mentioned . . . : They had changed the description of God's Messenger in their Scripture. They made him white and tall while the Prophet was brown and of medium height. They had said to their followers and companions: 'Look at the description of the prophet who will be sent at the end of time; his description does not match that of this [man].' The Jewish rabbis and doctors used to gain some worldly benefits from the Jewish people and so they were afraid of losing this gain if they were ever to show the real description."

---

[80]And they say, 'The Fire shall not touch us except for a number of days.' Say, 'Have you taken a promise from God? If so, God will never break His promise. Or do you ascribe to God what you do not know?'

[81]Certainly whoever commits misdeeds and is besieged by his iniquity—such shall be the inmates of the Fire, and they will remain in it [forever].

2:80–81 Wāḥidī explains these verses with a story about a particular belief of the Jews in Medina: "God's Messenger came to Medina and found the Jews saying: 'This worldly life will last seven thousand years. And for every one thousand years of the days of this worldly life people will be tormented in hell fire for one day of the days of the Afterlife. Thus, the torment will last for only seven days.'"

This passage (cf. Q 3:24) may be connected to a tradition by which the Talmud identifies three groups on the Day of Judgment, one of which will suffer only a temporary punishment in Gehinnom:

> It has been taught: Beth Shammai [said], There will be three groups at the Day of Judgment—one of thoroughly righteous, one of thoroughly wicked, and one of intermediate. The thoroughly righteous will forthwith be inscribed definitively as entitled to everlasting life; the thoroughly wicked will forthwith be inscribed definitively as doomed to Gehinnom. . . . The intermediate will go down to Gehinnom and squeal and rise again, as it says, "And I will bring the third part through the fire, and will refine them as silver is refined, and will try them as gold is tried. They shall call on my name and I will

answer them" [Zec 13:9] Of them, too, Hannah said, "The Lord killeth and maketh alive, he bringeth down to the grave and bringeth up" [1Sa 2:6]. (b. Rosh Hashanah 16b–17a)

Later in the same passage (b. Rosh Hashanah 17a) the Talmud makes a distinction between Israelites and Gentiles who sin—who suffer for only twelve months—and those who reject the community and suffer eternally.

———

⁸²And those who have faith and do righteous deeds—they shall be the inhabitants of paradise; they shall remain in it [forever].

⁸³When We took a pledge from the Children of Israel, [saying]: 'Worship no one but God, do good to your parents, relatives, orphans, and the needy, speak kindly to people, maintain the prayer, and give the *zakāt,'* you turned away, except a few of you, and you were disregardful.

2:83 On the Qur'ān and the Ten Commandments, see commentary on 17:22–39 (with further references). On kindness to orphans, see commentary on 107:2 (with further references).

———

⁸⁴And when We took a pledge from you, [saying]: 'You shall not shed your [own people's] blood, and you shall not expel your folks from your homes,' you pledged, and you testify [to this pledge of your ancestors]. ⁸⁵Then there you were, killing your folks and expelling a part of your folks from their homes, backing one another against them in sin and aggression! If they came to you as captives, you would ransom them, though their expulsion itself was forbidden you. What! Do you believe in part of the Book and deny another part? So what is the requital of those of you who do that except disgrace in the life of this

world? And on the Day of Resurrection, they shall be consigned to the severest punishment. And God is not oblivious of what you do.

[86]They are the ones who bought the life of this world for the Hereafter; so their punishment shall not be lightened, nor will they be helped.

[87]Certainly We gave Moses the Book and followed him with the apostles, and We gave Jesus, the son of Mary, clear proofs and confirmed him with the Holy Spirit. Is it not that whenever an apostle brought you that which was not to your liking, you would act arrogantly; so you would impugn a group [of them], and slay a[nother] group?

2:87 *Tafsīr al-Jalālayn,* in line with the majority opinion of Islamic tradition, identifies the Holy Spirit here as the angel Gabriel. However, of the four times "Holy Spirit" appears in the Qur'ān, it is associated with Jesus three times (Q 2:87, 253; 5:110), always with the expression "We confirmed [or better, 'supported'] him with the Holy Spirit." (The fourth case, 16:102, suggests that the Qur'ān was revealed through this same Spirit.) Thus the Qur'ān seems to reflect here the Christian notion of a close relationship between God, the Spirit, and Christ, even while it refutes the divinity of Christ (for God's sending the Holy Spirit down upon Jesus, see Luk 3:21–22; cf. Mat 3:16–17, 4:1; Mar 1:9–11, 12; Joh 1:32). The way the Qur'ān introduces "Holy Spirit" with *ayyadnāhu bi* ("We supported him with") in all three cases involving Jesus may reflect a Christian notion of the Holy Spirit as the "Paraclete" (Joh 14:16, 26; 15:26; 16:7). Greek *paraklètos* means "called to the side of" or idiomatically "advocate" (Latin *advocatus*).

The Qur'ānic term for Holy Spirit (*rūḥ al-qudus*), a juxtaposition of two nouns, may owe something to Syriac *rūḥā d-qūdshā.* However, it might also be compared to the (few) Sabaean (South Arabian) Christian inscriptions, such as that (known as CIH 541) at the Ma'rib dam, which refers to the Holy Spirit as *rḥ qds* (see the online *Corpus of South Arabian Inscriptions,* CIH 541, l. 3; and Robin, "Du paganisme," 147).

In this verse the Qur'ān again accuses the Israelites of killing the prophets (on which see commentary on 3:181–82, with further references).

[88]And they say, 'Our hearts are uncircumcised.' Rather, God has cursed them for their unfaith, so few of them have faith.

2:88 Here and in 4:155 the Qur'ān has the Jews themselves declare that their "hearts are uncircumcised." *Tafsīr al-Jalālayn* understands this same phrase to mean "our hearts are encased" and relates a tradition by which the Jews of Medina used this phrase to tell Muḥammad that their hearts "cannot comprehend what you say." The Qur'ān is here reapplying the metaphor of an uncircumcised heart in the Bible and later Christian anti-Jewish polemic. Several passages of the Old Testament accuse the Israelites of being uncircumcised of heart, even while they are circumcised in the flesh (Jer 9:26; cf. also Lev 26:41; Deu 10:16). This metaphor becomes central to Christian rhetoric. It is cited (along with the accusation that the Jews killed their prophets, an accusation raised by the Qur'ān in the previous verse) by Stephen in his speech before the Sanhedrin in Acts: "You stubborn people, with uncircumcised hearts and ears. You are always resisting the Holy Spirit, just as your ancestors used to do" (Act 7:51; cf. Rom 2:29). Subsequently it becomes a central trope in Syriac Christian anti-Jewish polemic, seen with Aphrahat (d. ca. 345) and Ephrem, among others:

> So it is known that whoever does not circumcise the foreskin of his heart, then also the circumcision of his flesh is of no value to him. (Aphrahat, *Homilies (On Circumcision)*, trans. Neusner, 23).

> Ask yourself, you fool, about the observance of the Law.
> What can circumcision do for a sin that lies within?
> Sin lies inside the heart;
> And you circumcise your foreskin! (Ephrem, *Sermones de fide*, 28, homily 3, ll. 233–37)

The Qur'ān, however, is not interested in the play on circumcision of the flesh or the heart but instead has the Jews use this expression simply as a way of declaring that their hearts are covered. In this it is parallel to those passages where the Qur'ān declares that God has cast veils on the hearts of unbelievers (6:25; 17:45–46; 18:57; 41:5) or made their ears deaf (2:7; 6:25; 31:7; 41:44). On the cursing of the Jews in particular, see commentary on 5:13–14 (with further references).

⁸⁹And when there came to them a Book from God, confirming that which is with them—and earlier they would pray for victory over the pagans—so when there came to them what they recognized, they denied it. So may the curse of God be on the faithless!

⁹⁰Evil is that for which they have sold their souls, by defying what God has sent down, out of envy that God should bestow His grace on any of His servants that He wishes. Thus they earned wrath upon wrath, and there is a humiliating punishment for the faithless.

⁹¹When they are told, 'Believe in what God has sent down,' they say, 'We believe in what was sent down to us,' and they disbelieve what is besides it, though it is the truth confirming what is with them. *Say,* 'Then why would you kill the prophets of God formerly, should you be faithful?'

⁹²Certainly Moses brought you manifest proofs, but then you took up the Calf in his absence and you were wrongdoers.

2:89–92 Islamic tradition generally holds these verses to be a condemnation of the Jews of Medina for their rejection of Muḥammad. Wāḥidī explains (on v. 89) that before the coming of Islam, the Jews of the region would pray that God might send forth a prophet. He continues: "But when the Prophet [Muḥammad] was sent forth, they disbelieved in him. It is due to this that God revealed [Q 2:89]." However, this passage follows immediately the mention of Moses and Jesus and an allusion to the Jewish rejection of Jesus (v. 87). It may accordingly refer to the denial of the revelation given to Jesus. On the golden calf (v. 92) in the Qurʾān, see commentary on 20:83–98 (with further references).

⁹³And when We took covenant with you and raised the Mount above you, [declaring], 'Hold on with power to what We have

given you, and do listen!' They said, 'We hear, and disobey,' and their hearts had been imbued with [the love of] the Calf, due to their unfaith. *Say,* 'Evil is that to which your faith prompts you, should you be faithful!'

2:93 The phrase "We hear and disobey," in Arabic *samiʿnā wa-ʿaṣaynā* (cf. 4:46), seems to be an intentional play on the Hebrew version of Deuteronomy 5:27: "Go nearer yourself and listen to everything that the Lord our God may say, and then tell us everything that the Lord our God has told you; we shall listen and put it into practice (*we-shāmaʿnū wa-ʿāsinū*)!" (cf. Exo 24:7). The Qurʾān uses a version of this phrase on three other occasions (Q 2:285; 5:7; 24:51)—but in the positive sense ("We hear and obey")—for the followers of its own prophet. See also commentary on 24:51.

The Arabic verb translated as "imbued" normally means "drank." By using this verb, the Qurʾān alludes to Exodus 32:19–20, where Moses compels the Israelites who had worshipped the golden calf to drink water in which powder from the calf had been mixed (cf. 20:97, where the ashes of the calf are instead scattered into the sea). Bell recognizes the allusion and translates "and they were made to drink the calf in their hearts for their unbelief." On the golden calf episode in the Qurʾān, see commentary on 20:83–98 (with further references).

---

⁹⁴*Say,* 'If the abode of the Hereafter were exclusively for you with God, and not for other people, then long for death, should you be truthful.'

2:94 The view attributed to the Jews here may be compared to the prophecy given to Daniel that the angel Michael (cf. Q 2:98 below) will protect the Israelites to the exclusion of all other people on the Day of Judgment:

At that time Michael will arise—the great Prince, defender of your people. That will be a time of great distress, unparalleled since nations first came into existence. When that time comes, your own people will be spared—all those whose names are found written in the Book. (Dan 12:1)

[95]But they will not long for it ever because of what their hands have sent ahead, and God knows best the wrongdoers. [96]Surely, you will find them the greediest of all people for life—even the idolaters. Each of them is eager to live a thousand years, though it would not deliver him from the punishment, were he to live [that long]. And God sees best what they do.

[97]*Say,* 'Whoever is an enemy of Gabriel [should know that] it is he who has brought it down on your heart with the will of God, confirming what has been [revealed] before it, and as a guidance and good news for the faithful.' [98][*Say,*] 'Whoever is an enemy of God, His apostles and His angels and Gabriel and Michael, [let him know that] God is indeed the enemy of the faithless.'

[99]We have certainly sent down manifest signs to *you,* and no one denies them except transgressors.

2:97–99 The identification of Gabriel as the agent, or messenger, of this revelation matches Gabriel's role as a messenger to Daniel (Dan 8:16; 9:21–27) in the Old Testament and to Zechariah (Luk 1:19) and Mary (Luk 1:26) in the New Testament.

[100]Is it not that whenever they made a covenant, a part of them would cast it away? Rather, the majority of them do not have faith.

[101]And when there came to them an apostle from God, confirming that which is with them, a part of those who were given the Book cast the Book of God behind their back, as if they did not know [that it is God's Book].

2:101 On the metaphor of "casting the Book of God behind their back," see commentary on 3:187

---

¹⁰²And they followed what the devils pursued during Solomon's reign—and Solomon was not faithless but it was the devils who were faithless—teaching the people magic and what was sent down to the two angels at Babylon, Hārūt and Mārūt, who would not teach anyone [the occult] without telling [him], 'We are only a test, so do not be faithless.' But they would learn from those two that with which they would cause a split between man and his wife—though they could not harm anyone with it except with God's leave. They would learn that which would harm them and bring them no benefit; though they certainly knew that anyone who buys it has no share in the Hereafter. Surely, evil is that for which they sold their souls, had they known!

2:102 The opening of this verse is an implicit accusation that the Jews (who are the subject of this section of Sura 2) practice magic as it was practiced in Solomon's time. In exegetical Jewish works, including the *Second Targum of Esther,* the glory of Solomon's realm (and the temple he constructed) is attributed to his mastery of magic (on this see also commentary on 34:12–13):

> All the kingdoms feared him, nations and languages were obedient to him; devils, demons, and ferocious beasts, evil spirits and accidents, were delivered into his hands. (*Second Targum of Esther,* 1:3, p. 269).

However, the Qurʾān, in line with the Talmud (b. Shabbat 56b), insists that Solomon remained faithful to God (pace 1 Kings, esp. chap. 11).

The Qurʾān also refers here to magic being sent down in Babylon, and indeed Babylon generally has a symbolic value as a center of astrology and magic in classical, Jewish, and Christian sources. Of particular interest in this context is the tradition of Jewish magic bowls from Babylon, which date from around the time of the Qurʾān's composition (see *Aramaic Bowl Spells*).

The names of the two angels, Hārūt and Mārūt, are shaped by the Qurʾān's interest in proper names that rhyme (e.g., Ṭālūt/Saul and Jālūt/Goliath; ʿĪsā/Jesus and Mūsā/Moses). Syriac *hertā* ("squabble, brawl, strife") may be behind Hārūt and Syriac *mertā* ("bitterness") behind Mārūt.

The idea that fallen angels revealed secrets to humans which led to their moral corruption is a central theme of the first part of the Book of Enoch with its fallen angel Azaz'el:

> And secondly the Lord said to Raphael, "Bind Azaz'el hand and foot (and) throw him into the darkness!" And he made a hole in the desert which was in Duda'el and cast him there; he threw on top of him rugged and sharp rocks. And he covered his face in order that he may not see light; and in order that he may be sent into the fire on the great day of judgment. . . . And the whole earth has been corrupted by Azaz'el's teaching of his (own) actions; and write upon him all sin. (1 Enoch 10:4–6, 8; cf. also *Pseudo-Clementines* 8:14)

The reference to "that with which they would cause a split between a man and his wife" may be connected to the story of the two wicked elders in Babylon (the same city where Hārūt and Mārūt are found in the Qur'ān) in the Greek story of Susanna, wife of Joakim (a story found as Daniel 13 in Catholic and Orthodox Bibles), according to which the elders falsely accuse Susanna of fornication (thereby seeking to "split" a man from his wife).

On the expression "no share in the Hereafter," see commentary on 2:200.

---

[103]Had they been faithful and Godwary, the reward from God would have been better, had they known!

[104]O you who have faith! Do not say *Rā'inā,* but say *Unẓurnā,* and listen! And there is a painful punishment for the faithless.

2:104 A number of academic scholars point out that *rā'inā* (Ar. "watch over us"; cf. 4:46) is close to Hebrew *rā'*, "evil." Horovitz ("Jewish Proper Names," 204, following Geiger, *Was hat Mohammed,* 17; *Judaism and Islam,* 12–13) argues that through the influence of Jews in Medina this word must have taken on a secondary, pejorative, sense because of its proximity to Hebrew *rā'*. Therefore Muḥammad commanded his followers to use *unẓurnā* ("look at us") instead. His theory is close to the traditional Islamic explanation of this verse, found, for example, with Wāḥidī:

> This is because the Arabs used to employ this expression [*ra'ina*], so when the Jews heard them using it with the Prophet they liked it. This same expression

in the parlance of the Jews had the connotation of vile abusive language. They said: "Before, we used to abuse Muḥammad secretly. Now, you can abuse him openly because this expression is used in their speech."

Alternatively the Qur'ān may simply be instructing its audience in what way they should ask God to watch over them, i.e. with the expression *unẓurnā* (cf. Ps. 16:1: "Protect me [Syr. *naṭrīn*], O God, in you is my refuge") and not with the expression *rā'inā*. A similar concern for particular locutions is also found in 2:58.

---

[105]Neither the faithless from among the People of the Book, nor the idolaters, like that any good be showered on you from your Lord; but God singles out for His mercy whomever He wishes, and God is dispenser of a mighty grace.

[106]For any verse that We abrogate or cause to be forgotten, We bring another better than it, or similar to it. Do you not know that God has power over all things? [107]Do you not know that to God belongs the kingdom of the heavens and the earth? And besides God you do not have any friend or helper.

[108]Would you question your Apostle as Moses was questioned formerly? Whoever changes faith for unfaith certainly strays from the right way.

[109]Many of the People of the Book are eager to turn you into unbelievers after your faith, out of their inner envy, [and] after the truth had become manifest to them. Yet excuse [them] and forbear until God issues His edict. Indeed, God has power over all things.

[110]And maintain the prayer and give the *zakāt*. Any good that you send ahead for your own souls, you shall find it with God. God indeed watches what you do.

[111]And they say, 'No one will enter paradise except one who is a Jew or Christian.' Those are their [false] hopes! *Say,* 'Produce

your evidence, should you be truthful.' [112]Certainly whoever submits his will to God and is virtuous, he shall have his reward with his Lord, and they will have no fear, nor shall they grieve.

[113]The Jews say, 'The Christians stand on nothing,' and the Christians say, 'The Jews stand on nothing,' though they follow the [same] Book. So said those who had no knowledge, [words] similar to what they say. God will judge between them on the Day of Resurrection concerning that about which they used to differ.

[114]Who is a greater wrongdoer than those who deny access to the mosques of God lest His Name be celebrated therein, and try to ruin them? Such ones may not enter them, except in fear. There is disgrace for them in this world, and a great punishment in the Hereafter.

[115]To God belong the east and the west: so whichever way you turn, there is the face of God! God is indeed all-bounteous, all-knowing.

[116]And they say, 'God has offspring.' Immaculate is He! No, to Him belongs whatever there is in the heavens and the earth. All are obedient to Him, [117]the Originator of the heavens and the earth. When He decides on a matter, He just says to it, 'Be!' and it is.

2:116–17 On the Qur'ān's denial that God would beget a son (or offspring), cf. 4:171; 9:30; 10:68; 17:111; 18:4; 19:35, 88–93; 21:26; 23:91; 25:2; 39:4; 43:81; 72:3; 112:3. It is not clear that the Qur'ān means in each of these cases specifically to invoke Christian doctrine on the divinity of Christ (on this see further commentary on 21:21–29).

The opening of verse 116 is literally "And they say, 'God has taken a son (or offspring).'" The verb "taken" (*ittakhadha*) is the same used in verse 54, where the Qur'ān speaks of the Israelites' "taking up the Calf." Various scholars have argued that the Qur'ān's use of this verb reflects the influence of some heterodox Christology, whether "Adoptionist," Arian, or Nestorian. Yet the Qur'ān here is deliberately using the same verb it uses to express the way that the wives of Potiphar (Q 12:21) and Pharaoh (Q 28:9) adopt Joseph and Moses, respectively. Thus the Qur'ān here means to belittle Christians for thinking of God in a human way.

This passage might be seen as a refutation of Hebrews 1:5 (which quotes Psa 2:7 and is related to Exo 4:22): "To which of the angels, then, has God ever said: You are my Son, today I have fathered you, or: I shall be a father to him and he a son to me?" (Heb 1:5; cf. Psa 2:7; Mat 28:18; Act 13:33; Heb 5:5; 1Pe 3:21b–22).

On God's creating through the word "Be!" (v. 117), see commentary on 36:82 (with further references).

———————————

[118]Those who have no knowledge say, 'Why does not God speak to us, or come to us a sign?' So said those who were before them, [words] similar to what they say. Alike are their hearts. We have certainly made the signs clear for a people who have certainty.

2:118 The demand of unbelievers to hear a divine voice, or to see a sign, is reminiscent of the New Testament (n.b. the phrase "So said those who were before them"). The unbelievers of the Qur'ān demand a sign, as the scribes and Pharisees demanded a sign of Jesus. The Qur'ān here has God conclude, "We have certainly made the signs clear for a people who have certainty." In the New Testament Jesus insists that the unbelievers will receive no sign (Mat 12:38; 16:4; Mar 8:12; Luk 11:29; Joh 6:30) and do not hear the voice of God (Joh 5:37–38)—for only the sheep hear the voice of the Good Shepherd (Joh 10:3, 27).

———————————

[119]Indeed, We have sent *you* with the truth, as a bearer of good news and as a warner, and *you* will not be questioned concerning the inmates of hell.

[120]Never will the Jews be pleased with *you,* nor the Christians, unless *you* followed their creed. *Say,* 'Indeed, it is the guidance

of God which is the [true] guidance.' And should *you* follow their desires after the knowledge that has come to *you, you* will not have against God any friend or helper.

¹²¹Those to whom We have given the Book follow it as it ought to be followed: they have faith in it. As for those who deny it—it is they who are the losers.

¹²²O Children of Israel, remember My blessing which I bestowed upon you, and that I gave you an advantage over all the nations. ¹²³Beware of the Day when no soul shall compensate for another, neither will any ransom be accepted from it, nor will any intercession benefit it, nor will they be helped.

2:122–23 These two verses are almost identical to 2:47–48. See commentary on those verses.

---

¹²⁴When his Lord tested Abraham with certain words, and he fulfilled them, He said, 'I am making you the Imam of mankind.' Said he, 'And from among my descendants?' He said, 'My pledge does not extend to the unjust.'

2:124–29 *overview* According to Islamic tradition, the following passage is set in Mecca. Muslim interpreters often explain that Abraham, Ishmael, and Hagar left Sarah and Isaac in Hebron and traveled into a deserted spot in the Arabian Desert, where Abraham and Ishmael built (or rebuilt) the Kaʿba. Afterward Abraham would leave Ishmael and Hagar behind and return to Sarah and Isaac. This passage might be compared with 14:35–41.

2:124 *Tafsīr al-Jalālayn* explains that God tested Abraham by giving him instructions on proper religious practice: "It is said that these included the rituals of the Pilgrimage, the rinsing of the mouth, snuffing up water into the nostrils [to clean them], cleaning of the teeth, trimming facial hair, combing of the hair, trimming the fingernails, shaving armpit and pubic hair, circumcision and washing one's private parts after elimination." Abraham was thus an imam (or "leader") inasmuch as believers were meant to imitate the example of Abraham in following these practices (which are, in fact, Islamic ritual practices).

It seems likely, however, that the "test" here is a reference to the way God tested Abraham (Gen 22:1; cf. Q 37:102–10) with the command to sacrifice his son. This would match well with what follows (vv. 125–28), which is closely connected with the story of the sacrifice in Genesis 22. On this see Witztum (*Syriac Milieu,* 171–72; "Foundations of the House," 33–34; Sinai, *Fortschreibung,* 139). When the divine voice of the Qur'ān declares that he is making Abraham "the Imam [or leader] of mankind," it reflects Genesis 22, where God rewards Abraham for his obedience (cf. also 37:109–10):

> [16]'I swear by my own self, the Lord declares, that because you have done this, because you have not refused me your own beloved son,
>
> [17]I will shower blessings on you and make your descendants as numerous as the stars of heaven and the grains of sand on the seashore. Your descendants will gain possession of the gates of their enemies. (Gen 22:16–17)

However, whereas Genesis has God promise to favor all of Abraham's descendants, the Qur'ān insists (end of v. 124) that this favor is only for the just.

---

[125]And [remember] when We made the House a place of reward for mankind and a sanctuary, [declaring], 'Take the venue of prayer from Abraham's Station.' We charged Abraham and Ishmael [with its upkeep, saying], 'Purify My House for those who go around it, [for] those who make it a retreat and [for] those who bow and prostrate.'

[126]When Abraham said, 'My Lord, make this a secure town, and provide its people with fruits—such of them as have faith in God and the Last Day,' He said, 'As for him who is faithless, I will provide for him [too] for a short time, then I will shove him toward the punishment of the Fire and it is an evil destination.'

[127]As Abraham raised the foundations of the House with Ishmael, [they prayed]: 'Our Lord, accept it from us! Indeed, You are the All-hearing, the All-knowing.

[128]'Our Lord, make us submissive to You, and [raise] from our progeny a nation submissive to You, show us our rites [of worship], and turn to us clemently. Indeed, You are the All-clement, the All-merciful."

2:125–28 Islamic tradition identifies the "House" (v. 125) as the Ka'ba in Mecca, "Abraham's station" (v. 125) as a small stone next to the Ka'ba (said to bear the footprint of Abraham still today), and the "town" (*balad* in v. 126) as Mecca. In verse 126 the Qur'ān has Abraham pray that God will make this "town" safe and will feed its people with "fruits" (a similar prayer is attributed to Abraham in 14:37; cf. also 106:4, which reports that God has "fed" the Quraysh). See further commentary on the related passage 14:35–41.

Notwithstanding the traditional connection of this verse to Mecca, it should be noted that the Qur'ān employs distinctly Biblical language here. Deuteronomy 12:5 alludes to Jerusalem as the "place" or "station" (Hb. *ha-māqōm*), whereas this Qur'ānic verse speaks of the "station" (Ar. *al-maqām*) of Abraham. The reference to Abraham raising the "foundations" of the "House" in verse 127 could correspond with the reference to his building an altar (in Hebron) in Genesis 13:18 or to his building an altar to God on Mt. Moriah in Genesis 22:9 (regarding which see commentary on 37:100–10). In Syriac Christian tradition the altar of Genesis 22 is connected explicitly with a sanctuary. The *Cave of Treasures* identifies the foundation of Jerusalem with the very moment of Abraham's sacrifice on that altar: "At the moment that Abraham raised Isaac, his son, on the altar, Jerusalem was founded" ([Or.], 30:1). This identification follows from 2 Chronicles 3:1, where an association is made between the site of Abraham's sacrifice, Mt. Moriah (Gen 22:2), and the site of the temple in Jerusalem: "Solomon then began building the house (Hb. *bēt*) of the Lord in Jerusalem on Mount Moriah where David his father had had a vision."

Joseph Witztum analyzes a number of pre-Qur'ānic authors who suggest that Isaac helped Abraham build an altar (see *Syriac Milieu*, 166–70) as the Qur'ān has Ishmael help him build the "house" (Ar. *bayt*). Jacob of Serugh even has Isaac assist Abraham in building a house (Syr. *baytā*):

Abraham approached and put down the fire with the knife / and began to build an altar for the Lord on the top of the mountain.

The master-builder of faith approached and / in order to build there a *house* for the mysteries which would take place.

And when Isaac gazed and saw what his father was doing, / he himself lifted stones in order to bring them forth to build the altar.

He had seen the priest building an altar for his own sacrifice / and stretched out his hand in order to finish [the building] with him untroubled.

For [Abraham] was the priest, the master-builder and the father of the lamb / Isaac was the sacrifice, the stone bearer and the son of the priest. (Jacob of Serugh, *On Abraham and His Types,* 4:90, ll. 4–13, trans. J. Witztum, in *Syriac Milieu,* 168)

Witztum argues that the Qur'ān transfers the imagery associated with Jerusalem in such traditions to Mecca (on this see Witztum, "Foundations of the House," 38).

The Abrahamic traditions in Mecca may also have some connections with Hebron. The Byzantine historian Sozomen (d. ca. 450) relates that the Arabs of his day (along with others) celebrated an annual festival at the Oak of Mamre, the spot near Hebron where by tradition the divine visitation to Abraham in Genesis 18 took place. This festival—not unlike the later Islamic pilgrimage—involved prayers, a well, animal sacrifices, offerings, abstaining from sexual relations, and sleeping in tents:

This place is now called Terebinthus, and is about fifteen stadia distant from Hebron, which lies to the south, but is two hundred and fifty stadia distant from Jerusalem. It is recorded that here the Son of God appeared to Abraham, with two angels, who had been sent against Sodom, and foretold the birth of his son. Here the inhabitants of the country and of the regions round Palestine, the Phoenicians, and the Arabians (*Arrabioi*), assemble annually during the summer season to keep a brilliant feast; and many others, both buyers and sellers, resort thither on account of the fair. Indeed, this feast is diligently frequented by all nations: by the Jews, because they boast of their descent from the patriarch Abraham; by the Pagans, because angels there appeared to men; and by Christians, because He who for the salvation of mankind was born of a virgin, afterwards manifested Himself there to a godly man. This place was moreover honored fittingly with religious exercises. Here some prayed to the God of all; some called upon the angels, poured out wine, burnt incense, or offered an ox, or he-goat, a sheep, or a cock. Each one made some beautiful product of his labor, and after carefully husbanding it through the entire year, he offered it according to promise as provision for that feast, both for himself and his dependents. And either from honor to the place, or from fear of Divine wrath, they all abstained from coming near their wives, although during the feast these were more than ordinarily studious of their beauty and adornment. Nor, if they chanced to appear and to take part in the public processions, did they act at all licentiously. Nor did they behave imprudently in any other respect, although the tents were contiguous to each other, and they all lay promiscuously together. The place is open country, and arable, and without houses, with the exception of the buildings around Abraham's old oak and the well he prepared. (Sozomen, *Ecclesiastical History* 2:4, p. 261)

It is possible that the celebration of an Abrahamic pilgrimage at this spot near Hebron was eventually transferred to Mecca. In 5:95–97 the Qur'ān describes rituals around a sanctuary, which it identifies as the *ka'ba* (whence the name given to the black building in Mecca).

———————

¹²⁹'Our Lord, raise amongst them an apostle from among them, who will recite to them Your signs and teach them the Book and wisdom and purify them. Indeed, You are the All-mighty, the All-wise.'

2:129 In this verse the Qur'ān has Abraham pray that God will send a prophet from among his descendants (cf. 61:6, which has Jesus predict the coming of Muḥammad). This prayer seems to be related to the manner in which Moses proclaims that God will send a prophet from his own people in Deuteronomy 18:15 ("The Lord your God will raise up a prophet like me; you will listen to him"; cf. Deu 18:18), a promise interpreted in Acts 3:22 as a reference to Jesus.

———————

¹³⁰And who will [ever] forsake Abraham's creed except one who debases himself? We certainly chose him in the [present] world, and in the Hereafter he will indeed be among the Righteous. ¹³¹When his Lord said to him, 'Submit,' he said, 'I submit to the Lord of all the worlds.' ¹³²Abraham enjoined this [creed] upon

his children, and [so did] Jacob, [saying], 'My children! God has indeed chosen this religion for you; so do not die except in complete surrender [to God].

¹³³Were you witnesses when death approached Jacob, when he asked his children, 'What will you worship after me?' They said, 'We will worship your God and the God of your fathers, Abraham, Ishmael, and Isaac, the One God, and to Him do we submit.'

2:132–33 The Qur'ān here (v. 133) counts Ishmael among the "fathers" of Jacob, although Ishmael was the brother of Jacob's father Isaac.

This passage reflects a tradition found in the *Targum Neofiti* on Deuteronomy 6:4 ("Listen, Israel: the Lord our God is the one . . ."). In the Hebrew Bible these are the words of God, through Moses, to the entire people of Israel. According to *Targum Neofiti,* however, these are also the words of the twelve sons in response to Jacob's (Israel's) dying wish that they deny the idol worship of Abraham's father:

> When the appointed time of our father Jacob arrived to be gathered in peace from the midst of the world, he gathered the twelve tribes and made them stand round about his bed of gold. Our father Jacob answered and said to them: From Abraham, my father's father, arose the blemished Ishmael and all the sons of Keturah, and from Isaac my father arose the blemished Esau, my brother. Perchance you worship the idols which Abraham's father worshiped, or perchance you worship the idols (which) Laban, my mother's brother, worshiped? Or do you worship the God of Jacob your father? The twelve tribes of Jacob answered together with a perfect heart and said, Listen to us, Israel our father, the Lord our God is one Lord; may his name be blessed for ever and ever. (*Targum Neofiti,* Deu 6:4).

¹³⁴That was a nation that has passed: for it there will be what it has earned, and for you there will be what you have earned, and you will not be questioned about what they used to do.

¹³⁵They say, 'Be either Jews or Christians so that you may be [rightly] guided.' *Say,* 'No, rather [we will follow] the creed of Abraham, a *ḥanīf,* and he was not one of the polytheists.'

2:135 Qarai leaves the Arabic term *ḥanīf*—which the Qur'ān frequently associates with Abraham—untranslated. It is often understood to mean "monotheist," but it may mean especially "gentile monotheist" ("gentile" in the sense of "neither a Jew nor a Christian"). On this see further commentary on 16:120–23.

---

[136]Say, 'We have faith in God and that which has been sent down to us, and that which was sent down to Abraham, Ishmael, Isaac, Jacob and the Tribes, and that which Moses and Jesus were given, and what the prophets were given from their Lord; we make no distinction between any of them and to Him do we submit.' [137]So if they believe in the like of what you believe in, then they are surely guided; but if they turn away, then [know that] they are only [steeped] in defiance. God shall suffice you against them, and He is the All-hearing, the All-knowing.

[138]'The baptism of God, and who baptizes better than God? And Him do we worship.'

2:138 It is likely that the Qur'ān is alluding to baptism here, but the Arabic word Qarai translates in this manner (*ṣibgha*) means more literally "dye." The Coptic Gospel of Philip (third century) speak of God "dyeing" those who are baptized (*Gospel of Philip* 61:12–20). A tradition in Wāḥidī on this verse explains: "When a child was born into the Christians, they used to baptize him on the seventh day by dipping him in holy water in order to purify him. They claimed that this baptism takes the place of circumcision. Upon doing this, they used to say: 'Now the child has become a true Christian,' and so God revealed this verse."

---

[139]*Say,* 'Will you argue with us concerning God, while He is our Lord and your Lord, and to us our deeds belong, and to you your deeds belong, and we worship Him dedicatedly?'

[140][Ask them,] 'Do you say that Abraham, Ishmael, Isaac, Jacob, and the Tribes were Jews or Christians?' *Say,* 'Is it you who know better, or God?' And who is a greater wrongdoer than someone who conceals a testimony that is with him from God? And God is not oblivious of what you do.

2:140 This verse should be compared to 3:67. The list of Biblical protagonists notably includes Ishmael, although it makes no mention of his sons (of which there were twelve according to Gen 25:12–16) . On the question of hiding or falsifying scripture (here "concealing a testimony"), see commentary on 4:46.

---

[141]That was a nation that has passed: for it there will be what it has earned, and for you there will be what you have earned, and you will not be questioned about what they used to do.

[142]The foolish among the people will say, 'What has turned them away from the *qiblah* [direction of prayer] they were following?' *Say,* 'To God belong the east and the west. He guides whomever He wishes to a straight path.'

[143]Thus We have made you a middle nation that you may be witnesses to the people, and that the Apostle may be a witness to you. We did not appoint the *qiblah you* were following, but that We may ascertain those who follow the Apostle from those who turn back on their heels. It was indeed a hard thing except for those whom God has guided. And God would not let your prayers go to waste. God is indeed most kind and merciful to mankind.

[144]We certainly see *you* turning *your* face about in the sky. We will surely turn *you* to a *qiblah* of *your* liking: so *turn* your face towards the Holy Mosque, and wherever you may be, turn your faces towards it! Indeed, those who were given the Book surely know that it is the truth from their Lord. And God is not oblivious of what they do.

¹⁴⁵Even if *you* bring those who were given the Book every [kind of] sign, they will not follow your *qiblah*. Nor shall you follow their *qiblah,* nor will any of them follow the *qiblah* of the other. And if you follow their desires, after the knowledge that has come to *you, you* will be one of the wrongdoers.

¹⁴⁶Those whom We have given the Book recognize him just as they recognize their sons, but a part of them indeed conceal the truth while they know.

2:146 On the question of hiding or falsifying scripture, see commentary on 4:46 (with further references).

---

¹⁴⁷This is the truth from *your* Lord; so do not *be* among the sceptics.

¹⁴⁸Everyone has a cynosure to which he turns; so take the lead in all good works. Wherever you may be, God will bring you all together. Indeed, God has power over all things.

¹⁴⁹Whencesoever *you* may go out, turn *your* face towards the Holy Mosque. It is indeed the truth from *your* Lord, and God is not oblivious of what you do. ¹⁵⁰And whencesoever *you* may go out, turn *your* face towards the Holy Mosque, and wherever you may be, turn your faces towards it, so that the people may have no allegation against you, neither those of them who are wrong-doers. So do not fear them, but fear Me, that I may complete My blessing on you and so that you may be guided.

2:150 The Qur'ān here has God declare: "So do not fear [wrongdoers], but fear Me" (cf. 5:3) in a way close to Matthew 10:28: "Do not be afraid of those who kill the body but cannot kill the soul; fear him rather who can destroy both body and soul in hell."

¹⁵¹Even as We sent to you an Apostle from among yourselves, who recites to you Our signs and purifies you, and teaches you the Book and wisdom, and teaches you what you did not know.

¹⁵²Remember Me and I will remember you, and thank Me, and do not be ungrateful to Me.

¹⁵³O you who have faith! Take recourse in patience and prayer; indeed God is with the patient.

¹⁵⁴Do not call those who were slain in God's way 'dead.' No, they are living, but you are not aware.

2:154 The standard Qur'ānic teaching on the afterlife is that humans go to heaven or hell only when their souls are again joined to their bodies on the Day of Resurrection (see, e.g., 50:16–35). However, the martyrs are here (cf. 3:157–58, 169–70, 195; 9:111; 36:26) promised the special favor of enjoying heaven right away. Muslim scholars accordingly wondered how the martyrs might exist in heaven without having been joined to their resurrected bodies. *Tafsīr al-Jalālayn* offers one answer: "Their spirits are, according to a hadith, contained in green birds that take wing freely wherever they wish in Paradise."

The Qur'ān suggests elsewhere (Q 3:157–58, 195) that the martyrs receive this special favor because their act of martyrdom wins them forgiveness of sin. As Tor Andrae has shown (*Les origines de l'islam et le christianisme*, 161ff.), the idea that martyrdom involves the absolution of sins is prominent in Syriac Christian texts such as the third-century *Didascalia* (chap. 20) and the *Treaty on the Martyrs* of Mar Isaï (d. late sixth cen.); the latter text also insists—much like the Qur'ān—that the martyrs are "living":

> The true martyrs who, by way of a death that covers their sins, demonstrate even more the beauty of their deeds and receive this glorious inheritance by virtue of their blood. By leaving this life they have prepared for their souls an honorable abode in paradise. It was thought that they are already dead, but by their death they have killed their sin, and *they are alive with God.* (Mar Isaï, *Treaty on the Martyrs*, 32)

It is worth noting, as well, that the Syriac Christian tradition, for example Severus of Antioch (d. ca. AD 540), generally portrays the martyrs as combatants who struggle with the devil, or pagans, and win a crown of glory as a sign of the triumph of their martyrdom:

When the treacherous crafty tyrant Julian, who surpassed and overcame all men in the wickedness of impiety, was persecuting the worship of God, and was concealing his injurious action by a pretense and a mask of mildness and gentleness, and was envious and bitter against the combatants on account of the crowns of martyrdom, and was by deceit making captive of many and sweeping them away, Juventinus and the valiant men with him, champions and soldiers of Christ, confuted and exposed him, in that they displayed and contended in a gallant conflict of combating prowess, and stripped off the cloak of his deceitfulness and gained crowns of victory and for the combats which they endured. (James of Edessa, *The Hymns of Severus of Antioch,* 153, p. 200)

---

[155]We will surely test you with a measure of fear and hunger and a loss of wealth, lives, and fruits; and *give* good news to the patient [156]—those who, when an affliction visits them, say, 'Indeed, we belong to God and to Him do we indeed return.' [157]It is they who receive the blessings of their Lord and [His] mercy, and it is they who are the [rightly] guided.

[158]Ṣafā and Marwah are indeed among God's sacraments. So whoever makes *hajj* to the House, or performs the *'umrah,* there is no sin upon him to circuit between them. Should anyone do good of his own accord, then God is indeed appreciative, all-knowing.

2:158 On "God's sacraments," see commentary on Q 22:26–37.

---

[159]Indeed, those who conceal what We have sent down of manifest proofs and guidance, after We have clarified it in the Book for mankind—they shall be cursed by God and cursed by the cursers.

2:159 On the question of hiding or falsifying scripture, see commentary on 4:46 (with further references).

---

^{160}except such as repent, make amends, and clarify—those I shall pardon, and I am the All-clement, the All-merciful.

^{161}Indeed, those who turn faithless and die faithless—it is they on whom shall be the curse of God, the angels and all mankind. ^{162}They will remain in it [forever] and their punishment shall not be lightened, nor will they be granted any respite.

^{163}Your god is the One God, there is no god except Him, the All-beneficent, the All-merciful.

^{164}Indeed, in the creation of the heavens and the earth, and the alternation of night and day, and the ships that sail at sea with profit to men, and the water that God sends down from the sky—with which He revives the earth after its death, and scatters therein every kind of animal—and the changing of the winds, and the clouds disposed between the sky and the earth, there are signs for a people who exercise their reason.

2:164 This verse (cf. 45:12–13) reflects the manner in which Psalm 104 praises God for creation (cr. Matthew Kuiper):

^{1}Bless the Lord, my soul, the Lord, my God, how great you are! Clothed in majesty and splendor,
^{2}wearing the light as a robe! You stretch out the heavens like a tent,
^{3}build your palace on the waters above, making the clouds your chariot, gliding on the wings of the wind,
^{4}appointing the winds your messengers, flames of fire your servants.
. . .
^{10}In the ravines you opened up springs, running down between the mountains,
^{11}supplying water for all the wild beasts; the wild asses quench their thirst,
^{12}on their banks the birds of the air make their nests, they sing among the leaves.
^{13}From your high halls you water the mountains, satisfying the earth with the fruit of your works:

¹⁴for cattle you make the grass grow, and for people the plants they need, to bring forth food from the earth. (Psa 104:1–4, 10–14; cf. Gen 1; Psa 19:1–4; Rom 1:20)

The Corpus Coranicum website here refers instead to 1 Enoch 2:1–5, which indeed speaks specifically of clouds and rain (1 Enoch 2:3). On heavenly bodies as signs, Speyer (*BEQ,* 20) refers to Isaiah 45:7; Psalms 104, 136; and Job 38:12.

---

¹⁶⁵Among the people are those who set up compeers besides God, loving them as if loving God—but the faithful have a more ardent love for God—though the wrongdoers will see, when they sight the punishment, that power, altogether, belongs to God, and that God is severe in punishment. ¹⁶⁶When those who were followed will disown the followers, and they will sight the punishment while all their means of recourse will be cut off, ¹⁶⁷and when the followers will say, 'Had there been another turn for us, we would disown them as they disown us [now]!' Thus shall God show them their deeds as regrets for themselves, and they shall not leave the Fire.

¹⁶⁸O mankind! Eat of what is lawful and pure in the earth, and do not follow in Satan's steps. He is indeed your manifest enemy. ¹⁶⁹He only prompts you to [commit] evil and indecent acts, and that you attribute to God what you do not know.

¹⁷⁰When they are told, 'Follow what God has sent down,' they say, 'No, we will follow what we have found our fathers following.' What, even if their fathers neither exercised their reason nor were guided?!

¹⁷¹The parable of the faithless is that of someone who shouts after that which does not hear [anything] except a call and cry: deaf, dumb, and blind, they do not exercise their reason.

¹⁷²O you who have faith! Eat of the good things We have provided you, and thank God, if it is Him that you worship.

¹⁷³He has forbidden you only carrion, blood, the flesh of the swine, and that which has been offered to other than God. But should someone be compelled, without being rebellious or transgressive, there shall be no sin upon him. God is indeed all-forgiving, all-merciful.

¹⁷⁴Indeed, those who conceal what God has sent down of the Book and sell it for a paltry gain—they do not ingest into their bellies [anything] except fire, and God shall not speak to them on the Day of Resurrection, nor shall He purify them, and there is a painful punishment for them.

2:172–74 Verses 172–73 emphasize the relatively moderate nature of dietary restrictions that God demands of the believers (v. 173: "He has forbidden you *only*"). In this way this passage is not unlike the declaration of the apostles in Jerusalem (Act 15):

> ²⁸It has been decided by the Holy Spirit and by ourselves not to impose on you any burden beyond these essentials:
> ²⁹you are to abstain from food sacrificed to idols, from blood, from the meat of strangled animals and from illicit marriages. Avoid these, and you will do what is right. Farewell. (Act 15:28–29)

Both passages are meant to draw a contrast with the restrictions imposed on the Jews (which, according to 4:160, were imposed as a punishment). This anti-Jewish tone continues in the following verse (174), where the Qur'ān accuses the Jews of concealing the truth about divine revelation (regarding which see commentary on 4:46, with further references).

---

¹⁷⁵They are the ones who bought error for guidance, and punishment for pardon: how patient of them to face the Fire!

¹⁷⁶That is so because God has sent down the Book with the truth, and those who differ about the Book are surely in extreme defiance.

[177]Piety is not to turn your faces to the east or the west; rather, piety is [personified by] those who have faith in God and the Last Day, the angels, the Book, and the prophets, and who give their wealth, for the love of Him, to relatives, orphans, the needy, the traveler and the beggar, and for [the freeing of] the slaves, and maintain the prayer and give the *zakāt,* and those who fulfill their covenants, when they pledge themselves, and those who are patient in stress and distress, and in the heat of battle. They are the ones who are true [to their covenant], and it is they who are the Godwary.

2:177 On kindness to orphans, see commentary on 107:2 (with further references).

---

[178]O you who have faith! Retribution is prescribed for you regarding the slain: freeman for freeman, slave for slave, and female for female. But if one is granted any extenuation by his brother, let the follow up [for the blood-money] be honourable, and let the payment to him be with kindness. That is a remission from your Lord and a mercy; and should anyone transgress after that, there shall be a painful punishment for him.

[179]There is life for you in retribution, O you who possess intellects! Maybe you will be Godwary!

2:178–79 As Michael Pregill points out (*QSC,* 69), this passage (cf. 5:45) reflects not so much the Biblical lex talionis (Exo 21:23–25; Lev 24:19–20; Deu 19:21) as much as the new interpretation of the lex talionis offered in Matthew 5. In both cases the point is the moderation ("a remission . . . and a mercy"; v. 178) of a strict law.

[38]'You have heard how it was said: Eye for eye and tooth for tooth.
[39]But I say this to you: offer no resistance to the wicked. On the contrary, if anyone hits you on the right cheek, offer him the other as well. (Mat 5:38–39; cf. Luk 6:29)

¹⁸⁰Prescribed for you, when death approaches any of you and he leaves behind any property, is that he make a bequest for his parents and relatives, in an honourable manner—an obligation on the Godwary. ¹⁸¹And should anyone alter it after hearing it, its sin shall indeed lie on those who alter it. God is indeed all-hearing, all-knowing. ¹⁸²But should someone, fearing deviance or sin on the testator's behalf, set things right between them, there is no sin upon him. God is indeed all-forgiving, all-merciful.

¹⁸³O you who have faith! Prescribed for you is fasting as was prescribed for those who were before you, so that you may be Godwary. ¹⁸⁴That for known days. But should any of you be sick or on a journey, let it be a [similar] number of other days. Those who find it straining shall be liable to atonement by feeding a needy person. Should anyone do good of his own accord, that is better for him, and to fast is better for you, should you know.

¹⁸⁵The month of Ramaḍān is one in which the Qur'ān was sent down as guidance to mankind, with manifest proofs of guidance and the Criterion. So let those of you who witness it fast [in] it, and as for someone who is sick or on a journey, let it be a [simi-lar] number of other days. God desires ease for you, and He does not desire hardship for you, and so that you may complete the number, and magnify God for guiding you, and that you may give thanks.

2:185 Islamic tradition understands this verse (cf. 44:2–3; 97:1) as a de-scription of the way the Qur'ān—a complete book which existed physically in heaven from all time—was sent down with the angel Gabriel from the highest heaven to the lowest heaven during the holy month of Ramadan.

In fact the Qur'ān uses the expression *qur'ān* (related to the Syr. term *qeryānā,* designating a church lectionary) to speak of certain discrete oral revelations rather than the book that was eventually given the title "Qur'ān." The refer-ence in this verse to the revelation of the *qur'ān and* the *furqān* (the word Qarai renders as "Criterion," but in one case [Q 8:41] as "Separation") matches 2:53, where the Qur'ān speaks of the revelation of the "Book" (here, too, a physical book is not intended but an oral revelation) and the *furqān* (on this term, cf. 3:3–4; 8:29, 41; 21:48; 25:1). The Qur'ān uses a number of different expressions (e.g., *furqān, ḥikma, ḥukm, kitāb, qur'ān, dhikr*) to describe revelations which God gives to prophets.

---

¹⁸⁶When My servants ask *you* about Me, [*tell* them that] I am indeed nearmost. I answer the supplicant's call when he calls Me. So let them respond to Me and have faith in Me, so that they may fare rightly.

¹⁸⁷You are permitted on the night of the fast to go into your wives: they are a garment for you, and you are a garment for them. God knew that you would betray yourselves, so He pardoned you and excused you. So now consort with them and seek what God has ordained for you, and eat and drink until the white streak becomes manifest to you from the dark streak at the crack of dawn. Then complete the fast until nightfall, and do not consort with them while you dwell in confinement in the mosques. These are God's bounds, so do not approach them. Thus does God clarify His signs for mankind so that they may be Godwary.

2:187 Our translator, in line with certain traditions of medieval exegesis (including *Tafsīr al-Jalālayn*), renders an Arabic expression here which literally refers to "thread" (Ar. *khayṭ*) as "streak." The translation of Droge—"until a white thread may be discerned from a black thread at the dawn"—is more accurate. The Qur'ān seems to be following a tradition known from the Mishna Berakoth 1:2 (cf. b. Berakoth 9b), which explains that the *Shema* prayer can be recited for one's morning obligation from the time that one can distinguish between blue and white wool (see *BEQ* 459; Geiger, *Judaism and Islam,* 68).

On the Biblical connection with the expression "God's bounds" (*ḥudūd Allāh*), see commentary on 58:4 (with further references).

---

[188]Do not eat up your wealth among yourselves wrongfully, nor proffer it to the judges in order to eat up a part of the people's wealth sinfully, while you know [that it is immoral to do so].

[189]They question *you* concerning the new moons. *Say,* 'They are timekeeping signs for the people and [for the sake of] *hajj*.'

It is not piety that you enter the houses from their rear; rather, piety is [personified by] one who is Godwary, and enter the houses from their doors, and be wary of God, so that you may be felicitous.

[190]Fight in the way of God those who fight you, but do not transgress. Indeed, God does not like transgressors. [191]And kill them wherever you confront them, and expel them from where they expelled you, for persecution is graver than killing. But do not fight them near the Holy Mosque unless they fight you therein; but if they fight you, kill them; such is the requital of the faithless. [192]But if they desist, God is indeed all-forgiving, all-merciful.

[193]Fight them until persecution is no more, and religion becomes [exclusively] for God. Then if they desist, there shall be no reprisal except against the wrongdoers.

[194]A sacred month for a sacred month, and all sanctities require retribution. So should anyone aggress against you, assail him in the manner he assailed you, and be wary of God, and know that God is with the Godwary.

[195]Spend in the way of God, and do not cast yourselves with your own hands into destruction; and be virtuous. Indeed, God loves the virtuous.

[196]Complete the *hajj* and the *'umrah* for God's sake, and if you are prevented, then [make] such [sacrificial] offering as is feasible. And do not shave your heads until the offering reaches its [assigned] place. But should any of you be sick, or have a hurt in his head, let the atonement be by fasting, or charity, or sacrifice. And when you have security—for those who enjoy [release from

the restrictions] by virtue of their *'umrah* until the *hajj*—let the offering be such as is feasible.

As for someone who cannot afford [the offering], let him fast three days during the *hajj* and seven when you return; that is [a period of] ten complete [days]. That is for someone whose family does not dwell by the Holy Mosque. And be wary of God, and know that God is severe in retribution.

¹⁹⁷The *hajj* [season] is in months well-known; so whoever decides on *hajj* [pilgrimage] therein, [should know that] there is to be no sexual contact, vicious talk, or disputing during the *hajj*. Whatever good you do, God knows it. And take provision, for Godwariness is indeed the best provision. So be wary of Me, O you who possess intellects!

¹⁹⁸There is no sin upon you in seeking your Lord's bounty [during the *hajj* season]. Then when you stream out of 'Arafāt remember God at the Holy Mashʿar, and remember Him as He has guided you, and earlier you were indeed among the astray.

¹⁹⁹Then stream out from where the people stream out, and plead to God for forgiveness; indeed God is all-forgiving, all-merciful. ²⁰⁰And when you finish your rites, remember God as you would remember your fathers, or with a more ardent remembrance. Among the people there are those who say, 'Our Lord, give us in this world,' but for such there is no share in the Hereafter.

2:200 The expression "for such there is no share in the Hereafter" (Ar. *mā lahu fī l-ākhirati min khalāq*) is close to the Hebrew expression (found in Mishnah *Sanhedrin* 10:2) "no share (*ḥēleq*) in the world to come" (cf. 2:102, at the end).

---

²⁰¹And among them there are those who say, 'Our Lord, give us good in this world and good in the Hereafter, and save us from the

punishment of the Fire.' [202]Such shall partake of what they have earned, and God is swift at reckoning.

[203]Remember God in the appointed days. Then whoever hastens off in a couple of days, there is no sin upon him, and whoever delays, there is no sin upon him—that for one who has been Godwary—and be wary of God and know that toward Him you will be mustered.

[204]Among the people is he whose talk about worldly life impresses you, and he holds God witness to what is in his heart, though he is the staunchest of enemies. [205]If he were to wield authority, he would try to cause corruption in the land and to ruin the crop and the stock, and God does not like corruption. [206]And when he is told, 'Be wary of God,' conceit seizes him sinfully; so let hell suffice him, and it is surely an evil resting place!

[207]And among the people is he who sells his soul seeking the pleasure of God, and God is most kind to [His] servants.

2:206–7 In verse 206 (and in seventy-six other verses) the Qur'ān uses *jahannam* to refer to hell, a term related to Hebrew *gē hinnōm* (i.e., "the valley of Hinnom"), a valley south of Jerusalem where fires were kept to burn refuse and the bodies of animals and criminals. It is used in the Gospels (Gk. *geenna,* or Syr. *ghennā*) and in Jewish rabbinic literature, as the place of fiery eschatological punishment (i.e., hell; cf. Mat 5:29–30, 10:28, 18:9; Mar 9:43–47; Luk 12:5).

The Qur'ān's praise of the one who is ready to sell himself to please God (v. 207) seems to be (in light of 2:244–45; 4:74; 9:111) an allusion to those who fight and die in the holy war.

---

[208]O you who have faith! Enter into submission, all together, and do not follow in Satan's steps; he is indeed your manifest enemy. [209]And should you stumble after the manifest proofs that have come to you, know that God is all-mighty, all-wise.

²¹⁰Do they await anything but that God['s command] should come to them in the shades of the clouds, with the angels, and the matter be decided [once for all]? To God all matters are returned. ²¹¹Ask the Children of Israel how many a manifest sign We had given them. Whoever changes God's blessing after it has come to him, indeed God is severe in retribution.

²¹²Worldly life has been glamorized for the faithless, and they ridicule the faithful. But those who are Godwary shall be above them on the Day of Resurrection, and God provides for whomever He wishes without any reckoning.

²¹³Mankind were a single community; then God sent the prophets as bearers of good news and warners, and He sent down with them the Book with the truth, that it may judge between the people concerning that about which they differed, and none differed in it except those who were given it, after clear proofs had come to them, out of envy among themselves. Then God guided those who had faith to the truth of what they differed in, by His will, and God guides whomever He wishes to a straight path.

2:213 Regarding the Qur'ān's statements on the division of humanity into different communities, see commentary on 10:19 (with further references).

———————————

²¹⁴Do you suppose that you will enter paradise though there has not yet come to you the like of [what befell] those who went before you? Stress and distress befell them and they were convulsed until the apostle and the faithful who were with him said, 'When will God's help [come]?' Behold! God's help is indeed near!

²¹⁵They ask *you* as to what they should spend. *Say,* 'Whatever wealth you spend, let it be for parents, relatives, orphans, the

needy, and the traveler.' God indeed knows whatever good that you may do.

2:215 On kindness to orphans, see commentary on 107:2 (with further references).

---

²¹⁶Warfare has been prescribed for you, though it is repulsive to you. Yet it may be that you dislike something which is good for you, and it may be that you love something which is bad for you, and God knows and you do not know.

²¹⁷They ask *you* concerning warfare in the holy month. *Say,* 'It is an outrageous thing to fight in it, but to keep [people] from God's way, and to be unfaithful to Him, and [to keep people from] the Holy Mosque, and to expel its people from it are more outrageous with God. And persecution is graver than killing. They will not cease fighting you until they turn you away from your religion, if they can. And whoever of you turns away from his religion and dies faithless—they are the ones whose works have failed in this world and the Hereafter. They shall be the inmates of the Fire, and they shall remain in it [forever].

²¹⁸Indeed, those who are faithful and those who have migrated and waged *jihād* in the way of God—it is they who expect God's mercy, and God is all-forgiving, all-merciful.

²¹⁹They ask *you* concerning wine and gambling. *Say,* 'There is a great sin in both of them, and some profits for the people, but their sinfulness outweighs their profit.'

And they ask *you* as to what they should spend. *Say,* 'All that is surplus.' Thus does God clarify His signs for you so that you may reflect.

2:219 Qarai renders here Arabic *maysir* as "gambling"; it is traditionally identified as a specific game of chance played with arrows. However, in all three cases where this term appears in the Qur'ān (including at 5:90–91, which traditionally is seen as abrogating 2:219), it appears immediately after "wine" (Ar. *khamr*). While it is possible that the Qur'ān means to deal with "wine" and "gambling" together (although note that the Arabic word translated as "profits," *manāfiʿ*, means rather "advantages"), it is possible that this entire phrase refers to alcohol. The expression "*al-khamr* and *al-maysir*" may reflect an expression in the Aramaic translation (*Targum Onqelos*) of Leviticus 10:9: "You, together with your sons, should not drink any wine (*ḥmar*) or any intoxicating drink (*mrawē*)" (*Targum Onqelos,* Lev 10:9, trans. 19). *Maysir,* however, is not cognate to *mrawē*. For a different perspective, see the comments of Zellentin (*Qur'ān's Legal Culture,* 118–25).

---

²²⁰about the world and the Hereafter.

And they ask *you* concerning the orphans. *Say,* 'It is better to set right their affairs, and if you intermingle with them, they are of course your brothers: God knows those who cause corruption from those who set things right, and had God wished He would have put you to hardship.' God is indeed all-mighty, all-wise.

²²¹Do not marry idolatresses until they embrace faith. A faithful slave girl is better than an idolatress, though she should impress you. And do not marry [your daughters] to idolaters until they embrace faith. A faithful slave is better than an idolater, though he should impress you. Those invite [others] to the Fire, but God invites to paradise and pardon, by His will, and He clarifies His signs for the people so that they may take admonition.

²²²They ask *you* concerning [intercourse during] menses. *Say,* 'It is hurtful.' So keep away from wives during the menses, and do not approach them till they are clean. And when they become clean, go into them as God has commanded you. God indeed loves the penitent and He loves those who keep clean.

[223]Your women are a tillage for you, so come to your tillage whenever you like, and send ahead for your souls, and be God-wary, and know that you will encounter Him; and give good news to the faithful.

[224]Do not make God an obstacle, through your oaths, to being pious and Godwary, and to bringing about concord between people. And God is all-hearing, all-knowing. [225]God will not take you to task for what is unconsidered in your oaths, but He will take you to task for what your hearts have incurred, and God is all-forgiving, all-forbearing.

[226]For those who forswear their wives there shall be a waiting [period] of four months. And if they recant, God is indeed all-forgiving, all-merciful. [227]But if they resolve on divorce, God is indeed all-hearing, all-knowing.

[228]Divorced women shall wait by themselves for three periods of purity [after menses], and it is not lawful for them to conceal what God has created in their wombs if they believe in God and the Last Day; and their husbands have a greater right to restore them during this [duration], if they desire reconcilement. The wives have rights similar to the obligations upon them, in accordance with honourable norms; and men have a degree above them, and God is all-mighty and all-wise.

2:228 As Geiger notes (*Judaism and Islam,* 69), the notion of waiting three months (cf. 65:4) before marriage has a basis in the Talmud (m. Yevamot 4:10).

––––––––––

[229][Revocable] divorce may be only twice; then [let there be] either an honourable retention, or a kindly release. It is not lawful for you to take back anything from what you have given them,

unless the couple fear that they may not maintain God's bounds. But if you fear they would not maintain God's bounds, there is no sin upon them in what she may give to secure her own release. These are God's bounds, so do not transgress them, and whoever transgresses the bounds of God—it is they who are the wrongdoers.

[230]And if he divorces her, she will not be lawful for him thereafter until she marries a husband other than him; then if he divorces her, there is no sin upon them to remarry if they think that they can maintain God's bounds. These are God's bounds, which He clarifies for a people who have knowledge.

2:229–30 On the Biblical connection with the expression "God's bounds" (*ḥudūd Allāh*), see commentary on 58:4 (with further references).

———————

[231]When you divorce women and they complete their term [of waiting], then either retain them honourably or release them honourably, and do not retain them maliciously in order that you may transgress; and whoever does that certainly wrongs himself. Do not take the signs of God in derision, and remember God's blessing upon you, and what He has sent down to you of the Book and wisdom, to advise you therewith. Be wary of God, and know that God has knowledge of all things.

[232]When you divorce women and they complete their term [of waiting], do not hinder them from [re]marrying their husbands, when they honourably reach mutual consent. Herewith are advised those of you who believe in God and the Last Day. That will be more decent and purer for you, and God knows and you do not know.

[233]Mothers shall suckle their children for two full years—that for such as desire to complete the suckling—and on the father shall be their maintenance and clothing, in accordance with honourable norms. No soul is to be tasked except according to its capacity: neither the mother shall be made to suffer harm on her child's account, nor the father on account of his child, and on the [father's] heir devolve [duties and rights] similar to that. And if the couple desire to wean, with mutual consent and consultation, there will be no sin upon them. And if you want to have your children wet-nursed, there will be no sin upon you so long as you pay what you give in accordance with honourable norms, and be wary of God and know that God watches what you do.

2:233 The idea that a woman should suckle her children for two years (cf. 31:14) has a basis in the Talmud (b. Ketubbot 60a). On the Qur'ān's declaration "Neither the mother shall be made to suffer harm on her child's account," see Deuteronomy 24:16: "Parents may not be put to death for their children, nor children for parents, but each must be put to death for his own crime."

---

[234]As for those of you who die leaving wives, they shall wait by themselves four months and ten days, and when they complete their term, there will be no sin upon you in respect of what they may do with themselves in accordance with honourable norms. And God is well aware of what you do.
[235]There is no sin upon you in what you may hint in proposing to [recently widowed] women, or what you may secretly cherish within your hearts. God knows that you will be thinking of them, but do not make troth with them secretly, unless you say honourable words, and do not resolve on a marriage tie until the pre-

scribed term is complete. Know that God knows what is in your hearts, so beware of Him; and know that God is all-forgiving, all-forbearing.

[236]There is no sin upon you if you divorce women while you have not yet touched them or settled a dowry for them. Yet provide for them—the well-off according to his capacity, and the poorly-off according to his capacity—with a sustenance that is honourable, an obligation on the virtuous.

[237]And if you divorce them before you touch them, and you have already settled a dowry for them, then [pay them] half of what you have settled, unless they forgo it, or someone in whose hand is the marriage tie forgoes it. And to forgo is nearer to God-wariness; so do not forget graciousness among yourselves. God indeed watches what you do.

[238]Be watchful of your prayers, and [especially] the middle prayer, and stand in obedience to God; [239]and should you fear [a danger], then [pray] on foot or mounted, and when you are safe, remember God, as He taught you what you did not know.

[240]Those of you who die leaving wives shall bequeath for their wives providing for a year, without turning them out; but if they leave, there is no sin upon you in respect of what they may do with themselves in accordance with honourable norms. And God is all-mighty, all-wise.

[241]For the divorced women there shall be a provision, in accordance with honourable norms—an obligation on the Godwary. [242]Thus does God clarify His signs to you so that you may exercise your reason.

[243]Have you not regarded those who left their homes in thousands, apprehensive of death, whereupon God said to them, 'Die,' then He revived them? God is indeed gracious to mankind, but most people do not give thanks.

2:243 This passage may ultimately be connected to Ezekiel 37:5–10, which has God raise up (through the prophecy of Ezekiel) a "great, immense army" (v. 10) from bones (note that the Qur'ān regularly uses "thousands" [*ulūf*] or "thousand" [*alf*] with the general meaning of a great number; cf., e.g., 8:65–66; 22:47; 32:5; 97:3). There is nothing in Ezekiel, however, on people leaving their homes.

The peculiar locution in which the Qur'ān has God say "die"—and then is said to revive those who have died—may reflect the promise of everlasting life which the Qur'ān makes to the martyrs in the following verses (vv. 244–245). The Qur'ān could be suggesting in this verse (cf. 4:100) that those who migrate for the sake of God receive the same reward as those who die in the holy war for the sake of God.

---

²⁴⁴Fight in the way of God, and know that God is all-hearing, all-knowing. ²⁴⁵Who is it that will lend God a good loan that He may multiply it for him severalfold? God tightens and expands [the means of life], and to Him you shall be brought back.

2:245 The Qur'ān's reference to a "loan" here may allude to giving one's life in holy war. See commentary on 9:111 (with further references).

---

²⁴⁶Have you not regarded the elite of the Israelites after Moses, when they said to their prophet, 'Appoint for us a king, that we may fight in the way of God.' He said, 'May it not be that you will not fight if fighting were prescribed for you?' They said, 'Why should we not fight in the way of God, when we have been expelled from our homes and [separated from] our children?' So when fighting was prescribed for them, they turned back except a few of them, and God knows well the wrongdoers. ²⁴⁷Their prophet said to them, 'God has appointed Saul as king for you.' They said, 'How can he have kingship over us, when

we have a greater right to kingship than him, as he has not been given ample wealth?' He said, 'God has indeed chosen him over you, and enhanced him vastly in knowledge and physique, and God gives His kingdom to whomever He wishes, and God is all-bounteous, all-knowing.'

2:246–47 1 Samuel 8:4–5 relates that the elders of the Israelites assembled and decided to request that Samuel appoint a king for them (the Qur'ān may be alluding to this assembly with its reference to the "elite" [lit. "assembly" or "council"; Ar. *mala'*] of Israel in v. 246). They explain: "No! We are determined to have a king, so that we can be like the other nations, with our own king to rule us and lead us and fight our battles" (1Sa 8:19–20). The Qur'ān also has the Israelites proclaim their desire for a king for the sake of war, but laments that they are then unwilling to fight (perhaps a reference to 1Sa 11, where the Israelites in Jabesh beg a foreign invader for a peace treaty).

Samuel's reply, that God has "enhanced [Saul] vastly in knowledge and physique"—though not in wealth—reflects 1 Samuel 9–10, which describes the physical appearance of Saul ("head and shoulders taller than anyone else"; 1 Sa 10:2), his financial limitations, and the gift of prophecy given to him. The large size of Saul is reflected in the name the Qur'ān gives to him, Ṭālūt, which may be from the Arabic root *ṭ-w-l.* meaning "height" (see *FV,* 204).

---

²⁴⁸Their prophet said to them, 'Indeed, the sign of his kingship shall be that the Ark will come to you, bearing tranquillity from your Lord and the relics left behind by the House of Moses and the House of Aaron, borne by the angels. There is indeed a sign in that for you, should you be faithful.'

2:248 The Qur'ān seems to imply that Saul will bring forth the ark as a sign of his kingship. In the Biblical account the ark is lost to the Philistines before Saul becomes king, and then—after it brings all sorts of woes on the Philistines—installed at Kiriath-Jearim (1Sa 7:2). It is David, not Saul, who eventually brings the ark to Jerusalem (2Sa 6; 1Ch 13:5–6; see *BEQ,* 367).

Our translator relates that the ark will come "bearing tranquility [Ar. *sakīna*] from your Lord" (cf. 9:26, 40; 48:4, 18, 26). The Arabic root of *sakīna* means "to dwell" *or* "to be peaceful, calm" (and in other passages—9:26, 40, and 48:4, 18, 26—it may have a meaning of "tranquility"). Yet the Qur'ān states clearly here that this *sakīna* is *in* the ark (*fīhi*). This follows the usage of Aramaic texts which speak of God's *shekīntā* (i.e., his dwelling or presence) residing in the ark (see *FV,* 174) . *Targum Onqelos* on Exodus 25:8 has God declare "Let them make before Me a sanctuary and I will let my presence [*shekīntā*] rest among them" (see also b. *Sotah,* 13a). The Arabic phrase "bearing a *sakīna* from your Lord" thus seems to be a locution expressing "bearing your Lord's presence" (in the ark).

The "relics left behind" are the items God commanded Moses to put in the ark: the tablets of the Law (Exo 25:16, 21; 40:20; cf. Deu 10:2, 5; 1Ki 8:9), manna (Exo 16:33), and Aaron's rod (Num 17:25; cf. Heb 9:4). The reference to angels seems to reflect the design of the ark, which had an angelic figure on either side with outstretched wings (Exo 25:18–20; 22; cf. Num 7:89; 1Ki 8:6–7; 1Ch 28:18; 2Ch 5:7–8).

---

[249]As Saul set out with the troops, he said, 'God will test you with a stream: anyone who drinks from it will not belong to me, but those who do not drink from it will belong to me, barring someone who draws a scoop with his hand.' But they drank from it, [all] except a few of them. So when he crossed it along with the faithful who were with him, they said, 'We have no strength today against Goliath and his troops.' Those who were certain they will encounter God said, 'How many a small party has overcome a larger party by God's will! And God is with the patient.'

2:249 This passage is close to a Biblical account that does not involve Saul at all, but rather Gideon (cf. *BEQ,* 368; Bell 1:52):

[5]So Gideon took the people down to the waterside, and the Lord said to him, 'All those who lap the water with their tongues, as a dog laps, put these on one side. And all those who kneel down to drink, put these on the other side.' [6]The number of those who lapped with their hands to their mouth was three hundred; all the rest of the people had knelt to drink.

⁷the Lord then said to Gideon, 'With the three hundred who lapped the water, I shall rescue you and put Midian into your power. Let the people as a whole disperse to their homes.' (Jdg 7:5–7)

This is not the only case of the Qurʾān transferring (or mixing) Biblical traditions. One might compare the presentation of Mary the mother of Jesus as the sister of Aaron (hence Moses) and daughter of ʿImrān (see commentary on 3:33, with further references) or the appearance of Haman in Egypt instead of Persia (see commentary on 28:38, with further references).

²⁵⁰So when they marched out for [encounter with] Goliath and his troops, they said, 'Our Lord, pour patience upon us, make our feet steady, and assist us against the faithless lot.' ²⁵¹Thus they routed them with God's will, and David killed Goliath, and God gave him kingdom and wisdom, and taught him whatever He liked. Were it not for God's repelling the people by means of one another, the earth would surely have been corrupted; but God is gracious to the world's people.

2:250–51 The Qurʾān follows here the narrative of 1 Samuel, by which Saul leads Israel against the Philistines but David defeats Goliath, the Philistine champion: "Thus David triumphed over the Philistine with a sling and a stone; he hit the Philistine [Goliath] and killed him, though he had no sword in his hand" (1Sa 17:50). The declaration (v. 251) that God gave "kingdom and wisdom" to David may have a precedent in 2 Samuel 14, such as verse 20: "Your servant Joab did this to approach the matter indirectly, but my lord [David] has the wisdom of the Angel of God; he knows everything that happens on earth!'" Cf. 21:79; 38:20. On wisdom (Ar. *ḥikma*) otherwise in the Qurʾān, see commentary on 3:48.

²⁵²These are the signs of God which We recite for *you* in truth, and *you* are indeed one of the apostles.

²⁵³These are the apostles, some of whom We gave an advantage over others: of them are those to whom God spoke and some of them He raised in rank, and We gave Jesus, son of Mary, manifest proofs and strengthened him with the Holy Spirit.

Had God wished, those who succeeded them would have not fought one another, after clear proofs had come to them. But they differed. There were among them those who had faith and there were those who were faithless, and had God wished, they would not have fought one another; but God does whatever He desires.

2:253 On the phrase "some of whom We gave an advantage over others," *Tafsīr al-Jalālayn* comments, "Namely Muḥammad." Yet this verse (cf. 2:87) is best understood in light of its context in Sura 2, namely the story of Israel and Israel's relationship with the prophets, especially Moses and Jesus. The prophets given an "advantage" are presumably Moses—to whom God spoke (on this see Num 12:4–8; cf. 4:164; 7:143)—and Jesus, who is distinguished by his relationship to the Holy Spirit (notably at his baptism, see Mat 3:16; Mar 1:10; Luk 3:22; Joh 1:32). On the Holy Spirit in the Qur'ān, see commentary on 2:87 and 16:102 (with further references).

The second part of this verse seems to allude to the split between Jews and Christians ("those who succeeded them") over Jesus (cf. 61:14), who brought "manifest proofs" (cf. the first part of the verse) which the Christians accepted but the Jews rejected (cf. 61:6). *Tafsīr al-Jalālayn,* however, identifies "those who were faithless" as the Christians, commenting, "Some disbelieved, as the Christians did after Jesus."

---

²⁵⁴O you who have faith! Spend out of what We have provided you before there comes a day on which there will be no bargaining, neither friendship, nor intercession. And the faithless—they are the wrongdoers.

²⁵⁵God—there is no god except Him—is the Living One, the All-sustainer. Neither drowsiness befalls Him nor sleep. To Him belongs whatever is in the heavens and whatever is on the earth.

Who is it that may intercede with Him except with His permission? He knows what is before them and what is behind them, and they do not comprehend anything of His knowledge except what He wishes. His seat embraces the heavens and the earth and He is not wearied by their preservation, and He is the All-exalted, the All-supreme.

2:255 In Daniel 6:27 (26) the Persian king Darius identifies the God of Israel as "the living God, he endures forever (*elāhā ḥayyā w-qayyām l-ʿālmīn*)." Here the Qurʾān describes God (*allāh*) as the "Living One [*al-ḥayy*], the All-sustainer [*al-qayyūm*]" (cf. 3:2; 20:111).

As Bell (*Commentary,* 1:53) notes, the Qurʾān uses turns of phrase common in the Psalms here. In the expression "neither drowsiness befalls Him nor sleep" the Qurʾān follows Psalm 121:4, using two Arabic terms (*sina, nawm*) cognate to two Hebrew terms in this verse: "You see—he neither sleeps (*lō yānūm*) nor slumbers (*lō yīshān*), the guardian of Israel" (cf. also Isa 40:28). The mention of God's "seat" or "throne" (*kursī*) at the end of the verse might be compared to Psalm 103:19 (cf. also Isaiah 66:1): "The Lord has fixed his throne in heaven, his sovereign power rules over all." Nöldeke-Schwally (*History,* 1:184) argue that this verse might be a translation of a Jewish or Christian hymn.

---

²⁵⁶There is no compulsion in religion: rectitude has become distinct from error. So one who disavows satanic entities and has faith in God has held fast to the firmest handle for which there is no breaking; and God is all-hearing, all-knowing.

2:256 On the term for "satanic entities" (*ṭāghūt*), see commentary on 4:51–52 (with further references).

---

²⁵⁷God is the friend of the faithful: He brings them out of darkness into light. As for the faithless, their friends are satanic

entities, who drive them out of light into darkness. They shall be the inmates of the Fire, and they will remain in it [forever].

2:257 "Jesus then said: The light will be with you only a little longer now. Go on your way while you have the light, or darkness will overtake you, and nobody who walks in the dark knows where he is going." (Joh 12:35; cf. Joh 12:46). Cf. Q 2:17; 5:16. On the term for "satanic entities" (*ṭāghūt*), see commentary on 4:51–52 (with further references).

---

²⁵⁸Have you not regarded him who argued with Abraham about his Lord, [only] because God had given him kingdom? When Abraham said, 'My Lord is He who gives life and brings death,' he replied, 'I [too] give life and bring death.' Abraham said, 'God indeed brings the sun from the east; now you bring it from the west.' Thereat the faithless one was dumbfounded. And God does not guide the wrongdoing lot.

2:258 *Tafsīr al-Jalālayn* rightly identifies "him who argued with Abraham about his Lord" as Nimrod. While in the Bible Nimrod appears only as a "mighty hunter" (see Gen 10:8–9; 1Ch 1:10), in later Jewish and Christian tradition he becomes a mighty king who organized the building of the Tower of Babel. This verse appears to be related to a tradition in *Genesis Rabbah* which has Abraham (as a child) argue with King Nimrod over proper worship (on Abraham's conflict with his father and his father's people over idolatry, see commentary on 26:69–93, with further references):

> [Abraham's father Terah] seized him and delivered him to Nimrod. "Let us worship the fire!" he [Nimrod] proposed. "Let us rather worship water, which extinguishes the fire," replied he. "Then let us worship water!" "Let us rather worship the clouds which bear the water!" "Then let us worship the clouds!" "Let us rather worship the winds which disperse the clouds." "Then let us worship the wind?" "Let us rather worship human beings, who withstand the wind." "You are just bandying words," he exclaimed; "we will worship nought but the fire." (*Genesis Rabbah*, 38:13)

Speyer wonders (*BEQ*, 141) if the Qur'ān's detail regarding the sun's changing directions may be connected to a report in the Talmud (b. Sanhedrin, 90a) that one should not follow a prophet who teaches idolatry even if he makes the sun stand still.

――――――――――

²⁵⁹Or him who came upon a township as it lay fallen on its trellises. He said, 'How will God revive this after its death?!' So God made him die for a hundred years, then He resurrected him. He said, 'How long did you remain?' Said he, 'I have remained a day or part of a day.' He said, 'No, you have remained a hundred years. Now look at your food and drink which have not rotted! Then look at your ass! [This was done] that We may make you a sign for mankind. And now look at the bones, how We raise them up and then clothe them with flesh!' When it became evident to him, he said, 'I know that God has power over all things.'

2:259 As in the previous verse the Qur'ān here uses a narrative from Biblical tradition to illustrate its teaching that God alone has power over life and death (cf. 2:28, 243; 3:156; 7:158; 9:116; 10:56; 15:23; 23:80; 30:19). "Township" here translates the Arabic *qarya* (cf. 2:58) and refers to Jerusalem. This verse is related to an anecdote found in the *Paraleipomena of Jeremiah* (a Jewish text, also known as 4 Baruch, from the second century AD) by which Abimelech (see Jer 38:7–13) is made to fall asleep just before the destruction of Jerusalem by the Babylonians and is awoken sixty-six years later:

> But Abimelech took the figs in the burning heat; and coming upon a tree, he sat under its shade to rest a bit. And leaning his head on the basket of figs, he fell asleep and slept for 66 years; and he was not awakened from his slumber. And afterward, when he awoke from his sleep, he said: I slept sweetly for a little while but my head is heavy because I did not get enough sleep. . . . And as he sat, he saw an old man coming from the field; and Abimelech said to him: I say to you, old man, what city is this? And he said to him: It is Jerusalem. And Abimelech said to him: "Where is Jeremiah the priest, and Baruch the secretary, and all the people of this city, for I could not find them? And the old man said to him: Are you not from this city, seeing that you remember

Jeremiah today, because you are asking about him after such a long time? For Jeremiah is in Babylon with the people; for they were taken captive by king Nebuchadnezzar, and Jeremiah is with them to preach the good news to them and to teach them the word." (*Paraleipomena of Jeremiah,* 5:1–3, 15–19)

The manner in which the Qur'ān has God speak of His power to clothe bones with flesh in the second part of the verse may be related to the vision of a valley full of bones in Ezekiel 37 (see commentary on 2:243). This verse is closely related to the passage in Q 18 on the People of the Cave (see commentary on 18:9–26).

---

²⁶⁰And when Abraham said, 'My Lord! Show me how You revive the dead,' He said, 'Do you not believe?' He said, 'Yes indeed, but in order that my heart may be at rest.' He said, 'Catch four of the birds and cut them into pieces, and place a part of them on every mountain, then call them; they will come to you hastening. And know that God is all-mighty and all-wise.'

2:260 Here the Qur'ān again (as in 2:258, 259) illustrates God's power over life and death by referring to a Biblical tradition. The tradition is related to Genesis 15, where Abram (i.e., Abraham) is commanded to sacrifice four animals:

⁹He said to him, 'Bring me a three-year-old heifer, a three-year-old she-goat, a three-year-old ram, a turtledove and a young pigeon.'
¹⁰He brought him all these, split the animals down the middle and placed each half opposite the other; but the birds he did not divide.
¹¹And whenever birds of prey swooped down on the carcases, Abram drove them off. (Gen 15:6–11)

In the Qur'ān the animals become four birds (*Tafsīr al-Jalālayn* identifies them as a peacock, an eagle, a raven, and a cock). Tellingly, in both Genesis 15 and in the Qur'ān (cf. 2:258) Abraham has already demonstrated his faith and seeks merely a confirmation of that which God has told to him. Only the Qur'ān, however, has Abraham show interest in the resurrection of the body. Abraham's demand for a sign might be compared with that of the disciples of Jesus in 5:112. The turn of phrase "that my heart be at rest" (*li-yaṭma'inna qalbī*) with which Abraham responds is found in the response of the disciples to Jesus in 5:113.

²⁶¹The parable of those who spend their wealth in the way of God is that of a grain which grows seven ears, in every ear a hundred grains. God enhances severalfold for whomever He wishes, and God is all-bounteous, all-knowing.

²⁶²Those who spend their wealth in the way of God and then do not follow up what they have spent with reproaches and affronts, they shall have their reward near their Lord, and they will have no fear, nor will they grieve.

²⁶³A polite reply [to the needy] and forgiving [their annoyance] is better than a charity followed by affront. God is all-sufficient, most forbearing.

²⁶⁴O you who have faith! Do not render your charities void by reproaches and affronts, like those who spend their wealth to be seen by people and have no faith in God and the Last Day. Their parable is that of a rock covered with soil: a downpour strikes it, leaving it bare. They have no power over anything they have earned, and God does not guide the faithless lot.

²⁶⁵The parable of those who spend their wealth seeking God's pleasure and to confirm themselves [in their faith], is that of a garden on a hillside: the downpour strikes it, whereupon it brings forth its fruit twofold; and if it is not a downpour that strikes it, then a shower, and God watches what you do.

2:261–65 In these verses the Qurʾān seems to build on the Gospel parable of the sower. Verse 2:264 reflects the seed which falls on rock, and verses 261 and 265 reflect the conclusion of that parable (e.g., Luk 8:8) which compares believers to a crop which grows abundantly:

⁴With a large crowd gathering and people from every town finding their way to him, he told this parable:

⁵'A sower went out to sow his seed. Now as he sowed, some fell on the edge of the path and was trampled on; and the birds of the air ate it up.

⁶Some seed fell on rock, and when it came up it withered away, having no moisture.

⁷Some seed fell in the middle of thorns and the thorns grew with it and choked it.

⁸And some seed fell into good soil and grew and produced its crop a hundred-fold.' Saying this he cried, 'Anyone who has ears for listening should listen!' (Luk 8:4–8; cf. Mat 13:1–9; Mar 4:1–9)

On verse 264, see also commentary on 4:38.

²⁶⁶Would any of you like to have a garden of palm trees and vines, with streams running in it, with all kinds of fruit for him therein, and old age were to strike him while he had weakly offspring; whereupon a fiery hurricane were to hit it, whereat it lies burnt? Thus does God clarify His signs for you so that you may reflect.

²⁶⁷O you who have faith! Spend of the good things you have earned [through trade and the like] and of what We bring forth for you from the earth, and do not be of the mind to give the bad part of it, for you yourselves would not take it, unless you ignore it. And know that God is all-sufficient, all-laudable.

²⁶⁸Satan frightens you of poverty and prompts you to [commit] indecent acts. But God promises you His forgiveness and grace, and God is all-bounteous, all-knowing.

²⁶⁹He grants wisdom to whomever He wishes, and he who is given wisdom, is certainly given an abundant good, and none takes admonition except those who possess intellect.

²⁷⁰God indeed knows whatever charity you may give, or vows that you may vow, and the wrongdoers have no helpers. ²⁷¹If you disclose your charities, that is well, but if you hide them and give them to the poor, that is better for you, and it will atone for some of your misdeeds, and God is well aware of what you do.

2. al-Baqara, *The Heifer*   *105*

²⁷²It is not up to *you* to guide them; rather, it is God who guides whomever He wishes.

Whatever wealth you spend, it is for your own benefit, as you do not spend but to seek God's pleasure, and whatever wealth you spend will be repaid to you in full and you will not be wronged.

²⁷³[The charities are] for the poor who are straitened in the way of God, not capable of moving about in the land [for trade]. The unaware suppose them to be well-off because of their reserve. You recognize them by their mark; they do not ask the people importunately. And whatever wealth you may spend, God indeed knows it.

²⁷⁴Those who give their wealth by night and day, secretly and openly, they shall have their reward near their Lord, and they will have no fear, nor will they grieve.

2:270–274, The notion that God knows of those who give alms (even if they do so secretly) reflects Matthew 6:1–4, esp. verse 4: "Your almsgiving must be secret, and your Father who sees all that is done in secret will reward you."

———————

²⁷⁵Those who exact usury will not stand but like one deranged by the Devil's touch. That is because they say, 'Trade is just like usury.' While God has allowed trade and forbidden usury. Whoever relinquishes [usury] on receiving advice from his Lord shall keep [the gains of] what is past, and his matter will rest with God. As for those who resume, they shall be the inmates of the Fire and they will remain in it [forever].

²⁷⁶God brings usury to naught, but makes charities flourish. God does not like any sinful ingrate.

²⁷⁷Indeed, those who have faith, do righteous deeds, maintain the prayer and give the *zakat,* they shall have their reward near their Lord, and they will have no fear, nor will they grieve.

[278]O you who have faith! Be wary of God and abandon [all claims to] what remains of usury, should you be faithful. [279]And if you do not, then be informed of a war from God and His apostle. And if you repent, then you will have your principal, neither harming others, nor suffering harm. [280]If [the debtor] is in straits, let there be a respite until the time of ease; and if you remit [the debt] as charity, it will be better for you, should you know. [281]And beware of a day in which you will be brought back to God. Then every soul shall be recompensed fully for what it has earned, and they will not be wronged.

[282]O you who have faith! When you contract a loan for a specified term, write it down. Let a writer write with honesty between you, and let not the writer refuse to write as God has taught him. So let him write, and let the one who incurs the debt dictate, and let him be wary of God, his Lord, and not diminish anything from it. But if the debtor be feeble-minded, or weak, or incapable of dictating himself, then let his guardian dictate with honesty, and take as witness two witnesses from your men, and if there are not two men, then a man and two women—from those whom you approve as witnesses—so that if one of the two defaults the other will remind her. The witnesses must not refuse when they are called, and do not consider it wearisome to write it down, whether it be a big or small sum, [as a loan lent] until its term. That is more just with God and more upright in respect to testimony, and the likeliest way to avoid doubt, unless it is an on-the-spot deal you transact between yourselves, in which case there is no sin upon you not to write it. Take witnesses when you make a deal, and let no harm be done to the writer or witness, and if you did that, it would be sinful of you. Be wary of God and God will teach you, and God has knowledge of all things.

²⁸³If you are on a journey and cannot find a writer, then a retained pledge [shall suffice]. And if one of you entrusts [an asset] to another, let him who is trusted deliver his trust, and let him be wary of God, his Lord. And do not conceal your testimony; anyone who conceals it, his heart will indeed be sinful. And God knows well what you do.

²⁸⁴To God belongs whatever is in the heavens and the earth. Whether you disclose what is in your hearts or hide it, God will bring you to account for it. Then He will forgive whomever He wishes and punish whomever He wishes, and God has power over all things.

²⁸⁵The Apostle and the faithful have faith in what has been sent down to him from his Lord. Each [of them] has faith in God, His angels, His scriptures and His apostles. [They declare,] 'We make no distinction between any of His apostles.' And they say, 'We hear and obey. Our Lord, forgive us, and toward You is the return.'

2:285 The declaration attributed to the believers here (cf. 5:7; 24:51), "We hear and obey" might be compared to that attributed to the Jews in 2:93 and 4:46, where they are made to say "We hear and disobey" (cf. also 8:21). See commentary on 2:93.

———————

²⁸⁶God does not task any soul beyond its capacity. Whatever [good] it earns is to its own benefit, and whatever [evil] it incurs is to its own harm.

'Our Lord! Do not take us to task if we forget or make mistakes! Our Lord! Do not place upon us a burden as You placed on those who were before us! Our Lord! Do not lay upon us what we

have no strength to bear! Excuse us, forgive us, and be merciful
to us! You are our Master, so help us against the faithless lot!'

2:286 The idea here is close to that of Paul in 1 Corinthians: "None of the
trials which have come upon you is more than a human being can stand. You can
trust that God will not let you be put to the test beyond your strength, but with
any trial will also provide a way out by enabling you to put up with it" (1Co
10:13; cf. *BEQ,* 451).

3. *Āl ʿImrān*, The Family of ʿImrān

In the Name of God, the All-beneficent, the All-merciful.

¹*Alif, Lām, Mīm.*

²God—there is no god except Him—is the Living One, the All-sustainer. ³He has sent down to *you* the Book with the truth, confirming what was [revealed] before it, and He had sent down the Torah and the Evangel ⁴before as guidance for mankind, and He has sent down the Criterion. Indeed, there is a severe punishment for those who deny the signs of God, and God is all-mighty, avenger.

3:3–4 Islamic tradition associates the Torah with a scripture, or revelation, given to Moses, and the "Evangel" or "Gospel" (Ar. *Injīl*) with a scripture, or revelation, given to Jesus. These are assumed to have been Islamic scriptures similar to the Qurʾān. Unlike the Qurʾān, however, the Torah and the Gospel were lost or corrupted. The Old and New Testaments are thus falsified versions of Islamic scriptures. However, the Qurʾān could be using the term "Torah" (from Hb. *tōrāh*) to refer to the Hebrew Bible (and not only to a theorized Islamic scripture), and it could be using the singular *Injīl* (from Gk. *euaggelion*, probably through Ethiopic *wāngel*) to refer to the New Testament (indeed in 5:47 and 7:157 the Qurʾān seems to use *Injīl* to refer to the Christian scriptures). On the term rendered here as "Criterion" (Ar. *furqān*), see commentary on 2:53.

⁵Nothing is indeed hidden from God in the earth or in the sky.
⁶It is He who forms you in the wombs [of your mothers] however He wishes. There is no god except Him, the All-mighty, the
All-wise.

3:6 On the verb rendered here as "forms" (*ṣawwara*), see commentary on
40:64 (with further references).

⁷It is He who has sent down to *you* the Book. Parts of it are definitive verses, which are the mother of the Book, while others are
ambiguous. As for those in whose hearts is deviance, they pursue
what is metaphorical in it, pursuing misguidance and aiming at
its [mis]interpretation. But no one knows its interpretation except God and those firmly grounded in knowledge; they say, 'We
believe in it; all of it is from our Lord.' Only those who possess
intellect take admonition.
⁸[They say,] 'Our Lord! Do not make our hearts swerve after
You have guided us, and bestow Your mercy on us. Indeed, You
are the All-munificent. ⁹Our Lord! You will indeed gather mankind on a day in which there is no doubt. God indeed does not
break His promise.'
¹⁰As for the faithless, neither their wealth nor their children
shall avail them anything against God; it is they who will be fuel
for the Fire; ¹¹as in the case of Pharaoh's clan and those who were
before them, who denied Our signs. So God seized them for their
sins, and God is severe in retribution.
¹²Say to the faithless, 'You shall be overcome and mustered
toward hell, and it is an evil resting place.'
¹³There was certainly a sign for you in the two hosts that met:
one host fighting in the way of God and the other faithless, who

saw them as visibly twice as many. God strengthens whomever He wishes with His help. There is indeed a moral in that for those who have insight.

[14]The love of [worldly] allures, including women and children, accumulated piles of gold and silver, horses of mark, livestock and farms, has been made to seem decorous to mankind. Those are the wares of the life of this world, but goodness of one's ultimate destination lies with God. [15]*Say,* 'Shall I inform you of something better than that? For those who are Godwary there will be gardens near their Lord, with streams running in them, to remain in them [forever], and chaste mates, and God's pleasure.' And God watches His servants.

3:15 On the description of paradise here (including the reference to "chaste mates"), see commentary on 2:25.

---

[16]Those who say, 'Our Lord! Indeed, we have faith. So forgive us our sins, and save us from the punishment of the Fire.' [17][They are] patient and truthful, obedient and charitable, and they plead for [God's] forgiveness at dawns.

[18]God, maintainer of justice, the Almighty and the All-wise, besides whom there is no god, bears witness that there is no god except Him, and [so do] the angels and those who possess knowledge.

[19]Indeed, with God religion is Islām, and those who were given the Book did not differ except after knowledge had come to them, out of envy among themselves. And whoever denies God's signs [should know that] God is swift at reckoning.

3:19 With "Islām" the Qurʾān here presumably means "submission" (the meaning of the Arabic term *islām*) and not Islam as a proper name (it was presumably verses such as this—and 3:85, and 5:3—which led later Muslims to name their religion "Islam"). The statement "those who were given the Book" (i.e., earlier revelations) differed after "knowledge [again, an allusion to divine revelation] had come to them" (cf. 2:213, 253; 3:105; 10:93; 42:14; 45:17; 98:4) is a reference to the religious disputes between Christians and Jews, and among Christians, testified by the literature of religious polemic in the Late Antique Near East.

---

²⁰If they argue with *you,* say, 'I have submitted my will to God, and [so has] he who follows me.' And *say* to those who were given the Book and the uninstructed ones, 'Do you submit?' If they submit, they will certainly be guided; but if they turn away, *your* duty is only to communicate, and God watches His servants.

3:20 The Arabic word *ummiyyūn* is rendered here as "uninstructed ones"; *Tafsīr al-Jalālayn* explains this term as a reference to "Arab idolaters." In fact, the word is related to *umma,* "nation," and means "gentiles" in the sense of those people to whom God has not yet given part of the divine revelation, or "Book." See commentary on 2:78–79 (with further references).

---

²¹Those who deny God's signs and kill the prophets unjustly and kill those who call for justice from among the people, inform them of a painful punishment.

3:21 On the killing of the prophets, an accusation which the Qurʾān makes against the Jews, see commentary on 3:181–82 (with further references).

---

²²They are the ones whose works have failed in this world and the Hereafter, and they will have no helpers.

²³Have *you* not regarded those who were given a share of the Book, who are summoned to the Book of God in order that it may

judge between them, whereat a part of them refuse to comply and they are disregardful? [24]That is because they say, 'The Fire shall not touch us except for numbered days,' and they have been misled in their religion by what they used to fabricate.

3:24 See commentary on 2:80–81. *Tafsīr al-Jalālayn* remarks here, "They said, 'the Fire shall not touch us, except for a number of days,' that is, for forty days [only], the length of time their forefathers worshipped the calf, after which it would end."

---

[25]But how will it be [with them] when We gather them on a day in which there is no doubt, and every soul shall be recompensed fully for what it has earned, and they will not be wronged?

[26]*Say,* 'O God, Master of all sovereignty! You give sovereignty to whomever You wish, and strip of sovereignty whomever You wish; You make mighty whomever You wish, and You degrade whomever You wish; all choice is in Your hand. Indeed, You have power over all things.'

3:26 "The Lord makes poor and rich, he humbles and also exalts" (1Sa 2:7; cf. Luk 1:52).

---

[27]'You make the night pass into the day and You make the day pass into the night. You bring forth the living from the dead and You bring forth the dead from the living, and provide for whomever You wish without reckoning.'

[28]The faithful should not take the faithless for protectors [and allies] instead of the faithful, and God will have nothing to do with those who do that, except out of caution, when you are wary

of them. God warns you to beware of [disobeying] Him, and toward God is the return.

²⁹*Say,* 'Whether you hide what is in your hearts or disclose it, God knows it, and He knows whatever there is in the heavens and whatever there is in the earth; and God has power over all things.'

³⁰The day when every soul will find present whatever good it has done; and as for the evil it has done, it will wish there were a far distance between it and itself. God warns you to beware of [disobeying] Him, and God is most kind to [His] servants.

³¹*Say,* 'If you love God, then follow me; God will love you and forgive you your sins, and God is all-forgiving, all-merciful.'

³²*Say,* 'Obey God and the Apostle.' But if they turn away, indeed God does not like the faithless.

³³Indeed, God chose Adam and Noah, and the progeny of Abraham and the progeny of Imran[,] above all the nations;

3:33 The name 'Imrān (v. 33) seems to correspond with Biblical Amram, the father of Moses, Aaron, and Miriam (the Hebrew form of "Mary") (cf. Num 26:59; 1Ch 5:29; also Exo 15:20). Here (cf. Q 66:12), however, he appears as the father of Mary, the mother of Jesus. The Qur'ān thus conflates the two Marys, as it does when it describes Mary as "sister of Aaron" (Q 19:28; note how in that same Sura, 19:53, Moses is named the "brother of Aaron"). The conflation is likely a confusion (on this see Geiger, *Judaism and Islam,* 136–37), although some scholars argue that it is an intentional way to emphasize Mary's connection to the temple in Jerusalem where (according to the tradition which the Qur'ān follows in this passage) she was raised. The fourth century Syriac Christian Aphrahat draws a parallel between the two Marys: "Miriam stood on the edge of the river when Moses was floating in the water; and Mary bare Jesus, after the Angel Gabriel had made the annunciation to her" (*Demonstrations* 21:10).

---

³⁴some of them are descendants of the others, and God is all-hearing, all-knowing.

³⁵When the wife of Imran said, 'My Lord, I dedicate to You in consecration what is in my belly. Accept it from me; indeed You are the All-hearing, the All-knowing.' ³⁶When she bore her, she said, 'My Lord, I have borne a female [child]'—and God knew better what she had borne, and the male [child she expected] was no match for the female [child she had borne]—'and I have named her Mary, and I commend her and her offspring to Your care against [the evil of] the outcast Satan.'

3:35–36 The Qurʾān follows closely here the *Protoevangelium of James,* a Greek Christian work written in the late second century and translated into Syriac in the fifth century. In the *Protoevangelium* Mary's mother (Anna; Hb. "Hannah") is barren, but when she laments, God sends an angel from heaven to announce that she will bear a child. In thanksgiving Anna proclaims that she will consecrate the child to the service of God in the Jerusalem temple. The scene recapitulates that of Hannah in 1 Samuel with an important exception: whereas the Old Testament Hannah asks God for a son (as "males belong to the Lord"; Exo 13:12), Anna (like the wife of ʿImrān in the Qurʾān) declares to God her readiness to accept a son or a daughter (cf. Q 3:36):

> And behold an angel of the Lord came to her and said: "Anna, Anna, the Lord has heard your prayer. You shall conceive and bear, and your offspring shall be spoken of in the whole world. And Anna said: "As the Lord my God lives, if I bear a child, *whether male or female,* I will bring it as a gift to the Lord my God, and it shall serve him all the days of its life." (*Protoevangelium* 4.1, emphasis added)

The manner in which the Qurʾān has Mary's mother commend Mary and her "descendants" (i.e., Jesus) to God's protection from the devil may allude to the Christian doctrine that Mary and Jesus were free from sin. On the reference to Satan as an "outcast" (Ar. *rajīm*), see commentary on 15:26–35.

———————

³⁷Thereupon her Lord accepted her with a gracious acceptance, and made her grow up in a worthy fashion, and He charged Zechariah with her care.

Whenever Zechariah visited her in the sanctuary, he would find provisions with her. He said, 'O Mary, from where does this come for you?' She said, 'It comes from God. God provides whomever He wishes without reckoning.'

3:37 The Qurʾān follows here a tradition also found in the *Protoevangelium of James* in which Mary is brought to the Jerusalem temple, under the guardianship of Zechariah, once she is weaned. Mary then remains enclosed in a chamber in the temple, where she receives food "from the hand of an angel" (*Protoevangelium* 8.1):

> And when the child was three years old, Joachim said: "Let us call the undefiled daughters of the Hebrews, and let each one take a lamp, and let these be burning, in order that the child may not turn back and her heart be enticed away from the Temple of the Lord." And he did so until they went up to the Temple of the Lord. And the priest took her and kissed her and blessed her, saying: "The Lord has magnified your name among all generations; because of you the Lord at the end of the days will manifest his redemption to the children of Israel."
>
> And he placed her on the third step of the altar, and the Lord God put grace upon the child, and she danced for joy with her feet, and the whole house of Israel loved her.
>
> And her parents went down wondering, praising and glorifying the almighty God because the child did not turn back [to them]. And Mary was in the Temple nurtured like a dove and received food from the hand of an angel. (*Protoevangelium* 7.2–8.1)

The term rendered by the Qurʾān as "sanctuary," Arabic *miḥrāb*, has been thought to be related to a Semitic root (*ḥ.r.m.*) which is generally used for a sacred space, or temple (e.g., the *ḥarām* of Mecca). However, Christian Robin has shown ("Du paganisme," 152–53) that in South Arabian or Sabaean inscriptions *miḥrāb* is used for an important building. It is in this sense that the Qurʾān uses the term (although in later Islamic usage it also refers to the prayer niche in mosques). Here *miḥrāb* refers to the Jerusalem temple, where Zechariah is found in the Gospel of Luke when an angel announces to him the promise of a son (cf. Luk 1:5–20). In 3:39 and 19:11 *miḥrāb* also has the meaning of "temple," whereas in 34:13 (pl. *maḥārib*) and 38:21 it seems to mean "palace." All of these are consistent with the South Arabian origin of the term.

³⁸Thereat Zechariah supplicated his Lord. He said, 'My Lord! Grant me a good offspring from You! You indeed hear all supplications.'

³⁹Then, as he stood praying in the sanctuary the angels called out to him: 'God gives you the good news of John, as a confirmer of a Word of God, eminent and chaste, a prophet, and one of the righteous.'

⁴⁰He said, 'My Lord, how shall I have a son while old age has overtaken me and my wife is barren?' Said He, 'So it is that God does whatever He wishes.'

3:38–40 This passage alludes to Luke's account of the annunciation of John to Zechariah, who was serving as a priest in the tabernacle of the Temple (Luk 1:5–13; discussed in commentary on 19:2–6).

Here (v. 39) the Qurʾān has God announce to Zechariah that his son, that is, John (cf. 19:7; 21:90), will be "a confirmer of a Word of God." This alludes to the turn of phrase ("word from Him") with which the angels describe Jesus to Mary in the annunciation in verse 45. To *Tafsīr al-Jalālayn* the Qurʾān describes Jesus as a word "because he was created through the *word* 'Be'" (see v. 47). In fact the Qurʾān seems to be using the language of John 1, which has John (the Baptist) announce the coming of Jesus, the Word of God:

> ¹⁴The Word became flesh, he lived among us, and we saw his glory, the glory that he has from the Father as only Son of the Father, full of grace and truth. ¹⁵John witnesses to him. He proclaims: 'This is the one of whom I said: He who comes after me has passed ahead of me because he existed before me.' (Joh 1:14–15)

The description (v. 39) of John the Baptist as "chaste" may reflect the Gospel portrait of John as a solitary figure who lived in the wilderness (Mat 3:1; Mar 1:4–6; Luk 3:2).

⁴¹He said, 'My Lord, grant me a sign.' Said He, 'Your sign is that you will not speak to people for three days except in gestures.

Remember your Lord much often, and glorify Him morning and evening.'

3:41 This verse (cf. 19:10–11) might be compared with Luke 1:18–20 (see also commentary on 19:7–11), but note that in the Qurʾān Zechariah's muteness is not a punishment but a "sign" granted to him:

> [18]Zechariah said to the angel, 'How can I know this? I am an old man and my wife is getting on in years.'
> [19]The angel replied, 'I am Gabriel, who stand in God's presence, and I have been sent to speak to you and bring you this good news.
> [20]Look! Since you did not believe my words, which will come true at their appointed time, you will be silenced and have no power of speech until this has happened.' (Luk 1:18–20)

---

[42]And when the angels said, 'O Mary, God has chosen you and purified you, and He has chosen you above the world's women.

3:42 The Qurʾān might be following Luke's narrative here in its description of Mary when it has the angels declare to Mary, God has "chosen you above the world's women":

> [41]Now it happened that as soon as Elizabeth heard Mary's greeting, the child leapt in her womb and Elizabeth was filled with the Holy Spirit.
> [42]She gave a loud cry and said, 'Of all women you are the most blessed, and blessed is the fruit of your womb. (Luk 1:41–42)

Tafsīr al-Jalālayn, presumably in deference to those traditions which make one of the Prophet's wives or daughters equal or superior to Mary, remarks that the Qurʾān only means that Mary is superior to "the inhabitants of [her] time."

---

[43]O Mary, be obedient to your Lord, and prostrate and bow down with those who bow [in worship].'

⁴⁴These accounts are from the Unseen, which We reveal to *you,* and *you* were not with them when they were casting lots [to see] which of them would take charge of Mary's care, nor were *you* with them when they were contending.

3:44 Islamic tradition understands verse 3:44 as something like a flashback to the moment when Zechariah was chosen to be Mary's guardian (he already appears as her guardian in v. 37). The word translated here as "lots" (Ar. *aqlām*) is generally understood as "pens" (it does have this meaning elsewhere: 31:27; 68:1; 96:4). *Tafsīr al-Jalālayn* relates that men cast quills into water to choose who would have the "custodianship of Mary" (other traditions relate that when the pen of Zechariah went motionless, or floated upstream, he was designated Mary's custodian). In fact the Qurʾān is following the chronology of Mary's life as found in the *Protoevangelium.* The contest is over who will marry Mary, and it involves not pens but rods, or reeds. The Arabic *aqlām* comes from Greek *kalamos* (and it is a *kalamos,* "reed," that soldiers put in the right hand of Christ in Mat 27:29):

> And Joseph threw down his axe and went out to meet them. And when they were gathered together, they took the rods and went to the high priest. The priest took the rods from them and entered the Temple and prayed. When he had finished the prayer he took the rods, and went out (again) and gave them to them: but there was no sign on them. Joseph received the last rod, and behold, a dove came out of the rod and flew on to Joseph's head. And the priest said to Joseph: "Joseph, to you has fallen the good fortune to receive the virgin of the Lord; take her under your care." (*Protoevangelium* 9.1)

---

⁴⁵When the angels said, 'O Mary, God gives you the good news of a Word from Him whose name is Messiah, Jesus son of Mary, distinguished in the world and the Hereafter, and one of those brought near [to God]. ⁴⁶He will speak to the people in the cradle and in adulthood, and will be one of the righteous.'

⁴⁷She said, 'My Lord, how shall I have a child seeing that no human has ever touched me?' He said, 'So it is that God creates

whatever He wishes. When He decides on a matter He just says to it "Be!" and it is.

3:45–47 The Qurʾān here has "angels" speak to Mary, whereas in the Gospel of Luke (and in Q 19:17–21) only one angel does so (the same change takes place with Zechariah—one angel in Luke 1 and "angels" in Q 3:39). Otherwise the Qurʾān seems to follow Luke:

> [31]Look! You are to conceive in your womb and bear a son, and you must name him Jesus.
> [32]He will be great and will be called Son of the Most High. The Lord God will give him the throne of his ancestor David;
> [33]he will rule over the House of Jacob for ever and his reign will have no end.'
> [34]Mary said to the angel, 'But how can this come about, since I have no knowledge of man?'
> [35]The angel answered, 'The Holy Spirit will come upon you, and the power of the Most High will cover you with its shadow. And so the child will be holy and will be called Son of God. (Luk 1:31–35)

The Qurʾān's use of "Messiah" to refer to Jesus has none of the sense of the Hebrew word *māshīaḥ* ("anointed one" and, idiomatically, "the awaited savior"). Instead, the Qurʾān seems to make this word a proper name of Jesus.

It is curious that the Qurʾān has the angels—who are speaking to Mary—refer to Jesus as "Jesus, son of Mary."

The reference in verse 46 to Jesus' speaking "to the people in the cradle" (cf. 5:110; 19:29) refers to a tradition found in the Latin *Gospel of Pseudo-Matthew* (likely written in the early seventh century). On this see further commentary on 19:16–26.

The description of God's ability to create by speaking may allude to the manner of God's creation described in Genesis 1 (see also commentary on 36:82). The description of Jesus as a "word" follows from the Christian theological language connected to John 1:1: "In the beginning was the Word: the Word was with God and the Word was God" (see also commentary on 3:38–40). On the Qurʾān's denial that God would beget a son, see commentary on 2:116–17 (with further references).

---

[48]He will teach him the Book and wisdom, the Torah and the Evangel,

3:48 This verse is related to 5:110. On Torah and Evangel, see commentary on 3:3–4. The suggestion of Horovitz (*KU*, 71–73) that "wisdom" refers to "pre-Mosaic" revelations is not to be followed (see also commentary on 3:79–80). None of these four terms ("Book," "wisdom," "Torah," "Evangel") should be associated with any particular scripture or revelation. "Torah" and "Evangel" mean generally the revelations given to Moses and Jesus respectively (cf. 3:3, 65; 5:46, 66; 7:157), while Book and wisdom (cf. 2:129, 151, 231; 3:81, 164; 4:54, 113; 5:110; 6:89; 45:16; 62:2) are general and overlapping terms for divine revelation.

Regarding "wisdom" (*ḥikma*), one should note that the Qurʾān also refers to revelation as a *ḥukm* given by God (e.g., 3:79; 12:22, where Qarai translates "judgment," and 13:37, where he translates "dispensation"; cf. also 6:89; 19:12; 21:74, 79; 26:21; 28:14; 45:16; 52:48; 60:10; 68:48; 76:24).

————————

⁴⁹and [he will be] an apostle to the Children of Israel, [and he will declare,] "I have certainly brought you a sign from your Lord: I will create for you the form of a bird out of clay, then I will breathe into it, and it will become a bird by God's leave. I heal the blind and the leper and I revive the dead by God's leave. I will tell you what you have eaten and what you have stored in your houses. There is indeed a sign in that for you, should you be faithful.

3:49 Jesus is here made to address the Israelites directly as in 5:72 and 61:6. The miracle of Jesus' creating a bird (or birds) from clay, and his bringing it to life with his breath (cf. 5:110), is known from the apocryphal *Childhood of the Savior* (second century AD; commonly, and erroneously, referred to as the Infancy Gospel of Thomas). In the Christian context the point is to have Jesus create a living thing in the way that God creates Adam (Gen 2:7):

¹When the boy Jesus was five years old, he was playing at the ford of a rushing stream. And he gathered the disturbed water into pools and made them pure and excellent, commanding them by the character of his word alone and not by means of a deed.
²Then, taking soft clay from the mud, he formed twelve sparrows. It was the Sabbath when he did these things, and many children were with him.

³And a certain Jew, seeing the boy Jesus with the other children doing these things, went to his father Joseph and falsely accused the boy Jesus, saying that, on the Sabbath he made clay, which is not lawful, and fashioned twelve sparrows.

⁴And Joseph came and rebuked him, saying, "Why are you doing these things on the Sabbath?" But Jesus, clapping his hands, commanded the birds with a shout in front of everyone and said, "Go, take flight, and remember me, living ones." And the sparrows, taking flight, went away squawking. (*Childhood of the Savior* 1:1–4)

The Qurʾān has Jesus declare that he does this (and most, but not all, of the following miracles) "by God's leave," and therefore implies that these miracles are not signs of his divinity. Still, it might be noted that with this miracle the Jesus of the Qurʾān acts like the God of the Qurʾān, who creates Adam (Q 15:29; 38.72) and Jesus (Q 21:91) with his breath.

For Jesus' healing the blind, see: Mat 9:27–30, 12:22, 15:30–31, 20:30–34; Mar 8:22–26; Luk 18:35–43; Joh 9:1–7. For Jesus' healing lepers, see Mat 8:2–3; Mar 1:40–41; Luk 5:12–13. For Jesus' raising the dead, see Mar 5:38–42; cf. also Joh 11:17–44: The clairvoyant miracles alluded to at the end of the verse ("I will tell you what you have eaten and what you have stored in your houses") are not attested in earlier Gospels (and are missing from the parallel verse 5:110), but they seem to reflect a Christian perspective which has the divine Jesus know the unseen.

---

⁵⁰[I come] to confirm [the truth of] that which is before me of the Torah, and to make lawful for you some of the things that were forbidden you. I have brought you a sign from your Lord; so be wary of God and obey me.

3:50 On Jesus' confirming the Torah, see Q 5:46; 61:6. On Jesus' bringing signs to Israel, see Q 43:63; 61:6.

The idea in this verse that Jesus permitted some of the things which were once forbidden may be related to those Qurʾānic passages which explain that certain things were forbidden to the Israelites only because of their wrongdoing (cf. also Gospel passages such as Mat 15:17–20 and Mar 7:18–23; cr. Matthew

Kuiper). As Holger Zellentin argues (*Qurʾān's Legal Culture,* 140ff.) in this the Qurʾān seems to reflect an idea found in the Syriac *Didascalia* (based on Ezekiel 20:23–25) that God imposed additional burdensome laws—a second law—upon the Jews. See further commentary on 4:160 (with further references).

The final phrase in the Qurʾānic verse ("so be wary of God and obey me"), which is given to Jesus also in 43:63, is a refrain used by various prophets in Qurʾān 26 (vv. 108, 110, 126, 131, 144, 150, 163, 179).

⁵¹God is indeed my Lord and your Lord; so worship Him. This is a straight path."'

3:51 On the declaration "Worship God, my Lord and your Lord," which the Qurʾān attributes to Jesus on several occasions (5:72, 117; 19:36; 43:64) see commentary on 43:63–65.

⁵²When Jesus sensed their faithlessness, he said, 'Who will be my helpers [on the path] toward God?' The Disciples said, 'We will be helpers of God. We have faith in God, and you be witness that we have submitted [to Him]. ⁵³Our Lord, we believe in what You have sent down, and we follow the apostle, so write us among the witnesses.'

⁵⁴Then they plotted [against Jesus], and God also devised, and God is the best of devisers.

3:52–54 The term in verse 52 (cf. 61:14) rendered as "helpers" is *anṣār.* It might have been chosen because of its relationship to the Qurʾānic term for Christians: *naṣārā.* Also in this verse the Qurʾān has the disciples of Jesus call themselves *muslimūn* "submitted [to God]" (cf. 5:111).

According to the traditional Islamic understanding, the disciples were faithful companions of Jesus (*Tafsīr al-Jalālayn* calls them "Jesus's intimates and the first to believe in him"). V. 54, however, might imply that the disciples plotted against God. To avoid this conclusion, most commentators argue that the pronoun "they" in this verse refers to the Israelites (Jews) who rejected Jesus when they plotted against him and attempted to crucify him (Qarai implies as much by adding the words "against Jesus"). God proved himself to be the best of "plotters" or "devisers" (*khayru l-mākirīn;* cf. Q 7:99; 8:30; note that the same verb is translated differently in this latter verse) when he rescued Jesus from this plot (but on this see commentary on 4:157). *Tafsīr al-Jalālayn* relates "God says: And they, the disbelievers among the Children of Israel, schemed, against Jesus, by assigning someone to assassinate him; and God schemed, by casting the likeness of Jesus onto the person who intended to kill him, and so they killed him, while Jesus was raised up into heaven; and God is the best of schemers, most knowledgeable of him [Jesus]."

The way the disciples respond to the call of Jesus in verse 53, by declaring their belief in him, might be compared to the way that Christians in 5:83 are said to respond to the revelation given to the Qurʾān's Prophet.

---

⁵⁵When God said, 'O Jesus, I shall take you[r soul], and I shall raise you up toward Myself, and I shall clear you of [the calumnies of] the faithless, and I shall set those who follow you above the faithless until the Day of Resurrection. Then to Me will be your return, whereat I will judge between you concerning that about which you used to differ.

3:55 Our translator has God here say to Jesus: "I shall take your soul." The Arabic term (*tawaffā*) behind the translation is regularly used in the Qurʾān to refer to the manner by which God separates soul from body at death, that is, His taking one's life (note, for example, the prayer in 7:126: "Lord! Pour patience upon us, and *grant us to die [tawaffanā] as muslims.*") However, according to the standard Islamic teaching (see commentary on 4:157), Jesus did not die but was taken up to heaven body and soul (cf. 4:158). Thus, *Tafsīr al-Jalālayn* paraphrases this passage: "'O Jesus, I am gathering you, seizing you, and raising you to Me, away from the world *without death.*" Not all translators agree with this idea; Asad translates "shall cause thee to die."

The second part of this verse seems to have God promise that those who followed Jesus (i.e., Christians) will be set above those who did not (i.e., Jews). This is in harmony with an idea prevalent in early Christian sources, including Syriac fathers such as Jacob of Serugh, by which the Jews were punished for their rejection of Christ:

> The kings have levelled Jerusalem and brought down its walls / Who is it who has cut off the unction of the priests which exists no more?
>
> He is above in heaven, He who hates you and strikes you. / Yet if you wish to confess His Son He will be calm (Jacob of Serugh, *Homélies contre les juifs,* 146, homily 5, ll. 167–70)

Some Muslim interpreters, however, are wary of the idea that this verse would suggest a special favor given to Christians. Hilali-Khan translates: "I will make those who follow you (Monotheists, who worship none but God) superior to those who disbelieve [in the Oneness of God, or disbelieve in some of His Messengers, e.g., Muḥammad, ʿIsa (Jesus), Musa (Moses), etc."

———————

⁵⁶As for the faithless, I will punish them with a severe punishment in the world and the Hereafter; and they will have no helpers.' ⁵⁷But as for those who have faith and do righteous deeds, He will pay them in full their rewards, and God does not like the wrongdoers.

⁵⁸These that We recite to *you* are from the signs and the Wise Reminder.

⁵⁹Indeed, the case of Jesus with God is like the case of Adam: He created him from dust, then said to him, 'Be,' and he was.

3:59 According to the standard Islamic interpretation, in this verse the Qurʾān is refuting the idea that Jesus is the divine Son of God because he has no father (by pointing out that Adam, too, had no father). Wāḥidī embeds this interpretation in a story about Christians from the southern Arabian city of Najrān who visited the Prophet Muḥammad one day: "Two monks from Najran came to see the Prophet and he invited them to surrender to God. One of them said: 'We have surrendered to God before you.' He said: 'You lie! Three things prevent you from surrendering to God: your worship of the cross, eating pork and your claim that God has a son.' They said: 'Then who is the father of Jesus?' The Prophet was not in the habit of giving hasty answers but waited for God's answer instead. Then God revealed this verse."

Elsewhere in the Qurʾān God creates Adam (15:29; 38:72) and Jesus (21:91) by his breath, but here he does so by speaking. Elsewhere (see commentary on 36:82, with further references), the Qurʾān declares that whenever God wants to create something he simply says "Be" (see also 2:117; 3:47, with reference to Jesus; 19:35, perhaps with reference to Jesus). On the creation of humans from dust, see commentary on 11:61 (with further references).

---

⁶⁰This is the truth from *your* Lord, so do not be among the skeptics.

⁶¹Should anyone argue with *you* concerning him, after the knowledge that has come to *you,* say, 'Come! Let us call our sons and your sons, our women and your women, our souls and your souls, then let us pray earnestly and call down God's curse upon the liars.'

⁶²This is indeed the true account, for sure. There is no god but God, and indeed God is the All-mighty, the All-wise.

⁶³But if they turn away, indeed God knows best the agents of corruption.

⁶⁴*Say,* 'O People of the Book! Come to a common word between us and you: that we will worship no one but God, that we will not ascribe any partner to Him, and that some of us will not take some others as lords besides God.'

But if they turn away, *say,* 'Be witnesses that we have submitted [to God].'

3:64 The opening of this verse ("O People of the Book!") marks a discrete section of the Sura. Where our translator has a "common word," the Arabic seems to mean "balanced," that is, "reasonable" (cf. the use of *sawāʾ* in 8:58; 21:109). Indeed the verse is full of the language which the Qurʾān employs elsewhere (cf. 3:80; 5:72; 9:31) against Jews and Christians; in other words, this verse is not an invitation to some sort of theological compromise but a reproach of Jews and Christians. Thereby it acts as an introduction to the following verses. The end of the verse ("But if they turn away, say, 'Be witnesses that we are *muslims*'") is parallel to the words of Jesus' disciples in 3:52; 5:111.

---

[65]O People of the Book! Why do you argue concerning Abraham? Neither the Torah nor the Evangel were sent down until [long] after him. Do you not exercise your reason? [66]Ah! You are • the ones who argue about that of which you have knowledge. But why do you argue about that of which you have no knowledge? And God knows and you do not know. [67]Abraham was neither a Jew nor a Christian. Rather, he was a *ḥanīf,* a muslim, and he was not one of the polytheists.

[68]Indeed, the nearest of all people to Abraham are those who follow him and this prophet and those who have faith, and God is the friend of the faithful.

3:65–68 This passage is parallel to Q 2:139–41. In Romans (cf. also Gal 4:21–26) Paul presents the faith of Abraham (who lived before the Jewish law was given to Moses on Mt. Sinai) as a prophetic anticipation of Christian faith:

> [2]If Abraham had been justified because of what he had done, then he would have had something to boast about. But not before God:
> [3]does not scripture say: Abraham put his faith in God and this was reckoned to him as uprightness? (Rom 4:2–3)

Later Christians, such as Eusebius (d. ca. 340), are more explicit still, comparing the religion of Abraham with that of Christians:

> It was by faith towards the Logos of God, the Christ who had appeared to him, that he was justified, and gave up the superstition of his fathers, and his

former erroneous life, and confessed the God who is over all to be one; and Him he served by virtuous deeds, not by the worship of the law of Moses, who came later. . . . It is only among Christians throughout the whole world that the manner of religion which was Abraham's can actually be found in practice. (Eusebius, *Ecclesiastical History,* 1:4:13–14)

Here the Qurʾān responds to this claim by insisting that Abraham was neither a Jew nor a Christian (cf. 2:133, 140). On the term *ḥanīf* (v. 67), see commentary on 16:120–23 (with further references).

---

⁶⁹A group of the People of the Book were eager to lead you astray; yet they lead no one astray except themselves, but they are not aware.

⁷⁰O People of the Book! Why do you deny God's signs while you testify [to their truth]? ⁷¹O People of the Book! Why do you mix the truth with falsehood, and conceal the truth while you know [it]?

⁷²A group of the People of the Book say, 'Believe in what has been sent down to the faithful at the beginning of the day, and disbelieve at its end, so that they may turn back [from their religion].' ⁷³[They say], 'Do not believe anyone except him who follows your religion.'

Say, 'Guidance is indeed the guidance of God.'

[They say.] '[Do not believe] that anyone may be given the like of what you were given, or that he may argue with you before your Lord.'

Say, 'All grace is indeed in God's hand; He grants it to whomever He wishes, and God is all-bounteous, all-knowing. ⁷⁴He singles out for His mercy whomever He wishes, and God is dispenser of a mighty grace.'

⁷⁵Among the People of the Book is he who if you entrust him with a quintal will repay it to you, and among them is he who, if

you entrust him with a dinar will not repay it to you unless you stand persistently over him. That is because they say, 'We have no obligation to the non-Jews.' But they attribute lies to God, and they know [it].

3:75 Our translator implies that the Qurʾān here is referring specifically to the Jews (who say, "We have no obligation to non-Jews") and accusing them of dishonesty. Yet the word he translates as "non-Jews" (Ar. *ummiyyīn*) refers to those who are not People of the Book (i.e., neither Jews nor Christians, regarding which see commentary on 2:78–79, with further references). As Speyer mentions (*BEQ*, 451), this verse might be related to the parable of the unforgiving servant in Matthew 18:23–35.

⁷⁶Yes, whoever fulfills his commitments and is wary of God— God indeed loves the Godwary.

⁷⁷There shall be no share in the Hereafter for those who sell God's covenant and their oaths for a paltry gain, and on the Day of Resurrection God will not speak to them, nor will He [so much as] look at them, nor will He purify them, and there is a painful punishment for them.

⁷⁸There is indeed a group of them who alter their tone while reading out some text [that they have themselves authored], so that you may suppose it to be from the Book, though it is not from the Book, and they say, 'It is from God,' though it is not from God, and they attribute lies to God, and they know [it].

3:78 Behind Qarai's "alter their tone while reading out some text" is the Arabic *yalwūna alsinatahum bi-l-kitābi* (cf. 4:46). The "text" (Ar. *kitāb*) the Qurʾān alludes to is divine revelation. This is Asad's understanding when he translates "distort the Bible with their tongues." On scriptural falsification see commentary on 4:46 (with further references).

[79]It does not behoove any human that God should give him the Book, judgement and prophethood, and then he should say to the people, 'Be my servants instead of God.' Rather [he would say], 'Be a godly people, because of your teaching the Book and because of your studying it.' [80]And he would not command you to take the angels and the prophets for lords. Would he call you to unfaith after you have submitted [to God]?

3:79–80 J. Horovitz argues that with "Book, judgement (*ḥukm*), and prophethood" (cf. 6:89; 45:16; for just "prophethood and book," see 29:27; 57:26; see also 3:48 for "book and wisdom [*ḥikma*]"), the Qurʾān intends the three parts of the Hebrew Bible ("Torah, Prophets, and Writings"; see Horovitz, *KU*, 72ff.). More likely they are general and overlapping terms for divine revelation. According to the Qurʾān here, someone who has received these gifts from God ("Book, judgement, and prophethood") would not tell people to worship him (cf. 5:116–17); rather, he would tell them to be *rabbāniyyīn*, which Qarai translates as "godly people." This term is sometimes thought to mean "rabbis" in other contexts (e.g., Q 5:44, 63). The term is possibly derived from Jewish Aramaic *rabbānī* ("my master"; see *FV*, 136–39 and Ambros, 107), but could also be derived from Syriac *rabbān* ("our master").

It could be that the Qurʾān is alluding to Jesus in verse 79 (Asad calls this an "obvious reference to Jesus"), but verse 80 suggests that the Qurʾān is generally concerned with the worship of anything but God as God. On the worship of angels, see 4:172; 34:40–42 (here also *jinn*). See also 9:31, where the Qurʾān accuses Jews and Christians of taking their religious leaders to be gods.

[81]When God took a compact concerning the prophets, [He said,] 'Inasmuch as I have given you [the knowledge] of the Book and wisdom, should an apostle come to you thereafter confirming what is with you, you shall believe in him and help him.' He said, 'Do you pledge and accept My covenant on this condition?' They

said, 'We pledge.' Said He, 'Then be witnesses, and I, too, am among witnesses along with you.'

3:81 Here as elsewhere the "Book and wisdom" should not be identified with specific scriptures, but rather as two general terms for revelation (see commentary on 3:48, with further references).

---

⁸²Then whoever turns away after that—it is they who are the transgressors.

⁸³Do they seek a religion other than that of God, while to Him submits whoever there is in the heavens and the earth, willingly or unwillingly, and to Him they will be brought back?

⁸⁴*Say,* 'We have faith in God and in what has been sent down to us, and what was sent down to Abraham, Ishmael, Isaac, Jacob and the Tribes, and what Moses, Jesus and the prophets were given by their Lord. We make no distinction between any of them, and to Him do we submit.'

⁸⁵Should anyone follow a religion other than Islam, it shall never be accepted from him, and he will be among the losers in the Hereafter.

⁸⁶How shall God guide a people who have disbelieved after their faith and [after] bearing witness that the Apostle is true, and [after] manifest proofs had come to them? God does not guide the wrongdoing lot.

3:86 Wāḥidī reports here a number of traditions which connect this verse to certain Muslims in the time of the Prophet who left their religion but then, hearing this verse, returned to it. Asad, however, argues that Jews and Christians are intended. Cf. 2:159.

⁸⁷Their requital is that there shall be upon them the curse of God, the angels, and all mankind. ⁸⁸They will remain in it [forever], and their punishment will not be lightened, nor will they be granted any respite, ⁸⁹except such as repent after that and make amends, for God is all-forgiving, all-merciful.

⁹⁰Indeed, those who turn faithless after their faith, and then advance in faithlessness, their repentance will never be accepted, and it is they who are the astray.

⁹¹Indeed, those who turn faithless, and die faithless, a world of gold will not be accepted from any of them should he offer it for ransom. For such there will be a painful punishment, and they will have no helpers.

⁹²You will never attain piety until you spend out of what you hold dear, and whatever you may spend of anything, God indeed knows it.

⁹³All food was lawful to the Children of Israel except what Israel had forbidden himself before the Torah was sent down. *Say,* 'Bring the Torah and read it, if you are truthful.' ⁹⁴So whoever fabricates lies against God after that—it is they who are the wrongdoers.

⁹⁵*Say,* 'God has spoken the truth; so follow the creed of Abraham, a *ḥanīf,* and he was not one of the polytheists.

3:93–95 Genesis 9:3 has God say to Noah and his sons, "Every living thing that moves will be yours to eat, no less than the foliage of the plants. I give you everything." That Israel (i.e. Jacob) forbade himself a certain food may be a reference to the prohibition of the "thigh sinew" connected to the story of his wrestling with a figure at Jabbok (see Gen 32:33). The Qurʾān here suggests that one should return to the example of Israel's grandfather Abraham (although of course the Qurʾān does have certain food prohibitions, notably pork, blood, and carrion: 2:173; 5:3; 6:145; 16:115). On the term *ḥanīf* (v. 95), see commentary on 16:120–23 (with further references).

⁹⁶Indeed, the first house to be set up for mankind is the one at Bakkah, blessed and a guidance for all nations. ⁹⁷In it are manifest signs [and] Abraham's Station, and whoever enters it shall be secure. And it is the duty of mankind toward God to make pilgrimage to the House—for those who can afford the journey to it—and should anyone renege [on his obligation], God is indeed without need of the creatures.

3:96–97 In 2:127 the Qurʾān describes how Abraham and Ishmael "raised the Foundations of the House." In my commentary on 2:125–28, I suggest that "the House" may not be the present-day Kaʿba in Mecca (see 48:24) but rather Hebron or Jerusalem. Here the Qurʾān speaks of pilgrimage to the "House" and locates it in "Bakkah." Commentators (and translators) as a rule identify Bakkah as Mecca (although there is no evidence outside of Islamic tradition for this identification). Qarai and Asad both add notes explaining that "Bakkah" is another form of the word "Mecca," and Hilali-Khan put "Mecca" in parentheses in their translation.

Tafsīr al-Jalālayn recounts, "When [the Jews] said, 'Our direction of prayer came before yours,' the following was revealed: The first house, for worship, established for the people, on earth, was that at Bakkah (a variant of Makka [Mecca], so called because it 'crushes' [*tabukku*] the necks of tyrants); it was built by the angels before the creation of Adam, and after it the Aqsā [in Jerusalem] was built, a period of forty years separating them."

Bakkah may in fact be a reference to the "valley of Bākā," located in the southern part of Jerusalem and mentioned in Psalm 84:6 specifically in connection with pilgrimage:

⁵Blessed those who find their strength in you, whose hearts are set on pilgrimage.
⁶As they pass through the Valley of the Balsam [*ʿēmeq ha-bākā*], they make there a water-hole, and—a further blessing—early rain fills it.
⁷They make their way from height to height, God shows himself to them in Zion. (Psa 84:5–7)

⁹⁸*Say,* 'O People of the Book! Why do you deny the signs of God, while God is witness to what you do?'

[99]*Say,* 'O People of the Book! why do you bar the faithful from the way of God, seeking to make it crooked, while you are witnesses [to its truthfulness]? And God is not oblivious of what you do.'

3:99 On the accusation against the People of the Book that they "bar the faithful" from the way to God, see 4:160; 9:34; 11:19; 14:3.

───────────────

[100]O you who have faith, if you obey a part of those who were given the Book, they will turn you back, after your faith, into faithless ones. [101]And how would you be faithless while the signs of God are recited to you and His Apostle is in your midst? Whoever takes recourse in God is certainly guided to a straight path.

[102]O you who have faith! Be wary of God with the wariness due to Him and do not die except in the state of submission [to God and His Apostle]. [103]Hold fast, all together, to God's cord, and do not be divided [into sects]. Remember God's blessing upon you when you were enemies, then He brought your hearts together, so you became brothers with His blessing. And you were on the brink of a pit of Fire, whereat He saved you from it. Thus does God clarify His signs for you so that you may be guided.

[104]There has to be a nation among you summoning to the good, bidding what is right, and forbidding what is wrong. It is they who are the felicitous.

[105]Do not be like those who became divided [into sects] and differed after manifest signs had come to them. For such there will be a great punishment

3:105 The Qurʾān might here be referring to the Israelites who disagreed over Jesus and were divided into two sects: Jews and Christians (cf. 61:6, also see 6:159; 30:32; 42:14). The Qurʾān regularly refers to the divisions between them (see 2:113; 3:19; 9:30; 23:53). The Qurʾān is also aware of divisions among Christians, and presents these divisions as the mark of a divine punishment (cf. 5:14; 19:37).

---

[106]on the day when [some] faces will turn white and [some] faces will turn black. As for those whose faces turn black, [they will be told], 'Did you disbelieve after your faith? So taste the punishment because of what you used to disbelieve.' [107]But as for those whose faces become white, they shall dwell in God's mercy, and they will remain in it [forever].

[108]These are the signs of God which We recite to *you* in truth, and God does not desire any wrong for the creatures.

[109]To God belongs whatever is in the heavens and whatever is in the earth, and to God all matters are returned.

[110]You are the best nation [ever] brought forth for mankind: you bid what is right and forbid what is wrong, and have faith in God. And if the People of the Book had believed, it would have been better for them. Among them [some] are faithful, but most of them are transgressors.

[111]They will never do you any harm, except for some hurt; and if they fight you, they will turn their backs [to flee], then they will not be helped. [112]Wherever they are found, abasement is stamped upon them, except for an asylum from God and an asylum from the people. They have earned the wrath of God, and poverty has been stamped upon them. That, because they would deny the signs of God and kill the prophets unjustly. That, because they would disobey and commit transgression.

3:110–12 The declaration here (v. 110) that the Qurʾān's community is the "best nation" might be compared to similar language used elsewhere for Israel: 2:47; 2:122; 7:140; 44:32; 45:16. A number of New Testament passages, such as

1 Peter 2 (which paraphrases Exo 19:5–6), contend that the blessings which God had given to Israel are now given to the Christian community:

> ⁹But you are a chosen race, a kingdom of priests, a holy nation, a people to be a personal possession to sing the praises of God who called you out of the darkness into his wonderful light.
>
> ¹⁰Once you were a non-people and now you are the People of God; once you were outside his pity; now you have received pity. (1Pe 2:9–10)

On the reference to the killing of the prophets (v. 112), see commentary on 3:181–82 (with further references).

---

¹¹³Yet they are not all alike. Among the People of the Book is an upright nation; they recite God's signs in the watches of the night and prostrate.

¹¹⁴They have faith in God and the Last Day, and bid what is right and forbid what is wrong, and they are active in [performing] good deeds. Those are among the righteous. ¹¹⁵Whatever good they do, they will not go unappreciated for it, and God knows well the Godwary.

3:113–15 The allusion to an "upright nation" in verse 113 (cf. the allusion to a small group of Israelites in 5:13) among the People of the Book might be compared to Paul's allusion in Romans 11:5 to a "remnant, set aside by grace." Islamic tradition usually connects the "upright nation" with certain Jews who converted to Islam. Wāḥidī relates about verse 113: "When ʿAbd Allah ibn Salam, Thaʿlabah ibn Saʿyah, Usayd ibn Saʿyah, Asad ibn ʿUbayd and other Jews embraced Islam, the Jewish rabbis said: 'Only the evil amongst us believed in Muḥammad, for had they been among our best they would not have abandoned the religion of their forefathers.' They also said to them: 'You incurred a great loss when you have exchanged the religion of your forefathers with another religion.' God then revealed this verse."

For his part, Blachère (91) wonders if the Qurʾān could be referring to the Christian community: "The term *umma* ['nation'] can hardly be right for a small group of believers. Perhaps we must imagine Christians here."

[116]As for the faithless, neither their wealth nor their children will avail them anything against God. They shall be the inmates of the Fire, and they will remain in it [forever].

[117]The parable of what they spend in the life of this world is that of a cold wind that strikes the tillage of a people who wronged themselves, destroying it. God does not wrong them, but they wrong themselves.

[118]O you who have faith! Do not take your confidants from others than yourselves; they will spare nothing to ruin you. They are eager to see you in distress. Hatred has already shown itself from their mouths, and what their breasts hide [within] is yet worse. We have certainly made the signs clear for you, should you exercise your reason.

[119]Ah! You are the ones who bear love towards them, while they do not love you, though you believe in all the Books. When they meet you, they say, 'We believe,' but when they are alone, they bite their fingertips at you out of rage. Say, 'Die of your rage!' God indeed knows well what is in the breasts. [120]If some good befalls you, it upsets them, but if some ill befalls you, they rejoice at it. Yet if you are patient and Godwary, their guile will not harm you in any way. God indeed encompasses what they do.

[121]When *you* left your family at dawn to settle the faithful in their positions for battle—and God is all-hearing, all-knowing. [122]When two groups among you were about to lose courage— though God is their protector, and in God alone let all the faithful put their trust.

[123]Certainly God helped you at Badr, when you were weak [in the enemy's eyes]. So be wary of God so that you may give thanks.

[124]When *you* were saying to the faithful, 'Is it not enough for you that your Lord should aid you with three thousand angels sent down?' [125]Yes, if you are steadfast and Godwary, and should they come at you suddenly, your Lord will aid you with five thousand angels sent in [to the scene of battle]. [126]God did not appoint it but as a good news for you and to reassure with it your hearts; and victory comes only from God, the All-mighty, the All-wise, [127]that He may cut down a section of the faithless, or subdue them, so that they retreat disappointed.

[128]*You* have no hand in the matter, whether He accepts their repentance or punishes them, for they are indeed wrongdoers. [129]To God belongs whatever there is in the heavens and the earth: He forgives whomever He wishes and punishes whomever He wishes, and God is all-forgiving, all-merciful.

3:123–29 Islamic tradition understands "Badr" here as a reference to the story of a victorious battle at a site (between Mecca and Medina) of this name described in the biography of Muḥammad. *Tafsīr al-Jalālayn* explains that God revealed verse 123 after the Muslims were later defeated at Uhud, to remind them of God's graces to them at Badr: "When they were defeated, the following was revealed as a way of reminding them of God's favour."

The references to three thousand, and then to five thousand angels (cf. 8:9, which mentions one thousand), however, suggest some influence of the Biblical book of Joshua. In Joshua 7 the Israelites attack the Canaanite city of Ai with three thousand men and are defeated (Jos 7:3–5). In Joshua 8 (after the wrong-doer Aachen is killed), the Israelites attack Ai with five thousand men and are victorious (Jos 8:12; cf. Lev 26:7–8; Jos 23:10) (cr. Matthew Kuiper).

---

[130]O you who have faith! Do not exact usury, twofold and sev-eralfold, and be wary of God so that you may be felicitous. [131]Beware of the Fire which has been prepared for the faithless, [132]and obey God and the Apostle so that you may be granted [His] mercy.

¹³³Hasten towards your Lord's forgiveness and a paradise as vast as the heavens and the earth, prepared for the Godwary ¹³⁴— those who spend in ease and adversity, and suppress their anger, and excuse [the faults of] the people, and God loves the virtuous; ¹³⁵and those who, when they commit an indecent act or wrong themselves, remember God, and plead [to God seeking] forgiveness for their sins—and who forgives sins except God?—and who knowingly do not persist in what [sins] they have committed.

3:135 The point of the rhetorical question—"and who forgives sins except for God"—might be to reject the Christian claim that Christ forgives sins (see Mat 9:3–8; Mar 2:7; Luk 5:21, 7:48–49).

¹³⁶Their reward is forgiveness from their Lord, and gardens with streams running in them, to remain in them [forever]. How excellent is the reward of the workers!

3:136 On the streams of paradise, see commentary on 2:25 (with further references).

¹³⁷Certain [Divine] precedents have passed before you. So travel through the land and observe how was the fate of the deniers. ¹³⁸This is an explanation for mankind, and a guidance and advice for the Godwary. ¹³⁹Do not weaken or grieve: you shall have the upper hand, should you be faithful. ¹⁴⁰If wounds afflict you, like wounds have already afflicted those people; and We make such vicissitudes rotate among mankind, so that God may ascertain those who have faith, and that He may take martyrs from among you, and God does

not like the wrongdoers. [141]And so that God may purge [the hearts of] those who have faith and that He may wipe out the faithless.

[142]Do you suppose that you would enter paradise, while God has not yet ascertained those of you who have waged *jihād* and He has not ascertained the steadfast?

[143]Certainly you were longing for death before you had encountered it. Then certainly you saw it, as you were looking on.

[144]Muḥammad is but an apostle; [other] apostles have passed before him. If he dies or is slain, will you turn back on your heels? Anyone who turns back on his heels will not harm God in the least, and soon God will reward the grateful.

[145]No soul may die except by God's leave, at an appointed time. Whoever desires the reward of this world, We will give him of it; and whoever desires the reward of the Hereafter, We will give him of it; and soon We will reward the grateful.

[146]How many a prophet there has been with whom a multitude of godly men fought. They did not falter for what befell them in the way of God, neither did they weaken, nor did they abase themselves; and God loves the steadfast. [147]All that they said was, 'Our Lord, forgive our sins and our excesses in our affairs, make our feet steady, and help us against the faithless lot.' [148]So God gave them the reward of this world and the fair reward of the Hereafter; and God loves the virtuous.

3:146–48 On the notion that God rewards martyrs with eternal life, see 2:154 (and commentary on that verse).

―――――――――

[149]O you who have faith! If you obey the faithless, they will turn you back on your heels, and you will become losers. [150]God is indeed your Master, and He is the best of helpers.

¹⁵¹We shall cast terror into the hearts of the faithless because of their ascribing partners to God, for which He has not sent down any authority, and their refuge shall be the Fire, and evil is the [final] abode of the wrongdoers.

¹⁵²God certainly fulfilled His promise to you when you were slaying them with His leave, until you lost courage, disputed about the matter, and disobeyed after He showed you what you loved. Some among you desire this world, and some among you desire the Hereafter. Then He turned you away from them so that He might test you.

Certainly He has excused you, for God is gracious to the faithful. ¹⁵³When you were fleeing without paying any attention to anyone, while the Apostle was calling you from your rear, He requited you with grief upon grief, so that you may not grieve for what you lose nor for what befalls you, and God is well aware of what you do.

¹⁵⁴Then He sent down to you safety after grief—a drowsiness that came over a group of you—while another group, anxious only about themselves, entertained false notions about God, notions of [pagan] ignorance. They say, 'Do we have any role in the matter?' *Say,* 'The matter indeed belongs totally to God.' They hide in their hearts what they do not disclose to *you.*

They say, 'Had we any role in the matter, we would not have been slain here.' *Say,* 'Even if you had remained in your houses, those destined to be slain would have set out toward the places where they were laid to rest, so that God may test what is in your breasts, and that He may purge what is in your hearts, and God knows well what is in the breasts.'

3:154 On the expression "notions of [pagan] ignorance," see commentary on 48:26 (with further references).

¹⁵⁵Those of you who fled on the day when the two hosts met, only Satan had made them stumble because of some of their deeds. Certainly God has excused them, for God is all-forgiving, all-forbearing.

¹⁵⁶O you who have faith! Do not be like the faithless who say of their brethren, when they travel in the land or go into battle, 'Had they stayed with us they would not have died or been killed,' so that God may make it a regret in their hearts. But God gives life and brings death, and God watches what you do.

¹⁵⁷If you are slain in the way of God, or die, forgiveness and mercy from God are surely better than what they amass. ¹⁵⁸If you die or are slain, you will surely be mustered toward God.

3:157–58 Here the Qurʾān suggests that those who die fighting in holy war will have their sins forgiven. It also suggests (since "forgiveness and mercy" is better than the worldly pleasures amassed by those who do not fight) that this forgiveness will be their ticket to paradise (where they will have heavenly pleasures; cf. 2:154; 3:169, 195; 4:74, 100; 9:111; 22:58–59; 47:4–6). In this the Qurʾān is in conversation with Christian tradition, by which martyrs receive absolution from their sins and a privileged place in heaven for the sake of their sacrifice. This idea is seen already in Revelation (2:10). It is also evident in many pious martyr accounts, such as that which Eusebius tells of St. Potamiaena. Eusebius explains how St. Potamiaena, after her death, returned to visit the Roman soldier who treated her well before her death and later converted to Christianity, to announce to him his own imminent martyrdom: "Potamiaena appeared to him by night, wreathing his head with a crown and saying that she had called upon the Lord for him and obtained what she requested, and that before long she would take him to herself." (Eusebius, *Ecclesiastical History,* 6:5:6, 2:27). See also commentary on 2:154; 3:169–70 (with further references).

¹⁵⁹It is by God's mercy that *you* are gentle to them; had *you* been harsh and hardhearted, they would have surely scattered

from around you. So *excuse* them and *plead* for forgiveness for them, and *consult* them in the affairs, and once *you* are resolved, put *your* trust in God. Indeed, God loves those who trust in Him.

¹⁶⁰If God helps you, no one can overcome you, but if He forsakes you, who will help you after Him? So in God alone let all the faithful put their trust.

¹⁶¹A prophet may not breach his trust, and whoever breaches his trust will bring his breaches on the Day of Resurrection; then every soul shall be recompensed fully for what it has earned, and they will not be wronged.

¹⁶²Is he who follows [the course of] God's pleasure like him who earns God's displeasure and whose refuge is hell, an evil destination? ¹⁶³They have ranks with God, and God watches what they do.

¹⁶⁴God certainly favoured the faithful when He raised up among them an apostle from among themselves to recite to them His signs, and to purify them and teach them the Book and wisdom, and earlier they had indeed been in manifest error.

3:164 "From their own brothers I shall raise up a prophet like yourself" (Deu 18:18).

––––––––––

¹⁶⁵What, when an affliction visits you—while you have inflicted twice as much—do you say, 'How is this?'! *Say,* 'This is from your own souls.' Indeed, God has power over all things.

¹⁶⁶What befell you on the day when the two hosts met, was by God's permission, so that He may ascertain the faithful, ¹⁶⁷and ascertain the hypocrites. [When] they were told: 'Come, fight in the way of God, or defend [yourselves], they said, 'If we knew any fighting, we would have surely followed you.' That day they were

nearer to unfaith than to faith. They say with their mouths what is not in their hearts, and God knows well whatever they conceal.

168Those who said of their brethren, while they themselves sat back: 'Had they obeyed us, they would not have been killed.' *Say,* 'Then keep death off from yourselves, if you are truthful.'

169Do not suppose those who were slain in the way of God to be dead; no, they are living and provided for near their Lord, 170exulting in what God has given them out of His grace, and rejoicing for those who have not yet joined them from [those left] behind them, that they will have no fear, nor will they grieve.

3:169–70 The Qurʾān again (cf. 2:154–57; 3:157–58) has God speak of the fate of the martyrs. In this verse the Qurʾān has God promise that the martyrs are alive *now*, in the heavenly garden, where they are "provided for," or literally, "given nourishment" (cf. 52:17–28). This reflects in part Revelation, with its description of martyrs "sealed" (Rev 7:4) and alive in heaven: "When he broke the fifth seal, I saw underneath the altar the souls of all the people who had been killed on account of the Word of God, for witnessing to it" (Rev 6:9; cf. Rev 2:10; 7:9). The doctrine of the immediate retribution of the martyrs is prominent in the writings of certain Syriac church fathers. On this see further commentary on 2:154 (with further references).

As the bodies of the martyrs are buried on earth, Muslim scholars were led by this verse to wonder how they might be able to eat the "nourishment" given to them in paradise. Wāḥidī relates a tradition by which they are given the bodies of birds to do so: "Ibn ʿAbbas who reported that the Messenger of God said: When your brothers were killed at Uhud, God placed their spirits inside green birds which go to the rivers of Paradise and eat of its fruits and reach to lamps hanging in the shade of the Throne. When they tasted the wholesomeness of their food, drink and abode, they said: 'Who would inform our brothers, on our behalf, that we are being provided in Paradise, so that they do not shy away from Jihad or shirk away from war?' God said: 'I will inform them on your behalf,' and so He revealed [this verse]."

171They rejoice in God's blessing and grace, and that God does not waste the reward of the faithful.

¹⁷²Those who responded to God and the Apostle [even] after they had been wounded—for those of them who have been virtuous and Godwary there shall be a great reward. ¹⁷³—Those to whom the people said, 'All the people have gathered against you, so fear them.' That only increased them in faith, and they said, 'God is sufficient for us, and He is an excellent trustee.' ¹⁷⁴So they returned with God's blessing and grace, untouched by any harm. They pursued the pleasure of God, and God is dispenser of a great grace. ¹⁷⁵That is only Satan frightening [you] of his followers! So fear them not, and fear Me, should you be faithful.

¹⁷⁶*Do not grieve* for those who are active in unfaith; they will not hurt God in the least: God desires to give them no share in the Hereafter, and there is a great punishment for them. ¹⁷⁷Those who have bought unfaith for faith will not hurt God in the least, and there is a painful punishment for them. ¹⁷⁸Let the faithless not suppose that the respite We grant them is good for their souls: We give them respite only that they may increase in sin, and there is a humiliating punishment for them.

3:178 Geiger (*Judaism and Islam,* 57–58) traces the notion that God would let sinners prosper in this life (that they might be punished more severely in the next) to a rabbinic theodicy based in part on Proverbs 14:12: "There are ways that some think straight, but they lead in the end to death."

———————————

¹⁷⁹God will not leave the faithful in your present state, until He has separated the bad ones from the good. God will not acquaint you with the Unseen, but God chooses whomever He wishes from His apostles. So have faith in God and His apostles; and if you are faithful and Godwary, there shall be a great reward for you.

¹⁸⁰Let the stingy not suppose that [their grudging] what God has given them out of His bounty is good for them; no, it is bad

for them. They will be collared with what they grudge on the Day of Resurrection. To God belongs the heritage of the heavens and the earth, and God is well aware of what you do.

[181]God has certainly heard the remark of those who said, 'God is poor and we are rich.' We will record what they have said, and their killing of the prophets unjustly, and We shall say, 'Taste the punishment of the burning. [182]That is because of what your hands have sent ahead, and because God is not tyrannical to His servants.'

3:181–82 Wāḥidī explains the phrase "God is poor and we are rich" with a story in which a Jew of Medina named Finḥās refuses the demand of Muḥammad's companion Abū Bakr to accept Islam and give alms, explaining: "O Abū Bakr, you claim that our Lord is asking us to lend Him our wealth. Yet, it is only the poor who borrow from the rich. And if what you say is true, it follows that God is poor and we are rich, for if He were rich He would not ask us to lend Him our wealth." Although this tradition seems to be a pious legend, it is presumably the case that the Qurʾān has Jews in mind, in light of the following accusation of "killing the prophets" (cf. 2:87, 91; 3:21, 112, 183; 4:155; 5:70), a standard theme in the Qurʾān's anti-Jewish polemics.

Only two brief passages of the Old Testament have the Israelites kill a prophet (2Ch 24:20–21 and Jer 26:20–23). In 1 Kings, however, Elijah refers to the Israelites' murder of the prophets:

> [9]There he went into a cave and spent the night there. Then the word of the Lord came to him saying, 'What are you doing here, Elijah?'
> [10]He replied, 'I am full of jealous zeal for the Lord Sabaoth, because the Israelites have abandoned your covenant, have torn down your altars and put your prophets to the sword. I am the only one left, and now they want to kill me.' (1Ki 19:9–10; cf. Rom 11:3)

In Nehemiah 9:26 the Israelites, in the time of Ezra, confess that their ancestors killed the prophets. In Matthew, Jesus accuses the Israelites of killing the prophets: "So! Your own evidence tells against you! You are the children of those who murdered the prophets!" (Mat 23:3), and then again (later in that same chapter):

[35]and so you will draw down on yourselves the blood of every upright person that has been shed on earth, from the blood of Abel the holy to the blood of Zechariah son of Barachiah whom you murdered between the sanctuary and the altar.

[36]In truth I tell you, it will all recoil on this generation.

[37]Jerusalem, Jerusalem, you that kill the prophets and stone those who are sent to you! How often have I longed to gather your children together, as a hen gathers her chicks under her wings, and you refused! (Mat 23:35–37; cf. Luk 11:47–48, 13:34–35; 1Th 2:14–15; Heb 11:32–37a)

Stephen also makes this accusation before the Sanhedrin in Acts: "Can you name a single prophet your ancestors never persecuted? They killed those who foretold the coming of the Upright One, and now you have become his betrayers, his murderers" (Act 7:52).

Unlike the canonical Old Testament, the *Lives of the Prophets* (a text which was once thought to be Jewish in origin but which, as David Satran has argued, is thoroughly Christian), describes the murder of many of the prophets of Israel at the hands of their own people. According to the *Lives,* three of the four Major Prophets of the Old Testament were killed by the Jews:

"[Isaiah] died after he was sawn in two by Manasseh and was buried beneath the oak of Rogel . . ." "[Jeremiah] died in Tahpanhes (Daphne) in Egypt when he was stoned by the people. He is buried in the area of the residence of Pharaoh, since the Egyptians honored him . . ." "[Ezekiel] is from the land of Arira, of the priests, and he died in the land of the Chaldeans during the captivity, when he had prophesied many things to those in Judea. The leader of the people of Israel there killed him, when he was rebuked by him for worshipping idols." (*Lives of the Prophets,* 121–23)

The theme of Jews as killers of the prophets is especially popular among the Syriac Christian authors such as Ephrem:

[The Jews] slaughter the prophets / like innocent lambs.

Doctors came to them / and they became for them a butcher. (Ephrem, *Sermons on Faith,* 3:379–82)

---

[183]*Tell* those who say, 'God has pledged us not to believe in any apostle unless he brings us an offering consumed by fire,'

'Apostles before me certainly did bring you manifest signs and what you speak of. Then why did you kill them, if you are truthful?'

3:183 In light of the reference to killing prophets at the end of this verse the opponents being quoted are presumably Jews (see commentary on 3:181–82). The reference to "an offering consumed by fire" may be an allusion to the narrative of Elijah's sacrifice in 1 Kings 18 (cf. Lev 9:24; Jdg 6:21, 13:20):

> [36]At the time when the offering is presented, Elijah the prophet stepped forward. 'Lord, God of Abraham, Isaac and Israel,' he said, 'let them know today that you are God in Israel, and that I am your servant, that I have done all these things at your command.
> [37]Answer me, Lord, answer me, so that this people may know that you, the Lord, are God and are winning back their hearts.'
> [38]Then the Lord's fire fell and consumed the burnt offering and the wood and licked up the water in the trench.
> [39]When all the people saw this they fell on their faces. 'The Lord is God,' they cried, 'the Lord is God!' (1Ki 18:36–39)

[184]But if they deny *you,* [other] apostles have been denied before *you,* who came with manifest signs, holy writs, and an illuminating scripture.

3:184 In this verse the arguments against the Jews begun in verse 181 are continued. "Holy writs" here is translated from the Arabic *al-zubur* (cf. 16:44; 35:25), the plural of *al-zabūr* that is used elsewhere (Q 4:163; 17:55; 21:105) in the Qurʾān to refer to the scripture given to David, that is, the Psalms. Translators are divided over how to render this word here. Some (like our translator) consider it to refer generally to divine books (Yusuf Ali: "Books of dark prophecies" (!); Hilali-Khan, "Scripture"; Asad: "books of divine wisdom"), while others consider it a reference to the Psalms (Pickthall, Arberry). *Zabūr/zubur* is perhaps related to the Syriac word for the Psalms (*mazmūrā;* on this see Jeffery, *FV,* 149), although Ambros (120) argues that it is connected to epigraphic South Arabian.

¹⁸⁵Every soul shall taste death, and you will indeed be paid your full rewards on the Day of Resurrection. Whoever is delivered from the Fire and admitted to paradise has certainly succeeded. The life of this world is nothing but the wares of delusion.

3:185 On the phrase "Every soul shall taste death," see commentary on 44:56 (with further references). This verse might be compared to 1 Corinthians 3:11–16.

¹⁸⁶You will surely be tested in your possessions and your souls, and you will surely hear much affront from those who were given the Book before you and from the polytheists; but if you are patient and Godwary, that is indeed the steadiest of courses. ¹⁸⁷When God made a covenant with those who were given the Book: 'You shall explain it for the people, and you shall not conceal it,' they cast it behind their backs and sold it for a paltry gain. How evil is what they buy!

3:187 The Qurʾān's rhetoric here seems to be directed principally against the Jews. The particular idiom that they have "cast [the Book] behind their backs" may reflect Nehemiah 9:26, where the Israelites confess to casting the Torah behind their backs (and to killing the prophets—see Q 3:181, 183): "But they grew disobedient, rebelled against you and thrust your law behind their backs; they slaughtered your prophets who had reproved them to bring them back to you, and committed monstrous impieties" (Neh 9:26; cr. Andrew O'Connor). On the accusation of concealing the Book, see commentary on 4:46 (with further references).

¹⁸⁸Do not suppose those who brag about what they have done, and love to be praised for what they have not done—do not

suppose them saved from punishment, and there is a painful punishment for them.

[189]To God belongs the kingdom of the heavens and the earth, and God has power over all things.

[190]Indeed, in the creation of the heavens and the earth and the alternation of night and day, there are signs for those who possess intellect. [191]Those who remember God standing, sitting, and lying on their sides, and reflect on the creation of the heavens and the earth [and say], 'Our Lord, You have not created this in vain! Immaculate are You! Save us from the punishment of the Fire.

3:191 "You shall tell them to your children, and keep on telling them, when you are sitting at home, when you are out and about, when you are lying down and when you are standing up" (Deu 6:7).

---

[192]Our Lord, whoever that You make enter the Fire will surely have been disgraced by You, and the wrongdoers will have no helpers. [193]Our Lord, we have indeed heard a summoner calling to faith, declaring, "Have faith in your Lord!" So we believed. Our Lord, forgive us our sins and absolve us of our misdeeds, and make us die with the pious. [194]Our Lord, give us what You have promised us through Your apostles, and do not disgrace us on the Day of Resurrection. Indeed, You do not break Your promise.'

[195]Then their Lord answered them, 'I do not waste the work of any worker among you, whether male or female; you are all on the same footing. So those who migrated and were expelled from their homes, and were tormented in My way, and those who fought and were killed—I will surely absolve them of their misdeeds and I will admit them into gardens with streams running in

them, as a reward from God, and God—with Him is the best of rewards.'

3:195 On the Christian subtext of the reference to the martyr's reward in this passage, see commentary on 2:154; 3:169–70 (with further references). As Speyer mentions (*BEQ,* 451), the particular idea that those who "migrated" will also be rewarded with eternal life (cf. 4:100) may be connected to Matthew 19:29: "And everyone who has left houses, brothers, sisters, father, mother, children or land for the sake of my name will receive a hundred times as much, and also inherit eternal life." On the streams of paradise, see commentary on 2:25 (with further references).

—————————

[196]Never be misled by the bustle of the faithless in the towns. [197]It is a trivial enjoyment; then their refuge is hell, and it is an evil resting place.

[198]But those who are wary of their Lord—for them shall be gardens with streams running in them, to remain in them [forever], a hospitality from God; and what is with God is better for the pious.

[199]Among the People of the Book there are indeed those who have faith in God and in what has been sent down to you, and in what has been sent down to them. Humble toward God, they do not sell the signs of God for a paltry gain. They shall have their reward near their Lord; indeed God is swift at reckoning.

[200]O you who have faith! Be patient, stand firm, and close [your] ranks, and be wary of God so that you may be felicitous.

4. *AL-NISĀʾ*, THE WOMEN

In the Name of God, the All-beneficent, the All-merciful.

¹O mankind! Be wary of your Lord who created you from a single soul, and created its mate from it, and, from the two of them, scattered numerous men and women. Be wary of God, in whose Name you adjure one another and of [severing the ties with] blood relations. God is indeed watchful over you.

²Give the orphans their property, and do not replace the good with the bad, and do not eat up their property [by mingling it] with your own property, for that is indeed a great sin.

³If you fear that you may not deal justly with the orphans, then marry [other] women that you like, two, three, or four. But if you fear that you may not treat them fairly, then [marry only] one, or [marry from among] your slave-women. That makes it likelier that you will not be unfair.

⁴Give women their dowries, handing it over [to them]; but if they remit anything of it of their own accord, then consume it as [something] lawful and wholesome.

⁵Do not give the feeble-minded your property which God has assigned you to manage: provide for them out of it and clothe them, and speak to them honourable words.

⁶Test the orphans when they reach the age of marriage. Then if you discern in them maturity, deliver to them their property. And do not consume it lavishly and hastily lest they should grow up. As for him who is well-off, let him be abstemious, and as for him who is poor, let him eat in an honourable manner. And when you deliver to them their property, take witnesses over them, and God suffices as reckoner.

⁷Men have a share in the heritage left by parents and near relatives, and women have a share in the heritage left by parents and near relatives, whether it be little or much, a share ordained [by God].

⁸And when the division is attended by relatives, the orphans and the needy, provide for them out of it, and speak to them honourable words. ⁹Let those fear [the result of mistreating orphans] who, were they to leave behind weak offspring, would be concerned on their account. So let them be wary of God, and let them speak upright words.

¹⁰Those who consume the property of orphans wrongfully, only ingest fire into their bellies, and soon they will enter the Blaze.

4:1–10 In the first verse of this Sura the Qur'ān alludes to the Biblical tradition of the creation of Adam and Eve (cf. 6:98; 7:189; 16:72; 30:21; 35:11; 39:6). The translation of Hilali-Khan makes this more explicit: "O mankind! Be dutiful to your Lord, Who created you from a single person (Adam), and from him (Adam) He created his wife [Hawwa, Eve], and from them both He created many men and women." By reminding the audience that the creation of man and woman was accomplished by God's will, this verse introduces the following section which presents God's will for the proper relationship of men and women.

In verse 3 the question of marrying multiple wives is raised with attention to the problem of dealing justly with them (cf. 4:129), a concern also in Exodus 21:10–11:

¹⁰If he takes another wife, he must not reduce the food, clothing or conjugal rights of the first one.

[11]Should he deprive her of these three things she will leave a free woman, without paying compensation.

Verse 3 also mentions marrying slave women (cf. 4:25; Deu 21:10–14). In the verses that follow the Qurʾān focuses on the proper rules of marriage (cf. 4:24–25; 5:5; 60:10) and on the importance of caring for widows and orphans (on this see commentary on 107:2, with further references). This latter concern reflects Biblical tradition (Exo 22:21–23; Deu 10:18, 14:29, 24:17–21, 26:12–13; Psa 68:5, 146:9; Isa 1:17; James 1:27) and later Syriac Christian tradition, as in the *Didascalia* (esp. chap. 17, 160–61).

Yahuda argues that the term in verse 2 for "sin" (*ḥūb*) and the verb in verse 3 for "be unfair" (*taʿūlū*) derive from Hebrew, but they may both come from Syriac instead (cf. Syr. *ḥawbā*, "sin," and *ʿawlā*, "injustice, iniquity").

---

[11]God enjoins you concerning your children: for the male shall be the like of the share of two females, and if there be [two or] more than two females, then for them shall be two-thirds of what he leaves; but if she be alone, then for her shall be a half; and for each of his parents a sixth of what he leaves, if he has children; but if he has no children, and his parents are his [sole] heirs, then it shall be a third for his mother; but if he has brothers, then a sixth for his mother, after [paying off] any bequest he may have made or any debt [he may have incurred]. Your parents and your children—you do not know which of them is likelier to be beneficial for you. This is an ordinance from God. God is indeed all-knowing, all-wise.

[12]For you shall be a half of what your wives leave, if they have no children; but if they have children, then for you shall be a fourth of what they leave, after [paying off] any bequest they may have made or any debt [they may have incurred]. And for them [it shall be] a fourth of what you leave, if you have no children; but if you have children, then for them shall be an eighth of what you leave, after [paying off] any bequest you may have made or

any debt [you may have incurred]. If a man or woman is inherited by siblings and has a brother or a sister, then each of them shall receive a sixth; but if they are more than that, then they shall share in one third, after [paying off] any bequest he may have made or any debt [he may have incurred] without prejudice. [This is] an enjoinment from God, and God is all-knowing, all-forbearing.

¹³These are God's bounds, and whoever obeys God and His Apostle, He shall admit him to gardens with streams running in them, to remain in them [forever]. That is the great success.

4:13 On the Biblical connection with the expression "God's bounds" (*ḥudūd Allāh*), see commentary on 58:4 (with further references). On the streams of paradise, see commentary on 2:25 (with further references).

---

¹⁴But whoever disobeys God and His Apostle and transgresses the bounds set by God, He shall make him enter a Fire, to remain in it [forever], and there will be a humiliating punishment for him.

¹⁵Should any of your women commit an indecent act, produce against them four witnesses from yourselves, and if they testify, detain them in [their] houses until death finishes them, or God decrees a course for them.

¹⁶Should two among you commit it, chastise them both; but if they repent and reform, let them alone. God is indeed all-clement, all-merciful.

¹⁷[Acceptance of] repentance by God is only for those who commit evil out of ignorance and then repent promptly. It is such whose repentance God will accept, and God is all-knowing, all-wise. ¹⁸But [acceptance of] repentance is not for those who go on committing misdeeds: when death approaches any of them,

he says, 'I repent now.' Nor is it for those who die while they are faithless. For such We have prepared a painful punishment.

¹⁹O you who have faith! It is not lawful for you to inherit women forcibly, and do not press them to take away part of what you have given them, unless they commit a gross indecency. Consort with them in an honourable manner; and should you dislike them, maybe you dislike something while God invests it with an abundant good.

²⁰If you desire to take a wife in place of another, and you have given one of them a quintal [of gold], do not take anything away from it. Would you take it by way of calumny and flagrant sin?! ²¹How could you take it back, when you have known each other, and they have taken from you a solemn covenant?

²²Do not marry any of the women whom your fathers had married, excluding what is already past. That is indeed an indecency, an outrage and an evil course.

²³Forbidden to you are your mothers, your daughters and your sisters, your paternal aunts and your maternal aunts, your brother's daughters and your sister's daughters, your [foster] mothers who have suckled you and your sisters through fosterage, your wives' mothers, and your stepdaughters who are under your care [born] of the wives whom you have gone into—but if you have not gone into them there is no sin upon you, and the wives of your sons who are from your own loins, and that you should marry two sisters at one time, excluding what is already past; indeed God is all-forgiving, all-merciful—

²⁴and married women, excepting your slave women. This is God's ordinance for you.

As to others than these, it is lawful for you to seek [temporary union with them] with your wealth, in wedlock, not in license. For the enjoyment you have had from them thereby, give them their dowries, by way of settlement, and there is no sin upon you in what you may agree upon after the settlement. God is indeed all-knowing, all-wise.

4:21–24 This passage may be the Qur᾽ān's effort to articulate regulations on sexual relations along the lines of Leviticus 18:1–20 and 20:11–21.

———————

²⁵As for those of you who cannot afford to marry faithful free women, then [let them marry] from what you own, from among your faithful slave-women. Your faith is best known [only] to God; you are all [on a] similar [footing]. So marry them with their masters' permission, and give them their dowries in an honourable manner—[such of them] as are chaste women, not licentious ones or those who take paramours. But should they commit an indecent act on marrying, there shall be for them [only] half the punishment for free women. This is for those of you who fear falling into fornication; but it is better that you be continent, and God is all-forgiving, all-merciful.

²⁶God desires to explain [the laws] to you and guide you to the customs of those who were before you, and to turn toward you clemently, and God is all-knowing, all-wise.

²⁷God desires to turn toward you clemently, but those who pursue their [base] appetites desire that you fall into gross waywardness. ²⁸God desires to lighten your burden, for man was created weak.

4:28 The Qur᾽ān's declaration here (cf. 8:66) might be seen as following the declaration of Christ in Matthew that his "burden" is light:

²⁸'Come to me, all you who labour and are overburdened, and I will give you rest.
²⁹Shoulder my yoke and learn from me, for I am gentle and humble in heart, and you will find rest for your souls.
³⁰Yes, my yoke is easy and my burden light.' (Mat 11:28–30)

²⁹O you who have faith! Do not eat up your wealth among yourselves unrightfully, but it should be traded by mutual consent. And do not kill yourselves. Indeed, God is most merciful to you. ³⁰And whoever does that in aggression and injustice, We will soon make him enter the Fire, and that is easy for God.

³¹If you avoid the major sins that you are forbidden, We will absolve you of your misdeeds and admit you to a noble abode.

³²Do not covet the advantage which God has given some of you over others. To men belongs a share of what they have earned, and to women a share of what they have earned. And ask God for His bounty. Indeed, God has knowledge of all things.

³³For everyone We have appointed heirs to what the parents and near relatives leave, as well as those with whom you have made a compact; so give them their share [of the heritage]. Indeed, God is witness to all things.

³⁴Men are the managers of women, because of the advantage God has granted some of them over others, and by virtue of their spending out of their wealth. Righteous women are obedient and watchful in the absence [of their husbands] of what God has enjoined [them] to guard. As for those [wives] whose misconduct you fear, [first] advise them, and [if ineffective] keep away from them in the bed, and [as the last resort] beat them. Then if they obey you, do not seek any course [of action] against them. Indeed, God is all-exalted, all-great.

³⁵If you fear a split between the two of them, then appoint an arbiter from his relatives and an arbiter from her relatives. If they desire reconcilement, God shall reconcile them. God is indeed all-knowing, all-aware.

³⁶Worship God and do not ascribe any partners to Him, and be good to parents, the relatives, the orphans, the needy, the near neighbour and the distant neighbour, the companion at your side,

the traveler, and your slaves. God indeed does not like those who are arrogant and boastful.

4:36 On kindness to orphans, see commentary on 107:2 (with further references).

---

³⁷Those who are [themselves] stingy and bid [other] people to be stingy, too, and conceal what God has given them out of His bounty—We have prepared a humiliating punishment for the faithless ³⁸and those who spend their wealth to be seen by people, and believe neither in God nor in the Last Day. As for him who has Satan for his companion—an evil companion is he!

4:38 Cf. 2:264. As Rudolph mentions (16), the spirit of this verse may be related to Matthew 6:1–4:

¹'Be careful not to parade your uprightness in public to attract attention; otherwise you will lose all reward from your Father in heaven.
²So when you give alms, do not have it trumpeted before you; this is what the hypocrites do in the synagogues and in the streets to win human admiration. In truth I tell you, they have had their reward.
³But when you give alms, your left hand must not know what your right is doing;
⁴your almsgiving must be secret, and your Father who sees all that is done in secret will reward you.

---

³⁹What harm would it have done them had they believed in God and the Last Day, and spent out of what God has provided them? God knows them well.

⁴⁰Indeed, God does not wrong [anyone] [even to the extent of] an atom's weight, and if it be a good deed He doubles it[s reward], and gives from Himself a great reward.

⁴¹So how shall it be, when We bring a witness from every nation and We bring *you* as a witness to them? ⁴²On that day those who were faithless and disobeyed the Apostle will wish the earth were levelled with them, and they will not conceal any matter from God.

⁴³O you who have faith! Do not approach prayer when you are intoxicated, [not] until you know what you are saying, nor [enter mosques] in the state of ritual impurity until you have washed yourselves, except while passing through. But if you are sick or on a journey, or any of you has come from the toilet, or you have touched women, and you cannot find water, then make your ablution on clean ground and wipe a part of your faces and your hands. God is indeed all-excusing, all-forgiving.

4:43 The notion that one should not pray when drunk may seem obvious enough, although Geiger (*Judaism and Islam,* 67) notes that it has a precedent in the Talmud (b. Berakoth 31b; Eruvin 64). He also notes (*Judaism and Islam,* 68) that the Qur'ān here seems to follow the way the Talmud (b. Berakoth 15a) allows for ablution with "earth" as an exception to ablution by water. Cf. 5:6.

⁴⁴Have you not regarded those who were given a share of the Book, who purchase error and desire that you [too] should lose the way? ⁴⁵But God knows your enemies better, and God suffices as friend, and God suffices as helper.

⁴⁶Among the Jews are those who pervert words from their meanings and say, 'We hear and disobey' and 'Hear without listening!' and '*Rā'inā,*' twisting their tongues and reviling the faith. But had they said, 'We hear and obey' and 'Listen' and '*Unẓurnā,*' it would have been better for them and more upright. But God has cursed them for their faithlessness, so they will not believe except a few.

4:46 The Arabic behind "pervert words from their meanings" is *yuḥarrifūna al-kalima 'an mawāḍi'ihi.* From *yuḥarrifūna* comes the Arabic noun *taḥrīf,* the term used by Islamic tradition to describe the accusation that Jews and Christians falsified Islamic revelations allegedly given to them (the Torah and the Gospel, respectively) and wrote in their place the Hebrew Bible and the New Testament. On this verse *Tafsīr al-Jalālayn* focuses on the Jews and explains, "Some, group, from among the Jews distort, alter, the words, that God revealed in the Torah pertaining to the descriptions of Muḥammad."

However, neither here nor elsewhere (cf. 2:42, 59, 75, 79, 140, 146, 159, 174; 3:71, 78, 187; 5:13–15, 41; 6:91; 7:162) does the Qur'ān argue that the Bible of the Jews and Christians is falsified (5:47 and 10:94 actually suggest that the Bible is reliable). Instead, the Qur'ān argues that the Jews (in particular) have hidden or misrepresented (by "twisting their tongues") their revelation. Hence Qarai's rendering ("pervert words from their meanings") is accurate.

The Qur'ān's argument follows from the insistence of Christians that the Jews failed to find the predictions of Jesus Christ—or allusions to God's son—in the Old Testament, a position already seen with Paul in 2 Corinthians.

> [14]But their minds were closed; indeed, until this very day, the same veil remains over the reading of the Old Testament: it is not lifted, for only in Christ is it done away with.
> [15]As it is, to this day, whenever Moses is read, their hearts are covered with a veil,
> [16]and this veil will not be taken away till they turn to the Lord. (2Co 3:14–16)

This position is especially important to the Syriac Christian fathers (who develop in a particular way a tradition of reading the Old Testament Christologically), such as Isaac of Antioch (d. late fifth century) and Jacob of Serugh (d. 521):

> Let us take for ourselves a scripture / that we inquire of it concerning us and you.
> And from the treasury of your books bring forth / the invalidation of your observances. (Isaac of Antioch, *Homily against the Jews,* 50, ll. 439–42)

> The scribe of your people has hidden the truth / Your teachers have not openly declared the reality.
> Whether or not they know it, they have hidden reality. / They will not show you the image of the Son in their texts. (Jacob of Serugh, *Homélies contre les juifs,* 156, homily 5, ll. 305–8)

On the phrase "We hear and disobey," see commentary on 2:93 and 24:51. Behind the phrase "Hear without listening" which the Qur᾽ān attributes to the Jews may be Isaiah 6:9 (quoted by Jesus in Mat 13:14), where the prophet says, "Listen and listen, but never understand," although the Qur᾽ān seems to attribute this to all of the Jews. On the terms *Rā ῾inā* and *Unẓurnā* and their connections to Hebrew and Syriac, see commentary on 2:104. On the cursing of the Jews, see commentary on 5:13–14 (with further references).

---

⁴⁷O you who were given the Book! Believe in what We have sent down confirming what is with you, before We blot out the faces and turn them backwards, or curse them as We cursed the People of the Sabbath, and God's command is bound to be fulfilled.

4:47 The reference to blotting out faces seems to be an allusion to the manner God in the Qur᾽ān curses "the People of the Sabbath" by transforming them into monkeys (cf. 2:65–66; 7:163–66) or pigs and monkeys (5:60). *Tafsīr al-Jalālayn* comments here: "O you who have been given the Scripture, believe in what We have revealed, of the Qur᾽ān, confirming what is with you, of the Torah, before We obliterate faces, erasing the eyes, noses and eyebrows in them, and turn them inside out, and make them like the napes of the neck, a flat plate, or curse them, by transforming them into apes, as We cursed, [as] We transformed, those of the Sabbath." In one of the less fortunate notes in his otherwise masterful Qur᾽ān commentary, Rudi Paret notes here: "The ugly rear-ends of baboons can actually be compared with faces."

Muhammad Asad, who does not like the idea that God would punish sinners by deforming them physically, translates "lest We efface your hopes and bring them to an end—just as We rejected those people who broke the Sabbath: for God's will is always done." On the People of the Sabbath, see commentary on 7:163–66 (with further references).

---

⁴⁸Indeed, God does not forgive that a partner should be ascribed to Him, but He forgives anything besides that to whomever He

wishes. Whoever ascribes partners to God has indeed fabricated [a lie] in great sinfulness.

4:48 Regarding this verse (a doublet with 4:116), see the commentary on 4:116–17 (with further references).

---

⁴⁹Have you not regarded those who style themselves as pure? Indeed, it is God who purifies whomever He wishes, and they will not be wronged [so much as] a single date-thread.

⁵⁰*Look,* how they fabricate lies against God! That suffices for a flagrant sin.

⁵¹Have *you* not regarded those who were given a share of the Book, believing in idols and satanic entities and saying of the pagans: 'These are better guided on the way than the faithful'? ⁵²They are the ones whom God has cursed, and whomever God curses, you will never find any helper for him.

4:51–52 The word translated in verse 52 as "idols," *jibt,* is perhaps derived from the Ethiopic (Ge'ez) *gəbt,* "new, foreign, strange." The meaning "idol" would be connected to the Ethiopic of Psalm 81:9: "You shall have no strange gods [Ethiopic *amlakä gəbt*], shall worship no alien god." Note also that Hebrew *ṣlāmīm* ("idols") in 2 Chronicles 23:17 and 24:18 (Gk. *eidola*) is translated in Ethiopic as *amaləktä gəbt* "new, alien gods"(cf. also Deu 32:17).

The word translated here as "satanic entities," *ṭāghūt* (cf. 2:256, 257; 4:60, 76; 5:60; 16:36; 39:17; an invariable term that appears with both plural and singular meaning), is derived ultimately from Aramaic *ṭāʿū(thā)* ("idols") (e.g., Isa 10:11). However, in light of its pairing with *jibt,* here it may derive from the Ethiopic form thereof, *taʿōt* (on this see Manfred Kropp, "Beyond Single Words" and Nöldeke, *Neue Beiträge,* 48). In the Qurʾān *ṭāghūt* often seems to mean something like "demons."

The declaration in verse 52, "They are the ones whom God has cursed," is likely an allusion specifically to the Jews (see commentary on 5:13–14, with further references). Thus, in these two verses the Qur'ān seems to be accusing the Jews of idolatry and demon worship.

---

⁵³Do they have a share in sovereignty? If so, they will not give the people [so much as] a speck on a date-stone!

⁵⁴Or do they envy those people for what God has given them out of His bounty? We have certainly given the progeny of Abraham the Book and wisdom, and We have given them a great sovereignty. ⁵⁵Of them are some who believe in him, and of them are some who deter [others] from him; and hell suffices for a blaze!

4:54–55 The phrase "great sovereignty" in verse 54 may refer to the kings of Israel, as the Qur'ān insists that God gave sovereignty (*mulk*) to Saul (Q 2:247), David (Q 38:26), and Solomon (Q 38:35–36).

---

⁵⁶Indeed, We shall soon make those who deny Our signs enter a Fire: as often as their skins become scorched, We shall replace them with other skins, so that they may taste the punishment. God is indeed all-mighty, all-wise.

⁵⁷As for those who have faith and do righteous deeds, We shall admit them into gardens with streams running in them, to remain in them forever. In it there will be chaste mates for them, and We shall admit them into a deep shade.

4:57 On the Qur'ānic paradise, see commentary on 2:25 (with further references).

---

⁵⁸Indeed, God commands you to deliver the trusts to their [rightful] owners, and to judge with fairness when you judge be-

tween people. Excellent indeed is what God advises you. God is indeed all-hearing, all-seeing.

⁵⁹O you who have faith! Obey God and obey the Apostle and those vested with authority among you. And if you dispute concerning anything, refer it to God and the Apostle, if you have faith in God and the Last Day. That is better and more favourable in outcome.

⁶⁰Have *you* not regarded those who claim that they believe in what has been sent down to *you* and what was sent down before *you*? They desire to seek the judgment of satanic entities, though they were commanded to reject them, and Satan desires to lead them astray into far error.

4:60 On the term for "satanic entities" (*ṭāghūt*), see commentary on 4:51–52 (with further references).

———

⁶¹When they are told, 'Come to what God has sent down and [come] to the Apostle,' *you* see the hypocrites keep away from *you* aversely. ⁶²But how will it be when an affliction visits them because of what their hands have sent ahead? Then they will come to *you*, swearing by God, 'We desired nothing but goodwill and comity.' ⁶³They are the ones whom God knows as to what is in their hearts. So *let* them alone, and advise them, and *speak* to them concerning themselves far-reaching words.

⁶⁴We did not send any apostle but to be obeyed by God's leave. Had they, when they wronged themselves, come to *you* and pleaded to God for forgiveness, and the Apostle had pleaded forgiveness for them, they would have surely found God clement and merciful. ⁶⁵But no, by *your* Lord! They will not believe until they make *you* a judge in their disputes, then do not find

within their hearts any dissent to *your* verdict and submit in full submission.

⁶⁶Had We prescribed for them, [commanding]: 'Slay [the guilty among] your folks or leave your habitations,' they would not have done it except a few of them. And if they had done as they were advised, it would have been better for them and stronger in confirming [their faith]. ⁶⁷Then We would have surely given them from Us a great reward, ⁶⁸and We would have guided them to a straight path.

⁶⁹Whoever obeys God and the Apostle—they are with those whom God has blessed, including the prophets and the truthful, the martyrs and the righteous, and excellent companions are they! ⁷⁰That is the grace of God, and God suffices as knower [of His creatures].

⁷¹O you who have faith! Take your precautions, then go forth in companies, or go forth en masse.

⁷²Among you is indeed he who drags his feet, and should an affliction visit you, he says, 'It was certainly God's blessing that I did not accompany them!' ⁷³But should a bounty from God come to you, he will say—as if there were no [tie of friendship and] affection between you and him—'I wish I were with them so that I had achieved the great success!'

⁷⁴Let those who sell the life of this world for the Hereafter fight in the way of God; and whoever fights in the way of God, and then is slain, or he subdues [the enemy], We shall soon give him a great reward.

4:74 The "great reward" of the martyrs (cf. 3:169ff.; 4:100; 9:111; 22:58; 47:4–6) alluded to here is forgiveness of sins (cf. 3:157, 195; 4:98ff.) and immediate entry into the heavenly paradise (whereas other souls will wait for the Day of Judgment). On this see commentary on 2:154 (with further references). On martyrdom as a loan or transaction, see 2:245; 9:111; 61:10–12.

---

[75]Why should you not fight in the way of God and the oppressed men, women, and children, who say, 'Our Lord, bring us out of this town whose people are oppressors, and appoint for us a protector from Yourself, and appoint for us a helper from Yourself'?

[76]Those who have faith fight in the way of God, and those who are faithless fight in the way of satanic entities. So fight the allies of Satan; indeed the stratagems of Satan are always flimsy.

4:76 On the Arabic term rendered "satanic entities" (*ṭāghūt*), see commentary on 4:51–52 (with further references).

---

[77]Have you not regarded those who were told, 'Keep your hands off [from warfare], and maintain the prayer and give the *zakāt'*? But when fighting was prescribed for them, behold, a part of them feared those people as if fearing God, or were even more afraid, and they said, 'Our Lord! Why did You prescribe fighting for us? Why did You not respite us for a short time?!'

Say, 'The enjoyments of this world are trifle and the Hereafter is better for the Godwary, and you will not be wronged so much as a single date-thread. [78]Wherever you may be, death will overtake you, even if you were in fortified towers.'

If any good befalls them, they say, 'This is from God;' and when an ill befalls them, they say, 'This is from *you.*' *Say,* 'All is from God.' What is the matter with these people that they would not understand any matter?

[79]Whatever good befalls *you* is from God; and whatever ill befalls *you* is from *yourself.* We sent *you* as an apostle to mankind, and God suffices as witness.

4:79 The insistence that all good things come from God is close to the spirit of James 1:17: "All that is good, all that is perfect, is given us from above; it comes down from the Father of all light; with him there is no such thing as alteration, no shadow caused by change" (cr. Andrew O'Connor).

---

⁸⁰Whoever obeys the Apostle certainly obeys God; and as for those who turn their backs [on *you*], We have not sent *you* to keep watch over them.

⁸¹They profess obedience [to *you*], but when they go out from *your* presence, a group of them conspire overnight [to do] something other than what *you* say. But God records what they conspire overnight. So *disregard* them and put *your* trust in God, for God suffices as trustee.

⁸²Do they not contemplate the Qurʾān? Had it been from [someone] other than God, they would have surely found much discrepancy in it.

⁸³When a report of safety or alarm comes to them, they immediately broadcast it; but had they referred it to the Apostle or to those vested with authority among them, those of them who investigate would have ascertained it. And were it not for God's grace upon you and His mercy, you would have surely followed Satan, [all] except a few.

⁸⁴So *fight* in the way of God: *you* are responsible only for *yourself,* but *urge* on the faithful [to fight]. Maybe God will curb the might of the faithless, for God is greatest in might and severest in punishment.

⁸⁵Whoever intercedes for a good cause shall receive a share of it, and whoever intercedes for an evil cause shall share its burden, and God has supreme authority over all things.

4:85 Speyer (*BEQ*, 460) connects this verse to b. Bava Qamma 92a: "One who solicits mercy for his fellow while he himself is in need of the same thing, [will be answered first]."

---

[86]When you are greeted with a salute, greet with a better one than it, or return it; indeed God takes account of all things.

[87]God—there is no god except Him—will surely gather you on the Day of Resurrection, in which there is no doubt; and who is more truthful in speech than God?

[88]Why should you be two groups concerning the hypocrites, while God has made them relapse [into unfaith] because of their deeds? Do you desire to guide someone God has led astray? Whomever God leads astray, you will never find any way for him.

[89]They are eager that you should disbelieve just as they have disbelieved, so that you all become alike. So do not make friends [with anyone] from among them, until they migrate in the way of God. But if they turn their backs, seize them and kill them wherever you find them, and do not take from among them friends or helpers, [90]excepting those who join a people between whom and you there is a treaty, or such as come to you with hearts reluctant to fight you, or to fight their own people. Had God wished, He would have imposed them upon you, and then they would have surely fought you. So if they keep out of your way and do not fight you and offer you peace, then God does not allow you any course [of action] against them.

[91]You will find others desiring to be secure from you and from their own people; yet whenever they are called back to polytheism, they relapse into it. So if they do not keep out of your way, nor offer you peace, nor keep their hands off [from fighting], then

seize them and kill them wherever you confront them, and it is such against whom We have given you a clear sanction.

⁹²A believer may not kill another believer, unless it is by mistake. Anyone who kills a believer by mistake should set free a believing slave and pay blood-money to his family, unless they remit it in charity. If he belongs to a people who are hostile to you but is a believer, then a believing slave is to be set free. And if he belongs to a people with whom you have a treaty, the blood-money is to be paid to his family and a believing slave is to be set free. He who does not afford [freeing a slave] must fast for two successive months as a penance from God, and God is all-knowing, all-wise.

⁹³Should anyone kill a believer intentionally, his requital shall be hell, to remain in it [forever]; God shall be wrathful at him and curse him and He will prepare for him a great punishment.

⁹⁴O you who have faith! When you issue forth in the way of God, try to ascertain: do not say to someone who offers you peace, 'You are not a believer,' seeking the transitory wares of the life of this world. But with God are plenteous gains. You too were such earlier, but God did you a favour. Therefore, do ascertain. God is indeed well aware of what you do.

⁹⁵Not equal are those of the faithful who sit back—excepting those who suffer from some disability—and those who wage *jihād* in the way of God with their possession and persons. God has graced those who wage *jihād* with their possessions and persons by a degree over those who sit back; yet to each God has promised the best reward, and God has graced those who wage *jihād* over those who sit back with a great reward: ⁹⁶ranks from Him, forgiveness and mercy, and God is all-forgiving, all-merciful.

⁹⁷Indeed, those whom the angels take away while they are wronging themselves, they ask, 'What state were you in?' They

reply, 'We were oppressed in the land.' They say, 'Was not God's earth vast enough so that you might migrate in it?' The refuge of such shall be hell, and it is an evil destination. [98]Except those oppressed among men, women and children, who have neither access to any means nor are guided to any way. [99]Maybe God will excuse them, for God is all-excusing, all-forgiving.

[100]Whoever migrates in the way of God will find many havens and plenitude in the earth. And whoever leaves his home migrating toward God and His Apostle, and is then overtaken by death, his reward shall certainly fall on God, and God is all-forgiving, all-merciful.

4:100 On the reward for migration, see commentary on 3:195.

---

[101]When you journey in the land, there is no sin upon you in shortening the prayers if you fear that the faithless may trouble you; indeed the faithless are your manifest enemies.

[102]When *you* are among them, leading them in prayers, let a group of them stand with *you,* carrying their weapons. And when they have done the prostrations, let them withdraw to the rear, then let the other group which has not prayed come and pray with *you,* taking their precautions and [bearing] their weapons. The faithless are eager that you should be oblivious of your weapons and your baggage, so that they could assault you all at once. But there is no sin upon you, if you are troubled by rain or are sick, to set aside your weapons; but take your precautions. God has indeed prepared a humiliating punishment for the faithless.

[103]When you have finished the prayers, remember God, standing, sitting and lying down; and when you feel secure, perform

the [complete] prayers, for the prayer is indeed a timed prescription for the faithful.

¹⁰⁴Do not slacken in the pursuit of those people. If you are suffering, they are also suffering like you, but you expect from God what they do not expect, and God is all-knowing, all-wise.

¹⁰⁵Indeed, We have sent down to you the Book with the truth, so that *you* may judge between the people by what God has shown *you; do not be* an advocate for the traitors, ¹⁰⁶and *plead* to God for forgiveness; indeed God is all-forgiving, all-merciful.

¹⁰⁷And *do not plead* for those who betray themselves; indeed God does not like those who are treacherous and sinful.

¹⁰⁸They try to hide [their real character] from people, but they do not try to hide from God, though He is with them when they conspire overnight with a discourse that He does not approve of. And God encompasses whatever they do.

¹⁰⁹Aha! There you are, pleading for them in the life of this world! But who will plead for them with God on the Day of Resurrection, or will be their defender?

¹¹⁰Whoever commits evil or wrongs himself and then pleads to God for forgiveness, will find God all-forgiving, all-merciful.

¹¹¹Whoever commits a sin, commits it only against himself; and God is all-knowing, all-wise.

4:111 On the notion that no soul shall carry another's burden, see commentary on 82:19 (with further references).

---

¹¹²Whoever commits an iniquity or sin and then accuses an innocent person of it, is indeed guilty of calumny and a flagrant sin.

¹¹³Were it not for God's grace and His mercy on *you,* a group of them were bent on leading *you* astray; but they do not mis-

lead anyone except themselves and they cannot do *you* any harm. God has sent down to *you* the Book and wisdom, and He has taught *you* what *you* did not know, and great is God's grace upon *you*.

[114]There is no good in much of their secret talks, excepting someone who enjoins charity or what is right or reconciliation between people, and whoever does that, seeking God's pleasure, soon We shall give him a great reward.

[115]Whoever defies the Apostle, after the guidance has become clear to him, and follows a way other than that of the faithful, We shall abandon him to his devices and We will make him enter hell, and it is an evil destination.

[116]Indeed, God does not forgive that any partner should be ascribed to Him, but He forgives anything besides that to whomever He wishes. And whoever ascribes partners to God has certainly strayed into far error.

[117]They invoke none but females besides Him, and invoke none but some froward Satan,

4:116–17 Verse 116 (cf. 4:48) illustrates the theological concern at the heart of the Qur'ān's message: the greatest sin is to belittle God; any offense against humans, even murder (see vv. 92–93), can be forgiven, but the offense against God of belittling his sovereignty cannot. Verse 117 alludes to one example of such an insult: the description of certain angels as daughters of God (cf. 6:100; 16:57; 17:40; 37:150; 43:19; 53:27). On this see further commentary on 43:16–19. Regarding the unforgiveable sin of verse 116, one might compare Deuteronomy 13:7–9, which makes "incitement to idolatry" a capital crime, and the Gospel passages on "blasphemy against the Holy Spirit":

[31]And so I tell you, every human sin and blasphemy will be forgiven, but blasphemy against the Spirit will not be forgiven.
[32]And anyone who says a word against the Son of man will be forgiven; but no one who speaks against the Holy Spirit will be forgiven either in this world or in the next. (Mat 12:31–32; cf. Mar 3:28–30; Luk 12:8–10).

On calling upon Satan (v. 117), see commentary on 14:22 (with further references).

---

[118]whom God has cursed, and who said, 'I will surely take a settled share of Your servants, [119]and I will lead them astray and give them [false] hopes, and prompt them to slit the ears of cattle, and I will prompt them to alter God's creation.' Whoever takes Satan as a friend instead of God has certainly incurred a manifest loss. [120]He makes them promises and gives them [false] hopes, yet Satan does not promise them anything but delusion.

[121]The refuge of such shall be hell, and they will not find any escape from it.

[122]As for those who have faith and do righteous deeds, We will admit them into gardens with streams running in them, to remain in them forever—a true promise of God, and who is truer in speech than God?

4:122 On the streams of paradise, see commentary on 2:25 (with further references).

---

[123]It will be neither after your hopes nor the hopes of the People of the Book: whoever commits evil shall be requited for it, and he will not find for himself any friend or helper besides God. [124]And whoever does righteous deeds, whether male or female, should he be faithful—such shall enter paradise and they will not be wronged [so much as] the speck on a date-stone.

[125]Who has a better religion than him who submits his will to God, being virtuous, and follows the creed of Abraham, a *ḥanīf*? And God took Abraham for a dedicated friend.

4:125 On the term *ḥanīf* and its association with Abraham, see commentary on 16:120–23 (with further references). In this verse the Qur'ān speaks of God's "taking" Abraham as a "dedicated friend" (Ar. *khalīl*). Muhammad Asad renders the last phrase of this verse as "seeing that God exalted Abraham with His love." In Isaiah 41:8 and 2 Chronicles 20:7 Abraham is referred to as the "friend" or "beloved" (Hb. *ōhab*) of God. James 2 alludes to this by referring to Abraham as God's *philos* ("friend" or "beloved"): "In this way the scripture was fulfilled: Abraham put his faith in God, and this was considered as making him upright; and he received the name 'friend of God'" (Jam 2:21–23).

Wāḥidī explains the Qur'ān's description of Abraham as God's friend with a story in which God miraculously changes grains of sand into wheat at a time of a great famine. Abraham's wife, Sarah, finds the wheat and bakes bread while Abraham is still sleeping. The story concludes: "When Abraham woke up, he smelt the odour of food, and he asked: 'O Sarah, where did you get this food?' She said: 'It is from your Egyptian friend.' He said: 'No, it is rather from my friend God.' On that day God chose Abraham as friend."

---

[126]To God belongs whatever is in the heavens and whatever is on the earth, and God encompasses all things.

[127]They seek *your* ruling concerning women. *Say,* 'God gives you a ruling concerning them and what is announced to you in the Book concerning girl orphans—whom you do not give what has been prescribed for them, and yet you desire to marry them—and about the weak among children: that you should maintain the orphans with justice, and whatever good you do, indeed God knows it well.

[128]If a woman fears misconduct or desertion from her husband, there is no sin upon the couple if they reach a reconciliation between themselves; and reconcilement is better. The souls are prone to greed; but if you are virtuous and Godwary, God is indeed well aware of what you do.

[129]You will not be able to be fair between wives, even if you are eager to do so. Yet do not turn away from one altogether, leaving

her as if in a suspense. But if you are conciliatory and Godwary, God is indeed all-forgiving, all-merciful.

[130]But if they separate, God will suffice each of them out of His bounty, and God is all-bounteous, all-wise.

[131]To God belongs whatever is in the heavens and whatever is on the earth. We have certainly enjoined those who were given the Book before you, and you, that you should be wary of God. But if you are faithless, [you should know that] to God belongs whatever is in the heavens and whatever is on the earth, and God is all-sufficient, all-laudable.

[132]To God belongs whatever is in the heavens and whatever is on the earth, and God suffices as trustee.

[133]If He wishes, He will take you away, O mankind, and bring others [in your place]; God has the power to do that.

[134]Whoever desires the reward of this world, [should know that] with God is the reward of this world and the Hereafter, and God is all-hearing, all-seeing.

[135]O you who have faith! Be maintainers of justice and [honest] witnesses for the sake of God, even if it should be against yourselves or [your] parents and near relatives, and whether it be [someone] rich or poor, for God has a greater right over them. So do not follow [your] desires, lest you should be unfair, and if you distort [the testimony] or disregard [it], God is indeed well aware of what you do.

[136]O you who have faith! Have faith in God and His Apostle and the Book that He has sent down to His Apostle and the Book He had sent down earlier. Whoever disbelieves in God and His angels, His Books and His apostles and the Last Day, has certainly strayed into far error.

[137]As for those who believe and then disbelieve, then believe [again] and then disbelieve and then increase in disbelief, God will never forgive them, nor will He guide them to any [right] way.

¹³⁸Inform the hypocrites that there is a painful punishment for them ¹³⁹—those who take the faithless for allies instead of the faithful. Do they seek honour with them? [If so,] all honour belongs to God.

¹⁴⁰Certainly He has sent down to you in the Book that when you hear God's signs being disbelieved and derided, do not sit with them until they engage in some other discourse, or else you [too] will be like them. God will indeed gather the hypocrites and the faithless in hell all together ¹⁴¹—those who lie in wait for you: if there is a victory for you from God, they say, 'Were we not with you?' But if the faithless get a share [of victory], they say, 'Did we not prevail upon you and defend you against the faithful?' God will judge between you on the Day of Resurrection, and God will never provide the faithless any way [to prevail] over the faithful.

¹⁴²The hypocrites seek to deceive God, but it is He who outwits them. When they stand up for prayer, they stand up lazily, showing off to the people and not remembering God except a little, ¹⁴³wavering in between: neither with these, nor with those. And whomever God leads astray, you will never find any way for him.

4:142–43 As Speyer mentions (*BEQ,* 452), the Qur'ān condemns the ostentatious prayer of "hypocrites" in a way similar to Matthew 6:5: "And when you pray, do not imitate the hypocrites: they love to say their prayers standing up in the synagogues and at the street corners for people to see them. In truth I tell you, they have had their reward." On "hypocrites" in the Qur'ān, see commentary on 63:1.

———

¹⁴⁴O you who have faith! Do not take the faithless for allies instead of the faithful. Do you wish to give God a clear sanction against yourselves?

¹⁴⁵Indeed, the hypocrites will be in the lowest reach of the Fire, and you will never find any helper for them, ¹⁴⁶except for those who repent and reform and hold fast to God and dedicate their religion [exclusively] to God. Those are with the faithful, and soon God will give the faithful a great reward.

¹⁴⁷Why should God punish you if you give thanks and be faithful? And God is appreciative, all-knowing.

¹⁴⁸God does not like the disclosure of [anyone's] evil [conduct] in speech except by someone who has been wronged, and God is all-hearing, all-knowing.

¹⁴⁹Whether you disclose a good [deed that you do] or hide it, or excuse an evil [deed], God is indeed all-excusing, all-powerful.

¹⁵⁰Those who disbelieve in God and His apostles and seek to separate God from His apostles, and say, 'We believe in some and disbelieve in some' and seek to take a way in between ¹⁵¹—it is they who are truly faithless, and We have prepared for the faithless a humiliating punishment.

¹⁵²But those who have faith in God and His apostles and make no distinction between any of them—them He will soon give their rewards, and God is all-forgiving, all-merciful.

¹⁵³The People of the Book ask *you* to bring down for them a Book from the heaven. Certainly they asked Moses for [something] greater than that, for they said, 'Show us God visibly,' whereat a thunderbolt seized them for their wrongdoing. Then they took up the Calf [for worship] after all the clear proofs that had come to them. Yet We excused that, and We gave Moses a manifest authority.

¹⁵⁴We raised the Mount above them for the sake of their covenant, and We said to them, 'Enter while prostrating at the gate' and We said to them, 'Do not violate the Sabbath,' and We took a solemn covenant from them.

¹⁵⁵Then because of their breaking their covenant, their denial of God's signs, their killing of the prophets unjustly and for their saying, 'Our hearts are uncircumcised' . . . Indeed, God has set a seal on them for their unfaith, so they do not have faith except a few.

4:153–55 These three verses are parallel to 2:51–56 and 2:83–93. The demand of the Israelites to see God "openly," alluded to in verse 153 (cf. 2:55), is related to Exodus 19:21 and traditions in *Exodus Rabbah* (see commentary on 2:55–56). The translation "thunderbolt" (Ar. *ṣā'iqa*) of verse 153 is uncertain (cf. 2:19; where the plural *ṣawā'iq* is rendered "thunderclaps"). On the golden calf (v. 153; cf. 7:148; 20:85–98), see commentary on 20:83–98. Regarding the "raising of the Mount" (v. 154; cf. 2:93; 7:171), see commentary on 2:63. On the command to enter the gate (v. 154), see commentary on 2:58–59. Concerning the Qur'ān's doctrine on the Sabbath (v. 154; cf. 2:65; 4:47), see commentary on 7:163–66 and 16:124.

The reference to the Israelites' breaking of the covenant (v. 155) seems to be connected to the golden calf episode (cf. 2:93; 5:13; n.b. 4:153 in reference to this episode). On the killing of the prophets (v. 155), see commentary on 3:181-82 (with further references).

Finally, in verse 155 the Qur'ān speaks of God's, "setting a seal on" (Arabic *ṭ.b.* ʿ) the hearts of the Jews. In the Qur'ān's anti-Jewish polemic the heart is an important topos generally (cf. 2:88; 5:13). In 4:155, as in 2:88, the Qur'ān has the Jews declare that their hearts are "uncircumcised." While this turn of phrase reflects a Biblical topos (cf. Lev 26:41; Jer 9:25; Act 7:51; Rom 2:28–29), the point is that their hearts are "covered" (i.e., they refuse to listen to the words of prophets). The expression that God has "set a seal" on the hearts of the Jews (v. 155) is like that employed elsewhere for the way God keeps unbelievers from believing in the message of the Qur'ān. On this see commentary on 7:101 (with further references). The Qur'ān's point is that Jewish unbelief is a punishment from God and not their own doing.

In a similar way the Syriac Christian *Didascalia*—while discussing the abomination of the golden calf—insists that God hardened the hearts of the Israelites:

However, in not one of them did they abide, but they again provoked the Lord to anger. On this account He yet added to them by the second legislation a blindness worthy of their works. . . . Indeed the Lord judged them with a just judgment and did to them thus because of their evil, and *hardened their heart* like that of Pharaoh. (*Didascalia,* chap. 26, 245–46)

4:155–62 *overview* In this section (which overlaps with the previous section) the Qurʾān offers a list of Israelite transgressions to demonstrate their infidelity to God: breaking the covenant (v. 155); denying God's signs (v. 155); killing the prophets (v. 155; see commentary on 3:181, with further references); having "uncircumcised" hearts (v. 155; see commentary on 2:88); calumny against Mary (v. 156); boasting of killing of Jesus (v. 157); usury (v. 161, see commentary on that verse, with further references); and consuming the wealth of others (v. 161). This list leads to a final condemnation in verse 161: "And We have prepared a painful punishment for the faithless among them." Those Jews who believe in the Qurʾān's Prophet, however, will be saved (v. 162).

[156]And for their faithlessness and their uttering a monstrous calumny against Mary,

4:156 This verse continues the list of the Jews' transgressions begun in v. 155. The term translated in verse 156 as "monstrous calumny" (Ar. *buhtān*) is derived from Syriac *buhtānā* ("calumny"). The Qurʾān is likely accusing the Jews of claiming that Mary begot Jesus through illicit relations. The Qurʾān might be responding to Jewish traditions found in certain manuscripts of the Babylonian Talmud (in passages later edited under the pressure of Christian censorship) which seem to report that Mary had a lover named Pandera who fathered Jesus (b. Shabbat 104b; Sanhedrin, 67a). See Schäfer, "Jesus in the Talmud," 133–34.

[157]and for their saying, 'We killed the Messiah, Jesus son of Mary, the apostle of God'—though they did not kill him nor crucify him, but so it was made to appear to them. Indeed, those who differ concerning him are in doubt about him: they do not have any knowledge of that beyond following conjectures, and certainly they did not kill him.

4:157 This verse is usually understood by Muslim scholars to mean that God changed someone to look like Jesus and that this other person was mistakenly killed by the Jews, whereas Jesus escaped death entirely (this understanding is influenced by a reading of 3:54, which has God "devise," or "plot" in a response to those who plotted against Jesus). *Tafsīr al-Jalālayn* explains, "The one slain and crucified, who was an associate of theirs [the Jews], was given the resemblance, of Jesus. In other words, God cast his [Jesus's] likeness to him and so they thought it was him [Jesus]." Compare also the translation of Hilali-Khan: "but the resemblance of 'Isa (Jesus) was put over another man (and they killed that man)."

In fact the verse does not deny that Jesus was crucified or that he died—it only denies that the Jews killed him. The reason for this denial is quite particular to the Qur'ān: the insistence that God is the one who gives life and death (see 2:258; 3:156; 7:158; 9:116; passim). In describing the manner in which God causes death, the Qur'ān elsewhere uses the verb *tawaffā* (see, e.g., 6:60; 10:46, 104; 13:40; passim). This is the verb that the Qur'ān has God use to announce that God himself will cause Jesus to die (Q 3:55) and that Jesus uses (Q 5:117) after his ascension into heaven to speak of how God *caused* him to die.

Thus, with this verse the Qur'ān means not to deny the death of Jesus but to use the Israelites' claim of having killed Jesus, a prophet of God, as an example—along with the others mentioned in this section (vv. 155–61) of Jewish perfidy (it is connected in particular to the Qur'ān's description of the Jews as "killers of the prophets" in v. 155). In this it is comparable to those passages in the Acts of the Apostles where the Crucifixion is presented as the climax of a long history of Israelite infidelity:

> [14]It was you who accused the Holy and Upright One, you who demanded that a murderer should be released to you
> [15]while you killed the prince of life. God, however, raised him from the dead, and to that fact we are witnesses. (Act 3:14–15; cf. Act 4:8–12)

---

[158]Indeed, God raised him up toward Himself, and God is all-mighty, all-wise.

[159]There is none among the People of the Book but will surely believe in him before his death; and on the Day of Resurrection he will be a witness against them.

4:158–59 According to standard Islamic tradition God raised Jesus up to heaven (v. 158) before he was taken to be crucified. There is no reason, however, why this verse could not be understood in light of the New Testament traditions on the ascension such as that in Acts 1:7–11.

Verse 159 causes no little confusion among Muslim commentators, as it is not clear whether "his" death refers to that of one "among the People of the Book" or to that of Jesus. According to the first view each Jew and Christian, at the moment just before death, has a vision that leads him or her to believe in Jesus (as a Muslim prophet), although this belief is too late to save them from damnation. According to the second view, Jesus—who escaped death during his first stay on earth—will return to earth in the End Times. After his descent to earth all Jews and Christians will convert to Islam so that by the time Jesus dies, just before the Day of Resurrection, all of the People of the Book will believe in Jesus (as a Muslim prophet). This second, eschatological tradition may be in part a response to 4:159 (since a story was needed that explained how all the Jews and Christians would believe in the Muslim Jesus before his death).

The latter part of this verse seems to be related to the Christian tradition that Jesus will act as a judge on the last day, as in Matthew 25:31–32 (cf. Mat 16:27–28; Mar 8:38–9:1; 13:24–27; Luk 9:26–27, 21:27; Joh 5:27). The Qur'ān, which insists that Jesus is not divine, makes him only a witness on that day.

---

¹⁶⁰Due to the wrongdoing of the Jews, We prohibited them certain good things that were permitted to them [earlier], and for their barring many [people] from the way of God,

4:160 In Matthew 19:7–8 Jesus describes a provision of Mosaic Law—divorce—as a reflection of God's reduced expectations of the Israelites in light of their hard-heartedness. Here the idea is reversed. The restrictive dietary laws of Mosaic Law are described as a punishment for their wrongdoing. On this theme, see 3:50, 93; 6:146; 16:118; 16:124. On the specific foods forbidden to the Jews, see commentary on 6:145–46.

As Holger Zellentin has shown (*Qur'ān's Legal Culture,* 140ff.), the idea that the Mosaic Law is in part a punishment given to the Jews is connected to an idea found in the Syriac Christian *Didascalia,* by which God first established an easy law at Mt. Sinai. When the Israelites impiously worshipped the golden calf, God then established a second, difficult law as a punishment:

Therefore the Lord became angry, and in the heat of His anger—(yet) with the mercy of His goodness—He bound them with the second legislation, and laid heavy burdens upon them and a hard yoke upon their neck. And He says now no longer: "If you shall make," as formerly, but he said: "Make an altar, and sacrifice continually," as though He had need of these things.

Therefore He laid upon them continual burnt offerings as a necessity, and caused them to abstain from meats through distinction of meats. Indeed, from that time were animals discerned, and clean flesh and unclean, from that time were separations, and purifications, and baptisms and sprinklings. And from that time were sacrifices, and offerings, and tables. (*Didascalia,* chap. 26, 227)

This passage in the *Didascalia* is in turn based in part on Ezekiel 20:23–25:

[23]Once again, however, I pledged them my word that I would scatter them throughout the nations and disperse them in foreign countries,
[24]because they had not followed my judgements but had rejected my laws and profaned my Sabbaths, their eyes being fastened on the foul idols of their ancestors.
[25]And for this reason I gave them laws that were not good and judgements by which they could never live.

On the Qur'ān's expression "barring . . . from the way of God," see commentary on 9:34–35.

---

[161]and for their taking usury—though they had been forbidden from it—and for eating up the wealth of the people wrongfully. And We have prepared a painful punishment for the faithless among them.

4:161 Exodus 22:24 forbids the taking of interest ("If you lend money to any of my people, to anyone poor among you, you will not play the usurer with him: you will not demand interest from him") (cf. Lev 25:35–37; Deu 23:20). Luke 6:35 develops the ethical principle: "Instead, love your enemies and do good to them, and lend without any hope of return. You will have a great reward, and you will be children of the Most High, for he himself is kind to the ungrateful and the wicked." The Syriac *Didascalia* condemns usury with a term (Syr. *rebītā*) that is cognate to the Arabic word (*ribā*) that the Qur'ān employs for usury here:

> Again the apostles constituted: whoever lends and takes usury (*rebītā*) and is occupied in merchandise and covetousness shall not serve again and shall not remain in the ministry. (*Didascalia* chap. 3, p. 39)

---

¹⁶²But as for those who are firmly grounded in knowledge from among them and faithful, they believe in what has been sent down to *you,* and what was sent down before *you*—those who maintain the prayer, give the *zakāt,* and believe in God and the Last Day—them We shall give a great reward.

¹⁶³We have indeed revealed to *you* as We revealed to Noah and the prophets after him, and [as] We revealed to Abraham, Ishmael, Isaac, Jacob, and the Tribes, Jesus and Job, Jonah, Aaron and Solomon—and We gave David the Psalms—¹⁶⁴and apostles that We have recounted to *you* earlier and apostles We have not recounted to *you*—and to Moses God spoke directly—¹⁶⁵apostles, as bearers of good news and warners, so that mankind may not have any argument against God, after the [sending of the] apostles, and God is all-mighty, all-wise.

4:163–65 The list of (exclusively Biblical) prophets here might be compared to others: 2:136; 3:84; 6:84–86; 21:48–91; 33:7; 42:13; 37:75–148. The place of Jesus in the middle of the list of prophets (in between "the tribes" and Job) of verse 163 does not follow the order of the Bible or any traditional chronological order. His name might appear in this place because of the Qur'ān's concern with rhyme, if it is assumed that this long verse could be divided into shorter, rhyming verses: "tribes" (Ar. *asbāṭ*) and Solomon (Ar. *sulaymān*) would be at the end of verses; Jesus (Ar. *ʿīsā*) would be at the beginning of a verse in a position of prominence parallel to that of Noah and David.

The declaration at the end of verse 163, "We gave David the Psalms" (*zabūr;* elsewhere the plural *zubur* is used for scripture generally; on this see commentary on 17:55, with further references), reflects the traditional Jewish and Christian idea that David is the principal author of the Psalms. This idea is evident already in the Midrash (*Avot* 6:9) and New Testament texts (e.g., Mar 12:36–37), which attribute lines in the Psalms to David. God's direct speech to Moses (v. 164) reflects Numbers 12:4–8 (cf. Exo 33:11; Deu 5:4–5). See also commentary on 2:253 (with further references).

---

¹⁶⁶But God bears witness to what He has sent down to *you*—He sent it down with His knowledge—and the angels bear witness [too], and God quite suffices as witness.

¹⁶⁷Indeed, those who are faithless and bar [others] from the way of God, have certainly strayed into far error. ¹⁶⁸Indeed, those who are faithless and do wrong, God will never forgive them, nor will He guide them to any way, ¹⁶⁹except the way to hell, to remain in it forever, and that is easy for God.

¹⁷⁰O mankind! The Apostle has certainly brought you the truth from your Lord. So have faith! That is better for you. And if you are faithless, [you should know that] to God belongs whatever is in the heavens and the earth, and God is all-knowing, all-wise.

¹⁷¹O People of the Book! Do not exceed the bounds in your religion, and do not attribute anything to God except the truth. The Messiah, Jesus son of Mary, was only an apostle of God, and His Word that He cast toward Mary and a spirit from Him. So have faith in God and His apostles, and do not say, '[God is] a trinity.' Relinquish [such a creed]! That is better for you. God is but the One God. He is far too immaculate to have any son. To Him belongs whatever is in the heavens and whatever is on the earth, and God suffices as trustee.

4:171 In 3:45 the angels announce to Mary that the child whom she will bear, Jesus, is a "word from God." Here Jesus is a word "cast into" (pace Qarai: "toward") Mary. That Jesus is called a "spirit from" God is connected to 21:91 and 66:12, which have God describe how he breathed his spirit into Mary or into "her body" to create Jesus. Qarai's translation here, "do not say, '[God is] a trinity'" (cf. 5:73, 116), reflects the common Islamic interpretation of this verse. However, the Qur'ān here has simply "Do not say *'three.'*" This verse is an important example (along with v. 48 of this Sura) of the Qur'ān's concern with divine sublimity, or the dignity of God. The critique of Christians here is not predicated on abstract rationality, but rather on the jealousy of the Qur'ān's God, who insists that he alone be worshipped (cf. 2:116; 6:100ff.; 10:68; 19:88–95; 25:2; 39:3–5; 43:81ff.). This theological emphasis is not unlike that found in Exodus 34 (among other Old Testament passages):

> [12]Take care you make no pact with the inhabitants of the country which you are about to enter, or they will prove a snare in your community.
> [13]You will tear down their altars, smash their cultic stones and cut down their sacred poles,
> [14]for you will worship no other god, since the Lord's name is the Jealous One; he is a jealous God. (Exo 34:12–14; cf. Ex 20:5; Deu 4:23–25, 5:9, 6:15; Jos 24:19–20)

An alternative reading here, proposed by Luxenberg, would modify the initial phrase *lā taghlū fī dīnikum* ("do not exceed the bounds in your religion"; cf. 5:77) to *lā ta'lū fī dīnikum,* following the Syriac idiom *a'li b-dīnā,* "to err in one's judgment, to make a mistake." The initial phrase would then read: "O People of the Book! Do not err in your judgment!" (See C. Luxenberg "Neudeutung der arabischen Inschrift im Felsendom," 136–37).

---

[172]The Messiah would never disdain being a servant of God, nor would the angels brought near [to Him]. And whoever disdains His worship and is arrogant, He will gather them all toward Him.

4:172 In this verse (in which the theme of v. 171 is continued) the Qur'ān insists that Jesus and the angels recognize God's divine right and that they consider themselves only servants of God (regarding which see 19:30; 43:59). This verse might be viewed as a sort of reply to Philippians 2:3–9, where, according to the traditional Christian understanding of this passage, Paul presents Jesus as the Son of God who was willing to empty himself of his divine dignity to become a servant, and, even more, to die the death of a criminal:

[5]Make your own the mind of Christ Jesus:
[6]Who, being in the form of God, did not count equality with God something to be grasped.
[7]But he emptied himself, taking the form of a slave, becoming as human beings are; and being in every way like a human being. (Phi 2:5–7)

———————

[173]As for those who have faith and do righteous deeds, He will pay them in full their rewards, and He will enhance them out of His grace. But those who are disdainful and arrogant, He will punish them with a painful punishment, and they will not find besides God any friend or helper.

[174]O mankind! Certainly a proof has come to you from your Lord, and We have sent down to you a manifest light.

[175]As for those who have faith in God and hold fast to Him, He will admit them to His mercy and grace, and He will guide them on a straight path to Him.

[176]They ask *you* for a ruling. *Say,* 'God gives you a ruling concerning the *kalālah:* If a man dies and has no children [or parents], but has a sister, for her shall be a half of what he leaves, and he shall inherit from her if she has no children. If there be two sisters, they shall receive two-thirds of what he leaves. But if there be [several] brothers and sisters, for the male shall be like the share of two females. God explains [the laws] for you lest you should go astray, and God has knowledge of all things.'

5. *AL-MĀʾIDA*, THE TABLE

In the Name of God, the All-beneficent, the All-merciful.

¹O you who have faith! Keep your agreements. You are permitted animals of grazing livestock, except for what is [now] announced to you, disallowing game while you are in pilgrim sanctity. Indeed, God decrees whatever He desires.

²O you who have faith! Do not violate God's sacraments, neither the sacred month, nor the offering, nor the necklaces, nor those bound for the Sacred House who seek their Lord's bounty and [His] pleasure. But when you emerge from pilgrim sanctity you may hunt for game. Ill feeling for a people should not lead you to transgress, because they barred you from [access to] the Sacred Mosque. Cooperate in piety and Godwariness, but do not cooperate in sin and aggression, and be wary of God. God is indeed severe in retribution.

³You are prohibited carrion, blood, the flesh of swine, and what has been offered to other than God, and the animal strangled or beaten to death, and that which dies by falling or is gored to death, and that which is mangled by a beast of prey—barring that which you may purify—and what is sacrificed on stone altars [to

idols], and that you should divide by raffling with arrows. All that is transgression.

Today the faithless have despaired of your religion. So do not fear them, but fear Me. Today I have perfected your religion for you, and I have completed My blessing upon you, and I have approved Islam as your religion.

But should anyone be compelled by hunger, without inclining to sin, then God is indeed all-forgiving, all-merciful.

5:3 The particular restrictions on food at the opening of this verse (cf. 2:173; 6:145; 16:115) reflect dietary codes of the Pentateuch: carrion (Exo 22:30; Lev 17:15, 22:8; Deu 14:21), blood (Gen 9:4; Lev 3:17; Deu 12:16, 23), and pork (Lev 11:7; Deu 14:8). They have also been compared to the instructions given to new converts to Christianity in Acts 15:29 (and 21:25), but the addition of pork is notable.

Cuypers argues (*Banquet*, 87) that the Qurʾān's two references in the middle of this verse to "today" are reminiscent of the way Deuteronomy (see esp. Deu 26:16–19) speaks regularly of "today" in its narrative of God's covenant with Israel.

⁴They ask *you* as to what is lawful for them. *Say*, 'All the good things are lawful for you.' As for what you have taught hunting dogs [to catch], teaching them by what God has taught you, eat of what they catch for you and mention God's Name over it, and be wary of God. God is indeed swift at reckoning.

⁵Today all the good things have been made lawful for you—the food of those who were given the Book is lawful for you, and your food is lawful for them—and the chaste ones from among faithful women, and chaste women of those who were given the Book before you, when you have given them their dowries, in

wedlock, not in license, nor taking paramours. Should anyone renounce his faith, his works shall fail and he will be among the losers in the Hereafter.

5:5–11 *overview* Cuypers (*Banquet,* 61–64) makes this section of *al-Māʾida* comparable to those passages in Deuteronomy in which God prepares the Israelites for their entry into the promised land by reminding them of their religious obligations. Verse 5 (which begins with "Today"; cf. 5:3) might be compared with Deuteronomy 26:16–18:

> [16]'the Lord 'your God commands you *today* to observe these laws and customs; you must keep and observe them with all your heart and with all your soul.
> [17] *'Today* you have obtained this declaration from the Lord: that he will be your God, but only if you follow his ways, keep his statutes, his commandments, his customs, and listen to his voice.
> [18]And *today* the Lord has obtained this declaration from you: that you will be his own people—as he has said—but only if you keep all his commandments. (Deu 26:16–18)

---

[6]O you who have faith! When you stand up for prayer, wash your faces and your hands up to the elbows, and wipe a part of your heads and your feet up to the ankles. If you are *junub,* purify yourselves. But if you are sick, or on a journey, or any of you has come from the toilet, or you have touched women, and you cannot find water, then make *tayammum* with clean ground and wipe a part of your faces and your hands with it. God does not desire to put you to hardship, but He desires to purify you and to complete His blessing upon you so that you may give thanks.

5:6 On washing with sand (*tayammum*) instead of water, see commentary on 4:43.

⁷Remember God's blessing upon you and His covenant with which He has bound you when you said, 'We hear and obey.' And be wary of God. Indeed, God knows well what is in the breasts.

5:7 On the declaration attributed to the believers, "We hear and obey," see commentary on 2:93; 24:51 (with further references). This verse has the believers take the place of the Israelites who in Exodus (note esp. 24:7)—but *not* in the Qurʾān (see 2:93; 4:46)—declare that they will obey God.

⁸O you who have faith! Be maintainers of justice, as witnesses for God's sake, and ill feeling for a people should never lead you to be unfair. Be fair; that is nearer to Godwariness, and be wary of God. God is indeed well aware of what you do. ⁹God has promised those who have faith and do righteous deeds forgiveness and a great reward. ¹⁰As for those who are faithless and deny Our signs, they shall be the inmates of hell.

¹¹O you who have faith! Remember God's blessing upon you when a people set out to extend their hands against you, but He withheld their hands from you, and be wary of God, and in God alone let all the faithful put their trust. ¹²Certainly God took a pledge from the Children of Israel, and We raised among them twelve chiefs. And God said, 'I am with you! Surely, if you maintain the prayer and give the *zakāt* and have faith in My apostles and support them and lend God a good loan, I will surely absolve you of your misdeeds, and I will surely admit you into gardens with streams running in them. But whoever of you disbelieves after that has certainly strayed from the right way.'

5:12 The reference to the twelve leaders (Ar. *naqīb;* Qarai translates "chiefs") of Israel may be related to Numbers 13, where God has Moses choose twelve men (one from each tribe) to reconnoiter Canaan, or to the appointment of elders to assist Moses (Exo 18:24–25; Num 11:16–17). However, the point of this verse is to offer to the believers (who have just, in v. 7, consented to a covenant with God) the negative example of the Israelites who broke their covenant with God (already in v. 7 the Qurʾān alludes to the infidelity of the Israelites). In this light it seems likely that the Qurʾān is referring generally to the division of Israel into twelve tribes. On the streams of paradise, see commentary on 2:25 (with further references).

——————

¹³Then We cursed them because of their breaking their covenant and made their hearts hard: they pervert words from their meanings, and have forgotten a part of what they were reminded. *You* will not cease to learn of some of their treachery, excepting a few of them. Yet excuse them and forbear. Indeed, God loves the virtuous.

¹⁴Also We took their pledge from those who say, 'We are Christians;' but they forgot a part of what they were reminded. So We stirred up enmity and hatred among them until the Day of Resurrection, and God will soon inform them concerning what they had been doing.

5:13–14 The contrast between the polemic against the Jews in verse 13 and the less violent polemic against the Christians in verse 14 should not be missed. Both the Jews and the Christians "have forgotten a part of what they were reminded" (perhaps a reference to forgetting "predictions" of Muḥammad [cf. 7:157; 61:6]; this phrase, or a similar version thereof, also appears in 6:44; 7:165; 25:18). However, only in regard to the Jews is it said, "We cursed them" (cf. 2:88; 4:46; 5:60, 64, 78) and "made their hearts hard" (cf. Rom 9:18), and "they pervert words from their meanings" (cf. 4:46; 5:41; 2:75); only the Jews are accused of treachery.

In certain passages the Old Testament (e.g., Isa 24:5–6; Jer 11:3) declares that those who break the covenant are cursed. On the curse of the Jews, see the Gospel report of Jesus' symbolic cursing of a fig tree (see Mar 11:12–22; cf. Mat 21:18–21) and see Galatians 3 (quoting Deu 27:26):

> ⁹So it is people of faith who receive the same blessing as Abraham, the man of faith.
> ¹⁰On the other hand, all those who depend on the works of the Law are under a curse, since scripture says: Accursed be he who does not make what is written in the book of the Law effective, by putting it into practice. (Gal 3:9–10)

Note also chapter 26 of the *Didascalia,* which associates a "second legislation" (given to Israel after their sin of worshipping the golden calf) with a curse:

> And in the Gospel again He said: "This people's heart is waxed gross and their eyes they have shut, and their ears they have stopped, lest at any time they should be converted; but blessed are your eyes that see, and your ears that hear" [cf. Mat 13:15–16]. Indeed you have been released from the bonds, and relieved of the second legislation, and freed from bitter slavery, and a curse has been taken off and removed from you. (*Didascalia,* chap. 26, 228).

On the accusation of scriptural falsification, alluded to with the phrase "they pervert words from their meanings," see commentary on 4:46, with further references.

Regarding verse 14, it is tempting to see the way in which the Qurʾān has God say of the Christians, "So We stirred up enmity and hatred among them until the Day of Resurrection," as a reflection of the strife between the principal Christian communities of the Late Antique Near East. However, precisely the same is said of the Jews in 5:64 (and a variation of this phrase is applied to Abraham's people in 60:4).

---

¹⁵O People of the Book! Certainly Our Apostle has come to you, clarifying for you much of what you used to hide of the Book, and excusing many [an offense of yours]. Certainly there has come to you a light from God and a manifest Book. ¹⁶With it God guides those who pursue His pleasure to the ways of peace,

and brings them out from darkness into light by His will, and
guides them to a straight path.

5:15–16 As Cuypers points out (*Banquet,* 113–14), verses 15–16 (note also
33:46, where the Qur'ān's Prophet is compared to a "lamp"; see also 4:174)
seem to be related to the Canticle of Zechariah in Luke's Gospel (see Luk 1:76–
79, which develops Isa 9:1). One might also compare the imagery of light in
John's prologue (Joh 1:6–9; cf. Mat 4:16). Verse 16 is related to Q 2:257 (both
are close to John 12:35–36, 46).

---

¹⁷They are certainly faithless who say, 'God is the Messiah,
son of Mary.' *Say,* 'Who can avail anything against God should
He wish to destroy the Messiah, son of Mary, and his mother, and
everyone upon the earth?' To God belongs the kingdom of the
heavens and the earth, and whatever is between them. He creates
whatever He wishes and God has power over all things.

5:17 The declaration (v. 17; cf. 5:72) "God is the Messiah" would not have
been said by Christians (who would say "Christ is God" but not "God is Christ").
This wording should not be seen as the heterodox Christology of some heretical
group (or, as *Tafsīr al-Jalālayn* reports, as the declaration of Jacobite Christians)
but as the Qur'ān's *reductio ad absurdum* of Christian doctrine.

---

¹⁸The Jews and the Christians say, 'We are God's children and
His beloved ones.' *Say,* 'Then why does He punish you for your
sins?' No, you are humans from among His creatures. He forgives
whomever He wishes and punishes whomever He wishes, and to
God belongs the kingdom of the heavens and the earth and whatever is between them, and toward Him is your return.

5:18 The Qur'ān here has the Jews and Christians declare that they are the children (or "sons," Ar. *abnā'*) and "beloved ones" of God. The phrase reflects both Old Testament references to Israel (e.g., Deu 14:1–2) and a number of New Testament passages:

> [12]But to those who did accept him he gave power to become children of God, to those who believed in his name
> [13]who were born not from human stock or human desire or human will but from God himself. (Joh 1:12–13)

> [16]The Spirit himself joins with our spirit to bear witness that we are children of God.
> [17]And if we are children, then we are heirs, heirs of God and joint-heirs with Christ, provided that we share his suffering, so as to share his glory. (Rom 8:16–17; cf. Rom 9:8)

This verse is also close to a declaration in the Mishnah, which the Qur'ān seems to refute: "Israelites are beloved as they are called the sons of God" (m. Avot 3:14). Elsewhere the Qur'ān denies on principle that God could have sons or daughters (2:116–17; 6:100; 9:30; 10:68; 17:40; passim).

---

[19]O People of the Book! Certainly Our Apostle has come to you, clarifying [the Divine teachings] for you after a gap in [the appearance of] the apostles, lest you should say, 'There did not come to us any bearer of good news nor any warner.' Certainly there has come to you a bearer of good news and warner. And God has power over all things.

5:19 On the reference here to a "gap" in the appearance of apostles (or "messengers"), *Tafsīr al-Jalālayn* comments: "O People of the Scripture, there has verily come to you Our Messenger, Muḥammad, making clear to you, the laws of religion, after an interval between the messengers, for there was no messenger between him and Jesus, an interval of 569 years." The twentieth-century Indian translator Yusuf Ali adds in a note: "The six hundred years (in round figures) between Christ and Muḥammad were truly the dark ages of the world.

Religion was corrupted; the standard of morals fell low; many false systems and heresies arose; and there was a break in the succession of prophets until the advent of Muḥammad."

―――――――――

²⁰When Moses said to his people, 'O my people, remember God's blessing upon you when He appointed prophets among you and made you kings, and gave you what none of the nations were given. ²¹O my people, enter the Holy Land which God has ordained for you, and do not turn your backs, or you will turn losers.'

²²They said, 'O Moses, there are a tyrannical people in it. We will not enter it until they leave it. But once they leave it, we will go in.'

²³Said two men from among those who were Godfearing and whom God had blessed: 'Go at them by the gate! For once you have entered it, you will be the victors. Put your trust in God alone, should you be faithful.'

²⁴They said, 'O Moses, we will never enter it so long as they remain in it. Go ahead, you and your Lord, and fight! We will be sitting right here.'

²⁵He said, 'My Lord! I have no power over [anyone] except myself and my brother, so part us from the transgressing lot.'

²⁶He said, 'It shall be forbidden them for forty years: they shall wander about in the land. So do not grieve for the transgressing lot.'

5:20–26 In Numbers 13:31–33 some of the Israelites who had been sent to reconnoiter Canaan (an incident perhaps alluded to in 5:12), report their terror at discovering a race of giants who live there:

> ³¹But the men who had been with him said, 'We cannot attack these people; they are stronger than we are.'

³²And they began disparaging to the Israelites the country they had reconnoitred, saying, 'The country we have been to reconnoitre is a country that devours its inhabitants. All the people we saw there were of enormous size. ³³We saw giants there too (the Anakim, descended from the Giants). We felt like grasshoppers, and so we seemed to them.

The Qurʾān refers to the fear of the Israelites in verse 22. The "two men" of the following verse are Joshua and Caleb, who encourage the Israelites (Num 14:5–9) to trust that God will lead them to victory nonetheless. God's punishment of the Israelites, that they will wander in the desert for forty more years, is referred to in verse 26 (cf. Num 14:26–35).

---

²⁷Relate to them truly the account of Adam's two sons. When the two of them offered an offering, it was accepted from one of them and not accepted from the other. [One of them] said, 'Surely I will kill you.'

[The other one] said, 'God accepts only from the Godwary. ²⁸Even if you extend your hand toward me to kill me, I will not extend my hand toward you to kill you. Indeed, I fear God, the Lord of all the worlds. ²⁹I desire that you earn [the burden of] my sin and your sin, to become one of the inmates of the Fire, and such is the requital of the wrongdoers.'

³⁰So his soul prompted him to kill his brother and he killed him, and thus became one of the losers. ³¹Then God sent a crow, exploring in the ground, to show him how to bury the corpse of his brother. He said, 'Woe to me! Am I unable to be [even] like this crow and bury my brother's corpse?' Thus he became regretful.

5:27–31 The Qurʾān differs dramatically from the account of Cain and Abel in Genesis 4 by adding a dialogue which has Abel declare his refusal to lift his hand against his brother and insist on his readiness to die at his brother's hand (v. 28). In Genesis the two brothers do not speak to each other at all (although

Cain speaks to God after his murder of Abel). The conversation between Cain and Abel is close to that found in Palestinian Targums, such as *Targum Neofiti* (see Yahuda, 292–93; Witztum, *Syriac Milieu*, 127–28).

Witztum (*Syriac Milieu*, 125–53) shows that the Qurʾānic dialogue of the brothers is related to a series of Syriac Christian texts which describe a dialogue between Cain and Abel, including a "Syriac Dialogue Poem on Abel and Cain" (dated by S. Brock to "no later than the fifth century"; Brock, "Two Syriac Dialogue Poems," 333), an unpublished *Homily on Cain and Abel* by Isaac of Antioch (d. late fifth century) and the *Life of Abel* of Symmachus (fl. late fifth/ early sixth century). Unlike the Qurʾān, the "Syriac Dialogue Poem" has Abel implore Cain not to kill him (at one point declaring, "Adam will be angry if you kill me / Spare your mother: let not the young shoot / which sprang from her be cut off" [344]). The passivity of Abel before Cain in the Qurʾān reflects a comparison made in both the *Homily on Cain and Abel* and the *Life of Abel* between the death of Abel and that of Christ. The *Life of Abel* has Abel die with his "hands and arms stretched out" and remarks that in that act, "Him whose hands and arms were stretched out on the wood [of the cross] was clearly depicted" (Symmachus, *Life of Abel*, trans. Brock, 477; see Witztum, *Syriac Milieu* 150).

The notion of Abel as willing victim seems out of place with other Qurʾānic passages that, as a rule, have the wrongdoers destroyed by God and the righteous vindicated. The Qurʾān finds a way to justify it by having Abel declare (v. 29) that he wants Cain to bear the sin of both of them, despite the Qurʾānic doctrine elsewhere that no person can bear the burden of another (regarding which see commentary on 82:19, with further references).

The Qurʾān's allusion to a raven's (or crow's) scratching the earth (v. 31) is related to a tradition found in a number of Jewish and Christian texts, including the rabbinic *Pirqe de-Rabbi Eliezer* (ch. 21), which reports that a raven taught Adam (not Cain) how to bury Abel by digging the earth and burying another bird. Witztum (*Syriac Milieu*, 115–22), examines a number of these traditions (including the *Midrash Tanhuma*—which has Cain do the burying but involves "pure birds" instead of ravens). He concludes, however, that none of these texts are clearly pre-Qurʾānic and that a textual comparison "seems to support the primacy of the tradition as preserved in the Qurʾān" (Witztum, *Syriac Milieu*, 120).

———————

[32]That is why We decreed for the Children of Israel that whoever kills a soul, without [its being guilty of] manslaughter or

corruption on the earth, is as though he had killed all mankind, and whoever saves a life is as though he had saved all mankind. Our apostles certainly brought them clear signs, yet even after that many of them commit excesses on the earth.

5:32 A connection between this verse and the account of Abel's murder which precedes it is suggested by "that is why" (Ar. *min ajal dhālika*). The nature of the connection between the two, however, is clear only in light of a discussion in the Mishnah over the reason Genesis 4:10 speaks of the shedding of Abel's "bloods" (pl., Hb. *dāmīm*) and not his "blood" (sing.):

> For so we have found concerning Cain that slew his brother, for it is written: *The bloods of your brother cry.* It says not 'The blood of your brother,' but *The bloods of your brother*—his blood and the blood of his posterity. Another explanation: *Bloods of your brother*—because his blood was cast over the trees and stones. *For this reason* man was created one and alone in the world: to teach that whosoever destroys a single soul is regarded as though he destroyed a complete world, and whosoever saves a single soul is regarded as though he saved a complete world. (m. Sanhedrin 4:5, trans. Danby)

The precept that killing one soul is like killing all souls is directly linked here to the creation of man "one and alone in the world," but the larger context is the discussion of the "bloods" of Abel. The Qurʾān seems to have picked up on that larger context. It is also noteworthy that the Qurʾān refers to God's decreeing (Ar. *katabnā ʿalā*) something for Israel which is found not in the Bible but in the Mishnah. And it should not be missed that all of this is connected to the Qurʾān's anti-Jewish polemic: the decree "whoever kills a soul" is imposed *only* on the Israelites, whom the Qurʾān (anachronistically) blames for the murder of Abel (see further Witztum, *Syriac Milieu,* 122–24).

---

³³Indeed, the requital of those who wage war against God and His Apostle, and try to cause corruption on the earth, is that they shall be slain or crucified, or shall have their hands and feet cut off on opposite sides, or be banished from the land. That is a disgrace for them in this world, and there is a great punishment for

them in the Hereafter, ³⁴excepting those who repent before you capture them, and know that God is all-forgiving, all-merciful.

³⁵O you who have faith! Be wary of God, and seek the means of recourse to Him, and wage *jihād* in His way, so that you may be felicitous.

³⁶If the faithless possessed all that is on the earth, and as much of it besides, to redeem themselves with it from the punishment of the Day of Resurrection, it shall not be accepted from them, and there is a painful punishment for them.

5:36 As Speyer (*BEQ*, 452) indicates, this is close to Matthew 16:26: "What, then, will anyone gain by winning the whole world and forfeiting his life? Or what can anyone offer in exchange for his life?" (cf. Mar 8:36; Luk 9:25).

---

³⁷They would long to leave the Fire, but they shall never leave it, and there is a lasting punishment for them.

³⁸As for the thief, man or woman, cut off their hands as a requital for what they have earned. [That is] an exemplary punishment from God, and God is all-mighty, all-wise. ³⁹But whoever repents after his wrongdoing and reforms, God shall accept his repentance. God is indeed all-forgiving, all-merciful.

⁴⁰Do you not know that to God belongs the kingdom of the heavens and the earth? He punishes whomever He wishes, and forgives whomever He wishes, and God has power over all things.

⁴¹O Apostle! Do not grieve for those who are active in [promoting] unfaith, such as those who say, 'We believe' with their mouths, but whose hearts have no faith, and the Jews who eavesdrop with the aim of [telling] lies [against you] and eavesdrop for other people who do not come to you. They pervert words

from their meanings, [and] say, 'If you are given this, take it, but if you are not given this, beware!' Yet whomever God wishes to mislead, *you* cannot avail him anything against God. They are the ones whose hearts God did not desire to purify. There is disgrace for them in this world, and there is a great punishment for them in the Hereafter.

⁴²Eavesdroppers with the aim of [telling] lies, consumers of illicit gains—if they come to *you,* judge between them, or disregard them. If *you* disregard them, they will not harm *you* in any way. But if *you* do judge, judge between them with justice. Indeed, God loves the just.

⁴³And how should they make *you* a judge, while with them is the Torah, in which is God's judgement? Yet in spite of that, they turn their backs [on Him] and they are not believers.

⁴⁴We sent down the Torah containing guidance and light. The prophets, who had submitted, judged by it for the Jews, and so did the rabbis and the scribes, as they were charged to preserve the Book of God and were witnesses to it.

So do not fear the people, but fear Me, and do not sell My signs for a paltry gain. Those who do not judge by what God has sent down—it is they who are the faithless.

⁴⁵In it We prescribed for them: a life for a life, an eye for an eye, a nose for a nose, and an ear for an ear, a tooth for a tooth, and retaliation for wounds. Yet whoever remits it out of charity, that shall be an atonement for him. Those who do not judge by what God has sent down—it is they who are the wrongdoers.

5:45 Note Leviticus 24:19–20:

¹⁹Anyone who injures a neighbour shall receive the same in return,
²⁰broken limb for broken limb, eye for eye, tooth for tooth. As the injury inflicted, so will be the injury suffered. (Lev 24:19–20; cf. Exo 21:24–25; Deu 19:21; cf. 16:126).

⁴⁶We followed them with Jesus son of Mary to confirm that which was before him of the Torah, and We gave him the Evangel containing guidance and light, confirming what was before it of the Torah, and as guidance and advice for the Godwary.

⁴⁷Let the people of the Evangel judge by what God has sent down in it. Those who do not judge by what God has sent down— it is they who are the transgressors.

⁴⁸We have sent down to *you* the Book with the truth, confirming what is before it of the Book and as a guardian over it. So *judge* between them by what God has sent down, and *do not follow* their desires against the truth that has come to *you*.

For each [community] among you We had appointed a code [of law] and a path, and had God wished He would have made you one community, but [His purposes required] that He should test you with respect to what He has given you.

So take the lead in all good works. To God shall be the return of you all, whereat He will inform you concerning that about which you used to differ.

⁴⁹*Judge* between them by what God has sent down, and *do not follow* their desires. Beware of them lest they should beguile *you* from part of what God has sent down to *you*. But if they turn their backs [on *you*], then know that God desires to punish them for some of their sins, and indeed many of those people are transgressors.

⁵⁰Do they seek the judgement of [pagan] ignorance? But who is better than God in judgement for a people who have certainty?

5:41–50 On the expression "they pervert words from their meanings" (v. 41; cf. 3:176), see commentary on 4:46 (with further references). Wāḥidī explains verse 43 with a well-known story involving Muḥammad and an adulterous Jew in Medina:

One day, the Messenger of God passed by a Jewish man who had just been flogged and had his face darkened with coal. He summoned the Jews and asked them: 'Is this what your Scripture decrees as punishment for the adulterer?' 'Yes!' they replied. He then summoned one of their doctors and asked him: 'I implore you by God who has sent the Torah to Moses, is this what your Scripture decrees as punishment for the adulterer.' He said: 'No! And if you had not implored me by God, I would not tell you. . . . The Messenger of God said: 'O God! I am the first to reapply your command after they had suspended it.' And he ordered that the Jewish man be stoned.

While scholars conventionally connect this passage to Muḥammad's conflict with the Jews of Medina, the Qurʾān also shows concern here for Christians (instructing them in in v. 47 to judge by the "Evangel").

Cuypers (*Banquet,* 223–56) argues that this section of *al-Māʾida* is structured in a concentric pattern (a rhetorical element typical of Semitic scriptures) similar to Lev 24:13–23 (cf. Exo 21:23–25; Deu 19:21). In both cases the moral principle, the lex talionis, lies at the center (Q 5:45; Lev 24:20; cf. Q 2:178–79). The Qurʾān's allusion to the possibility of showing mercy by abdicating the victim's right to vengeance ("Yet whoever remits it out of charity," v. 45) reflects something of the spirit of Matthew 5:38–39:

> [38]'You have heard how it was said: Eye for eye and tooth for tooth.
> [39]But I say this to you: offer no resistance to the wicked. On the contrary, if anyone hits you on the right cheek, offer him the other as well (cf. Luk 6:29)

On the allusion to different communities (v. 48), see commentary on 10:19 (with further references). On the expression "[pagan] ignorance" (v. 50), see commentary on 48:26 (with further references).

———————

[51]O you who have faith! Do not take the Jews and the Christians for allies: they are allies of each other. Any of you who allies with them is indeed one of them. Indeed, God does not guide the wrongdoing lot. [52]Yet *you* see those in whose hearts is a sickness rushing to them, saying, 'We fear lest a turn of fortune should visit us.'

Maybe God will bring about a victory or a command from Him, and then they will be regretful for what they kept secret in their hearts, ⁵³and the faithful will say, 'Are these the ones who swore by God with solemn oaths that they were with you?!' Their works have failed, and they have become losers.

⁵⁴O you who have faith! Should any of you desert his religion, God will soon bring a people whom He loves and who love Him, [who will be] humble towards the faithful, stern towards the faithless, waging *jihād* in the way of God, not fearing the blame of any blamer. That is God's grace which He grants to whomever He wishes, and God is all-bounteous, all-knowing.

⁵⁵Your guardian is only God, His Apostle, and the faithful who maintain the prayer and give the *zakāt* while bowing down. ⁵⁶Whoever takes God, His Apostle and the faithful for his guardians [should know that] the confederates of God are indeed victorious.

⁵⁷O you who have faith! Do not take as allies those who take your religion in derision and play, from among those who were given the Book before you and the infidels, and be wary of God, should you be faithful.

5:57 "Do not harness yourselves in an uneven team with unbelievers; how can uprightness and law-breaking be partners, or what can light and darkness have in common?" (2Co 6:14).

---

⁵⁸When you call to prayer, they take it in derision and play. That is because they are a people who do not reason.

⁵⁹*Say,* 'O People of the Book! Are you vindictive toward us for any reason except that we have faith in God and in what has been sent down to us and in what was sent down before, and that most of you are transgressors?'

⁶⁰*Say,* 'Shall I inform you concerning something worse than that as a requital from God? Those whom God has cursed and with whom He is wrathful, and turned some of whom into apes and swine, and worshipers of satanic entities. Such are in a worse situation and more astray from the right way.'

5:60 In 2:65–66 and 7:163–66 the Qurʾān has God curse a people who violate the Sabbath by saying to them, "Be you spurned apes" (see commentary on 7:163–66). In 4:47 the Qurʾān alludes to the cursing of the "People of the Sabbath" and has God tell his audience to believe lest he "blot out . . . faces and turn them backwards." Here the Qurʾān reports that God made (*jaʿala*) people into apes *and* swine, but without any explicit reference to the People of the Sabbath. It is possible that the mention of pigs here is connected somehow to the anecdote of the Gerasene demoniac (Luk 8:26–33; cf. Mat 8:28–34; Mar 5:1–20), in which Jesus sends demons into a herd of swine. On the cursing of the Jews, see commentary on 5:13–14 (with further references). On the term for "satanic entities" (*ṭāghūt*), see commentary on 4:51–52 (with further references).

-----

⁶¹When they come to you, they say, 'We believe.' Certainly they enter with disbelief and leave with it, and God knows best what they have been concealing. ⁶²*You* see many of them actively engaged in sin and aggression and consuming illicit gains. Surely, evil is what they have been doing. ⁶³Why do not the rabbis and the scribes forbid them from sinful speech and consuming illicit gains? Surely, evil is what they have been working.

⁶⁴The Jews say, 'God's hand is tied up.' Tied up be their hands, and cursed be they for what they say! No, His hands are wide open: He bestows as He wishes.

Surely many of them will be increased in rebellion and unfaith by what has been sent to *you* from your Lord, and We have cast enmity and hatred amongst them until the Day of Resurrection.

Every time they ignite the flames of war, God puts them out. They seek to cause corruption on the earth, and God does not like the agents of corruption.

5:64 Both Rudolph (*Abhängigkeit,* 13) and Hirschfeld (*New Researches,* 134) wonder whether the opening phrase of this passage is connected to Numbers 11:23, in which God asks Moses: "Is the arm of the Lord so short?" On the cursing of the Jews see commentary on 5:13–14 (with further references).

---

⁶⁵Had the People of the Book believed and been Godwary, We would have absolved them of their misdeeds and admitted them into gardens of bliss. ⁶⁶Had they observed the Torah and the Evangel, and what was sent down to them from their Lord, they would have drawn nourishment from above them and from beneath their feet. There is an upright group among them, but what many of them do is evil.

⁶⁷O Apostle! Communicate that which has been sent down to *you* from *your* Lord, and if *you* do not, *you* will not have communicated His message, and God will protect *you* from those people. Indeed, God does not guide the faithless lot.

⁶⁸*Say,* 'O People of the Book! You do not stand on anything until you observe the Torah and the Evangel and what has been sent down to you from your Lord.'

Surely many of them will be increased in rebellion and unfaith by what has been sent down to *you* from your Lord. So *do not grieve* for the faithless lot.

⁶⁹Indeed, the faithful, the Jews, the Sabaeans, and the Christians—those who have faith in God and the Last Day and act righteously—they will have no fear, nor will they grieve.

5:69 On this verse see commentary on 2:62, to which it is closely related (see also 22:17).

---

⁷⁰Certainly We took a pledge from the Children of Israel and We sent apostles to them. Whenever an apostle brought them that which was not to their liking, they would impugn a part of them and a part they would slay.

5:70 On the Qurʾānic description of the Jews as killers of the prophets, see commentary on 3:181 (with further references).

---

⁷¹They supposed there would be no testing, so they became blind and deaf. Thereafter God accepted their repentance, yet [again] many of them became blind and deaf, and God watches what they do.

⁷²They are certainly faithless who say, 'God is the Messiah, son of Mary.' But the Messiah had said, 'O Children of Israel! Worship God, my Lord and your Lord. Indeed, whoever ascribes partners to God, God will forbid him [entry into] paradise and his refuge will be the Fire, and the wrongdoers will not have any helpers.'

5:72 On the Qurʾān's condemnation here of those who say that "God is the Messiah, son of Mary," see commentary on 5:17. On Jesus as a messenger to the Israelites, see 3:49; 43:59; 61:6. Here, and on four other occasions (Q 3:51; 5:117; 19:36; 43:64) the Qurʾān has Jesus declare, "Worship God, my Lord and your Lord," a phrase which has some similarity to John 20:17. On this see commentary on 43:63–65.

⁷³They are certainly faithless who say, 'God is the third [person] of a trinity,' while there is no god except the One God. If they do not desist from what they say, a painful punishment shall befall the faithless among them.

5:73 Most translators, including Qarai, imagine that the Qurʾān is here concerned with the Trinity (Yusuf Ali, Hilali-Khan, and Asad also do so). Yet the Arabic here is *thālithu thalātha,* lit. "third of three" (cf. 4:171) This formulation suggests that the Qurʾān's concern in this verse, as in the previous verse, is Christ ("one of three" persons of the Trinity). In other words, vv. 72–73 should be thought of as one unit; in both cases the Qurʾān is speaking of those who declare that "God is Christ." See further Griffith, "Syriacisms in the Arabic Qurʾān." *Tafsīr al-Jalālayn* (thinking of 5:116) comments that the Qurʾān means to condemn those who say that God is one of three gods, "the other two being Jesus and his mother." On the possibility that the author of the Qurʾān thought of the Trinity as "Father, Mother, and Son" see commentary on 5:116–19.

⁷⁴Will they not repent to God and plead to Him for forgiveness? Yet God is all-forgiving, all-merciful.

⁷⁵The Messiah, son of Mary, is but an apostle. Certainly [other] apostles have passed before him, and his mother was a truthful one. Both of them would eat food. Look how We clarify the signs for them, and yet, look, how they go astray!

5:75 Qarai renders the Arabic word *ṣiddīqa* here "truthful one" based on the meaning of the Arabic root. In this he follows classical commentaries such as *Tafsīr al-Jalālayn,* which defines *ṣiddīq* as "extremely truthful." It could be that with this term the Qurʾān is referring to Mary's honesty in regard to the divine origin of her baby, in the face of those who accused her of conceiving the baby illegitimately (cf. 4:156; 19:27); in 66:12 Mary is said to have confirmed (*ṣaddaqat*) the words of her Lord. It is also possible that the meaning of *ṣiddīqa* is connected to Hebrew or Aramaic *ṣaddīq,* meaning "righteous" or "pious" (see

Ambros, 159). This would fit the Qur'ān's use of this same term to describe Joseph (Q 12:46), Abraham (Q 19:41) and Idrīs (19:56) (see also 4:69; 57:19). On eating food as a sign of humanity, see 21:8; 25:7 (also 23:51). Here (see also commentary on 5:116–19) the Qur'ān seems to assume that Christians consider Jesus and Mary to be divine.

---

⁷⁶*Say, 'Do you worship, besides God, what has no power to bring you any benefit or harm, while God—He is the All-hearing, the All-knowing?!'*

5:76 On the description of anything which unbelievers worship other than God as powerless see commentary on 10:18 (with further references).

---

⁷⁷*Say, 'O People of the Book! Do not unduly exceed the bounds in your religion and do not follow the myths of a people who went astray in the past and led many astray, and [themselves] strayed from the right path.'*
⁷⁸*The faithless among the Children of Israel were cursed on the tongue of David and Jesus son of Mary. That, because they would disobey and commit transgressions.*

5:78 *Tafsīr al-Jalālayn* connects the mention of David's and Jesus' cursing of the Israelites to 5:60, explaining that the reference to monkeys there is connected to the story of the People of the Sabbath (Q 2:65–66; 7:163–66), and the reference to pigs there is connected to the story of the table from heaven (Q 5:111–15). However, David does not appear in the passages on the People of the Sabbath and Jesus does not curse the Israelites in the passage on the table from heaven.

As for the reference to David in the present verse, one instead might note Psalm 109 (traditionally attributed to David) in which the Psalmist curses his enemies: "He had a taste for cursing; let it recoil on him! No taste for blessing;

let it never come his way!" (v. 17). Regarding Jesus, one might note passages such as Matthew 23:33–36, in which Jesus condemns the scribes and Pharisees for their infidelity to their God. On the cursing of the Jews see commentary on 5:13–14 (with further references).

---

⁷⁹They would not forbid one another from the wrongs that they committed. Surely, evil is what they had been doing.

⁸⁰*You* see many of them allying with the faithless. Surely evil is what they have sent ahead for their own souls, as God is displeased with them and they shall remain in punishment [forever]. ⁸¹Had they believed in God and the Prophet and what has been sent down to him, they would not have taken them for allies. But most of them are transgressors.

⁸²Surely, you will find the Jews and the polytheists to be the most hostile of all people towards the faithful, and surely you will find the nearest of them in affection to the faithful to be those who say 'We are Christians.' That is because there are priests and monks among them, and because they are not arrogant. ⁸³When they hear what has been revealed to the Apostle, you see their eyes fill with tears because of the truth that they recognize.

They say, 'Our Lord, we believe; so write us down among the witnesses. ⁸⁴Why should we not believe in God and the truth that has come to us, eager as we are that our Lord should admit us among the righteous people?'

⁸⁵So, for what they said, God requited them with gardens with streams running in them, to remain in them [forever], and that is the reward of the virtuous.

⁸⁶But as for those who are faithless and deny Our signs—they shall be the inmates of hell.

5:82–86 Wāḥidī relates four stories meant to provide a context for this passage. All of the stories involve the figure of the Negus, the Christian Ethiopian king to whom, according to medieval Islamic tradition, the Prophet sent some of his followers in the Meccan period. In the first two stories some of those followers (after they arrive in Ethiopia) recite a passage of the Qurʾān to the Negus and the priests and monks (n.b. the wording of v. 82) accompanying him. Wāḥidī continues, "Whenever they read a verse, the tears rolled down their cheeks due to the truth which they recognized" (cf. 5:83; 17:107–9, 19:58). In the next two stories the Negus sends some of his followers (priests and monks) to the Prophet in Mecca, who recites to them a passage of the Qurʾān. According to one of these, the Ethiopian priests and monks declare, "How similar is this to what used to be revealed to Jesus!" and begin to weep. These stories should all be seen as pious legends meant to explain this passage.

Otherwise this passage is meant to distinguish Christians, some of whom recognize the Qurʾān's prophet, from the Jews, who are categorically opposed to him (they are, with the polytheists, "the most hostile" to the believers). On the streams of paradise (v. 85), see commentary on 2:25 (with further references).

———

[87]O you who have faith! Do not prohibit the good things that God has made lawful for you, and do not transgress. Indeed, God does not like the transgressors. [88]Eat the lawful and good things that God has provided you, and be wary of God in whom you have faith.

[89]God will not take you to task for what is frivolous in your oaths; but He will take you to task for what you pledge in earnest. The atonement for it is to feed ten needy persons with the average food you give to your families, or their clothing, or the freeing of a slave. He who cannot afford [any of these] shall fast for three days. That is the atonement for your oaths when you vow. But keep your oaths. Thus does God clarify His signs for you so that you may give thanks.

5:89 Speyer (*BEQ*, 442) connects the manner in which the Qurʾān offers an allowance for those unable to fulfill the full conditions of atonement to Leviticus 5:11; 12:8 (cf. Deu 23:21–23) (cr. Andrew O'Connor).

---

⁹⁰O you who have faith! Indeed, wine, gambling, idols and the divining arrows are abominations of Satan's doing, so avoid them, so that you may be felicitous. ⁹¹Indeed, Satan seeks to cast enmity and hatred among you through wine and gambling, and to hinder you from the remembrance of God and from prayer. Will you, then, relinquish?

5:90–91 In both verses the word *maysir* is rendered in Qarai's translation "gambling," but it may mean "intoxicating drink" (see commentary on 2:219).

---

⁹²Obey God and obey the Apostle, and beware; but if you turn your backs, then know that Our Apostle's duty is only to communicate in clear terms.

⁹³There will be no sin upon those who have faith and do righteous deeds in regard to what they have eaten [in the past] so long as they are Godwary and faithful and do righteous deeds, and are further Godwary and faithful, and are further Godwary and virtuous. And God loves the virtuous.

⁹⁴O you who have faith! God will surely test you with some of the game within the reach of your hands and spears, so that God may know those who fear Him in secret. So whoever transgresses after that, there is a painful punishment for him.

⁹⁵O you who have faith! Do not kill any game when you are in pilgrim sanctity. Should any of you kill it intentionally, its atonement will be the counterpart from cattle of what he has killed, as

judged by two just men among you, brought to the Kaʿba as an offering, or an atonement by feeding needy persons, or its equivalent in fasting, that he may taste the untoward consequence of his conduct. God has excused what is already past; but should anyone resume, God will take vengeance on him, for God is almighty, avenger.

⁹⁶You are permitted the game of the sea and its food, a provision for you and for the caravans, but you are forbidden the game of the land so long as you remain in pilgrim sanctity, and be wary of God toward whom you will be gathered.

⁹⁷God has made the Kaʿba, the Sacred House, a [means of] sustentation for mankind, and [also] the sacred month, the offering and the garlands, so that you may know that God knows whatever there is in the heavens and the earth and that God has knowledge of all things.

⁹⁸Know that God is severe in retribution, and that God is all-forgiving, all-merciful.

⁹⁹The Apostle's duty is only to communicate and God knows whatever you disclose and whatever you conceal.

¹⁰⁰*Say,* 'The good and the bad are not equal, though the abundance of the bad should amaze you.' So be wary of God, O you who possess intellect, so that you may be felicitous!

¹⁰¹O you who have faith! Do not ask about things which, if they are disclosed for you, will upset you. Yet if you ask about them while the Qurʾān is being sent down, they shall be disclosed to you. God has excused it, and God is all-forgiving, all-forbearing. ¹⁰²Certainly some people asked about them before you and then came to disbelieve in them.

¹⁰³God has not prescribed any such thing as *Baḥīrah, Sāʾibah, Waṣīlah,* or *Ḥām;* but those who are faithless fabricate lies against God and most of them do not exercise their reason.

5:103 Qarai keeps four Arabic words untranslated in this verse—"*Baḥīrah, Sāʾibah, Waṣīlah,* or *Ḥām*"—because of the medieval Islamic tradition that the Qurʾān is referring to particular camels (for which there are no English equivalents) used for pagan rituals. *Tafsīr al-Jalālayn* quotes a tradition which explains: "The *baḥīra* is that [camel] whose milk is consecrated to idols and whom no human may milk; the *sāʾiba* is the one they would leave to roam freely for their gods and was forbidden to bear any load; the *waṣīla* is the young she-camel that would give birth to a young female, as its first offspring, followed by another female, bearing one after the other without a male in between: she would then be left to roam freely for their idols; the *hām* is the mature male camel, which after completing a certain number of copulations with a female, would then be consigned to [the pagans'] idols and be exempt from bearing any load, and they would call it *hāmī;* but the disbelievers invent lies against God, in this matter, by attributing [the sanctioning of] such [practices] to Him."

---

[104]When they are told, 'Come to what God has sent down and [come] to the Apostle,' they say, 'What we have found our fathers following is sufficient for us.' What, even if their fathers did not know anything and were not guided?!

[105]O you who have faith! Take care of your own souls. Those who are astray cannot hurt you if you are guided. To God will be the return of you all, whereat He will inform you concerning what you have been doing.

[106]O you who have faith! When death approaches any of you, the witness between you, while making a bequest, shall be two just men from among yourselves, or two from among others if you are journeying in the land and the affliction of death visits you. You shall detain the two of them after the prayer, and, if you have any doubt, they shall vow by God, 'We will not sell it for any gain, even if it were a relative, nor will we conceal the testimony of God, for then we would be among the sinners.'

[107]But if it is found that both of them were guilty of sin, then two others shall stand up in their place from among those nearest in kinship to the claimants and swear by God: 'Our testimony is truer than their testimony, and we have not transgressed, for then we would be among the wrongdoers.'

[108]That makes it likelier that they give the testimony in its genuine form, or fear that other oaths will be taken after their oaths. Be wary of God and listen, and God does not guide the transgressing lot.

[109]The day God will gather the apostles and say, 'What was the response given to you?' They will say, 'We have no knowledge. Indeed, You know best all that is Unseen.'

[110]When God will say, O Jesus son of Mary, remember My blessing upon you and upon your mother, when I strengthened you with the Holy Spirit, so you would speak to the people in the cradle and in adulthood, and when I taught you the Book and wisdom, the Torah and the Evangel, and when you would create from clay the form of a bird with My leave, and you would breathe into it and it would become a bird with My leave; and you would heal the blind and the leper with My leave, and you would raise the dead with My leave; and when I held off [the evil of] the Children of Israel from you when you brought them clear proofs, whereat the faithless among them said, 'This is nothing but plain magic.'

5:109–10 The Qurʾān seems to set these two verses at the end of time. Whereas in 3:49 Jesus announces to the Israelites the miracles that he will perform, here the Qurʾān has God speak to Jesus the miracles he has already performed. This apocalyptic setting is interrupted by the episode of the table (vv. 111–15) but returns with the conversation between God and Jesus that begins in verse 116.

On the Holy Spirit in the Qurʾān, see commentary on 2:87 and 16:102 (with further references). The miracle of Jesus' speaking "in the cradle," though not in the New Testament, is found in early Christian texts such as the *Gospel of*

Pseudo-Matthew (on this see commentary on 19:16–26, with further references). On the creation of a bird from clay, see commentary on 3:49. On the Israelites' accusation that Jesus performed magic, see 61:6. The opening section of 5:110 parallels 3:48.

---

¹¹¹And when I inspired the Disciples, [saying], 'Have faith in Me and My apostle,' they said, 'We have faith. Be witness that we have submitted [to God].'

¹¹²When the Disciples said, 'O Jesus son of Mary! Can your Lord send down to us a table from the sky?' Said he, 'Be wary of God, if you be faithful.'

¹¹³They said, 'We desire to eat from it, and our hearts will be at rest: we shall know that you have told us the truth, and we will be among witnesses to it.'

¹¹⁴Said Jesus son of Mary, 'O God! Our Lord! Send down to us a table from the heaven, to be a festival for us, for the first ones among us and the last ones and as a sign from You, and provide for us; for You are the best of providers.'

¹¹⁵God said, 'I will indeed send it down to you. But should any of you disbelieve after this, I will indeed punish him with a punishment such as I do not punish anyone in all creation.'

5:111–15 In verse 111 the disciples of Jesus (the Qur'ānic word, *ḥawāriyyūn*, comes from the Ethiopic word *ḥawāryā* meaning idiomatically "apostle"; see Ambros, 308) receive a direct revelation from God. This seems to contradict the Islamic doctrine that only prophets receive direct revelations; hence *Tafsīr al-Jalālayn* explains, "That is, I commanded them by the tongue of Jesus."

The episode of the table (vv. 112ff.) has the disciples make a demand for a sign from Jesus (cf. the demand of Abraham in 2:260). It is often imagined to be connected to the Gospel passages on the multiplication of the loaves and fish, or the passage in Acts 10:9–16 in which a sheet filled with animals for Peter to eat comes down from the sky. In fact, it is closely connected to the discourse on the bread of life in John 6. As in the episode of the table in the Qur'ān, in John 6 the followers of Jesus demand a sign, saying: "What *sign* will you yourself do, the sight of which will make us believe in you? What work will you do?" (Joh 6:30). They then refer to manna: "Our fathers ate manna in the desert; as scripture says: He gave them bread from heaven to eat" (Joh 6:31).

John 6 is thus connected to Psalm 78, which laments the infidelity of the Israelites in general and, in particular, their impertinent demand for a "banquet" in the desert during the Exodus (v. 19). The word for "banquet" translates the Hebrew word (*shulḥān*) for table. Notably in the Ethiopic Bible *shulḥān* is translated *mā'edd*. This, presumably, is the source of the Qur'ānic word *al-mā'ida:*

> [18]they deliberately challenged God by demanding food to their hearts' content.
> [19]They insulted God by saying, 'Can God make a banquet (Ethiopic *mā'edd*) in the desert?' (Psa 78:18–19)

In Islamic tradition the disciples are held to be faithful followers of Jesus. However, this passage, which makes the disciples similar to the crowds of John 6, suggests that they are less than faithful (see also commentary on 3:52–54).

---

[116]And when God will say, 'O Jesus son of Mary! Was it you who said to the people, "Take me and my mother for gods besides God"?' He will say, 'Immaculate are You! It does not behoove me to say what I have no right to. Had I said it, You would certainly have known it: You know whatever is in my self, and I do not know what is in Your Self. Indeed, You know best all that is Unseen. [117]I did not say to them [anything] except what You had commanded me [to say]: "Worship God, my Lord and your Lord." And I was a witness to them so long as I was among them. But when You had taken me away, You Yourself were watchful over them, and You are witness to all things. [118]If You punish them, they are indeed Your servants; but if You forgive them, You are indeed the All-mighty, the All-wise.'

[119]God will say, 'This day truthfulness shall benefit the truthful. For them there will be gardens with streams running in them, to remain in them forever. God is pleased with them and they are pleased with Him. That is the great success.'

5:116–19 In verse 116 the Qurʾānic scene shifts back to the eschatological hour, as though the conversation between God and Jesus begun in verse 110 is resumed. The issue at hand in this final passage of the Sura is the eternal fate of Christians, which is left as an open question (v. 118).

According to some scholars, verse 116 suggests that the Qurʾān (or more simply, Muḥammad) was influenced by the presence in the Arabian Peninsula of heretical Christians who believed in Mary's divinity. Some scholars justify this idea with the notion that in the Byzantine period the Arabian desert was something a like a refuge for Christians who disagreed with Chalcedonian doctrine (to support this notion, scholars sometimes quote a tradition—unreliably ascribed to various Byzantine historians—that Arabia is "haeresium ferax," the "bearer" [or "mother"] or heresies). Others note the reference in Epiphanius's (d. 403) heresiographical work *Panarion* to a group of women in the Arabian desert who considered Mary a goddess and offered her cakes of bread (Gk. *collyrida;* for which reason Epiphanius names this group the Collyridians).

None of this speculation is necessary. Verse 116 need not be a precise record of the doctrines held by the Christians in the Qurʾān's immediate context. However, this verse does seem to suggest that the Qurʾān's author thought of the Trinity as "Father, Mother, Son" (God, Mary, Jesus). This conclusion also seems to be suggested by 5:75 (see commentary) and by the absence of any connection in the Qurʾān between the Holy Spirit and the Christian teaching of the Trinity.

The end of verse 116—"You know whatever is in myself"—corresponds to the end of verse 109, in which not only Jesus but all of the prophets declare, "We have no knowledge. Indeed, You know best all that is Unseen."

The phrase in 5:117, "Worship God, my Lord and your Lord" (cf. 3:51; 5:72; 19:36; 43:63–65) is connected to John 20:17. In John Christ speaks after the resurrection, whereas in the Qurʾān he speaks (apparently) after God has raised him to heaven. The following phrase in Q 5:117—in which Jesus declares, "I was a witness to them so long as I was among them"—seems to be connected to John 17, especially verse 12: "While I was with them, I kept those you had given me true to your name. I have watched over them and not one is lost except one who was destined to be lost, and this was to fulfil the scriptures."

On the streams of paradise (v. 119), see commentary on 2:25 (with further references).

———————

[120]To God belongs the kingdom of the heavens and the earth and whatever there is in them, and He has power over all things.

6. *AL-AN'ĀM,* THE CATTLE

In the Name of God, the All-beneficent, the All-merciful.

¹All praise belongs to God who created the heavens and the earth and made darkness and light. Yet the faithless equate [others] with their Lord.

6:1 "I form the light and I create the darkness, I make well-being, and I create disaster, I, the Lord, do all these things" (Isa 45:7).

---

²It is He who created you from clay, then ordained the term [of your life]—the specified term is with Him—and yet you are in doubt.

6:2 Here the Qur'ān speaks of the creation of Adam from clay. In Genesis 2:7 Adam is created from the earth (*hā-ādām*). The Qur'ān's report that he was created specifically from clay (*ṭīn;* cf. 7:12; 15:26, 28, 33; 17:61; 23:12; 32:7; 37:11; 38:71, 76; 55:14; in 3:59 he is created instead from "dirt," or *turāb*) may reflect an idea of God as potter (n.b. 55:14, which refers to potter's clay).

---

³He is God in the heavens and on the earth: He knows your secret and your overt [matters], and He knows what you earn.

⁴There did not come to them any sign from among the signs of their Lord, but that they have been disregarding it. ⁵They have certainly denied the truth when it came to them, but soon there will come to them the news of what they have been deriding.

⁶Have they not regarded how many a generation We have destroyed before them whom We had granted power in the land in respects that We did not grant you, and We sent abundant rains for them from the sky and made streams run for them? Then We destroyed them for their sins, and brought forth another generation after them.

⁷Had We sent down to you a Book on paper so they could touch it with their [own] hands, [still] the faithless would have said, 'This is nothing but plain magic.'

⁸They say, 'Why has not an angel been sent down to him?' Were We to send down an angel, the matter would surely be decided, and then they would not be granted any respite.

⁹Had We made him an angel, We would have surely made him a man, and We would have still confounded them just as they confound [the truth now].

6:8–9 On the expectation of unbelievers that divine messages would be brought by an angel, see commentary on 6:50 (with further references).

———————

¹⁰Apostles were certainly derided before *you*. Then those who ridiculed them were besieged by what they used to deride.

¹¹*Say,* 'Travel through the land and see how was the fate of the deniers.'

¹²*Say,* 'To whom belongs whatever there is in the heavens and the earth?' *Say,* 'To God. He has made mercy binding for Himself. He will surely gather you on the Day of Resurrection, in

which there is no doubt. Those who have ruined their souls will not have faith.'

[13]To Him belongs whatever abides in the night and the day, and He is the All-hearing, the All-knowing.

[14]*Say,* 'Shall I take for guardian [anyone] other than God, the originator of the heavens and the earth, who feeds and is not fed?'

Say, 'I have been commanded to be the foremost of those who submit [to God], and [told,] "Never be one of the polytheists."'

6:14 This verse seems to anticipate the account later in this Sura (vv. 74–83) of Abraham's vision of the stars, sun, and moon, an account based on Jewish and Christian stories of Abraham's childhood (see further commentary on 6:74–83).

---

[15]*Say,* 'Indeed, should I disobey my Lord, I fear the punishment of a tremendous day.'

[16]Whoever is spared of it on that day, He will have certainly been merciful to him, and that is a manifest success.

[17]Should God visit you with some distress there is no one to remove it except Him; and should He bring you some good, then He has power over all things. [18]And He is the All-dominant over His servants, and He is the All-wise, the All-aware.

[19]*Say,* 'What thing is greatest as witness?' *Say,* 'God! [He is] witness between me and you, and this Qurʾān has been revealed to me in order that I may warn you thereby and whomever it may reach.'

'Do you indeed bear witness that there are other gods besides God?' *Say,* 'I do not bear witness [to any such thing].' *Say,* 'Indeed, He is the One God, and I disown whatever you associate [with Him].'

²⁰Those whom We have given the Book recognize him just as they recognize their own sons. Those who have ruined their souls will not have faith.

6:20 *Tafsīr al-Jalālayn* explains: "Those to whom We have given the Scripture recognise him, that is, Muḥammad, by the descriptions of him in their Scripture, as they recognise their sons." Most translators (e.g., Yusuf Ali, Pickthall, Asad, Arberry), however, understand the pronoun which Qarai renders as "him" as a reference to Muḥammad's book ("it"), and indeed this is the meaning suggested by a parallel expression in 2:146. One should not, however, think of the book as the Qurʾān (which could not yet have been a complete book when this verse was proclaimed) but rather as Muḥammad's revelations generally, his "heavenly Book" (on this point see commentary on 2:53).

---

²¹Who is a greater wrongdoer than him who fabricates lies against God or denies His signs? Indeed, the wrongdoers will not be felicitous.

²²On the day when We gather them all together, We shall say to those who ascribed partners [to God], 'Where are your partners that you used to claim?' ²³Then their only excuse will be to say, 'By God, our Lord, we were not polytheists.'

²⁴Look, how they forswear themselves, and what they used to fabricate has forsaken them!

²⁵There are some of them who prick up their ears at *you,* but We have cast veils on their hearts lest they should understand it and a deafness into their ears; and though they should see every sign, they will not believe in it. When they come to *you,* to dispute with *you,* the faithless say, 'These are nothing but myths of the ancients.'

6:25 On the Qurʾān's report here (18:57 is parallel) that God has "cast veils on" the hearts of the unbelievers, see commentary on 17:45–46 (with further references). On the expression "myths of the ancients," see commentary on 68:15 (with further references).

---

²⁶They dissuade [others] from [following] him, and [themselves] avoid him; yet they destroy no one but themselves, but they are not aware.

²⁷Were *you* to see when they are brought to a halt by the Fire, whereupon they will say, 'Alas, were we to be sent back [into the world], we would not deny the signs of our Lord, and we would be among the faithful!' ²⁸Indeed, what they used to hide before has now become evident to them. But were they to be sent back they would revert to what they were forbidden, and they are indeed liars.

²⁹They say, 'There is nothing but our life of this world, and we will not be resurrected.'

³⁰Were *you* to see when they are brought to a halt before their Lord. He will say, 'Is this not a fact?' They will say, 'Yes, by our Lord!' He will say, 'So taste the punishment because of what you used to deny.'

³¹They are certainly losers who deny the encounter with God. When the Hour overtakes them suddenly, they will say, 'Alas for us, for what we neglected in it!' And they will bear their burdens on their backs. Behold, evil is what they bear!

³²The life of the world is nothing but play and diversion, and the abode of the Hereafter is surely better for those who are God-wary. Will you not exercise your reason?

³³We certainly know that what they say grieves *you*. Yet it is not *you* that they deny, but it is God's signs that the wrongdoers impugn.

³⁴Apostles were certainly denied before *you,* yet they patiently bore being denied and tormented until Our help came to them.

Nothing can change the words of God, and there have certainly come to *you* some of the accounts of the apostles.

6:34 On the expression "Nothing can change the words of God," see commentary on 6:115 (with further references).

———————

35And should their aversion be hard on *you,* find, if you can, a tunnel into the ground, or a ladder into the heaven, that *you* may bring them a sign. Had God wished, He would have brought them together on guidance. So *do not be* one of the ignorant.

6:35 On the notion of a ladder leading from earth to heaven (and its Biblical subtext), see commentary on 52:38.

———————

36Only those who listen will respond [to *you*]. As for the dead, God will resurrect them, then they will be brought back to Him.

37They say, 'Why has not a sign been sent down to him from his Lord?' *Say,* 'God is indeed able to send down a sign,' but most of them do not know.

38There is no animal on land nor bird that flies with its wings, but they are communities like yourselves. We have not omitted anything from the Book. Then they will be mustered toward their Lord.

39Those who deny Our signs are deaf and dumb, in a manifold darkness. God leads astray whomever He wishes, and whomever He wishes He puts him on a straight path.

40*Say,* 'Tell me, should God's punishment overtake you, or should the Hour overtake you, will you supplicate anyone other than God, if you are truthful? 41No, Him you will supplicate, and

He will remove that for which you supplicated Him, if He wishes, and you will forget what you ascribe [to Him] as partners.'

[42]We have certainly sent [apostles] to nations before *you,* then We seized them with hardship and distress so that they might entreat [Us]. [43]Then why did they not entreat when Our punishment overtook them! But their hearts had hardened and Satan had made what they had been doing seem decorous to them.

[44]So when they forgot what they had been admonished of, We opened for them the gates of all [good] things. When they became proud of what they were given, We seized them suddenly, whereat they became despondent. [45]Thus the wrongdoing lot were rooted out, and all praise belongs to God, the Lord of all the worlds.

6:42–45 This passage is connected to the Qur'ān's historical vision, according to which God has sent prophets to various peoples to warn them of God's wrath. As a rule the peoples reject these prophets and are destroyed by God (n.b. v. 45 and cf., e.g., 7:59–93; 11:25–100; 26:10–191). The principal exception to this rule is the story of Jonah (see commentary on 37:139–48, with further references).

———————

[46]*Say,* 'Tell me, should God take away your hearing and your sight and set a seal on your hearts, which god other than God can restore it for you?' *Look,* how We paraphrase the signs variously; nevertheless they turn away.

[47]*Say,* 'Tell me, should God's punishment overtake you suddenly or visibly, will anyone be destroyed except the wrongdoing lot?'

[48]We do not send the apostles except as bearers of good news and warners. As for those who are faithful and righteous, they will have no fear, nor will they grieve. [49]But as for those who deny Our signs, the punishment shall befall them because of the transgressions they used to commit.

⁵⁰*Say,* 'I do not say to you that I possess the treasuries of God, nor do I know the Unseen, nor do I say to you that I am an angel. I follow only what is revealed to me.'

Say, 'Are the blind one and the seer equal? So will you not reflect?'

6:50 On several occasions the Qurʾān has unbelievers, including Noah's people (Q 23:24), the people of ʿĀd and Thamūd (Q 41:14), and all those to whom a prophet has been sent (Q 14:10), express a conviction that God should send revelation to humans through angels, and not through human prophets. In this verse, as elsewhere (Q 6:8–9, 91, 111, 158; 14:9–11; 15:7; 17:94–95; 22:75; 23:24), the Qurʾān has its own opponents ask why an angel was not sent to them. Behind such passages might be Biblical accounts of angels' delivering divine messages (see, e.g., Gen 21:17–18; Jdg 6:11–20; Mat 28:2–6; Luk 2:9–10; Act 8:26; Rev 1:1).

---

⁵¹*Warn* by its means those who fear being mustered toward their Lord, besides whom they will have neither friend nor intercessor, so that they may be Godwary.

⁵²*Do not drive away* those who supplicate their Lord morning and evening, desiring His face. Neither are *you* accountable for them in any way, nor are they accountable for *you* in any way, so that *you* should drive them away and thus become one of the wrongdoers.

⁵³Thus do We test them by means of one another so that they should say, 'Are these the ones whom God has favoured from among us?!' Does not God know best the grateful?!

⁵⁴When those who have faith in Our signs come to *you, say,* 'Peace to you! Your Lord has made mercy incumbent upon Himself: whoever of you commits an evil [deed] out of ignorance and then repents after that and reforms, then He is indeed all-forgiving, all-merciful.'

⁵⁵Thus do We elaborate the signs, so that the way of the guilty may be brought to light.

⁵⁶*Say,* 'I have been forbidden to worship those whom you invoke besides God.' *Say,* 'I do not follow your desires, for then I will go astray, and I will not be among the [rightly] guided.'

⁵⁷*Say,* 'I indeed stand on a manifest proof from my Lord and you have denied it. What you seek to hasten is not up to me. Judgement belongs only to God; He expounds the truth and He is the best of judges.'

⁵⁸*Say,* 'If what you seek to hasten were with me, the matter would have been decided between you and me, and God knows best the wrongdoers.'

⁵⁹With Him are the treasures of the Unseen; no one knows them except Him. He knows whatever there is in land and sea. No leaf falls without His knowing it, nor is there a grain in the darkness of the earth, nor anything fresh or withered but it is in a manifest Book.

6:59 The Arabic here for "treasures" (of the Unseen) is literally "keys" (*mafātīḥ*). This expression is related to Matthew 16:19. See commentary on 39:63 (with further references). On the reference to a leaf falling, Rudolph (*Abhängigkeit,* 14) wonders whether there is a connection with Mat 10:29: "Can you not buy two sparrows for a penny? And yet not one falls to the ground without your Father knowing."

------

⁶⁰It is He who takes your souls by night, and He knows what you do by day, then He reanimates you therein so that a specified term may be completed. Then to Him will be your return, whereat He will inform you concerning what you used to do.

⁶¹He is the All-dominant over His servants, and He sends guards to [protect] you. When death approaches anyone of you,

Our messengers take him away and they do not neglect [their duty].

6:61 The Arabic rendered here as "guards" (*ḥafaẓa*) may mean "observers" (angels who keep watch, not those who protect). Elsewhere (13:11; 82:10–11; 86:4), this same root is used in a way that suggests such angels are "observers." This is in line with the Qurʾān's teaching that there are angels assigned to humans to write down their deeds (10:21; 43:80). See further commentary on 82:10–12.

---

⁶²Then they are returned to God, their real master. Behold, all judgement belongs to Him and He is the swiftest of reckoners.

⁶³*Say,* 'Who delivers you from the darkness of land and sea, [when] you invoke Him suppliantly and secretly: "If He delivers us from this, we will surely be among the grateful"?'

⁶⁴*Say,* 'It is God who delivers you from them and from every distress, [but] then you ascribe partners [to Him].'

⁶⁵*Say,* 'He is able to send you a punishment from above you or from under your feet, or confound you as [hostile] factions, and make you taste one another's violence.'

Look, how We paraphrase the signs variously so that they may understand!

⁶⁶*Your* people have denied it, though it is the truth. *Say,* 'It is not my business to watch over you.'

⁶⁷For every prophecy there is a [preordained] setting, and soon you will know.

⁶⁸When you see those who gossip impiously about Our signs, avoid them until they engage in some other discourse; but if Satan makes you forget, then, after remembering, do not sit with the wrongdoing lot. ⁶⁹Those who are Godwary are in no way accountable for them, but this is merely for admonition's sake, so that they may beware.

[70]Leave alone those who take their religion for play and diversion and whom the life of this world has deceived, and admonish with it, lest any soul should perish because of what it has earned: It shall not have any friend besides God, nor any intercessor; and though it should offer every kind of ransom, it will not be accepted from it. They are the ones who perish because of what they have earned; they shall have boiling water for drink and a painful punishment for what they used to deny.

[71]*Say,* 'Shall we invoke besides God that which can neither benefit us nor harm us, and turn back on our heels after God has guided us, like someone seduced by the devils and bewildered in the land, who has companions that invite him to guidance, [saying,] "Come to us!"?'

Say, 'It is God's guidance which is [true] guidance, and we have been commanded to submit to the Lord of all the worlds,

6:71 On the description of anything that unbelievers worship other than God as powerless, see commentary on 10:18 (with further references).

———————

[72]and told, "Maintain the prayer and be wary of Him; it is He toward whom you will be gathered."'

[73]It is He who created the heavens and the earth with consummate wisdom, and the day He says [to something], 'Be!' it is. His word is the truth, and to Him belongs all sovereignty on the day when the Trumpet will be blown. Knower of the sensible and the Unseen, He is the All-wise, the All-aware.

6:73 On the trumpet blast, see commentary on 78:18 (with further references). On God's creating through the word "Be!" see commentary on 36:82 (with further references).

---

⁷⁴When Abraham said to Azar, his father, 'Do you take idols for gods? Indeed, I see you and your people to be in clear error.'

⁷⁵Thus did We show Abraham the dominions of the heavens and the earth, that he might be of those who possess certitude. ⁷⁶When night darkened over him, he saw a star and said, 'This is my Lord!' But when it set, he said, 'I do not like those who set.'

⁷⁷Then, when he saw the moon rising, he said, 'This is my Lord!' But when it set, he said, 'Had my Lord not guided me, I would surely have been among the astray lot.'

⁷⁸Then, when he saw the sun rising, he said, 'This is my Lord! This is bigger!' But when it set, he said, 'O my people, I indeed disown what you take as [His] partners.' ⁷⁹'Indeed, I have turned my face toward Him who originated the heavens and the earth, as a *ḥanīf,* and I am not one of the polytheists.'

⁸⁰His people argued with him. He said, 'Do you argue with me concerning God, while He has guided me for certain? I do not fear what you ascribe to Him as [His] partners, excepting anything that my Lord may wish. My Lord embraces all things in [His] knowledge. Will you not then take admonition?'

⁸¹'How could I fear what you ascribe [to Him] as partners, when you do not fear ascribing partners to God for which He has not sent down any authority to you? So [tell me,] which of the two sides has a greater right to safety, if you know? ⁸²Those who have faith and do not taint their faith with wrongdoing—it is they for whom there will be safety, and they are the [rightly] guided.'

⁸³This was Our argument that We gave to Abraham against his people. We raise in rank whomever We wish. *Your* Lord is indeed all-wise, all-knowing.

6:74–83 In this passage the Qurʾān develops a tradition on Abraham that is prominent in earlier Jewish and Christian exegetical works. The tradition seems to have been inspired by speculation on two Biblical passages: Genesis 15:4–6, which has God tell Abraham to examine the stars of the sky, and Deuteronomy 4:19:

> When you raise your eyes to heaven, when you see the sun, the moon, the stars—the entire array of heaven—do not be tempted to worship them and serve them. The Lord your God has allotted these to all the other peoples under heaven. (Deu 4:19)

These passages shaped the way Jewish and Christian authors told the story of Abraham's childhood in Ur (Gen 11:31). According to a tradition found in the *Apocalypse of Abraham* (a work of Jewish origin, usually dated to the first or second century AD) and *Genesis Rabbah* (38:19), Abraham's father, Terah (the Qurʾān names him Āzar, perhaps through a confusion with the name of Abraham's servant, Eliezer, who appears in the Targums, the Septuagint, and the Peshitta of Gen 15:2) is himself a "manufacturer of idols" (cf. Jos 24:2).

Jubilees (which has Terah reject idol worship) relates that Abraham observed the stars one night, looking for a sign that would tell what the rain for the upcoming year would be like. As he observed the stars he came to the realization that there is only one god, the creator. Thus, he became a monotheist by observing nature, and without receiving revelation:

> And he was sitting alone making observations [of the stars] and a voice came into his heart saying, "All the signs of the stars and the signs of the sun and the moon are all under the Lord's control. Why am I seeking [them out]? If He wishes, He will make it rain morning and evening, and if He desires He will not make it fall, for everything is under His control." (*Jubilees,* 12:16–7)

The *Apocalypse of Abraham* has Abraham himself recount this experience:

> So I would call the sun nobler than the earth, since with its rays it illumines the inhabited world and the various airs. But I would not make it into a god either, since its course is obscured both at night and by the clouds. Nor, again, would I call the moon and the stars gods, since they too in their times at night can darken their light. (*Apocalypse of Abraham* 7:8–10; cf. also Josephus, *Jewish Antiquities:* I, 7:1)

On Abraham's preaching to his father and his people see commentary on 26:69–93 (with further references). On Abraham as a *ḥanīf,* see commentary on 16:120–23 (with further references).

---

[84]And We gave him Isaac and Jacob and guided each of them. And Noah We had guided before, and from his offspring David

and Solomon, Job, Joseph, Moses and Aaron—thus do We reward the virtuous—

6:84 On the possibility that the Qurʾān considers both Isaac and Jacob to be sons of Abraham, see commentary on 29:27 (with further references).

---

⁸⁵and Zechariah, John, Jesus and Ilyās—each of them among the righteous—

6:85 On Elijah (Ilyās), see commentary on 37:123–32.

---

⁸⁶and Ishmael, Elisha, Jonah and Lot—each We preferred over all the nations—⁸⁷and from among their fathers, descendants and brethren—We chose them and guided them to a straight path.

⁸⁸That is God's guidance: with it He guides whomever He wishes of His servants. But were they to ascribe any partners [to God], what they used to do would not avail them.

⁸⁹They are the ones whom We gave the Book, judgement and prophethood. So if these disbelieve in them, We have certainly entrusted them to a people who will never disbelieve in them.

6:89 On the combination of "Book," "judgment," and "prophethood," see commentary on Q 45:16–17 (with further references).

---

⁹⁰They are the ones whom God has guided. So follow their guidance.

Say, 'I do not ask you any recompense for it. It is just an admonition for all the nations.'

6:90 On the idea that a true prophet does not seek a reward, see commentary on 34:47 (with further references).

---

⁹¹They did not regard God with the regard due to Him when they said, 'God has not sent down anything to any human.' *Say,* 'Who had sent down the Book that was brought by Moses as a light and guidance for the people, which you make into parchments that you display, while you conceal much of it, and [by means of which] you were taught what you did not know, [neither] you nor your fathers?'

Say, 'God!' Then *leave* them to play around in their impious gossip.

6:91 On the expectation of unbelievers that divine messages would be brought by an angel, see commentary on 6:50 (with further references).

The Qurʾān returns here to a theme that is prominent in this Sura, namely, the argument of its opponents that true revelation is brought by someone who has gone up to heaven and returned with divine knowledge, or with a celestial book, or by an angel who has come down from heaven; the Qurʾān also replies to this argument in verses 50 and 109 (cf. also v. 158). While verse 7 refers to the idea that God could have sent down a *qirṭās* (sing.) from heaven, here the Qurʾān speaks of the *qarāṭīs* (pl.) that its opponents display (in the first case Qarai translates as "paper" and in verse 91 as "parchments"; the term is used in later Arabic texts for "papyrus"). Verse 35 alludes to a tunnel and to a ladder by which one could ascend to heaven and return with a miraculous sign. Verse 37 (and again v. 109) notes the objection of the Qurʾān's opponents that Muḥammad does not perform miracles. Verse 50 has the Prophet insist that he does not receive revelation in the way they expect it to be given. Verse 91 is meant to prove that God can reveal (and has revealed) things in the way that the Qurʾān's Prophet claims to receive revelation.

As Patricia Crone ("Angels versus Humans," 332) notes, the Jewish (and Christian) understanding of the revelation to Moses is that he entered into the divine realm when he ascended to the top of Mount Sinai (for which reason he did not eat) and received the Torah:

R. Joshua b. Levi also said: When Moses ascended on high, the ministering angels spake before the Holy One, blessed be He, 'Sovereign of the Universe!

What business has one born of woman amongst us?' 'He has come to receive the Torah,' answered He to them. (b. Shabbat, 88b)

Similarly, in apocalyptic works the prophets, or visionaries, ascend to heaven and return to earth with a divine message. This is the case with the para-Biblical books of Enoch, and in the New Testament with the apostle John in the Book of Revelation: "Then, in my vision, I saw a door open in heaven and heard the same voice speaking to me, the voice like a trumpet, saying, 'Come up here: I will show you what is to take place in the future'" (Rev 4:1). In other words, the perspective of the Qur'ān's opponents on revelation seems to match that of Jews and Christians.

The reference to the Qur'ān's opponents' display of "parchments" with Moses's scripture implies that they are not pagans but likely Jews (although this is supposed to be a "Meccan" Sura and there should be no Jews in Mecca). As Paret (*Kommentar,* 147) notes, this is further complicated by the beginning of this verse, which seems to address not Jews but those who reject entirely the possibility of revelation.

---

[92]Blessed is this Book that We have sent down, confirming what was [revealed] before it, so that *you* may warn the Mother of Cities and those around it. Those who believe in the Hereafter believe in it, and they are watchful of their prayers.

[93]Who is a greater wrongdoer than him who fabricates lies against God, or says, 'It has been revealed to me,' while nothing was revealed to him, and says, 'I will bring the like of what God has sent down'?

Were *you* to see when the wrongdoers are in the throes of death, and the angels extend their hands [saying]: 'Give up your souls! Today you will be requited with a humiliating punishment because of what you used to attribute to God untruly, and for your being disdainful towards His signs.'

[94]'Certainly you have come to Us alone, just as We created you the first time, and left behind whatever We had bestowed on you. We do not see your intercessors with you—those whom you claimed to be [Our] partners in [deciding] you[r] [fate]. Certainly

all links between you have been cut, and what you used to claim has forsaken you!'

⁹⁵God is indeed the splitter of the grain and the pit. He brings forth the living from the dead and He brings forth the dead from the living. That is God! Then where do you stray?

6:95 "In all truth I tell you, unless a wheat grain falls into the earth and dies, it remains only a single grain; but if it dies it yields a rich harvest" (Joh 12:24).

---

⁹⁶Splitter of the dawn, He has made the night for rest, and the sun and the moon for calculation. That is the ordaining of the Allmighty, the All-knowing.

⁹⁷It is He who made the stars for you, so that you may be guided by them in the darkness of land and sea. We have certainly elaborated the signs for a people who have knowledge.

⁹⁸It is He who created you from a single soul, then there is the [enduring] abode and the place of temporary lodging. We have certainly elaborated the signs for a people who understand.

⁹⁹It is He who sends down water from the sky, and brings forth with it every kind of growing thing. Then, from it We bring forth vegetation from which We produce the grain in clusters and from the palm-tree, from its blossoms, low-hanging clusters [of dates] and gardens of grapes, olives and pomegranates, similar and dissimilar. Look at its fruit as it fructifies and ripens. There are indeed signs in that for a people who have faith.

¹⁰⁰They make the jinn partners of God, though He has created them, and carve out sons and daughters for Him without any knowledge. Immaculate is He and far above what they allege [concerning Him]!

6:100 The jinn are understood by Islamic tradition to be a class of beings created from fire, and distinct from demons, humans, and angels. It seems more likely that jinn is another name for demons (on this see commentary on 6:112). The Qurʾān here accuses humans of associating the jinn with God. On the worship of jinn, see 6:128; 34:41; 37:158; 72:6. Note that in 18:50, where the Qurʾān explicitly names the devil "one of the jinn," it also warns against taking the devil's offspring as "masters" instead of God.

On this verse Wāḥidī relates: "This verse was revealed about the atheists who claimed that God and Satan were two brothers; that God was the creator of human beings, beasts and cattle whereas Satan was the creator of vipers, predatory animals and scorpions."

101The originator of the heavens and the earth—how could He have a child when He has had no spouse? He created all things and He has knowledge of all things.

6:101 The argument that God could have no son (or "child") may be directed against Christians, although in the previous verse the Qurʾān argues against those who invent sons and daughters for God, suggesting that *walad* here means "offspring" (hence Blachère's "enfants"), not "son." The way in which the Qurʾān argues in simplistic, literal terms (God has no spouse; he thus does not have sex and could not have a child; cf. 72:3) suggests either a misunderstanding of the Biblical metaphor of God's children or (more likely) a straw-man argument.

102That is God, your Lord, there is no god except Him, the creator of all things; so worship Him. He watches over all things. 103The eyesights do not perceive Him, yet He apprehends the eyesights, and He is the All-attentive, the All-aware. 104[*Say,*] 'Insights have already come to you from your Lord. So whoever sees, it is to the benefit of his own soul, and whoever remains blind, it is to its detriment, and I am not a keeper over you.'

[105]Thus do We paraphrase the signs variously, lest they should say, '*You* have received instruction,' and so that We may make it clear for people who have knowledge.

[106]*Follow* that which has been revealed to *you* from your Lord, there is no god except Him, and *turn* away from the polytheists. [107]Had God wished they would not have ascribed partners [to Him]. We have not made *you* a caretaker for them, nor is it your duty to watch over them.

[108]Do not abuse those whom they invoke besides God, lest they should abuse God out of hostility, without any knowledge. That is how We have made their conduct seem decorous to every people. Then their return will be to their Lord and He will inform them concerning what they used to do.

[109]They swear by God with solemn oaths that were a sign to come to them they would surely believe in it. *Say*, 'The signs are only from God,' and what will bring home to you that they will not believe even if they came?

[110]We transform their hearts and their visions as they did not believe in it the first time, and We leave them bewildered in their rebellion.

[111]Even if We had sent down angels to them and the dead had spoken to them, and We had gathered all things before them manifestly, they would [still] not believe unless God wished, but most of them are ignorant.

6:111 On the expectation of unbelievers that divine messages would be brought by an angel, see commentary on 6:50 (with further references).

The point about the futility of sending one of the dead to the unbelievers (cf. 7:44–50; 23:99–100) is close to that in the New Testament parable of the rich man and Lazarus, which concludes with Abraham declaring, "If they will not listen either to Moses or to the prophets, they will not be convinced even if someone should rise from the dead" (Luk 16:31).

---

¹¹²That is how for every prophet We have assigned the devils from among humans and jinn as enemies, who inspire each other with seductive statements to deceive [the people]. Had *your* Lord wished, they would not have done it. So *leave* them with what they fabricate,

6:112 According to Islamic tradition God created three classes of beings: angels (from light), humans (from dirt or clay), and jinn (from fire). A fourth class (demons) evolved when some of the angels fell from heaven. Academic scholars have generally followed the notion that the jinn are a different class of beings from the fallen angels, and sometimes have proposed that the Qur'ān inherited the idea of jinn from pre-Islamic, pagan Arab superstition.

This verse, however, suggests that things are different. "Demons" (Ar. *shayāṭīn,* related to Hb. *śāṭān* and Syr. *sāṭānā,* "Satan") can be either humans or jinn. In other words, the jinn *are* the fallen angels. Some of them (like some humans) are opposed to God (and thus called *shayāṭīn*), and some of them (like some humans) believe in God. This matches Q 18:50, which makes the devil himself (Iblīs) "one of the jinn," and Q 72, according to which some of the jinn believe in God (cf. James 2:19). See further commentary on 72:1–14.

---

¹¹³so that the hearts of those who do not believe in the Hereafter may incline towards it, and so that they may be pleased with it and commit what they commit.

¹¹⁴[*Say,*] 'Shall I seek a judge other than God, while it is He who has sent down to you the Book [whose contents have been] well-elaborated?' Those We have given the Book know that it has been sent down from your Lord with the truth; so do not be one of the skeptics.

¹¹⁵The word of *your* Lord has been fulfilled in truth and justice. Nothing can change His words, and He is the All-hearing, the All-knowing.

6:115 "Sky and earth will pass away, but my words will never pass away" (Mat 24:35; cf. Isa 40:8; cr. Andrew O'Connor). Cf. 6:34; 10:64; 17:77; 18:27.

---

¹¹⁶If you obey most of those on the earth, they will lead you astray from the way of God. They follow nothing but conjectures and they do nothing but make surmises.

¹¹⁷*Your* Lord knows best those who stray from His way, and He knows best those who are guided.

¹¹⁸Eat from that over which God's Name has been mentioned, if you are believers in His signs. ¹¹⁹Why should you not eat that over which God's Name has been mentioned, while He has already elaborated for you whatever He has forbidden you, excepting what you may be compelled to [eat in an emergency]? Indeed, many mislead [others] by their fancies, without possessing any knowledge. Indeed, *your* Lord knows best the transgressors.

¹²⁰Renounce outward sins and the inward ones. Indeed, those who commit sins shall be requited for what they used to commit.

¹²¹Do not eat [anything] of that over which God's Name has not been mentioned, and that is indeed transgression. Indeed, the satans inspire their friends to dispute with you, and if you obey them, you will indeed be polytheists.

¹²²Is he who was lifeless, then We gave him life and provided him with a light by which he walks among the people, like one who dwells in a manifold darkness which he cannot leave? What they have been doing is thus presented as decorous to the faithless.

[123]Thus have We installed in every town its major criminals so that they may plot therein. Yet they do not plot except against themselves, but they are not aware. [124]When a sign comes to them, they say, 'We will not believe until we are given the like of what was given to God's apostles.' God knows best where to place His apostleship! Soon the guilty will be visited by a degradation and severe punishment from God because of the plots they used to devise.

[125]Whomever God desires to guide, He opens his breast to Islam, and whomever He desires to lead astray, He makes his breast narrow and straitened as if he were climbing to a height. Thus does God lay [spiritual] defilement on those who do not have faith.

[126]This is the straight path of *your* Lord. We have already elaborated the signs for a people who take admonition. [127]For them shall be the abode of peace near their Lord and He will be their friend because of what they used to do.

[128]On the day that He will gather them all together, [He will say], 'O community of the jinn! You made many followers among humans.' Their friends from among the humans will say, 'Our Lord, we took advantage of each other, and we completed our term You had appointed for us.' He will say, 'The Fire is your abode, to remain in it [forever], except what God may wish.' *Your* Lord is indeed all-wise, all-knowing.

6:128 This verse illustrates the Qurʾān's use of the term "jinn" to refer generally to fallen angels, who seek to lead humans astray but who can recognize the truth of divine revelation (on this see commentary on 6:112 and 72:1–14).

---

[129]That is how We make wrongdoers one another's friends because of what they used to perpetrate.

¹³⁰'O community of the jinn and humans! Did there not come to you apostles from yourselves, recounting to you My signs and warning you of the encounter of this Day?' They will say, 'We do bear witness against ourselves.' The life of this world had deceived them, and they will testify against themselves that they had been faithless.

¹³¹This is because your Lord would never destroy the towns unjustly while their people were unaware.

¹³²For everyone there are ranks in accordance with what they have done, and your Lord is not oblivious of what they do.

¹³³Your Lord is the All-sufficient dispenser of mercy. If He wishes, He will take you away and make whomever He wishes succeed you, just as He produced you from the descendants of another people.

¹³⁴Indeed, what you are promised will surely come and you will not be able to thwart it.

¹³⁵*Say,* 'O my people, act according to your ability; I too am acting. Soon you will know in whose favour will be the outcome of that abode. Indeed, the wrongdoers will not prosper.'

¹³⁶They dedicate to God a portion of what He has created of the crops and cattle and say, 'This is for God,' so do they maintain, 'and this is for our partners.' But what is for their partners does not reach God, and what belongs to God reaches their partners. Evil is the judgement that they make.

¹³⁷That is how to many of the polytheists those whom they ascribe as partners [to God] present the slaying of their children as decorous that they may ruin them and confound their religion for them. Had God wished, they would not have done it. So *leave* them with what they fabricate.

6:137 Islamic tradition explains this verse (cf. 6:140; also 6:151 and 17:31, which connect the killing of children to indigence) with stories of the pagan

Meccans burying their children alive (*Tafsīr al-Jalālayn* explains: "And thus . . . those associates of theirs, from among the *jinn,* have adorned for many of the idolaters the slaying of their children, by burying them alive."). It is possible, however, that the Qurʾān is here in conversation with those Biblical passages which condemn the sacrifice of children to other gods, notably Deuteronomy 12:31: "This is not the way to treat the Lord your God. For in honor of their gods they have done everything detestable that the Lord hates; yes, in honor of their gods, they even burn their own sons and daughters as sacrifices!" (Deu 12:31; cf. Lev 18:21; 2Ki 16:3, 17:31; Jer 32:35). One might also note the warning against killing children in the early Christian text known as the *Didache:*

> Thou shalt not corrupt boys, thou shalt not commit fornication, [thou shalt not steal,] thou shalt not deal in magic, thou shalt do no sorcery, thou shalt not murder a child by abortion nor kill them when born . . . thou shalt not speak evil, thou shalt not cherish a grudge, thou shalt not be double-minded nor double-tongued. (2:2)

---

[138]They say, 'These cattle and tillage are a taboo: none may eat them except whom we wish,' so they maintain, and there are cattle whose backs are forbidden and cattle over which they do not mention God's Name, fabricating a lie against Him. Soon He will requite them for what they used to fabricate.

[139]And they say, 'That which is in the bellies of these cattle is exclusively for our males and forbidden to our wives. But if it be still-born, they will all share it.' Soon He will requite them for their allegations. He is indeed all-wise, all-knowing.

[140]They are certainly losers who slay their children foolishly without any knowledge, and forbid what God has provided them, fabricating lies against God. They have certainly gone astray and are not guided.

6:140 On the slaying of children, see commentary on 6:137.

¹⁴¹It is He who produces gardens trellised and without trellises, and palm-trees and crops of diverse produce, olives and pomegranates, similar and dissimilar. Eat of its fruits when it fructifies, and give its due on the harvest day, and be not wasteful; indeed He does not like the wasteful.

¹⁴²Of the cattle [some] are for burden and [some] for slaughter. Eat of what God has provided you and do not follow in Satan's footsteps; he is indeed your manifest enemy.

¹⁴³Eight mates: two of sheep and two of goats. *Say,* 'Is it the two males that He has forbidden or the two females, or what is contained in the wombs of the two females? Inform me with knowledge, should you be truthful.'

¹⁴⁴And two of camels and two of oxen. *Say,* 'Is it the two males that He has forbidden or the two females, or what is contained in the wombs of the two females? Were you witnesses when God enjoined this upon you?' So who is a greater wrongdoer than him who fabricates lies against God to mislead the people without any knowledge? Indeed, God does not guide the wrongdoing lot.

¹⁴⁵*Say,* 'I do not find in what has been revealed to me that anyone should be forbidden to eat anything except carrion or spilt blood, or the flesh of swine—for that is indeed unclean—or an impiety offered to other than God.' But should someone be compelled, without being rebellious or aggressive, indeed your Lord is all-forgiving, all-merciful.

¹⁴⁶To the Jews We forbade every animal having an undivided hoof, and of oxen and sheep We forbade them their fat, except what is borne by their backs, or the entrails, or what is attached to the bones. We requited them with that for their rebelliousness, and We indeed speak the truth.

6:145–46 This section (beginning with v. 136) of Q 6 involves polemic against certain ritual practices of the Qur'ān's opponents followed by a declaration of the Qur'ān's own ritual food laws (v. 145). Thereafter (v. 146) the Qur'ān adds a polemic against the strict dietary laws of the Jews, citing specific food restrictions close to those laid out in Leviticus ("undivided hoof," however, is not an obvious rendition of Arabic *dhū ẓufur* in v. 146):

> [2]"Speak to the Israelites and say: "Of all animals living on land these are the creatures you may eat:
> [3]"You may eat any animal that has a cloven hoof, divided into two parts, and that is a ruminant. (Lev 11:2–3; cf. Deu 14:6)

> [23]"Speak to the Israelites and say: "You may not eat the fat of ox, sheep or goat.
> [24]The fat of an animal that has died a natural death or been savaged by beasts may be used for any other purpose, but you are not to eat it.
> [25]Anyone who eats the fat of an animal offered as food burnt for the Lord will be outlawed from his people. (Lev 7:23–25; cf. 3:3–5, 14–15)

The Qur'ān presents these restrictions as a punishment for Jewish rebelliousness (On this see commentary on 4:160, with further references).

---

[147]But if they impugn *you, say,* 'Your Lord is dispenser of an all-embracing mercy, but His punishment will not be averted from the guilty lot.'

[148]The polytheists will say, 'Had God wished we would not have ascribed any partner [to Him], nor our fathers, nor we would have forbidden anything.' Those who were before them had impugned likewise until they tasted Our punishment.

Say, 'Do you have any [revealed] knowledge that you can produce for us? You follow nothing but conjectures, and you do nothing but make surmises.'

[149]*Say,* 'To God belongs the conclusive argument. Had He wished, He would have surely guided you all.'

[150]*Say,* 'Bring your witnesses who may testify that God has forbidden this.' So if they testify, do not testify with them, and do not

follow the desires of those who deny Our signs, and those who do not believe in the Hereafter and equate [others] with their Lord.

[151]*Say,* 'Come, I will recount what your Lord has forbidden you: That you shall not ascribe any partners to Him, and you shall be good to the parents, you shall not kill your children due to penury—We will provide for you and for them—you shall not approach indecencies, the outward among them and the inward ones, and you shall not kill a soul [whose life] God has made inviolable, except with due cause. This is what He has enjoined upon you so that you may exercise your reason.

[152]Do not approach the orphan's property, except in the best [possible] manner, until he comes of age. Observe fully the measure and the balance with justice.' We task no soul except according to its capacity.

'And when you speak, be just, even if it were a relative; and fulfill God's covenants. This is what He enjoins upon you so that you may take admonition.'

[153]'This indeed is my straight path, so follow it, and do not follow [other] ways, for they will separate you from His way. This is what He enjoins upon you so that you may be Godwary.'

6:151–53 Scholars often connect this passage (closely related to 17:22–39; cf. also 25:67–72) to the Ten Commandments (Exo 20; Deu 5), although the Qurʾān does not refer to them here, or count in any way on its audience's knowledge of them. On the command "You shall not kill your children due to penury" (v. 151), see commentary on 6:137 (with further references). Regarding the Ten Commandments and the Qurʾān, see commentary on 17:22–39 (with further references).

On the use of proper "measuring" as an example of righteousness (v. 152), see commentary on Q 83:1–3 (with further references).

When the Qurʾān declares that God does not "task" a soul "except according to its capacity" (v. 152; cf. 2:233, 286; 7:42; 23:62; 65:7), it is close to (see

Speyer, *BEQ,* 452) 1 Corinthians 10:13: "None of the trials which have come upon you is more than a human being can stand. You can trust that God will not let you be put to the test beyond your strength, but with any trial will also provide a way out by enabling you to put up with it."

---

¹⁵⁴Then We gave Moses the Book, completing [Our blessing] on him who is virtuous, and as an elaboration of all things, and as guidance and mercy, so that they may believe in the encounter with their Lord.

¹⁵⁵And this Book We have sent down is a blessed one; so follow it and be Godwary so that you may receive [His] mercy.

6:154–55 These two verses are closely connected to Psalm 19, which is a reflection on the revelation of the Law to Moses:

⁷The Law of the Lord is perfect, refreshment to the soul; the decree of the Lord is trustworthy, wisdom for the simple.
⁸The precepts of the Lord are honest, joy for the heart; the commandment of the Lord is pure, light for the eyes. (Psa 19:7–8)

Psalm 19:7 describes that law as "perfect" (Hb. *temīmā*), whereas 6:154 describes the Book given to Moses as "completing" (or perhaps, "perfecting"; Ar. *tamāman*). See *BEQ,* 297.

---

¹⁵⁶Lest you should say, 'The Book was sent down only to two communities before us, and we were indeed unaware of their studies,' ¹⁵⁷or [lest] you should say, 'If the Book had been sent down to us, we would have surely been better-guided than them.'

There has already come to you a manifest proof from your Lord and guidance and mercy. So who is a greater wrongdoer than him who denies the signs of God and turns away from them? Soon We shall requite those who turn away from Our signs with a terrible punishment because of what they used to evade.

¹⁵⁸Do they await anything but that the angels should come to them, or *your* Lord should come, or some of *your* Lord's signs should come? The day when some of *your* Lord's signs do come, faith will not benefit any soul that had not believed beforehand and had not earned some goodness in its faith. *Say,* 'Wait! We too are waiting!'

6:158 On the expectation of unbelievers that divine messages would be brought by an angel, see commentary on 6:50 (with further references). Rudolph (*Abhängigkeit,* 15) suggests that the second part of this verse is connected to James 2:17.

---

¹⁵⁹Indeed, those who split up their religion and became sects, *you* will not have anything to do with them. Their matter rests only with God; then He will inform them concerning what they used to do.

6:159 On the Qur'ān's allusions to those who have divided into sects, see commentary on 5:13–14.

---

¹⁶⁰Whoever brings virtue will receive [a reward] ten times its like; but whoever brings vice will not be requited except with its like, and they will not be wronged.

¹⁶¹*Say,* 'My Lord has indeed guided me to a straight path, the upright religion, the creed of Abraham, a *ḥanīf,* and he was not one of the polytheists.'

6:161 On Abraham as a *ḥanīf,* see commentary on 16:120–23 (with further references).

---

[162]*Say,* 'Indeed, my prayer and my worship, my life and my death are for the sake of God, the Lord of all the worlds. [163]He has no partner, and I have been commanded [to follow] this [creed], and I am the first of those who submit [to God].'

[164]*Say,* 'Shall I seek a Lord other than God, while He is the Lord of all things?'

No soul does evil except against itself, and no bearer shall bear another's burden; then your return will be to your Lord, whereat He will inform you concerning that about which you used to differ.

6:164 On the notion that no soul shall carry another's burden, see commentary on 82:19 (with further references).

---

[165]It is He who has made you successors on the earth, and raised some of you in rank above others so that He may test you with respect to what He has given you. *Your* Lord is indeed swift in retribution, and He is indeed all-forgiving, all-merciful.

7. *AL-AʿRĀF*, THE ELEVATIONS

In the Name of God, the All-beneficent, the All-merciful.

¹*Alif, Lām, Mīm, Ṣād.*

²[This is] a Book that has been sent down to *you* and as admonition for the faithful; so let there be no disquiet in *your* heart on its account that *you* may warn thereby.

³Follow what has been sent down to you from your Lord, and do not follow any masters besides Him. Little is the admonition that you take!

⁴How many a town We have destroyed! Our punishment came to it at night, or while they were taking a midday nap. ⁵When Our punishment overtook them, their cry was only that they said, 'We have indeed been wrongdoers!'

⁶We will surely question those to whom the apostles were sent, and We will surely question the apostles. ⁷Then We will surely recount to them with knowledge, for We had not been absent.

⁸The weighing [of deeds] on that Day is a truth. As for those whose deeds weigh heavy in the scales—it is they who are the felicitous. ⁹As for those whose deeds weigh light in the scales—it is they who have ruined their souls, because they used to wrong Our signs.

¹⁰Certainly We have established you on the earth and made in it [various] means of livelihood for you. Little do you thank.

¹¹Certainly We created you, then We formed you, then We said to the angels, 'Prostrate before Adam.' So they [all] prostrated, but not Iblis: he was not among those who prostrated.

¹²Said He, 'What prevented you from prostrating, when I commanded you?'

'I am better than him,' he said. 'You created me from fire and You created him from clay.'

7:11–12 While the story of the angels' prostration before Adam is not found in the Bible, it emerges from speculation on Psalm 8:4–6:

⁴What are human beings that you spare a thought for them, or the child of Adam that you care for him?
⁵Yet you have made him little less than a god, you have crowned him with glory and beauty,
⁶made him lord of the works of your hands, put all things under his feet. (cf. Job 7:17; Psa 144:3–4; Heb 2:6–9)

Certain rabbinic interpreters (e.g., b. Sanhedrin 38b) understood this passage of the Psalms to be the words of angels upon the creation of man. A tradition in *Genesis Rabbah* develops instead Isaiah 2:22, which it takes as a divine admonition to angels who (noticing the glory of Adam who is created in the image of God) rush to worship him. God intervenes by having Adam (cf. Gen 2:21) fall asleep:

When the Lord created Adam, the angels mistook him [for a divine being]. What did the Holy One, blessed be He, do? He caused sleep to fall upon him, and so all knew that he was [but mortal] man. Thus it is written, "Have no more to do with humankind, which has only breath in its nostrils. How much is this worth?" [Isa 2:22] (*Genesis Rabbah,* 8:9)

A number of early Christian traditions have God (as He does in the Qurʾān) instead command the angels to prostrate before Adam. From a Christian perspective this angelic worship of Adam anticipates the worship of Christ described in Philippians (Phi 2:9–11; cf. Heb 1:6). In the Syriac Christian work *Cave of Treasures*—as in the Qurʾān (v. 12)—the angels prostrate before Adam, but the devil refuses to do so, with the explanation that he is made from fire while Adam is made from dirt:

God formed Adam with his holy hands, in His image and in His likeness. When the angels saw the image and the glorious appearance of Adam, they trembled at the beauty of his figure. . . . Moreover, the angels and celestial powers heard the voice of God saying to Adam "See, I have made you king, priest and prophet, Lord, leader and director of all those made and created. To you alone have I given these and I give you authority over everything I have created." When the angels and the archangels, the thrones and dominions, the cherubims and seraphims, that is when all of the celestial powers heard this voice, all of the orders bent their knees and prostrated before him. (*Cave of Treasures* [Oc.], 2:12–13, 22–25)

When the leader of the lesser order saw the greatness given to Adam, he became jealous of him and did not want to prostrate before him with the angels. He said to his hosts, 'Do not worship him and do not praise him with the angels. It is proper that you should worship me, since I am fire and spirit, not that I worship something that is made of dirt. (*Cave of Treasures* [Oc.], 3:1–2)

On the prostration of the angels before Adam, see 2:34; 15:29–33; 17:61–62; 18:50; 20:116; 38:71–78.

Muslim commentators of course did not follow this Adam-Christ typology and were anxious to explain why God would command the angels to bow before Adam (indeed some Muslim mystics, notably al-Ḥallāj [d. 309/922], argue that the devil did the right thing by refusing to do so). *Tafsīr al-Jalālayn* explains that the prostration of angels before Adam was only "a bow of salutation." According to a second explanation, Adam was only the direction of prayer (or *qibla*) for the angels (as a niche in mosques today indicates the direction of Mecca toward which Muslims are to pray) who were actually prostrating before God. A third explanation is based on the final words of 2:30 ("Indeed I know what you do not know") and the tradition (see commentary on 2:30) that God sent angels to fight against the jinn, the first inhabitants of earth who had become violent. The devil, according to this explanation, was the captain of those angels and had become arrogant after defeating the jinn. God commanded the angels to bow before Adam because he "knew" that the devil would refuse. The command, in other words, was a ruse to expose the devil's pride.

On the Arabic word for "formed" in verse 11, see commentary on 40:64 (with further references).

----

¹³'Get down from it!' He said. 'It is not for you to be arrogant therein. Be gone! You are indeed among the degraded ones.'

7:13–25 *overview* This passage illustrates the cosmological vision of the Qurʾān, a vision shared with Syriac Christian texts such as Ephrem's *Hymns on Paradise* (on this see commentary on 2:25), by which the Garden of Eden lies atop a cosmic mountain, at the lowest level of heaven. Accordingly the Qurʾān has God tell the devil to "go down" twice: first (v. 13) from a higher level of heaven where the angels dwell to the garden of paradise, and second (v. 24) from paradise into the earthly realm.

---

[14]He said, 'Respite me till the day they will be resurrected.'

[15]Said He, 'You are indeed among the reprieved.'

[16]'As You have consigned me to perversity,' he said, 'I will surely lie in wait for them on Your straight path. [17]Then I will come at them from their front and rear, and from their right and left, and You will not find most of them to be grateful.'

[18]Said He, 'Begone hence, blameful and banished! Whoever of them follows you, I will surely fill hell with you all.'

7:14–18 The Qurʾān's account (see also commentary on 15:36–43; 17:62–65; 38:79–85) of the way in which God agrees to the devil's plan to tempt humanity (v. 18) is not unlike that in Job:

[8]So the Lord asked him, 'Did you pay any attention to my servant Job? There is no one like him on the earth: a sound and honest man who fears God and shuns evil.'

[9]'Yes,' Satan said, 'but Job is not God-fearing for nothing, is he?

[10]Have you not put a wall round him and his house and all his domain? You have blessed all he undertakes, and his flocks throng the countryside.

[11]But stretch out your hand and lay a finger on his possessions: then, I warrant you, he will curse you to your face.'

[12]'Very well,' the Lord said to Satan, 'all he has is in your power. But keep your hands off his person.' So Satan left the presence of the Lord. (Job 1:8–12)

However, the Qurʾān insists that the devil is granted only a respite (cf. 17:61–65; 38:79–85) and suggests that the devil will be punished on the Day of Resurrection (Q 7:14; cf. 26:94–95). To this end it is worth noting how the New

Testament suggests at times that the devil has been given dominion on earth (but will be destroyed at the end of time, as in Rev 20:10):

> ¹And you were dead, through the crimes and the sins
> ²which used to make up your way of life when you were living by the principles of this world, obeying the ruler who dominates the air, the spirit who is at work in those who rebel. (Eph 2:1–2; cf. Mat 4:8–9; Luk 4:5–7; Joh 12:31, 14:30, 16:11; 2Co 4:4)

---

¹⁹[Then He said to Adam,] 'O Adam, dwell with your mate in paradise and eat thereof whence you wish; but do not approach this tree, lest you should be among the wrongdoers.'

²⁰Then Satan tempted them, to expose to them what was hidden from them of their nakedness, and he said, 'Your Lord has only forbidden you from this tree lest you should become angels, or lest you become immortals.' ²¹And he swore to them, 'I am indeed your well-wisher.' ²²Thus he brought about their fall by deception.

So when they tasted of the tree, their nakedness became apparent to them, and they began to stitch over themselves with the leaves of paradise.

Their Lord called out to them, 'Did I not forbid you from that tree, and tell you, "Satan is indeed your manifest enemy?"'

7:19–22 Whereas Genesis refers only to a snake in the Garden of Eden, the Qurʾān, like Syriac Christian texts including *Cave of Treasures* and Ephrem's *Hymns on Paradise* (following Rev 12:9), and unlike most Jewish texts, puts Satan there. In this verse Satan speaks to both Adam and Eve, whereas in 20:120 (cf. also 2:36) Satan speaks only to Adam. Also, whereas 20:121 makes Adam responsible for their sin, here (v. 22; cf. 2:36) Satan is blamed. In this passage the Qurʾān has God declare the devil an "enemy" after Adam (and Eve) eat from the tree, which in 20:117 God does instead after the devil refuses to prostrate to Adam.

Genesis has God command Adam not to eat from the "tree of the knowledge of good and evil" and refers to a separate tree, the "tree of life" (Gen 2:16–17; 3:21–24). The Qurʾān has God tell both Adam and Eve, "Do not *approach* this tree" (v. 19; cf. 2:35) and nowhere refers to a second tree. Elsewhere (Q 20:120), the Qurʾān speaks of the "tree of immortality," presumably an allusion to the "tree of life" (note also how in 7:19 there is an allusion to Adam becoming like an angel, that is, immortal). Like the Qurʾān, the "Oriental" version of *Cave of Treasures* makes no mention of the "tree of the knowledge of good and evil" but rather connects the sin of Adam and Eve with the "tree of life." It does so to make a parallel between the one tree of life and the one cross of salvation (*Cave of Treasures* [Or.], 4:2–5; on this see Witztum, *Syriac Milieu,* 81–83, who refers to the work of E. Beck, "Iblis und Mensch," 235, and M. Radscheit, "Der Höllenbaum," 113–14).

Genesis (3:7) relates that Adam and Eve "*realized* that they were naked" once they ate from the tree; that is, it implies that Adam and Eve were naked form the moment of their creation but only figured this out later. However, according to a number of Jewish (see, e.g., *Genesis Rabbah* 20:12) and Christian exegetical traditions, Adam and Eve were not created naked. The Christian *Cave of Treasures* relates that until their fall, "Adam and Eve were in paradise, clothed with glory (*shūbḥā*) and shining with their gloriousness, for three hours" (*Cave of Treasures* [Oc.], 3:14–15; see Witztum, *Syriac Milieu,* 93; Beck, "Iblis und Mensch," 237). In other words, they *became* naked when they ate from the tree.

In his *Hymns on Paradise* (3:15) Ephrem declares that their garments of holiness (*qūdshā*) and glory (*shūbḥā*) disappeared the very moment they ate from the tree. Seeing their nakedness they hastened to make a rough replacement with fig leaves (Gen 3:7). Eventually God provided them with a garment of skin (Gen 3:21; according to *Cave of Treasures,* the "skin of trees," i.e., bark).

As Joseph Witztum shows (*Syriac Milieu,* 93–107), the Qurʾān is in conversation with these traditions on the garments of Adam and Eve when it reports that Satan sought to tempt them in order to "expose to them what was hidden from them of their nakedness." The Qurʾān means, in other words, that Satan was eager to strip Adam and Eve of the "royal vestments" with which God had clothed them.

---

²³They said, 'Our Lord, we have wronged ourselves! If You do not forgive us and have mercy upon us, we will surely be among the losers.'

²⁴He said, 'Get down, being enemies of one another! On the earth shall be your abode and sustenance for a time.'

²⁵He said, 'In it you will live, and in it you will die, and from it you will be raised [from the dead].'

7:23–25 Here Adam and Eve seek forgiveness from God (v. 23). God commands "them"—presumably Adam, Eve, and Satan—to leave the garden (v. 24) but comforts Adam and Eve with a promise that they will rise from the dead (v. 25). Verse 24, which has God declare that they will be "enemies of one another" seems to reflect Genesis 3:15, where God explains that He will "put enmity" between the serpent and the woman. The allusion to the "earth" in verse 25 may be connected with Genesis 3:17 ("Accursed be the soil because of you. Painfully will you get your food from it as long as you live").

This passage also reflects the cosmological vision of early Syriac Christian sources in which paradise is on the top of a cosmic mountain, above the earth, and thus has God cry out, "Go *down*" (on this see commentary on 2:25).

The idea that God forgave Adam is found in the *Life of Adam and Eve*. This text has God assure Adam that, if he should live a life of righteousness, he will be resurrected and return to paradise (cf. 7:24–25):

> Adam said again to God, "My Lord, I beseech you, give me of the tree of life, so that I may eat before I shall have gone forth from the Garden." God said to Adam, "You cannot take of it in your lifetime, because I have given an order to the Seraphs to guard it round about with weapons because of you, lest you should eat more of it and become immortal and say, 'Behold, I shall not die;' and you will be boastful of it and be victorious in the war which the enemy has made with you. Rather, when you go out of the Garden, guard yourself from slander, from harlotry, from adultery, from sorcery, from the love of money, from avarice and from all sins. Then, you shall arise from death, in the resurrection which is going to take place. At that time, I will give you of the tree of life and you will be eternally undying.' (*Life of Adam and Eve*, Armenian version, trans. Anderson and Stone, 28:2–4)

---

²⁶'O Children of Adam! We have certainly sent down to you garments to cover your nakedness, and for adornment. Yet the

garment of Godwariness—that is the best.' That is [one] of God's signs, so that they may take admonition.

²⁷'O Children of Adam! Do not let Satan tempt you, like he expelled your parents from paradise, stripping them of their garments to show them their nakedness. Indeed, he sees you—he and his hosts—whence you do not see them. We have indeed made the devils friends of those who have no faith.'

7:26–27 In verse 26 Qarai translates Arabic *rīsh* as "adornment" (he again uses "adornment" in v. 31 to translate Ar. *zīna*). *Rīsh,* however, means "feathers," and other translators follow the literal meaning (Arberry: "We have sent down on you a garment to cover your shameful parts, and feathers"). Qarai seems to follow the opinion of exegetes that *rīsh* can metaphorically mean any sort of decorative apparel (since, according to one tradition, the Bedouins considered feathers a symbol of luxury).

However, as this verse follows the report of Adam and Eve's losing their heavenly garment (v. 22) and the report of their expulsion from paradise (vv. 23–25; see also v. 27), it may be connected to Genesis 3:21, which mentions that God made "tunics of skin" for Adam and Eve before they left the garden. Jewish and Christian sources include a wide range of ideas about these tunics. We read the following opinions in *Genesis Rabbah,* for example:

R. Eleazar said: They were of goats' skin. R. Joshua said: Of hares' skin. R. Jose b. R. Hanina said: It was a garment made of skin with its wool. Resh Lakish said: It was of Circassian wool, and these were used [later] by firstborn children. R. Samuel b. Nahman said: [They were made from] the wool of camels and the wool of hares. (*Genesis Rabbah,* 20:12)

It could be that the Qur'ān is contributing one further idea: feathers.

———————

²⁸When they commit an indecency, they say, 'We found our fathers practising it and God has enjoined it upon us.'

Say, 'Indeed, God does not enjoin indecencies. Do you attribute to God what you do not know?'

²⁹*Say*, 'My Lord has enjoined justice,' and [He has enjoined,] 'Set your heart [on Him] at every occasion of prayer, and invoke Him, putting your exclusive faith in Him. Even as He brought you forth in the beginning, so will you return.'

³⁰He has guided a part [of mankind] and a part has deserved [to be consigned to] error, for they took the devils for masters instead of God, and supposed that they were guided.

³¹O Children of Adam! Put on your adornment on every occasion of prayer, and eat and drink, but do not waste; indeed He does not like the wasteful.

³²*Say*, 'Who has forbidden the adornment of God, which He has brought forth for His servants, and the good things of [His] provision?'

Say, 'These are for the faithful in the life of this world, and exclusively for them on the Day of Resurrection.' Thus do We elaborate the signs for a people who have knowledge.

³³*Say*, 'My Lord has forbidden only indecencies, the outward among them and the inward ones, and sin and undue aggression, and that you should ascribe to God partners for which He has not sent down any authority, and that you should attribute to God what you do not know.'

³⁴There is a [preordained] time for every nation: when their time comes, they shall not defer it by a single hour nor shall they advance it.

7:34 Speyer (*BEQ*, 453) compares this verse to Acts 17:26: "From one single principle he not only created the whole human race so that they could occupy the entire earth, but he decreed the times and limits of their habitation."

---

³⁵O Children of Adam! If there come to you apostles from yourselves, recounting to you My signs, then those who are Godwary

and righteous will have no fear, nor will they grieve. [36]But those who deny Our signs and disdain them, they shall be the inmates of the Fire and they shall remain in it [forever].

[37]So who is a greater wrongdoer than him who fabricates lies against God, or denies His signs? Their share, as decreed in the Book, shall reach them. When Our messengers come to take them away, they will say, 'Where is that which you used to invoke besides God?' They will say, 'They have forsaken us,' and they will testify against themselves that they were faithless.

[38]He will say, 'Enter the Fire, along with the nations of jinn and humans who passed before you!' Every time that a nation enters [hell], it will curse its sister [nation]. When they all join in it, the last of them will say about the first of them, 'Our Lord, it was they who led us astray; so give them a double punishment of the Fire.' He will say, 'It is double for each [of you], but you do not know.' [39]And the first of them will say to the last of them, 'You have no merit over us! So taste the punishment because of what you used to perpetrate.'

[40]Indeed, those who deny Our signs and disdain them—the gates of the heaven will not be opened for them, nor shall they enter paradise until the camel passes through the needle's eye, and thus do We requite the guilty.

7:40 In the Synoptic Gospels Jesus uses the metaphor of the camel and the eye of the needle to describe how difficult it is for the rich to enter heaven:

> [23]Then Jesus said to his disciples, 'In truth I tell you, it is hard for someone rich to enter the kingdom of Heaven.
> [24]Yes, I tell you again, it is easier for a camel to pass through the eye of a needle than for someone rich to enter the kingdom of Heaven.' (Mat 19:23–24; cf. Mar 10:25; Luk 18:25)

The Qurʾān applies this metaphor instead to those who reject the signs of God.

⁴¹They shall have hell for their resting place, and over them shall be sheets [of fire], and thus do We requite the wrongdoers.

⁴²As for those who have faith and do righteous deeds—We task no soul except according to its capacity—they shall be the inhabitants of paradise and they shall remain in it [forever]. ⁴³We will remove whatever rancour there is in their breasts, and streams will run for them.

They will say, 'All praise belongs to God, who guided us to this. Had not God guided us, we would have never been guided. Our Lord's apostles had certainly brought the truth.' The call will be made to them: 'This is paradise, which you have been given to inherit because of what you used to do!'

⁴⁴The inhabitants of paradise will call out to the inmates of the Fire, 'We found what our Lord promised us to be true; did you find what your Lord promised you to be true?' 'Yes,' they will say. Then a caller will announce in their midst, 'May God's curse be on the wrongdoers!' ⁴⁵—Those who bar [others] from the way of God, and seek to make it crooked, and disbelieve in the Hereafter.

⁴⁶There will be a veil between them. And on the Elevations will be certain men who recognize each of them by their mark. They will call out to the inhabitants of paradise, 'Peace be to you!' (They will not have entered it, though they would be eager to do so. ⁴⁷When their look is turned toward the inmates of the Fire, they will say, 'Our Lord, do not put us among the wrongdoing lot!')

⁴⁸The occupants of the Elevations will call out to certain men whom they recognize by their marks, 'Your rallying did not avail you, nor what you used to disdain. ⁴⁹Are these the ones concerning whom you swore that God will not extend them any mercy?' 'Enter paradise! You shall have no fear, nor shall you grieve.'

⁵⁰The inmates of the Fire will call out to the inhabitants of paradise, 'Pour on us some water, or something of what God has provided you.' They will say, 'God has forbidden these two to the faithless!'

7:44–50 It is unclear in this passage if the "occupants of the Elevations" are in an especially "high" place in heaven or rather in a space between heaven and hell. Geiger (*Judaism and Islam,* 50–51) thinks it is the later.

As pointed out by Bell (*Commentary,* 1:231–33) and Rudolph (*Abhängigkeit,* 15), this passage seems to have a particular relationship with the story in Luke of the rich man and Lazarus (cf. 6:111). One might compare in particular verse 46 (with its mention of a "veil," Ar. *ḥijāb*) with Luk 16:26 and verse 50 (which has the damned ask for water) with Luk 16:24:

²⁴So he cried out, "Father Abraham, pity me and send Lazarus to dip the tip of his finger in *water* and cool my tongue, for I am in agony in these flames."
²⁵Abraham said, "My son, remember that during your life you had your fill of good things, just as Lazarus his fill of bad. Now he is being comforted here while you are in agony.
²⁶But that is not all: between us and you *a great gulf* has been fixed, to prevent those who want to cross from our side to yours or from your side to ours." (Luk 16:24–26)

---

⁵¹Those who took their religion for diversion and play and whom the life of the world had deceived. So today We will forget them as they forgot the encounter of this day of theirs, and used to impugn Our signs.

⁵²Certainly We have brought them a Book which We have elaborated with knowledge, as guidance and mercy for a people who have faith. ⁵³Do they await anything but its fulfillment? The day when its fulfillment comes, those who had forgotten it before will say, 'Our Lord's apostles had certainly brought the truth. Do we

have any intercessors to intercede for us, or could we be returned [to the world], so that we may act differently from what we used to?'!' They have already ruined their souls, and what they used to fabricate has forsaken them.

⁵⁴Your Lord is indeed God, who created the heavens and the earth in six days, and then settled on the Throne. He draws the night's cover over the day, which pursues it swiftly, and [He created] the sun, the moon, and the stars, [all of them] disposed by His command. Lo! All creation and command belong to Him. Blessed is God, the Lord of all the worlds.

7:54 On the creation of the heavens and the earth in six days, see commentary on 41:9–12 (with further references). Here (and in 10:3; 25:59; 32:4; 57:4) God "settles" on His throne after creating. Regarding this sequence, see commentary on 32:4 (with further references). The references to sun, moon, and stars here might be compared to Jeremiah 31:35: "The Lord who provides the sun to shine by day, who regulates moon and stars to shine by night, who stirs the sea, making its waves roar, he whose name is the Lord Sabaoth, says this."

---

⁵⁵Supplicate your Lord, beseechingly and secretly. Indeed, He does not like the transgressors. ⁵⁶Do not cause corruption on the earth after its restoration, and supplicate Him with fear and hope: indeed God's mercy is close to the virtuous.

⁵⁷It is He who sends forth the winds as harbingers of His mercy. When they bear [rain-]laden clouds, We drive them toward a dead land and send down water on it, and with it We bring forth all kinds of crops. Thus shall We raise the dead; maybe you will take admonition.

⁵⁸The good land—its vegetation comes out by the permission of its Lord, and as for that which is bad, it does not come out

except sparsely. Thus do We paraphrase the signs variously for a people who give thanks.

7:58 This verse might reflect the parable of the sower (Mar 4:2–9; cf. Mat 13:3–9), although it is not clear that the Qur'ān is using "land" metaphorically for humans.

---

⁵⁹Certainly We sent Noah to his people. He said, 'O my people, worship God! You have no other god besides Him. I indeed fear for you the punishment of a tremendous day.'

7:59–137 *overview* Here the Qur'ān relates a series of accounts involving prophets, unbelievers, and divine punishment. This series, or a version thereof, is found principally in four Suras (cf. also 37:75–148, a series of narratives involving only Biblical characters):

   7: Noah, vv. 59–64; Hūd, 65–72; Ṣāliḥ, 73–79; Lot, 80–84; Shuʿayb, 85–93; Moses, 103–62
   11: Noah, vv. 25–49; Hūd, 50–60; Ṣāliḥ, 61–66; Abraham and Lot, 69–83; Shuʿayb, 84–95; Moses, 96–99
   26: Moses, vv. 10–68; Abraham, 69–102; Noah, 105–22; Hūd, 123–40; Ṣāliḥ, 141–59; Lot, 160–75; Shuʿayb, 176–91.
   54: Noah, vv. 9–17; Hūd, 18–20; Ṣāliḥ, 23–32; Lot, 33–40; Moses, 41–42

In each case the Qur'ān means to teach a lesson about divine punishment, not to describe the history of salvation. In this regard the Qur'ān is closer in spirit to 2 Peter 2, which alludes to the stories of Noah and Lot for the sake of moral exhortation, than it is to Old Testament narratives. Ultimately, however, these accounts are best understood in light of the Qur'ān's own prophetology; that is, the Qur'ān projects the image and message of its own prophet on earlier figures to convince its audience to accept and obey Muḥammad (and avoid the fate of earlier doomed peoples).

The Moses accounts (Q 7:103–62; 11:96–99; 26:10–68; 54:41–42) of these Suras do not follow closely the formulaic structure of the other prophetic stories. See commentary on 20:9–16 (on the call of Moses); 26:18–29 (on the confrontation with Pharaoh); 28:7ff. (on the childhood and early life of Moses); 40:23ff. (on Pharaoh and Haman).

[60]The elite of his people said, 'Indeed, we see you to be in manifest error.'

[61]He said, 'O my people, I am not in error. Rather, I am an apostle from the Lord of all the worlds. [62]I communicate the messages of my Lord to you and I am your well-wisher, and I know from God what you do not know. [63]Do you consider it odd that a reminder from your Lord should come to you through a man from among yourselves, to warn you so that you may be Godwary and so that you may receive His mercy?'

[64]But they impugned him. So We delivered him and those who were with him in the ark, and We drowned those who impugned Our signs. They were indeed a blind lot.

[65]To [the people of] ʿĀd [We sent] Hūd, their kinsman. He said, 'O my people, worship God! You have no other god besides Him. Will you not then be wary [of Him]?'

7:69 Geiger (*Judaism and Islam,* 88–91) thinks that Hūd is the Biblical Eber (Gen 10:21, 24, 25; passim) and associates the punishment of his people with the scattering of the people at the Tower of Babel, but this is not certain.

[66]The elite of his people who were faithless said, 'Indeed, we see you to be in folly, and indeed we consider you to be a liar.'

[67]He said, 'O my people, I am not in folly. Rather, I am an apostle from the Lord of all the worlds. [68]I communicate to you the messages of my Lord and I am a trustworthy well-wisher for you. [69]Do you consider it odd that that a reminder from your Lord should come to you through a man from yourselves, to warn you? Remember when He made you successors after the people of Noah, and increased you vastly in creation. So remember God's bounties so that you may be felicitous.'

7:69 As Bell mentions (*Commentary*, 1:238) the declaration of Hūd (to his people)—"and increased you vastly in creation"—might suggest a notion that the people of Hūd were giants. In Q 26:130 we read how Hūd declares that ʿĀd acted like *jabbārīn*, which could be cognate to Hebrew *gibbōrīm*, meaning "giants." It is possible that the people of ʿĀd are meant to be the antediluvian *nephilīm* of Genesis 6:4. *Tafsīr al-Jalālayn* reports that the tallest of them was a hundred feet.

———————

⁷⁰They said, 'Have you come to [tell] us that we should worship God alone and abandon what our fathers have been worshiping? Then bring us what you threaten us with, if you are truthful.'

⁷¹He said, 'Punishment and wrath from your Lord has become due against you. Do you dispute with me regarding names which you have named—you and your fathers—for which God has not sent down any authority? So wait! I too am waiting along with you.'

⁷²Then We delivered him and those who were with him by a mercy from Us, and We rooted out those who impugned Our signs and were not faithful.

⁷³To [the people of] Thamūd [We sent] Ṣāliḥ, their kinsman. He said, 'O my people, worship God! You have no other god besides Him. There has certainly come to you a clear proof from your Lord. This she-camel of God is a sign for you. Let her alone to graze [freely] in God's land, and do not cause her any harm, for then you shall be seized by a painful punishment. ⁷⁴Remember when He made you successors after [the people of] ʿĀd, and settled you in the land: you build palaces in its plains, and hew houses out of the mountains. So remember God's bounties, and do not act wickedly on the earth, causing corruption.'

⁷⁵The elite of his people who were oppressors said to those who were oppressed—to those among them who had faith—'Do you know that Ṣāliḥ has been sent by his Lord?' They said, 'We indeed believe in what he has been sent with.'

⁷⁶Those who were oppressors said, 'We indeed disbelieve in what you have believed.'

⁷⁷So they hamstrung the She-camel and defied the command of their Lord, and they said, 'O Ṣāliḥ, bring us what you threaten us with, if you are one of the apostles.'

⁷⁸Thereupon the earthquake seized them and they lay lifeless prostrate in their homes. ⁷⁹So he abandoned them [to their fate], and said, 'O my people! Certainly I communicated to you the message of my Lord, and I was your well-wisher, but you did not like well-wishers.'

⁸⁰And Lot, when he said to his people, 'What! Do you commit an outrage none in the world ever committed before you?! ⁸¹Indeed, you come to men with desire instead of women! You are indeed a dissolute lot.'

⁸²But the only answer of his people was that they said, 'Expel them from your town! They are indeed a puritanical lot.'

⁸³Thereupon We delivered him and his family, except his wife; she was one of those who remained behind. ⁸⁴Then We poured down upon them a rain [of stones]. So observe how was the fate of the guilty!

7:80–84 In Genesis 19:7 Lot condemns the "wicked" behavior of the Sodomites (cf. vv. 80–81 above); otherwise the Qurʾān's brief reference to the story of Lot for the purpose of moral exhortation is closer to 2 Peter 2:6–8 than to Genesis (see further commentary on 29:28–35). On Lot, see 11:69–83; 15:57–74; 26:160–75; 27:54–58; 29:28–35; 37:133–38; 54:33–40 and commentary on 15:57–74 and 29:28–35. On Lot's wife, see commentary on 27:54–58 (with further references).

---

⁸⁵To [the people of] Midian [We sent] Shuʿayb, their townsman. He said, 'O my people, worship God! You have no other

god besides Him. There has come to you a clear proof from your Lord. Observe fully the measure and the balance, do not cheat the people of their goods, and do not cause corruption in the land after its restoration. That is better for you, if you are faithful.

7:85 Geiger (*Judaism and Islam*, 137–42) identifies Shuʿayb with Jethro, the father-in-law of Moses, who in the account of Exodus (3:1) is a priest of Midian.

On the use of proper "measuring" as an example of righteousness, see commentary on Q 83:1–3 (with further references).

---

[86]And do not lie in wait on every road to threaten and bar those who have faith in Him from the way of God, seeking to make it crooked. Remember when you were few and He multiplied you, and observe how was the fate of the agents of corruption. [87]If a group of you have believed in what I have been sent with, and a group have not believed, be patient until God judges between us, and He is the best of judges.'

[88]The elite of his people who were oppressors said, 'O Shuʿayb, we will surely expel you and the faithful who are with you from our town, or else you shall revert to our creed.'

He said, 'What! Even if we should be unwilling?! [89]We would be fabricating a lie against God if we revert to your creed after God had delivered us from it. It does not behoove us to return to it, unless God, our Lord, should wish so. Our Lord embraces all things in [His] knowledge. In God alone we have put our trust.' 'Our Lord! Judge justly between us and our people, and You are the best of judges!'

[90]The elite of his people who were faithless said, 'If you follow Shuʿayb, you will indeed be losers.'

[91]So the earthquake seized them and they lay lifeless prostrate in their homes. [92]Those who impugned Shuʿayb became as if they

had never lived there. Those who impugned Shuʿayb were themselves the losers.

⁹³So he abandoned them [to their fate] and said, 'O my people! Certainly I communicated to you the messages of my Lord, and I was your well-wisher. So how should I grieve for a faithless lot?'

⁹⁴We did not send a prophet to any town without visiting its people with stress and distress so that they might entreat [for God's forgiveness]. ⁹⁵Then We changed the ill [conditions] to good until they multiplied [in numbers] and said, 'Adversity and ease befell our fathers [too].' Then We seized them suddenly while they were unaware.

⁹⁶If the people of the towns had been faithful and Godwary, We would have opened to them blessings from the heaven and the earth. But they impugned [Our apostles]; so We seized them because of what they used to perpetrate.

⁹⁷Do the people of the towns feel secure from Our punishment overtaking them at night while they are asleep?

⁹⁸Do the people of the towns feel secure from Our punishment overtaking them at midday while they are playing around?

⁹⁹Do they feel secure from God's devising? No one feels secure from God's devising except the people who are losers.

¹⁰⁰Does it not dawn upon those who inherited the earth after its [former] inhabitants that if We wish We will punish them for their sins and set a seal on their hearts so they would not hear?

¹⁰¹These are the towns some of whose accounts We recount to *you*. Their apostles certainly brought them clear proofs, but they were not the ones to believe in what they had impugned earlier. Thus does God put a seal on the hearts of the faithless.

7:101 The Qurʾān's allusion to God's sealing of hearts (cf. 2:7; 6:46; 4:155; 9:87; 10:74; 16:108; 30:59; 40:35; 45:23; 47:16; 63:3) reflects Biblical passages such as Exodus 4:21: "The Lord said to Moses, 'Think of the wonders I have given you power to perform, once you are back in Egypt! You are to perform them before Pharaoh, but I myself shall make him obstinate [lit. "harden his heart"], and he will not let the people go'" (Exo 4:21; cf. Exo 7:3; 14:17; Jos 11:18–20; Isa 6:9–13; Rom 9:18).

---

[102]We did not find in most of them any [loyalty to] covenants. Indeed, We found most of them to be transgressors.

[103]Then We sent Moses after them with Our signs to Pharaoh and his elite, but they wronged them. So observe how was the fate of the agents of corruption!

[104]And Moses said, 'O Pharaoh, I am indeed an apostle from the Lord of all the worlds. [105]It behooves me to say nothing about God except the truth. I certainly bring you a clear proof from your Lord. So let the Children of Israel go with me.'

7:103–4 On Moses's confrontation with Pharaoh, see commentary on 26:18–29 and 26:30–45 (with further references).

---

[106]He said, 'If you have brought a sign, produce it, if you are truthful.'

[107]Thereat he threw down his staff, and behold, it became a manifest python. [108]Then he drew out his hand, and behold, it was [bright and] white to the onlookers.

7:106–8 In Exodus 4, God instructs Moses to perform the two miracles alluded to here, but in front of the Israelites and not in front of Pharaoh:

[1]Moses replied as follows, 'But suppose they will not believe me or listen to my words, and say to me, "the Lord has not appeared to you"?'

²the Lord then said, 'What is that in your hand?' 'A staff,' he said.
³'Throw it on the ground,' said the Lord. Moses threw it on the ground; the staff turned into a snake and Moses recoiled from it.
⁴the Lord then said to Moses, 'Reach out your hand and catch it by the tail.' He reached out his hand, caught it, and in his hand it turned back into a staff.
⁵'Thus they may believe that the Lord, the God of their ancestors, the God of Abraham, the God of Isaac and the God of Jacob, has appeared to you.'
⁶Next, the Lord said to him, 'Put your hand inside your tunic.' He put his hand inside his tunic, then drew it out again: and his hand was diseased, white as snow.
⁷the Lord then said, 'Put your hand back inside your tunic.' He put his hand back inside his tunic and when he drew it out, there it was restored, just like the rest of his flesh. (Exo 4:1–7)

The Qurʾān seems to allude to Moses's "diseased" hand by describing it as "white" (v. 108), although Muhammad Asad explains the reference to his white hand by commenting: "endowed with transcendent luminosity in token of his prophethood—and not, as stated in the Bible (Exodus iv, 6), 'leprous as snow.'"

In Exodus God speaks to Moses of three miracles to be performed before the Israelites: the staff and serpent, the leprous hand, and the turning of the Nile's water into blood (Exo 4:1–9). However, Moses and Aaron perform only two miracles, and in front of Pharaoh: Aaron (not Moses) throws down his staff, which turns into a serpent (Exo 7:10–12), and the next day, they turn the water of the Nile into blood (Exo 7:16–21). However, the idea that Moses worked all of these miracles in front of the Egyptians could be inferred from Exodus 4:21 (which has God declare that Moses will perform wonders before Pharaoh). On this see Geiger, *Judaism and Islam* (125), who refers to the *Pirqe de-Rabbi Eliezer* (48) and Witztum, *Syriac Milieu* (28–30), who also (following Samuel Lee) notes a potentially relevant comment in Ephrem's *Commentary on Genesis*. On Moses's miracles before Pharaoh, see also commentary on 20:17–24 and 26:30–45.

---

¹⁰⁹The elite of Pharaoh's people said, 'This is indeed an expert magician; ¹¹⁰he seeks to expel you from your land.' 'So what do you advise?'

7:109–10 Here Pharaoh's advisers declare Moses a threat to the Egyptian people (in 26:34–35 these words are attributed to Pharaoh himself). This passage may reflect the Biblical story of Esther, in which Haman, adviser to the Persian king Ahasuerus, plots the downfall of Mordechai and the massacre of the Jews of Persia (see Est 3:8–11). In this regard it is telling that the Qurʾān elsewhere (28:8, 38; 40:24, 36) gives the name Haman to an adviser of Pharaoh.

---

¹¹¹They said, 'Put him and his brother off for a while, and send heralds to the cities ¹¹²to bring you every expert magician.'

¹¹³And the magicians came to Pharaoh. They said, 'We shall indeed have a reward if we were to be the victors?'

¹¹⁴He said, 'Of course! And you shall indeed be among those near [to me].'

¹¹⁵They said, 'O Moses, will you throw [first], or shall we throw?'

¹¹⁶He said, 'Throw [yours].' So when they threw, they bewitched the people's eyes and overawed them, producing a tremendous magic.

¹¹⁷And We signalled to Moses: 'Throw down your staff.' And behold, it was swallowing what they had faked.

7:115–17 On the Qurʾānic account of Moses in Pharaoh's court and its relationship to the Exodus narrative, see commentary on 26:30–45 (with further references).

---

¹¹⁸So the truth came out, and what they had wrought was reduced to naught. ¹¹⁹Thereat they were vanquished, and retreated, humiliated.

¹²⁰And the magicians fell down in prostration. ¹²¹They said, 'We have believed in the Lord of all the worlds, ¹²²the Lord of Moses and Aaron.'

¹²³Pharaoh said, 'Do you profess faith in Him before I may permit you? It is indeed a plot you have devised in the city to expel its people from it. Soon you will know [the consequences]! ¹²⁴Surely I will cut off your hands and feet on opposite sides and then I will crucify all of you.'

¹²⁵They said, 'We will indeed return to our Lord. ¹²⁶You are vindictive toward us only because we believed in the signs of our Lord when they came to us.' 'Our Lord! Pour patience upon us, and grant us to die as *muslims.*'

7:120–26 The conversion of the magicians in Pharaoh's court here seems to develop themes found in two passages of Exodus. In the first (8:14–15), Pharaoh's magicians recognize a plague as the work of God, while in the second (10:7) they encourage Pharaoh to accept the demands of Moses:

> ¹⁴By their spells the magicians tried to produce mosquitoes in the same way but failed, and there were mosquitoes on man and beast.
> ¹⁵So the magicians said to Pharaoh, 'This is the finger of God.' But Pharaoh was obstinate and, as the Lord had foretold, refused to listen to them. (Exo 8:14–15)

> ⁷At which, Pharaoh's officials said to him, 'How much longer are we to be tricked by this fellow? Let the people go and worship the Lord their God. Do you not finally realise that Egypt is on the brink of ruin?' (Exo 10:7)

On the belief of Pharaoh's magicians in Moses and his God, see 20:70–73; 26:46–51.

On the (anachronistic) way that the Qurʾān has Pharaoh threaten to crucify his unfaithful magicians (crucifixion was not yet known in ancient Egypt), Jeffery (*FV,* 197) writes: "Muḥammad seems to have considered [that Crucifixion] was a favourite pastime of Pharaoh." On Pharaoh and crucifixion, see 20:71; 26:49.

¹²⁷The elite of Pharaoh's people said, 'Will you leave Moses and his people to cause corruption in the land, and to abandon you and your gods?' He said, 'We will kill their sons and spare their women, and indeed we are dominant over them.'

7:127 The first part of this verse has the "elite" (lit., the "council," Ar. *mala ʾ*) express a different conviction from the "magicians" of verses 120–26 who have just professed their faith in Moses's God. On the second part of the verse (the killing of male Israelites), see commentary on 40:25 (with further references).

¹²⁸Moses said to his people, 'Turn to God for help and be patient. The earth indeed belongs to God, and He makes whomever of His servants He wishes to inherit it, and the outcome will be in favour of the Godwary.'

7:128 "Moses said to the people, 'Do not be afraid! Stand firm, and you will see what the Lord will do to rescue you today: the Egyptians you see today you will never see again" (Exo 14:13).

¹²⁹They said, 'We were tormented before you came to us and [also] after you came.' He said, 'Maybe your Lord will destroy your enemy and make you successors in the land, and then He will see how you act.'

7:129 "For evil-doers will be annihilated, while those who hope in the Lord shall have the land for their own" (Psa 37:29; cf. Q 21:105).

¹³⁰Certainly We afflicted Pharaoh's clan with droughts and loss of produce, so that they may take admonition. ¹³¹But whenever any good came to them, they would say, 'This is our due.' But if any ill visited them, they took it for ill omens attending Moses and those who were with him. (Behold! The cause of their ill omens is indeed from God, but most of them do not know.)

¹³²And they said, 'Whatever sign you may bring us to bewitch us, we are not going to believe you.'

¹³³So We sent against them a flood and locusts, lice, frogs and blood, as distinct signs. But they acted arrogantly, and they were a guilty lot.

7:133 The Qurʾān here seems to refer to five plagues (cf. Exo 7–10), one of which is a flood (*ṭūfān;* cf. Exo 14). Elsewhere (Q 17:101) the Qurʾān has God refer to nine signs which He gave Moses to show to Pharaoh (cf. also the allusions in 43:48–50).

¹³⁴Whenever a plague fell upon them, they would say, 'O Moses, invoke your Lord for us by the covenant He has made with you. If you remove the plague from us, we will certainly believe in you and let the Children of Israel go along with you.'

¹³⁵But when We had removed the plague from them until a term that they should have completed, behold, they broke their promise.

7:134–35 The Qurʾān here reflects the cycle by which Pharaoh agrees to let the Israelites go if only the plagues will cease, and then withdraws his agreement once they do cease (cf. 43:50). This is seen, for example, in Exodus 8:11 (after the plague of frogs): "But once Pharaoh saw that there had been a respite, he became obstinate and, as the Lord had foretold, refused to listen to them." Verse

134 seems to be anachronistic in that it has Pharaoh refer to the covenant that God made with Moses, although the covenant is not made until after the Exodus (cr. Andrew O'Connor).

---

^{136}So We took vengeance on them and drowned them in the sea, for they impugned Our signs and were oblivious to them.

7:136 "Sea" is the rendering of *yamm,* which is not the typical Arabic term but is instead closely related to a common word for "sea" in Syriac (*yammā*) and other Semitic languages. The Qur'ān uses *yamm* for "river" or "sea" (in reference to the Nile River [20:39; 28:7], the Sea of Reeds or Red Sea [7:136; 20:78; 28:40; 51:40], and the river from the account of the golden calf [20:97]), that is, only in accounts of Moses. On this see Witztum, *Syriac Milieu,* 281n4.

On the crossing of the Red Sea or Sea of Reeds in the Qur'ān, see commentary on 26:52–59 (with further references).

---

^{137}We made the people who were oppressed heirs to the east and west of the land which We had blessed, and *your* Lord's best word [of promise] was fulfilled for the Children of Israel because of their patience, and We destroyed what Pharaoh and his people had built and whatever they used to erect.

^{138}We carried the Children of Israel across the sea, whereat they came upon a people attending to certain idols that they had. They said, 'O Moses, make for us a god like the gods that they have.'

He said, 'You are indeed an ignorant lot. ^{139}What they are engaged in is indeed bound to perish, and what they have been doing shall come to naught.'

^{140}He said, 'Shall I find you a god other than God, while He has graced you over all the nations?'

7:138–40 The Qurʾān reflects here an episode from Exodus according to which God warns the Israelites not to worship the gods of the idolatrous peoples they will encounter:

> [23]My angel will precede you and lead you to the home of the Amorites, the Hittites, the Perizzites, the Canaanites, the Hivites and the Jebusites, whom I shall exterminate.
> [24]You will not bow down to their gods or worship them or observe their rites, but throw them down and smash their cultic stones. (Exo 23:23–24; cf. Exo 34:11–33)

---

[141]And when We delivered you from Pharaoh's clan who inflicted on you a terrible torment, slaughtering your sons and sparing your women, and there was a great test in that from your Lord.

[142]We made an appointment with Moses for thirty nights, and completed them with ten [more]; thus the tryst of his Lord was completed in forty nights.

And Moses said to Aaron, his brother, 'Be my successor among my people, and set things right and do not follow the way of the agents of corruption.'

7:142 Here the Qurʾān has Moses say to his brother Aaron, "Be my *khalīfa*," which Qarai renders as "Be my successor." *Khalīfa*, however, is better understood here as "vice-gerent" or "representative" (cf. the translation of Asad: "Take thou my place among my people"). Although the Qurʾān places the designation of Aaron as Moses's representative after the flight from Egypt (and the covenant on Sinai), it seems to be related to Exodus 4: (Moses's initial encounter with God on Sinai), where God says to Moses: "[Aaron] will speak to the people in your place; he will be your mouthpiece, and you will be as the god inspiring him" (Exo 4:14–16; cf. Exo 7:1–2).

---

[143]When Moses arrived at Our tryst and his Lord spoke to him, he said, 'Lord, show [Yourself] to me, that I may look at You!' He

said, 'You shall not see Me. But look at the mountain: if it abides in its place, then you will see Me.' So when his Lord disclosed Himself to the mountain, He levelled it, and Moses fell down swooning. When he recovered, he said, 'Immaculate are You! I turn to You in penitence, and I am the first of the faithful.'

¹⁴⁴He said, 'O Moses, I have chosen you over the people with My messages and My speech. So take what I give you and be among the grateful.'

7:143–44 Qarai (as in v. 142) here has "tryst," but the Arabic is *mīqāt,* meaning something closer to "appointment" (or "appointed time"). This passage (cf. 2:55; 4:153, which have all the Israelites impiously seek to see God; and 28:38, which has Pharaoh do so) reflects Exodus 33:18ff. (on God's speaking to Moses, see commentary on 2:253, with further references):

¹⁸He then said, 'Please show me your glory.'
¹⁹the Lord said, 'I shall make all my goodness pass before you, and before you I shall pronounce the name [YHWH]; and I am gracious to those to whom I am gracious and I take pity on those on whom I take pity.
²⁰But my face,' he said, 'you cannot see, for no human being can see me and survive.' (Exo 33:18–20)

---

¹⁴⁵We wrote for him in the Tablets advice concerning all things and an elaboration of all things, [and We said], 'Hold on to them with power, and bid your people to hold on to the best of [what is in] them. Soon I shall show you the abode of the transgressors. ¹⁴⁶Soon I shall turn away from My signs those who are unduly arrogant in the earth: though they should see every sign, they will not believe in it, and if they see the way of rectitude they will not follow it, and if they see the way of error they will follow it. That is because they impugn Our signs and are oblivious to them.'

¹⁴⁷Those who deny Our signs and the encounter of the Hereafter, their works have failed. Shall they be requited except for what they used to do?

7:145–47 The Qurʾān alludes here (v. 145) to God's giving the Ten Commandments to Moses. Verse 145 has God write things down on tablets, whereas in Deuteronomy 27:8 God commands Moses to do so ("On these stones you must write all the words of this Law; cut them carefully"; see also Exo 20:1–17; Deu 5:4–21). The allusion to human infidelity in verses 146–47 may be connected to the infidelity of the Israelites in the desert (on which see Deu 9:6–7). On the Ten Commandments and the Qurʾān, see commentary on 17:22–39 (with further references).

---

¹⁴⁸The people of Moses took up in his absence a calf [cast] from their ornaments—a body that gave out a lowing sound. Did they not regard that it did not speak to them, nor did it guide them to any way? They took it up [for worship] and they were wrongdoers.

¹⁴⁹But when they became remorseful and realised they had gone astray, they said, 'Should our Lord have no mercy on us, and forgive us, we will be surely among the losers.'

7:148–49 On the golden calf episode in the Qurʾān, and in particular the Qurʾān's report that the calf "gave out a lowing sound" (v. 148), see commentary on 20:83–98.

---

¹⁵⁰When Moses returned to his people, angry and indignant, he said, 'Evil has been your conduct in my absence! Would you hasten on the edict of your Lord?'

He threw down the tablets and seized his brother by the head, pulling him towards himself. He said, 'Son of my mother, indeed this people thought me to be weak, and they were about to kill me. So do not let the enemies gloat over me, and do not take me with the wrongdoing lot.'

7:150 The way the Qurʾān has Moses grab Aaron "by the head" (here and in 20:94) shows that the Qurʾān shares the Biblical tradition of Moses's righteous anger at his brother's sin:

²¹Moses then said to Aaron, 'What have these people done to you for you to have brought so great a sin on them?'
²²Aaron replied, 'My lord should not be so angry. You yourself know what a bad state these people are in!
²³They said to me, "Make us a god to go at our head; for that Moses, the man who brought us here from Egypt—we do not know what has become of him." (Exo 32:21–23)

Here (and 20:94) the Qurʾān has Aaron refer to Moses as "son of my mother," the only appearances of this phrase in the Qurʾān. *Tafsīr al-Jalālayn* explains this unusual appellation by commenting that Aaron meant to calm Moses's anger by referring to their mother, being convinced that an appeal to a mother (as opposed to a father) would have a special emotional impact.

---

¹⁵¹He said, 'My Lord, forgive me and my brother and admit us into Your mercy, for You are the most merciful of the merciful. ¹⁵²Indeed, those who took up the calf [for worship] shall be overtaken by their Lord's wrath and abasement in the life of the world.'

Thus do We requite the fabricators [of lies]. ¹⁵³Yet [to] those who commit misdeeds, but repent after that and believe—indeed, after that, your Lord shall surely be all-forgiving, all-merciful.

¹⁵⁴When Moses's indignation abated, he picked up the tablets whose inscriptions contained guidance and mercy for those who are in awe of their Lord.

¹⁵⁵Moses chose seventy men from his people for Our tryst, and when the earthquake seized them, he said, 'My Lord, had You wished, You would have destroyed them and me before. Will You destroy us for what fools amongst us have done? It is only Your test by which You lead astray whomever You wish and guide

whomever You wish. You are our master, so forgive us and have mercy on us, for You are the best of those who forgive.

7:154–55 Whereas verse 154 alludes to Exodus 34, in which God gives the tablets of the Law to Moses for the second time, verse 155 begins a new episode related to the report in Numbers 11 (which is set after the departure of the Israelites from Mt. Sinai) that Moses appointed seventy elders to be present at one of his encounters with God (Qarai translates "tryst"; the Arabic word is *mīqāt,* meaning "appointment"; Yahuda [289] argues that it is related to Hebrew *mo'ēd,* "appointed time"):

> [24]Moses went out and told the people what the Lord had said. Then he collected seventy of the people's elders and stationed them round the Tent.
> [25]the Lord descended in the cloud. He spoke to him and took some of the spirit that was on him and put it on the seventy elders. When the spirit came on them they prophesied—but only once. (Num 11:24–25)

To explain the abrupt transition between verses 154 and 155, Yahuda (289) proposes that "Muhammad was told consecutively" different stories about the wanderings of the Israelites and then retold them together.

Thereafter the Qur'ān speaks of a *rajfa* which "seized" the Israelites (in 2:55 the Israelites are killed by a *ṣā'iqa*—according to Qarai, a "thunderbolt"). *Rajfa* is the term the Qur'ān uses earlier in this same Sura (v. 78) to refer to the calamity with which God struck Thamūd (and again in 29:37, the unbelieving people of Midian). Qarai translates *rajfa* as "earthquake," and one thereby assumes that the Israelites have been killed by this *rajfa* (but then one wonders why Moses subsequently begs to save their lives). The context here implies, as suggested by the *Commentary* of Bell (1:252), that the Qur'ān may be referring to the coming of the spirit (Hb. *rūaḥ;* Syr. *rūḥā*) upon the elders in Numbers 11:24–25 (cr. Michael Novick).

The manner in which Moses implores God in verse 155 not to destroy all of the Israelites because of what the "fools" have done follows from Numbers 11:1–2, where Moses demands that God not destroy the Israelites for their ingratitude.

———————

[156]And appoint goodness for us in this world and the Hereafter, for indeed we have come back to You.'

Said He, 'I visit My punishment on whomever I wish, but My mercy embraces all things. Soon I shall appoint it for those who are Godwary and give the *zakāt* and those who believe in Our signs ¹⁵⁷—those who follow the Apostle, the untaught prophet, whose mention they find written with them in the Torah and the Evangel, who bids them to do what is right and forbids them from what is wrong, makes lawful to them all the good things and forbids them from all vicious things, and relieves them of their burdens and the shackles that were upon them—those who believe in him, honour him, and help him and follow the light that has been sent down with him, they are the felicitous.'

¹⁵⁸*Say,* 'O mankind! I am the Apostle of God to you all, [of Him] to whom belongs the kingdom of the heavens and the earth. There is no god except Him. He gives life and brings death.'

So have faith in God and His Apostle, the untaught prophet, who has faith in God and His words, and follow him so that you may be guided.

7:156–58 In verse 156 the Qurʾān has God declare that His "mercy [*raḥma*] embraces all things." This might be compared to Psalm 145:9, which explains that God's "tenderness [or "mercy"; Hb. *raḥam*] embraces all his creatures."

The context of these three verses is unclear. God's response to Moses's address begins in verse 156 and continues in 157. However, verse 157 also seems to be about Muḥammad and addressed to his audience (presumably the reference to the "Evangel"—i.e., Jesus' revelation—would make sense to the Qurʾān's own audience but not to Moses). Verse 158 seems to address Muḥammad directly.

Verse 157 reports that Muḥammad will make the burdens of the law easier for his followers (he "relieves them of their burdens"; cf. 2:286). Speyer (*BEQ,* 453) compares this to Matthew 11:30, where Jesus declares: "Yes, my yoke is easy and my burden light."

In verses 157–58 our translation renders the Arabic term *ummī* as "untaught," but a better translation is "gentile" (on this see commentary on 2:78–79, with further references). Finally, the use of "light" (Ar. *nūr*) for Muḥammad in v. 157

(cf. 5:15–16) calls to mind the language used in the Gospels (especially notable in John 1) for Jesus.

159Among the people of Moses is a nation who guide [the people] by the truth and do justice thereby.

7:159 Speyer (*BEQ,* 274) suggests that this verse (and 10:83) is connected to Exodus 32:26, which reports that only one tribe (the Qurʾān has *umma,* "nation"), namely the tribe of Levi, rallied to Moses after the sacrilege of the golden calf.

160We split them up into twelve tribal communities, and when his people asked him for water, We revealed to Moses, [saying], 'Strike the rock with your staff,' whereat twelve fountains gushed forth from it. Every tribe came to know its drinking-place. We shaded them with clouds and We sent down to them manna and quails: 'Eat of the good things We have provided you.' And they did not wrong Us, but they used to wrong [only] themselves.

7:160 The opening of this verse, with its mention of the division of the Israelites, is close to 7:168. The latter part of the verse is close to 2:57 (see commentary on that verse, and cf. 20:80). The Qurʾān alludes here to a number of Pentateuchal narratives: the twelve springs at Elim (Exo 15:27; Num 33:9; unlike the Bible, the Qurʾān makes it explicit that the twelve springs are meant to match the twelve tribes.); Moses's striking the rock to release water at Meribah (Num 20:10ff.); the appearance of the Lord's presence in a cloud (Exo 13:21); the provision of manna (Exo 16:9ff.) and quails (Num 11:31ff.). The allusion to these events in the context of exhortation might be compared to the Psalms. Psalm 106 (vv. 32–33) alludes to the waters of Meribah, and Psalm 78 alludes to the manna and quails:

23Even so he gave orders to the skies above, he opened the sluice-gates of heaven;

²⁴he rained down manna to feed them, he gave them the wheat of heaven;
²⁵mere mortals ate the bread of the Mighty, he sent them as much food as they could want.
²⁶He roused an east wind in the heavens, despatched a south wind by his strength;
²⁷he rained down meat on them like dust, birds thick as sand on the seashore,
²⁸tumbling into the middle of his camp, all around his dwelling-place.
²⁹They ate as much food as they wanted, he satisfied all their cravings. (Psa 78:23–29)

---

¹⁶¹When they were told, 'Settle in this town and eat thereof whence you wish, and say, "Relieve [us of the burden of our sins]," and enter while prostrating at the gate, that We may forgive your iniquities, and soon We shall enhance the virtuous,' ¹⁶²the wrongdoers changed that saying with other than what they had been told. So We sent against them a plague from the sky because of the wrongs they used to commit.

7:161–62 See commentary on the parallel passage at 2:58–59.

---

¹⁶³Ask them about the town that was situated on the seaside, when they violated the Sabbath, when their fish would come to them on the Sabbath day, visibly on the shore, but on days when they were not keeping Sabbath they would not come to them. Thus did We test them because of the transgressions they used to commit.

¹⁶⁴When a group of them said, 'Why do you advise a people whom God will destroy or punish with a severe punishment?' They said, 'As an excuse before your Lord, and [with the hope] that they may be Godwary.'

¹⁶⁵So when they forgot what they had been reminded of, We delivered those who forbade evil [conduct] and seized the

wrongdoers with a terrible punishment because of the transgressions they used to commit.

¹⁶⁶When they defied [the command pertaining to] what they were forbidden from, We said to them, 'Be you spurned apes.'

7:163–66 Here and elsewhere (cf. 2:65; 4:47) the Qurʾān speaks of God's cursing those who broke the Sabbath. The idea of a curse for breaking the Sabbath is based ultimately on Numbers 15 (32–36), which relates how a man caught gathering wood on the Sabbath was stoned to death. In 2:65, as in this passage (v. 166), the Qurʾān mentions that God cursed the Sabbath breakers by commanding them to be apes. 5:60 includes a declaration that God made some people into "apes and swine," although it is not clear if the reference to swine should be connected to the punishment of the Sabbath breakers (see commentary on 4:47; 5:60). In the present passage the Qurʾān explains why this people broke the Sabbath, namely because they were tempted by fish that would appear to them on the Sabbath but not on other days. This explanation reflects an account in the Talmud (Qiddushin 72a) set in Babylon:

> Today they have turned away from the Almighty: a fishpond overflowed on the Sabbath, and they went and caught the fish on the Sabbath, whereat R. Aḥi son of R. Josiah declared the ban against them, and they renounced Judaism. (b. Qiddushin, 72a)

The idea of God's punishing an unfaithful people by transforming them into apes may be related to a second passage in the Babylonian Talmud (b. Sanhedrin, 109a) that has God punish the conspirators behind the Tower of Babel by turning them into apes (among other things):

> They split up into three parties. One said, "Let us ascend and dwell there"; the second said, "Let us ascend and serve idols"; and the third said, "Let us ascend and wage war [with God]." The party which proposed, "Let us ascend, and dwell there"—the Lord scattered them; the one that said, "Let us ascend and wage war" were turned to *apes,* spirits, devils, and night-demons. (b. Sanhedrin, 109a)

---

¹⁶⁷And when *your* Lord proclaimed that He would surely send against them, until the Day of Resurrection, those who would

inflict a terrible punishment on them. *Your* Lord is indeed swift in retribution, and indeed He is all-forgiving, all-merciful.

¹⁶⁸We dispersed them into communities around the earth: some of them were righteous, and some of them otherwise, and We tested them with good and bad [times] so that they may come back.

7:168 The term rendered here as "dispersed" (Ar. *qaṭṭaʿnāhum*) is closer to "divided." It is the same verb that appears in verse 160 for the division of Israel into twelve tribes (it is also used for the wrongful way in which humans divide up communities; see 21:93; 23:53). As this verse is in the middle of a section on the transgressions of the Jews, and God's punishment of them, it may be a reference to the diaspora of the Israelites.

---

¹⁶⁹Then they were succeeded by an evil posterity which inherited the Book: they grab the transitory gains of this lower world and say, 'It will be forgiven us.' And if similar transitory gains were to come their way, they would grab them too. Was not the covenant of the Book—and they have studied what is in it—taken with them that they shall not attribute anything except truth to God?

The abode of the Hereafter is better for those who are God-wary. Do you not exercise your reason?

¹⁷⁰As for those who hold fast to the Book and maintain the prayer—We do not waste the reward of those who set things right.

¹⁷¹When We plucked the mountain [and held it] above them as if it were a canopy (and they thought it was about to fall on them): 'Hold on with power to what We have given you and remember that which is in it, so that you may be Godwary.'

¹⁷²When *your* Lord took from the Children of Adam their descendants from their loins, and made them bear witness over

themselves, [He said to them,] 'Am I not your Lord?' They said, 'Yes indeed! We bear witness.' [This,] lest you should say on the Day of Resurrection, 'We were indeed unaware of this,' [173]or lest you should say, 'Our fathers ascribed partners [to God] before [us] and we were descendants after them. Will You then destroy us because of what the falsifiers did?'

[174]Thus do We elaborate the signs, so that they may come back.

7:171–74 The idea in verse 171 of the mountain—Mt. Sinai—being lifted above the Israelites reflects a tradition in the Babylonian Talmud. On this see commentary on 2:63. On the term translated here as "canopy" (Ar. *ẓulla*), Ya-huda (284) argues that it means something closer to a jar (inverted).

Most commentators see no connection between verse 171 and what follows (vv. 172–74). For example, in a note at the end of verse 171 Muhammad Asad comments, "This is the end, so far as this *surah* is concerned, of the story of the children of Israel." In fact, verses 172–74 reflect an opinion expressed in the Babylonian Talmud (Shevu'ot 39a) that the covenant on Mt. Sinai (cf. v. 171) was made between God and all later generations, not only those who stood on the base of the mountain:

> When [Moses] adjured Israel, he said to them: 'Know that not according to your own minds do I adjure you, but according to the mind of the Omnipres-ent, and my mind;' as it is said: Neither with you only do I make this covenant and this oath, but with Him that stands here with us. From those words we know that those who were standing by Mount Sinai were adjured; the com-ing generations, and proselytes who were later to be proselytised, how do we know that they too were adjured at that time? Because it is said: And also with him that is not here with us this day. (b. Shevu'ot 39a)

The declaration in verse 172 in which all humanity is made to testify that God will be their Lord also reflects Joshua 24:22: "Joshua then said to the people, 'You are witnesses to yourselves that you have chosen the Lord, to serve him.' They replied, 'Witnesses we are!'"

———

[175]*Relate* to them an account of him to whom We gave Our signs, but he cast them off. Thereupon Satan pursued him, and he

became one of the perverse. [176]Had We wished, We would have surely raised him by their means, but he clung to the earth and followed his [base] desires. So his parable is that of a dog: if you make for it, it lolls out its tongue, and if you let it alone, it lolls out its tongue. Such is the parable of the people who impugn Our signs. So *recount* these narratives, so that they may reflect.

7:175–76 It is not evident what person the Qurʾān has in mind here, although it is tempting to think of Judas, who, regretting his betrayal of Jesus, hanged himself (Mat 27:5). Bell (*Commentary* 1:260–61) thinks that this passage has a Christian origin but wonders whether it is connected instead to 2 Timothy 4:10 (which speaks of Demas, who deserted Paul); 1 Timothy 1:20 (which speaks of men whom Paul "handed over to Satan"), or to Philippians 3:2 ("Beware of dogs! Beware of evil workmen! Beware of self-mutilators!").

Wāḥidī recounts several traditions on this passage. The first tradition identifies the person who "became one of the perverse" (v. 175) as Balaam, a gentile prophet who sets off to curse the Israelites despite God's warning not to do so (although he does not ultimately curse them; see Num 22–24). A second tradition involves the poet Umayya Ibn Abī al-Ṣalt:

> This verse was revealed about Umayyah ibn Abi al-Salt al-Thaqafi who had studied the Scriptures and knew that God was about to send a messenger at around that time, hoping to be himself that messenger. When God sent Muḥammad, he envied him resentfully and disbelieved in him.

A third tradition involves an Israelite woman who turns into a dog, and then back into a woman:

> This verse is about a man who was given three prayers [to be] answered. This man had a wife called al-Basus who loved him, and from her he had children. One day she said to him: 'Let one of those answered prayers of yours be for me.' He said: 'One is for you, what do you wish for?' She said: 'Ask God to make me the most beautiful woman among the Children of Israel.' [He did and] when she knew that there was no one like her, she shunned him and wanted something else. The man prayed to God to make her a barking dog. And so, two prayers were wasted. Then, her children came to him and said: 'We cannot stand this, our mother has become a barking dog and people are insulting us because of her. Pray that God restores her to her initial state.' The man prayed and she became as she was before.'

¹⁷⁷Evil is the parable of the people who deny Our signs and used to wrong themselves. ¹⁷⁸Whomever God guides is rightly guided, and whomever He leads astray—it is they who are the losers.

¹⁷⁹Certainly We have winnowed out for hell many of the jinn and humans: they have hearts with which they do not understand, they have eyes with which they do not see, they have ears with which they do not hear. They are like cattle; rather, they are more astray. It is they who are the heedless.

7:179 The turns of phrase in this verse reflect Biblical language (cf. 2:7; 7:194–95; 22:46; see Rudolph, *Abhängigkeit,* 11–12):

"Now listen to this, stupid, brainless people who have eyes and do not see, who have ears and do not hear!" (Jer 5:21; cf. Deu 29:4; Psa 115:4–8; 135:15–18; Isa 6:10; Eze 12:2; Mar 8:18; Rom 11:8):

¹¹He told them, 'To you is granted the secret of the kingdom of God, but to those who are outside everything comes in parables,
¹²so that they may look and look, but never perceive; listen and listen, but never understand; to avoid changing their ways and being healed.' (Mar 4:11–12; cf. Mat 13:10–17; Act 28:27)

¹⁸⁰To God belong the Best Names, so supplicate Him by them, and abandon those who commit sacrilege in His names. Soon they shall be requited for what they used to do.

¹⁸¹Among those We have created are a nation who guide by the truth and do justice thereby.

¹⁸²As for those who impugn Our signs, We will draw them imperceptibly [into ruin], whence they do not know. ¹⁸³And I will grant them respite, for My devising is indeed sure.

¹⁸⁴Have they not reflected that there is no madness in their companion [and that] he is just a manifest warner? ¹⁸⁵Have they not contemplated the dominions of the heavens and the earth and whatever things God has created, and that maybe their time has already drawn near? So what discourse will they believe after this?! ¹⁸⁶Whomever God leads astray has no guide, and He leaves them bewildered in their rebellion.

¹⁸⁷They question *you* concerning the Hour, when will it set in? *Say,* 'Its knowledge is only with my Lord: none except Him shall manifest it at its time. It will weigh heavy on the heavens and the earth. It will not overtake you but suddenly.' They ask *you* as if *you* were in the know of it. *Say,* 'Its knowledge is only with God, but most people do not know.'

7:187 "But as for that day and hour, nobody knows it, neither the angels of heaven, nor the Son, no one but the Father alone" (Mat 24:36; cf. Mat 24:44, 50, 25:13; Mar 13:32; Luk 12:40, 46; Act 1:7; Rev 3:3).

---

¹⁸⁸*Say,* 'I have no control over any benefit for myself, nor [over] any harm, except what God may wish. Had I known the Unseen, I would have acquired much good, and no ill would have befallen me. I am only a warner and bearer of good news to a people who have faith.'

¹⁸⁹It is He who created you from a single soul, and made from it its mate, so that he might find comfort with her. So when he had covered her, she bore a light burden and passed [some time] with it. When she had grown heavy, they both invoked God, their Lord: 'If You give us a healthy [child], we will be surely grateful.'

¹⁹⁰Then when He gave them a healthy [child], they ascribed partners to Him in what He had given them. Far is God above [having] any partners that they ascribe [to Him]!

7:189–90 Here the Qurʾān suggests that Adam and Eve, after a son was born to them, fell away from the proper worship of God by associating other things with him. Wāḥidī explains this verse with a story involving the devil: "Initially, all the children of Adam and Eve died in their infancy. And so, Satan whispered to them: 'If a boy is born to you, call him ʿAbd al-Harith [the slave of al-Harith].' The name of Satan was, prior to that, al-Harith. Adam and Eve did as he asked them to do."

Regarding this passage, Speyer (*BEQ*, 79) alludes to a Talmudic passage (b. Sanhedrin, 56b) which (in the context of a discussion of the laws given to Noah) relates that God prohibited Adam idolatry (which could suggest that he had been idolatrous earlier).

---

¹⁹¹Do they ascribe [to Him] partners that create nothing and have been created themselves, ¹⁹²and who can neither help them, nor help themselves? ¹⁹³If you call them to guidance, they will not follow you: it is the same to you whether you call them or whether you are silent.

¹⁹⁴Indeed, those whom you invoke besides God are creatures like you. So invoke them: they should answer you, if you are truthful. ¹⁹⁵Do they have any feet to walk with? Do they have any hands to grasp with? Do they have any eyes to see with? Do they have any ears to hear with?

Say, 'Invoke your partners [that you ascribe to God] and try out your stratagems against me without granting me any respite. ¹⁹⁶My protector is indeed God who has sent down the Book, and He takes care of the righteous. ¹⁹⁷Those whom you invoke besides Him can neither help you, nor help themselves. ¹⁹⁸If you call them to guidance, they will not hear. *You* see them observing *you,* but they do not perceive.'

7:194–98 This passage reflects Psalm 115:4–8 (cf. 19:42, which puts similar words into the mouth of Abraham). See commentary on 37:88–96.

———————

[199] *Adopt* [a policy of] excusing [the faults of people], *bid* what is right, and *turn away* from the ignorant.

[200] Should a temptation from Satan disturb *you,* invoke the protection of God; indeed He is all-hearing, all-knowing. [201] When those who are Godwary are touched by a visitation of Satan, they remember [God] and, behold, they perceive. [202] But their brethren, they draw them into perversity, and then they do not spare [any harm].

[203] When *you* do not bring them a sign, they say, 'Why do *you* not improvise one?'

Say, 'I only follow what is revealed to me from my Lord; these are insights from your Lord, and guidance and mercy for people who have faith.'

[204] When the Qur'ān is recited, listen to it and be silent, maybe you will receive [God's] mercy.

[205] And remember *your* Lord morning and evening, beseechingly and reverentially, within *your* heart, without being loud, and *do not be* among the heedless. [206] Indeed, those who are [stationed] near *your* Lord do not disdain to worship Him. They glorify Him and prostrate to Him.

7:206 This verse (cf. 13:13; 21:19; 40:7; 41:38; 42:5; 69:17) offers a vision of angels' worshipping God that might be compared to Psalm 148 (esp. 1–5) and John's vision of heaven in Revelation 5:11–12.

8. *AL-ANFĀL*, THE SPOILS

In the Name of God, the All-beneficent, the All-merciful.

¹They ask *you* concerning the *anfāl. Say,* 'The *anfāl* belong to God and the Apostle.' So be wary of God and settle your differences, and obey God and His Apostle, if you are faithful.

8:1–19 *overview* Classical and modern commentators alike inevitably connect these verses (as well as vv. 42ff. and again 67ff.) with the story of the Battle of Badr and its spoils (*anfāl*). It is possible, however, that much (or all) of that story was written to explain these verses. The manner in which particular turns of phrase in the Qurʾān provoked commentators to tell such stories is seen in the comments of Wāḥidī on a phrase in verse 17—"And you did not throw when you threw, rather it was God who threw." He relates: "Most Qurʾānic commentators are of the opinion that [this] verse was revealed about the handful of valley dust that the Messenger of God threw on the idolaters on the Day of Badr. In that occasion he threw the handful of dust and said: 'Let the faces be distorted,' and some of this dust went into the eyes of every single idolater." In my opinion this tradition (like the other traditions Wāḥidī reports) is less a memory of "what really happened" and more a story invented to explain an unclear turn of phrase.

---

²The faithful are only those whose hearts tremble [with awe] when God is mentioned, and when His signs are recited to them,

they increase their faith, and who put their trust in their Lord, maintain the prayer and spend out of what We have provided them. ⁴It is they who are truly faithful. They shall have ranks near their Lord, forgiveness and a noble provision.

⁵As your Lord brought *you* out from *your* home with a judicious purpose, a part of the faithful were indeed reluctant. ⁶They disputed with you concerning the truth after it had become clear, as if they were being driven towards death while they looked on.

⁷When God promised you [victory over] one of the two companies, [saying], 'It is for you,' you were eager that it should be the one that was unarmed. But God desires to confirm the truth with His words and to root out the faithless, ⁸so that He may confirm the truth and bring falsehood to naught, though the guilty should be averse.

⁹When you appealed to your Lord for help, He answered you: 'I will aid you with a thousand angels in a file.'

¹⁰God did not appoint it but as a good news and to reassure your hearts. Victory comes only from God. God is indeed all-mighty, all-wise.

¹¹When He covered you with drowsiness as a [sense of] security from Him, and sent down water from the sky to purify you with it, and to repel from you the defilement of Satan, and to fortify your hearts, and to make [your] feet steady with it.

¹²Then your Lord signalled to the angels: 'I am indeed with you; so steady the faithful. I will cast terror into the hearts of the faithless. So strike their necks, and strike their every limb joint!'

¹³That, because they defied God and His Apostle. And whoever defies God and His Apostle, God is indeed severe in retribution. ¹⁴'Taste this, and [know] that for the faithless is the punishment of the Fire.'

¹⁵O you who have faith! When you encounter the faithless advancing [for battle], do not turn your backs [to flee] from them.

¹⁶Whoever turns his back [to flee] from them that day—unless [he is] diverting to fight or retiring towards another troop—he shall certainly earn God's wrath, and his refuge shall be hell, an evil destination.

¹⁷You did not kill them; rather, it was God who killed them; and *you* did not throw when *you* threw, rather, it was God who threw, that He might test the faithful with a good test from Himself. God is indeed all-hearing, all-knowing.

¹⁸Such is the case, and [know] that God undermines the stratagems of the faithless.

¹⁹If you sought a verdict, the verdict has already come to you; and if you cease [your belligerence against the Prophet and his followers], it is better for you; but if you resume, We [too] shall return and your troops will never avail you though they should be ever so many, and [know] that God is with the faithful.

²⁰O you who have faith! Obey God and His Apostle, and do not turn away from him while you hear [him]. ²¹Do not be like those who say, 'We hear,' though they do not hear. ²²Indeed, the worst of beasts in God's sight are the deaf and dumb who do not exercise their reason. ²³Had God known any good in them, He would have surely made them hear, and were He to make them hear, they would turn away, being disregardful.

²⁴O you who have faith! Answer God and the Apostle when he summons you to that which will give you life. Know that God intervenes between a man and his heart and that you will be mustered toward Him. ²⁵And beware of a punishment which shall not visit the wrongdoers among you exclusively, and know that God is severe in retribution. ²⁶Remember when you were few, abased in the land, and feared lest the people should despoil you, and He gave you refuge, and strengthened you with His help

and provided you with all the good things so that you may give thanks.

²⁷O you who have faith! Do not betray God and the Apostle, and do not betray your trusts knowingly. ²⁸Know that your possessions and children are only a test, and that God—with Him is a great reward.

²⁹O you who have faith! If you are wary of God, He will appoint a criterion for you, and absolve you of your misdeeds and forgive you, for God is dispenser of a mighty grace.

8:29 "Criterion" here is Qarai's rendering of *furqān,* in light of the Arabic meaning of the root *f.r.q.:* "to divide" (and indeed almost all translators, and most classical commentators, conceive of something similar). However, *furqān* here seems to have a meaning closer to the Aramaic or Syriac term (*purqānā*) from this same root, namely "salvation" or "redemption." Thus, we might render the passage in question as "If you are wary of [or simply "fear"] God, He shall save you [*yaj'alu la-kum furqānan*]." The authors of *Tafsīr al-Jalālayn* (without recognizing the Aramaic origin of *furqān*) seem to realize from context that this must be the case and relate: "He will grant you a [means of] separation, between yourselves and what you fear, so that you will be delivered." For *furqān* see commentary on 2:53, with further references.

---

³⁰When the faithless plotted against *you* to take *you* captive, or to kill or expel *you*—they plotted and God devised, and God is the best of devisers.

³¹When Our signs are recited to them, they say, 'We have heard already. If we want, we [too] can say like this. These are nothing but myths of the ancients.'

8:31 On the expression "myths of the ancients," see commentary on 68:15 (with further references).

---

³²And when they said, 'O God, if this be the truth from You, rain down upon us stones from the sky, or bring us a painful punishment.'

8:32 The topos of unbelievers' demanding a sign from heaven is common in the Gospels, as in Matthew 16:1: "The Pharisees and Sadducees came, and to put him to the test they asked if he would show them a sign from heaven" (cf. Mar 8:11; Luk 11:16). The way the Qur'ān has its opponents demand that stones rain down from heaven may harken back to the story of the destruction of Sodom (regarding which see Q 7:84; 11:82; 15:74; 25:40; 26:173; 27:58; 51:33ff; cf. the allusions to that story in Luk 17:28–30; Mat 11:23–24).

---

³³But God will not punish them while *you* are in their midst, nor will God punish them while they plead for forgiveness. ³⁴What [excuse] have they that God should not punish them, when they bar [the faithful] from the Holy Mosque, and they are not its custodians? Its custodians are only the Godwary, but most of them do not know. ³⁵Their prayer at the House is nothing but whistling and clapping. So taste the punishment because of what you used to deny. ³⁶Indeed, the faithless spend their wealth to bar from the way of God. Soon they will have spent it, then it will be a cause of regret to them, then they will be overcome, and the faithless will be gathered toward Hell, ³⁷so that God may separate the bad ones from the good, and place the bad on one another and pile them up together, and cast them into hell. It is they who are the losers.

8:36–37 It is not clear here (cf. 3:179) why the Qur'ān speaks about both bad and good among the faithless (as a rule it considers all the faithless to be bad). The idea that the bad and the good will be separated by God in a sort of eschatological triage is close that that of the parable of the wheat and tares (or darnel) in Mat 13:25–40 (cf. Mat 25:32–46).

---

³⁸*Say* to the faithless, if they cease [their belligerence against the Muslims], what is already past shall be forgiven them. But if they resume [their hostilities], the precedent of the predecessors has already come to pass.

³⁹Fight them until persecution is no more, and religion becomes exclusively for God. So if they desist, God indeed watches what they do. ⁴⁰But if they turn away, then know that God is your Master: an excellent master and an excellent helper!

⁴¹Know that whatever thing you may come by, a fifth of it is for God and the Apostle, for the relatives and the orphans, for the needy and the traveler, if you have faith in God and what We sent down to Our servant on the Day of Separation, the day when the two hosts met; and God has power over all things.

8:41 The Arabic behind "Day of Separation" is *yawm al-furqān*. This turn of phrase reflects the Syriac expression *yawmā d-purqānā*, "Day of Redemption," which appears in the Peshitta translation of Isaiah 49:8a: "Thus says the Lord: At the time of my favour I have answered you, on the day of salvation [Sy. *yawmā d-purqānā*] I have helped you." For more on the term *furqān*, see commentary on 2:53 (with further references).

---

⁴²When you were on the nearer side, and they on the farther side, while the caravan was below you, and had you agreed together on an encounter, you would have certainly failed to keep the tryst, but [it was] in order that God may carry through a matter that was bound to be fulfilled, so that he who perishes might

perish by a clear proof, and he who lives may live on by a clear proof, and God is indeed all-hearing, all-knowing.

⁴³When God showed them to you as few in *your* dream, and had He shown them as many, you would have lost heart, and disputed about the matter. But God spared you. He knows well indeed what is in the breasts. ⁴⁴And when He showed them to you as few in your eyes, when you met them [on the battlefield], and He made you [appear] few in their eyes, [it was] in order that God may carry through a matter that was bound to be fulfilled, and to God all matters are returned.

⁴⁵O you who have faith! When you meet a host [in battle], stand firm and remember God much so that you may prosper. ⁴⁶Obey God and His Apostle and do not dispute, or you will lose heart and your power will be gone. And be patient; indeed God is with the patient.

⁴⁷Do not be like those who left their homes vainly and to show off to the people, and to bar [other people] from the way of God, and God encompasses what they do.

⁴⁸When Satan made their deeds seem decorous to them, and said [to the faithless], 'None from among those people will defeat you today, and I will stand by you.' But when the two hosts sighted each other, he took to his heels, saying, 'Indeed, I am quit of you. I see what you do not see. Indeed, I fear God and God is severe in retribution.'

⁴⁹When the hypocrites said, and [also] those in whose hearts is a sickness, 'Their religion has deceived them.' But whoever puts his trust in God, then God is indeed all-mighty, all-wise.

⁵⁰Were you to see when the angels take away the faithless, striking their faces and their backs, [saying], 'Taste the punishment of the burning. ⁵¹That is because of what your hands have sent ahead, and God is not tyrannical to His servants.'

⁵²Like the precedent of Pharaoh's clan and those who were before them, who denied God's signs, so God seized them for their sins. God is indeed all-strong, severe in retribution.

8:52 Here, and in verse 54, the Qur'ān seems to make the destruction of the Egyptians a paradigmatic case of God's wrath against an unbelieving people. This may follow from Biblical verses such as 1 Samuel 6:6: "Why should you be as stubborn as Egypt and Pharaoh were? After he had brought disasters on them, did they not let the people leave?" (cr. Andrew O'Connor).

———————

⁵³That is because God never changes a blessing that He has bestowed on a people unless they change what is in their own souls, and God is all-hearing, all-knowing:

⁵⁴Like the precedent of Pharaoh's clan and those who were before them, who impugned the signs of their Lord; so We destroyed them for their sins and We drowned Pharaoh's clan, and they were all wrongdoers.

8:54 See commentary on 8:52.

———————

⁵⁵Indeed, the worst of beasts in God's sight are those who are faithless; so they will not have faith. ⁵⁶—Those with whom *you* made a treaty and who violated their treaty every time, and who are not Godwary. ⁵⁷So if *you* confront them in battle, *treat* them [in such a wise] as to disperse those who are behind them, so that they may take admonition. ⁵⁸And if *you* fear treachery from a people, *break off* [the treaty] with them in a like manner. Indeed, God does not like the treacherous. ⁵⁹Let the faithless not suppose

that they have outmaneuvered [God]. Indeed, they cannot frustrate [His power].

[60]Prepare against them whatever you can of [military] power and war-horses, awing thereby the enemy of God and your enemy, and others besides them, whom you do not know, but God knows them. And whatever you spend in the way of God will be repaid to you in full and you will not be wronged.

[61]If they incline toward peace, *you* [too] incline toward it and put *your* trust in God. Indeed, He is the All-hearing, the All-knowing.

[62]But if they desire to deceive *you,* God is indeed sufficient for you. It is He who strengthened *you* with His help and with the means of the faithful, [63]and united their hearts. Had *you* spent all [wealth] that is on the earth, *you* could not have united their hearts, but God united them together. He is indeed all-mighty, all-wise.

[64]O Prophet! Sufficient for *you* is God and those of the faithful who follow *you.* [65]O Prophet! Urge on the faithful to fight: If there be twenty steadfast men among you, they will overcome two hundred; and if there be a hundred of you, they will overcome a thousand of the faithless, for they are a lot who do not understand.

[66]Now God has lightened your burden, knowing that there is weakness in you. So if there be a hundred steadfast men among you, they will overcome two hundred; and if there be a thousand, they will overcome two thousand, by God's leave, and God is with the steadfast.

8:65–66 The promise that smaller numbers will overcome greater numbers may be related to Leviticus 26:7–8:

> [7]You will pursue your enemies and they will fall before your sword; [8]five of you pursuing a hundred of them, one hundred pursuing ten thousand; and your enemies will fall before your sword. (Lev 26:7–8; cf. Deu 32:30)

Verse 66 is closely related to Q 4:28 (see commentary on that verse for its possible relation to Matthew 11).

---

⁶⁷A prophet may not take captives until he has thoroughly deci-mated [the enemy] in the land. You desire the transitory gains of this world, while God desires [for you] [the reward of] the Hereafter, and God is all-mighty, all-wise. ⁶⁸Had it not been for a prior decree of God, there would have surely befallen you a great punishment for what you took. ⁶⁹Avail yourselves of the spoils you have taken, as lawful and good, and be wary of God. God is indeed all-forgiving, all-merciful.

8:67–69 Wāḥidī cites several traditions that connect these verses with a dis-pute over what to do with the Meccan prisoners captured at Badr. For example:

> "The Messenger of God consulted Abu Bakr regarding the prisoners of Badr, and the latter said: 'They are your people and clan, let them go!' But when he consulted ʿUmar, the latter said: 'Kill them.' The Messenger of God freed them in exchange for a ransom. God then revealed (It is not for any prophet to have captives until he hath made slaughter in the land) up to his words [Avail yourselves of the spoils you have taken]. When the Prophet met ʿUmar, he said to him: 'We almost incurred a misfortune as a result of opposing your view!'"

The way the Qurʾān reprimands its Prophet for taking prisoners is reminiscent of the story of Saul in I Samuel. Saul, who is in fact acts as a prophet (1 Samuel 10:11) is commanded to annihilate all of Amalek, but he keeps the best an-imals, and Amalek's king Agag, as spoils, for which he is reprimanded (1Sa 15:10–28).

---

⁷⁰O Prophet! *Say* to the captives who are in *your* hands, 'If God finds any good in your hearts, He will give you [something which is] better than what has been taken away from you, and He will

forgive you, and God is all-forgiving, all-merciful.' [71]But if they seek to betray *you,* then they have already betrayed God earlier, and He gave [*you*] power over them, and God is all-knowing, all-wise.

[72]Indeed, those who have believed and migrated and waged *jihād* with their possessions and persons in the way of God, and those who gave [them] shelter and help—they are heirs of one another. As for those who have believed but did not migrate, you have no heirship in relation to them whatsoever until they migrate. Yet if they ask your help for the sake of religion, it is incumbent on you to help them, excepting against a people with whom you have a treaty, and God watches what you do.

[73]As for the faithless, they are allies of one another. Unless you do the same, there will be strife in the land and great corruption.

[74]Those who have believed, migrated, and waged *jihād* in the way of God, and those who gave them shelter and help, it is they who are truly faithful. For them shall be forgiveness and a noble provision. [75]Those who believed afterwards and migrated, and waged *jihād* along with you, they belong with you; but the blood relatives are more entitled to inherit from one another in the Book of God. Indeed, God has knowledge of all things.

9. *AL-TAWBA*, REPENTANCE

¹[This is] a [declaration of] repudiation by God and His Apostle [addressed] to the polytheists with whom you had made a treaty:

9:1 Q 9 is the only Sura that is missing the divine invocation "In the Name of God, the All-beneficent, the All-merciful" (known as the *basmala*). Its absence suggests an intimate connection between the previous Sura. Indeed it is possible that the two Suras were originally one unit.

²Travel [unmolested] in the land for four months, but know that you cannot frustrate God, and that God will disgrace the faithless.

³[This is] an announcement from God and His Apostle to all the people on the day of the greater *hajj:* that God and His Apostle repudiate the polytheists: If you repent that is better for you; but if you turn your backs [on God], know that you cannot frustrate God, and inform the faithless of a painful punishment ⁴(excluding the polytheists with whom you have made a treaty, and who did not violate any [of its terms] with you, nor backed anyone against you. So fulfill the treaty with them until [the end of] its term. Indeed, God loves the Godwary).

⁵Then, when the sacred months have passed, kill the polytheists wherever you find them, capture them and besiege them, and

lie in wait for them at every ambush. But if they repent, maintain the prayer and give the *zakāt,* then let them alone. God is indeed all-forgiving, all-merciful.

⁶If any of the polytheists seeks asylum from *you, grant* him asylum until he hears the Word of God. Then *convey* him to his place of safety. That is because they are a people who do not know.

⁷How shall the polytheists have any [valid] treaty with God and His Apostle?! (Excluding those with whom you made a treaty at the Holy Mosque; so long as they are steadfast with you, be steadfast with them. Indeed, God loves the Godwary.) ⁸How? For if they get the better of you, they will observe toward you neither kinship nor covenant. They please you with their mouths while their hearts spurn you, and most of them are transgressors. ⁹They have sold the signs of God for a paltry gain, and have barred [the people] from His way. Evil indeed is what they have been doing. ¹⁰They observe toward a believer neither kinship nor covenant, and it is they who are the transgressors.

¹¹Yet if they repent and maintain the prayer and give the *zakāt,* then they are your brethren in faith. We elaborate the signs for a people who have knowledge. ¹²But if they break their pledges after their having made a treaty and revile your religion, then fight the leaders of unfaith—indeed they have no [commitment to] pledges—maybe they will desist.

¹³Will you not make war on a people who broke their pledges and resolved to expel the Apostle, and opened [hostilities] against you initially? Do you fear them? But God is worthier of being feared by you, should you be faithful. ¹⁴Make war on them so that God may punish them by your hands and humiliate them and help you against them, and heal the hearts of a faithful folk ¹⁵and

remove rage from their hearts, and God turns clemently to whomever He wishes, and God is all-knowing, all-wise

¹⁶Do you suppose that you will be let off while God has not yet ascertained those of you who wage *jihād* and those who do not take anyone as [their] confidant besides God and His Apostle and the faithful? God is well aware of what you do.

¹⁷The polytheists may not maintain God's mosques while they are witness to their own unfaith. Their works have failed and they shall remain in the Fire [forever]. ¹⁸Only those shall maintain God's mosques who believe in God and the Last Day, and maintain the prayer and give the *zakāt,* and fear no one except God. They, hopefully, will be among the guided.

¹⁹Do you regard the providing of water to *ḥajj* pilgrims and the maintenance of the Holy Mosque as similar [in worth] to someone who has faith in God and [believes in] the Last Day and wages *jihād* in the way of God? They are not equal with God, and God does not guide the wrongdoing lot.

²⁰Those who have believed and migrated, and waged *jihād* in the way of God with their possessions and persons have a greater rank near God, and it is they who are the triumphant. ²¹Their Lord gives them the good news of His mercy and [His] pleasure, and for them there will be gardens with lasting bliss, ²²to remain in them forever. With God indeed is a great reward.

²³O you who have faith! Do not befriend your fathers and brothers if they prefer unfaith to faith. Those of you who befriend them—it is they who are the wrongdoers. ²⁴*Say,* 'If your fathers and your sons, your brethren, your spouses, and your kinsfolk, the possessions that you have acquired, the business you fear may suffer, and the dwellings you are fond of, are dearer to you than God and His Apostle and to waging *jihād* in His way, then

wait until God issues His edict, and God does not guide the transgressing lot.

9:24 As Speyer (*BEQ*, 453) notes, this verse is close to Matthew 10:37: "No one who prefers father or mother to me is worthy of me. No one who prefers son or daughter to me is worthy of me" (cf. Luk 14:26).

---

[25]God has already helped you in many situations, and on the day of Ḥunayn, when your great number impressed you, but it did not avail you in any way, and the earth became narrow for you in spite of its expanse, whereupon you turned your backs [to flee]. [26]Then God sent down His composure upon His Apostle and upon the faithful, and He sent down hosts you did not see, and He punished the faithless, and that is the requital of the faithless.

9:26 On the term that Qarai translates as "composure" (Ar. *sakīna*), see commentary on 2:248 (with further references).

---

[27]Then God will turn clemently after that to whomever He wishes. God is indeed all-forgiving, all-merciful.

[28]O you who have faith! The polytheists are indeed unclean: so let them not approach the Holy Mosque after this year. Should you fear poverty, God will enrich you out of His bounty if He wishes. God is indeed all-knowing, all-wise.

[29]Fight those from among those who were given the Book who do not have faith in God nor [believe] in the Last Day, nor forbid what God and His Apostle have forbidden, nor practise the true religion, until they pay the tribute out of hand, degraded.

9:29 This verse is generally understood—in light of its reference to "those who were given the Book"—to legislate how Muslims are to deal with Jewish and Christian communities (and thus to mark a shift from v. 28, which is generally understood to refer to pagans). Yet Jews and Christians by definition believe in God and (for the most part) in the Last Day. Moreover, it is not clear how this verse could establish conditions under which Muslims are to wage war against Jews and Christians (how indeed could Muslims fight against *only* those Jews and Christians who don't believe in God and leave the rest alone?).

---

[30]The Jews say, 'Ezra is the son of God,' and the Christians say, 'Christ is the son of God.' That is an opinion that they mouth, imitating the opinions of the faithless of former times. May God assail them, where do they stray?!

9:30 The name rendered by Qarai as "Ezra" (Hb. *'ezrā*) is *'uzayr*. However, Jews do not consider Ezra "son of God" in any way parallel to the way Christians consider Christ the "Son of God" (and indeed Ezra is far from the most important personality in Jewish teaching). To explain the place of Ezra in this verse, scholars sometimes refer to the Talmud. According to one opinion cited therein: "Had Moses not preceded him, Ezra would have been worthy of receiving the Torah for Israel" (b. Sanhedrin 21b). Others refer to the apocryphal work 4 Ezra (or 2 Esdras), which has God refer to the messiah as "my son" (4Ez 7:28–29; cf. 4Ez 14:9–10).

It is possible that the Qur'ān does not mean Ezra with *'uzayr* (both Hamidullah and Paret leave *'uzayr* untranslated). One possibility is that *'uzayr* is the name of an angel. The *Book of Watchers* (the first part of 1 Enoch; see 8:1–2) accuses an angel named Azaz'el (*'z'zl*) or Azael (*'z'l*) of teaching impious things to humans (and later describes his fall from heaven). It is possible that the Qur'ān is accusing the Jews of having recourse to this (evil) angel, the name of which was emended from something like *'azayl* to Arabic *'uzayr,* assuming that the "l" was misread, or misheard, as "r." The description of an angel as "son of God" was indeed known among Jews from the classical and Late Antique period. Philo (*On Husbandry,* 51) describes the logos of God as an archangel and the "son of God." In the Rabbinic work *Sefer Hekhalot* (perhaps from the sixth or seventh century AD) the angel Metatron is presented as Enoch transformed, and is described as a second god. One might also note the reference to angel worship in Colossians 2:16–18 (see commentary on 17:40). On this see Patricia Crone's "The *Book of Watchers* in the Qur'ān," 36–48.

---

³¹They have taken their scribes and their monks as lords besides God, and also Christ, Mary's son; though they were commanded to worship only the One God, there is no god except Him; He is far too immaculate to have any partners that they ascribe [to Him]!

9:31 This verse is parallel to the Qur'ān's accusation elsewhere that the Christians and Jews turn their prophets or angels into gods (on this see esp. 3:80); here it accuses them of turning their religious leaders into gods. It is not evident that the Qur'ān is critiquing Christian doctrine on Christ in this verse. While Qarai translates "and also Christ, Mary's son," the Arabic text might be read (by putting *al-masīḥ* in the genitive) as "besides God and Christ, Mary's son." This reading not only better matches the syntax of the verse but also focuses attention on the question of Jewish and Christian religious leaders.

This verse is thus related to Q 3:64, where the believers tell the People of the Book to agree not to "take each other as lords besides God." In verse 9:31 (and again in verse 34), there is a particular polemic directed at the religious leaders of the Jews and Christians, whom the Qur'ān holds responsible for keeping people from the proper worship of God. Indeed both Jewish texts, such as the Mishnah, and Christian texts, such as the *Didascalia,* emphasize the importance of obeying religious leaders (cr. Holger Zellentin):

> Let the honour of thy disciple be as dear to thee as thine own, and the honour of thy colleague as the reverence for thy teacher (*rab*), and the reverence for thy teacher (*rab*) as the fear of heaven. (m. Avot 4:12)

> "The bishop is a servant of the word and mediator, but to you a teacher, and your father after God. . . . This is your chief and your leader and he is a mighty king to you. He guides in the place of the Almighty. But let him be honored by you as God, because the bishop sits for you in the place of the Almighty God." (*Didascalia,* chap. 9, p. 100)

The hyperbolic quality of the Qur'ān's rhetoric is evident here; the Qur'ān is not worried about heretical sects which actually worship their scribes and monks. Rather, it is employing satire for the sake of its religious apologetics. An echo might be heard of the polemics of Jesus in the Gospels against the scribes and Pharisees (see Mat 23:2–4; Mar 12:38–39; Luk 11:42–44, 20:46).

The end of this verse represents a particularly vigorous polemic against Jews and Christians, when it proclaims *subḥānahu ʿammā yushrikūn:* "He is far too immaculate to have any partners that they ascribe [to Him]!" In other words, this verse suggests that Jews and Christians are *mushrikūn,* a term otherwise thought to be a label for pagans.

---

³²They desire to put out the light of God with their mouths, but God is intent on perfecting His light though the faithless should be averse.

³³It is He who has sent His Apostle with guidance and the religion of truth, that He may make it prevail over all religions, though the polytheists should be averse.

³⁴O you who have faith! Indeed, many of the scribes and monks wrongfully eat up the people's wealth, and bar [them] from the way of God. Those who treasure up gold and silver, and do not spend it in the way of God, inform them of a painful punishment ³⁵on the day when these shall be heated in hellfire and therewith branded on their foreheads, their sides and their backs [and told]: 'This is what you treasured up for yourselves! So taste what you have treasured!'

9:34–35 Here we can again (cf. 9:31) hear the echo of Jesus' polemic against the scribes and the Pharisees, presented most dramatically in Matthew (see, e.g., Mat 23:15–17). On this see Emran El-Badawi, *The Qur'ān and the Aramaic Gospel Traditions* (chap. 4). The Qur'ān seems to substitute "scribes and monks" for the "scribes and Pharisees" of Matthew. As mentioned by Speyer (*BEQ*, 453), the reference to the "gold and silver" stored up by the avaricious which will inflict pain on their bodies in the afterlife seems very close to that in James 5:3: "All your gold and your silver are corroding away, and the same corrosion will be a witness against you and eat into your body. It is like a fire which you have stored up for the final days." Holger Zellentin ("*Aḥbār* and *Ruhbān*," 281) notes how the *Didascalia* (94) warns bishops not to "swallow" the gifts of their flocks, but to share them with those in want. Zellentin also refers to the warning of Jesus in the Gospels against scribes who "devour" (in the Syriac Peshitta the word is "eat") the property of widows. See Mark 12:40; Luke 20:47.

---

[36]Indeed, the number of months with God is twelve months in God's Book, the day when He created the heavens and the earth. Of these, four are sacred. That is the upright religion. So do not wrong yourselves during them.

Fight all the polytheists, just as they fight you together, and know that God is with the Godwary.

[37]*Nasī* [intercalation] is indeed an increase in unfaith, whereby the faithless are led [further] astray. They allow it in one year and forbid it another year, so as to fit in with the number which God has made inviolable, thus permitting what God has forbidden. Their evil deeds appear to them as decorous, and God does not guide the faithless lot.

[38]O you who have faith! What is the matter with you that when you are told: 'Go forth in the way of God,' you sink heavily to the ground? Are you pleased with the life of this world instead of the Hereafter? But the wares of the life of this world are insignificant compared with the Hereafter.

9:38 On the Qur'ān's comparison here of this world and the next, see commentary on Q 13:26.

---

[39]If you do not go forth, He will punish you with a painful punishment and replace you with another people, and you will not hurt Him in the least, and God has power over all things. [40]If you

do not help him, then God did certainly help him when the faithless expelled him as one of two [refugees], when the two of them
were in the cave, and he said to his companion, 'Do not grieve;
God is indeed with us.' Then God sent down His composure upon
him and strengthened him with hosts you did not see, and He
made the word of the faithless the lowest, and the word of God is
the highest, and God is all-mighty, all-wise.

9:40 On the term Qarai translates as "composure" (Ar. *sakīna*), see commentary on 2:248 (with further references).

---

⁴¹Go forth, whether [armed] lightly or heavily, and wage *jihād*
with your possessions and persons in the way of God. That is
better for you, should you know. ⁴²Were it an accessible gain or a
short journey, they would have surely followed *you;* but the distance seemed too far to them. Yet they will swear by God: 'If we
could, we would have surely gone forth with you.' They [merely]
destroy themselves, and God knows that they are indeed liars.
    ⁴³May God excuse *you!* Why did *you* grant them leave [to stay
behind] before those who told the truth were evident to *you* and
you had ascertained the liars?
    ⁴⁴Those who believe in God and the Last Day do not ask *your*
leave [exempting them] from waging *jihād* with their possessions
and their persons, and God knows best the Godwary. ⁴⁵Only those
seek a leave [of exemption] from you who do not believe in God
and the Last Day and whose hearts are in doubt, so they waver in
their doubt.
    ⁴⁶Had they desired to go forth, they would have surely made
some preparations for it; but God was averse to arouse them, so
He held them back, and it was said [to them], 'Be seated with
those who sit back.' ⁴⁷Had they gone forth with you, they would

have only added to your troubles, and they would have spread rumours in your midst, seeking to cause sedition among you. They have some spies among you, and God knows best the wrongdoers. [48]They certainly sought to cause sedition earlier and upset the matters for *you,* until the truth came and God's command prevailed, much as they were averse.

[49]Among them there are some who say, 'Give me leave, and do not put me to temptation.' Behold, they have already fallen into temptation and indeed hell besieges the faithless.

[50]If some good should befall *you,* it upsets them; but if an adversity befalls *you,* they say, 'We had already taken our precautions in advance,' and they go away boasting. [51]*Say,* 'Nothing will befall us except what God has ordained for us. He is our Master, and in God alone let all the faithful put their trust.' [52]*Say,* 'Do you await anything to befall us except one of the two excellent things? But we await that God will visit on you a punishment, from Him, or by our hands. So wait! We too are waiting along with you.'

[53]*Say,* 'Spend willingly or unwillingly, it shall never be accepted from you; for you are indeed a transgressing lot.' [54]Nothing stops their charities from being accepted except that they have no faith in God and His Apostle and do not perform the prayer except lazily, and do not spend but reluctantly. [55]So let not their wealth and children impress you: God only desires to punish them with these in the life of this world, and that their souls may depart while they are faithless.

[56]They swear by God that they belong with you, but they do not belong with you. Rather, they are a frightened lot. [57]If they could find a refuge, or a hideout or a hole [to creep into], they would turn to it in frantic haste.

[58]There are some of them who blame *you* regarding [the distribution of] the charities: if they are given from them, they are pleased, but if they are not given from them, behold, they are

displeased. [59][It would have been better] if they had been pleased with what God and His Apostle gave them, and had said, 'God is sufficient for us; God and His Apostle will give us out of His grace. Indeed, we beseech God.'

[60]The charities are only for the poor and the needy and those employed to collect them, and those whose hearts are to be reconciled, and for [the freedom of] the slaves and the debtors, and [to be spent]in the way of God, and for the traveler. [This is] an ordinance from God, and God is all-knowing, all-wise.

[61]Among them are those who torment the Prophet, and say, 'He is an ear.' *Say,* 'An ear that is good for you. He has faith in God and trusts the faithful, and is a mercy for those of you who have faith.' As for those who torment the Apostle of God, there is a painful punishment for them.

[62]They swear to you by God to please you; but God and His Apostle are worthier that they should please Him, should they be faithful. [63]Do they not know that whoever opposes God and His Apostle, there awaits him the Fire of hell, to remain in it [forever]? That is a great disgrace.

[64]The hypocrites are apprehensive lest a *sūrah* should be sent down against them, informing them about what is in their hearts. *Say,* 'Go on deriding. God will indeed bring out what you are apprehensive of.'

[65]If *you* question them [regarding their conduct], they will surely say, 'We were just gossiping and amusing ourselves.' *Say,* 'Were you deriding God, His signs, and His apostles? [66]Do not make excuses. You have disbelieved after your faith.' If We do forgive a group among you, We will punish another group, for they have been guilty.

[67]The hypocrites, men and women, are all alike: they bid what is wrong and forbid what is right, and are tight-fisted. They have forgotten God, so He has forgotten them. The hypocrites are

indeed the transgressors. [68]God has promised the hypocrites, men and women, and the faithless, the Fire of hell, to remain in it [forever]. That suffices them. God has cursed them, and there is a lasting punishment for them.

[69][Hypocrites! Your case is] similar to those who were before you, who were more powerful than you and more abounding in wealth and children: they enjoyed their share [of worldly existence]; you too enjoy your share, just like those who were before you enjoyed their share, and you have gossiped [impiously] as they gossiped. They are the ones whose works have failed in this world and the Hereafter, and it is they who are the losers.

[70]Has there not come to them the account of those who were before them—the people of Noah, 'Ād, and Thamūd, and the people of Abraham, the inhabitants of Midian, and the towns that were overturned? Their apostles brought them manifest proofs. So it was not God who wronged them, but it was they who used to wrong themselves.

9:70 In this verse the Qur'ān alludes to God's destruction of those peoples who rejected his messengers, and thereby gives its audience a good reason not to reject the latest messenger. The list of the peoples (cf. the slightly different lists in 14:9; 22:42–44) who have been destroyed concludes with a reference to *al-mu'tafikāt* (Qarai: "towns that were overturned"; cf. 53:53, 69:9). This Arabic term is likely related to the use of the root *h-p-k* in both the Hebrew and Aramaic versions of Genesis 19:25 ("He overthrew [Hb. *wayyahapōk;* Am. *wahpak*] those cities and the whole plain, with all the people living in the cities and everything that grew there") to indicate how God "overthrew" Sodom and Gomorrah—indeed Qur'ān 11:82 relates that God "overturned" Lot's city. This is, in other words, likely a reference to the people of Lot. The reference to "the people of Abraham" in this verse is curious inasmuch as the Qur'ān never mentions the punishment, or destruction, of his people. The Qur'ān may be referring to a tradition found in the Christian text *Apocalypse of Abraham* (8:1–6), by which God consumes with fire the house of idols in which Abraham's own father, Terah, works, killing him and all those inside.

For more detail on the "punishment story" of Noah, see commentary on 11:25–39; on the "punishment story" of "the towns that were overturned" (i.e., Lot), see commentary on 11:69–73.

---

⁷¹But the faithful, men and women, are friends of one another: they bid what is right and forbid what is wrong and maintain the prayer, give the *zakāt,* and obey God and His Apostle. It is they to whom God will soon grant His mercy. God is indeed all-mighty, all-wise.

⁷²God has promised the faithful, men and women, gardens with streams running in them, to remain in them [forever], and good dwellings in the Gardens of Eden. Yet God's pleasure is greater [than all these]; that is the great success.

9:72 The Qur'ān here (see also 13:23; 16:31; 18:31; 19:61; 20:76; 35:33; 38:50; 40:8; 61:12; 98:8) follows the teaching of Syriac Christian fathers such as Ephrem that paradise *is* the Garden of Eden. In his *Hymns on Paradise* (9:1a) Ephrem writes: "In the world there is struggle / in Eden a crown of glory."

Muhammad Asad, however, follows the medieval lexicographers who seek an Arabic etymology for the word (*ʿadn*). He adds an interpretation based on Hebrew, and translates "perpetual bliss" instead of Eden (Asad, *The Message of the Qurʾān,* 790n25 [on 38:49]). On the streams of paradise, see commentary on 2:25 (with further references).

---

⁷³O Prophet! Wage *jihād* against the faithless and the hypocrites, and be severe with them. Their refuge shall be hell, and it is an evil destination.

⁷⁴They swear by God that they did not say it. But they certainly did utter the word of unfaith and renounced faith after their *islām.* They contemplated what they could not achieve, and they were

vindictive only because God and His Apostle had enriched them out of His grace. Yet if they repent, it will be better for them; but if they turn away, God will punish them with a painful punishment in this world and the Hereafter, and they will not find any friend or helper in this land.

[75]Among them are those who made a pledge with God: 'If He gives us out of His bounty, we will surely give the *zakāt* and we will be among the righteous.' [76]But when He gave them out of His bounty, they begrudged it and turned away, being disregardful.

[77]So He caused hypocrisy to ensue in their hearts until the day they will encounter Him, because of their going back on what they had promised God and because of the lies they used to tell. [78]Do they not know that God knows their secret [thoughts] and [hears] their secret talks and that God is knower of all that is Unseen?

[79]Those who blame the voluntary donors from among the faithful concerning the charities and ridicule those who do not find [anything] except [what] their means [permit], God will put them to ridicule and there is a painful punishment for them.

[80]Whether *you* plead forgiveness for them or do not plead forgiveness for them, even if *you* plead forgiveness for them seventy times, God will never forgive them because they defied God and His Apostle; and God does not guide the transgressing lot.

9:80 The Qur'ān here seems to transform the message of forgiveness in Matthew 18:21–22:

> [21]Then Peter went up to him and said, 'Lord, how often must I forgive my brother if he wrongs me? As often as seven times?'
> [22]Jesus answered, 'Not seven, I tell you, but seventy-seven times.

Whereas Jesus teaches Peter that one is to forgive without limit (using seventy-seven as a symbolic number), the Qur'ān teaches the Prophet that God will never forgive unbelievers, no matter how many times he were to ask for their forgiveness (using seventy as a symbolic number).

---

[81]Those who were left behind boasted for sitting back against [the command of] the Apostle of God, and were reluctant to wage *jihād* with their possessions and persons in the way of God, and they said, 'Do not go forth in this heat.' *Say,* The fire of hell is severer in heat, should they understand. [82]So let them laugh a little; much will they weep as a requital for what they used to perpetrate.

[83]If God brings *you* back [from the battlefront] to a group of them and they seek *your* permission to go forth, *say,* 'You shall never go forth with me, and you shall not fight with me against any enemy. You were indeed pleased to sit back the first time, so sit back with those who stay behind.'

[84]And never *pray* over any of them when he dies, nor *stand* at his graveside. They indeed defied God and His Apostle and died as transgressors. [85]Let not their possessions or their children impress *you.* God only desires to punish them with these in this world, and that their souls may depart while they are faithless.

[86]When a *sūrah* is sent down [declaring]: 'Have faith in God, and wage *jihād* along with His Apostle, the affluent among them ask *you* for leave, and say, 'Let us remain with those who sit back.' [87]They are pleased to be with those who stay back, and their hearts have been sealed. So they do not understand.

[88]But the Apostle and the faithful who are with him wage *jihād* with their possessions and persons, and to such belong all the blessings, and it is they who are the felicitous. [89]God has prepared for them gardens with streams running in them, to remain in them [forever]. That is the great success.

9:89 On the streams of paradise, see commentary on 2:25 (with further references).

---

⁹⁰Some of the Bedouins who sought to be excused came, so that they may be granted leave [to stay back]; while those who lied to God and His Apostle sat back. Soon a painful punishment will visit the faithless among them.

9:90 "Bedouins" here (cf. also 9:97–99, 101, 120; 33:20; 48:11, 16; 49:14) is a translation of *al-a'rāb* ("the Arabs"). The meaning seems to follow from the use in various Semitic languages of the root *'-r-b* to refer to nomads or dwellers of the wilderness (and not only to Arabs or Arabic speakers). In the Hebrew Bible the cognate Hebrew terms reflect this use. "Arabs" are simply nomads of the wilderness, and "Arabia" is the wilderness in which they roam. Note, for example, Ezekiel 27:21, "Arabia and all the sheikhs of Kedar were your customers; they paid in lambs, rams and he-goats"; and Isaiah 13, which describes the ruins of Babylon with the remark "Never again will anyone live there or reside there for all generations to come. Never again will the Arab pitch his tent there, or the shepherds bring their flocks to rest" (Isa 13:19–20; cf. also 2Ch 22:1; Jer 25:24).

---

⁹¹There is no blame on the weak, nor on the sick, nor on those who do not find anything to spend, so long as they are sincere to God and His Apostle. There is no [cause for] blaming the virtuous, and God is all-forgiving, all-merciful. ⁹²Nor [is there any blame] on those to whom, when they came to *you* to provide them with a mount, *you* said, 'I do not find any mount for you,' and they turned back, their eyes flowing with tears, grieved because they did not find any means to spend.

⁹³The blame lies only on those who ask *your* leave [to stay behind] though they are well-off. They are pleased to be with those

who stay back; God has set a seal on their hearts, so they do not know [the outcome of their conduct].

⁹⁴They will offer you excuses when you return to them. *Say,* 'Do not make excuses; we will never believe you. God has informed us of your state of affairs. God and His Apostle will observe your conduct, then you will be returned to the Knower of the sensible and the Unseen, and He will inform you concerning what you used to do.'

⁹⁵When you return to them, they will swear to you by God, so that you may leave them alone. So leave them alone. They are indeed filth, and their refuge shall be hell, a requital for what they used to perpetrate. ⁹⁶They swear to you that you may be reconciled to them. But even if you are reconciled to them, God will not be reconciled to the transgressing lot.

⁹⁷The Bedouins are more obdurate in unfaith and hypocrisy, and more apt to be ignorant of the precepts that God has sent down to His Apostle, and God is all-knowing, all-wise.

⁹⁸Among the Bedouins are those who regard what they spend as a loss, and they watch for a reversal of your fortunes. Theirs shall be an adverse turn of fortune, and God is all-hearing, all-knowing.

⁹⁹Yet among the Bedouins are [also] those who believe in God and the Last Day, and regard what they spend as [a means of attaining] nearness to God and the blessings of the Apostle. Now, it shall indeed bring them nearness, and God will admit them into His mercy. God is indeed all-forgiving, all-merciful.

¹⁰⁰The early vanguard of the Emigrants and the Helpers and those who followed them in virtue—God is pleased with them and they are pleased with Him, and He has prepared for them gardens with streams running in them, to remain in them forever. That is the great success.

9:100 On the streams of paradise, see commentary on 2:25 (with further references).

---

[101]There are hypocrites among the Bedouins around you and among the people of Madīnah, steeped in hypocrisy. *You* do not know them; We know them, and We will punish them twice, then they shall be consigned to a great punishment.

[102][There are] others who have confessed to their sins, having mixed up righteous conduct with other that was evil. Maybe God will accept their repentance. God is indeed all-forgiving, all-merciful. [103]*Take* charity from their possessions to cleanse them and purify them thereby, and bless them. *Your* blessing is indeed a comfort to them, and God is all-hearing, all-knowing.

9:103 The notion that giving alms "cleanses" one reflects Tobit 12:9, which speaks of almsgiving as "purging" (Gk. *katharizō*) sin. (cr. Andrew Geist).

---

[104]Do they not know that it is God who accepts the repentance of His servants and receives the charities, and that it is God who is the All-clement, the All-merciful?

[105]*Say,* 'Go on working: God will see your conduct, and His Apostle and the faithful [as well], and you will be returned to the Knower of the sensible and the Unseen, and He will inform you concerning what you used to do.'

[106][There are] others waiting God's edict: either He will punish them, or turn to them clemently, and God is all-knowing, all-wise.

[107]As for those who took to a mosque for sabotage and defiance, and to cause division among the faithful, and for the pur-

pose of ambush [to be used] by those who have fought God and His Apostle before—they will surely swear, 'We desired nothing but good,' and God bears witness that they are indeed liars. [108]*Do not stand* in it ever!

A mosque founded on Godwariness from the [very] first day is worthier that *you* stand in it [for prayer]. Therein are men who love to keep pure, and God loves those who keep pure. [109]Is he who founds his building on Godwariness and [the pursuit of God's] pleasure better-off or someone who founds his building on the brink of a collapsing bank which collapses with him into the fire of hell? God does not guide the wrongdoing lot.

[110]The building they have built will never cease to be [a source of] disquiet in their hearts until their hearts are cut into pieces, and God is all-knowing, all-wise.

9:109–10 The Qur'ān here uses language that reflects the parable of a house built on sand in Matthew 7 (cf. *BEQ,* 454):

[24]'Therefore, everyone who listens to these words of mine and acts on them will be like a sensible man who built his house on rock.

[25]Rain came down, floods rose, gales blew and hurled themselves against that house, and it did not fall: it was founded on rock.

[26]But everyone who listens to these words of mine and does not act on them will be like a stupid man who built his house on sand.

[27]Rain came down, floods rose, gales blew and struck that house, and it fell; and what a fall it had!' (Mat 7:24–27)

---

[111]Indeed, God has bought from the faithful their souls and their possessions for paradise to be theirs: they fight in the way of God, kill, and are killed. A promise binding upon Him in the Torah and the Evangel and the Qur'ān. And who is truer to his promise than

God? So rejoice in the bargain you have made with Him, and that is the great success.

9:111 The point of this verse is that those who are prepared to give their lives to God in the holy war are promised paradise as a payment for their services (cf. 2:245; 4:74; 61:10–12). The idea that the martyrs have a special assurance of paradise follows from the Qur'ān's teaching elsewhere that the act of martyrdom involves forgiveness of sin. This teaching is close to that of the Syriac fathers (see commentary on 2:154, with further references). It is curious that the Qur'ān insists that the promise of heaven for holy warriors is found in the Torah and the Gospel (or "Evangel"); heaven is not found in the Torah and holy war is not found in the Gospels.

The notion that God possesses the believers, having bought them, is central to Paul's argument in 1 Corinthians for sexual morality: "You are not your own property, then; you have been bought at a price. So use your body for the glory of God" (1Co 6:20; cf. 1Co 7:21–23; 1Pe 1:18–19)

---

¹¹²[The faithful are] penitent, devout, celebrators of God's praise, wayfarers, who bow [and] prostrate [in prayer], bid what is right and forbid what is wrong, and keep God's bounds—and *give* good news to the faithful.

¹¹³The Prophet and the faithful may not plead for the forgiveness of the polytheists, even if they should be [their] relatives, after it has become clear to them that they will be the inmates of hell.

¹¹⁴Abraham's pleading forgiveness for his father was only to fulfill a promise he had made him. So when it became clear to him that he was an enemy of God, he repudiated him. Indeed, Abraham was most plaintive and forbearing.

9:113–14 Here the Qur'ān first (v. 113) insists that its prophet not pray for the unbelievers and then (v. 114) explains why Abraham prayed for his unbelieving father (in 26:86 the Qur'ān quotes his prayer), namely that he had promised to do so, an explanation which follows from the dialogue between Abraham and his father elsewhere. In 19:47 Abraham declares to his father: "I shall plead with my Lord to forgive you" (another version of this declaration is found in 60:4).

Behind the Qur'ān's discussion of Abraham's prayer for his father is a real concern to convince believers not to have sympathy for unbelievers, even unbelieving family members (see 58:22), something which presumably reflects an expression of Muḥammad's own desire that his followers break off all ties with those who have not accepted his message. The choice of Abraham to illustrate this principle is connected to the Jewish and Christian midrashic traditions which make his father Terah a maker of idols in Ur and Abraham a faithful monotheist who seeks to convince Terah to abandon idolatry. This scenario is found, for example, in the *Apocalypse of Abraham:*

> Listen, Terah, my father, I shall seek in your presence the God who created all the gods which we consider! For who is it, or which one is it, who colored heaven and made the sun golden, who has given light to the moon and the stars with it, who has dried the earth in the midst of many waters, who set you yourself among the elements, and who now has chosen me in the distraction of my mind? Will he reveal himself by himself to us? He is the God! (*Apocalypse of Abraham* 7:11–12)

The Qur'ān's interest in describing the way fidelity to God divides a son from his father (or, in the case of Noah in 11:42–47, a father from his son) may also be connected to the insistence of Jesus in the Gospels that his message will divide families (Mat 10:34–37; cf. Luk 12:51–53; 14:25).

Wāḥidī relates three stories meant to explain this passage. The first two have Muḥammad visit his uncle Abū Ṭālib on his deathbed and attempt unsuccessfully to convince him to profess a belief in Islam. When Abū Ṭālib dies without doing so, Muḥammad begins praying that he will be forgiven and God, to stop him from doing so, reveals these verses. In a third story, related on the authority of Muḥammad's companion Ibn Masʿūd, Muḥammad weeps at his mother's grave when he learns that God will not forgive his mother (for being a polytheist). He declares: "The words of God . . . were revealed and I was seized by the tenderness which a son has toward his mother. This is the reason why I wept."

---

[115]God does not lead any people astray after He has guided them, until He has made clear for them what they should beware of. Indeed, God has knowledge of all things.

[116]Indeed, to God belongs the kingdom of the heavens and the earth. He gives life and brings death. And besides God you do not have any friend or helper.

[117]Certainly God turned clemently to the Prophet and the Emigrants and the Helpers, who followed him in the hour of difficulty, after the hearts of a part of them were about to swerve. Then He turned clemently to them—indeed He is most kind and merciful to them [118]—and to the three who were left behind. When the land became narrow for them with [all] its expanse, and their own souls weighed heavily on them, and they knew that there was no refuge from God except in Him, then He turned clemently toward them so that they might be penitent. Indeed, God is the All-clement, the All-merciful.

[119]O you who have faith! Be wary of God, and be with the Truthful.

[120]It is not fitting for the people of Madīnah and the Bedouins around them to hang back behind the Apostle of God and prefer their own lives to his life. That is because they neither experience any thirst, nor fatigue, nor hunger, in the way of God, nor do they tread any ground enraging the faithless, nor do they gain any ground against an enemy but a righteous deed is written for them on its account. Indeed, God does not waste the reward of the virtuous.

[121]And neither do they incur any expense, big or small, nor do they cross any valley, but it is written to their account, so that God may reward them by the best of what they used to do.

[122]Yet it is not for the faithful to go forth en masse. But why should not a group from each of their sections go forth to become learned in religion and to warn their people when they return to them, so that they may beware?

¹²³O you who have faith! Fight the faithless who are in your vicinity, and let them find severity in you, and know that God is with the Godwary.

¹²⁴Whenever a *sūrah* is sent down, there are some of them who say, 'Which of you did it increase in faith?' As for those who have faith, it increases them in faith, and they rejoice. ¹²⁵But as for those in whose heart is a sickness, it only adds defilement to their defilement, and they die while they are faithless. ¹²⁶Do they not see that they are tried once or twice every year? Yet they neither repent, nor do they take admonition. ¹²⁷Whenever a *sūrah* is sent down, they look at one another: 'Is anybody observing you?' Then they slip away. God has turned their hearts away [from the truth], for they are a people who do not understand.

¹²⁸There has certainly come to you an apostle from among yourselves. Grievous to him is your distress; he has deep concern for you and is most kind and merciful to the faithful.

¹²⁹But if they turn their backs [on *you*], *say,* 'God is sufficient for me. There is no god except Him. In Him alone I have put my trust and He is the Lord of the Great Throne.'

10. *YŪNUS*, JONAH

In the Name of God, the All-beneficent, the All-merciful.

¹*Alif, Lām, Rā.* These are the signs of the Wise Book.

²Does it seem odd to these people that We have revealed to a man from among themselves, [declaring], 'Warn mankind and give good news to the faithful that they are in good standing with their Lord'? The faithless say, 'This is indeed a plain magician.'

³Your Lord is indeed God, who created the heavens and the earth in six days, and then settled on the Throne, directing the command. There is no intercessor, except after His leave. That is God, your Lord! So worship Him. Will you not then take admonition?

10:3 On the creation of the heavens and the earth in six days, see commentary on 41:9–12 (with further references). Here (and in 7:54; 10:3; 25:59; 32:4) God "settles" onto his throne after creating. Regarding this sequence, see commentary on 32:4 (with further references).

---

⁴To Him will be the return of you all; [that is] God's true promise. Indeed, He originates the creation, then He will bring it back

so that He may reward with justice those who have faith and do righteous deeds. As for the faithless, they shall have boiling water for drink and a painful punishment because of what they used to deny.

⁵It is He who made the sun a radiance and the moon a light, and ordained its phases that you might know the number of years and the calculation [of time]. God did not create all that except with consummate wisdom. He elaborates the signs for a people who have knowledge.

⁶Indeed, in the alternation of night and day, and whatever God has created in the heavens and the earth, there are surely signs for a people who are Godwary.

⁷Indeed, those who do not expect to encounter Us and who are pleased with the life of this world and satisfied with it, and those who are oblivious of Our signs ⁸—it is they whose refuge shall be the Fire because of what they used to do.

⁹Indeed, those who have faith and do righteous deeds, their Lord guides them by the means of their faith. Streams will run for them in gardens of bliss.

10:9 On the streams of paradise, see commentary on 2:25 (with further references).

¹⁰Their call therein will be, 'O God! Immaculate are You!' and their greeting therein will be, 'Peace!' and their concluding call, 'All praise belongs to God, the Lord of all the worlds.'

¹¹Were God to hasten ill for mankind with their haste for good, their term would have been over. But We leave those who do not expect to encounter Us bewildered in their rebellion.

[12]When distress befalls man he supplicates Us, [lying] on his side, sitting, or standing; but when We remove his distress, he passes on as if he had never supplicated Us concerning the distress that had befallen him. What they have been doing is thus presented as decorous to the transgressors.

[13]Certainly We destroyed the generations [that have passed] before you when they perpetrated wrongs: their apostles brought them manifest proofs, but they would not have faith. Thus do We requite the guilty lot. [14]Then We made you successors on the earth after them so that We may observe how you will act.

[15]When Our manifest signs are recited to them, those who do not expect to encounter Us say, 'Bring a Qur'ān other than this, or alter it.' *Say,* 'I may not alter it of my own accord. I follow only what is revealed to me. Indeed, should I disobey my Lord, I fear the punishment of a tremendous day.' [16]*Say,* 'Had God [so] wished, I would not have recited it to you, nor would He have made it known to you, for I have dwelled among you for a lifetime before it. Do you not exercise your reason?'

[17]So who is a greater wrongdoer than him who fabricates lies against God, or denies His signs? The guilty will indeed not prosper.

[18]They worship besides God that which neither causes them any harm, nor brings them any benefit, and they say, 'These are our intercessors with God.' *Say,* 'Will you inform God about something He does not know in the heavens or on the earth?' Immaculate is He and far above [having] any partners that they ascribe [to Him]!

10:18 As Speyer points out (*BEQ,* 445), the language the Qur'ān uses here (cf. 5:76; 6:71; 10:106; 13:16; 20:89; 21:66; 22:12; 25:3, 55; 26:72–73; 34:42) reflects Biblical passages which condemn idolatry, such as Jeremiah 2:11: "Does a nation change its gods?—and these are not gods at all! Yet my people have exchanged their Glory for the Useless One!" (cf. Jer 16:19; also Isa 44:10). Islamic tradition connects this verse to the stories of Meccan idol worship in the biography of the Prophet. *Tafsīr al-Jalālayn* writes, "And they worship, besides God, that is, other than Him, that which can neither hurt them, should they not worship it, nor profit them, if they do worship it—and these are the idols; and they say, of them: 'These are our intercessors with God.'"

---

¹⁹Mankind were but a single [religious] community; then they differed. And were it not for a prior decree of your Lord, decision would have been made between them concerning that about which they differ.

10:19 In certain places the Qur'ān declares that God himself desires humans to be divided into different communities (5:48; 11:118; 16:93; 42:8; 43:33). Here, however, the division into different communities seems to be a departure from God's original plan (cf. 2:213).

---

²⁰They say, 'Why has not some sign been sent down to him from his Lord?' *Say,* '[The knowledge of] the Unseen belongs only to God. So wait. I too am waiting along with you.'

10:20 The request of unbelievers, or hypocrites, for a sign (cf. commentary on 2:118; 6:37; 13:7; 20:133; 21:5; 29:50) is a prominent topos in the Gospels:

³⁸Then some of the scribes and Pharisees spoke up. 'Master,' they said, 'we should like to see a sign from you.'
³⁹He replied, 'It is an evil and unfaithful generation that asks for a sign! The only sign it will be given is the sign of the prophet Jonah. (Mat 12:38–39; cf. Mar 8:11–12; 16:1; Luk 11:16, 29–32)

²¹When We let people taste [Our] mercy after a distress that has befallen them, behold, they scheme against Our signs! *Say,* 'God is more swift at devising.' Indeed, Our messengers write down what you scheme.

²²It is He who carries you across land and sea. When you are in the ships and they sail along with them with a favourable wind, being joyful on its account, there comes upon them a tempestuous wind and waves assail them from every side, and they think that they are besieged, they invoke God putting exclusive faith in Him, 'If You deliver us from this, we will surely be among the grateful.'

10:22 The Bible contains several (presumably interrelated) passages in which sailors, caught in a storm, call out to God (or, in one case, to Jesus) and are saved. These include, as Speyer (*BEQ,* 448; also Rudolph, *Abhängigkeit,* 11) mentions, Psalm 107:23–28:

> ²³Voyagers on the sea in ships, plying their trade on the great ocean,
> ²⁴have seen the works of the Lord, his wonders in the deep.
> ²⁵By his word he raised a storm-wind, lashing up towering waves.
> ²⁶Up to the sky then down to the depths! Their stomachs were turned to water;
> ²⁷they staggered and reeled like drunkards, and all their skill went under.
> ²⁸They cried out to the Lord in their distress, he rescued them from their plight.

One might also compare the story of Jonah (esp. 1:4–5) and that of Jesus' calming the storm (Mar 4:36–39; cf. Mat 8:23–27; Luk 8:22–25).

²³But when He delivers them, behold, they commit violations on the earth unduly! O mankind! Your violations are only to your own detriment. [These are] the wares of the life of this world; then to Us will be your return, whereat We will inform you concerning what you used to do.

²⁴The parable of the life of this world is that of water which We send down from the sky. It mingles with the earth's vegetation from which humans and cattle eat. When the earth puts on its lustre and is adorned, and its inhabitants think they have power over it, Our edict comes to it, by night or day, whereat We turn it into a mown field, as if it did not flourish the day before. Thus do We elaborate the signs for a people who reflect.

²⁵God invites to the abode of peace, and He guides whomever He wishes to a straight path.

²⁶Those who are virtuous shall receive the best reward and an enhancement. Neither dust nor abasement shall overcast their faces. They shall be the inhabitants of paradise, and they shall remain in it [forever].

²⁷For those who have committed misdeeds, the requital of a misdeed shall be its like, and they shall be overcast by abasement. They shall have no one to protect [them] from God. [They will be] as if their faces were covered with dark patches of the night. They shall be the inmates of the Fire, and they shall remain in it [forever].

²⁸On the day when We gather them all together, We shall say to those who ascribe partners [to God], 'Stay where you are—you and your partners!' Then We shall set them apart from one another, and their partners will say, 'It was not us that you worshiped. ²⁹God suffices as a witness between you and us. We were indeed unaware of your worship.' ³⁰There every soul will examine what it has sent in advance, and they will be returned to God, their real master, and what they used to fabricate will forsake them.

³¹*Say,* 'Who provides for you out of the heaven and the earth? Who controls [your] hearing and sight, and who brings forth the living from the dead and brings forth the dead from the living, and who directs the command?' They will say, 'God.' *Say,* 'Will you not then be wary [of Him]?'

³²That, then, is God, your true Lord. So what is there after the truth except error? Then where are you being led away?

³³Thus the word of *your* Lord became due against those who transgress: that they shall not have faith.

³⁴*Say,* 'Is there anyone among your partners who originates the creation and then brings it back?' *Say,* 'God originates the creation, then He will bring it back.' Then where do you stray?

³⁵*Say,* 'Is there anyone among your partners who may guide to the truth?' *Say,* 'God guides to the truth. Is He who guides to the truth worthier to be followed, or he who is not guided unless he is shown the way? What is the matter with you? How do you judge?'

³⁶Most of them just follow conjectures; indeed conjecture is no substitute for the truth. God indeed knows best what they do.

³⁷This Qur'ān could not have been fabricated by anyone besides God; rather, it is a confirmation of what was [revealed] before it, and an elaboration of the Book, there is no doubt in it, from the Lord of all the worlds.

³⁸Do they say, 'He has fabricated it?' *Say,* 'Then bring a *sūrah* like it, and invoke whomever you can, besides God, if you are truthful.' ³⁹They indeed impugn something whose knowledge they do not comprehend, and whose explanation has not yet come to them. Those who were before them impugned likewise. So observe how was the fate of the wrongdoers!

⁴⁰Some of them believe in it, and some of them do not believe in it, and your Lord best knows the agents of corruption.

⁴¹If they impugn *you, say,* 'My deeds belong to me and your deeds belong to you: you are absolved of what I do and I am absolved of what you do.'

⁴²There are some of them who prick up their ears at *you.* But can *you* make the deaf hear even if they do not exercise their reason? ⁴³There are some of them who observe *you.* But can *you* guide the blind even if they do not see?

⁴⁴Indeed, God does not wrong people in the least; rather, it is people who wrong themselves. ⁴⁵On the day He will gather them [it will be] as if they had not remained [in the world] except for an hour of the day getting acquainted with one another. They are certainly losers who deny the encounter with God, and they are not guided.

⁴⁶Whether We show *you* a part of what We promise them, or take *you* away [before that], [in any case] their return will be to Us, and God is witness to what they do.

⁴⁷There is an apostle for every nation; so when their apostle comes, judgement is made between them with justice, and they are not wronged.

⁴⁸They say, 'When will this promise be fulfilled, should you be truthful?' ⁴⁹*Say,* 'I have no control over any benefit for myself nor [over] any harm except what God may wish. There is a time for every nation: when their time comes, they shall not defer it by a single hour nor shall they advance it.'

⁵⁰*Say,* 'Tell me, should His punishment overtake you by night or day, [you will not be able to avert it]; so what part of it do the guilty seek to hasten?' ⁵¹'What! Do you believe it when it has befallen? Now? While you would seek to hasten it [earlier]?!' ⁵²Then it will be said to those who were wrongdoers, 'Taste the everlasting punishment. Shall you be requited except for what you used to earn?'

⁵³They inquire of *you,* 'Is it true?' *Say,* 'Yes! By my Lord, it is true, and you cannot frustrate [Him].' ⁵⁴Were any soul that has done wrong to possess whatever there is on the earth, it would surely offer it for ransom. They will hide their remorse when they sight the punishment and judgement will be made between them with justice and they will not be wronged.

⁵⁵Behold, to God indeed belongs whatever is in the heavens and the earth. Behold, God's promise is indeed true, but most of

them do not know. ⁵⁶It is He who gives life and brings death, and to Him you shall be brought back.

⁵⁷O mankind! There has certainly come to you an advice from your Lord, and cure for what is in the breasts, and guidance and mercy for the faithful.

⁵⁸*Say,* 'In God's grace and His mercy—let them rejoice in that! It is better than what they amass.'

⁵⁹*Say,* 'Have you regarded what God has sent down for you of [His] provision, whereupon you have made some of it unlawful and [some] lawful?' *Say,* 'Did God give you the sanction [to do so], or do you fabricate lies against God?' ⁶⁰What is the idea of those who fabricate lies against God [concerning their own situation] on the Day of Resurrection? God is indeed gracious to mankind, but most of them do not give thanks.

⁶¹You do not engage in any work, neither do you recite any part of the Qurʾān, nor do you perform any deed without Our being witness over you when you are engaged therein. Not an atom's weight in the earth or in the heaven escapes *your* Lord, nor [is there] anything smaller than that nor bigger, but it is in a manifest Book.

⁶²Behold! The friends of God will indeed have no fear nor will they grieve ⁶³—those who have faith and are Godwary. ⁶⁴For them is good news in the life of this world and in the Hereafter. (There is no altering the words of God.) That is the great success.

10:64 On the expression "There is no altering the words of God," see commentary on 6:115 (with further references).

---

⁶⁵*Do not grieve* at their remarks; indeed all might belongs to God; He is the All-hearing, the All-knowing. ⁶⁶Behold, to God indeed belongs whoever is in the heavens and whoever is on the

earth. Those who invoke partners besides God—what do they pursue? They merely follow conjectures and they only make surmises.

⁶⁷It is He who made the night for you, that you may rest in it, and the day to provide visibility. There are indeed signs in that for people who listen.

⁶⁸They say, 'God has offspring!' Immaculate is He! He is the All-sufficient. To Him belongs whatever is in the heavens and whatever is in the earth. You have no authority for this [statement]. Do you attribute to God what you do not know?

⁶⁹*Say,* 'Indeed, those who fabricate lies against God will not prosper.' ⁷⁰[Their life will be] a brief enjoyment in this world; then to Us shall be their return, then We shall make them taste the severe punishment because of what they used to deny.

⁷¹*Relate* to them the account of Noah when he said to his people, 'O my people! If my stay [among you] be hard on you and [also] my reminding you of God's signs, [for my part] I have put my trust in God alone. So conspire together, along with your partners, leaving nothing vague in your plan; then carry it out against me without giving me any respite. ⁷²If you turn your back [on me], I do not ask any reward from you; my reward lies only with God and I have been commanded to be of those who submit [to Him].'

⁷³But they impugned him. So We delivered him and those who were with him in the ark and We made them the successors, and We drowned those who impugned Our signs. So observe how was the fate of those who were warned!

⁷⁴Then after him We sent [other] apostles to their people. They brought them clear proofs, but they would not believe something they had impugned before. Thus do We seal the hearts of the transgressors.

10:71–74 Here, as elsewhere, the Qur'ān—unlike the Bible—has Noah preach to his people (thus making him one of the prophets who warned people of divine destruction). The idea that Noah preached to his people before the flood is found both in Jewish sources, such as the Babylonian Talmud, and in Christian sources, such as Jacob of Serugh's *Homily on the Flood.* For more detail on the role of Noah in the Qur'ān, see commentary on 71:1–28 (with further references). On the idea that a true prophet does not seek a reward (v. 72), see commentary on 34:47 (with further references).

---

⁷⁵Then, after them, We sent Moses and Aaron with Our signs to Pharaoh and his elite, but they acted arrogantly and they were a guilty lot. ⁷⁶When the truth came to them from Us, they said, 'This is indeed plain magic!'

⁷⁷Moses said, 'Do you say of the truth when it comes to you [that it is magic]? Is this magic? Magicians do not prosper.'

⁷⁸They said, 'Have you come to us to turn us away from what we found our fathers following, so that supremacy may be yours in the land? We will not believe in the two of you.'

⁷⁹Pharaoh said, 'Bring me every expert magician.' ⁸⁰So when the magicians came, Moses said to them, 'Throw down what you have to throw.' ⁸¹So when they threw down [their sticks and ropes], Moses said, 'What you have produced is magic. Presently, God will indeed bring it to naught. Indeed, God does not foster the efforts of those who cause corruption. ⁸²God will confirm the truth with His words, though the guilty should be averse.'

⁸³But none believed in Moses except some youths from among his people for the fear of Pharaoh and his elite that he would persecute them. For Pharaoh was indeed a tyrant in the land, and indeed he was an unrestrained [despot].

⁸⁴And Moses said, 'O my people! If you have faith in God, put your trust in Him, if you have submitted [to Him].' ⁸⁵Whereat

they said, 'In God alone we have put our trust.' 'Our Lord! Do not make us a [means of] test for the wrongdoing lot, [86]and deliver us by Your mercy from the faithless lot.'

10:75–86 Here and elsewhere (cf. 7:109–26; 20:56–70; 26:30–45; 27:10–13; 28:31–33), the Qur'ān has Moses and Aaron confront Pharaoh and his sorcerers. This confrontation is based ultimately on Exodus 7:

> [10]Moses and Aaron went to Pharaoh and did as the Lord had ordered. Aaron threw down his staff in front of Pharaoh and his officials, and it turned into a serpent.
> [11]Then Pharaoh in his turn called for the sages and sorcerers, and by their spells the magicians of Egypt did the same.
> [12]Each threw his staff down and these turned into serpents. But Aaron's staff swallowed up theirs.
> [13]Pharaoh, however, remained obstinate and, as the Lord had foretold, refused to listen to Moses and Aaron.
> [14]the Lord then said to Moses, 'Pharaoh is adamant. He refuses to let the people go. (Exo 7:10–14)

The Qur'ān's presentation of this scene is shaped according to its prophetology, by which a prophet is accused of being a magician (v. 81; cf. 5:110, 6:7, 7:109, passim) and only a small group of the prophet's people believe in him (v. 83; cf. 7:159). In verse 83 Qarai (following classical opinions) renders *illā dhurriyyatun min qawmihi* as "except some youths from among his people," although this phrase means simply "except for a group of descendants from his people."

Bell suggests (*Commentary* 1:343) that verse 78 is related to Exodus 2:14. On Moses in Pharaoh's court, see also commentary on 26:30–45.

––––––––––––

[87]We revealed to Moses and his brother [saying], 'Settle your people in the city, and let your houses face each other, and maintain the prayer, and give good news to the faithful.'

[88]Moses said, 'Our Lord! You have given Pharaoh and his elite glamour and wealth in the life of this world, our Lord, that they

may lead [people] astray from Your way! Our Lord! Blot out their wealth and harden their hearts so that they do not believe until they sight the painful punishment.'

⁸⁹Said He, 'Your supplication has already been granted. So be steadfast and do not follow the way of those who do not know.'

10:88–89 The reference to God's hardening Pharaoh's heart reflects the report in Exodus that God made Pharaoh stubborn (lit.: "the Lord hardened Pharaoh's heart," Hb. *yeḥazzēq yhwh et-lēb parʿō*):

> ¹¹And the magicians could not compete with Moses in the matter of the boils, for the magicians were covered with boils like all the other Egyptians.
> ¹²But the Lord made Pharaoh stubborn and, as the Lord had foretold to Moses, he did not listen to them. (Exo 9:11–12; cf. Exo 9:34–35; 10:1–2)

---

⁹⁰We carried the Children of Israel across the sea, whereat Pharaoh and his troops pursued them, out of defiance and aggression. When overtaken by drowning, he called out, 'I do believe that there is no god except Him in whom the Children of Israel believe, and I am one of those who submit [to Him]!' ⁹¹[He was told,] 'What! Now? When you have been disobedient heretofore and were among the agents of corruption?! ⁹²So today We shall deliver your body so that you may be a sign for those who come after you.' Many of the people are indeed oblivious to Our signs.

10:90–92 The belief of Pharaoh here follows from verse 88, which has Moses pray that Pharaoh will not believe until he sees the chastisement which God has prepared for him. In verse 90, he sees the chastisement and believes. The conversion of Pharaoh may be a development of Exodus 15:11, which seems to have Pharaoh (Exo 15:9 begins, "The enemy boasted . . .") confess in the God of Israel: "Lord, who is like you, majestic in sanctity, who like you among the holy ones, fearsome of deed, worker of wonders." Speyer (*BEQ,* 291), following Geiger (*Was hat Mohammed,* 160), notes that the *Pirqe de-Rabbi Eliezer* (43) makes the attribution of these words to Pharaoh explicit. In any case this episode should be seen as an illustration of the Qur'ānic doctrine (see 4:18; 6:158; 32:29; 40:84–85) that God will not accept the repentance of sinners at the moment of their death (n.b. v. 91). Speyer (*BEQ*) also points out similar Qur'ānic passages wherein opponents of a prophet come to faith; of these the most notable is the conversion of the Queen of Sheba (Q 27:44). A closer antecedent to the conversion of Pharaoh is the way the Mishnah discusses Pharaoh's repentance:

> It is said, and Pharaoh said, "Who is the Lord that I should hearken unto his voice to let Israel go?" [Exo 5:2]. But when he was smitten what did he say? "The Lord is righteous" [Exo 9:27]. (m. Yadayim 4:8)

The idea of the deliverance of Pharaoh's body (v. 92) as "a sign for those who come after" might be connected to the preservation of the body of Lot's wife, who in the Biblical account (Gen 19:26) is turned into a pillar of salt, a tradition that implies that her body remained as a memorial of divine wrath for later generations (see Luk 17:32). It is not, however, a creation of the Qur'ān. The question of Pharaoh's survival appears in an opinion found in the (late fourth century AD) *Mekilta de-Rabbi Ishmael* (cr. Gavin McDowell):

> And the waters returned and covered the chariot, etc. [Exo 14:27]. Even Pharaoh, according to the words of R. Judah, as it is said, "The chariots of Pharaoh and his force, etc." [Exo 15:4]. R. Nehemiah says: *Except for Pharaoh.* About him it says, "However, for this purpose I have let you live" [Exo 9:16]. Others say that in the end Pharaoh went down and drowned, as it is said, "Then went the horse of Pharaoh, etc." [Exo 15:19]. (*Beshallah* 7)

According to *Tafsīr al-Jalālayn,* the angel Gabriel devised a way to keep Pharaoh from imploring God's mercy: "[Pharaoh] reiterated this [his submission to God] so that it might be accepted from him, but it was not; and Gabriel thrust mud from the sea into his mouth, lest [God's] mercy embrace him." On the drowning of Pharaoh and his army, see commentary on 54:41–42 (with further references).

---

[93]Certainly We settled the Children of Israel in a worthy settlement and We provided them with all the good things, and they

did not differ until [after] the knowledge had come to them. Your Lord will indeed judge between them on the Day of Resurrection concerning that about which they used to differ.

⁹⁴So if *you* are in doubt about what We have sent down to *you,* ask those who read the Book [revealed] before *you.* The truth has certainly come to *you* from *your* Lord; so do not be among skeptics.

10:94 In this verse, God seems to suggest to Muḥammad that he question Jews and Christians when he is in doubt (cf. 16:43). *Tafsīr al-Jalālayn,* however, reports: "The Prophet said, 'I have no doubt, nor will I question.'"

———————————

⁹⁵And do not be of those who impugn the signs of God, [for] then you shall be among the losers.

⁹⁶Indeed, those against whom your Lord's judgement has become due will not have faith ⁹⁷until they sight the painful punishment, even though every sign were to come to them.

⁹⁸Why has there not been any town except the people of Jonah that might believe, so that its belief might benefit it? When they believed, We removed from them the punishment of disgrace in the life of this world and We provided for them for a time.

⁹⁹Had your Lord wished, all those who are on earth would have believed. Would *you* then force people until they become faithful?

10:98–99 The description of the people of Nineveh as "Jonah's people" matches Qurʾānic prophetology, by which a prophet his sent to his own people. It does not match the Biblical account, at the heart of which is the identity of Nineveh as the enemy of Jonah's people, Israel. The idea (v. 98) that Nineveh was the only people to repent (see Jon 3:4–10) and be saved also does not match the Old Testament (see, for example, the story of Hezekiah and Jerusalem in Isa

36–37). Instead it reflects the way in which the New Testament authors have Jesus use Nineveh as a special example to his own generation.

> On Judgement Day the men of Nineveh will appear against this generation and be its condemnation, because when Jonah preached they repented; and, look, there is something greater than Jonah here. (Luk 11:32; cf. Mat 12:39–41; 16:4)

On Jonah in the Qur'ān, see commentary on 37:139–48 (see also 21:87–88).

———————

¹⁰⁰No soul may have faith except by God's leave, and He lays defilement on those who do not exercise their reason.

¹⁰¹*Say,* 'Observe what is in the heavens and the earth.' But neither signs nor warnings avail a people who have no faith. ¹⁰²Do they await anything except the like of the days of those who passed away before them? *Say,* 'Then wait! I too am waiting along with you.' ¹⁰³Then We will deliver Our apostles and those who have faith. Thus it is a must for Us to deliver the faithful.

¹⁰⁴*Say,* 'O people! If you are in doubt about my religion, then [know that] I do not worship those whom you worship besides God. Rather, I worship only God, who causes you to die, and I have been commanded to be among the faithful, ¹⁰⁵and that: "*Dedicate* yourself to the religion, as a *ḥanīf,* and never *be* one of the polytheists.

10:105 On *ḥanīf,* see commentary on 16:120–23 (with further references).

———————

¹⁰⁶Nor *invoke* besides God that which neither benefits *you* nor can do *you* any harm. For if *you* do so, *you* will indeed be among the wrongdoers."'

10:106 On the description of anything which unbelievers worship other than God as powerless, see commentary on 10:18 (with further references).

---

[107]Should God visit *you* with some distress, there is no one to remove it except Him; and should He desire any good for *you,* none can stand in the way of His grace: He grants it to whomever He wishes of His servants, and He is the All-forgiving, the All-merciful.

[108]*Say,* 'O mankind! The truth has already come to you from your Lord. Whoever is guided, is guided only for [the good of] his own soul, and whoever goes astray, goes astray only to its detriment, and it is not my business to watch over you.'

[109]*Follow* that which is revealed to *you,* and *be* patient until God issues [His] judgement, and He is the best of judges.

11. *Hūd*, Hūd

In the Name of God, the All-beneficent, the All-merciful.

¹*Alif, Lām Rā*. [This is] a Book, whose signs have been made definitive and then elaborated, from One [who is] all-wise, all-aware, ²declaring: 'Worship no one but God. I am indeed a warner to you from Him and a bearer of good news. ³Plead with your Lord for forgiveness, then turn to Him penitently. He will provide you with a good provision for a specified term and grant His grace to every meritorious person. But if you turn your backs [on Him], indeed I fear for you the punishment of a terrible day. ⁴To God will be your return, and He has power over all things.'

⁵Behold, they fold up their breasts to hide [their secret feelings] from Him. Behold, when they draw their cloaks over their heads, He knows whatever they keep secret and whatever they disclose. He knows well indeed whatever is in the breasts.

⁶There is no animal on the earth, but that its sustenance lies with God, and He knows its [enduring] abode and its temporary place of lodging. Everything is in a manifest Book.

⁷It is He who created the heavens and the earth in six days— and His Throne was [then] upon the waters—that He may test you [to see] which of you is best in conduct.

Yet if you *say,* 'You will indeed be raised up after death,' the faithless will surely say, 'This is nothing but plain magic.'

11:7 On the creation of the heavens and the earth in six days, see commentary on 41:9–12 (with further references). The Qurʾān's vision of God's throne hanging above the waters seems to reflect Psalm 104, which speaks of the palace of God above the waters (cf. also Rev 4:3; on God's throne, see also commentary on 69:17):

> ¹Bless the Lord, my soul, the Lord, my God, how great you are! Clothed in majesty and splendour,
> ²wearing the light as a robe! You stretch out the heavens like a tent,
> ³build your palace on the waters above, making the clouds your chariot, gliding on the wings of the wind. (Psa 104:1–3)

---

⁸And if We defer their punishment until a certain time, they will surely say, 'What holds it back?' Behold, on the day that it overtakes them it shall not be turned away from them, and they will be besieged by what they used to deride.

⁹If We let man taste a [breath of] mercy from Us and then withdraw it from him, he becomes despondent and ungrateful. ¹⁰And if We let him have a taste of Our blessings after adversities have befallen him, he will surely say, 'All ills have left me,' indeed being boastful and vain, ¹¹excepting those who are patient and do righteous deeds. For such there will be forgiveness and a great reward.

¹²[Look out] lest *you* should disregard aught of what has been revealed to *you,* and be upset because they say, 'Why has not a treasure been sent down to him, or [why does] not an angel accompany him?' *You* are only a warner, and God watches over all things.

[13]Do they say, 'He has fabricated it?' *Say,* 'Then bring ten *sūrahs* like it, fabricated, and invoke whomever you can, besides God, if you are truthful.' [14]But if they do not respond to you, know that it has been sent down by God's knowledge, and that there is no god except Him. Will you, then, submit [to God]?

[15]As for those who desire the life of this world and its glitter, We will recompense them fully for their works therein, and they will not be underpaid in it. [16]They are the ones for whom there will be nothing in the Hereafter except Fire: what they had accomplished in the world has failed, and their works have come to naught.

[17]Is he who stands on a clear proof from his Lord and whom a witness of his own [family] follows? And before him there was the Book of Moses, a guide and mercy. It is they who have faith in it, and whoever denies him from among the factions, the Fire is their tryst. So do not be in doubt about it; it is the truth from your Lord, but most people do not have faith.

[18]Who is a greater wrongdoer than him who fabricates lies against God? Such shall be presented before their Lord and the witnesses will say, 'It is these who lied against their Lord.' Behold! The curse of God is upon the wrongdoers [19]—those who bar [others] from the way of God and seek to make it crooked, and disbelieve in the Hereafter. [20]They cannot frustrate [God] on the earth, nor do they have any protectors besides God. For them the punishment shall be doubled, for they could neither listen, nor did they use to see. [21]They are the ones who have ruined their souls, and what they used to fabricate has forsaken them. [22]Undoubtedly, they are the ones who will be the biggest losers in the Hereafter.

[23]Indeed, those who have faith and do righteous deeds and are humble before their Lord—they shall be the inhabitants of paradise, and they shall remain in it [forever].

²⁴The parable of the two parties is that of those who are blind and deaf and those who see and hear. Are they equal in comparison? Will you not then take admonition?

²⁵Certainly We sent Noah to his people [to declare]: 'I am indeed a manifest warner to you:

11:25–98 *overview* On the punishment stories in the Qur'ān (and their connection to Biblical narratives), see commentary on 7:59–137 and 26:10–191. In my commentary here I focus only on the account of Noah, which in this Sura contains several unique features.

---

²⁶worship none but God. Indeed, I fear for you the punishment of a painful day.'

²⁷But the elite of the faithless from among his people said, 'We do not see you to be anything but a human being like ourselves, and we do not see anyone following you except the simpleminded riffraff from our midst. Nor do we see that you have any merit over us. Indeed, we consider you to be liars.'

²⁸He said, 'O my people! Tell me, should I stand on a clear proof from my Lord, and He has granted me His own mercy— though it should be lost on you—shall we force it upon you while you are averse to it? ²⁹O my people! I do not ask you any material reward for it. My reward lies only with God. But I will not drive away those who have faith. They will indeed encounter their Lord. But I see that you are an ignorant lot. ³⁰O my people! Who would come to my help against God were I to drive them away? Will you not then take admonition? ³¹I do not say to you that I possess the treasuries of God, neither do I know the Unseen. I do not claim to be an angel, neither do I say of those who are despicable in your eyes that God will not grant them any good—

God knows best what is in their hearts—for then I would indeed be a wrongdoer.'

³²They said, 'O Noah, you have disputed with us already, and you have disputed much with us. Now bring us what you threaten us with, if you are truthful.

³³He said, 'God will indeed bring it on you if He wishes, and you cannot frustrate [Him]. ³⁴My exhorting will not benefit you, much as I may seek to exhort you, if God desires to consign you to perversity. He is your Lord, and to Him you will be returned.'

³⁵Do they say, 'He has fabricated it?' *Say,* 'Should I have fabricated it, then my guilt will lie upon me, and I am absolved of your guilty conduct.'

³⁶It was revealed to Noah: 'None of your people will believe except those who already have faith; so do not sorrow for what they used to do. ³⁷Build the ark before Our eyes and by Our revelation, and do not plead with Me for those who are wrongdoers: they shall indeed be drowned.'

³⁸As he was building the ark, whenever the elders of his people passed by him, they would ridicule him. He said, 'If you ridicule us [today], we will ridicule you [tomorrow] just as you ridicule us [now]. ³⁹Soon you will know who will be overtaken by a punishment that will disgrace him, and on whom a lasting punishment will descend.'

11:25–39 In its various Noah accounts (cf. 7:59–64; 10:71–74; 23:23–30; 26:105–22; 54:9–17; 71:1–28) the Qurʾān emphasizes not the flood but the confrontation of Noah with his unbelieving people *before* the flood. The manner in which the Qurʾān describes this confrontation contrasts fundamentally with the Genesis account of the flood, which does not have Noah pronounce a single word until *after* he leaves the ark. However, the idea that Noah preached to his people (even if that preaching is not recorded in Genesis) is found already with the author of 2 Peter, who names Noah the "preacher of uprightness" (2Pe 2:5).

Later Jewish and Christian texts develop a portrait of Noah as a preacher who warned his people of the coming disaster. Ephrem and Jacob of Serugh, along with other Syriac fathers, report that his preaching went on for one hundred years. Ephrem reports that during this time people mocked him (cf. Q 11:38):

> Although Noah was an example to that generation by his righteousness and had, in his uprightness, announced to them the flood during that one hundred years, they still did not repent. So Noah said to them, "Some of all flesh will come to be saved with me in the ark." But they mocked him, "How will all the beasts and birds that are scattered throughout every corner of the earth come from all those regions." (Ephrem, *Commentary on Genesis,* 6:9)

For more detail, see commentary on 71:1–28 (with further references). On the idea that a true prophet does not seek a reward (11:29), see commentary on 34:47 (with further references).

———————

⁴⁰When Our edict came and the oven gushed [a stream of water], We said, 'Carry in it a pair of every kind [of animal], along with your family—except those [of them] against whom the edict has already been given—and those who have faith.' And none believed with him except a few.

⁴¹He said, 'Board it: In the Name of God it shall set sail and cast anchor. My Lord is indeed all-forgiving, all-merciful.' ⁴²And it sailed along with them amid waves [rising] like mountains.

Noah called out to his son, who stood aloof, 'O my son! 'Board with us, and do not be with the faithless!' ⁴³He said, 'I will take refuge on a mountain; it will protect me from the flood.' He said, 'There is none today who can protect from God's edict, except someone upon whom He has mercy.' Then the waves came between them, and he was among those who were drowned.

⁴⁴Then it was said, 'O earth, swallow your water! O sky, leave off!' The waters receded; the edict was carried out, and it settled on [Mount] Judi. Then it was said, 'Away with the wrongdoing lot!'

⁴⁵Noah called out to his Lord, and said, 'My Lord! My son is indeed from my family, and Your promise is indeed true, and You are the fairest of all judges.' ⁴⁶Said He, 'O Noah! He is indeed not of your family. He is indeed [a personification of] unrighteous conduct. So do not ask Me [something] of which you have no knowledge. I advise you lest you should be among the ignorant.' ⁴⁷He said, 'My Lord! I seek Your protection lest I should ask You something of which I have no knowledge. If You do not forgive me and have mercy upon me I will be among the losers.'

⁴⁸It was said, 'O Noah! Disembark in peace from Us and with [Our] blessings upon you and upon nations [to descend] from those who are with you, and nations whom We shall provide for, then a painful punishment from Us shall befall them.'

11:40–48 In this passage—and only here—the Qur'ān describes a son of Noah (*Tafsīr al-Jalālayn* gives him the name Canaan, the name of the son of Noah's son Ham in Genesis 9) who refuses to get in the ark with his father and (apparently) drowns with the unbelievers. With this account the Qur'ān is evidently interested in insisting that ties of faith are more important than ties of family (regarding which cf. 33:4–5 and 46:15–18). To this end it has God tell Noah earlier (v. 40) that those of his family against whom "the edict" is given should not enter the ark. Note also that when Noah implores God to have mercy on his son (v. 45), God replies to Noah that his son is not (or should not be considered to be) part of his family (presumably because he is an unbeliever).

This account is a departure from Genesis, by which Noah has three sons—Ham, Japheth, and Shem—who all enter the ark. It emerges instead from a section of Ezekiel in which the point is made that merit is not passed down from father to son (regarding which, see Deu 24:16). Ezekiel 14 and Ezekiel 18 both advance the argument that if a righteous man has an unrighteous son, this son will not be saved because of the father's righteousness. Tellingly, Ezekiel 14:20 invokes the figure of Noah (along with Daniel and Job—all three are figures who are praised by the Bible for their righteousness in the midst of trials) to make this point (cf. Q 11:45):

¹³'Son of man, when a country sins against me by being unfaithful and I point my finger at it and destroy its supply of food, inflicting famine on it and denuding it of human and animal,

¹⁴even if the three men, Noah, Daniel and Job, were living in it, they would save no one but themselves by their uprightness declares the Lord.

. . .

²⁰even if Noah and Daniel and Job were living there, as I live—declares the Lord—they would be able to save neither son nor daughter, only themselves by their uprightness.
(Eze 14:13–14, 20; cf. Eze 18:10–13)

The Qur'ān seems to make the hypothetical son of Noah in Ezekiel into a real son (one might compare how the hypothetical characters in Nathan's parable become real characters in the Qur'ān; see commentary on 38:21–26). It may have known of this passage from Ezekiel through its use by Syriac fathers such as Jacob of Serugh in their arguments against the Jewish notion of "merits of the fathers" (Hb. *zekhut avot*):

The soul of the father and the soul of the son both belong to the Lord; / it is the soul of the sinner from which vengeance shall be sought, *as it is written* / a just father will not profit a sinning son (cf. Eze 18:4); / *as it is written* he will save neither a son nor a daughter (cf. Eze 14:16). (Jacob of Serugh, *Homélies contre les juifs,* 164–65, homily 6, ll. 111–14)

The Qur'ānic notion that Noah's son tried to save himself by seeking refuge on a mountain may be connected to a tradition in *Cave of Treasures,* which describes how the unrighteous sons of Seth sought in vain to climb the cosmic mountain of paradise after they failed to get aboard the ark:

The children of Seth ran to the ark and begged Noah to open the door of the ark for them. When they saw the waves which surrounded them from every side they were overcome with great anxiety and sought to climb the mountain of paradise but they could not. (*Cave of Treasures* [Or.] 18:12–13)

On the oven (v. 40) from which the waters of the flood gushed, see 23:27; and see commentary on 23:23–30.

---

⁴⁹These are accounts of the Unseen which We reveal to *you.* Neither *you* nor *your* people used to know them before this. So *be* patient. The outcome will indeed be in favour of the Godwary.

⁵⁰And to 'Ād [We sent] Hūd, their kinsman. He said, 'O my people! Worship God. You have no other god besides Him: you

have merely fabricated [the deities that you worship]. ⁵¹'O my people! I do not ask you any reward for it. My reward lies only with Him who originated me. Do you not exercise your reason? ⁵²'O my people! Plead with your Lord for forgiveness, then turn to Him penitently: He will send copious rains for you from the sky, and add power to your [present] power. So do not turn your backs [on Him] as guilty ones.'

⁵³They said, 'O Hūd, you have not brought us any clear proof. We are not going to abandon our gods for what you say, and we are not going to believe you. ⁵⁴All we say is that some of our gods have visited you with some evil.'

He said, 'I call God to witness—and you too be [my] witnesses—that I repudiate what you take as [His] partners ⁵⁵besides Him. Now try out your stratagems against me, together, without granting me any respite. ⁵⁶Indeed, I have put my trust in God, my Lord and your Lord. There is no living being but He holds it by its forelock. My Lord is indeed on a straight path. ⁵⁷But if you turn your backs [on me], then [know that] I have communicated to you whatever I was sent to you with. My Lord will make another people succeed you, and you will not hurt God in the least. My Lord is indeed watchful over all things.'

⁵⁸When Our edict came, We delivered Hūd and the faithful who were with him, by mercy from Us, and We delivered them from a harsh punishment.

⁵⁹Such were [the people of] 'Ād: they disputed the signs of their Lord and disobeyed His apostles, and followed the dictates of every stubborn tyrant. ⁶⁰So they were pursued by a curse in this world and on the Day of Resurrection. Behold! 'Ād indeed defied their Lord. Now, away with 'Ād, the people of Hud!

⁶¹And to Thamūd [We sent] Ṣāliḥ, their kinsman. He said, 'O my people! Worship God. You have no other god besides Him.

He brought you forth from the earth and made it your habitation. So plead with Him for forgiveness, then turn to Him penitently. My Lord is indeed nearmost [and] responsive.'

11:61 The reference to humans' creation, "from the earth" (Ar. *arḍ;* cf. 6:2; 15:26; 23:12; 32:7; 35:11; 37:11) reflects Genesis 2:7 ("The Lord God shaped man from the soil of the ground and blew the breath of life into his nostrils, and man became a living being") and (as *Tafsīr al-Jalālayn* recognizes) is connected to the Qur'ānic passages (3:59; 7:12; 38:71, 76) that describe the creation of Adam from clay (*ṭīn*) or dust (*turāb*).

———————

⁶²They said, 'O Ṣāliḥ! Before this, you were a source of hope to us. Do you forbid us to worship what our fathers have been worshiping? We have indeed grave doubts concerning that to which you invite us.'

⁶³He said, 'O my people! Tell me, should I stand on a clear proof from my Lord, and He has granted me His own mercy, who will protect me from God should I disobey Him? For then you will increase me in nothing but loss. ⁶⁴O my people! This she-camel of God is a sign for you. Let her graze [freely] in God's land, and do not cause her any harm, for then you will be seized by a prompt punishment.'

⁶⁵But they hamstrung her, whereupon he said, 'Enjoy yourselves in your homes for three days: that is a promise not to be belied!'

⁶⁶So when Our edict came, We delivered Ṣāliḥ and the faithful who were with him by mercy from Us and from the [punishment and] disgrace of that day. *Your* Lord is indeed the All-strong, the All-mighty.

⁶⁷The Cry seized those who were wrongdoers, and they lay lifeless prostrate in their homes, ⁶⁸as if they had never lived there.

Behold! Thamūd indeed defied their Lord. Now, away with Thamūd!

⁶⁹Certainly Our messengers came to Abraham with the good news, and said, 'Peace!' 'Peace!' He replied. Presently, he brought [for them] a roasted calf. ⁷⁰But when he saw their hands not reaching out for it, he took them amiss and felt a fear of them. They said, 'Do not be afraid. We have been sent to the people of Lot.'

⁷¹His wife, standing by, laughed as We gave her the good news of [the birth of] Isaac, and of Jacob after Isaac. ⁷²She said, 'Oh, my! Shall I, an old woman, bear [children], and [while] this husband of mine is an old man?! That is indeed an odd thing!'

⁷³They said, 'Are you amazed at God's dispensation? [That is] God's mercy and His blessings upon you, members of the household. He is indeed all-laudable, all-glorious.'

11:69–73 In this passage (cf. 15:51–56; 29:31–35; 51:24–34) the Qur'ān develops the tradition found in Genesis 18 of the three mysterious visitors to Abraham who deliver the news that he and his wife Sarah will miraculously have a son in their old age.

> ¹The Lord appeared to him at the Oak of Mamre while he was sitting by the entrance of the tent during the hottest part of the day.
> ²He looked up, and there he saw three men standing near him. As soon as he saw them he ran from the entrance of the tent to greet them, and bowed to the ground.
> . . .
> ⁹'Where is your wife Sarah?' they asked him. 'She is in the tent,' he replied.
> ¹⁰Then his guest said, 'I shall come back to you next year, and then your wife Sarah will have a son.' Sarah was listening at the entrance of the tent behind him.
> ¹¹Now Abraham and Sarah were old, well on in years, and Sarah had ceased to have her monthly periods.
> ¹²So Sarah laughed to herself, thinking, 'Now that I am past the age of childbearing, and my husband is an old man, is pleasure to come my way again?'

¹³But the Lord asked Abraham, 'Why did Sarah laugh and say, "Am I really going to have a child now that I am old?"
¹⁴Nothing is impossible for the Lord. I shall come back to you at the same time next year and Sarah will have a son.' (Gen 18:1–2, 8–14)

Genesis suggests that it was God Himself who appeared to Abraham, whereas the Qur'ān speaks only of messengers, or guests. Genesis also (18:8) reports that these visitors ate the food Sarah prepared for them, whereas the Qur'ān (v. 70) reports that they do not eat. In this the Qur'ān follows the manner in which Jewish and Christian sources read this story. Justin Martyr (*Dialogue with Trypho,* chap. 57) makes the visitors out to be angels, as does Ephrem (*Commentary on Genesis,* 5:15). *Genesis Rabbah* (48:9) agrees that the visitors were angels and adds that they only *pretended* to eat (and this in order to conform with human customs, 48:14). *Targum Neofiti* on Genesis 18:8 relates: "They seemed to [Abraham] as if they were eating and as if they were drinking."

Unlike Genesis the Qur'ān mentions the laughter of Sarah (who is referred to only as "Abraham's wife") *before* it mentions the annunciation of Isaac. Qarai, however, recognizes that the Qur'ān means to say that Sarah laughed *because* of the annunciation (despite the Qur'ān's syntax); hence he translates "His wife, standing by, laughed *as* We gave her the good news." The "as" in his translation renders the Arabic word *wa*—which most translators render differently: "And his wife was standing [there], and she laughed: *But* we gave her glad tidings of Isaac, and after him, of Jacob" (Yusuf Ali) or "And his wife was standing by; she laughed, *therefore* We gave her the glad tidings of Isaac, and, after Isaac, of Jacob" (Arberry). These translations reflect the various manners by which the classical exegetes attempted to understand why Sarah laughed. According to *Tafsīr al-Jalālayn,* Sarah laughed because she was happy that Lot's people would be punished for their unrighteousness ("at the good tiding of their destruction").

However, Qarai is right that the Qur'ān means—like the Bible—that Sarah laughed upon hearing the annunciation. It mentions her laughter first only because of its adherence here to a rhyme scheme with *ī* or *ū* as the final vowel. The phrase "she laughed" (Ar. *ḍaḥikat*) does not match this scheme. Neither, for that matter, does "Isaac" (Ar. *isḥāq*). Thus the Qur'ān includes Isaac's son Jacob (Ar. *ya'qūb*) in the annunciation, so that it preserves the rhyme. The connection between the addition of the name of Jacob here and the rhyme scheme is still clearer in light of a comparison with the other two passages (Q 15:53; 51:28) that mention the annunciation. Each of these speaks only of a son (not a son and a grandson).

---

⁷⁴So when the awe had left Abraham and the good news had reached him, he pleaded with Us concerning the people of Lot. ⁷⁵Abraham was indeed most forbearing, plaintive [and] penitent.

⁷⁶ 'O Abraham, let this matter alone! Your Lord's edict has already come, and an irrevocable punishment shall overtake them.'

⁷⁷When Our messengers came to Lot, he was distressed on their account and in a predicament for their sake, and he said, 'This is a terrible day!'

⁷⁸Then his people came running toward him, and they had been committing vices aforetime. He said, 'O my people, these are my daughters: they are purer for you. Be wary of God and do not humiliate me with regard to my guests. Is there not a right-minded man among you?'

⁷⁹They said, 'You already know that we have no interest in your daughters, and you surely know what we want.'

⁸⁰He said, 'If only I had the power to deter you, or could take refuge in a mighty support!'

⁸¹They said, 'O Lot, we are messengers of your Lord. They will never get at you. Set out with your family in a watch of the night, and none of you shall turn round, except your wife; indeed she will be struck by what strikes them. Indeed, their tryst is the dawn. Is not the dawn [already] near?'

⁸²So when Our edict came, We made its topmost part its nethermost, and We rained on it stones of laminar shale, ⁸³sent from *your* Lord [for the transgressors], never far from the wrongdoers.

11:74–83 The Qurʾān here follows the sequence of Genesis 18–19, whereby the story of the visitors to Abraham is followed by Abraham's intercession before God over the fate of Sodom (Q 11:74–76; cf. 29:32), and the subsequent destruction of Sodom and its sister cities:

²²While the men left there and went to Sodom, the Lord remained in Abraham's presence.

²³Abraham stepped forward and said, 'Will you really destroy the upright with the guilty? (Gen 18:22–23)

The same sequence is found also in 15:51–77; 29:31–35, and 51:24–47 (and in the brief reference in 22:43). On Lot in the Qurʾān, see commentary on 15:57–74 and 54:33–39 (with further references). On Lot's wife, see commentary on 27:54–58 (with further references).

Verse 78 follows Genesis 19:8, where Lot offers his daughters to the mob outside his door "to treat as they please." However, according to most Islamic commentaries, Lot had marriage in mind. *Tafsīr al-Jalālayn* paraphrases the passage, "These are my daughters, they are purer for you," as "Here are my daughters, *marry them;* they are purer for you."

---

⁸⁴And to Midian [We sent] Shuʿayb, their townsman. He said, 'O my people! Worship God. You have no other god besides Him. Do not diminish the measure or the balance. I indeed see that you are faring well, but I fear for you the punishment of a besieging day.' ⁸⁵'O my people! Observe fully the measure and the balance with justice, and do not cheat the people of their goods, and do not act wickedly on the earth, causing corruption.' ⁸⁶'What remains of God's provision is better for you, should you be faithful, and I am not a keeper over you.'

⁸⁷They said, 'O Shuʿayb, does your worship require that we abandon what our fathers have been worshiping, or that we should not do with our wealth whatever we wish? You are indeed a gentle and sensible [person].'

⁸⁸He said, 'O my people! Have you considered, should I stand on a clear proof from my Lord, who has provided me a good provision from Himself? I do not wish to oppose you by what I forbid you. I only desire to put things in order, as far as I can, and my success lies only with God: in Him alone I have put my trust, and to Him I turn penitently. ⁸⁹O my people, do not let your

defiance toward me lead you to be visited by the like of what was visited on the people of Noah, or the people of Hūd, or the people of Ṣāliḥ; and the people of Lot are not far from you. ⁹⁰Plead with your Lord for forgiveness, then turn to Him penitently. My Lord is indeed all-merciful, all-affectionate.'

⁹¹They said, 'O Shuʿayb, we do not understand much of what you say. We indeed see that you are weak amongst us, and were it not for your tribe, we would have stoned you, and you are not a formidable [hindrance] for us.'

⁹²He said, 'O my people! Is my tribe more formidable in your sight than God, to whom you pay no regard? My Lord indeed encompasses whatever you are doing. ⁹³O my people! Act according to your ability; I too am acting. Soon you will know who will be overtaken by a punishment that will disgrace him, and who is a liar. So be on the watch; I too will be watching along with you.'

⁹⁴When Our edict came, We delivered Shuʿayb and the faithful who were with him by mercy from Us. And the Cry seized those who were wrongdoers, whereat they lay lifeless prostrate in their homes, ⁹⁵as if they had never lived there. Now, away with Midian!—just as Thamūd was done away with!

⁹⁶Certainly We sent Moses with Our signs and a clear authority ⁹⁷to Pharaoh and his elite, but they followed Pharaoh's dictates, and Pharaoh's dictates were not right-minded.

⁹⁸On the Day of Resurrection he will lead his people and conduct them into the Fire: an evil goal for the incoming! ⁹⁹They are pursued by a curse in this [world], as well as on the Day of Resurrection; evil is the award conferred [upon them]!

¹⁰⁰These are from the accounts of the townships which We recount to *you*. Of them there are some that still stand, and some that have been mown down. ¹⁰¹We did not wrong them, but they wronged themselves. When your Lord's edict came, their gods whom they would invoke besides God were of no avail to them

in any wise, and they did not increase them in anything but ruin. [102]Such is the seizing of *your* Lord when He seizes the townships that are wrongdoing. His seizing is indeed painful and severe.

[103]There is indeed a sign in that for those who fear the punishment of the Hereafter. That is a day on which all mankind will be gathered, and it is a day witnessed [by all creatures]. [104]We do not defer it but for a determinate term. [105]The day it comes, no one shall speak except by His leave. [On that day,] some of them will be wretched and [some] felicitous.

[106]As for the wretched, they shall be in the Fire: their lot therein will be groaning and wailing. [107]They will remain in it for as long as the heavens and the earth endure—except what *your* Lord may wish; indeed your Lord does whatever He desires.

[108]As for the felicitous, they will be in paradise. They will remain in it for as long as the heavens and the earth endure—except what *your* Lord may wish—an endless bounty.

[109]So do not be in doubt about what these worship: they worship just as their fathers worshiped before, and We shall surely pay them their full share, undiminished.

[110]Certainly We gave Moses the Book, but differences arose about it, and were it not for a prior decree of *your* Lord, a decision would have been made between them; indeed they are in grave doubt concerning it.

11:110 On the disputes which arose over the book of Moses, see commentary on 41:45. On revelation to Moses generally, see 7:117, 160; 10:87; 20:13, 77; 25:35; 26:10, 52, 63; 28:30, 43; 32:23; 37:114–17.

-----

[111]*Your* Lord will indeed recompense everyone fully for their works. He is indeed well aware of what they do. [112]So *be* stead-

fast, just as *you* have been commanded—[*you*] and whoever has turned [to God] with *you*—and do not overstep the bounds. Indeed, He watches what you do.

¹¹³Do not incline toward the wrongdoers, lest the Fire should touch you, and you will not have any protector besides God; then you will not be helped.

¹¹⁴*Maintain* the prayer at the two ends of the day, and during the early hours of the night. Indeed, good deeds efface misdeeds. That is an admonition for the mindful. ¹¹⁵And *be* patient; indeed God does not waste the reward of the virtuous.

¹¹⁶Why were there not among the generations before you a remnant [of the wise] who might forbid corruption in the land, except a few of those whom We delivered from among them? Those who were wrongdoers pursued [gratification] in the means of affluence they had been granted, and they were a guilty lot. ¹¹⁷*Your* Lord would never destroy the townships unjustly while their inhabitants were bringing about reform.

¹¹⁸Had *your* Lord wished, He would have made mankind one community; but they continue to differ,

11:118 Regarding the Qurʾān's statements on the division of humanity into different communities, see commentary on 10:19 (with further references).

---

¹¹⁹except those on whom *your* Lord has mercy—and that is why He created them—and the word of *your* Lord has been fulfilled: 'I will surely fill hell with jinn and humans, all together!'

¹²⁰Whatever that We relate to *you* of the accounts of the apostles are those by which We strengthen *your* heart, and there has come to *you* in this [*sūrah*] the truth and an advice and admonition for the faithful.

[121]*Say* to those who do not have faith, 'Act according to your ability; we too are acting. [122]And wait! We too are waiting.'

[123]To God belongs the Unseen of the heavens and the earth, and to Him all matters are returned. So *worship* Him and *trust* in Him. *Your* Lord is not oblivious of what you do.

12. *YŪSUF*, JOSEPH

In the Name of God, the All-beneficent, the All-merciful.

¹*Alif, Lām, Rā.* These are the signs of the Manifest Book. ²Indeed, We have sent it down as an Arabic Qur'ān so that you may exercise your reason.

³We will recount to *you* the best of narratives in what We have revealed to *you* of this Qur'ān, and prior to it *you* were indeed among those who are unaware [of it].

⁴When Joseph said to his father, 'Father! I saw eleven planets, and the sun and the moon: I saw them prostrating themselves before me,' ⁵he said, 'My son, do not recount your dream to your brothers, lest they should devise schemes against you. Satan is indeed man's manifest enemy. ⁶That is how your Lord will choose you and teach you the interpretation of dreams, and complete His blessing upon you and upon the house of Jacob, just as He completed it earlier for your fathers, Abraham and Isaac. Your Lord is indeed all-knowing and all-wise.'

12:4–6 According to Genesis Joseph had two prophetic dreams:

⁵Now Joseph had a dream, and he repeated it to his brothers, who then hated him more than ever.

[6]'Listen,' he said, 'to the dream I had.

[7]We were binding sheaves in the field, when my sheaf suddenly rose and stood upright, and then your sheaves gathered round and bowed to my sheaf.'

[8]'So you want to be king over us,' his brothers retorted, 'you want to lord it over us?' And they hated him even more, on account of his dreams and of what he said.

[9]He had another dream which he recounted to his brothers. 'Look, I have had another dream,' he said. 'There were the sun, the moon and eleven stars, bowing down to me.'

[10]He told his father and brothers, and his father scolded him. 'A fine dream to have!' he said to him. 'Are all of us then, myself, your mother and your brothers, to come and bow to the ground before you?'

[11]His brothers held it against him, but his father pondered the matter. (Gen 37:5–11)

The Qur'ān mentions only one dream, that which involves "eleven stars" (in Qur'ānic Arabic the word *kawkab* means "stars," not "planets"). Of note here is the way Joseph's father Jacob reacts upon hearing of his son's dream. He does not scold Joseph, as the Biblical Jacob does. Instead he warns Joseph not to tell the dream to his brothers ("lest they should devise schemes against you"). This reaction reflects how Syriac Christian scholars read the Genesis story (see Witztum, *Syriac Milieu,* 196–97; and before Witztum, see Näf, 58). One of the homilies attributed to Narsai (d. 503) has Jacob warn Joseph not to tell his brothers of this dream "lest there be envy among your brothers and they kill you" (Pseudo-Narsai, *Homilies on Joseph,* 522–23; trans. J. Witztum, *Syriac Milieu,* 193–94).

The *Syriac History of Joseph* (attributed to Basil of Caesarea [d. 379] but likely an original, fifth-century Syriac composition) has Jacob predict great things for Joseph (cf. Q 12:6):

> But Jacob was amazed and wondered at the dreams of Joseph [cf. Gen 37:11]. And he said to himself, "These dreams that have been seen by my son Joseph, they are not false dreams, rather they are true dreams. He has been shown them by God and something great will be done by God with Joseph." (*Syriac History of Joseph,* 3:3–4)

---

[7]In Joseph and his brothers there are certainly signs for the seekers. [8]When they said, 'Surely Joseph and his brother are dearer to our father than [the rest of] us, though we are a hardy

band. Our father is indeed in plain error.' ⁹'Kill Joseph or cast him away into some [distant] land, so that your father's attention may be exclusively towards you, and you may thereafter become a righteous lot.'

¹⁰One of them said, 'Do not kill Joseph, but throw him into the recess of a well so that some caravan may pick him up, if you are to do [anything].'

¹¹They said, 'Father! Why is it that you do not trust us with Joseph? We are indeed his well-wishers. ¹²Let him go with us tomorrow so that he may eat lots of fruits and play, and we will indeed take [good] care of him.'

12:8–12 As Joseph Witztum (*Syriac Milieu,* 197–200) shows, this passage suggests that Joseph's brothers conceived a murderous plot against Joseph even before they left their father's house (in v. 12 they propose taking Joseph away). This sequence contradicts that of Genesis, by which the idea of killing Joseph occurs to them only once they see him coming to Dothan from a distance:

> ¹⁸They saw him in the distance, and before he reached them they made a plot to kill him.
> ¹⁹'Here comes that dreamer,' they said to one another.
> ²⁰'Come on, let us kill him now and throw him down one of the storage-wells; we can say that some wild animal has devoured him. Then we shall see what becomes of his dreams.' (Gen 37:18–20)

As Witztum points out, certain Syriac texts such as Pseudo-Narsai's *Homilies on Joseph* have the brothers conceive of a plot to kill Joseph upon hearing of his dreams:

> Then the brothers of righteous Joseph heard these [dreams]; / they were smitten with envy and they planned to do away with him.
> When righteous Jacob saw that they were biting [Joseph] / he sent them to pasture the flock at Shechem. (Pseudo-Narsai, *Homilies on Joseph,* 523; trans. from: J. Witztum, *Syriac Milieu,* 199)

Pseudo-Narsai's description of the brothers' "biting" Joseph fits with the typological presentation of them as wolves (see Witztum, *Syriac Milieu,* 199, n. 45; Heal, 159; see further below). The way in which the Qur'ān has the brothers coax their father Jacob into allowing Joseph to come with them (v. 11) also has no precedent in Genesis, which has Jacob send Joseph to them at a later point (Gen 37:13).

---

¹³He said, 'It really upsets me that you should take him away, and I fear the wolf may eat him while you are oblivious of him.'

¹⁴They said, 'Should the wolf eat him while we are a hardy band, then we will indeed be losers!'

¹⁵So when they took him away and conspired to put him into the recess of a well, We revealed to him, '[A day will come when] you will surely inform them about this affair of theirs while they are not aware [of your identity].'

12:13–15 In verse 13 Jacob expresses his fear that a wolf might devour Joseph, and two verses later the brothers (deceitfully) report that this is precisely what has taken place. The wolf, as Witztum demonstrates, is a departure from the Joseph account in Genesis, which has Jacob declare only that a "wild animal" has devoured him:

> ³²Then they sent off the decorated tunic and had it taken to their father, with the message, 'This is what we have found. Do you recognise it as your son's tunic or not?'
> ³³He recognised it and cried, 'My son's tunic! A wild animal has devoured him! Joseph has been torn to pieces!' (Gen 37:32–33)

The appearance of a wolf in the Qurʾānic account is a sign of the prominence of Christian retellings of the Joseph account in the Qurʾān's milieu. Whereas some Jewish retellings identify the "wild animal" of Genesis as a bear, they do not identify it as a wolf (perhaps, as Witztum points out, because the beloved full brother of Joseph, Benjamin, is compared to a wolf in Gen 49:27). However, Pseudo-Narsai makes Joseph into a prototype of Christ. He thus compares Joseph to a lamb (as Christ was a lamb) and the brothers to wolves (predators of lambs):

> The wolves (*dēbē*) rose, grabbed the lamb, and dragged him, / saying to him: "relate to us the dreams you saw." (Pseudo-Narsai, *Homilies on Joseph,* 527; English trans. from Witztum, *Syriac Milieu,* 202)

¹⁶In the evening, they came weeping to their father. ¹⁷They said, 'Father! We had gone racing and left Joseph with our things, whereat the wolf ate him. But you will not believe us even if we spoke truly.' ¹⁸And they produced sham blood on his shirt.

He said, 'No, your souls have made a matter seem decorous to you. Yet patience is graceful, and God is my resort against what you allege.'

12:16–18 In Genesis Jacob is fooled by the brothers of Joseph when they tell him Joseph has been killed by a wild animal (and show him the false blood on his shirt that is stained with the blood of a goat they have slaughtered):

> ³¹They took Joseph's tunic and, slaughtering a goat, dipped the tunic in the blood.
> ³²Then they sent off the decorated tunic and had it taken to their father, with the message, 'This is what we have found. Do you recognise it as your son's tunic or not?'
> ³³He recognised it and cried, 'My son's tunic! A wild animal has devoured him! Joseph has been torn to pieces!' (Gen 37:31–33)

The reference to false ("sham") blood in Qur'ān 12:18 follows this. However, the Qur'ān, unlike Genesis, relates that Jacob does not believe the brothers and thus does not mourn Joseph. As Witztum shows (see *Syriac Milieu,* 207–9; also Näf, 66–67) Jacob's prescience in the Qur'ān reflects traditions in a number of Syriac texts. In Pseudo-Narsai's *Homilies on Joseph,* Jacob recognizes that the blood on the cloak is that of an animal, not that of a human (see Heal, *Tradition,* 152). In a homily attributed to Balai (fl. early fifth century), Jacob wonders why the cloak is intact if indeed Joseph had been devoured by animals (on this see Witztum, 209).

Tafsīr al-Jalālayn preserves a similar opinion: "They slaughtered a lamb and dabbed it [his shirt] with its blood—but they forgot to tear it [the shirt]—and they said that it was his blood. He, Jacob, said, when he saw that it [the shirt] was undamaged and realised that they were lying."

¹⁹There came a caravan, and they sent their water-drawer, who let down his bucket. 'Good news!' he said. 'This is a young boy!'

So they hid him as [a piece of] merchandise, and God knew best what they were doing. [20]And they sold him for a cheap price, a few dirhams, for they set small store by him.

12:19–20 As Geiger notes (*Judaism and Islam,* 117) the idea that someone would send down a bucket for water into the pit where Joseph languished contradicts Genesis 37:24, which insists that the pit was dry. Otherwise these two verses generally follow the narrative of that chapter:

> [26]Then Judah said to his brothers, 'What do we gain by killing our brother and covering up his blood?
>
> [27]Come, let us sell him to the Ishmaelites, then we shall not have laid hands on him ourselves. After all, he is our brother, and our own flesh.' His brothers agreed.
>
> [28]Now some Midianite merchants were passing, and they pulled Joseph out of the well. They sold Joseph to the Ishmaelites for twenty shekels of silver, and these men took Joseph to Egypt. (Gen 37:26–28)

---

[21]The man from Egypt who had bought him said to his wife, 'Give him an honourable place [in the household]. Maybe he will be useful to us, or we may adopt him as a son.'

Thus did We establish Joseph in the land and that We might teach him the interpretation of dreams. God has [full] command of His affairs, but most people do not know.

12:21 The way the Qur'ān here has Potiphar declare that he and his wife might adopt Joseph as a son differs from the narrative in Genesis, by which Potiphar simply makes Joseph his "personal attendant":

> [1]Now Joseph had been taken down into Egypt. Potiphar the Egyptian, one of Pharaoh's officials and commander of the guard, bought him from the Ishmaelites who had taken him down there.
>
> [2]the Lord was with Joseph, and everything he undertook was successful. He lodged in the house of his Egyptian master,

³and when his master saw how the Lord was with him and how the Lord made everything he undertook successful,

⁴he was pleased with Joseph and made him his personal attendant; and his master put him in charge of his household, entrusting him with all his possessions. (Gen 39:1–4)

This contrast is best explained through the influence of 28:9, where the wife of Pharaoh declares, regarding Moses, precisely the same thing: "Maybe he will benefit us, or we will adopt him as a son." The parallel between Qur'ān 28 and 12 is illustrated in detail by Witztum (*Syriac Milieu,* 285, 291–92; note that in Exodus it is Pharaoh's daughter, not his wife, who adopts Moses).

---

²²When he came of age, We gave him judgement and [sacred] knowledge, and thus do We reward the virtuous.

²³The woman in whose house he was, solicited him. She closed the doors and said, 'Come!!' He said, 'God forbid! He is indeed my Lord; He has given me a good abode. Indeed, the wrongdoers do not prosper.'

²⁴She certainly made for him; and he would have made for her [too] had he not beheld the proof of his Lord. So it was, that We might turn away from him all evil and indecency. He was indeed one of Our dedicated servants.

²⁵They raced to the door, and she tore his shirt from behind, and they ran into her husband at the door. She said, 'What is to be the requital of him who has evil intentions for your wife except imprisonment or a painful punishment?' ²⁶He said, 'It was she who solicited me.'

A witness of her own household testified [saying]: 'If his shirt is torn from the front, she tells the truth and he lies. ²⁷But if his shirt is torn from behind, then she lies and he tells the truth.'

²⁸So when he saw that his shirt was torn from behind, he said, 'This is [a case] of you women's guile! Your guile is great indeed!

²⁹Joseph, let this matter alone, and you, woman, plead for forgiveness for your sin, for you have indeed been erring.'

12:23–29 In Genesis 39 Potiphar accepts the deceitful account of his wife and throws Joseph into prison without giving him a chance to defend himself:

> ¹⁷Then she told him the same tale, 'The Hebrew slave you brought to us burst in on me to make a fool of me.
> ¹⁸But when I screamed, he left his tunic beside me and ran away.'
> ¹⁹When his master heard his wife say, 'This was how your slave treated me,' he became furious.
> ²⁰Joseph's master had him arrested and committed to the gaol where the king's prisoners were kept. And there in gaol he stayed. (Gen 39:17–20)

In the Qur'ān, however, Joseph is vindicated when an anonymous figure points out that he must have been fleeing from Potiphar's wife since his shirt is torn from behind. Joseph is later thrown into prison (see v. 35) but for no evident reason. As Witztum explains (*Syriac Milieu,* 211–17; cf. Näf, 70), the idea that Potiphar recognized Joseph's innocence seems to have begun with the conviction of Jewish and Christian exegetes that imprisonment would be too mild of a punishment for the crime of which Joseph was accused: attempted rape of his master's wife. Witztum writes, "The audience no doubt wondered why he escaped a more severe sentence" (216). An explanation was found (see, e.g., *Genesis Rabbah* 87:9) in having Potiphar recognize Joseph's innocence. The manner by which Potiphar discovered Joseph's innocence in the Qur'ān—through an examination of his shirt—is found already in Syriac Christian sources such as the homilies of Narsai (*Homily on Joseph,* 2:279) and Pseudo-Narsai (541–42, trans. Witztum, *Syriac Milieu,* 215). This element is missing from Jewish sources.

The way the Qur'ān (v. 24) has Joseph resist Potiphar's wife ("he would have made for her [too] had he not beheld the proof of his Lord") has an antecedent in Jewish tradition, but not in Christian tradition. A passage in the Babylonian Talmud relates how Potiphar's wife and Joseph "planned to sin together" until Joseph's father Jacob appeared to him in a vision:

> That day was their feast-day, and they had all gone to their idolatrous temple; but she had pretended to be ill because she thought, I shall not have an opportunity like today for Joseph to associate with me. And she caught him by his garment, saying etc. At that moment his father's image came and appeared to him through the window and said: "Joseph, thy brothers will have their names inscribed upon the stones of the ephod and thine amongst theirs; is it

thy wish to have thy name expunged from amongst theirs and be called an associate of harlots?" (b. *Sotah,* 36b)

This vision, evidently, is the "proof" to which the Qur'ān refers in verse 24 (see further J. Kugel, *In Potiphar's House,* 107–12, who shows how this is connected to Gen 49:24). A reflection of this tradition is preserved by *Tafsīr al-Jalālayn:* "Ibn 'Abbās said, 'Jacob was made to appear before him, and he struck [Joseph's] breast, whereupon his [sexual] desire withdrew [from his body] through his fingernails."

---

³⁰Some of the townswomen said, 'The chieftain's wife has solicited her slave boy! He has captivated her love. Indeed, we see her to be in plain error.' ³¹When she heard of their machinations, she sent for them and arranged a repast, and gave each of them a knife, and said [to Joseph], 'Come out before them.' So when they saw him, they marvelled at him and cut their hands [absent-mindedly], and they said, 'Good heavens! This is not a human being! This is but a noble angel!'

³²She said, 'He is the one on whose account you blamed me. Certainly I did solicit him, but he was continent, and if he does not do what I bid him, he will surely be imprisoned and humbled.'

³³He said, 'My Lord! The prison is dearer to me than to what they invite me. If You do not turn away their schemes from me, I will incline towards them and become one of the ignorant.'

³⁴So his Lord answered him and turned away their stratagems from him. Indeed, He is the All-hearing, the All-knowing.

³⁵Then it appeared to them, after they had seen all the signs [of his innocence], that they should confine him for some time.

12:30–35 The Qur'ān's reference to a gathering of women is not found in the Genesis account of Joseph or in most early Jewish and Christian sources. However, James Kugel (*In Potiphar's House,* 32ff.) draws attention to an

Aramaic poem that may predate the Qurʾān which describes how Potiphar's
wife brought together "the neighboring ladies." Only some versions of this
poem include the detail of the ladies cutting their hands (instead of fruit they
were given) upon beholding Joseph's beauty, and Kugel suggests (40) that both
the Qurʾān and the "bloody" versions of this poem are later developments on an
earlier, simpler poem.

All of these midrashic developments seem to be a response to a phrase in
Genesis 39:7: the Hebrew *aḥar ha-debārīm ha-ēlleh,* lit. "after these things"
or "after these words." The gathering of the ladies, their conversation, and the
cutting of their hands upon seeing Joseph, are meant to be the "things" (or the
"words") of Genesis 39:7. This story also explains why Potiphar's wife, in Genesis 39:14, calls out "*See,* [Potiphar] has brought among us a Hebrew to insult
us" (Gen 39:14 RSV). The reference to "seeing" led to a story about *seeing* Joseph (Kugel, *In Potiphar's House,* 50ff.) and the reference to "us"—instead of
"me"—was the seed sown in the exegetical mind which blossomed into a story
about Potiphar's wife *and* her friends (see Kugel, *In Potiphar's House,* 46).

As Witztum points out (*Syriac Milieu,* 215–16), the homilies on Joseph by
Narsai and Pseudo-Narsai relate—like the Qurʾān—that Potiphar knew of Joseph's innocence yet nevertheless threw him into prison (v. 35). According to
Narsai (*Homily on Joseph,* 2:279) Potiphar did so because of his jealousy, while
according to Pseudo-Narsai (*Homilies on Joseph,* 542) he did so because his
wife demanded that Joseph be sent away. The Qurʾān seems to develop its own
explanation, namely that Potiphar's wife once again sought to have relations
with Joseph, and that this time she threatened him with imprisonment should he
refuse (v. 32). It then has Joseph choose prison over fornication (v. 33).

---

³⁶There entered the prison two youths along with him. One of
them said, 'I dreamt that I am pressing grapes.' The other said,
'I dreamt that I am carrying bread on my head from which the
birds are eating.' 'Inform us of its interpretation,' [they said], 'for
indeed we see you to be a virtuous man.'

³⁷He said, 'Before the meals you are served come to you I will
inform you of its interpretation. That is among things my Lord
has taught me. Indeed, I renounce the creed of the people who

have no faith in God and who [also] disbelieve in the Hereafter. ³⁸I follow the creed of my fathers, Abraham, Isaac and Jacob. It is not for us to ascribe any partner to God. That is by virtue of God's grace upon us and upon all mankind, but most people do not give thanks. ³⁹O my prison mates! Are different masters better, or God, the One, the All-paramount? ⁴⁰You do not worship besides Him but [mere] names that you and your fathers have coined, for which God has not sent down any authority. Dispensation belongs only to God. He has commanded you to worship none except Him. That is the upright religion, but most people do not know.

⁴¹O my prison mates! As for one of you, he will serve wine to his master, and as for the other, he will be crucified and vultures will eat from his head. The matter about which you inquire has been decided.'

12:36–41 The Qur'ān has the baker crucified (v. 41), whereas Genesis has him hanged (Gen 40:22), although crucifixion was first practiced long after the traditional dates of Joseph's life:

⁶When Joseph came to them in the morning, he saw that they looked gloomy, ⁷and he asked the two officials who were in custody with him in his master's house, 'Why these sad looks today?'
⁸They replied, 'We have each had a dream, but there is no one to interpret it.' 'Are not interpretations God's business?' Joseph asked them. 'Tell me about them.'
. . .
²⁰And so it happened; the third day was Pharaoh's birthday and he gave a banquet for all his officials. Of his officials he lifted up the head of the chief cup-bearer and the chief baker,
²¹the chief cup-bearer by restoring him to his cup-bearing, so that he again handed Pharaoh his cup;
²²and by hanging the chief baker, as Joseph had explained to them. (Gen 40:6–8, 20–22)

42Then he said to the one whom he knew would be delivered from among the two: 'Mention me to your master.' But Satan caused him to forget mentioning [it] to his master. So he remained in the prison for several years.

12:42 The manner in which the Qurʾān (unlike Genesis, cf. Gen 40:23: "But the chief cup-bearer did not remember Joseph; he had forgotten him") blames Satan for the cupbearer's forgetting Joseph is connected to other Qurʾānic passages (Q 6:68; 18:63; 58:19) which make Satan responsible for man's forgetfulness.

43[One day] the king said, 'I saw [in a dream] seven fat cows being devoured by seven lean ones, and seven green ears and [seven] others [that were] dry. O courtiers, give me your opinion about my dream, if you can interpret dreams.' 44They said, '[These are] muddled dreams, and we do not know the interpretation of such dreams.'

45Said the one of the two who had been delivered [from the prison], remembering [Joseph] after a long time: 'I will inform you of its interpretation; so let me go [to meet Joseph in the prison].'

46'Joseph,' [he said], 'O truthful one, give us your opinion concerning seven fat cows who are eaten by seven lean ones, and seven green ears and [seven] others dry, that I may return to these people so that they may know [the truth of the matter].'

47He said, 'You will sow for seven consecutive years. Then leave in the ear whatever [grain] you harvest, except a little that you eat. 48Then after that there will come seven hard years which will eat up whatever you have set aside for them—all except a little which you preserve [for seed]. 49Then after that there will come a year wherein the people will be granted relief and provided with rains therein.'

12:43–49 The Qurʾān has Joseph offer the interpretation of Pharaoh's dreams from prison (only later, in v. 50, is he summoned to Pharaoh), while in Genesis Joseph offers the interpretation of Pharaoh's dreams in his presence:

> [14]Then Pharaoh had Joseph summoned, and they hurried him from the dungeon. He shaved and changed his clothes, and presented himself before Pharaoh.
>
> [15]Pharaoh said to Joseph, 'I have had a dream, and there is no one to interpret it. But I have heard it said of you that you can interpret a dream the instant you hear it.'
>
> [16]'Not I,' Joseph replied to Pharaoh, 'God will give Pharaoh a favourable answer.'
>
> . . .
>
> [25]Joseph said to Pharaoh, 'Pharaoh's dreams are one and the same: God has revealed to Pharaoh what he is going to do.
>
> [26]The seven fine cows are seven years and the seven ripe ears of grain are seven years; it is one and the same dream.
>
> [27]The seven gaunt and lean cows coming up behind them are seven years, as are the seven shrivelled ears of grain scorched by the east wind: there will be seven years of famine. (Gen 41:14–16, 25–27)

The Arabic behind "truthful one" in verse 46 is *ṣiddīq* and may come from Hebrew *ṣaddīq,* "pious, righteous"—(see Ambros, 159) a typical description of Joseph in midrash. This could also be behind other uses of this term: for Mary (5:75) and generally (4:69; 57:19).

---

[50]The king said, 'Bring him to me!'

When the messenger came to him, he said, 'Go back to your master, and ask him about the affair of the women who cut their hands. My Lord is indeed well aware of their stratagems.'

[51]The king said, 'What was your business, women, when you solicited Joseph?' They said, 'Heaven be praised! We know of no evil in him.' The prince's wife said, 'Now the truth has come to light! It was I who solicited him, and he is indeed telling the truth.'

[52][Joseph said], ['I initiated] this [inquiry], that he may know that I did not betray him in his absence, and that God does not further the schemes of the treacherous.'

⁵³'Yet I do not absolve my [own carnal] soul, for the [carnal] soul indeed prompts [men] to evil, except inasmuch as my Lord has mercy. My Lord is indeed all-forgiving, all-merciful.'

12:50–53 The Qur'ān has Potiphar's wife return to the scene to confess her guilt. As Witztum points out, in Genesis she does not say anything further after her accusations against Joseph in front of Potiphar (Gen 39:19). By reintroducing Potiphar's wife the Qur'ān is following a tradition found in Syriac homilies on Joseph (see Witztum's full discussion of these sources: *Syriac Milieu*, 217–22). For example, the *Commentary on Genesis* of Ephrem has Potiphar's wife confess her guilt to her husband:

> To show you that [Joseph] is not evil, I will now speak the truth which is contrary to my previous lie. I was enamored of Joseph when I falsely accused him. I made assault on his clothing because I was overcome by his beauty. (35:8)

It should be noted that Qarai attributes the declarations in verses 52–53 to Joseph (this is also the perspective of *Tafsīr al-Jalālayn*). However, the Qur'ān's relationship with Syriac texts such as the *Commentary on Genesis* suggests that these are the contrite declarations of Potiphar's wife.

---

⁵⁴The king said, 'Bring him to me, I will make him my favourite.' Then, when he had spoken with him, he said, 'Indeed, today [onwards] you will be honoured and trustworthy with us.'

⁵⁵He said, 'Put me in charge of the country's granaries. I am indeed fastidious [and] well-informed.'

⁵⁶That is how We established Joseph in the land that he may settle in it wherever he wished. We confer Our mercy on whomever We wish, and We do not waste the reward of the virtuous.

12:54–56 Note Genesis 41:39–41:

³⁹So Pharaoh said to Joseph, 'Since God has given you knowledge of all this, there can be no one as intelligent and wise as you.

⁴⁰You shall be my chancellor, and all my people shall respect your orders; only this throne shall set me above you.'

⁴¹Pharaoh said to Joseph, 'I hereby make you governor of the whole of Egypt.' (Gen 41:39–41)

————————————

⁵⁷And the reward of the Hereafter is surely better for those who have faith and are Godwary.

⁵⁸[After some years] the brothers of Joseph came and entered his presence. He recognized them, but they did not recognize him.

⁵⁹When he had furnished them with their provision, he said, 'Bring me a brother that you have through your father. Do you not see that I give the full measure and that I am the best of hosts? ⁶⁰But if you do not bring him to me, then there will be no rations for you with me, and don't [ever] approach me.'

⁶¹They said, 'We will solicit him from his father. [That] we will surely do.'

⁶²He said to his servants, 'Put their money [back] into their saddlebags. Maybe they will recognize it when they return to their folks, and maybe they will come back [again].'

12:58–62 Note Genesis 42:

⁷As soon as Joseph saw his brothers he recognised them. But he did not make himself known to them, and he spoke harshly to them. 'Where have you come from?' he asked. 'From Canaan to get food,' they replied.

⁸Now when Joseph recognised his brothers, but they did not recognise him,

. . .

¹⁸On the third day Joseph said to them, 'Do this and you will live, for I am a man who fears God.

¹⁹If you are honest men, let one of your brothers be detained where you are imprisoned; the rest of you, go and take supplies home for your starving families.

²⁰But you must bring your youngest brother back to me; in this way, what you have said will be verified, and you will not have to die!' And this is what they did.

. . .

²⁵Joseph gave the order to fill their panniers with grain, to put back each man's money in his sack, and to give them provisions for the journey. This was done for them. (Gen 42:7–8, 18–20, 25)

----

⁶³So when they returned to their father, they said, 'Father, the measure has been withheld from us, so let our brother go with us so that we may obtain the measure, and we will indeed take [good] care of him.'

⁶⁴He said, 'Should I trust you with him just as I trusted you with his brother before? Yet God is the best of protectors, and He is the most merciful of merciful ones.'

⁶⁵And when they opened their baggage, they found their money restored to them. They said, 'Father, what [more] do we want?! This is our money, restored to us! We will get provisions for our family and take care of our brother, and add another camel-load of rations. These are meagre rations.'

12:63–65 Genesis has one of the brothers discover that his money has been returned to him while they are still on the way back to Canaan (Gen 42:27–28); the others find their money bags later, in the presence of their father (Gen 42:35). The Qur'ān (12:65) has all of the brothers make this discovery in Canaan, in the presence of their father. Moreover, whereas Genesis has the brothers distressed at the discovery (Gen 42:28, 35), knowing that they might be accused of stealing supplies, the Qur'ān has them rejoice that they have both supplies and money ("Father, what [more] do we want?! This is our money, restored to us").

Witztum (*Syriac Milieu*, 225) points out that a parallel to their reaction is found in the sixth-century Greek work (generally thought to incorporate Syriac elements) of Romanos the Melodist, who in his hymn on Joseph has the brothers say to Jacob: "Father, why do you groan? Behold the joy we have found in the bags, the cost of the grain. Stop wailing!" (Romanus, *De Joseph,* 1:228; cf. Witztum, *Syriac Milieu,* 225).

⁶⁶He said, 'I will not let him go with you until you give me a [solemn] pledge by God that you will surely bring him back to me, unless you are made to perish.' When they had given him their [solemn] pledge, he said, 'God is witness over what we say.' ⁶⁷And he said, 'My sons, do not enter by one gate, but enter by separate gates, though I cannot avail you anything against God. Sovereignty belongs only to God. In Him alone I have put my trust; and in Him alone let all the trusting put their trust.'

12:67 The way the Qur'ān has Jacob tell his sons to enter by separate gates reflects a tradition found in Jewish midrash, notably *Genesis Rabbah,* but not in the Syriac sources:

> And Jacob said to his sons: "Why should ye be conspicuous?" "My sons," said he to them: "Ye are all strong and brotherly [friends]: do not enter through one gate and do not all stand in the same place, because of the [evil] eye." (*Genesis Rabbah,* 91:6)

⁶⁸When they entered whence their father had bidden them, it did not avail them anything against God, but only fulfilled a wish in Jacob's heart. He had indeed the knowledge of what We had taught him, but most people do not know. ⁶⁹When they entered into the presence of Joseph, he set his brother close to himself, and said, 'I am indeed your brother, so do not sorrow for what they used to do.'

12:69 The Qur'ān has Joseph reveal his identity to Benjamin here, although in Genesis Joseph reveals his identity only later (Gen 45), after Joseph's cup has been found with Benjamin. Witztum points out (226–28) that the Qur'ān seems to be developing a theme in Syriac Christian texts such as the *Homilies on Joseph* of Pseudo-Narsai, which has Joseph take Benjamin aside to comfort him. In the Qurʾān Joseph simply reveals the truth to Benjamin.

---

⁷⁰When he had furnished them with their provisions, he put the drinking-cup into his brother's saddlebag. Then a herald shouted: 'O [men of the] caravan! You are indeed thieves!'

⁷¹They said, as they turned towards them, 'What are you missing?'

⁷²They said, 'We miss the king's goblet.' 'Whoever brings it shall have a camel-load [of grain],' [said the steward], 'I will guarantee that.'

⁷³They said, 'By God! You certainly know that we did not come to make trouble in this country, and we are not thieves.'

⁷⁴They said, 'What shall be its requital if you [prove to] be lying?'

⁷⁵They said, 'The requital for it shall be that he in whose saddlebag it is found shall give himself over as its requital. Thus do we requite the wrongdoers.'

12:74–75 By having the brothers declare here that the one in whose bag the goblet is found "shall give himself over" (that is, become a slave or a prisoner) the Qurʾān differs from the declaration of the brothers in Genesis 44:9, where the brothers recommend death for the guilty party. This reflects how Syriac Christian authors sought to reconcile Genesis 44:9 with the following verse, wherein Joseph's chamberlain both says "it shall be as you say" and "the one on whom it is found shall become my slave (Gen 44:10)." See Witztum's discussion of this in *Syriac Milieu*, 229–30.

For example, and as Witztum points out (*Syriac Milieu*, 230), the *Homilies on Joseph* of Pseudo-Narsai has all the brothers express their willingness to become slaves should the cup be found:

He [the steward] said to them: "And if I do find it what shall happen?" / They all said: "We shall all be slaves to your lord." Pseudo-Narsai, *Homilies on Joseph*, 590; trans.: J. Witztum, *Syriac Milieu*, 230)

⁷⁶Then he began with their sacks, before [opening] his brother's sack. Then he took it out from his brother's sack.

Thus did We devise for Joseph's sake. He could not have held his brother under the king's law unless God willed [otherwise]. We raise in rank whomever We please, and above every man of knowledge is One who knows best.

⁷⁷They said, 'If he has stolen [there is no wonder]; a brother of his had stolen before.'

Thereupon Joseph kept the matter to himself and he did not disclose it to them. He said, 'You are in a worse state! And God knows best what you allege.'

12:77 There is no parallel in Genesis for the brothers' remark here, in regard to Benjamin: "If he has stolen [there is no wonder] a brother of his had stolen before." *Tafsīr al-Jalālayn* explains: "Joseph—he had stolen a golden idol from his maternal grandfather [i.e., Laban, the father of Rachel] and smashed it, lest he worship it. But Joseph kept it secret in his soul and did not disclose it, manifest it, to them." In Genesis 31 it is not Joseph but Rachel—mother of Joseph and Benjamin (but not the other brothers)—who steals Laban's idols:

³⁴Now Rachel had taken the household idols and put them inside a camel cushion, and was sitting on them. Laban went through everything in the tent but found nothing.
³⁵Then Rachel said to her father, 'Do not look angry, my lord, because I cannot rise in your presence, for I am as women are from time to time.' Laban searched but did not find the idols. (Gen 31:34–35)

At the root of the Qur'ān's description of Joseph as a thief might be Syriac texts such as the *Syriac History of Joseph* (see 41:1–8), which have the brothers (after the cup is found with Benjamin's things) malign Benjamin as the son of a thief (Rachel) and brother of a liar (Joseph—whom the brothers consider a liar on account of his dreams). The Qur'ān seems to conflate the two originally distinct insults into one. For a more detailed discussion of this, see Witztum, *Syriac Milieu*, 231–34.

---

[78]They said, 'O emir! Indeed, he has a father, a very old man; so take one of us in his place. Indeed, we see that you are a virtuous man.'

[79]He said, 'God forbid that we should detain anyone except him with whom we found our wares, for then we would indeed be wrongdoers.'

[80]When they had despaired of [moving] him, they withdrew to confer privately. The eldest of them said, 'Don't you know that your father has taken a [solemn] pledge from you by God, and earlier you have neglected your duty in regard to Joseph? So I will never leave this land until my father permits me, or God passes a judgement for me and He is the best of judges. [81]Go back to your father, and say, "Father! Your son has indeed committed theft, and we testified only to what we knew, and we could not have forestalled the unseen. [82]Ask [the people of] the town we were in and the caravan with which we came. We indeed speak the truth."'

12:78–82 The Qur'ān has the eldest of the brothers (*kabīruhum*) speak beginning in verse 80, although in Genesis (44:18ff.) it is not Reuben (the eldest) but Judah—the last of Jacob's children from Leah—who speaks. *Tafsīr al-Jalālayn* recognizes this and relates that by "eldest" the Qur'ān must mean either Reuben or "the most senior of them . . . *in opinion*—Judah."

---

[83]He said, 'No, your souls have made a matter seem decorous to you. Yet patience is graceful. Maybe God will bring them all [back] to me. Indeed, He is the All-knowing, the All-wise.'

[84]He turned away from them and said, 'Alas for Joseph!' His eyes had turned white with grief, and he choked with suppressed agony.

⁸⁵They said, 'By God! You will go on remembering Joseph until you wreck your health or perish.' ⁸⁶He said, 'I complain of my anguish and grief only to God. I know from God what you do not know.' ⁸⁷'Go, my sons, and look for Joseph and his brother, and do not despair of God's mercy. Indeed, no one despairs of God's mercy except the faithless lot.'

⁸⁸Then, when they entered into his presence, they said, 'O emir! Distress has befallen us and our family, and we have brought [just] a meagre sum. Yet grant us the full measure and be charitable to us! God indeed rewards the charitable.'

⁸⁹He said, 'Have you realized what you did to Joseph and his brother, when you were ignorant?'

⁹⁰They said, 'Are you really Joseph?!'

He said, 'I am Joseph, and this is my brother. Certainly God has shown us favour. Indeed, if one is Godwary and patient, God does not waste the reward of the virtuous.'

⁹¹They said, 'By God, God has certainly preferred you over us, and we have indeed been erring.'

⁹²He said, 'There shall be no reproach on you today. God will forgive you and He is the most merciful of the merciful.

12:83–92 Regarding the phrase "His eyes had turned white with grief" (v. 84), *Tafsīr al-Jalālayn* recounts: "And his eyes turned white, their dark colour was effaced and became white on account of his tears, with grief, for him, such that he was [filled] with suppressed agony, anguished and grief-stricken, but not manifesting his grief." In fact (and as Witztum [*Syriac Milieu*, 223–24] points out) the Qurʾān seems to mean that Jacob became blind (Hilali-Khan translate, to this end, "And he lost his sight because of the sorrow that he was suppressing"), since in verse 93 the Qurʾān has Joseph tell his brothers to put his shirt on Jacob's face, explaining "he will regain his sight" (and indeed in v. 96 they do so and he regains his sight.) See further commentary on 12:93–96.

This Qurʾānic sequence is not easy to follow. It begins with the brothers in Canaan with Jacob, and continues in Egypt, where Joseph reveals his identity to them. The sequence differs from the sequence in Genesis, which instead has the brothers recall to Joseph (in Egypt) their conversation with Jacob back in Canaan:

> [1]Then Joseph could not control his feelings in front of all his retainers, and he exclaimed, 'Let everyone leave me.' No one therefore was present with him while Joseph made himself known to his brothers,
> [2]but he wept so loudly that all the Egyptians heard, and the news reached Pharaoh's palace.
> [3]Joseph said to his brothers, 'I am Joseph. Is my father really still alive?' His brothers could not answer him, they were so dumbfounded at seeing him.
> [4]Then Joseph said to his brothers, 'Come closer to me.' When they had come closer to him he said, 'I am your brother Joseph whom you sold into Egypt.
> [5]But now, do not grieve, do not reproach yourselves for having sold me here, since God sent me before you to preserve your lives. (Gen 45:1–5)

---

[93]Take this shirt of mine and cast it upon my father's face; he will regain his sight, and bring me all your folks.'

[94]As the caravan set off, their father said, 'I sense the scent of Joseph, if you will not consider me a dotard.'

[95]They said, 'By God, you persist in your inveterate error.'

[96]When the bearer of good news arrived, he cast it on his face, and he regained his sight. He said, 'Did I not tell you, "I know from God what you do not know?"'

12:93–96 It is not clear where the "caravan" set off from (v. 94; most classical commentators have it setting off from Egypt), and indeed it is not easy to follow the Qur'ānic sequence in this section (vv. 94–95 seem to interrupt the sequence regarding the shirt in v. 93 and v. 96).

The Qur'ān here describes how Joseph's garment miraculously cured his father Jacob from his blindness. The Qur'ān seems to have developed the idea that Jacob became blind (and was subsequently healed) by interpreting literally certain metaphorical Syriac expressions (see the full discussion in Witztum, *Syriac Milieu*, 223–24). One might compare, for example, the *Syriac History of Joseph:*

And they spread out the coat in front of Jacob, and when he saw it, the light of his eyes grew dim, and the strength of his limbs vanished away. (*Syriac History of Joseph*, 12:1; cf. also 9:8a; 51:1–2)

Genesis relates that Joseph gave garments to his brothers along with other items which they were to give to their father Jacob (45:22–23; in *Jubilees* [43:22] and the Latin Vulgate Joseph sends also clothing to Jacob). Genesis 45:27 also notes that Jacob's spirit "revived" upon seeing the wagons Joseph had sent from Egypt. The Qur'ān's report that a garment sent by Joseph healed Jacob's blindness seems to be a development of these passages (see Witztum, *Syriac Milieu*, 235–37).

According to *Tafsīr al-Jalālayn* the shirt which healed Jacob came from paradise: "This was the shirt of Abraham, the one he wore when he was thrown into the fire [cf. 21:68–70, 29:24, 37:97–98]; he [Joseph] had it around his neck when he was at the bottom of the well. It [the shirt] had come from heaven: Gabriel commanded him [Joseph] to send it off [to Jacob] saying that the scent of Paradise lingers in it, and whenever it is cast upon a sufferer, it heals him."

---

⁹⁷They said, 'Father! Plead [with God] for forgiveness of our sins! We have indeed been erring.'

⁹⁸He said, 'I shall plead with my Lord to forgive you; indeed He is the All-forgiving, the All-merciful.'

12:97–98 In Genesis the brothers never ask Jacob's forgiveness for their crimes against Joseph (they ask Joseph's forgiveness after Jacob's death and explain that Jacob told them to do so: Gen 50:15–17). The Qur'ān, however, has the brothers ask Jacob to pray that God will forgive them. Witztum argues (*Syriac Milieu*, 238–39) that the Qur'ān's report is anticipated by the Syriac homily on Joseph of Balai, which has Jacob pray to God for the brothers' forgiveness (Balai, 108–9).

---

⁹⁹When they entered into the presence of Joseph, he set his parents close to himself, and said, 'Welcome to Egypt, in safety, God willing!'

12:99 The Qur'ān has Joseph bring both of his parents to Egypt, but according to Genesis his mother had already died (Gen 35:19) giving birth to his brother Benjamin. Geiger argues (*Judaism and Islam,* 117) that Muḥammad did so in order that Joseph's initial dream (Q 12:4), which has both of his parents symbolically bow before him, would be fulfilled. *Tafsīr al-Jalālayn* is aware of the problem regarding Rachel (namely that she should be dead) here and relates: "His father and his mother—or his maternal aunt."

---

¹⁰⁰And he seated his parents high upon the throne, and they fell down prostrate before him. He said, 'Father! This is the fulfillment of my dream of long ago, which my Lord has made come true. He was certainly gracious to me when He brought me out of the prison and brought you over from the desert after that Satan had incited ill feeling between me and my brothers. My Lord is indeed all-attentive in bringing about what He wishes. Indeed, He is the All-knowing, the All-wise.'

¹⁰¹'My Lord! You have granted me a share in the kingdom, and taught me the interpretation of dreams. Originator of the heavens and earth! You are my guardian in this world and the Hereafter! Let my death be in submission [to You], and unite me with the Righteous.'

12:100–101 Regarding verse 100 *Tafsīr al-Jalālayn* is concerned with the idea that Jacob (a "Muslim" prophet who should know how to act piously) bows down (the Arabic word is *sujjad,* related to a word used for an element of Islamic prayer) before a human (when this is the sort of thing a Muslim should do only before God). *Tafsīr al-Jalālayn* explains: "And he raised his parents, he seated them next to him, upon the throne, and they fell down, that is, his parents and brothers, prostrating before him—a prostration that was [actually] a bowing down, not placing their foreheads down [on the ground]; this was their standard [form of] greeting at that time." Muhammad Asad deals with the reference to the prostration of Joseph's parents by noting the opinion of Fakhr al-Dīn al-Rāzī (d. 606/1209): "The personal pronoun in 'before *him*' relates to God, since it is inconceivable that Joseph would have allowed his parents to prostrate themselves before himself." Debate on this passage is often connected to debate over the angels' prostrating before Adam (see commentary on 7:11–12, with further references).

———

¹⁰²These are accounts from the Unseen which We reveal to *you,* and *you* were not with them when they conspired together and schemed. ¹⁰³Yet, however eager *you* should be, most people will not have faith. ¹⁰⁴*You* do not ask them any reward for it: it is just a reminder for all the nations.

12:104 On the idea that a true prophet does not seek a reward, see commentary on 34:47 (with further references).

———

¹⁰⁵How many a sign there is in the heavens and the earth that they pass by while they are disregardful of it! ¹⁰⁶And most of them do not believe in God without ascribing partners to Him.

¹⁰⁷Do they feel secure from being overtaken by a blanket punishment from God, or being overtaken suddenly by the Hour, while they are unaware?

¹⁰⁸*Say,* 'This is my way. I summon to God with insight—I and he who follows me. Immaculate is God, and I am not one of the polytheists.'

¹⁰⁹We did not send [any apostles] before *you* except as men to whom We revealed from among the people of the towns. Have they not traveled through the land so that they may observe how was the fate of those who were before them? And the abode of the Hereafter is surely better for those who are Godwary. Do you not exercise your reason?

[110]When the apostles lost hope and they thought that they had been told lies, Our help came to them and We delivered whomever We wished, and Our punishment will not be averted from the guilty lot.

[111]There is certainly a moral in their accounts for those who possess intellect. This [Qur'ān] is not a fabricated discourse; rather, it is a confirmation of what was [revealed] before it, and an elaboration of all things, and guidance and mercy for people who have faith.

13. *al-Raʿd*, Thunder

_____

In the Name of God, the All-beneficent, the All-merciful.

¹*Alif, Lām, Mīm, Rā.* These are the signs of the Book. That which has been sent down to *you* from *your* Lord is the truth, but most people do not believe [in it].

²It is God who raised the heavens without any pillars that you see, and then presided over the Throne. He disposed the sun and the moon, each moving for a specified term. He directs the command, [and] elaborates the signs that you may be certain of encountering your Lord.

13:2 On the Qurʾān's vision of God's raising the heavens without any pillars see commentary on Q 31:10. On God's "presiding" (Qarai translates the expression as "settling" elsewhere; it can imply "sitting") over the throne, see commentary on 32:4 (with further references).

_____

³It is He who has spread out the earth and set in it firm mountains and streams, and of every fruit He has made in it two kinds. He draws the night's cover over the day. There are indeed signs in that for people who reflect.

⁴In the earth are neighbouring terrains [of diverse kinds] and vineyards, farms, and date palms growing from the same root and from diverse roots, [all] irrigated by the same water, and We give some of them an advantage over others in flavour. There are indeed signs in that for a people who exercise their reason.

⁵If *you* are to wonder [at anything], then wonderful is their remark, 'When we have become dust, shall we be [ushered] into a new creation?' They are the ones who defy their Lord; they shall have iron collars around their necks, they shall be the inhabitants of the Fire, and they will remain in it [forever].

13:5 The way the Qurʾān makes a case specifically for the resurrection of the body here and elsewhere (cf. 17:49, 98; 19:66; 23:35, 82; 32:10, 34:7; 36:78; 37:15, 53; 46:17; 50:3; 56:47) hardly reflects the traditional idea that Mecca was filled with pagans (this Sura is traditionally dated to the late Meccan period). If the Qurʾān were concerned with pagans, presumably it would need to defend its entire eschatological teaching, including the idea that there is a heaven like a garden and a hell that is a place of torture.

Notably, at the moment of the Qurʾān's origins the Syriac father Babai the Great (d. 628) was arguing against the Christians of his day who followed the doctrine of Ḥenana of Adiabene (d. 610). Babai accuses these Christians of denying the resurrection of the body (cr. Tommaso Tesei):

> However all of these followers of Ḥenana even in our day rise up for their destruction. These people deny not only the resurrection of the body of our Lord, but also the general resurrection of the bodies of all men. They believe in the redemption of all souls in the future and they believe that their redemption is when they are freed from the prison of the body in which they are confined. But in truth the bodies of these evil ones will rise in the resurrection of judgment and they will be handed over to eternal punishment with Satan their father, whose deception they have accepted. (Babai the Great, *Liber de unione*, 195).

⁶They would press *you* for evil sooner than for good, though there have already gone by exemplary punishments before them.

Your Lord is indeed forgiving to mankind despite their wrongdoing, and *your* Lord is indeed severe in retribution.

⁷The faithless say, 'Why has not some sign been sent down to him from his Lord?' *You* are only a warner, and there is a guide for every people.

⁸God knows what every female carries [in her womb], and what the wombs reduce and what they increase, and everything is by [precise] measure with Him, ⁹the Knower of the sensible and the Unseen, the All-great, the All-sublime.

¹⁰It is the same [to Him] whether any of you speaks secretly, or does so loudly, or whether he lurks in the night, or is open to view in daytime. ¹¹He has guardian angels, at his front and rear, who guard him by God's command.

Indeed, God does not change a people's lot, unless they change what is in their souls. And when God wishes to visit ill on a people, there is nothing that can avert it, and they have no protector besides Him.

¹²It is He who shows you the lightning, inspiring fear and hope, and He produces the clouds heavy [with rain]. ¹³The Thunder celebrates His praise, and the angels [too], in awe of Him, and He releases the thunderbolts and strikes with them whomever He wishes. Yet they dispute concerning God, though He is great in might.

13:13 On the image of angels' praising God, see commentary on 7:206 (with further references).

———————

¹⁴[Only] to Him belongs the true invocation; and those whom they invoke besides Him do not answer them in any wise—like someone who stretches his hands towards water [desiring] that it should reach his mouth, but it does not reach it—and the invocations of the faithless only go awry.

¹⁵To God prostrates whoever there is in the heavens and the earth, willingly or unwillingly, and their shadows at sunrise and sunset.

13:15 See commentary on 16:49 (with further references).

---

¹⁶*Say,* 'Who is the Lord of the heavens and the earth?' *Say,* 'God!' *Say,* 'Have you, then, taken others besides Him for protectors, who have no control over their own benefit or harm?' *Say,* 'Are the blind one and the seer equal? Or, are darkness and light equal?' Have they set up for God partners who have created like His creation, so that the creations seemed confusable to them? *Say,* 'God is the creator of all things, and He is the One, the All-paramount.'

13:16 On the description of anything which unbelievers worship other than God as powerless, see commentary on 10:18 (with further references).

---

¹⁷He sends down water from the sky whereat the valleys are flooded to [the extent of] their capacity, and the flood carries along a swelling scum. A similar scum arises from what they smelt in the fire for the purpose of [making] ornaments or wares. That is how God compares truth and falsehood. As for the scum, it leaves as dross, and that which profits the people stays in the earth. That is how God draws comparisons.

¹⁸There shall be the best [of rewards] for those who answer [the summons of] their Lord. But as for those who do not answer Him, even if they possessed all that is on the earth and as much of it besides, they would surely offer it to redeem themselves with

it. For such there shall be an adverse reckoning, and their refuge shall be hell, and it is an evil resting place.

[19]Is someone who knows that what has been sent down to *you* from your Lord is the truth, like someone who is blind? Only those who possess intellect take admonition [20]—those who fulfill God's covenant and do not break the pledge solemnly made, [21]and those who join what God has commanded to be joined, fear their Lord, and are afraid of an adverse reckoning [22]—those who are patient for the sake of their Lord's pleasure, maintain the prayer, and spend secretly and openly out of what We have provided them, and repel [others'] evil [conduct] with good. For such will be the reward of the [ultimate] abode:

13:22 Speyer (*BEQ,* 454) compares this verse (cf. 23:96) with Romans 12:21: "Do not be mastered by evil, but master evil with good."

---

[23]the Gardens of Eden, which they will enter along with whoever is righteous from among their forebears, spouses and descendants, and the angels will call on them from every door:

13:23 By identifying paradise with the "Garden of Eden" the Qurʾān is participating in a tradition of eschatology or cosmology found among Jews writing in Hebrew (who refer to paradise as *gan ʿēden*) and among Syriac Christian fathers such as Ephrem for whom entering heaven is a return to the garden from which Adam and Eve were cast out. See also commentary on 2:25 and 9:72 (with further references).

---

[24]'Peace be to you, for your patience.' How excellent is the reward of the [ultimate] abode!

[25]But as for those who break God's compact after having pledged it solemnly, and sever what God has commanded to be

joined, and cause corruption on the earth—it is such on whom the curse will lie, and for them will be the ills of the [ultimate] abode.

²⁶God expands and tightens the provision for whomever He wishes. They boast of the life of this world, but compared with the Hereafter the life of this world is but a [trifling] enjoyment.

13:26 "More beautiful is one hour of the even-tempered spirit of the world to come, than all the life of this world" (m. Avot 1:3; cf. Q 9:38).

---

²⁷The faithless say, 'Why has not some sign been sent down to him from his Lord?' *Say,* 'Indeed, God leads astray whomever He wishes, and guides to Himself those who turn penitently [to Him] ²⁸—those who have faith and whose hearts find rest in the remembrance of God.' Behold! The hearts find rest solely in God's remembrance!

²⁹Those who have faith and do righteous deeds—happy are they and good is their [ultimate] destination.

³⁰Thus have We sent *you* to a nation before which many nations have passed away, so that *you* may recite to them what We have revealed to *you.* Yet they defy the All-beneficent. *Say,* 'He is my Lord; there is no god except Him; in Him alone I have put my trust, and to Him alone will be my return.'

³¹If only it were a Qur'ān whereby the mountains could be moved, or the earth could be toured, or the dead could be spoken to. . . . Indeed, all dispensation belongs to God.

Have not the faithful yet realised that had God wished He would have guided mankind all together? The faithless will continue to be visited by catastrophes because of their doings, or they will land near their habitations, until God's promise comes to pass. Indeed, God does not break His promise.

13:31 This verse might be contrasted with 59:21, which (unlike the present verse) insists that "this" Qurʾān indeed has the power to destroy a mountain. See commentary on that verse for further references to the Qurʾān and mountains.

---

[32]Apostles were certainly derided before *you*. But then I gave respite to those who were faithless, then I seized them; so how was My retribution?

[33]Is He who sustains every soul in spite of what it earns [comparable to the idols]? Yet they ascribe partners to God! *Say,* 'Name them!' Will you inform Him concerning something He does not know about on the earth, or concerning [what are] mere words? Indeed, their scheming is presented as decorous to the faithless, and they have been barred from the [right] way; and whomever God leads astray, has no guide. [34]There is a punishment for them in the life of this world, and the punishment of the Hereafter will surely be harder, and they have no defender against God.

[35]A description of the paradise promised to the Godwary: streams run in it, its fruits and shade are everlasting. Such is the requital of those who are Godwary, and the requital of the faithless is the Fire.

13:35 The image of the blessed enjoying food and shade in paradise (cf. 36:56; 56:30; 76:13; 77:41) reflects the imagery of Revelation 7 (itself a reflection of Isa 49:10 and Psa 121:6):

[15]That is why they are standing in front of God's throne and serving him day and night in his sanctuary; and the One who sits on the throne will spread his tent over them.
[16]They will never hunger or thirst again; sun and scorching wind will never plague them. (Rev 7:15–17)

On the streams of paradise, see commentary on 2:25 (with further references).

---

³⁶Those whom We have given the Book rejoice in what has been sent down to *you,* and some of the factions deny a part of it. *Say,* 'I have indeed been commanded to worship God and not to ascribe any partner to Him. To Him do I summon [all mankind] and to Him will be my return.'

³⁷Thus We have sent it down as a dispensation in Arabic; and should *you* follow their desires after the knowledge that has come to *you, you* shall have neither any friend nor defender against God.

³⁸Certainly We have sent apostles before *you,* and We appointed wives and descendants for them; and an apostle may not bring a sign except by God's leave.

There is a written [ordinance] for every time:
³⁹God effaces and confirms whatever He wishes and with Him is the Mother Book.

⁴⁰Whether We show *you* some of what We promise them or take *you* away [before that], *your* duty is only to communicate, and it is for Us to do the reckoning.

⁴¹Have they not seen how We visit the land diminishing it at its edges? God judges, and there is none who may repeal His judgement, and He is swift at reckoning.

⁴²Those who were before them [also] schemed; yet all devising belongs to God. He knows what every soul earns. Soon the faithless will know in whose favour the outcome of that abode will be.

⁴³The faithless say, '*You* have not been sent [by God].' *Say,* 'God suffices as a witness between me and you, and he who possesses the knowledge of the Book.'

14. *IBRĀHĪM*, ABRAHAM

In the Name of God, the All-beneficent, the All-merciful.

¹*Alif, Lām, Rā.* [This is] a Book We have sent down to *you* so that *you* may bring mankind out from darkness into light, by the command of their Lord, to the path of the All-mighty, the All-laudable ²—God, to whom belongs whatever is in the heavens and whatever is on the earth.

And woe to the faithless for a severe punishment ³—those who prefer the life of this world to the Hereafter, bar [others] from the way of God, and seek to make it crooked. They are in extreme error.

⁴We did not send any apostle except with the language of his people, so that he might make [Our messages] clear to them. Then God leads astray whomever He wishes, and He guides whomsoever He wishes, and He is the All-mighty, the All-wise.

⁵Certainly We sent Moses with Our signs: 'Bring your people out from darkness into light and remind them of God's [holy] days.' There are indeed signs in that for every patient and grateful [servant].

⁶When Moses said to his people, 'Remember God's blessing upon you when He delivered you from Pharaoh's clan who in-

flicted a terrible torment on you, and slaughtered your sons and spared your women, and in that there was a great test from your Lord. [7]And [remember] when your Lord declared, "If you are grateful, I will surely enhance you [in blessing], but if you are ungrateful, My punishment is indeed severe.'"

[8]And Moses said, 'Should you be faithless—you and everyone on the earth, all together—indeed God is all-sufficient, all-laudable.'

14:5–8 The expression "God's days" (Ar. *ayyām Allāh*) in verse 5 appears only here and at 45:14. Muhammad Asad explains in a note: "In view of 45:14, where the expression 'the Days of God' unmistakably points to His judgment at the end of time—it is only logical to assume that in the present context this expression bears the same significance: namely, God's final judgment of man on the Day of Resurrection." Hilali-Khan argue that "God's days" means the great works of God (described in verse 6). They therefore translate with the expression "the annals of God."

Hilali-Khan are most likely correct. The reference to God's "days" (cf. Hb. *milḥamōth YHWH*, "the battles of the Lord"; see 1Sa 25:28) reflects those Biblical passages that remind Israel of the miracles done in Egypt in order to convince them to remain faithful to God; thus Psalm 105:5: "Remember the marvels he has done, his wonders, the judgements he has spoken" (cf. Exo 13:3; Deu 5:15b; 7:18; 15:15; 16:12; 24:18; 26:16–19).

---

[9]Has there not come to you the account of those who were before you—the people of Noah, 'Ād and Thamūd, and those who were after them, whom no one knows [well] except God? Their apostles brought them clear proofs, but they did not respond to them, and said, 'We disbelieve in what you have been sent with. We have indeed grave doubts concerning that to which you invite us.'

[10]Their apostles said, 'Is there any doubt about God, the originator of the heavens and the earth?! He calls you to forgive you a part of your sins, and grants you respite until a specified time.'

They said, 'You are nothing but humans like us who desire to bar us from what our fathers used to worship. So bring us a clear authority.'

[11]Their apostles said to them, 'We are indeed just human beings like yourselves; but God favours whomever of His servants that He wishes. We may not bring you an authority except by God's leave, and in God alone let all the faithful put their trust.

14:9–11 Behind this conversation (which, as Muhammad Asad puts it, "represents the gist of the answers given by various communities to various prophets") is the expectation of those in the Qur'ān's context that divine messengers would be angels. On this see commentary on 6:50 (with further references).

———————

[12]And why should we not put our trust in God, seeing that He has guided us in our ways? Surely, we will put up patiently with whatever torment you may inflict upon us, and in God alone let all the trusting put their trust.'

[13]But the faithless said to their apostles, 'Surely we will expel you from our land, or you shall revert to our creed.'

Thereat their Lord revealed to them: 'We will surely destroy the wrongdoers, [14]and We will surely settle you in the land after them. This [promise] is for someone who is awed to stand before Me and fears My threat.'

14:14 This passage (cf. 14:45) suggests that the Qur'ān has a general idea that new peoples settle in the very places where earlier peoples have been punished for their wrongdoing. On this see commentary on 22:45–46.

———————

[15]They prayed for victory [against the infidels], and every stubborn tyrant was defeated, [16]with hell lying ahead of him, [where]

he shall be given to drink of a purulent fluid, [17]gulping it down, but hardly swallowing it: death will assail him from every side, but he will not die, and there is a harsh punishment ahead of him.

[18]A parable of those who defy their Lord: their deeds are like ashes over which the wind blows hard on a tempestuous day: they have no power over anything they have earned. That is extreme error.

14:18 "How different the wicked, how different! Just like chaff blown around by the wind" (Psa 1:4).

---

[19]Have *you* not regarded that God created the heavens and the earth with consummate wisdom? If He wishes, He will take you away and bring about a new creation, [20]and that is not a formidable thing for God.

[21]Together, they will be presented before God. Then, those who were oppressed will say to the oppressors, 'We were indeed your followers. So will you avail us against God's punishment in any wise?' They will say, 'Had God guided us, we would have surely guided you. It is the same to us whether we are restless or patient: there is no escape for us.'

[22]When the matter is all over, Satan will say, 'Indeed, God made you a promise that was true and I [too] made you a promise, but I failed you. I had no authority over you, except that I called you and you responded to me. So do not blame me but blame yourselves. I cannot respond to your distress calls, neither can you respond to my distress calls. I indeed disavow your taking me for [God's] partner aforetime. There is indeed a painful punishment for the wrongdoers.'

14:22 Here the Qur'ān has Satan rebuke humans for taking him as a partner of God. Although the idea of Satan's preaching to man is unique to the Qur'ān, the idea that some humans make Satan as their master is found in several New Testament passages, including 1 Timothy 5:15: "There are already some who have turned aside to follow Satan" (cf. Rev 2:9). Cf. 4:117, 18:50; 37:158.

---

²³Those who have faith and do righteous deeds will be admitted into gardens with streams running in them, to remain in them [forever], by the leave of their Lord. Their greeting therein will be 'Peace!'

14:23 On the streams of paradise, see commentary on 2:25 (with further references).

---

²⁴Have you not regarded how God has drawn a parable? A good principle is like a good tree: its roots are steady and its branches are on high. ²⁵It gives its fruit every season by the leave of its Lord. God draws these parables for mankind so that they may take admonition.

²⁶And the parable of a bad principle is that of a bad tree: uprooted from the ground, it has no stability.

²⁷God fortifies those who have faith with a constant creed in the life of this world and in the Hereafter, and God leads astray the wrongdoers, and God does whatever He wishes.

14:24–27 Qarai here renders as "good principle" and "bad principle," but the Arabic means simply "good word" (*kalima ṭayyiba*) and "bad word" (*kalima khabītha*). The allusions to good and bad trees reflects the New Testament parable of the bad and good tree (which is related to Psa 1:3 and Jer 17:5–8, regarding which see *BEQ*, 445):

¹⁷In the same way, a sound tree produces good fruit but a rotten tree bad fruit. ¹⁸A sound tree cannot bear bad fruit, nor a rotten tree bear good fruit. ¹⁹Any tree that does not produce good fruit is cut down and thrown on the fire. (Mat 7:17–19; cf. Luk 6:43–44)

---

²⁸Have you not regarded those who have changed God's blessing with ingratitude and landed their people in the house of ruin? ²⁹—hell, which they shall enter, and it is an evil abode! ³⁰They have set up equals to God to lead [people] astray from His way. *Say,* 'Enjoy [for a while], for indeed your destination is hellfire!'

³¹*Tell* My servants who have faith to maintain the prayer and to spend secretly and openly from what We have provided them before there comes a day on which there will be neither any bargaining nor friendship.

³²It is God who created the heavens and the earth, and He sends down water from the sky and brings forth with it crops for your sustenance. And He disposed the ships for you[r benefit] so that they may sail at sea by His command, and He disposed the rivers for you. ³³He disposed the sun and the moon for you, constant [in their courses], and He disposed the night and the day ³⁴and gave you all that you had asked Him. If you enumerate God's blessings, you will not be able to count them. Man is indeed most unfair and ungrateful!

³⁵When Abraham said, 'My Lord! Make this city a sanctuary, and save me and my children from worshiping idols. ³⁶My Lord! They have indeed misled many people. So whoever follows me indeed belongs with me, and as for those who disobey me, well, You are indeed all-forgiving, all-merciful. ³⁷Our Lord! I have settled part of my descendants in a barren valley, by Your sacred House, our Lord, that they may maintain the prayer. So make the

hearts of a part of the people fond of them, and provide them with fruits, so that they may give thanks. [38]Our Lord! You indeed know whatever we hide and whatever we disclose, and nothing is hidden from God on the earth or in the heaven. [39]All praise belongs to God, who gave me Ishmael and Isaac despite [my] old age. My Lord indeed hears all supplications. [40]My Lord! Make me a maintainer of prayer, and my descendants [as well]. Our Lord, accept my supplication. [41]Our Lord! Forgive me, my parents, and all the faithful, on the day when the reckoning is held.'

14:35–41 Muslim commentators generally identify the "city" (Ar. *balad*) of this verse with Mecca. *Tafsīr al-Jalālayn* paraphrases: "And, mention, when Abraham said, 'My Lord, make this land, Mecca, secure—God granted him this petition and thus made it [Mecca] a sanctuary in which no human blood is shed, no person is wronged, prey is not hunted and one which is never deserted in any of its parts.'"

This passage (and the related passage: 2:124–41) is connected to Biblical and post-Biblical traditions regarding the altar that Abraham (and, in some cases, Isaac) built on Mt. Moriah for sacrifice (see commentary on 2:125–28). In these traditions Mt. Moriah is connected with Jerusalem (as it is already in 2Ch 3:1).

In the present passage the Qur'ān might be transferring such traditions to an Arabian site, perhaps Mecca (regarding the history of scholarship on this passage, see Sinai, *Fortschreibung,* 108ff.). One might note to this effect how elsewhere the Qur'ān links the "House" with al-Ṣafā/al-Marwa (2:158) and Quraysh (106:3) respectively (cr. Joseph Witztum). An association with Mecca might also be suggested by the turn of phrase (14:37; cf. 2:126) rendered by Qarai as "barren valley" (Mecca is indeed barren). However, this turn of phrase (*ghayri dhī zarʿin*) might mean simply "an uncultivated valley." To explain the reference to fruits here, *Tafsīr al-Jalālayn* relates that when Abraham made this prayer God transferred the town of Ṭāʾif (which lies at a higher elevation and thus has a cooler climate and produces more crops) to Arabia. One might compare the prayer of Abraham in verse 37 with the description of the holy land in Leviticus 25:19: "The land will give its fruit, and you will eat your fill and live in security"; note that in Q 14:35 the Qur'ān has Abraham pray that "this city" will be secure (*āmin;* Qarai renders this as "sanctuary"). On the references to a "secure" city, see the chart in Sinai, *Fortschreibung,* 133. In other words, the Qurʾān might intend that Abraham prayed for the "valley" where he settled to become both fruitful and secure, when at first it was neither.

In any case, one should keep in mind the possibility that Mecca was chosen as a site of the "House" only later, precisely because it seemed to match certain turns of phrase in the Qurʾān. The original setting of this verse could be Hebron, the site of Abraham's tomb (which had become a Byzantine church and a pilgrimage site known to Arabs at the time of Islam's rise; see commentary on 2:125–28). Genesis 13:18 relates that Abraham built an altar to God in Hebron, and this Qurʾānic passage (along with 2:125–28) might be inspired by it. This idea would do away with the need to imagine that Abraham made the (long) trip to the Arabian desert with Hagar and Ishmael while he left Sarah and Isaac back in Palestine.

Q 2:124–41 describes how Abraham built a sanctuary with Ishmael and how they both prayed (vv. 127–29) to God; in this passage Abraham prays alone and refers both to Ishmael and to Isaac. See further commentary on 2:125–28.

---

⁴²Do not suppose that God is oblivious of what the wrongdoers are doing. He is only granting them respite until the day when the eyes will be glazed. ⁴³Scrambling with their heads upturned, there will be a fixed gaze in their eyes and their hearts will be vacant.

⁴⁴*Warn* the people of the day when the punishment will overtake them, whereat the wrongdoers will say, 'Our Lord! Respite us for a short time so that we may respond to Your call and follow the apostles.' [They will be told,] 'Did you not use to swear earlier that there would be no reverse for you, ⁴⁵while you dwelt in the dwellings of those who had wronged themselves [before] and it had been made clear to you how We had dealt with them [before you], and We had [also] cited examples for you?'

⁴⁶They certainly devised their plots, but their plots are known to God, and their plots are not such as to dislodge the mountains.

⁴⁷So do not suppose that God will break His promise to His apostles. Indeed, God is all-mighty, avenger. ⁴⁸The day when the

earth is turned into another earth and the heavens [as well], and they are presented before God, the One, the All-paramount

14:48 "Then I saw a new heaven and a new earth; the first heaven and the first earth had disappeared now, and there was no longer any sea" (Rev 21:1; cf. Isa 65:17; see *BEQ*, 454).

---

[49]—on that day you will see the guilty bound together in chains, [50]their garments made of pitch, and the Fire covering their faces, [51]so that God may reward every soul for what it has earned. God is indeed swift at reckoning.

[52]This is a proclamation for mankind, so that they may be warned thereby and know that He is indeed the One God, and those who possess intellect may take admonition.

15. *AL-ḤIJR*, THE ROCK

In the Name of God, the All-beneficent, the All-merciful.

¹*Alif, Lām, Rā.* These are the signs of the Book and a manifest Qurʾān.

²Much will the faithless wish that they had been muslims. ³Leave them to eat and enjoy and to be diverted by longings. Soon they will know. ⁴We did not destroy any town but that it had a known term. ⁵No nation can advance its time nor can it defer it.

⁶They said, 'O *you*, to whom the Reminder has been sent down, *you* are indeed crazy. ⁷Why do *you* not bring us the angels if *you* are truthful?!'

15:7 On the expectation of unbelievers that divine messages would be brought by an angel, see commentary on 6:50 (with further references).

---

⁸We do not send down the angels except with due reason, and then they will not be granted any respite.

⁹Indeed, We have sent down the Reminder, and, indeed, We will preserve it.

¹⁰Certainly We sent [apostles] before *you* to former communities, ¹¹and there did not come to them any apostle but that they used to deride him. ¹²That is how We let it pass through the hearts of the guilty: ¹³they do not believe in it, and the precedent of the ancients has already passed.

¹⁴Were We to open for them a gate of the heaven so that they could go on ascending through it, ¹⁵they would surely say, 'Indeed, a spell has been cast on our eyes; indeed, we are a bewitched lot.'

15:14–15 These two verses (along with those that follow) illustrate the Qurʾān's cosmology, according to which the world is flat and the sky is a physical barrier—separating heaven from earth—stretched out like a dome above the earth. Angels are able to travel along certain pathways, or *asbāb* (see 2:166; 18:84, 85, 89, 92; 22:15; 38:10; 40:37; on this see van Bladel, "Heavenly Cords"), which stretch between heaven and earth, but the sky blocks humans (and demons) from entering into heaven or listening to the heavenly council. In these two verses the Qurʾān declares that even if this barrier were broken, and the unbelievers could see directly into heaven through a door (v. 15), they still would not believe. This cosmology is common in Late Antiquity. The notion of a door through which humans might see the heavens—or indeed ascend to them—is found (among other places) in 1 Enoch (14) and Revelation:

> ¹Then, in my vision, I saw a door open in heaven and heard the same voice speaking to me, the voice like a trumpet, saying, 'Come up here: I will show you what is to take place in the future.'
> ²With that, I fell into ecstasy and I saw a throne standing in heaven, and the One who was sitting on the throne. (Rev 4:1–2)

¹⁶Certainly We have appointed houses in the heaven and adorned them for the onlookers, ¹⁷and We have guarded them from every outcast Satan, ¹⁸except someone who may eavesdrop, whereat there pursues him a manifest flame.

15:16–18 The Qur'ān imagines that the sky is a barrier which blocks the access of humans and ("outcast") demons to heaven (see commentary on 15:14–15), yet the demons nevertheless seek to pierce this barrier in order to hear the conversation of God with his angels in the divine council. Thus God has put the stars into this barrier (as though they were bright pins pushed into the ceiling of a tent) not only to produce wonder in those who see them but also to act as barriers against demons who seek to enter (or better, return to) heaven to spy on the divine council (and to get some useful information). The term Qarai renders here as "houses" is *burūj,* a term used in later Arabic for "constellations" (and other translators—e.g., Arberry, Asad, and Hamidullah [Yusuf Ali renders "zodiacal signs"]—translate it in this way). However, the better translation (offered by Paret) is the literal meaning of this term, namely, "towers" (*burūj* likely derives from Greek *pyrgos,* through Syriac *burgā*), as the Qur'ān means to describe them quite literally as guard towers. Cf. 37:6–10; 41:12; 67:5; 72:8–9.

---

¹⁹We spread out the earth, and cast in it firm mountains, and We grew in it every kind of balanced thing, ²⁰and made in it [various] means of livelihood for you and for those whom you do not provide for. ²¹There is not a thing but that its sources are with Us, and We do not send it down except in a known measure.

²²And We send the fertilizing winds and send down water from the sky providing it for you to drink and you are not maintainers of its resources.

²³Indeed, it is We who give life and bring death and We are the inheritors.

²⁴Certainly We know the predecessors among you and certainly We know the successors, ²⁵and indeed it is *your* Lord who will resurrect them. Indeed, He is all-wise, all-knowing.

²⁶Certainly We created man out of a dry clay [drawn] from an aging mud, ²⁷and We created the jinn earlier out of a piercing fire.

²⁸When your Lord said to the angels, 'Indeed, I am going to create a human out of a dry clay [drawn] from an aging mud. ²⁹So

when I have proportioned him and breathed into him of My spirit, then fall down in prostration before him.'

³⁰Thereat the angels prostrated, all of them together, ³¹but not Iblis: he refused to be among those who prostrated.

³²He said, 'O Iblis! What kept you from being among those who have prostrated?'

³³Said he, 'I will not prostrate before a human whom You have created out of a dry clay [drawn] from an aging mud.'

³⁴He said, 'Begone hence, for you are indeed an outcast, ³⁵and indeed the curse shall lie on you until the Day of Retribution.'

15:26–35 The Qur'ān here alludes to the account based on Genesis by which God created man from the earth (on this see commentary on 6:2, with further references) and breathed into him his spirit (v. 29; see commentary on 32:8–9, with further references). The idea that God first created the jinn from fire (v. 27) reflects Christian texts such as *Cave of Treasures* that speak of the creation of the devil from fire (and have him already present at the creation of Adam).

Regarding the Qur'ān's report that God commanded the angels to bow down to Adam, see commentary on 7:11–12 (with further references).

In verse 34 the Qur'ān refers to the devil as "an outcast." The Arabic term here (translated correctly by Qarai) is *rajīm* (cf. 3:36; 15:17; 16:98; 38:77; 81:25; cf. also 67:5) from the root *r-j-m* (perhaps through a borrowing from Ethiopic *ragama,* a root used in the Ethiopic Bible for the cursing of the serpent in Gen 3:14 and for the casting of the condemned into the fire with the devil in Mat 25.41), which in Arabic normally means "to stone." Muslim exegetes often connect this verse to the idea that the devil is "stoned"—perhaps because (see the commentary above, on 15:16–18) God (or an angel) throws meteorites at demons who try to sneak into heaven, or perhaps because Abraham threw stones at the devil when he appeared in Mecca (a tradition that lies behind the ritual of stoning pillars during the annual Islamic pilgrimage). In fact this passage is best understood in light of the Qur'ān's cosmology (cf. 15:16–18). In this passage the Qur'ān explains how the devil was *cast out* of heaven down (literally) to earth, where he causes humans so much trouble.

On the term in verse 34 which Qarai renders as "Retribution" (Ar. *dīn*), see commentary on 83:11 (with further references).

³⁶He said, 'My Lord! Respite me till the day they will be resurrected.'

³⁷Said He, 'You are indeed among the reprieved ³⁸until the day of the known time.'

³⁹He said, 'My Lord! As You have consigned me to perversity, I will surely glamorize [evil] for them on the earth, and I will surely pervert them, all ⁴⁰except Your dedicated servants among them.'

⁴¹He said, 'This is the path [leading] straight to Me. ⁴²Indeed, as for My servants you do not have any authority over them, except the perverse who follow you, ⁴³and hell is indeed the tryst of them all.

15:36–43 Here (vv. 36–38) the Qurʾān reports that God agreed to the devil's request that his punishment be delayed so that he might do his best to lead humans away from God. On this see commentary on 7:14–18 (with further references).

⁴⁴It has seven gates, and to each gate belongs a separate portion of them.'

15:44 Matthew 16:18 refers to the gates of hell. They are mentioned elsewhere in the Qurʾān (16:29; 39:72; 40:76) but only here are numbered at seven. This number may be a reflection, or inversion, of the Qurʾānic idea of seven heavens (see commentary on 67:3, with further references).

⁴⁵Indeed, the Godwary will be amid gardens and springs.

15:45 On the streams of paradise, see commentary on 2:25 (with further references).

⁴⁶[They will be told,] "Enter it in peace and safety!" ⁴⁷We will remove whatever rancour there is in their breasts; [intimate like] brothers, [they will be reclining] on couches, facing one another. ⁴⁸Therein neither weariness shall touch them, nor will they [ever] be expelled from it.

⁴⁹*Inform* my servants that I am indeed the All-forgiving, the All-merciful, ⁵⁰and that My punishment is a painful punishment.

⁵¹And *inform* them about the guests of Abraham,

15:51–77 *overview* The way in which the Qurʾān connects the annunciation of Isaac to Abraham (vv. 51–56) with the story of the punishment of Sodom and Gomorrah (the people of Lot; 15:57–77) reflects the way these two elements are connected in Genesis 18–19. This same sequence appears in 11:74–83; 22:43; 29:31–35; and 51:24–47.

---

⁵²when they entered into his presence and said, 'Peace!'

He said, 'We are indeed afraid of you.'

⁵³They said, 'Do not be afraid. Indeed, we give you the good news of a wise son.'

⁵⁴He said, 'Do you give me good news, though old age has befallen me? What is the good news that you bring me!?'

⁵⁵They said, 'We bring you good news in truth; so do not be despondent.'

⁵⁶He said, 'Who despairs of his Lord's mercy except the astray?!'

15:51–56 By "guests" of Abraham the Qurʾān means the three visitors of Genesis 18. *Tafsīr al-Jalālayn,* however, relates: "And tell them of the guests of Abraham, that is, the angels—there were twelve, ten or three of them, among them Gabriel." On the annunciation of Isaac to Abraham (and Sarah, who appears in the passages in 11 and 51), see commentary on 11:69–73 (with further references).

⁵⁷He said, 'O messengers, what is now your errand?'

⁵⁸They said, 'We have been sent toward a guilty people, ⁵⁹[who will all perish] except the family of Lot. We will indeed deliver all of them, ⁶⁰except his wife, [who], We have ordained, will indeed be among those who remain behind.'

⁶¹So when the messengers came to Lot's family, ⁶²he said, 'You are strangers [to me].'

⁶³They said, 'Indeed, we bring you what they used to doubt. ⁶⁴We bring you the truth, and indeed we speak truly. ⁶⁵Take your family in a watch of the night and follow in their rear, and none of you should turn around, and proceed as you are bidden.' ⁶⁶We apprised him of the matter that these will be rooted out by dawn.

⁶⁷The people of the city came, rejoicing. ⁶⁸He said, 'These are indeed my guests. Do not bring dishonour on me. ⁶⁹Be wary of God and do not humiliate me.'

⁷⁰They said, 'Did we not forbid you from [defending] strangers?'

⁷¹He said, 'These are my daughters, [marry them] if you should do anything.'

⁷²By *your* life, they were bewildered in their drunkenness. ⁷³So the Cry seized them at sunrise, ⁷⁴and We made its topmost part its nethermost, and rained on them stones of shale.

15:57–74 Qarai, following the majority of Islamic authorities, suggests that Lot offered his daughters *in marriage* to the mob which gathered outside of his house (v. 71). However, there is no mention of marriage in the Qurʾān, which simply follows Genesis 19 (v. 8) in having Lot offer his daughters in place of his guests to the crowd:

> ⁶Lot came out to them at the door and, having shut the door behind him,
> ⁷said, 'Please, brothers, do not be wicked.
> ⁸Look, I have two daughters who are virgins. I am ready to send them out to you, for you to treat as you please, but do nothing to these men since they are now under the protection of my roof.'

⁹But they retorted, 'Stand back! This fellow came here as a foreigner, and now he wants to play the judge. Now we shall treat you worse than them.' Then they forced Lot back and moved forward to break down the door. ¹⁰But the men reached out, pulled Lot back into the house with them, and shut the door. ¹¹And they dazzled those who were at the door of the house, one and all, with a blinding light, so that they could not find the doorway.

. . .

¹⁵When dawn broke the angels urged Lot on, 'To your feet! Take your wife and your two daughters who are here, or you will be swept away in the punishment of the city.' ¹⁶And as he hesitated, the men seized his hand and the hands of his wife and his two daughters—the Lord being merciful to him—and led him out and left him outside the city. ¹⁷When they had brought him outside, he was told, 'Flee for your life. Do not look behind you or stop anywhere on the plain. Flee to the hills or you will be swept away.' (Gen 19:6–11, 15–17)

The Qurʾān's report that the crowd was "bewildered in their drunkenness" (Q 15:72) refers to the "blinding light" which "dazzled" the mob (Gen 19:11) and allowed Lot's family to escape. Ephrem relates that the Sodomites became blind:

> They spread a veil, so to speak, over the sight of the Sodomites with the darkness that lay over their appearance. Then the men brought Lot inside with them and the Sodomites outside were afflicted with blindness. (Ephrem, *Commentary on Genesis,* 16:5)

The remark that the "topmost" part of the cities became their "nethermost" (v. 74) reflects the language in Genesis of God's "overthrowing" (Hb. *yahapōk;* Sy. *hfak*) the cities (Gen 19:25). See commentary on 9:70.

On Lot's guests and the destruction of Lot's people cf. 7:80–84; 11:74–83; 26:160–74; 27:54–58; 29:31–35; 37:133–38; 51:31–37; 54:33–39 and commentary on 54:33–39. On Lot's wife see commentary on 27:54–58 (with further references).

———

⁷⁵There are indeed signs in that for the percipient. ⁷⁶Indeed, it is on a standing road, ⁷⁷and there is indeed a sign in that for the faithful.

15:76–77 On the ruins of Lot's city, see commentary on 37:133–38 (with further references).

---

⁷⁸Indeed, the inhabitants of Aykah were [also] wrongdoers. ⁷⁹So We took vengeance on them, and indeed the two of them are on an open highway.

15:78–79 In 26:176–77 the "inhabitants of al-Ayka" are identified as those to whom the Prophet Shuʿayb was sent. The classical Islamic sources generally interpret al-Ayka to mean "the thicket," and Muslim and non-Muslim translations alike often reflect this (Arberry: "dwellers in the thicket"; Asad: "dwellers of the wooden dales"; Hilali-Khan: "dwellers of the wood"). As the Qurʾān elsewhere (Q 7:85, passim) relates that Shuʿayb was sent to Midian, the reference to "al-Ayka" is sometimes thought to reflect the geography or vegetation of Midian (on Midian, see also 20:40; 28:22–23, 45). On the "inhabitants of al-Ayka," see 26:176–89; 38:13; 50:14.

However, Gerd Puin ("Leuke Kome") notes that "al-Ayka" has also been read *layka;* indeed the initial *alif* is missing in 26:176 and 38:13 (but not here or 50:14) in the Cairo edition of the Qurʾān. This suggests that the reading *al-ayka* is a correction. Puin argues that *layka* refers to Leuke Kome, a port on the Arabian Red Sea coast connected to the Nabataean kingdom. Thereby he does away with the "thicket."

---

⁸⁰Certainly the inhabitants of Ḥijr denied the apostles. ⁸¹We had given them Our signs but they disregarded them. ⁸²They used to hew out dwellings from mountains feeling secure.

⁸³So the Cry seized them at dawn, ⁸⁴and what they used to earn did not avail them.

⁸⁵We did not create the heavens and the earth and whatever is between them except with consummate wisdom, and indeed the Hour is bound to come. So *forbear* with a graceful forbearance.

[86]Indeed, *your* Lord is the All-creator, the All-knowing. [87]Certainly We have given *you* [the *sūrah* of] the seven oft-repeated verses and the great Qur'ān.

15:87 Here Qarai renders the Arabic term *mathānī* as "oft-repeated verses"—a translation which implies that the Qur'ān is alluding to the seven verses of Q 1 (*al-Fātiḥa*). However, in 39:23 Qarai renders *mathānī* as "similar motifs." This latter verse—where *mathānī* is equated to a "discourse" (*ḥadīth*) suggests that it refers to a narrative or tale (it is likely related to the Syriac root *t.n.y.* which can mean "to narrate"). What the Qur'ān means here by specifically seven *mathānī* which are *separate* from the "recitation" (*qur'ān*) is unclear. Geiger (*Judaism and Islam,* 42–43) argues that the *mathānī* is related to Hebrew *mishnah,* but that hardly explains the Qur'ān's use of the term in this passage.

---

[88]Do not extend *your* glance toward what We have provided to certain groups of them, and do not grieve for them. Lower *your* wing to the faithful, [89]and *say,* 'I am a manifest warner [of punishment from God],' [90]like what We sent down on those who split into bands, [91]who represented the Qur'ān as magic. [92]By *your* Lord, We will question them all [93]concerning what they used to do.

[94]So *proclaim* what *you* have been commanded, and *turn away* from the polytheists. [95]We will indeed suffice *you* against the deriders [96]—those who set up another deity besides God. Soon they will know! [97]Certainly We know that *you* become upset because of what they say. [98]So celebrate the praise of *your* Lord and be among those who prostrate, [99]and worship *your* Lord until certainty comes to *you.*

16. *AL-NAḤL*, THE BEES

In the Name of God, the All-beneficent, the All-merciful.

¹God's edict is coming! So do not seek to hasten it. Immaculate is He and far above having any partners that they ascribe [to Him].

16:1–15 *overview* Speyer (*BEQ*, 448; see also Rudolph, *Abhängigkeit*, 10–11; Hirschfeld, *New Researches,* 76) suggests that the opening section of Sura 16 has a close relationship with Psalm 104, as suggested by the following table (cr. Andrew O'Connor):

Imagery	Q 16 verse	Psalm 104 verse
Angels with the spirit or wind	2	4
Livestock or cattle	5	14
Sending rain or water	10	13, 16
Giving water to drink	10	11
Donkeys	8	11
Crops or plants for people	11	14
The sun and moon	12	19
Day and night	12	20 (and 22)
The sea; things in it to eat	14	25
Ships on the sea	14	26
Mountains	15	6–7, 13, 18, 32

²He sends down the angels with the Spirit of His command to whomever He wishes of His servants: 'Warn [the people] that there is no god except Me; so be wary of Me.'

16:2 Qarai translates the Arabic word *amr* here as "command." However, it could be that behind this word is the Aramaic *mēmrā:* "Word/Logos" (notice the German translation of Paret: "mit dem Geist von seinem Logos"). On this see commentary on 42:52 (with further references).

³He created the heavens and the earth with consummate wisdom. He is above having any partners that they ascribe [to Him].

⁴He created man from a drop of [seminal] fluid, and, behold, he is an open contender!

⁵He created the cattle, in which there is warmth for you and [other] uses, and some of them you eat. ⁶There is in them a beauty for you when you bring them home for rest and when you drive them forth to pasture. ⁷And they bear your burdens to towns which you could not reach except by straining yourselves. Your Lord is indeed most kind and merciful. ⁸And horses, mules and asses, for you to ride them, and for pomp, and He creates what you do not know.

⁹With God rests guidance to the straight path, and some of the paths are devious, and had He wished He would have guided you all.

¹⁰It is He who sends down water from the sky: from it you get your drink and with it are [sustained] the plants wherein you pasture your herds. ¹¹With it He makes the crops grow for you and olives, date palms, vines, and fruits of all kinds. There is indeed a sign in that for people who reflect.

¹²He disposed the night and the day for you, and the sun, the moon and the stars are disposed by His command. There are indeed signs in that for people who exercise their reason.

¹³And [He disposed for your benefit] whatever He has created for you in the earth of diverse hues—there is indeed a sign in that for people who take admonition.

¹⁴It is He who disposed the sea [for your benefit] that you may eat from it fresh meat, and obtain from it ornaments which you wear, and *you* see the ships plowing through it, so that you may seek of His bounty and that you may give thanks.

¹⁵He cast firm mountains in the earth lest it should shake with you, and [made] streams and ways so that you may be guided ¹⁶— and the landmarks [as well]—and by the stars they are guided.

¹⁷Is He who creates like one who does not create? Will you not then take admonition?

¹⁸If you enumerate God's blessings, you will not be able to count them. God is indeed all-forgiving, all-merciful, ¹⁹and God knows whatever you hide and whatever you disclose.

²⁰Those whom they invoke besides God do not create anything and are themselves created. ²¹They are dead and lifeless and are not aware when they will be resurrected.

16:20–21 The reference to those who "are dead" in verse 21 could either be to whatever is wrongly invoked or to those who are doing the invoking. If it is the former, the Qur'ān could be accusing its opponents of worshipping the dead, perhaps dead prophets, which might be an argument against Jews and Christians (cf. 9:30). Cf. 27:65.

²²Your God is the One God. Those who do not believe in the Hereafter, their hearts are in denial [of the truth], and they are ar-

rogant. [23]Undoubtedly, God knows whatever they hide and whatever they disclose. Indeed, He does not like the arrogant. [24]When they are asked, 'What is it that your Lord has sent down?,' they say, 'Myths of the ancients,'

16:24 On the expression "myths of the ancients," see commentary on 68:15 (with further references).

———————

[25][with the result] that they will bear the full weight of their own burden on the Day of Resurrection, along with part of the burden of those whom they mislead without any knowledge. Behold! Evil is what they bear!

[26]Those who were before them [had also] schemed. Then God came at their edifice from the foundations and the roof fell down upon them from above and the punishment overtook them whence they were not aware.

16:26 This verse is sometimes thought to be an allusion to the Tower of Babel (Bell, *Commentary,* 435), but it is parallel to 27:50–52, which relates to the ruin of Thamūd's dwellings.

———————

[27]Then, on the Day of Resurrection He will disgrace them and say, 'Where are My "partners" for whose sake you used to defy [God]?' Those who were given knowledge will say, 'Indeed, today disgrace and distress pursue the faithless.' [28]—Those whom the angels take away while they were wronging themselves. Thereat they submit: 'We were not doing any evil!' 'Yes,' [the angels reply,] 'God indeed knows well what you used to do! [29]Enter

the gates of hell to remain in it [forever]. Evil is the [final] abode of the arrogant.'

³⁰But to those who were Godwary it will be said, 'What is it that your Lord has sent down?' They will say, 'Good.' For those who do good in this world there will be a good [reward], and the abode of the Hereafter is better, and the abode of the Godwary is surely excellent: ³¹the Gardens of Eden, which they will enter, with streams running in them. There they will have whatever they wish, and thus does God reward the Godwary ³²—those whom the angels take away while they are pure. They say [to them], 'Peace be to you! Enter paradise because of what you used to do.'

16:30–32 On the Garden of Eden as the heavenly paradise of believers in the Qur'ān, see commentary on 2:25 and 9:72 (with further references).

———————

³³Do they await aught except that the angels should come to them, or *your* Lord's edict should come? Those who were before them had acted likewise; God did not wrong them, but they used to wrong themselves. ³⁴So the evils of what they had earned visited them, and they were besieged by what they used to deride.

³⁵The polytheists say, 'Had God wished, we would not have worshiped anything besides Him—neither we, nor our fathers—nor forbidden anything without His sanction.' Those who were before them had acted likewise. Is the apostles' duty anything but to communicate in clear terms?

³⁶Certainly We raised an apostle in every nation [to preach:] 'Worship God and shun satanic entities.' Among them were some whom God guided, and among them were some who deserved to be in error. So travel through the land and observe how was the fate of the deniers.

16:36 On the term *ṭāghūt,* rendered as "satanic entities," see commentary on 4:51–52 (with further references).

---

³⁷Even if *you* are eager for them to be guided, indeed God does not guide those who mislead [others], and they will have no helpers.

³⁸They swear by God with solemn oaths that God will not resurrect those who die. Yes indeed, [He will], it is a promise binding upon Him, but most people do not know, ³⁹so that He may clarify for them what they differ about, and that the faithless may know that they were liars.

⁴⁰All that We say to a thing, when We will it, is to say to it 'Be!' and it is.

16:40 On God's creating through the word "Be!" see commentary on 36:82 (with further references).

---

⁴¹Those who migrate for the sake of God after they have been wronged, We will surely settle them in a good place in the world, and the reward of the Hereafter is surely greater, had they known ⁴²—Those who are patient and who put their trust in their Lord.

⁴³We did not send [any apostles] before *you* except as men to whom We revealed. Ask the People of the Reminder if you do not know.

16:43 The Qur'ān here insists that God sends only men as messengers (although elsewhere [3:39, 42] the Qur'ān does have angels as divine messengers). The expression "People of the Reminder" (Ahmed Ali translates as "keepers of the Oracles of God") is parallel to "People of the Book" (both "Reminder" [Ar.

dhikr] and "Book" [Ar. *kitāb*] have the meaning of "revelation" in the Qur'ān). In other words, the Qur'ān here instructs its audience to have recourse to Jews and Christians on religious matters. See the parallel verse 21:7; also 10:94; 17:101; 26:197.

---

⁴⁴[We sent them] with clear proofs and scriptures. We have sent down the Reminder to *you* so that *you* may clarify for these people that which has been sent down to them, so that they may reflect.

16:44 On the term rendered as "scriptures" (Ar. *zubur*), see commentary on 3:184 (with further references).

---

⁴⁵Do those who devise evil schemes feel secure that God will not make the earth swallow them, or the punishment will not overtake them whence they are not aware? ⁴⁶Or that He will not seize them in the midst of their bustle, whereupon they will not be able to frustrate [Him]? ⁴⁷Or that He will not visit them with attrition? Your Lord is indeed most kind and merciful.

⁴⁸Have they not regarded that whatever thing God has created casts its shadow to the right and the left, prostrating to God in utter humility? ⁴⁹To God prostrates whatever is in the heavens and whatever is on the earth, including animals and angels, and they are not arrogant.

16:49 In this verse (cf. 13:15; 17:44; 22:18) the Qur'ān seems to have God take the place of Jesus in Philippians 2, where Paul (quoting in part Isa 45:23–24) declares that all things in the heavens and on the earth bow down to Christ:

⁹And for this God raised him high, and gave him the name which is above all other names;
¹⁰so that all beings in the heavens, on earth and in the underworld, should bend the knee at the name of Jesus. (Phi 2:9–10)

One might also compare this verse to Revelation 5:3: "Then I heard all the living things in creation—everything that lives in heaven, and on earth, and under the earth, and in the sea, crying: To the One seated on the throne and to the Lamb, be all praise, honour, glory and power, for ever and ever."

———————

⁵⁰They fear their Lord above them, and do what they are commanded.

⁵¹God has said, 'Do not worship two gods. Indeed, He is the One God, so be in awe of Me [alone].' ⁵²To Him belongs whatever is in the heavens and the earth, and to Him belongs the enduring religion. Will you, then, be wary of other than God?

⁵³Whatever blessing you have is from God, and when a distress befalls you, you make entreaties to Him. ⁵⁴Then, when He removes the distress from you—behold, a part of them ascribe partners to their Lord, ⁵⁵being unthankful for what We have given them. So let them enjoy. Soon they will know!

⁵⁶They assign a share in what We have provided them to what they do not know. By God, you will surely be questioned concerning what you used to fabricate.

⁵⁷And they attribute daughters to God—immaculate is He— while they will have what they desire! ⁵⁸When one of them is brought the news of a female [newborn], his face becomes darkened and he chokes with suppressed agony. ⁵⁹He hides from the people out of distress at the news he has been brought: shall he retain it in humiliation, or bury it in the ground! Behold! Evil is the judgement that they make.

⁶⁰There is an evil description of those who do not believe in the Hereafter, and the loftiest description belongs to God, and He is the All-mighty, the All-wise. ⁶¹Were God to take mankind to task for their wrongdoing, He would not leave any living being upon it. But He respites them until a specified time; so when their

time comes they shall not defer it by a single hour nor shall they advance it.

⁶²They attribute to God what they dislike [for themselves], and their tongues assert the lie that the best reward [in the Hereafter] will be theirs. Undoubtedly, the Fire shall be their lot and they will be foremost [in entering it].

⁶³By God, We have certainly sent [apostles] to nations before *you.* But Satan made their deeds seem decorous to them. So he is their master today and there is a painful punishment for them.

⁶⁴We did not send down the Book to *you* except [for the purpose] that *you* may clarify for them what they differ about, and as guidance and mercy for people who have faith.

⁶⁵God sends down water from the sky with which He revives the earth after its death. There is indeed a sign in that for people who listen. ⁶⁶There is indeed a lesson for you in the cattle: We give you to drink pure milk, pleasant to those who drink, from what is in their bellies, from between [intestinal] waste and blood. ⁶⁷And from the fruits of date palms and vines you draw wine and goodly provision. There are indeed signs in that for people who exercise their reason.

⁶⁸And your Lord inspired the bee [saying]: 'Make your home in the mountains and on trees and the trellises that they erect. ⁶⁹Then eat from every [kind of] fruit and follow meekly the ways of your Lord.' There issues from its belly a juice of diverse hues, in which there is cure for the people. There is indeed a sign in that for people who reflect.

⁷⁰God has created you, then He takes you away, and there are some among you who are relegated to the nethermost age so that they know nothing after [having possessed] some knowledge. God is indeed all-knowing, all-powerful.

⁷¹God has granted some of you an advantage over others in [respect of] provision. Those who have been granted an advantage do not give over their provision to their slaves so that they become equal in its respect. What, do they dispute the blessing of God?

⁷²God made for you mates from your own selves and appointed for you children and grandchildren from your mates, and We provided you with all the good things. What, do they believe in falsehood while they deny the blessing of God?

⁷³They worship besides God what has no power to provide them with anything from the heavens and the earth, nor are they capable [of doing that]. ⁷⁴So do not draw comparisons for God: indeed, God knows and you do not know.

⁷⁵God draws a parable: a slave owned by a master, having no power over anything, and someone [a free man] whom We have provided with a goodly provision and he spends out of it secretly and openly. Are they equal? All praise belongs to God. But most of them do not know.

⁷⁶God draws [another] parable: Two men, one of whom is dumb, having no power over anything and who is a liability to his master: wherever he directs him he does not bring any good. Is he equal to someone who enjoins justice and is [steady] on a straight path?

⁷⁷To God belongs the Unseen of the heavens and the earth. The matter of the Hour is just like the twinkling of an eye, or [even] shorter. Indeed, God has power over all things.

16:77 This verse seems to include a turn of phrase which appears in 1 Corinthians:

⁵¹Now I am going to tell you a mystery: we are not all going to fall asleep,

⁵²but we are all going to be changed, instantly, *in the twinkling of an eye,* when the last trumpet sounds. The trumpet is going to sound, and then the dead will be raised imperishable, and we shall be changed. (1Co 15:51–52)

Note, however, that whereas the Greek expression in 1 Corinthians (*en ripē ophthalmou*) seems to mean "blinking of the eye," the Arabic expression of Q 16:77 (*lamḥi al-baṣar;* cf. Syr. *rfāf ʿaynā*) means something more like "glance of the eye."

---

⁷⁸God has brought you forth from the bellies of your mothers while you did not know anything. He invested you with hearing, sight, and the hearts, so that you may give thanks.

⁷⁹Have they not regarded the birds disposed in the air of the sky: no one sustains them except God. There are indeed signs in that for people who have faith.

16:79 "Look at the birds in the sky. They do not sow or reap or gather into barns; yet your heavenly Father feeds them. Are you not worth much more than they are?" (Mat 6:26; cf. Mat 10:29; see *BEQ,* 454).

---

⁸⁰It is God who has made your homes a place of rest for you, and He made for you homes out of the skins of the cattle which you find light and portable on the day of your shifting and on the day of your halt, and out of their wool, fur and hair [He has appointed] furniture and wares [enduring] for a while.

⁸¹It is God who made for you the shade from what He has created, and made for you retreats in the mountains, and made for you garments that protect you from heat, and garments that protect you from your [mutual] violence. That is how He completes His blessing upon you so that you may submit [to Him].

⁸²But if they turn their backs [on *you*], *your* duty is only to communicate in clear terms. ⁸³They recognize the blessing of God and then deny it, and most of them are faithless.

⁸⁴The day We shall raise up a witness from every nation, the faithless will not be permitted [to speak], nor will they be asked to propitiate [God]. ⁸⁵And when the wrongdoers sight the punishment, it shall not be lightened for them, nor will they be granted any respite. ⁸⁶When the polytheists sight their partners, they will say, 'Our Lord! These are our partners whom we used to invoke besides You.' But they will retort to them, 'You are indeed liars!' ⁸⁷They will submit to God on that day, and what they used to fabricate will forsake them. ⁸⁸Those who are faithless and bar from the way of God—We shall add punishment to their punishment because of the corruption they used to cause.

⁸⁹The day We raise in every nation a witness against them from among themselves, We shall bring *you* as a witness against these. We have sent down the Book to *you* as a clarification of all things and as guidance, mercy and good news for those who submit [to God].

⁹⁰Indeed, God enjoins justice and kindness, and generosity towards relatives, and He forbids indecency, wrongdoing, and aggression. He advises you so that you may take admonition.

⁹¹Fulfill God's covenant when you pledge, and do not break [your] oaths after pledging them solemnly and having made God a witness over yourselves. God indeed knows what you do.

⁹²Do not be like her who would undo her yarn, breaking it up after [spinning it to] strength, by making your oaths a means of [mutual] deceit among yourselves, so that one community may become more affluent than another community. God only tests you thereby, and on the Day of Resurrection He will clarify for you what you used to differ about. ⁹³Had God wished, He would have made you one community, but He leads astray whomever He wishes and guides whomever He wishes, and you will surely be questioned concerning what you used to do.

Regarding the Qur'ān's statements on the division of humanity into different communities, see commentary on 10:19 (with further references).

---

⁹⁴Do not make your oaths a means of [mutual] deceit among yourselves, lest feet should stumble after being steady and [lest] you suffer ill for barring from the way of God and face a great punishment.

⁹⁵Do not sell God's covenants for a paltry gain. What is with God is indeed better for you, should you know. ⁹⁶That which is with you will be spent [and gone], but what is with God shall last [forever], and We will surely pay the patient their reward by the best of what they used to do.

⁹⁷Whoever acts righteously, [whether] male or female, should he be faithful, We shall revive him with a good life and pay them their reward by the best of what they used to do.

⁹⁸When you recite the Qur'ān, seek the protection of God against the outcast Satan. ⁹⁹Indeed, he does not have any authority over those who have faith and put their trust in their Lord. ¹⁰⁰His authority is only over those who befriend him and those who make him a partner [of God].

¹⁰¹When We change a sign for another in its place—and God knows best what He sends down—they say, '*You* are only a fabricator.' Indeed, most of them do not know. ¹⁰²*Say,* the Holy Spirit has brought it down duly from your Lord to fortify those who have faith and as guidance and good news for those who submit [to God].

16:102 Most Muslim authorities (including *Tafsīr al-Jalālayn*) understand the reference to the Holy Spirit in this verse (in part because of 2:97–98) as a reference to the angel Gabriel (although Asad translates "holy inspiration" and Ahmed Ali "divine grace"). However, the other three appearances of the term "Holy Spirit" in the Qurʾān (Q 2:87, 253; 5:110) all occur in verses which declare that God "supported" Jesus with the Holy Spirit (cf. Mat 3:16; cf. Mar 1:10; Luke 3:22; Joh 1:32). These verses suggest that by "Holy Spirit" the Qurʾān does not mean an angel, and that the Qurʾān uses this expression in a manner parallel to the Bible (and perhaps the Jewish idea of *rūʾaḥ ha-qōdesh*) to mean a divine power. This idea matches the way the Qurʾān speaks of God's "Spirit," which is active in creation (Q 15:29; 32:9; 38:72) and revelation (Q 16:102; 26:192–93) at the command of God (Q 17:85). See further my commentary on 2:87 (cr. Mehdy Shaddel).

[103]We certainly know that they say, 'It is only a human that instructs him.' The language of him to whom they refer is non-Arabic, while this is a clear Arabic language.

16:103 The Qurʾān here refutes an accusation that someone—evidently a non-Arabic speaker—was the true source of its Prophet's proclamations. Wāḥidī offers a story to explain the accusation: "ʿAbd Allāh ibn Muslim . . . said: 'We owned two Christian youths from the people of ʿAyn Tamr, one called Yasar and the other Jabr. Their trade was making swords but they also could read the Scriptures in their own tongue. The Messenger of God used to pass by them and listen to their reading. As a result, the idolaters used to say: 'He is being taught by them!' To give them the lie, God revealed [this verse].'"

[104]Indeed, those who do not believe in the signs of God—God shall not guide them and there is a painful punishment for them. [105]Only those fabricate lies who do not believe in the signs of God, and it is they who are the liars.
[106]Excepting someone who is compelled [to recant his faith] while his heart is at rest in it, those who disbelieve in God after [affirming] their faith, and open up their breasts to unfaith, God's

wrath shall be upon them and there is a great punishment for them. [107]That, because they preferred the life of the world to the Hereafter and that God does not guide the faithless lot. [108]They are the ones God has set a seal on their hearts, and on their hearing and sight, and it is they who are the heedless. [109]Undoubtedly, they are the ones who will be the losers in the Hereafter.

[110]Thereafter *your* Lord will indeed be forgiving and merciful to those who migrated after they were persecuted, waged *jihād* and remained steadfast.

[111]The day [will come] when every soul will come pleading for itself and every soul will be recompensed fully for what it has done, and they will not be wronged.

[112]God draws a parable: There was a town secure and peaceful, its provision coming abundantly from every place. But it was ungrateful toward God's blessings. So God made it taste hunger and fear because of what they used to do.

16:112 *Tafsīr al-Jalālayn* identifies this town as Mecca (as do Hilali-Khan); hunger and security appear in 106:4 (in a Sura that refers to the Quraysh), but there the Qur'ān gives thanks to God that *he has saved them* from hunger and fear (here God has brought hunger and fear upon a town). Also, there is no reason to think of Mecca "tasting hunger and fear" in the context of the *sīra* until the latter part of Muḥammad's life, when he was no longer living there, and this is supposed to be a Meccan Sura (Bell solves the problem by making it a Medinan insertion). This verse could refer instead to the destruction of Jerusalem, either by the Babylonians (as recorded in 2Ch 36:15–19 retrospectively) or by the Romans (see, e.g., Mar 13:1–2; cf. Mat 24:1–2; Luke 21:5–6, predictively). Both events seem to be alluded to in Q 17:4–8.

---

[113]There had already come to them an apostle from among themselves, but they impugned him. So the punishment seized them while they were wrongdoers.

^{114}Eat out of what God has provided you as lawful and good, and give thanks for God's blessing, if it is Him that you worship. ^{115}He has forbidden you only carrion, blood, the flesh of the swine, and that which has been offered to other than God. But if someone is compelled [to eat any of that], without being rebellious or aggressive, God is indeed all-forgiving, all-merciful.

^{116}Do not say, asserting falsely with your tongues, 'This is lawful, and that is unlawful,' attributing lies to God. Indeed, those who attribute lies to God will not prosper. ^{117}[Their share of the present life is] a trifling enjoyment, and there will be a painful punishment for them.

^{118}We forbade to the Jews what We have recounted to *you* earlier, and We did not wrong them, but they used to wrong themselves.

16:118 A reference to the excessive laws of the Jews, given to them as a punishment. On this topic, see commentary on 4:160 (with further references).

---

^{119}Moreover, your Lord will indeed be forgiving and merciful to those who repent after having committed evil out of ignorance and reform themselves.

^{120}Indeed, Abraham was a nation [all by himself], obedient to God, a *ḥanīf,* and he was not a polytheist. ^{121}Grateful [as he was] for His blessings, He chose him and guided him to a straight path. ^{122}We gave him good in this world, and in the Hereafter he will indeed be among the Righteous. ^{123}Thereafter, We revealed to *you* [saying], 'Follow the creed of Abraham, a *ḥanīf,* who was not a polytheist.'

16:120–23 The Qur'ān here calls Abraham a "nation" (Ar. *umma*), a term which expresses the way a people would be descended from him, and thus reflects Genesis 18:

¹⁷Now the Lord had wondered, 'Shall I conceal from Abraham what I am going to do,

¹⁸as Abraham will become a great and powerful nation and all nations on earth will bless themselves by him? (Gen 18:17–18)

In the Qur'ān *ḥanīf* (seen here in vv. 120 and 123; cf. 2:135, 3:67, 3:95, 4:125, 6:79, 6:161, 10:105; 22:31; 98:5) is associated in particular with Abraham. Muslim scholars, and many academic scholars, understand it to mean "monotheist" (Pickthall: "by nature upright"; Yusuf Ali: "true in Faith"; Arberry: "man of pure faith"). This meaning is suggested by 22:31 and 98:5 where the related term *ḥunafā'* is used for devotion to God. The point of the Qur'ān, however, is also that Abraham believed in God *naturally,* independently from Jewish and Christian revelation (as he lived before Moses and Jesus: Q 3:65). Thus *ḥanīf* includes within it the sense of "gentile." Indeed a cognate of *ḥanīf* (*ḥanpē*) is used in this way to render "Greeks" (Gk. *Hellēnas*) in the Syriac New Testament (Joh 7:35; Act 18:4; Rom 1:16).

Here the Qur'ān's point is that Jews and the Christians do not follow the religion of Abraham. It thus uses Abraham to argue against the Jews and Christians as Paul uses Abraham to express his message about faith and law (see Rom 4, e.g., v. 13: "For the promise to Abraham and his descendants that he should inherit the world was not through the Law, but through the uprightness of faith").

———————

¹²⁴The Sabbath was only prescribed for those who differed about it. Your Lord will indeed judge between them on the Day of Resurrection concerning that about which they differ.

16:124 The Qur'ān's reference to the Sabbath here is related to its assessment of other aspects of Jewish law, namely that the excesses of that law are a punishment for Jewish infidelity. On this see commentary on 4:160 (with further references). New Testament passages such as Matthew 12 also criticize Jewish observance of the Sabbath, but they do so by challenging the very conception of the law:

⁵Or again, have you not read in the Law that on the Sabbath day the Temple priests break the Sabbath without committing any fault?
⁶Now here, I tell you, is something greater than the Temple.
⁷And if you had understood the meaning of the words: Mercy is what pleases me, not sacrifice, you would not have condemned the blameless.

⁸For the Son of man is master of the Sabbath. (Mat 12:5–8; cf. Mar 2:27–28; Luk 6:5)

In light of the New Testament, Syriac fathers such as Jacob of Serugh argue that Jews miss the spiritual meaning of the Sabbath:

Ceasing to work on the Sabbath, but not ceasing his wrongdoing / by keeping this observance he believes himself the friend of Moses. / O Jew, about the Sabbath it is in a spiritual manner / that one must be moved to speak thereof. / One should listen to the book of Moses with the ears of the soul / but what can I do for you who can hear only fleshly things? (Jacob of Serugh, *Homélies contre les juifs,* 86, homily 3, ll. 6–11)

Concerning the Qur'ānic view of the Sabbath (cf. 2:65; 4:47), see commentary on 7:163–66.

---

¹²⁵*Invite* to the way of *your* Lord with wisdom and good advice and dispute with them in a manner that is best. Indeed, *your* Lord knows best those who stray from His way, and He knows best those who are guided.

¹²⁶If you retaliate, retaliate with the like of what you have been made to suffer, but if you are patient, that is surely better for the steadfast.

16:126 One might compare this verse to Matthew 5:38–39:

³⁸'You have heard how it was said: Eye for eye and tooth for tooth.
³⁹But I say this to you: offer no resistance to the wicked. On the contrary, if anyone hits you on the right cheek, offer him the other as well.

Whereas Matthew offers a new moral code in place of the old, the Qur'ān still accepts the idea of *lex talionis* ("eye for an eye;" cf. Q 5:45) but recommends forgiveness.

---

¹²⁷So *be patient,* and *you* cannot be patient except with God['s help]. And *do* not grieve for them, nor *be* upset by their guile. ¹²⁸Indeed, God is with those who are Godwary and those who are virtuous.

17. *AL-ISRĀ'*, THE NIGHT JOURNEY

In the Name of God, the All-beneficent, the All-merciful.

¹Immaculate is He who carried His servant on a journey by night from the Sacred Mosque to the Farthest Mosque whose environs We have blessed, so that We might show him some of Our signs. Indeed, He is the All-hearing, the All-seeing.

17:1 The classical Islamic sources contain different stories meant to explain this verse. In almost all of these stories the "Sacred Mosque" is identified with Mecca (or the Ka'ba in particular). Some stories identify the "Furthest Mosque" as heaven itself, and others identify it as Jerusalem, relating that Muḥammad traveled there from Mecca on a miraculous beast named Burāq. *Tafsīr al-Jalālayn,* for example, quotes a tradition in which the Prophet explains: "I was brought al-Burāq, a white animal, larger than a donkey but smaller than a mule. . . . It set off carrying me until I reached the Holy House [of Jerusalem]." This tradition (like most stories of the Prophet's Night Journey) continues by relating that Muḥammad then ascended into heaven, where he met earlier prophets.

Whether the Sacred Mosque should be identified with Mecca (or the Ka'ba) is unclear (regarding this, see my commentary on 2:125–28). However, there is good Qur'ānic evidence (as argued by Neuwirth, "From the Sacred Mosque to the Remote Temple," see esp. 223–25) which supports the identification of the "Furthest Mosque" with Jerusalem, or at least with Palestine.

In this verse the Qur'ān describes this as a place "whose environs We have blessed." When the Qur'ān alludes to Biblical events that take place in Palestine it often describes the land as "blessed"—for example, the land of Abraham and Lot (21:71), the land of Solomon (Q 21:81), and the land to which the Israelites traveled after their liberation from Egypt (Q 7:137). Moreover, the Qur'ān's interest in Jerusalem continues in verses 4–8 of this Sura (and is seen again in v. 60).

---

²We gave Moses the Book and made it a guide for the Children of Israel, [saying,] 'Do not take any trustee besides Me'—³descendants of those whom We carried [in the ark] with Noah. He was indeed a grateful servant.

⁴We revealed to the Children of Israel in the Book: 'Twice you will cause corruption on the earth and you will perpetrate great tyranny.' ⁵So when the first occasion of the two [prophecies] came, We aroused against you Our servants possessing great might, and they ransacked [your] habitations, and the promise was bound to be fulfilled.

⁶Then We gave you back the turn [to prevail] over them, and We aided you with children and wealth, and made you greater in number, ⁷[saying,] 'If you do good, you will do good to your [own] souls, and if you do evil, it will be [evil] for them.' So when the occasion for the other [prophecy] comes, they will make your faces wretched, and enter the Temple just as they entered it the first time, and destroy utterly whatever they come upon.

⁸Maybe your Lord will have mercy on you, but if you revert, We [too] will revert, and We have made hell a prison for the faithless.

Q 17:4–8 This passage likely alludes to the two times Jerusalem was sacked and its temple destroyed, by the Babylonians (586 BC) and by the Romans (AD 70). Verse 4 apparently alludes to both calamities and indeed suggests that "the Book" contained predictions of these. This could follow from the way the Bible has each destruction prophesied: the first destruction in Leviticus 26:14–39, and the second in the various predictions of Christ (Mar 13:1–2; Mat 24:1–2; Luk 21:5–6).

By this reading verse 5 refers to the Babylonians' assault on Jerusalem and destruction of the temple under Nebuchadnezzar, verse 6 to the return of the Israelite exiles to Jerusalem (after the Persian defeat of the Babylonians in 539 BC), and verse 7 to the Roman destruction of the temple (tellingly referred to as a *masjid* in Arabic) under Titus. Qarai translates verse 7 as referring to future events (on this Bell agrees, *Commentary* 1:460; n.b. the same turn of phrase in 17:104), but it could be understood to refer to the past; that is, instead of "So when the occasion for the other [prophecy] comes" we might follow Droge's translation, "When the second promise came (to pass)." This reading is not absolutely clear from syntax, as the following phrase ("they will make your faces wretched") is in the subjunctive mood. For this reason Bell (who sees v. 8 as the apodosis to the *idhā* statement of v. 7) translates: "So when the promise of the second comes (to fulfillment), *that they may* disgrace you" (Droge has "to cause you distress") (cr. Joseph Witztum).

In any case the Qurʾān here reflects the Biblical theodicy associated with these events, namely that God handed Jerusalem over to Israel's enemies on account of the city's sins. This theodicy might be seen (among other places) in 2 Chronicles (36:15–20), which looks back at the destruction of the first temple, and in the predictions of Jesus regarding the destruction of the second temple (Mar 13:1–2; Mat 24:1–2; Luk 21:5–6).

---

⁹This Qurʾān indeed guides to what is most upright, and gives the good news to the faithful who do righteous deeds that there is a great reward for them.

¹⁰As for those who do not believe in the Hereafter, We have prepared a painful punishment for them.

¹¹Man prays for ill as [avidly as] he prays for good, and man is overhasty.

¹²We made the night and the day two signs. We effaced the sign of the night and made the sign of the day lightsome, so that you may seek from your Lord's bounty and that you may know the number of years and calculation [of time], and We have elaborated everything in detail.

17:12 Yahuda (302) argues that the description of the night and the day as signs is related to Genesis 1:14, where the sun and the moon are described as signs (Hb. *ōtōt*).

---

¹³We have strapped every person's karma to his neck, and We shall bring it out for him on the Day of Resurrection as a book that he will find wide open. ¹⁴'Read your book! Today your soul suffices as your own reckoner.'

17:13–14 Here (cf. 17:71; 18:49; 39:69; 78:29) the Qur'ān alludes to a register (not really "karma") of each individual's good or evil deeds, to be opened on the Day of Judgment. One might compare the appearance of similar books in Daniel and 1 Enoch (cf. *BEQ,* 434):

A stream of fire poured out, issuing from his presence. A thousand thousand waited on him, ten thousand times ten thousand stood before him. The court was in session and the books lay open. (Dan 7:10)

He shall read aloud regarding every aspect of your mischief, in the presence of the Great Holy One. Then your faces shall be covered with shame, and he will cast out every deed which is built upon oppression. (1 Enoch 97:6; cf. 90:20)

On the notion that no soul shall carry another's burden see commentary on 82:19 (with further references).

---

¹⁵Whoever is guided is guided only for [the good of] his own soul, and whoever goes astray, goes astray only to its detriment. No bearer shall bear another's burden.

We do not punish [any community] until We have sent [it] an apostle. ¹⁶And when We desire to destroy a town We command its affluent ones [to obey God]. But they commit transgression in it, and so the word becomes due against it, and We destroy it utterly.

¹⁷How many generations We have destroyed since Noah! Your Lord is sufficient as [a witness who is] a well-informed observer of His servants' sins.

¹⁸Whoever desires this transitory life, We expedite for him therein whatever We wish, for whomever We desire. Then We appoint hell for him, to enter it blameful and spurned.

¹⁹Whoever desires the Hereafter and strives for it with an endeavour worthy of it, should he be faithful—the endeavour of such will be well-appreciated. ²⁰To these and to those—to all We extend the bounty of *your* Lord, and the bounty of *your* Lord is not confined.

²¹Observe how We have given some of them an advantage over some others; yet the Hereafter is surely greater in respect of ranks and greater in respect of relative merit.

²²Do not set up another god besides God, or you will sit blameworthy, forsaken. ²³*Your* Lord has decreed that you shall not worship anyone except Him, and [He has enjoined] kindness to parents. Should any of them or both reach old age at your side, do not say to them, 'Fie!' And do not chide them, but speak to them noble words. ²⁴Lower the wing of humility to them mercifully, and say, 'My Lord! Have mercy on them, just as they reared me when I was [a] small [child]!' ²⁵Your Lord knows best what is in your hearts. Should you be righteous, He is indeed most forgiving toward penitents.

²⁶Give the relatives their [due] right, and the needy and the traveler [as well], but do not squander wastefully. ²⁷The wasteful are indeed brothers of satans, and Satan is ungrateful to his Lord. ²⁸And if you have to hold off from [assisting] them [for now], seeking your Lord's mercy which you expect [in the future], speak to them gentle words. ²⁹Do not keep your hand chained to your neck, nor open it altogether, or you will sit being blamewor-

thy and regretful. [30]Indeed, your Lord expands and tightens the provision for whomever He wishes. He is indeed a well-informed observer of His servants.

[31]Do not kill your children for the fear of penury: We will provide for them and for you. Killing them is indeed a great iniquity.

[32]Do not approach fornication. It is indeed an indecency and an evil way.

[33]Do not kill a soul [whose life] God has made inviolable, except with due cause, and whoever is killed wrongfully, We have certainly given his heir an authority. But let him not commit any excess in killing, for he enjoys the support [of law].

[34]Do not approach the orphan's property except in the best manner, until he comes of age.

Fulfill your covenants; indeed all covenants are accountable.

[35]When you measure, observe fully the measure, [and] weigh with an even balance. That is better and more favourable in outcome [in the Hereafter].

[36]Do not pursue anything that has not come to your knowledge. Indeed, hearing, eyesight and the heart—all these are accountable. [37]Do not walk exultantly on the earth. Indeed, you will neither pierce the earth, nor reach the mountains in height. [38]The evil of all these is detestable to your Lord.

[39]These are among [precepts] that your Lord has revealed to you of wisdom. Do not set up another god besides God, or you will be cast into hell, being blameworthy and banished [from His mercy].

17:22–39 Brinner ("An Islamic Decalogue," 76–80) argues that this passage (a condensed version of which appears in 6:151–53) involves an Islamic version of the Ten Commandments (Exo 20:1–17; Deu 5:4–21), adapted to an Arabian setting. He describes them as follows:

1. 17:22: Exodus 20:4 (third commandment)

2. 17:23–25: Exodus 20:3, 12 (second and fifth commandments)

3. 17:26–30: cf. Exodus 22:20–26/Deuteronomy 15:7–11 (Islamic addition)

4. 17:31: cf. Leviticus 18:21 (Islamic addition)

5. 17:32: Exodus 20:14 (seventh commandment)

6. 17:33: Exodus 20:13 (sixth commandment)

7. 17:34: cf. Exodus 20:21 (Islamic addition; on kindness to orphans, see commentary on 107:2, with further references)

8. 17:35: cf. Leviticus 19:35 and Deu 25:13–16 (Islamic addition; see commentary on Q 83:1–3)

9. 17:36: (Islamic addition)

10. 17:37–38: cf. Deuteronomy 8:14 (Islamic addition)

Angelika Neuwirth ("A Discovery of Evil in the Qur'ān?") argues that this is the earliest of three passages (including also 6:151–53 and 2:83–85) which present Qur'ānic versions of the Ten Commandments. The Qur'ān also seems to allude to the tablets on which the Ten Commandments were written in 7:145; cf. also 5:1–21; 25:67–72; 28:44–46.

---

[40]Did your Lord prefer you for sons, and [Himself] adopt females from among the angels? You indeed make a monstrous statement!

17:40 Traditionally scholars argue that this and similar verses (cf. 4:117; 6:100; 16:57; 37:149–53; 43:16–19; 53:21–22, 27) are directed against the pagan Meccans who worshipped certain female angels as daughters of God. However, it is equally possible that behind such passages are the doctrines of certain Jews who venerated the angels. Their existence is suggested by Paul's letter to the Colossians:

> [18]Do not be cheated of your prize by anyone who chooses to grovel to angels and worship them, pinning every hope on visions received, vainly puffed up by a human way of thinking. (Col 2:18)

Note, too, how the pagan Celsus, in his dialogue with Origen (written ca. 180) asserts that Jews "worship the heaven and the angels in it" (Origen, *Contra Celsum,* 5:6; Origen denies the assertion). Thus the Qur'ān might be criticizing here not pagans but Arabized Jews who likewise believed in the one God Allāh but considered some of his angels to be his "daughters." See further commentary on 43:16–19; Crone, "Religion of the Qur'ānic Pagans" (esp. 188–200).

----

⁴¹Certainly We have variously paraphrased [the principles of guidance] in this Qur'ān so that they may take admonition, but it increases them only in aversion.

⁴²*Say,* 'Were there [other] gods besides Him, as they say, they would have surely encroached on the Lord of the Throne. ⁴³Immaculate is He and preeminently far above what they say!'

⁴⁴The seven heavens glorify Him and the earth [too], and whoever is in them. There is not a thing but celebrates His praise, but you do not understand their glorification. He is indeed all-forbearing, all-forgiving.

17:44 On the seven heavens in the Qur'ān, see commentary on 67:3 (with further references). On all things praising God, see commentary on 16:49. The notion that humans are unable to understand the way creation glorifies God may owe something to Psalm 19:1–3:

> ¹The heavens declare the glory of God, the vault of heaven proclaims his handiwork,
> ²day discourses of it to day, night to night hands on the knowledge.
> ³No utterance at all, no speech, not a sound to be heard.

----

⁴⁵When *you* recite the Qur'ān, We draw a hidden curtain between *you* and those who do not believe in the Hereafter, ⁴⁶and We cast veils on their hearts, lest they should understand it, and a deafness into their ears. When *you* mention *your* Lord alone in the Qur'ān, they turn their backs in aversion.

17:45–46 The Qur'ān here speaks first of a "curtain" (*ḥijāb,* v. 45) which separates believers and unbelievers and then of "veils" (*akinna,* v. 46) which cover the hearts of the unbelievers when the revelation (*qurʾān*) is read. This latter declaration is close to Paul's description of the veil (Gk. *kalumma*) that covers the heart of the Jews when they hear the "Old Testament":

> ¹⁴But their minds were closed; indeed, until this very day, the same veil remains over the reading of the Old Testament: it is not lifted, for only in Christ is it done away with.
>
> ¹⁵As it is, to this day, whenever Moses is read, their hearts are covered with a veil,
>
> ¹⁶and this veil will not be taken away till they turn to the Lord. (2Co 3:14–16)

One might also compare Jesus' declaration that those "on the outside . . . listen, but never understand" (Mar 4:11–12; cf. Mat 13:13–15; Luk 8:10; Act 28:26–27—all of which recall Isa 6:9–10).

The Qurʾān speaks of veils over the hearts of unbelievers in 6:25; 18:57; 41:5 and of their deafness in 2:7; 6:25; 31:7; 41:44. The related expression "uncircumcised hearts" is used specifically for the Jews in 2:88; 4:155.

---

⁴⁷We know best what they listen for when they listen to *you,* and when they hold secret talks, when the wrongdoers say, '[If you follow him] You will be following just a bewitched man.' ⁴⁸*Look,* how they coin epithets for *you;* so they go astray, and cannot find a way.

⁴⁹They say, 'What, when we have become bones and dust, shall we really be raised in a new creation?' ⁵⁰*Say,* '[Yes, even if] you should become stones, or iron, ⁵¹or a creature more fantastic to your minds!' They will say, 'Who will bring us back?' *Say,* 'He who originated you the first time.' They will nod their heads at you and say, 'When will that be?' *Say,* 'Maybe it is near! ⁵²The day He calls you, you will respond to Him, praising Him, and you will think you remained [in the world] only for a little while.'

⁵³*Tell* My servants to speak in a manner which is the best. Indeed, Satan incites ill feeling between them, and Satan is indeed man's open enemy.

⁵⁴Your Lord knows you best. He will have mercy on you if He wishes, or punish you, if He wishes, and We did not send *you* to watch over them. ⁵⁵*Your* Lord knows best whoever is in the heavens and the earth. Certainly We gave some prophets an advantage over the others, and We gave David the Psalms.

17:55 The declaration "We gave David the Psalms" (*zabūr;* cf. 4:163; 21:105) reflects the traditional Jewish and Christian association of the Psalms with David, evident already in the Mishnah (m. Avot 6:9) and the New Testament (e.g., Mar 12:36–37). Elsewhere, however, the Qurʾān uses the plural *zubur* to mean generally "books" or "scriptures" (e.g., 3:184; 16:44; 23:53; 26:196; 35:25; 54:43; 54:52). The term *zabūr* is perhaps derived from Syriac *mazmūrā* or Hebrew *mizmōr* "Psalm" (see Jeffery, *FV,* 149), or from epigraphic South Arabian (see Ambros, 120).

---

⁵⁶*Say,* 'Invoke those whom you claim [to be gods] besides Him. They have no power to remove your distress, nor to bring about any change [in your state]. ⁵⁷They [themselves] are the ones who supplicate, seeking a recourse to their Lord, whoever is nearer [to Him], expecting His mercy and fearing His punishment.' *Your* Lord's punishment is indeed a thing to beware of.

⁵⁸There is not a town but We will destroy it before the Day of Resurrection, or punish it with a severe punishment. That has been written in the Book.

⁵⁹Nothing keeps Us from sending signs except that the former peoples denied them. We gave Thamūd the she-camel as an eye-opener, but they wronged her. We do not send the signs except for warning.

⁶⁰When We said to *you,* '*Your* Lord indeed encompasses those people,' We did not appoint the vision that We showed *you* except as a tribulation for the people and the tree cursed in the Qurʾān. We warn them, but it only increases them in their outrageous rebellion.

17:60 The vision (*ru'ya*) mentioned here is connected to the beginning of this Sura (v. 1) where the Qur'ān refers to God's taking His servant to a blessed land to "show him (*nuriyahu*) some of Our signs." That land is presumably Palestine or Jerusalem itself (see commentary on 17:1).

The Muslim commentators generally identify the "tree cursed in the Qur'ān [or better, *qur'ān*]" with a tree of hell, and point to Q 37:62–66, with its description of the *zaqqūm* tree. Wāḥidī relates here a story about Muḥammad's opponent Abū Jahl: "When the tree of al-Zaqqūm was mentioned in the Qur'ān, the Quraysh were threatened with it. Abū Jahl said: 'Do you know what this *zaqqūm,* with which Muḥammad threatens you, is?' They said: 'No!' He said: 'Meat and broth with cream. By God, if he let us put our hands on it we will devour it!' God revealed [this verse] saying: this tree is repulsive."

However, the Qur'ān nowhere uses the word "cursed" to describe the *zaqqūm* tree. The Gospels, however, describe Jesus' cursing of a fig tree (Mar 11:13–14; 20–22; Mat 21:19–21), a tree that serves in the Bible as a symbol of the temple and Jewish rituals generally (on this note, cf. 95:1; commentary on 95:1–3).

It could be that the "tree" is Israel and, moreover, that there is a connection with God's cursing of the Israelites in the Qur'ān (regarding which see commentary on 5:13–14, with further references). Thereby the vision (of Jerusalem) in this verse would be connected with the tree (representing the temple).

———————

⁶¹When We said to the angels, 'Prostrate before Adam,' they [all] prostrated, but not Iblis: he said, 'Shall I prostrate before someone whom You have created from clay?'

17:61 On the prostration of the angels before Adam (and the devil's refusal to prostrate), see commentary on 7:11–12 (with further references).

———————

⁶²Said he, 'Do You see this one whom You have honoured above me? If You respite me until the Day of Resurrection, I will surely lay my yoke on his progeny, [all] except a few.'

⁶³Said He, 'Begone! Whoever of them follows you, the hell shall indeed be your requital, an ample reward. ⁶⁴Instigate whomever of them you can with your voice, and rally against them your cavalry and infantry, and share with them in wealth and children, and make promises to them!' But Satan promises them nothing but delusion. ⁶⁵'As for My servants, you will have no authority over them.' And your Lord suffices as trustee.

17:62–65 On the respite which the devil requests and receives from God, see commentary on 7:14–18 (with further references).

---

⁶⁶Your Lord is He who drives for you the ships in the sea so that you may seek His bounty. He is indeed most merciful to you. ⁶⁷When distress befalls you at sea, those whom you invoke besides Him are forsaken. But when He delivers you to land, you are disregardful [of Him]. Man is very ungrateful.

⁶⁸Do you feel secure that He will not make the coastland swallow you, or He will not unleash upon you a rain of stones? Then you will not find any defender for yourselves.

⁶⁹Do you feel secure that He will not send you back into it another time and unleash against you a shattering gale and drown you because of your unfaith? Then you will not find for yourselves any redresser against Us.

⁷⁰Certainly We have honoured the Children of Adam and carried them over land and sea, and provided them with all the good things, and preferred them with a complete preference over many of those We have created.

⁷¹The day We shall summon every group of people along with their *imām,* then whoever is given his book in his right hand—

they will read their book, and they will not be wronged so much
as a single date-thread.

17:71 Here the Qurʾān speaks of the righteous receiving a book in their right
hand (also 69:19, 84:7; cf. 69:25, which speaks of the unrighteous receiving a
book in their left hand). However, 56:8 (also 56:27–40, 90) and 90:18 speak of
those who on the Day of Judgment are on the right side (cf. 56:9, also 56:51–56,
92–94, for those on the left side). This latter image is closer to Matthew 25:31–
46. See further commentary on 90:7–20.

---

⁷²But whoever has been blind in this [world], will be blind in
the Hereafter, and [even] more astray from the [right] way.
⁷³They were about to beguile *you* from what God has revealed
to *you* so that *you* may fabricate against Us something other than
that, whereat they would have befriended you. ⁷⁴Had We not fortified *you,* certainly *you* might have inclined toward them a bit.
⁷⁵Then We would have surely made *you* taste a double [punish-
ment] in this life and a double [punishment] after death, and then
you would have not found for *yourself* any helper against Us.
⁷⁶They were about to hound *you* out of the land, to expel *you*
from it, but then they would not have stayed after *you* but a little.
⁷⁷A precedent touching those We have sent before *you* from among
Our apostles, and *you* will not find any change in Our precedent.
⁷⁸*Maintain* the prayer [during the period] from the sun's decline till the darkness of the night, and [observe particularly] the
dawn recital. The dawn recital is indeed attended [by angels].
⁷⁹And *keep vigil* for a part of the night, as a supererogatory
[devotion] for *you.* It may be that *your* Lord will raise *you* to a
praiseworthy station.
⁸⁰And *say,* 'My Lord! 'Admit me with a worthy entrance, and
bring me out with a worthy departure, and render me a favourable
authority from Yourself.'

⁸¹And *say,* 'The truth has come, and falsehood has vanished. Falsehood is indeed bound to vanish.'

⁸²We send down in the Qur'ān that which is a cure and mercy for the faithful, and it increases the wrongdoers only in loss.

⁸³When We bless man, he is disregardful and turns aside; but when an ill befalls him, he is despondent.

⁸⁴*Say,* 'Everyone acts according to his character. Your Lord knows best who is better guided with regard to the way.'

⁸⁵They question *you* concerning the Spirit. *Say,* 'The Spirit is of the command of my Lord, and you have not been given of the knowledge except a few [of you].'

17:85 Qarai (cf. Arberry, Asad, Blachère) renders Arabic *amr* here as "command," but others (Hilali-Khan) understand it to mean "affair" (the verse would then mean that the true nature of the Spirit is known only to God). A third understanding is also possible, by which *amr* is related to Aramaic *mēmrā* ("word") and refers to the divine Logos. See commentary on 42:52 (with further references).

Muslim commentators generally identify the Qur'ān's references to the "Spirit" or the "Holy Spirit" (e.g., 2:87, 253; 5:110; 16:2,102; 19:17; 40:15; 42:52; 97:4) as references to the angel Gabriel. However, this passage and others (16:2; 40:15; 42:52; 97:4) suggest that it is something more (see further commentary on 2:87).

---

⁸⁶If We wish, We would take away what We have revealed to *you.* Then *you* would not find for yourself any defender against Us ⁸⁷except a mercy from *your* Lord. His grace has indeed been great upon *you.*

⁸⁸*Say,* 'Should all humans and jinn rally to bring the like of this Qur'ān, they will not bring its like, even if they assisted one another.'

⁸⁹We have certainly interspersed this Qur'ān with every [kind of] parable for the people, but most of these people are only bent on ingratitude.

⁹⁰They say, 'We will not believe *you* until *you* make a spring gush forth for us from the ground. ⁹¹Or until *you* have a garden of date palms and vines and *you* make streams gush through it. ⁹²Or until *you* cause the sky to fall in fragments upon us, just as *you* have averred. Or until *you* bring God and the angels [right] in front of us. ⁹³Or until *you* have a house of gold, or *you* ascend into the sky. And we will not believe *your* ascension until *you* bring down for us a book that we may read.'

Say, 'Immaculate is my Lord! Am I anything but a human apostle?!' ⁹⁴Nothing has kept these people from believing when guidance came to them, but their saying, 'Has God sent a human as an apostle?!' ⁹⁵*Say,* 'Had there been angels in the earth, walking around and residing [in it like humans do], We would have sent down to them an angel from the heaven as apostle.'

17:94–95 On the expectation of unbelievers that divine messages would be brought by an angel, see commentary on 6:50 (with further references).

⎯⎯⎯⎯⎯⎯⎯⎯⎯⎯

⁹⁶*Say,* 'God suffices as witness between me and you. He is indeed a well-informed observer of His servants.'

⁹⁷Whomever God guides is rightly guided, and whomever He leads astray—*you* will never find for them any protector besides Him. On the Day of Resurrection, We will muster them [scrambling] on their faces, blind, dumb, and deaf. Their refuge shall be hell. Whenever it subsides, We will intensify the blaze for them.

⁹⁸That is their requital because they denied Our signs and said, 'What, when we have become bones and dust, shall we really be raised in a new creation?'

⁹⁹Do they not see that God, who created the heavens and the earth, is able to create the like of them? He has appointed for them a term, in which there is no doubt; yet the wrongdoers are only bent on ingratitude.

¹⁰⁰*Say*, 'Even if you possessed the treasuries of my Lord's mercy, you would withhold them for the fear of being spent, and man is very niggardly.'

¹⁰¹Certainly We gave Moses nine manifest signs. So ask the Children of Israel. When he came to them, Pharaoh said to him, 'O Moses, indeed I think you are bewitched.'

¹⁰²He said, 'You certainly know that none has sent these [signs] as eye-openers except the Lord of the heavens and the earth, and I, O Pharaoh, indeed think you are doomed.'

17:101–2 Although this passage is sometimes taken as a reference to the Ten Commandments, the nine "signs" here (cf. 27:12) are more likely the two signs which Moses showed to Pharaoh (the snake turning into a staff [Q 7:107; 20:20; 26:32; 27:10; 28:31] and his hand turning white [Q 7:108; 20:22; 26:33; 27:12; 28:32]), along with seven of the ten plagues known from Exodus (drought [Q 7:130]: flood, locusts, lice, frogs, blood [Q 7:133], "anger" [and not "plague" as Qarai has it; 7:134]—perhaps the death of the firstborn). Cf. 27:12.

By "bewitched" the Qurʾān means to have Pharaoh declare that Moses's miracles took place through magic, not through the power of God. The Qurʾān makes this a common accusation against prophets (see 5:110; 6:7; 7:109, passim).

¹⁰³He desired to exterminate them from the land, so We drowned him and all those who were with him.

17:103 Note Exodus 14:21–23:

²¹Then Moses stretched out his hand over the sea, and the Lord drove the sea back with a strong easterly wind all night and made the sea into dry land. The waters were divided
²²and the Israelites went on dry ground right through the sea, with walls of water to right and left of them.
²³The Egyptians gave chase, and all Pharaoh's horses, chariots and horsemen went into the sea after them. (Exo 14:21–23)

---

¹⁰⁴After him We said to the Children of Israel, 'Take up residence in the land, and when the occasion of the other [promise] comes, We will gather you in mixed company.'

17:104 When read together with verse 103 this passage suggests that the Qur'ān has the Israelites settle not in the Biblical promised land (see Deu 30:15–18) but in Egypt. On this idea, which is proposed by Nicolai Sinai ("Inheriting Egypt"), see commentary on Q 26:52–59 (with further references).

---

¹⁰⁵With the truth did We send it down, and with the truth did it descend, and We did not send *you* except as a bearer of good news and warner. ¹⁰⁶We have sent the Qur'ān in [discrete] parts so that *you* may recite it for the people a little at a time, and We have sent it down piecemeal. ¹⁰⁷*Say,* 'Whether you believe in it or do not believe, indeed, when it is recited to those who were given knowledge before it, they fall down in prostration on their faces ¹⁰⁸and say, "Immaculate is our Lord! Our Lord's promise is indeed bound to be fulfilled." ¹⁰⁹Weeping, they fall down on their faces, and it increases them in humility.'

[110]*Say,* 'Invoke "God" or invoke "the All-beneficent." Whichever [of His names] you may invoke, to Him belong the Best Names.' Be neither loud in *your* prayer, nor murmur it, but follow a middle course between these, [111]and *say,* 'All praise belongs to God, who has neither any offspring, nor has He any partner in sovereignty, nor has He [made] any friend out of weakness,' and *magnify* Him with a magnification [worthy of Him].

18. *AL-KAHF*, THE CAVE

In the Name of God, the All-beneficent, the All-merciful.

[1]All praise belongs to God, who has sent down the Book to His servant and did not let any crookedness be in it, [2][a Book] upright, to warn of a severe punishment from Him, and to give good news to the faithful who do righteous deeds that there shall be for them a good reward, [3]to abide in it forever, [4]and to warn those who say, 'God has offspring.' [5]They do not have any knowledge of that, nor did their fathers. Monstrous is the utterance that comes out of their mouths, and they say nothing but a lie.

[6]*You* are liable to imperil *your* life out of grief for their sake if they do not believe this discourse. [7]Indeed, We have made whatever is on the earth an adornment for it that We may test them [to see] which of them is best in conduct. [8]And indeed We will turn whatever is on it into a barren plain.

[9]Do *you* suppose that the Companions of the Cave and the Inscription were among Our wonderful signs?

18:9–26 *overview* The Qur'ānic passage on the "Companions of the Cave" is a reflection on a Christian legend—generally known as the Sleepers of Ephesus—that was well known throughout the Christian communities of the Middle

East at the time of Islam's origins. The legend was most likely written in Greek in the fifth century AD. Syriac versions thereof were composed already in the sixth century. The Qur'ānic account is not a simple borrowing of the Christian legend and notably contains few if any Syriacisms, but it is presumably due to the prominence of this story among Christians in its context (Arabs or otherwise) that the Qur'ān's author knew of it.

The Christian legend opens in the time of the Christ-hating pagan emperor Decius (r. 249–51). The protagonists of the story are seven (or, in some traditions, eight; note the corresponding indecision in Q 18:22) Christian boys who refuse to offer incense at the altars of Zeus, Apollo, and Artemis (the patron god of Ephesus) as ordered by Decius. For this they are imprisoned, but they escape and flee to a cave outside a city. There God casts upon them a miraculous sleep (or a death). Two believers from the city, who know the location of the cave and believe that the boys would be raised, later inscribe a lead tablet with the boys' names and their story and post it next to the cave.

The boys "wake up" many years later during the reign of the Christ-loving emperor Theodosius II (r. 408–50). Thinking they are still living during the dark days of the pagan emperor, they cautiously send one of their members into the city. To his great surprise this scout discovers (after certain adventures) that Ephesus has become a Christian city. Eventually the emperor Theodosius himself comes to Ephesus to meet the miraculous boys. Upon doing so, he is convinced of the doctrine of the resurrection of the body (despite the teaching of some—labeled "Origenists"—who taught that only the soul is resurrected). After meeting the good emperor, the boys return to the cave and die (or "sleep") for good.

The Qur'ān, like the Christian authors who told this story, uses it to make a case for the doctrine of the resurrection of the body (n.b. esp. v. 21). Thus, this account should be compared to the story of the man and his donkey in 2:259. Yet the Qur'ān also frames this passage with an anti-Christian theological message (n.b. v. 4, which precedes the account, and v. 26, which concludes it).

18:9 The "inscription" here refers to the lead tablet inscribed by the two believers of Ephesus and posted at the entrance to the cave (see Griffith, "Christian Lore and the Arabic Qur'ān," 125–27), as described by Jacob of Serugh in his metrical homily on the "Sleepers of Ephesus":

> There were there two sophists, sons of the leading men, / and they reckoned
> that the Lord would resurrect them, / So they made tablets of lead and placed
> them beside them; / on them they wrote down the names of the children of

light, / and why the young men had gone to hide in the cave, / and at what time they had fled from the presence of the emperor Decius. (Jacob of Serugh, *Mēmrā on the Sleepers of Ephesus,* 25, ll. 67–72)

---

¹⁰When the youths took refuge in the Cave, they said, 'Our Lord! Grant us mercy from Yourself and help us on to rectitude in our affair.'

18:10

They ascended the mountain and went into the cave to spend the night there, / and they called upon the Lord with a plaintive voice, saying as follows; / We beg you good shepherd who has chosen his sheep, / preserve your flock from that wolf who is thirsting for our blood. (Jacob of Serugh, *Mēmrā on the Sleepers of Ephesus,* 23 (ll. 53–56)

---

¹¹So We put them to sleep in the Cave for several years. ¹²Then We aroused them that We might know which of the two groups better reckoned the period they had stayed.

¹³We relate to *you* their account in truth. They were indeed youths who had faith in their Lord, and We had enhanced them in guidance

18:12–13 See commentary on 18:25. Verse 13 might mark the beginning of a second version of this account.

---

¹⁴and fortified their hearts when they stood up and said, 'Our Lord is the Lord of the heavens and the earth. We will never in-

voke any god besides Him, for then we shall certainly have said an atrocious lie. ¹⁵These—our people—have taken gods besides Him. Why do they not bring any clear authority touching them? So who is a greater wrongdoer than he who fabricates lies against God? ¹⁶When you have dissociated yourselves from them and from what they worship except God, take refuge in the Cave. Your Lord will unfold His mercy for you, and He will help you on to ease in your affair.'

18:14–16

The emperor saw how admirable were their persons / and he spoke to them with blandishments, saying, / "Tell me boys, why have you transgressed my orders? / Come along and sacrifice, and I will make you leaders." / The son of the hyparchos opened his mouth, along with his seven companions, / "We will not worship deaf images, the work of (human) hands: / we have the Lord of heaven, and he will assist us. / It is him that we worship, and to him do we offer the purity of our hearts.

. . .

There was a rock cave on the top of the mountain / and the dear boys decided to hide there.

(Jacob of Serugh, *Mēmrā on the Sleepers of Ephesus,* 22, ll. 28–35, 46–47)

---

¹⁷*You* may see the sun, when it rises, slanting toward the right of their cave, and, when it sets, cut across them towards the left, and they are in a cavern within it. That is one of God's signs. Whomever God guides is rightly guided, and whomever He leads astray, *you* will never find for him any friend that can guide. ¹⁸You will suppose them to be awake, though they are asleep. We turn them to the right and to the left, and at the threshold their dog [lies] stretching its forelegs. If you come upon them, you will surely turn to flee from them and will be filled with a terror of them.

18:18 The presence of a dog in the Qurʾānic account of the Companions of the Cave poses a problem to Muslim interpreters. Why would a dog, a ritually unclean animal (Muslims are to wash seven times after contact with a dog's saliva), be found together with the pious companions of the cave? Why would a dog be inside their "house" when a well-known hadith relates that angels do not enter houses with dogs in them? Ibn Kathīr (*Tafsīr,* 3:72) resolves this problem by insisting that the dog actually remained outside of the cave, to protect them.

However, the dog poses no problem when the account of the Companions of the Cave is read in the light of the Qurʾān's Biblical subtext. In Jacob of Serugh's *mēmrā* on the Sleepers the boys describe themselves—using a Gospel metaphor—as sheep, Christ as their shepherd, and Decius as a wolf. Christ responds by sending a "watcher" to guard them. This watcher is presumably meant to be an angel (indeed the term "watcher" *ʿīrā* is used for certain angels in Syriac Christian texts), but the Qurʾān takes the metaphor used in Jacob's text literally and imagines it to be a dog (one might say a sheepdog):

> We beg you good shepherd who has chosen his sheep, / preserve your flock from that wolf who is thirsting for our blood. / He took their spirits and raise them up above, to heaven / and left a *watcher* to be guarding their limbs. (Jacob of Serugh, *Mēmrā on the Sleepers of Ephesus,* 23, ll. 55–60)

Indeed we know a dog already featured in Christian accounts of the legend from the report of a Byzantine traveler (also) named Theodosius who describes Ephesus as the city of "the seven sleeping brothers, and the dog Viricanus at their feet" (*The Pilgrimage of Theodosius,* 16).

---

[19]So it was that We aroused them [from sleep] so that they might question one another. One of them said, 'How long have you stayed [here]?' They said, 'We have stayed for a day, or part of a day.' They said, 'Your Lord knows best how long you have stayed. Send one of you to the city with this money. Let him observe which of them has the purest food and bring you provisions from there. Let him be attentive, and let him not make anyone aware about you. [20]Indeed, should they prevail over you, they will [either] stone you [to death] or force you back into their creed, and then you will never prosper.'

18:19–20 The declaration "day, or part of a day" (which also appears in the story of the man and his donkey in 2:259) is a distinctive Qurʾānic refrain to express its teaching that the dead will feel that only a moment has passed since their death at the moment of the resurrection.

As for the money, its place in the Qurʾān might seem curious (seeing that so many other details about the boys go unmentioned) but its importance is evident from the Christian account. Jacob describes how the boys take coins with them in order to make ends meet while they are out of Ephesus. It is one of these coins—which have the image of Decius, who was emperor when they fell asleep—with which one of them tries to buy food back in Ephesus. This leads a shopkeeper, at first, to suspect him of having found buried treasure. In the end, however, the people of Ephesus learn that the truth about the boy is still more amazing, and eventually they summon the emperor himself to meet him and his companions:

> He went out to the street to buy some bread to take it back with him / he took out and produced some of the small change he had in his purse. / The man who was selling took it and examined it; / he gave it to his companion, so that his [companion] too might examine it. / The small change passed through the hands of five people as they examined it, / [and they began] whispering amongst themselves over it. / The boy saw that they were whispering and he answered and said, /"Give me some bread if you are going to give me any; otherwise I am off." / The man who was selling came up and grabbed the boy: /"Tell me, boy, where are you from, and what is your country? / As for the treasure you have found, let us be sharers with you in it."
>
> . . . .
>
> Gossip fell on all streets of the Ephesians / that a boy has some treasure; and they immediately grabbed hold of him. / Word entered the holy church, reaching the bishop; / he sent and snatched him from their hands. (Jacob of Serugh, *Mēmrā on the Sleepers of Ephesus*, 27–28, ll. 111–19, 125–28a)

On the Companions' fear that they might be "stoned" (v. 20), see commentary on 26:105–16 (with further references).

---

²¹So it was that We let them come upon them, so that they might know that God's promise is indeed true, and that there is no doubt in the Hour. As they disputed among themselves about their matter, they said, 'Build a building over them. Their Lord

knows them best.' Those who had the say in their matter said, 'We will set up a place of worship over them.'

18:21 Here the Qur'ān turns immediately to the denouement of the Christian legend: after the story of the boys is known to the people of Ephesus, they summon the emperor Theodosius, who declares his intention to build a shrine over the bodies of the Sleepers in the midst of the city. The boys, however, respond that they will stay in the cave, as that is the place to which Jesus summoned them. It is on this occasion—exactly as the Qur'ān has it ("so that they might know that God's promise is indeed true") that the boys explain that they have been awoken only so that the emperor may believe in the resurrection of the body:

> Theodosius the emperor urged them to come down with him / in the midst of Ephesus, and he would build a shrine over their bodies. / They say in reply, "Here we shall be, for here we love; / the shepherd who chose us is the one who bade us be here. / For your sake has Christ our Lord awoken us / so that you might see and hold rim that the resurrection truly exists. (Jacob of Serugh, *Mēmrā on the Sleepers of Ephesus,* 30, ll. 177–82).

That there was indeed an ancient (pre-Qur'ānic) shrine in Ephesus is suggested by the account of the pilgrim Theodosius (*The Pilgrimage of Theodosius,* 16).

———

²²They will say, '[They are] three; their dog is the fourth of them,' and they will say, '[They are] five, their dog is the sixth of them,' taking a shot at the invisible. They will say, '[They are] seven, their dog is the eighth of them.' *Say,* 'My Lord knows best their number, and none knows them except a few.' So *do* not dispute concerning them except for a seeming dispute, and *do* not question about them any of them.

18:22 With this verse the context shifts to a later dispute over the number of companions in the Sleepers account. The Qur'ān's concern for such a dispute reflects the development of the legend among Christians. Some versions of this legend (e.g., Jacob's *mēmrā* and the *Ecclesiastical History* of John of Ephesus [d. 586]) report that there were eight companions, while others (e.g., the *Ecclesiastical History* of Zacharias of Mitylene [d. 536], and most other later versions), insist that there were only seven. The Qur'ān here attempts to resolve that dispute, by insisting that the number is known only to God (on this see Griffith, "Christian Lore and the Arabic Qur'ān," 129).

---

²³*Do* not say about anything, 'I will indeed do it tomorrow' ²⁴without [adding], 'God willing.' And when *you* forget, remember *your* Lord and *say,* 'Maybe my Lord will guide me to [something] more akin to rectitude than this.'

18:23–24 Note James 4:13–15:

¹³ Well now, you who say, 'Today or tomorrow, we are off to this or that town; we are going to spend a year there, trading, and make some money.'
¹⁴You never know what will happen tomorrow: you are no more than a mist that appears for a little while and then disappears.
¹⁵Instead of this, you should say, 'If it is the Lord's will, we shall still be alive to do this or that.' (Jam 4:13–15)

---

²⁵They remained in the Cave for three hundred years, and added nine more [to that number].

18:25 In contrast to the question of the number of Companions in the Cave (v. 22), the Qur'ān offers a precise answer here to the question of the number of years that the Companions remained in the cave. Its answer (309 years) does not match the chronology of the Christian story, which begins in the days of Decius (r. 249–51) and ends in the days of Theodosius II (r. 408–50). It may reflect instead a remark in Jacob's *mēmrā* on the Sleepers, according to which, by the reckoning of a wise (or actually not so wise) man of Ephesus, the emperor Decius would have been 372 years old had he been still alive at the time when the youth went to the city to buy food. See Jacob of Serugh, *Mēmrā on the Sleepers of Ephesus,* 29, ll. 147–48, 151–54.

---

²⁶*Say,* 'God knows best how long they remained. To Him belongs the Unseen of the heavens and the earth. How well does He see! How well does He hear! They have no guardian besides Him, and none shares with Him in His judgement.'

²⁷Recite what has been revealed to *you* from the Book of *your* Lord. Nothing can change His words, and *you* will never find any refuge besides Him.

18:27 On the expression "Nothing can change His words," see commentary on 6:115 (with further references).

---

²⁸Content *yourself* with the company of those who supplicate their Lord morning and evening, desiring His Face, and do not loose sight of them, desiring the glitter of the life of this world. And *do not obey* him whose heart We have made oblivious to Our remembrance and who follows his own desires, and whose conduct is [mere] profligacy. ²⁹And *say,* '[This is] the truth from your Lord: let anyone who wishes believe it, and let anyone who wishes disbelieve it.' We have indeed prepared for the wrongdoers a Fire whose curtains will surround them [on all sides]. If they cry out for help, they will be helped with a water like molten copper which will scald their faces. What an evil drink and how ill a resting place!

³⁰As for those who have faith and do righteous deeds—indeed We do not waste the reward of those who are good in deeds. ³¹For

such there will be the Gardens of Eden with streams running in them. They will be adorned therein with bracelets of gold and wear green garments of fine and heavy silk, reclining therein on couches. How excellent a reward and how good a resting place!

18:31 On the Garden of Eden as the heavenly paradise of believers in the Qurʾān, see commentary on 2:25 and 9:72 (with further references).

---

³²*Draw* for them the parable of two men for each of whom We had made two gardens of vines and We had surrounded them with date palms and placed crops between them. ³³Both gardens yielded their produce without stinting anything of it. And We had set a stream gushing through them.

³⁴He had abundant fruits, so he said to his companion as he conversed with him: 'I have more wealth than you, and am stronger with respect to numbers.' ³⁵He entered his garden while he wronged himself. He said, 'I do not think that this will ever perish, ³⁶and I do not think that the Hour will ever set in. And even if I am returned to my Lord I will surely find a resort better than this.'

³⁷His companion said to him as he conversed with him: 'Do you disbelieve in Him who created you from dust, then from a drop of [seminal] fluid, then fashioned you as a man? ³⁸But I [say], "He is God, my Lord" and I do not ascribe any partner to my Lord. ³⁹Why did you not say when you entered your garden, "[This is] as God has willed! There is no power except by God!" If you see that I have lesser wealth than you and [fewer] children, ⁴⁰maybe my Lord will give me [something] better than your garden and He will unleash upon it bolts from the sky, so that it becomes a bare

plain. ⁴¹Or its water will sink down, so that you will never be able to obtain it.'

⁴²And ruin closed in on his produce and as it lay fallen on its trellises he began to wring his hands for what he had spent on it. He was saying, 'I wish I had not ascribed any partner to my Lord.' ⁴³He had no party to help him besides God, nor could he help himself. ⁴⁴There, all authority belongs to God, the Real. He is best in rewarding and best in requiting.

18:32–44 This parable (cf. 3:117; 36:13–29; and esp. 68:17–33) is close to the parable of the rich fool in Luke 12:

> ¹⁶Then he told them a parable, 'There was once a rich man who, having had a good harvest from his land,
>
> ¹⁷thought to himself, "What am I to do? I have not enough room to store my crops."
>
> ¹⁸Then he said, "This is what I will do: I will pull down my barns and build bigger ones, and store all my grain and my goods in them,
>
> ¹⁹and I will say to my soul: My soul, you have plenty of good things laid by for many years to come; take things easy, eat, drink, have a good time."
>
> ²⁰But God said to him, "Fool! This very night the demand will be made for your soul; and this hoard of yours, whose will it be then?"
>
> ²¹So it is when someone stores up treasure for himself instead of becoming rich in the sight of God.' (Luk 12:16–21)

On the creation of humanity from dust (v. 37), see commentary on 11:61 (with further references).

⁴⁵*Draw* for them the parable of the life of this world: [It is] like the water We send down from the sky. Then the earth's vegetation mingles with it. Then it becomes chaff, scattered by the wind. And God has power over all things. ⁴⁶Wealth and children are an adornment of the life of the world, but lasting righteous deeds are better with *your* Lord in reward and better in hope.

18:46 Speyer (*BEQ*, 458) compares this verse to Mishnah Avot 6:9, which includes the story of a rabbi who insists that he will not accept certain gifts of gold since "in the hour of the departure of a man [from the world], there accompany him neither gold nor silver, nor precious stones nor pearls, but Torah and good deeds alone."

---

⁴⁷The day We shall set the mountains moving and *you* will see the earth in full view, We will muster them and We will not leave out anyone of them. ⁴⁸They will be presented before *your* Lord in ranks [and told]: 'Certainly you have come to Us just as We created you the first time. But you maintained that We will not appoint a tryst for you.'

⁴⁹The Book will be set up. Then *you* will see the guilty apprehensive of what is in it. They will say, 'Woe to us! What a book is this! It omits nothing, big or small, without enumerating it.' They will find present whatever they had done, and *your* Lord does not wrong anyone.

⁵⁰When We said to the angels, 'Prostrate before Adam,' they prostrated, but not Iblis. He was one of the jinn, so he transgressed against his Lord's command. Will you then take him and his offspring for masters in My stead, though they are your enemies? How evil a substitute for the wrongdoers!

18:50 On the account of the angelic prostration before Adam, see commentary on 7:11–12 (with further references). In this verse the Qur'ān suggests that the unbelievers take the devil and his "offspring" as rivals to God (cf. 4:117; 6:100; 14:22; 37:158; 6:100 and 37:158 have the unbelievers instead make the jinn associates of God). See commentary on 6:100, with further references.

Here the Qur'ān describes the devil (Iblīs) as "one of the jinn;" elsewhere the devil explains that he was (like the jinn) created from fire (cf. 7:12; 38:76). This troubles some Muslim commentators who take the position that the devil was a fallen angel (to solve this conflict they sometimes imagine that the devil came

from a "tribe" of angels named "Jinn"). It is likely, however, that the Qur'ān
conceives of the jinn not as a separate class of beings but precisely as fallen angels. In other words, the Qur'ān conceives of only two orders of beings: angels
(created from fire, among whom some fell and are known as *jinn* or *shayāṭīn*—
of these some came to believe in God [cf. 72]) and humans (created from dirt
or clay). Islamic tradition has the angels created from light but this is nowhere
mentioned in the Qur'ān. See also commentary on 72:1–14.

---

⁵¹I did not make them witness to the creation of the heavens
and the earth, nor to their own creation, nor do I take as assistants
those who mislead others.

⁵²The day He will say [to the polytheists], 'Call those whom
you maintained to be My partners,' they will call them, but they
will not respond to them, for We shall set an abyss between them.
⁵³The guilty will sight the Fire and know that they are about to fall
into it, for they will find no way to escape it.

⁵⁴We have certainly interspersed this Qur'ān with every kind of
parable for the people. But man is the most disputatious of creatures. ⁵⁵Nothing has kept these people from believing and pleading to their Lord for forgiveness when guidance came to them,
except [their demand] that the precedent of the ancients come to
pass for them, or that the punishment come to them, face to face.
⁵⁶We do not send the apostles except as bearers of good news and
warners, but those who are faithless dispute fallaciously to refute
thereby the truth, having taken in derision My signs and what
they are warned of.

⁵⁷Who is a greater wrongdoer than he who is reminded of the
signs of his Lord, whereat he disregards them and forgets what
his hands have sent ahead? We have indeed cast veils on their
hearts, lest they should understand it, and a deafness into their

ears; and if *you* invite them to guidance, they will never [let them-
selves] be guided.

18:57 On the reference here (cf. 6:25) to veils that cover (or contain) the
hearts of unbelievers, see commentary on 17:45–46 (with further references).

---

⁵⁸Your Lord is the All-forgiving dispenser of mercy. Were He
to take them to task because of what they have committed, He
would have surely hastened their punishment. But they have a
tryst, [when] they will not find a refuge besides Him.

⁵⁹Those are the towns that We destroyed when they were
wrongdoers, and We appointed a tryst for their destruction.

⁶⁰When Moses said to his lad, 'I will go on [journeying] until I
have reached the confluence of the two seas, or have spent a long
time [traveling].'

⁶¹So when they reached the confluence between them, they forgot their fish, which found its way into the sea, sneaking away.
⁶²So when they had passed on, he said to his lad, 'Bring us our
meal. We have certainly encountered much fatigue on this journey of ours.'

⁶³He said, 'Did you see?! When we took shelter at the rock, indeed
I forgot about the fish—and none but Satan made me forget to mention it!—and it made its way into the sea in an amazing manner!'

⁶⁴He said, 'That is what we were after!' So they returned, re-
tracing their footsteps.

18:60–64 Although the Qur'ān names the protagonist of this account "Moses," it is developing a tradition known from the stories told about Alexander
and his cook Andrew (*andreas*) and their quest for the fountain of life (itself a

development of older tales—beginning with ancient Near Eastern literature).
This account is part of a tradition that includes the Greek *Alexander Romance*
(fourth or fifth century AD), the Babylonian Talmud, and the Syriac Christian
Song of Alexander (ca. AD 630–35; the *Song* is falsely attributed to Jacob of
Serugh). Below I include passages from the *Song of Alexander,* which describes
how the cook discovers the fountain of life when his fish comes to life. In the
Song, the vocabulary used for bathing in the fountain of life is that used for
baptism, and the motif of the fish (which represents Christ) returning to life (cf.
18:61, 63) alludes to Christ's resurrection:

> The Macedonian king, the son of Philip spoke: / "I have determined to follow
> a great quest to reach the lands, / even the furthest lands, / to reach the seas,
> and the coasts, and the borders as they are; / Above all to enter and to see the
> land of darkness / if it is truly as I heard it is." (*Song of Alexander,* recension
> 1, p. 26, ll. 33–38)

> Then [Alexander's cook] came to the spring, which contained the life-
> giving water / he came close to it, in order to wash the fish in water, but it
> came alive and escaped;
> The poor man was afraid that the king would blame him / that he give
> back the [value of the] fish, which had come to life and which he did not stop.
> So he got down into the water, in order to catch it, but was unable / then he
> climbed out from there in order to tell the king that he had found [the spring]
> He called, but no one heard him, and so he went to a mountain from where
> they heard him / the king was glad when he heard about the spring.
> The king turned around in order to bathe [in the spring] as he had sought
> to do / and they went from the mountain in the middle of darkness, but they
> could not reach it. (Song of Alexander, recension 1, pp. 48–50, ll. 182–92)

The "confluence of the two seas" (*majma' al-baḥrayn*) in verse 60 is generally understood by Muslim commentators to be, as *Tafsīr al-Jalālayn* explains,
"the point where the Byzantine sea and the Persian sea meet." However, in light
of this episode's relationship to the Alexander literature, this phrase more likely
means the point at which the waters in the heavens and the waters on earth meet
(on this see Gen 1:6–7), that is, the end of the world (n.b. in this regard how
Alexander, or *Dhū l-Qarnayn,* goes to the westernmost [v. 86] and easternmost
[v.90] points on earth, something which reflects a flat earth.). As Tommaso Tesei
(*QSC,* 381–82) has shown, Syriac Christian authors such as Narsai (*Homélies
de Narsaï sur la création,* p. 528), use the expression "two seas" to refer to the

waters of heaven and the waters of earth. The Qur'ān also refers to "two seas" in 25:53 and 55:19.

---

⁶⁵[There] they found one of Our servants whom We had granted mercy from Ourselves and taught him knowledge from Our own.

18:65–82 *overview* The Qur'ān here connects the story of Alexander's quest for the fountain of life (vv. 60–64) with a story likewise known from pre-Islamic sources, making Moses the protagonist of both. The appearance of Moses in place of Alexander in the first story is unusual, and his appearance in the second story is jarring, inasmuch as he doesn't act much like a prophet therein. He is the disciple to the mysterious "servant of God" (known as al-Khiḍr in Islamic tradition) and not a particularly good disciple.

As Roger Paret demonstrates ("Un parallèle Byzantin à Coran XVIII, 59–81"), this latter story is connected to a tradition found in a manuscript (still unedited) which includes passages from the *Leimon* (or *Pratum Spirituale*) of John Moschus (d. 619) that are not found in the standard edition thereof. Most of these traditions present the theme of a sage who is upset by the methods of divine justice. One tradition (narrative 96; see T. Nissen, "Unbekannte Erzählungen aus dem *Pratum Spirituale*," 367) tells the story of an angel of God (equivalent to the mysterious "servant of God" in the Qur'ān) who acts in ways that mystify an old and pious monk. The angel steals a cup from a pious man, strangles the son of another pious man, and rebuilds the wall which belonged to an impious and inhospitable man. The angel explains that the cup which belonged to the first man had been stolen. The son of the second pious man was to grow up to be an evil sinner; by strangling this son the angel allowed him to die before he fell into sin. Beneath the wall of the impious man lay hidden treasure, and by rebuilding the wall, he kept the man from finding this treasure and using it for evil. These line up closely to the Qur'ānic "Moses and the servant of God" passage.

---

⁶⁶Moses said to him, 'May I follow you for the purpose that you teach me some of the probity you have been taught?'

⁶⁷He said, 'Indeed, you cannot have patience with me! ⁶⁸And how can you have patience about something you do not comprehend?'

⁶⁹He said, 'God willing, you will find me to be patient, and I will not disobey you in any matter.'

⁷⁰He said, 'If you follow me, do not question me concerning anything until I myself first mention it for you.'

⁷¹So they went on. When they boarded the boat, he made a hole in it. He said, 'Did you make a hole in it to drown its people? You have certainly done a monstrous thing!'

⁷²He said, 'Did I not say that you cannot have patience with me?'

⁷³He said, 'Do not take me to task for my forgetting, and do not be hard upon me.'

⁷⁴So they went on until they came upon a boy, whereupon he slew him. He said, 'Did you slay an innocent soul without [his having slain] anyone? You have certainly done a dire thing!'

18:74 *Tafsīr al-Jalālayn* notes that Muslim authorities have different ideas of how the "servant of God" killed this boy: "By slitting his throat with a knife while he lay down, or by tearing his head off with his hand, or by smashing his head against a wall."

⁷⁵He said, 'Did I not tell you that you cannot have patience with me?'

⁷⁶He said, 'If I question you about anything after this, do not keep me in your company. You already have enough excuse on my part.'

⁷⁷So they went on until they came to the people of a town. They asked its people for food, but they refused to extend them any

hospitality. There they found a wall which was about to collapse, so he erected it. He said, 'Had you wished, you could have taken a wage for it.'

⁷⁸He said, 'This is where you and I shall part. I will inform you about the interpretation of that over which you could not maintain patience. ⁷⁹As for the boat, it belonged to some poor people who work on the sea. I wanted to make it defective, for behind them was a king seizing every ship usurpingly. ⁸⁰As for the boy, his parents were faithful [persons], and We feared he would overwhelm them with rebellion and unfaith. ⁸¹So We desired that their Lord should give them in exchange one better than him in respect of purity and closer in mercy. ⁸²As for the wall, it belonged to two boy orphans in the city. There was a treasure under it belonging to them. Their father had been a righteous man. So your Lord desired that they should come of age and take out their treasure—as mercy from your Lord. I did not do that out of my own accord. This is the interpretation of that over which you could not maintain patience.'

⁸³They question *you* concerning Dhul Qarnayn. *Say,* 'I will relate to you an account of him.'

18:83–101 *overview* This episode is also related to legends connected to Alexander (it is presumably not a coincidence that two Alexander accounts appear in the same Sura in the Qur'ān), but in this case to the Syriac Christian *Neṣḥānā d-leh d-Aleksandrōs,* "The Victory of Alexander" (written ca. AD 630), a text traditionally known in English as the *Legend of Alexander.* In the commentary that follows I am indebted to the article of Kevin van Bladel: "The Legend of Alexander the Great in the Qur'ān 18:83–102."

⁸⁴We had indeed granted him power in the land and given him the means to all things.

18:83–84 The Qur'ān here refers to Alexander as *Dhū l-Qarnayn,* "the two-horned one." Alexander is represented on certain coins (for example those minted by King Lysimachus of Thrace around 300 BC) with the horns of the God Ammon. In the *Legend of Alexander* Alexander declares to God "thou hast made me horns upon my head" (as a symbol of his power) and makes Alexander a righteous figure who anticipates the coming of the Son of God:

> King Alexander bowed himself and did reverence, saying, "O God, Lord of kings and judges, thou who settest up kings and destroyest their power, I know in my mind that thou hast exalted me above all kings, and *thou hast made me horns upon my head,* wherewith I might thrust down the kingdoms of the world; give me power from thy holy heavens that I may receive strength greater than [that of] the kingdoms of the world and that I may humble them, and I will magnify thy name, O Lord, forever, and thy memorial shall be from everlasting to everlasting, and I will write the name of God in the charter of my kingdom, that there may be for Thee a memorial always. And if the Messiah, who is the Son of God, comes in my days, I and my troops will worship Him. (*Legend of Alexander,* trans. Budge, 146)

For his part Muhammad Asad declares that by *Dhū l-Qarnayn* the Qur'ān cannot mean Alexander, since Alexander was not a believer in the true God; he suggests that this account is simply a "parabolic discourse on faith and ethics."

---

⁸⁵So he directed a means. ⁸⁶When he reached the place where the sun sets, he found it setting over a warm sea, and by it he found a people.

We said, 'O Dhul Qarnayn! You will either punish them, or treat them with kindness.' ⁸⁷He said, 'As for him who is a wrongdoer, we will punish him. Then he shall be returned to his Lord and He will punish him with a dire punishment. ⁸⁸But as for him who has faith and acts righteously, he shall have the best reward, and we will assign him easy tasks under our command.'

18:85–88

And they put ships to sea and sailed on the sea four months and twelve days, and they arrived at the dry land beyond the eleven bright seas. And Alexander and his troops encamped, and he sent and called to him the governor who was in the camp, and said to him, "Are there any men here guilty of death?" They said to him, "We have thirty and seven men in bonds who are guilty of death." And the king said to the governor," Bring hither those evil doers."

. . .

And the men went, and came to the shore of the sea. Now Alexander thought within himself, "If it be true as they say, that everyone who comes near the foetid sea dies, it is better that these who are guilty of death should die," and when they had gone, and had arrived at the shore of the sea, they died instantly. And Alexander and his troops were looking at them when they died, for he and his nobles had ridden to see what would happen to them, and they saw that they died the moment that they reached the sea. And king Alexander was afraid and retired, and he knew that it was impossible for them to cross over to the place where were the ends of the heavens (*Legend of Alexander*, trans. Budge, 147–48)

---

[89]Then he directed another means. [90]When he reached the place where the sun rises, he found it rising on a people for whom We had not provided any shield against it. [91]So it was, and We were fully aware of whatever [means] he had.

18:89–91

"The place of [the sun's] rising is over the sea, and the people who dwell there, when he is about to rise, flee away and hide themselves in the sea, that they be not burnt by his rays." (*Legend of Alexander*, trans. Budge, 148)

---

[92]Thereafter he directed another means. [93]When he reached [the place] between the two barriers, he found between them a people who could hardly understand a word [of his language]. [94]They said, 'O Dhul Qarnayn! Gog and Magog are indeed causing

disaster in this land. Shall we pay you a tribute on condition that you build a barrier between them and us?'

⁹⁵He said, 'What my Lord has furnished me is better. Yet help me with some power, and I will make a bulwark between you and them. ⁹⁶Bring me pieces of iron!' When he had levelled up between the flanks, he said, 'Blow!' When he had turned it into fire, he said, 'Bring me molten copper to pour over it.' ⁹⁷So they could neither scale it, nor could they make a hole in it.

18:92–97 The Qur'ān here reflects the continuation of the *Legend of Alexander,* which relates how Alexander travelled to the north where he learned from the people there of how the Huns, who lived on the other side of a great mountain and were led by kings (among others) named Gog and Magog (cf. 18:94) frequently pour through a pass in that mountain to devastate the land. In response Alexander (cf. 18:95–97) builds a wall to "close up this breach":

> Alexander said to his troops, "Do ye desire that we should do something wonderful in this land?" They said to him, "As thy majesty commands we will do." The king said, " Let us make a gate of brass and close up this breach." His troops said, " As thy majesty commands we will do." And Alexander commanded and fetched three thousand smiths, workers in iron, and three thousand men, workers in brass. (*Legend of Alexander,* trans. Budge, 153)

————————————

⁹⁸He said, 'This is a [gift of] mercy from my Lord. But when the promise of my Lord is fulfilled, He will level it, and my Lord's promise is true.' ⁹⁹That day We will let them surge over one another, and the Trumpet will be blown, and We will gather them all, ¹⁰⁰and on that day We will bring hell into view visibly for the faithless ¹⁰¹—those whose eyes were blind to My remembrance and who could not hear.

18:98–101 Here the Qur'ān has *Dhū l-Qarnayn* predict that in the last days before the resurrection the bulwark he has built will be breached, a prediction which follows the way in which Alexander, in the Syriac *Legend,* predicts that the Huns will in the future break forth and "take captive the nations":

> Also I have written that, at the conclusion of eight hundred and twenty-six years, the Huns shall go forth by the narrow way which goes forth opposite Haloras, whence the Tigris goes forth like the stream which turns a mill, and they shall take captive the nations, and shall cut off the roads, and shall make the earth tremble by their going forth. And again I have written and made known and prophesied that it shall come to pass, at the conclusion of nine hundred and forty years, another king, when the world shall come to an end by the command of God the ruler of creation. Created things shall anger God, and sin shall increase, and wrath shall reign, and the sins of mankind shall mount up and shall cover the heavens, and the Lord will stir up in His anger the kingdoms that lie within this gate; for when the Lord seeks to slay men, he sends men against men, and they destroy one another. (*Legend of Alexander,* trans. Budge, 154)

On the trumpet blast, see commentary on 78:18 (with further references).

---

¹⁰²Do the faithless suppose that they have taken My servants for protectors in My stead? Indeed, We have prepared hell for the hospitality of the faithless.

¹⁰³*Say,* 'Shall we inform you about the biggest losers in their works? ¹⁰⁴Those whose efforts are misguided in the life of the world, while they suppose they are doing good.' ¹⁰⁵They are the ones who deny the signs of their Lord and encounter with Him. So their works have failed. On the Day of Resurrection We will not give them any weight. ¹⁰⁶That is their requital—hell—because of their unfaith and their deriding My signs and My apostles.

¹⁰⁷As for those who have faith and do righteous deeds, they will have the gardens of Firdaws for abode,

18:107 The word *firdaws* ("paradise" from Greek *paradeisos,* perhaps derived from Persian) appears only here and 23:11.

---

[108]to remain in them [forever]; they will not seek to leave them for another place.

[109]*Say,* 'If the sea were ink for the words of my Lord, the sea would be spent before the words of my Lord are finished, though We replenish it with another like it.'

18:109 See commentary on 31:27.

---

[110]*Say,* 'I am just a human being like you. It has been revealed to me that your God is the One God. So whoever expects to encounter his Lord, let him act righteously and not associate anyone with the worship of his Lord.'

19. *Maryam*, Mary

In the Name of God, the All-beneficent, the All-merciful.

¹*Kāf, Hā, Yā, 'Ayn, Ṣād.*

²[This is] an account of your Lord's mercy on Zechariah, His servant, ³when he called out to his Lord with a secret cry. ⁴He said, 'My Lord! Indeed, my bones have become feeble, and my head has turned white with age, yet never have I, my Lord, been unblessed in my supplications to You! ⁵Indeed, I fear my kinsmen, after me, and my wife is barren. So grant me from Yourself an heir ⁶who may inherit from me and inherit from the House of Jacob, and make him, my Lord, pleasing [to You]!'

19:2–6 This passage might be read in light of Luke 1. Both texts notably have Zechariah refer to the "House of Jacob" (Q 19:6 and Luk 1:33). Only the Qurʾān, however, has Zechariah pray to God for an heir (cf. 3:38–40; 21:89; Zechariah is also referred to in 6:85). The prayer of Zechariah in the Qurʾān might be shaped by 2:127–29, where Abraham and Ishmael pray for a nation, and a divine messenger, to be raised up from their progeny, or by the way in which Mary's mother dedicates her child to God in 3:35–36.

473

---

⁷'O Zechariah! Indeed, We give you the good news of a son, whose name is "John." Never before have We made anyone his namesake.'

⁸He said, 'My Lord! How shall I have a son, when my wife is barren and I am already advanced in age?'

⁹He said, 'So shall it be. Your Lord has said, "It is simple for Me." Certainly I created you before when you were nothing.'

¹⁰He said, 'My Lord! Appoint a sign for me.' He said, 'Your sign is that you will not speak to the people for three complete nights.'

¹¹So he emerged before his people from the Temple and signalled to them that they should glorify [God] morning and evening.

19:7–11 The Qur'ān here (cf. 3:39–40; 21:90) has God announce to Zechariah both that he will have a son and that this son will be named John (regarding his name cf. Luk 1:61). The Qur'ān is developing Luke 1, although it has God speak directly to Zechariah (unlike Luke, where it is the angel Gabriel, and unlike 3:39, where it is instead "angels"). Verses 8–9 (cf. 3:40) should be compared to Luke 1:18–19, but also understood in light of the similar words in the Qur'ān of Mary (Q 3:47; 19:20–21) and of Sarah (Q 11:72; 51:29–30) in their responses to divine annunciations of a miraculous baby boy. Whereas in Luke Zechariah becomes mute as a punishment for disbelieving the angel's message, in the Qur'ān (vv. 9–10; cf. 3:41) muteness is the answer to Zechariah's request for a sign:

> ¹¹Then there appeared to him the angel of the Lord, standing on the right of the altar of incense.
>
> ¹²The sight disturbed Zechariah and he was overcome with fear.
>
> ¹³But the angel said to him, 'Zechariah, do not be afraid, for your prayer has been heard. Your wife Elizabeth is to bear you a son and you shall name him John. ¹⁴ He will be your joy and delight and many will rejoice at his birth,
>
> . . .
>
> ¹⁸Zechariah said to the angel, 'How can I know this? I am an old man and my wife is getting on in years.'

[19]The angel replied, 'I am Gabriel, who stand in God's presence, and I have been sent to speak to you and bring you this good news.

[20]Look! Since you did not believe my words, which will come true at their appointed time, you will be silenced and have no power of speech until this has happened.'

[21]Meanwhile the people were waiting for Zechariah and were surprised that he stayed in the sanctuary so long.

[22]When he came out he could not speak to them, and they realised that he had seen a vision in the sanctuary. But he could only make signs to them and remained dumb. (Luk 1:11–13, 18-22)

---

[12]'O John!' [We said,] 'Hold on with power to the Book!' And We gave him judgement while still a child, [13]and compassion and purity from Us. He was Godwary

19:13 The name for John in Qur'ānic Arabic, *yaḥyā,* could also be pointed as *yuḥannā* (the Christian Arabic form of the name) in which case one might recognize the first word of this verse, *ḥanānan* ("compassion") as an allusion to his name.

---

[14]and good to his parents, not self-willed or disobedient. [15]Peace be to him, the day he was born, the day he dies, and the day he is raised alive!

19:15 Cf. 19:33, where Jesus calls peace upon himself.

---

[16]And *mention* in the Book Mary, when she withdrew from her family to an easterly place. [17]Thus did she seclude herself from

them, whereupon We sent to her Our Spirit and he became incarnate for her as a perfect human.

[18]She said, 'I seek the protection of the All-beneficent from you, should you be Godwary!'

[19]He said, 'I am only a messenger of your Lord that I may give you a pure son.'

[20]She said, 'How shall I have a child seeing that no human being has ever touched me, nor have I been unchaste?'

[21]He said, 'So shall it be. Your Lord says, "It is simple for Me, and so that We may make him a sign for mankind and mercy from Us, and it is a matter [already] decided."

[22]Thus she conceived him, then withdrew with him to a distant place. [23]The birth pangs brought her to the trunk of a date palm. She said, 'I wish I had died before this and become a forgotten thing, beyond recall.'

[24]Thereupon he called her from below her, [saying,] 'Do not grieve! Your Lord has made a spring to flow at your feet. [25]Shake the trunk of the palm tree, freshly picked dates will drop upon you. [26]Eat, drink and be comforted. Then if you see any human, say, "I have indeed vowed a fast to the All-beneficent, so I will not speak to any human today."'

19:16–26 The annunciation of Jesus in "an easterly place" (v. 16) could reflect an awareness that the temple (with which Mary was associated) was in the east of Jerusalem. The next verse (v. 17) speaks of how Mary hid behind a curtain or barrier (*ḥijāb;* Qarai renders "seclude herself"), which could suggest that she was in the temple when she conceived Jesus.

The Qur'ān here (cf. 3:45–47; 5:110) describes the birth of Jesus in a way that contrasts with the canonical Gospels but is closely related to two apocryphal Gospels. The first is the *Protoevangelium of James,* which (like the Qur'ān in v. 22) places the birth of Christ in a remote place:

> And they came half the way, and Mary said to him: "Joseph, take me down from the ass, for the child within me presses me, to come forth." And he took

her down there and said to her: "Where shall I take you and hide your shame? For the place is desert." And he found a cave there and brought her into it, and left her in the care of his sons and went out to seek for a Hebrew midwife in the region of Bethlehem. (*Protoevangelium of James,* 17:2–18:1)

The second is the *Gospel of Pseudo-Matthew* (a Latin text likely dating from the early seventh century, dependent on earlier traditions) which describes a miracle involving a palm tree and a spring, and Jesus' speaking as an infant (cf. Q 19:24–27; cf. vv. 30–33; 3:46; and commentary on 3:45–47; the miracle of the palm tree is already mentioned by Sozomen [d. 450]: *Ecclesiastical History* 5:21). However, the *Gospel of Pseudo-Matthew* makes these miracles part of the flight of the Holy Family to Egypt:

Now on the third day of their journey, as they went on, it happened that blessed Mary was wearied by too great heat of the sun in the desert, and seeing a palm tree, she said to Joseph, "I should like to rest a little in the shade of this tree." And Joseph led her quickly to the palm and let her dismount from her animal. And when blessed Mary had sat down, she looked up at the top of the palm tree and saw that it was full of fruits, and said to Joseph, "I wish someone would fetch some of these fruits of the palm tree." And Joseph said to her, "I wonder that you say this; for you see how high this palm tree is, and I wonder that you even think about eating of the fruits of the palm. I think rather of the lack of water, which already fails us in the skins, and we have nothing with which we can refresh ourselves and the animals."

Then the child Jesus, who was sitting with a happy countenance in his mother's lap, said to the palm, "Bend down your branches, O tree, and refresh my mother with your fruit." And immediately at this command the palm bent its head down to the feet of blessed Mary, and they gathered from it fruits with which they all refreshed themselves. But after they had gathered all its fruits, it remained bent down and waited to raise itself again at the command of him at whose command it had bent down. Then Jesus said to it, "Raise yourself, O palm, and be strong and join my trees which are in the paradise of my Father. And open beneath your roots a vein of water which is hidden in the earth, and let the waters flow so that we may quench our thirst from it." And immediately it raised itself, and there began to gush out by its root a fountain of water very clear, fresh, and completely bright. (*Gospel of Pseudo-Matthew,* 20:1–2)

The explanation for the contrast between the Qurʾān and the *Gospel of Pseudo-Matthew* has recently been offered by Stephen Shoemaker ("Christmas in the Qurʾān"; see also G. Dye, "Lieux saints communs"), who shows that the Kathisma church on the outskirts of Jerusalem (which may have served as a model for the Dome of the Rock; it was eventually used as a Marian shrine by Muslims and Christians alike) was a site where (in competition with the Church of the Nativity in Bethlehem) the birth of Jesus was commemorated *along with* the miracle of the palm tree and spring given to Mary during the flight to Egypt. Thus, it seems possible that the Qurʾān's author knew of the popular Palestinian traditions surrounding the Kathisma church.

The description of Jesus as a "sign" (v. 21) might be connected to Luke 2:34, which makes Jesus a "sign" (that will be "opposed").

---

²⁷Then, carrying him, she brought him to her people. They said, 'O Mary, you have certainly come up with an odd thing! ²⁸O kinswoman of the Aaronites! Your father was not an evil man, nor was your mother unchaste.'

²⁹Thereat she pointed to him. They said, 'How can we speak to one who is yet a baby in the cradle?'

³⁰He said, 'I am indeed a servant of God! He has given me the Book and made me a prophet. ³¹He has made me blessed, wherever I may be, and He has enjoined me to [maintain] the prayer and to [pay] the *zakāt* as long as I live, ³²and to be good to my mother, and He has not made me self-willed and wretched. ³³Peace to me the day I was born, the day I die, and the day I am raised alive.'

19:27–33 In verse 28 the Qurʾān has Mary's people refer to her as "sister of Aaron" (*ukhta hārūn*). Qarai, to avoid the suggestion that the Qurʾān has confused Mary with Miriam (the Hb. form of "Mary," Ar. *Maryam*), the sister of Aaron (and Moses; see Exo 15.20), translates "kinswoman of the Aaronites." Some scholars argue that the Qurʾān means intentionally to associate Mary with Aaron in a symbolic manner (perhaps because they are both associated with priestly service to the Lord—the *Protoevangelium of James* refers to Mary's upbringing in the temple). Yet the phrase "sister of Aaron" matches the Qurʾān's description of Mary elsewhere (3:33; 66:12) as the "daughter of ʿImrān" (Miriam, Aaron, and Moses are the children of Biblical Amram; see

1Ch 5:29). The Qur'ān thus departs from pre-Qur'ānic Christian tradition (e.g., in the *Protoevangelium of James*), which makes the father of Mary, mother of Jesus, Joachim. It is likely that the Qur'ān's author has confused and conflated the two Biblical figures named "Mary."

Otherwise this passage has the Israelites scrutinize Mary's claim that she conceived of the Holy Spirit (cf. 4:156 wherein the Israelites accuse Mary of fornication). This may be related to the skepticism of a woman named Salome in the *Protoevangelium of James:*

> [Joseph] went out to seek a Hebrew midwife in the region of Bethlehem . . .
> And he found one who was just coming down from the hill-country, and he
> took her with him, and said to the midwife: "Mary is betrothed to me; but she
> conceived of the Holy Spirit after she had been brought up in the Temple of
> the Lord. And the midwife went with him. . . . And the midwife came out of
> the cave, and Salome met her. And she said to her: "Salome, Salome, I have
> a new sight to tell you; a virgin has brought forth a thing which her nature
> does not allow." And Salome said: "As the Lord my God lives, unless I put
> (forward) my finger and test her condition, I will not believe that a virgin has
> brought forth. And Salome went in and made her ready to test her condition.
> And she cried out, saying: "Woe for my wickedness and my unbelief; for I
> have tempted the living God; and behold, my hand falls away from me, con-
> sumed by fire!" (*Protoevangelium of James,* 18:1; 19:1–20:1)

---

³⁴That is Jesus, son of Mary, a Word of the Real concerning whom they are in doubt. ³⁵It is not for God to take a son. Immaculate is He! When He decides on a matter, He just says to it, 'Be!' and it is.

³⁶[Jesus said,] 'God is indeed my Lord and your Lord. So worship Him. This is a straight path.'

³⁷But the factions differed among themselves. So woe to the faithless at the scene of a tremendous day. ³⁸How well they will hear and how well they will see on the day when they come to Us! But today the wrongdoers are in plain error. ³⁹While they are [yet] heedless and do not believe, *warn* them of the Day of Regret when the matter will have been decided.

⁴⁰Indeed, We shall inherit the earth and whoever there is on it, and to Us they will be brought back.

19:34–40 This section (cf. 5:116–17), as pointed out by Guillaume Dye ("Lieux saints communs," 13) and before him Richard Bell (*Commentary,* 1:506), has a different rhyme from what precedes and follows and may be a later interpolation. The anti-Christian character of verses 35–36 suggests that this section might be an effort to counter the Christian interpretation of the story of Jesus' speech as a child, namely that it is a miracle which redounds to his divinity. On the other hand the description of Jesus as the "Word of the Real" in v. 34 (*qawl al-ḥaqq;* cf. 3:45 and 4:171, which make Jesus a *kalima* [also "Word"] from God) seems to make Jesus an extraordinary prophet.

On the declaration "Worship God, my Lord and your Lord," which the Qur'ān attributes to Jesus on several occasions (3:51; 5:72, 117; 43:64) see commentary on 43:63–65. On God's creating through the word "Be!" (v. 35), see commentary on 36:82 (with further references).

———————

⁴¹And *mention* in the Book Abraham. He was indeed a truthful man and a prophet. ⁴²When he said to his father, 'Father! Why do you worship that which neither hears nor sees and is of no avail to you in any way? ⁴³Father! Indeed, a knowledge has already come to me, which has not come to you. So follow me that I may guide you to a right path. ⁴⁴Father! Do not worship Satan. Satan is indeed disobedient to the All-beneficent. ⁴⁵Father! I am indeed afraid that a punishment from the All-beneficent will befall you, and you will become Satan's accomplice.'

⁴⁶He said, 'Abraham! Are you renouncing my gods? If you do not desist, I will stone you. Get away from me for a long while.'

19:41–46 On Abraham's preaching to his father (vv. 42–45)—the Biblical Terah—(although in 6:74 he is given the name Āzar), see commentary on 26:69–93 (with further references). On Abraham's promise to pray for his father (v. 47, below), cf. 14:41; 60:4. See also commentary on 60:4 (with further references).

Abraham's declaration (v. 42) that his father's idols neither hear nor see reflects the language of Psalm 115:4–8 (see commentary on Q 37:88–96, with further references). On the way Abraham's father threatens him with stoning (of all possible punishments) in verse 46, see commentary on 26:105–16 (with further references).

---

⁴⁷He said, 'Peace be to you! I shall plead with my Lord to forgive you. He is indeed gracious to me. ⁴⁸I dissociate myself from you and whatever you invoke besides God. I will supplicate my Lord. Hopefully, I will not be unblessed in supplicating my Lord.'

⁴⁹So when he had left them and what they worshiped besides God, We gave him Isaac and Jacob, and each We made a prophet.

19:49 On the possibility that the Qur'ān considers both Isaac and Jacob to be sons of Abraham, see commentary on 29:27 (with further references).

---

⁵⁰And We gave them out of Our mercy, and conferred on them a worthy and lofty repute.

⁵¹And *mention* in the Book Moses. Indeed, he was exclusively dedicated [to God], and was an apostle and prophet. ⁵²We called him from the right side of the Mount and We drew him near [to Ourselves] for confidential discourse. ⁵³And We gave him out of Our mercy his brother Aaron, a prophet.

19:51–53 The Qur'ān regularly refers to Mt. Sinai simply as the "Mount" (Ar. *al-ṭūr*): cf. 2:63, 93; 4:154; 20:80; 23:20 ("Mount Sinai"); 28:29, 46; 52:1; 95:2 ("Mount Sinai"—with a different Arabic form). The notion that God came from the right side of the mountain (in 28:29 Moses sees a fire "on the side of a mountain," and in 28:30 he is spoken to "from the right bank of the valley"; cf. also 28:44) may be related to Deuteronomy 33:2:

He said, "The Lord came from Sinai, and dawned from Seir upon us; he shone forth from Mount Paran, he came from the ten thousands of holy ones, with flaming fire *at his right hand.*" (Deu 33:2 RSV).

---

⁵⁴And *mention* in the Book Ishmael. He was indeed true to his promise and an apostle and prophet.

19:54 Explaining the Qurʾān's declaration that Ishmael was "true to his promise" (which has no clear Biblical subtext) *Tafsīr al-Jalālayn* comments: "He never promised anything which he did not fulfil; he [once] waited for three days for someone whom he had promised [to meet]; or [it is said that he waited] an entire year until that person [finally] returned to the place in which he [Ishmael] was [supposed to have met the former]."

---

⁵⁵He used to bid his family to [maintain] the prayer and to [pay] the *zakāt,* and was pleasing to his Lord.

⁵⁶And *mention* in the Book Idrīs. He was indeed a truthful man and a prophet, ⁵⁷and We raised him to an exalted station.

19:56–57 The name Idrīs (mentioned only here and 21:85; in both places his name follows that of Ishmael) is often thought to be connected to Syriac *andraws* or *andrīs* (see Jeffery, *FV,* 52), from Greek *andreas.* It is possible that the Qurʾān has in mind here the cook of Alexander by that name who in the Syriac Christian Alexander Legend discovers the fountain of life (see commentary on 18:60–64) and thereby gains eternal life. Alternatively some link Q 19:57 with Enoch in light of Genesis 5 "Enoch walked with God, then was no more, because God took him" (Gen 5:22–24) and especially Hebrews 11:5: "It was because of his faith that Enoch was taken up and did not experience death: he was no more, because God took him; because before his assumption he was acknowledged to have pleased God." Muslim authorities also associate Idrīs with Enoch (*Tafsīr al-Jalālayn* calls Idrīs "Noah's great-grandfather"; Hilali-Khan put [Enoch] in brackets in their translation of v. 56).

---

⁵⁸They are the ones whom God has blessed from among the prophets of Adam's progeny, and from [the progeny of] those We carried with Noah, and from among the progeny of Abraham and Israel, and from among those that We guided and chose. When the signs of the All-beneficent were recited to them, they would fall down weeping in prostration.

19:58 This verse is one of two (along with 3:93) which reflects an awareness of the tradition in Genesis 32 of the changing of Jacob's name (cf. Gen 32:28–29).

---

⁵⁹But they were succeeded by an evil posterity who neglected the prayer and followed [their base] appetites. So they will soon encounter [the reward of] perversity, ⁶⁰barring those who repent, believe and act righteously. Such will enter paradise and they will not be wronged in the least. ⁶¹Gardens of Eden promised by the All-beneficent to His servants, [while they were still] unseen. His promise is indeed bound to come to pass.

19:61 On the Garden of Eden, see commentary on 2:25 and 9:72 (with further references).

---

⁶²Therein they will not hear vain talk, but only 'Peace!' Therein they will have their provision morning and evening. ⁶³This is the

paradise that We will give as inheritance to those of Our servants who are Godwary.

⁶⁴[O Gabriel, tell the Prophet,] 'We do not descend except by the command of *your* Lord. To Him belongs whatever is before us and whatever is behind us and whatever is in between that, and *your* Lord does not forget ⁶⁵—the Lord of the heavens and the earth and whatever is between them. So worship Him and be steadfast in His worship. Do *you* know anyone who might be His namesake?'

⁶⁶Man says, 'What? Shall I be brought forth alive [from the grave] when I have been dead?' ⁶⁷Does not man remember that We created him before when he was nothing? ⁶⁸By *your* Lord, We will surely gather them with the devils; then We will surely bring them up around hell [scrambling] on their knees. ⁶⁹Then from every group We shall draw whichever of them was more defiant toward the All-beneficent. ⁷⁰Then surely We will know best those who deserve most to enter it. ⁷¹There is none of you but will come to it: a [matter that is a] decided certainty with *your* Lord. ⁷²Then We will deliver those who are Godwary and leave the wrongdoers in it, fallen on their knees.

⁷³When Our clear signs are recited to them, the faithless say to the faithful, 'Which of the two groups is superior in station and better with respect to company?' ⁷⁴How many a generation We have destroyed before them who were superior in furnishings and appearance!

⁷⁵*Say,* 'Whoever abides in error, the All-beneficent shall prolong his respite until they sight what they have been promised: either punishment or the Hour.' Then they will know whose position is worse, and whose host is weaker.

⁷⁶God enhances in guidance those who are [rightly] guided, and lasting righteous deeds are better with your Lord in reward and better at the return [to God].

⁷⁷Have *you* not regarded him who denies Our signs and says, 'I will surely be given wealth and children'? ⁷⁸Has he come to know the Unseen, or taken a promise from the All-beneficent? ⁷⁹No indeed! We will write down what he says, and We will prolong his punishment endlessly. ⁸⁰We shall take over what he talks about from him and he will come to Us alone.

⁸¹They have taken gods besides God so that they may be a [source of] might to them. ⁸²No Indeed! Soon they will disown their worship, and they will be their opponents. ⁸³Have *you* not regarded that We unleash the devils upon the faithless to urge them vigorously?

⁸⁴So *do* not make haste against them; indeed We are counting for them, a counting [down]. ⁸⁵The day We shall gather the Godwary toward the All-beneficent, [arriving] on mounts, ⁸⁶and drive the guilty as a thirsty herd towards hell, ⁸⁷no one will have the power to intercede [with God], except him who has taken a covenant with the All-beneficent.

⁸⁸They say, 'The All-beneficent has offspring!'

⁸⁹You have certainly advanced something hideous! ⁹⁰The heavens are about to be rent apart at it, the earth to split open and the mountains to collapse into bits, ⁹¹that they should ascribe offspring to the All-beneficent! ⁹²It does not behoove the All-beneficent to have offspring. ⁹³There is none in the heavens and the earth but he comes to the All-beneficent as a servant. ⁹⁴Certainly He has counted them [all] and numbered them precisely, ⁹⁵and each of them will come to Him alone on the Day of Resurrection.

⁹⁶Indeed, those who have faith and do righteous deeds—the All-beneficent will endear them [to His creation].

⁹⁷We have indeed made it simple in *your* language so that *you* may give good news thereby to the Godwary and warn with it a disputatious lot.

⁹⁸How many a generation We have destroyed before them! Can you descry any one of them, or hear from them so much as a murmur?

20. *ṬĀ HĀ*, ṬĀ HĀ

In the Name of God, the All-beneficent, the All-merciful.

¹*Ṭā Hā!* ²We did not send down the Qur'ān to *you* that *you* should be miserable, ³but only as an admonition to him who fears [his Lord]. ⁴A sending down [of the Revelation] from Him who created the earth and the lofty heavens ⁵—the All-beneficent, settled on the Throne.

20:5 On God's "settling" on the throne, see commentary on 32:4 (with further references).

⁶To Him belongs whatever is in the heavens and whatever is on the earth, and whatever is between them and whatever is under the ground.
⁷Whether you speak loudly [or in secret tones,] He indeed knows the secret and what is still more hidden.
⁸God—there is no god except Him—to Him belong the Best Names.
⁹Did the story of Moses come to *you?* ¹⁰When he sighted a fire, he said to his family, 'Wait! Indeed, I descry a fire! Maybe I will bring you a brand from it, or find some guidance at the fire.'

¹¹So when he came to it, he was called, 'O Moses! ¹²I am indeed your Lord! So take off your sandals. You are indeed in the sacred valley of Ṭuwā. ¹³I have chosen you, so listen to what is revealed. ¹⁴I am indeed God—there is no god except Me. So worship Me and maintain the prayer for My remembrance. ¹⁵Indeed, the Hour is bound to come: I will have it hidden, so that every soul may be rewarded for its endeavour. ¹⁶So do not let yourself be distracted from it by those who do not believe in it and who follow their desires, or you will perish.'

20:9–16 This passage (cf. 19:52; 26:10–17; 27:7–12; 28:29–35, 46; 79:15–18) is the Qur'ān's development of "the call of Moses" scene in Exodus 3:

> ¹Moses was looking after the flock of his father-in-law Jethro, the priest of Midian; he led it to the far side of the desert and came to Horeb, the mountain of God.
>
> ²The angel of the Lord appeared to him in a flame blazing from the middle of a bush. Moses looked; there was the bush blazing, but the bush was not being burnt up.
>
> ³Moses said, 'I must go across and see this strange sight, and why the bush is not being burnt up.'
>
> ⁴When the Lord saw him going across to look, God called to him from the middle of the bush. 'Moses, Moses!' he said. 'Here I am,' he answered.
>
> ⁵'Come no nearer,' he said. 'Take off your sandals, for the place where you are standing is holy ground.
>
> ⁶I am the God of your ancestors,' he said, 'the God of Abraham, the God of Isaac and the God of Jacob.' At this Moses covered his face, for he was afraid to look at God. (Exo 3:1–6)

God's announcement to Moses "I am indeed *Allāh*" (v. 14) may be a declaration of his proper name (parallel to Exodus 3:14, which has the Biblical God reveals his name as YHWH).

It is also noteworthy that the Qur'ān has God predict the coming Hour of Judgment (v. 15), whereas there is nothing in Exodus of this. On the term Ṭuwā (v. 12), see commentary on 79:16. The burning bush episode appears in the present passage and in 27:7–12 and 28:29–35.

¹⁷'Moses, what is that in your right hand?'

¹⁸He said, 'It is my staff. I lean on it and with it I beat down leaves for my sheep, and I have other uses for it.'

¹⁹He said, 'Moses, throw it down.'

²⁰So he threw it down, and lo! it was a snake, moving swiftly.

²¹He said, 'Take hold of it and do not fear. We will restore it to its former state. ²²Now clasp your hand to your armpit: it will emerge white, without any harm—[this is yet] another sign ²³that We may show you some of Our great signs. ²⁴Go to Pharaoh. He has indeed rebelled.'

20:17–24 Here the Qur'ān reports that Moses's hand, when he pulled it out of his garment, was "white, without any harm." This seems to be a pointed response to the description of the miracle in Exodus 4:6, where Moses's hand is described as "leprous." Similarly the Aramaic *Targum Onqelos* omits the Biblical detail that Moses' hand was "leprous" and describes it only as "white as snow." Cf. 7:108; 26:33; 28:32. For more on the miracles of Moses's staff and hand, see commentary on 7:106–8 and 26:30–45.

²⁵He said, 'My Lord! Open my breast for me. ²⁶Make my task easy for me. ²⁷Remove the hitch from my tongue, ²⁸[so that] they may understand my speech. ²⁹Appoint for me a minister from my family, ³⁰Aaron, my brother. ³¹Strengthen my back through him ³²and make him my associate in my task, ³³so that we may glorify You greatly ³⁴and remember You much. ³⁵You are indeed watching us.'

³⁶He said, 'Moses, your request has been granted!

20:25–36 This episode reflects Exodus 4:

¹⁰Moses said to the Lord, 'Please, my Lord, I have never been eloquent, even since you have spoken to your servant, for I am slow and hesitant of speech.'
¹¹'Who gave a person a mouth?' the Lord said to him. 'Who makes a person dumb or deaf, gives sight or makes blind? Is it not I, the Lord?
¹²Now go, I shall help you speak and instruct you what to say.'
¹³'Please, my Lord,' Moses replied, 'send anyone you decide to send!'
¹⁴At this, the Lord's anger kindled against Moses, and he said to him, 'There is your brother Aaron the Levite, is there not? I know that he is a good speaker. Here he comes to meet you. When he sees you, his heart will be full of joy.' (Exo 4:10–14)

Tafsīr al-Jalālayn explains that the "hitch" (v. 27) in Moses's tongue was "the result of his having been burnt by a live coal which he had placed [accidentally] in his mouth as a child" (a tradition connected to Isa 6:6–7 and known from Jewish sources). On the designation of Aaron as Moses's assistant, see 25:35; 26:12–14; 28:34.

---

³⁷Certainly We have done you a favour another time, ³⁸when We revealed to your mother whatever was to be revealed: ³⁹"Put him in the casket and cast it into the river. Then the river will cast it on the bank, and he shall be picked up by an enemy of Mine and an enemy of his." And I made you endearing, and that you might be reared under My [watchful] eyes. ⁴⁰When your sister walked up [to Pharaoh's palace], saying, "Shall I show you someone who will take care of him?" Then We restored you to your mother, so that she might not grieve and be comforted. Then you slew a soul, whereupon We delivered you from anguish, and We tried you with various ordeals. Then you stayed for several years among the people of Midian. Then you turned up as ordained, O Moses!
⁴¹And I chose you for Myself.'

20:37–41 (cf. 28:7–13). The word *tābūt*, which the Qur'ān (v. 39) uses for the basket in which the baby Moses was placed, has the meaning of "casket" or "tomb" in modern Arabic (hence Qarai's peculiar translation; Asad translates "chest'"). The meaning of the term, however, is best understood in light of the Hebrew term *tēbā* (meaning simply "chest" or "ark") in Exodus 2:3 (in Aramaic, *tēbūtā,* used in the Targums both for Noah's basket and for the "ark of the covenant," in Ethiopic, *tābot*). Tellingly the Qur'ān also uses *tābūt* for the Ark of the Covenant (Q 2:248).

On Moses's being returned to his mother, see commentary on 28:12–13. On Moses's adoption by Pharaoh's wife, see commentary on 28:9. On the relationship between the Qur'ānic material on the nativity of Moses in Exodus, see commentary on 28:9, 12–13.

At the end of verse 40 the Qur'ān refers back to God's care for Moses during his upbringing in Egypt, Moses's murder of an Egyptian (Exo 2:12; on which cf. 28:15–19 and commentary on those verses), and his subsequent flight to Midian (Exo 2:13–22; 3:1–4). It then returns to the scene of God's commissioning of Moses to free Israel from Pharaoh (vv. 42ff.) On Moses's flight from Egypt, cf. 26:14; 26:19–21; 28:15–21 and see commentary on 28:15–19 (with further references). On Moses's sojourn in Midian, see commentary on 28:23–28.

---

⁴²'Go ahead, you and your brother, with My signs, and do not flag in My remembrance. ⁴³Both of you go to Pharaoh, for he has indeed rebelled. ⁴⁴Speak to him in a soft manner; maybe he will take admonition or fear.'

⁴⁵They said, 'Our Lord! We are indeed afraid that he will forestall us or will exceed all bounds.'

⁴⁶He said, 'Do not be afraid, for I will be with the two of you, hearing and seeing [whatever happens].

20:46 "'I shall be with you,' God said, 'and this is the sign by which you will know that I was the one who sent you. After you have led the people out of Egypt, you will worship God on this mountain.'" (Exo 3:12)

---

⁴⁷So approach him and say, "We are the apostles of your Lord. Let the Children of Israel go with us and do not torture them!

We certainly bring you a sign from your Lord, and may peace be upon him who follows guidance! ⁴⁸Indeed, it has been revealed to us that punishment shall befall those who impugn us and turn their backs [on us].'"

⁴⁹He said, 'Who is your Lord, Moses?'

20:49 "'Who is the Lord,' Pharaoh replied, 'for me to obey what he says and let Israel go? I know nothing of the Lord, and I will not let Israel go.'" (Exo 5:2)

———————

⁵⁰He said, 'Our Lord is He who gave everything its creation and then guided it.'

⁵¹He said, 'What about the former generations?'

⁵²He said, 'Their knowledge is with my Lord, in a Book. My Lord neither makes any error nor forgets.' ⁵³He, who made the earth for you a cradle and threaded for you therein ways, and sent down water from the sky and We brought forth with it various kinds of vegetation, [saying] ⁵⁴'Eat and pasture your cattle. There are indeed signs in that for those who have sense.' ⁵⁵From it did We create you, into it shall We return you, and from it shall We bring you forth another time.

⁵⁶Certainly We showed him all Our signs. But he impugned [them] and refused [to believe them]. ⁵⁷He said, 'Moses, have you come to us to expel us from our land with your magic? ⁵⁸Yet we [too] will bring you a magic like it! So fix a tryst between us and you, which neither we shall fail nor you, at a middle place.'

⁵⁹He said, 'Your tryst shall be the Day of Adornment, and let the people be assembled in early forenoon.'

20:56–59 The Qur'ān's declaration (v. 56) that Pharaoh refused all of God's signs (cf. 54:41–42; 79:20–22) is connected to the Biblical account by which

Pharaoh refused to be convinced by the marvels which Moses and Aaron performed before him. The Qur'ān's declaration is also shaped by its general notion that prophets come with signs.

The notion that Moses meant to expel the Egyptians by magic (v. 57; cf. 10:76; 20:63) may be related to the accusations of magic against Jesus (Q 61:6), or against Muḥammad himself (10:2; 38:4). In 51:52 the Qur'ān declares that all prophets are accused of being magicians. On the accusation that Moses was a magician, see 7:109, 132; 10:76–77; 17:101; 20:63; 26:34–35, 49; 27:13; 28:36, 48; 40:24; 43:49; 51:39.

"Tryst" (vv. 58, 59, 80) is Qarai's translation for "meeting" (Ar. *maw'id*).

---

⁶⁰Then Pharaoh withdrew [to consult privately], summoned up his guile, and then arrived [at the scene of the contest].

⁶¹Moses said to them, 'Woe to you! Do not fabricate lies against God, or He will obliterate you with a punishment. Whoever fabricates lies certainly fails.'

⁶²So they disputed their matter among themselves, and kept their confidential talks secret.

⁶³They said, 'These two are indeed magicians who intend to expel you from your land with their magic and to abolish your excellent tradition!

20:63 The reference to two magicians in verse 63 should be compared to 28:48 (see commentary on that verse). On the accusation against Moses (and Aaron) concerning magic see commentary on 20:56–59.

---

⁶⁴So summon up your ingenuity, then come in orderly ranks. Today those who have the upper hand will triumph!'

⁶⁵They said, 'O Moses! Will you throw, or shall we be the first to throw?'

⁶⁶He said, 'No, you throw down first.' Thereupon, behold, their ropes and staffs appeared to him by their magic to wriggle swiftly.

⁶⁷Then Moses felt a certain fear within his heart. ⁶⁸We said, 'Do not be afraid. Indeed, you will have the upper hand. ⁶⁹Throw down what is in your right hand, and it will swallow what they have conjured. What they have conjured is only a magician's trick, and the magician does not fare well wherever he may show up.'

20:67–69 It is Moses who throws down his staff here (cf. 26:45), whereas in Exodus (7:10) it is Aaron who does so. On the account of Moses in Pharaoh's court in the Qurʾān and its relationship to the Exodus narrative see commentary on 26:30–45 (with further references).

⁷⁰Thereat the magicians fell down prostrating. They said, 'We have believed in the Lord of Aaron and Moses!'

⁷¹He said, 'Did you believe him before I should permit you? He is indeed your chief who has taught you magic! Surely, I will cut off your hands and feet from opposite sides, and I will crucify you on the trunks of palm trees, and you will know which of us can inflict a severer and more lasting punishment.'

⁷²They said, 'We will never prefer you to the clear proofs which have come to us and to Him who originated us. Decide whatever you want to decide. You can only decide about the life of this world. ⁷³We have indeed believed in our Lord that He may forgive us our offences and the magic you compelled us to perform. God is better and more lasting.'

20:70–73 On the belief of Pharaoh's magicians in Moses and his God, see commentary on 7:120–26 (with further references).

⁷⁴Whoever comes to his Lord laden with guilt, for him shall be hell, where he will neither live nor die. ⁷⁵But whoever comes to Him with faith and he has done righteous deeds, for such shall be the highest ranks ⁷⁶—the Gardens of Eden with streams running in them, to abide in them [forever], and that is the reward of him who keeps pure.

20:76 On paradise as the Garden of Eden in the Qurʾān, see commentary on 2:25 and 9:72 (with further references).

⁷⁷We revealed to Moses, [saying], 'Set out with My servants at night and strike out for them a dry path through the sea. Do not be afraid of being overtaken, and have no fear [of getting drowned].

⁷⁸Then Pharaoh pursued them with his troops, whereat they were engulfed by what engulfed them of the sea. ⁷⁹Pharaoh led his people astray and did not guide them.

20:77–79 On the drowning of Pharaoh and his army, see commentary on 54:41–42 (with further references).

⁸⁰O Children of Israel! We delivered you from your enemy, and We appointed with you a tryst on the right side of the Mount and We sent down to you manna and quails: ⁸¹'Eat of the good things We have provided you, but do not overstep the bounds therein, lest My wrath should descend on you. And he on whom My wrath descends certainly perishes. ⁸²I indeed forgive those who repent, become faithful, act righteously, and thereafter follow guidance.'

20:80–82 On the notion that God came from the right side of the mountain, see commentary on 19:51–53 (with further references). On the quails and
manna, see commentary on 7:160 (with further references).

---

⁸³[God said,] 'O Moses, what has prompted you to hasten ahead
of your people?'

20:83–98 *overview* This passage is the Qur'ān's adaption of the Exodus story
of the golden calf (Exo 32; cf. Q 2:51–54, 92–93; 4:153; 7:148–52):

> ¹When the people saw that Moses was a long time before coming down the
> mountain, they gathered round Aaron and said to him, 'Get to work, make us
> a god to go at our head; for that Moses, the man who brought us here from
> Egypt—we do not know what has become of him.'
> ²Aaron replied, 'Strip off the gold rings in the ears of your wives and your
> sons and daughters, and bring them to me.'
> ³The people all stripped off the gold rings from their ears and brought them
> to Aaron.
> ⁴He received what they gave him, melted it down in a mould and with it
> made the statue of a calf. 'Israel,' the people shouted, 'here is your God who
> brought you here from Egypt!' (Exo 32:1–4)

Most traditional scholars identify the figure named *al-sāmirī* in this passage
as an unfaithful idolater among the Israelites (Sāmirī is usually connected to
an imagined Israelite tribe "Sāmira"). Academic scholars often understand this
name to mean "Samaritan" and conclude that the place of a Samaritan in this
account must reflect (ultimately) Jewish anti-Samaritan sentiment (along with
a desire to protect Aaron from the sin of idolatry). It has been considered (see,
e.g., Yahuda, 286ff.) to be an allusion to the account in 1 Kings 12 (see vv.
25–29; see esp. 1Ki 12:28/Exo 32:4 and Q 20:88) by which the Israelite king
Jeroboam, who reigned in Shechem (the center of Samaritan worship), set up
two calves for people to worship.

However, in the Biblical account it is Aaron who is responsible for the crime
of the golden calf, for which reason Michael Pregill (*QSC,* 229) argues that the
term *al-sāmirī* is best understood as an Arabic adaptation of Hebrew *shōmer,*
with the meaning "the watchman," and as a reference to Aaron (who was left to
watch over Israel while Moses was speaking with God on Mt. Sinai). This inter-

pretation makes sense of verse 95 ("What is your business, O Sāmirī!"), which seems to be the address of Moses to Aaron.

––––––––––––

⁸⁴He said, 'They are close upon my heels and I hurried on to You, my Lord, so that You may be pleased.'

⁸⁵He said, 'We indeed tried your people in your absence, and the Samiri has led them astray.'

20:85 Yahuda (286), noting the connection of Jeroboam with the worship of a calf in Samaria, compares this verse with 1 Kings 14:16: "He will abandon Israel for the sins which Jeroboam has committed and made Israel commit."

––––––––––––

⁸⁶Thereupon Moses returned to his people, indignant and grieved. He said, 'O my people! Did your Lord not give you a true promise? Did the period [of my absence] seem too long to you? Or did you desire that your Lord's wrath should descend on you and so you failed your tryst with me?'

20:86 Cf. Exo 32:21: "Moses then said to Aaron, 'What have these people done to you for you to have brought so great a sin on them?'"

––––––––––––

⁸⁷They said, 'We did not fail our tryst with you of our own accord, but we were laden with the weight of those people's ornaments, and we cast them [into the fire] and so did the Samiri throw.'

⁸⁸Then he produced for them a calf—a [lifeless] body with a low—and they said, This is your god and the god of Moses, so he

forgot! ⁸⁹Did thcy not see that it did not answer them, nor could it bring them any benefit or harm?

20:88–89 Here, unlike Exodus or other Biblical passages on the golden calf, the Qur'ān seems to report that the calf which al-Sāmirī fashioned "lowed"; that is, it came to life. *Tafsīr al-Jalālayn* explains here that al-Sāmirī did so with some of the dust from the angel Gabriel's horse (an interpretation shaped by the allusion in verse 96 to "the messenger's trail").

As Michael Pregill points out (*QSC,* 299), however, it is possible to understand the Arabic phrase here to mean "he produced for them the body of 'a calf which lows'" (instead of "he produced for them a calf—a [lifeless] body with a low"). This would obviate the need to imagine that the golden calf came to life, and the expression would be roughly parallel to Psalm 106:20, which alludes to the calf as "the image of a grass-eating bull."

The end of verse 88 ("so he forgot"), perhaps added for the sake of the rhyme, causes confusion among interpreter. Some argue that al-Sāmirī forgot (Moses's teaching). Others argue that these are the words of al-Sāmirī who accuses Moses of forgetting.

On the description of anything that unbelievers worship other than God as "powerless" (v. 89), see commentary on 10:18 (with further references).

⁹⁰Aaron had certainly told them earlier, 'O my people! You are only being tested by it. Indeed, your Lord is the All-beneficent. So follow me and obey my command!' ⁹¹They had said, 'We will keep on attending to it until Moses returns to us.'

⁹²He said, 'O Aaron! What kept you, when you saw them going astray, ⁹³from following me? Did you disobey my command?'

⁹⁴He said, 'O son of my mother! Do not grab my beard or my head! I feared lest you should say, "You have caused a rift among the Children of Israel, and did not heed my word [of advice]."'

⁹⁵He said, 'What is your business, O Samiri?'

⁹⁶He said, 'I saw what they did not see. I took a handful [of dust] from the messenger's trail and threw it. That is how my soul prompted me.'

⁹⁷He said, 'Begone! It shall be your [lot] throughout life to say, "Do not touch me!" There is indeed a tryst for you which you will not fail to keep! Now look at your god to whom you kept on attending. We will burn it down and then scatter it[s ashes] into the sea.

20:92–97 The Qurʾān continues its homiletic interpretation of the account of the golden calf in Exodus 32. Michael Pregill (*QSC,* 229) reads this Qurʾānic passage as all one dialogue between Moses and Aaron (who *is* al-Sāmirī), pace the assumption of classical exegetes and academic scholars alike that verses 92–94 are a conversation between Moses and Aaron and verses 95–97 a conversation between Moses and (a third figure named) al-Sāmirī.

Pregill's reading would explain why Moses reprimands Aaron (vv. 92–94; cf. 7:150). However, it implies a different understanding of verse 97. This verse is usually understood as a curse of exile against al-Sāmirī. To this end Hilali-Khan add to their translation of the phrase "Do not touch me" an explanatory comment in parentheses: "i.e., you will live alone exiled away from mankind." Some scholars argue that this phrase reflects somehow the Jewish prohibition of dealings with the Samaritans or the Samaritan concern for purity. According to Pregill, however, this verse is an allusion to the establishment of the priesthood, for which Aaron is a symbol (cf. 7:142). By declaring, "Do not touch me," Aaron signals his purified status as a priest. For his part, Yahuda (287) argues instead that Moses has afflicted al-Sāmirī with leprosy (as a punishment), and therefore (in line with Lev 13:45) al-Sāmirī has to call out to keep people from touching him.

The end of verse 97 alludes to the scattering of the ashes of the calf into the water in Deuteronomy 9:21 (cf. Q 2:93, which has the Israelites instead "drink" the calf as in Exo 32:20).

⁹⁸Your God indeed is God; there is no god except Him. He embraces all things in [His] knowledge.'

⁹⁹Thus do We relate to *you* some accounts of what is past. Certainly We have given *you* a Reminder from Ourselves. ¹⁰⁰Whoever disregards it shall bear a burden [of his denial] on the Day of Resurrection, ¹⁰¹remaining in it [forever]. Evil is their burden on the Day of Resurrection ¹⁰²—the day the Trumpet will be blown; on that day We will muster the guilty with blind eyes.

20:102 On the trumpet blast, see commentary on 78:18 (with further references).

---

¹⁰³They will whisper to one another: 'You have stayed only for ten [days].' ¹⁰⁴We know best what they will say, when the smartest of them in approach will say, 'You stayed only a day!'

¹⁰⁵They question *you* concerning the mountains. *Say,* 'My Lord will scatter them [like dust].' ¹⁰⁶Then He will leave it as a level plain. ¹⁰⁷*You* will not see any crookedness or unevenness in it.

20:105–7 Cf. "Let every valley be filled in, every mountain and hill be levelled, every cliff become a plateau, every escarpment a plain" (Isa 40:4).

---

¹⁰⁸On that day they will follow the summoner without meandering. Their voices will be muted before the All-beneficent, and *you* will hear nothing but a murmur. ¹⁰⁹Intercession will not avail that day except from him whom the All-beneficent allows and approves of his word.

¹¹⁰He knows what is before them and behind them, but they do not comprehend Him in their knowledge.

20:110 "You fence me in, behind and in front, you have laid your hand upon me. Such amazing knowledge is beyond me, a height to which I cannot attain" (Psa 139:5–6).

––––––––––

[111]All faces shall be humbled before the Living One, the All-sustainer, and those who bear [the burden of] wrongdoing will fail. [112]But whoever does righteous deeds, should he be faithful, will fear neither injustice or disparagement.

[113]Thus We have sent it down as an Arabic Qur'ān and We have paraphrased the warnings in it variously, so that they may be Godwary, or it may prompt them to remembrance. [114]So, exalted is God, the True Sovereign. *Do not hasten* with the Qur'ān before its revelation is completed for you, and *say,* 'My Lord! Increase me in knowledge.'

[115]Certainly We had enjoined Adam earlier, but he forgot, and We did not find any resoluteness in him. [116]When We said to the angels, 'Prostrate before Adam,' they prostrated, but not Iblis: he refused.

––––––––––

20:115–16 On the prostration of the angels before Adam, see commentary on 7:11–12 (with further references).

––––––––––

[117]We said, 'O Adam! This is indeed an enemy of yours and your mate's. So do not let him expel you from paradise, or you will be miserable. [118]You will neither be hungry in it nor naked. [119]You will neither be thirsty in it, nor suffer from [the heat of] the sun.'

[120]Then Satan tempted him. He said, 'O Adam! Shall I show you the tree of immortality and an imperishable kingdom?'

¹²¹So they both ate of it, and their nakedness became evident to them, and they began to stitch over themselves with the leaves of paradise. Adam disobeyed his Lord and went amiss.

20:117–21 The Qurʾān here (and elsewhere; cf. 2:36ff.; 7:19ff.) has Satan appear in the Garden of Eden to tempt Adam and Eve, whereas Genesis (3:2ff.) has only a serpent in the garden. This reflects the Christian association of the serpent with Satan. On this see commentary on 2:36. On Satan's temptation of Adam in the Qurʾān, see commentary on 7:19–22.

The Qurʾān has Satan tempt Adam and Eve with "the tree of immortality and an imperishable kingdom" (v. 120). This suggests that that the Qurʾān thinks of the "tree of life" as the forbidden tree, whereas Genesis makes "the tree of knowledge of good and evil" the forbidden tree (Gen 2:17) and refers later (3:22–24) to a different tree known as the "tree of life." On this see commentary on 7:19–22 (with further references).

¹²²Then his Lord chose him and turned to him clemently, and guided him.

20:122 The Qurʾān has God forgive Adam in a way that reflects Syriac Christian texts such as *Cave of Treasures*. On this see 2:38 and 7:22–25 and see commentary on 7:23–25 (with further references).

¹²³He said, 'Get down from it both of you, all together, being enemies of one another! Yet, should any guidance come to you from Me, those who follow My guidance will not go astray, nor will they be miserable.

20:123 The declaration "Get down from [the garden]," reflects a cosmology according to which the Garden of Eden is on a cosmic mountain, the top of which reaches into heaven. On this see commentary on 2:25 and 7:23–25 (with further references).

––––––––––

¹²⁴But whoever disregards My remembrance will have a wretched life, and We shall raise him blind on the Day of Resurrection.'

¹²⁵He will say, 'My Lord! Why have You raised me blind, though I used to see?' ²⁶He will say: 'So it is. Our signs came to you, but you forgot them, and so you will be forgotten today.'

¹²⁷Thus do We requite those who transgress and do not believe in the signs of their Lord, and the punishment of the Hereafter is severer and more lasting.

¹²⁸Does it not dawn upon them how many generations We have destroyed before them, amid [the ruins of] whose dwellings they walk? There are indeed signs in this for those who have good sense. ¹²⁹Were it not for a prior decree of *your* Lord and a stated time, [their doom] would have been immediate.

¹³⁰So *be patient* with what they say, and *celebrate* the praise of *your* Lord before the rising of the sun and before the sunset, and glorify Him in watches of the night and at the day's ends, so that *you* may be pleased.

¹³¹Do not extend *your* glance toward what We have provided certain groups of them as a glitter of the life of this world, in order that We may test them thereby. The provision of *your* Lord is better and more lasting. ¹³²And bid *your* family to prayer and be steadfast in maintaining it. We do not ask any provision of *you:* it is We who provide for *you,* and the ultimate outcome [in the Hereafter] belongs to Godwariness.

¹³³They say, 'Why does he not bring us a sign from his Lord?' Has there not come to them a clear proof in that which is in the former scriptures?

20:133 On the Arabic term behind "scriptures," *ṣuḥuf*, see commentary on 80:13–15 (with further references).

---

[134]Had We destroyed them with a punishment before it, they would have surely said, 'Our Lord! Why did You not send us an apostle so that we might have followed Your signs before we were abased and disgraced?'

[135]*Say,* 'Everyone [of us] is waiting. So wait! Soon you will know who are the people of the right path, and who is [rightly] guided.'

21. *AL-ANBIYĀ*, THE PROPHETS

In the Name of God, the All-beneficent, the All-merciful.

¹Mankind's reckoning has drawn near to them, yet they are disregardful in [their] obliviousness. ²There does not come to them any new reminder from their Lord but they listen to it as they play around, ³their hearts set on diversions. The wrongdoers secretly whisper together, [saying], 'Is this [man] not just a human being like yourselves? Will you give in to magic with open eyes?'

⁴He said, 'My Lord knows every word [spoken] in the heaven and on the earth, and He is the All-hearing, the All-knowing.'

⁵But they said, '[They are] muddled dreams!' 'He has indeed fabricated it!' 'He is indeed a poet!' 'Let him bring us a sign like those sent to the former generations.'

⁶No town that We destroyed before them believed. Will these then have faith [if they are sent signs]? ⁷We did not send [any apostles] before *you* except as men to whom We revealed. Ask the People of the Reminder if you do not know.

21:7 This verse has the Qur'ān tell its audience to consult with Jews and Christians ("People of the Reminder") to confirm that God sends men (not angels) as messengers. See further commentary on the parallel verse at 16:43 (with further references).

⁸We did not make them bodies that did not eat food, nor were they immortal. ⁹Then We fulfilled Our promise to them and We delivered them and whomever We wished, and We destroyed the transgressors. ¹⁰Certainly We have sent down to you a Book in which there is an admonition for you. Do you not exercise your reason?

¹¹How many a town We have smashed that had been wrongdoing, and We brought forth another people after it. ¹²So when they sighted Our punishment, behold, they ran away from it. ¹³'Do not run away! Return to the opulence you were given to enjoy and to your dwellings so that you may be questioned!'

¹⁴They said, 'Woe to us! We have indeed been wrongdoers!' ¹⁵That remained their cry until We turned them into a mown field, stilled [like burnt ashes].

¹⁶We did not create the heaven and the earth and whatever is between them for play. ¹⁷Had We desired to take up some diversion We would have taken it up with Ourselves, were We to do [so]. ¹⁸Indeed, We hurl the truth against falsehood, and it crushes its head, and behold, falsehood vanishes! And woe to you for what you allege [about God].

¹⁹To Him belongs whatever is in the heavens and the earth, and those who are near Him do not disdain to worship Him, nor do they become weary.

21:19 On the image of the angels' praising God, see commentary on 7:206 (with further references).

²⁰They glorify [Him] night and day, without flagging.

²¹Have they taken gods from the earth who raise [the dead]? ²²Had there been any gods in them other than God, they would surely have fallen apart. Clear is God, the Lord of the Throne, of what they allege [concerning Him].

²³He is not questioned concerning what He does, but they are questioned.

²⁴Have they taken gods besides Him? *Say,* 'Produce your evidence! This is a precept of those who are with me, and a precept of those [who went] before me.' But most of them do not know the truth and so they are disregardful. ²⁵We did not send any apostle before *you* but that We revealed to him that 'There is no god except Me; so worship Me.'

²⁶They say, 'The All-beneficent has offspring.' Immaculate is He! Indeed, they are [His] honoured servants. ²⁷They do not venture to speak ahead of Him, and they act by His command. ²⁸He knows what is before them and what is behind them, and they do not intercede except for someone He approves of, and they are apprehensive for the fear of Him. ²⁹Should any of them say, 'I am a god besides Him,' We will requite him with hell. Thus do We requite the wrongdoers.

21:21–29 In this passage the Qurʾān insists that there are no gods other than Allāh and condemns those who take earthly things as gods (v. 21). Verse 21 seems to mean literally that these supposed gods "raise [the dead]" (*yunshirūn*), although presumably the Qurʾān means only that the unbelievers *think* they can raise the dead. In verse 26 Qarai understands Arabic *walad* as a plural and translates "offspring" (a reading suggested by the plural "servants" at the end of the verse). Verse 27 suggests that the Qurʾān is concerned with those who consider angels to be God's offspring. It might be compared to Q 53:19–23 (see commentary on those verses). Verse 29 might be compared to the question posed by God to Christ in Q 5:116. See commentary on 2:116–17 (with further references).

On God as "Lord of the Throne" (v. 22), cf. 9:129; 23:86, 116; 27:26; 43:82.

---

³⁰Have the faithless not regarded that the heavens and the earth were interwoven and We unravelled them, and We made every living thing out of water? Will they not then have faith?

21:30 Here the Qur'ānic description of creation reflects the imagery of Genesis 1, which begins with a scene of watery chaos, until God begins to divide the waters and, eventually, land from water. The author of 2 Peter ("They deliberately ignore the fact that long ago there were the heavens and the earth, formed out of water and through water by the Word of God"; 2Pe 3:5) insists that the heavens and the earth were formed out of water, as does Ephrem in his *Commentary on Genesis* (1:10). On the creation of animals from water, see 24:45. On the creation of humans from water, see commentary on 24:41–45 (with further references).

---

³¹We set firm mountains in the earth lest it should shake with them, and We made in them broad ways so that they may be guided [to their destinations]. ³²We made the sky a preserved roof and yet they are disregardful of its signs. ³³It is He who created the night and the day, the sun and the moon, each swimming in an orbit.

³⁴We did not give immortality to any human before *you*. If *you* are fated to die, will they live on forever? ³⁵Every soul shall taste death, and We will test you with good and ill by way of test, and to Us you will be brought back.

21:35 On "tasting" death, see commentary on 44:56 (with further references).

³⁶Whenever the faithless see *you,* they only take *you* in derision: 'Is this the one who speaks ill of your gods?' And they dismiss the remembrance of the All-beneficent. ³⁷Man is a creature of haste. Soon I will show you My signs. So do not ask Me to hasten.

³⁸And they say, 'When will this promise be fulfilled, if *you* are truthful?' ³⁹If only the faithless knew about the time when they will not be able to keep the Fire off their faces and their backs, nor will they be helped! ⁴⁰Indeed, it will overtake them suddenly, dumbfounding them. So they will neither be able to avert it, nor will they be granted any respite.

⁴¹Apostles were certainly derided before *you;* but those who ridiculed them were besieged by what they had been deriding.

⁴²*Say,* 'Who can guard you, day and night, against [the punishment of] the All-beneficent [should He want to punish you]?' They are indeed disregardful of their Lord's remembrance.

⁴³Do they have gods besides Us to defend them? Neither can they help themselves, nor can they shield [the idolaters] from Us. ⁴⁴We have indeed provided for them and their fathers until they lived on for long years. Do they not see how We visit the land diminishing it at its edges? Are they the ones who will prevail?

⁴⁵*Say,* 'I indeed warn you by the means of revelation.' But the deaf do not hear the call when they are warned.

⁴⁶Should a whiff of your Lord's punishment touch them, they will surely say, 'Woe to us! We have indeed been wrongdoers!'

⁴⁷We shall set up just scales on the Day of Resurrection, and no soul will be wronged in the least. Even if it be the weight of a mustard seed We will produce it and We suffice as reckoners.

21:47 On the use of the New Testament expression "mustard seed" to represent a small amount, see commentary on 31:16.

⁴⁸Certainly We gave Moses and Aaron the Criterion, a light and reminder for the Godwary

21:48 Behind "the Criterion" is the Arabic term *furqān*. This translation (cf. Asad: "standard") reflects the Arabic root *f-r-q*, meaning "to separate" or "to divide." The Aramaic root (*p-r-q*), however, is related to salvation, or redemption, and *furqān* here (note its description as a "light and reminder") may be an allusion to the salvation offered by the law which God revealed to Israel. On *furqān*, see also commentary on 2:53 (with further references).

⁴⁹—those who fear their Lord in secret and are apprehensive of the Hour. ⁵⁰This [too] is a blessed reminder which We have sent down. Will you then deny it?

⁵¹Certainly We gave Abraham his rectitude aforetime, and We knew him

21:51–70 *overview* On Abraham's conflict with his father and his people, see commentary on 26:69–93 (with further references).

⁵²when he said to his father and his people, 'What are these images to which you keep on attending?'

⁵³They said, 'We found our fathers worshiping them.'

⁵⁴He said, 'Certainly you and your fathers have been in plain error.'

⁵⁵They said, 'Are you telling the truth, or are you [just] kidding?'

⁵⁶He said, 'Your Lord is indeed the Lord of the heavens and the earth, who originated them, and I bear witness to this. ⁵⁷By God,

I will devise a stratagem against your idols after you have gone away.'

⁵⁸So he broke them into pieces, all except the biggest of them, so that they might come back to it.

⁵⁹They said, 'Whoever has done this to Our gods?! He is indeed a wrongdoer!'

⁶⁰They said, 'We heard a young man speaking ill of them. He is called "Abraham."'

⁶¹They said, 'Bring him before the people's eyes so that they may bear witness [against him].'

⁶²They said, 'Was it you who did this to our gods, O Abraham?'

⁶³He said, 'No, it was this biggest one of them who did it! Ask them, if they can speak.'

⁶⁴Thereat they came to themselves and said [to one another], 'It is you indeed who are the wrongdoers!' ⁶⁵Then they hung their heads. [However, they said], 'You certainly know that they cannot speak.'

⁶⁶He said, 'Then, do you worship besides God that which cannot cause you any benefit or harm? ⁶⁷Fie on you and what you worship besides God! Do you not exercise your reason?'

21:51–67 The Qurʾān here refers to a midrashic tale found in several sources, including *Genesis Rabbah*, set during Abraham's childhood. According to this tale, Abraham's father, Terah, was an idol maker, and he counted on Abraham to help him with his work. However, the work in his father's idol shop confirmed Abaham's innate sense that the worship of idols was futile. One day, when he was left alone, he devised a plot to show the inanity of worshipping idols:

> Terah was a manufacturer of idols. He once went away somewhere and left Abraham to sell them in his place. A man came and wished to buy one. "How old are you?" Abraham asked him. "Fifty years," was the reply. "Woe to such a man!" he exclaimed, "you are fifty years old and would worship a day-old object!" At this he became ashamed and departed. On another occasion a

woman came with a plateful of flour and requested him, "Take this and offer it to them." So he took a stick, broke them, and put the stick in the hand of the largest. When his father returned he demanded, "What have you done to them?" "I cannot conceal it from you," he rejoined. "A woman came with a plateful of fine meal and requested me to offer it to them. One claimed, "I must eat first," while another claimed, "I must eat first." Thereupon the largest arose, took the stick, and broke them." "Why do you make sport of me," he cried out; "have they then any knowledge!" "Should not your ears listen to what your mouth is saying," he retorted. (*Genesis Rabbah,* 38:13)

Cf. 37:88–96. On Abraham's preaching to his father and his people, see commentary on 26:69–93 (with further references). On the description of anything unbelievers worship other than God (v. 66) as being powerless, see commentary on 10:18 (with further references).

---

⁶⁸They said, 'Burn him and help your gods, if you are to do anything!'

⁶⁹We said, 'O fire! Be cool and safe for Abraham!' ⁷⁰They plotted to harm him, but We made them the biggest losers.

21:68–70 The Qur'ān here (cf. 29:23–4; 37:97–101) follows the sequence of a midrashic tale on Abraham's childhood (see commentary on 21:51–67 for the beginning of the tale). Abraham's destruction of the idols in his father's shop leads his father (who is upset that his son has acted irreligiously and caused such trouble for the family business) to take him to Nimrod, the ruler of Abraham's city. In the Bible (Gen 10:8–9; 1Ch 1:10) Nimrod is a "mighty hunter" and king (see also Mic 5:5), but his character is developed in later exegesis. It is Nimrod who rules in the valley of Shinar and who organizes the building of the Tower of Babel. This he does to defy God (*Targum Neofiti* of Gen 10:9 relates that Nimrod "was mighty in sinning before the Lord") and to have an edifice that would survive a second flood. In this passage, which has Abraham end up in a furnace, the Qur'ān is following midrashic traditions such as that in *Genesis Rabbah:*

[Terah] seized him and delivered him to Nimrod. "Let us worship the fire!" he [Nimrod] proposed. "Let us rather worship water, which extinguishes the fire," replied he. "Then let us worship water!" "Let us rather worship the clouds which bear the water." "Then let us worship the clouds." "Let us rather worship the winds which disperse the clouds." "Then let us worship the wind." "Let us rather worship human beings, who withstand the wind." You are just bandying words, he exclaimed; "We will worship nought but the fire. Behold, I will cast you into it, and let your God whom you adore come and save you from it."

Now Haran was standing there undecided. If Abram is victorious, [thought he], I will say that I am of Abram's belief, while if Nimrod is victorious I will say that I am on Nimrod's side. When Abram descended into the fiery furnace and was saved, he [Nimrod] asked him, "Of whose belief are you?" "Of Abram," he replied. Thereupon he seized and cast him into the fire; his inwards were scorched and he died in his father's presence [cf. Gen 11:28]. (*Genesis Rabbah,* 38:13: cf. b. Pesahim 118a)

On the salvation of Abraham from the furnace, cf. 29:24–25 and 37:97–98. The casting of Abraham in fire (coming from the midrashic account) seems to contradict the threat that Abraham would be stoned (the more common threat against messengers in the Qur'ān) in 19:46.

Tafsīr al-Jalālayn explains how Abraham's people got him into the furnace: "Thus they gathered lots of firewood and lit a fire throughout it. They then tied up Abraham, placed him in a ballista and had him hurled into the fire."

---

⁷¹We delivered him and Lot toward the land which We have blessed for all nations. ⁷²And We gave him Isaac, and Jacob as well for a grandson, and each of them We made righteous. ⁷³We made them *imams,* guiding by Our command, and We revealed to them [concerning] the performance of good deeds, the maintenance of prayers, and the giving of *zakāt,* and they used to worship Us.

21:72–73 On the possibility that the Qur'ān considers both Isaac and Jacob to be sons of Abraham, see commentary on 29:27 (with further references). Here a word, *nāfila* ("addition"), is interpreted by Qarai as "grandson," to make the Qur'ān line up with the Biblical genealogy. In verse 73 Qarai does not translate the Arabic term *imam*s ("leaders"; cf. 32:24), used to describe Isaac and Jacob.

---

⁷⁴We gave judgement and knowledge to Lot and We delivered him from the town which used to commit vicious acts. They were indeed an evil and depraved lot. ⁷⁵And We admitted him into Our mercy. He was indeed one of the righteous.

⁷⁶And before that Noah; when he called out, We responded to him and delivered him and his family from the great agony. ⁷⁷We helped him against the people who impugned Our signs. They were indeed an evil lot; so We drowned them all.

⁷⁸And [remember] David and Solomon when they gave judgement concerning the tillage when the sheep of some people strayed into it by night, and We were witness to their judgement.

21:78 There is no clear antecedent for the Qur'ān's reference here to David and Solomon's judgment regarding a problem involving sheep getting into a field, or for why the Qur'ān would have both David and Solomon give a judgment on the same issue. Nevertheless, this case is meant to give an example of the "judgment and knowledge" which the Qur'ān attributes to both figures (v. 79).

---

⁷⁹We gave its understanding to Solomon, and to each We gave judgement and knowledge. We disposed the mountains and the birds to glorify [Us] with David, and We have been the doer [of these things].

21:79 The Qur'ān's declaration here (cf. 34:10; 38:18–19) that the "mountains and the birds" glorify God with David reflects the traditional Jewish and

Christian understanding of David as the principal author of the Psalms. It may reflect Psalm 148, which calls on nature to praise God:

> [7]Praise the Lord from the earth, sea-monsters and all the depths,
> [8]fire and hail, snow and mist, storm-winds that obey his word,
> [9]mountains and every hill, orchards and every cedar,
> [10]wild animals and all cattle, reptiles and winged birds. (Psa 148:7–10)

On Solomon's receiving "judgment and knowledge" from God, cf. 27:15. On David's receiving "judgment and knowledge" from God, see commentary on 2:250–51 (with further references).

---

[80]We taught him the making of coats of mail for you, to protect you from your [own] violence. Will you then be grateful?

21:80 This verse (cf. 24:10–11) is generally understood to mean that God taught David how to produce armor (hence Qarai's translation: "the making of coats of mail"), although the Arabic term (*labūs*) that Qarai renders "coats of mail" can mean simply "clothing," and the phrase Qarai renders as "from your own violence" could mean "from your own harm [*ba'sikum*]." Asad thus translates: "how to make garments [of God-consciousness] for you, [O men,] so that they might fortify you against all that may cause you fear."

---

[81]And [We disposed] for Solomon the tempestuous wind which blew by his command toward the land which We have blessed, and We have knowledge of all things. [82]Among the devils were some who dived for him and performed tasks other than that, and We were watchful over them.

21:81–82 Here the Qur'ān presents Solomon with divine powers, including control over the wind (v. 81) and control over spiritual beings, even demons (v. 82). This passage is closely connected to the way the author of the Wisdom of Solomon (traditionally understood to be Solomon himself, although the text likely dates to the first century BC) praises God for the understanding which He has been given of all things, including the forces of nature, and spirits:

> [17]He it was who gave me sure knowledge of what exists, to understand the structure of the world and the action of the elements,
> [18]the beginning, end and middle of the times, the alternation of the solstices and the succession of the seasons,
> [19]the cycles of the year and the position of the stars,
> [20]the natures of animals and the instincts of wild beasts, the powers of spirits and human mental processes, the varieties of plants and the medical properties of roots. (Wis 7:17–20)

Cf. 34:12–13 and 38:36–39. See commentary on 34:12–13.

---

[83]And [remember] Job, when he called out to his Lord, 'Distress has indeed befallen me, and You are the most merciful of the merciful.' [84]So We answered his prayer and removed his distress, and We gave him [back] his family along with others like them, as a mercy from Us and an admonition for the devout.

21:83–84 This passage reflects the Biblical book of Job, according to which Job, after the death of his family (and various other disasters) received new children, although Qarai's translation suggests that he received his same children back (this follows from medieval commentaries, including *Tafsīr al-Jalālayn,* which relate that God brought his children to life):

> [12]The Lord blessed Job's latter condition even more than his former one. He came to own fourteen thousand sheep, six thousand camels, a thousand yoke of oxen and a thousand she-donkeys.
> [13]He had seven sons and three daughters;
> [14]his first daughter he called 'Turtledove,' the second 'Cassia' and the third 'Mascara.'
> [15]Throughout the land there were no women as beautiful as the daughters of Job. And their father gave them inheritance rights like their brothers.

¹⁶After this, Job lived for another one hundred and forty years, and saw his children and his children's children to the fourth generation. (Job 42:12–16)

See 38:41–44 and commentary on that passage.

———————

⁸⁵And [remember] Ishmael, Idris, and Dhul-Kifl—each of them was among the patient. ⁸⁶We admitted them into Our mercy. They were indeed among the righteous.

21:85–86 On Idrīs see commentary on 19:56–57. "Dhū l-Kifl" (cf. 38:48) is an epithet meaning "the one who did [or received] double," but it is not clear who is meant thereby. Geiger (*Judaism and Islam,* 155) thinks he is Obadiah or Ezekiel; Torrey (*Jewish Foundation,* 72) identifies him as Joshua; Bell (*Commentary,* 555) as Tobit; Hilali-Khan as Isaiah.

———————

⁸⁷And [remember] Jonah, when he left in a rage thinking that We would not put him to hardship. Then he cried out in the darkness, 'There is no god except You! You are immaculate! I have indeed been among the wrongdoers!' ⁸⁸So We answered his prayer and delivered him from the agony, and thus do We deliver the faithful.

21:87–88 Here the Qur'ān, following the Biblical account of Jonah, alludes to the way in which Jonah left Jaffa on a boat headed west, after God had commanded him to head to Nineveh (to the east) to warn its people (the enemy of Israel) of impending punishment (something Jonah was not interested in doing). The Qur'ān then alludes to Jonah's repentant prayer in the belly of the big fish, and to God's commanding the fish to spit him up on the shore:

¹The word of the Lord was addressed to Jonah son of Amittai:

²'Up!' he said, 'Go to Nineveh, the great city, and proclaim to them that their wickedness has forced itself upon me.'
³Jonah set about running away from the Lord, and going to Tarshish. He went down to Jaffa and found a ship bound for Tarshish; he paid his fare and boarded it, to go with them to Tarshish, to get away from the Lord. (Jon 1:1–3)

¹Now the Lord ordained that a great fish should swallow Jonah; and Jonah remained in the belly of the fish for three days and three nights.
²From the belly of the fish, Jonah prayed to the Lord, his God

. . .

¹¹The Lord spoke to the fish, which then vomited Jonah onto the dry land. (Jon 2:1–2, 11)

On Jonah see commentary on 37:139–48 (with further references). Muslim commentators often imagine a different sequence of events. *Tafsīr al-Jalālayn* writes that Jonah "left in a rage" after he was mistreated by the people to whom he preached. Only then was he swallowed by a fish.

---

⁸⁹And [remember] Zechariah, when he cried out to his Lord, 'My Lord! Do not leave me without an heir and You are the best of inheritors.' ⁹⁰So We answered his prayer and gave him John, and cured for him his wife [of infertility]. They were indeed active in [performing] good works, and they would supplicate Us with eagerness and awe and were humble before Us.

21:89–90 On Zechariah, see 3:37–44; 6:85; 19:2–15 and commentary on 19:2–6, 7–11.

---

⁹¹And [remember] her who guarded her chastity, so We breathed into her of Our spirit, and made her and her son a sign for all the nations.

21:91 On Mary's virginal conception of Jesus, cf. 3:45–47; 19:17–34; 66:12. The Qur'ān, like the Gospel of Luke, has Mary conceive through the agency of and the parallel passage in God's spirit:

> ³⁴Mary said to the angel, 'But how can this come about, since I have no knowledge of man?'
> ³⁵The angel answered, 'The Holy Spirit will come upon you, and the power of the Most High will cover you with its shadow. And so the child will be holy and will be called Son of God. (Luk 1:34–35)

On the Spirit in the Qur'ān, see commentary on 2:87 (with further references).

<hr />

⁹²This community of yours is indeed one community and I am your Lord. So worship Me. ⁹³They have fragmented their religion among themselves, [but] everyone of them will return to Us.

21:92–93 This is possibly a reference to the discord among Christians or between Christians and Jews (cf. 2:113; 5:14). See commentary on the similar passage, 23:51–53.

<hr />

⁹⁴Whoever is faithful and does righteous deeds, his endeavour shall not go unappreciated, and We will indeed record it for him. ⁹⁵It is forbidden for [the people of] any town that We have destroyed [to return to the world]: they shall not return, ⁹⁶until when Gog and Magog are let loose and they race down from every slope,

21:96 Ezekiel 38:2 speaks of a king named Gog from the land of Magog ("Son of man, turn towards Gog, to the country of Magog, towards the paramount prince of Meshech and Tubal, and prophesy against him"), and Revelation alludes to an apocalyptic event in which two nations—Gog and Magog—will be unleashed to wreak havoc on earth before the apocalypse:

⁷When the thousand years are over, Satan will be released from his prison ⁸and will come out to lead astray all the nations in the four quarters of the earth, Gog and Magog, and mobilise them for war, his armies being as many as the sands of the sea. (Rev 20:7–8)

Traditions surrounding Gog and Magog subsequently became quite popular in Late Antiquity, in particular in Syriac texts such as the *Alexander Romance* and *Alexander Legend.* See further 18:92–97 and commentary on those verses (cr. Mehdy Shaddel).

---

⁹⁷and the true promise draws near [to its fulfilment], behold, the faithless will look on with a fixed gaze: 'Woe to us! We have certainly been oblivious of this! We have indeed, been wrongdoers!'

⁹⁸Indeed, you and what [idols] you worship besides God will be fuel for hell, and you will enter it. ⁹⁹Had they been gods, they would not have entered it, and they will all remain in it [forever]. ¹⁰⁰Their lot therein will be groaning, and they will not hear anything in it.

21:98–100 As Geiger (*Judaism and Islam,* 56) notes, the Talmud (b. Sukkah 29a) insists that false gods too are punished: "There is no nation which is smitten that its gods are not smitten together with it, as it is said, And against all the gods of Egypt I will execute judgments (Exo 12:12)."

---

¹⁰¹Indeed, those to whom there has gone beforehand [the promise of] the best reward from Us will be kept away from it. ¹⁰²They will not hear even its faint sound and they will remain [forever] in what their souls desire. ¹⁰³The Great Terror will not upset them, and the angels will receive them [saying]: 'This is your day which you were promised' ¹⁰⁴—the day We shall roll up the heaven like

rolling of the scrolls [meant] for writings. We will bring it back just as We began the first creation—a promise [binding] on Us. [That] indeed We will do.

21:104 The metaphor of the skies being rolled up like scrolls (cf. 39:67) is used in both Isaiah 34:4b ("The heavens will be rolled up like a scroll and all their array will fade away, as fade the leaves falling from the vine, as fade those falling from the fig tree") and Revelation 6:14 ("The sky disappeared like a scroll rolling up and all the mountains and islands were shaken from their places").

---

^{105}Certainly We wrote in the Psalms, after the Torah: 'My righteous servants shall indeed inherit the earth.'

21:105 Here Qarai renders as "Torah" the Arabic word *dhikr,* which means simply "remembrance." In this verse the Qur'ān seems to declare that it is quoting from the Psalms. However, while the quotation is evocative of material in Psalm 37, it is not a direct citation:

> ^{9}For evil-doers will be annihilated, while those who hope in the Lord shall have the land for their own (NRSV: "shall inherit the land").
> . . .
> ^{28}For the Lord loves justice and will not forsake his faithful. Evil-doers will perish eternally, the descendants of the wicked be annihilated,
> ^{29}but the upright shall have the land for their own (NRSV: "shall inherit the land"), there they shall live for ever. (Psa 37:9, 28–29)

One might also compare Mat 5:4: "Blessed are the gentle: they shall have the earth as inheritance." Cf. also 1 Enoch 5:7. On the term rendered here as "Psalms" (*zabūr,* pl. *zubur*), see commentary on 17:55 (with further references).

---

^{106}There is indeed in this a proclamation for a devout people.
^{107}We did not send *you* but as mercy to all the nations.

[108]*Say,* 'It has been revealed to me that your God is the One God. So will you submit?' [109]But if they turn away, *say,* 'I have proclaimed to you all alike, and I do not know whether what you have been promised is far or near. [110]He indeed knows whatever is spoken aloud and knows whatever you conceal. [111]I do not know—maybe it is a test for you and an enjoyment for a while.'

[112]He said, 'My Lord! Judge [between us and the polytheists] with justice.' 'Our Lord is the All-beneficent; [He is our] resort against what you allege.'

22. *AL-ḤAJJ*, THE PILGRIMAGE

In the Name of God, the All-beneficent, the All-merciful.

¹O mankind! Be wary of your Lord! The quake of the Hour is indeed a terrible thing. ²The day that you will see it, every suckling female will be unmindful of what she suckled, and every pregnant female will deliver her burden, and you will see the people drunk, yet they will not be drunken, but God's punishment is severe.

³Among the people are those who dispute about God without any knowledge and follow every froward devil, ⁴about whom it has been decreed that he will mislead those who take him for a friend and conduct them toward the punishment of the Blaze.

⁵O people! If you are in doubt about the resurrection, [consider that] We created you from dust, then from a drop of [seminal] fluid, then from a clinging mass, then from a fleshy tissue, partly formed and partly unformed, so that We may manifest [Our power] to you. We lodge in the wombs whatever We wish for a specified term, then We bring you forth as infants, then [We rear you] so that you may come of age. [Then] there are some of you who are taken away, and there are some of you who are relegated to the nethermost age, such that he knows nothing after [having possessed] some knowledge.

And you see the earth torpid, yet when We send down water upon it, it stirs and swells and grows every delightful kind [of plant].

22:5 On the creation of humanity from dust, see commentary on 11:61 (with further references). The Qurʾān here argues for God's ability to raise the bodies of the dead on the basis of God's initial creation of humans (i.e., Adam) from dust. This argument might be compared to the words of the mother in 2 Maccabees who comforts her son (soon to be killed for his faith) by arguing that his initial creation by God suggests God's power to bring him back to life:

> [22]'I do not know how you appeared in my womb; it was not I who endowed you with breath and life, I had not the shaping of your every part.
> [23]And hence, the Creator of the world, who made everyone and ordained the origin of all things, will in his mercy give you back breath and life, since for the sake of his laws you have no concern for yourselves.' (2Ma 7:22–23)

---

[6]All that is because God is the Reality and it is He who revives the dead, and He has power over all things, [7]and because the Hour is bound to come, there is no doubt in it, and God will resurrect those who are in the graves.

[8]Among the people are those who dispute concerning God without knowledge or guidance, or an enlightening scripture, [9]turning aside disdainfully to lead [others] astray from the way of God. For such there is disgrace in this world, and on the Day of Resurrection We will make him taste the punishment of the burning: [10]'That is because of what your hands have sent ahead, and because God is not tyrannical to the servants.'

[11]And among the people are those who worship God on the [very] fringe: if good fortune befalls him, he is content with it; but if an ordeal visits him he makes a turnabout, to become a loser in the world and the Hereafter. That is clear loss. [12]He invokes besides God that which can bring him neither benefit nor harm. That is extreme error.

22:12 On the description of anything unbelievers worship other than God as powerless, see commentary on 10:18 (with further references).

---

[13]He invokes someone whose harm is surely likelier than his benefit. An evil master indeed and an evil companion!

[14]God will indeed admit those who have faith and do righteous deeds into gardens with streams running in them. Indeed, God does whatever He desires.

22:14 On the streams that run "under" (Ar. *taḥt;* Qarai has "in") paradise, see commentary on 2:25 (with further references).

---

[15]Whoever thinks that God will not help him in this world and the Hereafter, let him stretch a rope to the ceiling and hang himself, and see if his artifice would remove his rage.

[16]Thus have We sent it down as clear signs, and indeed God guides whomever He desires.

[17]God will indeed judge between the faithful, the Jews, the Sabaeans, the Christians, the Magians and the polytheists on the Day of Resurrection. God is indeed witness to all things.

22:17 This is the only mention of the "Magians" (Zoroastrians) in the Qurʾān.

---

[18]Have you not regarded that whoever is in the heavens and whoever is on the earth prostrates to God, as well as the sun, the moon, and the stars, the mountains, the trees, and the animals and many humans? And many have come to deserve the punishment.

Whomever God humiliates will find none who may bring him honour. Indeed, God does whatever He wishes.

22:18 See commentary on 16:49 (with further references).

---

[19]These two contending groups contend concerning their Lord. As for those who are faithless, cloaks of fire will be cut out for them, and boiling water will be poured on their heads, [20]with which their skins and entrails will fuse, [21]and there will be clubs of iron for them. [22]Whenever they desire to leave it out of anguish, they will be turned back into it [and told]: 'Taste the punishment of the burning!'

[23]God will indeed admit those who have faith and do righteous deeds into gardens with streams running in them, adorned therein with bracelets of gold and pearl, and their dress therein will be silk.

22:23 On the rivers which run under (Ar. *taḥt;* Qarai has "in") paradise, see commentary on 2:25 (with further references).

---

[24]They have been guided to chaste speech, and guided to the path of the All-laudable.

[25]Indeed, those who are faithless and who bar from the way of God and the Sacred Mosque, which We have assigned for all people, the native and the visitor being equal therein—whoever wrongfully tries to commit violation in it, We shall make him taste a painful punishment.

²⁶When We settled for Abraham the site of the House, [saying], Do not ascribe any partners to Me, and purify My House for those who circle around it and those who stand [in it for prayer] and those who bow and prostrate themselves. ²⁷And proclaim the *ḥajj* to all the people: they will come to you on foot and on lean camels, coming from distant places, ²⁸that they may witness the benefits for them, and mention God's Name during the known days over the livestock He has provided them. So eat thereof, and feed the destitute and the needy. ²⁹Then let them do away with their untidiness, fulfill their vows, and circle around the Ancient House. ³⁰That, and whoever venerates the sacraments of God, that is better for him with his Lord.

You are permitted [animals of] grazing livestock, except for what will be recited to you. So avoid the abomination of idols and avoid false speech, ³¹as persons having pure faith in God, not ascribing partners to Him. Whoever ascribes partners to God is as though he had fallen from a height, then [his corpse] were devoured by vultures, or [his remains were] blown away by the wind, far and wide. ³²That, and whoever venerates the sacraments of God—indeed that arises from the Godwariness of hearts. ³³You may benefit from them until a specified time, then their place of sacrifice is by the Ancient House. ³⁴For every nation We have appointed a rite so that they might mention God's Name over the livestock He has provided them.

Your God is the One God, so submit to Him. And *give* good news to the humble ³⁵—those whose hearts tremble with awe when God is mentioned and who are patient through whatever visits them, and who maintain the prayer and spend out of what We have provided them.

³⁶We have appointed for you the [sacrificial] camels as part of God's sacraments. There is good for you in them. So mention the

Name of God over them as they stand, and when they have fallen on their flanks, eat from them and feed the self-contained needy and the mendicant. Thus have We disposed them for your benefit so that you may give thanks. ³⁷It is not their flesh or blood that reaches God; rather, it is your piety that reaches Him. Thus has He disposed them for your benefit so that you may magnify God for His guiding you. And *give* good news to the virtuous.

22:26–37 This passage is traditionally understood as the establishment of the Meccan pilgrimage on the basis of Abraham's precedent. The traditional authorities, however, are not sure whether to make this a Meccan or Medinan Sura (the Cairo edition makes it a Middle Medinan Sura but most classical Muslim authorities make it Meccan). Moreover, this passage never mentions Mecca itself; it is possible that the rituals of the *hajj* in Mecca, including circumambulation of the Kaʿba (v. 29) and the sacrifice of animals (vv. 34, 36) were developed later as scholars sought to interpret these verses (although the text in v. 33 suggests that the sacrifice should take place at the Kaʿba and not at Mina, where it is done today). On the possibility that the "House" (v. 26) or "Ancient House" (v. 33) which Abraham established was not in Mecca, see commentary on 2:125–28 and 14:35–41.

The term in verse 31 rendered here as "having pure faith in God" (*ḥunafāʾa li-Llah*) is connected to the description of Abraham as a *ḥanīf*, "a devoted, gentile monotheist" (see further commentary on 16:120–23).

In verses 32 and 36 the Qurʾān speaks of "sacraments of God" (*shaʿāʾir Allāh;* cf. 2:158; 5:2) These "sacraments" are rituals of religious importance (v. 32; see Ambros, 149). In 2:158 they are the circumambulation of al-Ṣafā and al-Marwa and in 22:36 the sacrifice of animals.

The idea of sacrifice here (v. 37) is close to numerous Biblical passages on sacrifice (Isa 1:11; Jer 6:20; Amo: 5:21–22; Mic 6:6–7). Especially close are 1 Samuel 15 and Matthew 9:

> To which, Samuel said: Is the Lord pleased by burnt offerings and sacrifices or by obedience to the Lord's voice? Truly, obedience is better than sacrifice, submissiveness than the fat of rams. (1Sa 15:22)

> Go and learn the meaning of the words: Mercy is what pleases me, not sacrifice. And indeed I came to call not the upright, but sinners. (Mat 9:13; cf. Mar 12:33; 1Sa 15:22; Hos 6:6; Pro 11:3)

³⁸God will indeed defend those who have faith. Indeed, God does not like any ingrate traitor. ³⁹Those who are fought against are permitted [to fight] because they have been wronged, and God is indeed able to help them ⁴⁰—those who were expelled from their homes unjustly only because they said, 'God is our Lord.' Had not God repulsed the people from one another, ruin would have befallen the monasteries, churches, synagogues and mosques in which God's Name is much invoked. God will surely help those who help Him. God is indeed all-strong, all-mighty.

22:40 The word translated here as "monasteries" is *ṣawāmi ʿ*, literally "hermit cells" (from Ethiopic *ṣōmā ʾt*). "Synagogues" is the rendering of *ṣalawāt,* which could simply mean "places of prayer" (with no special connection to Judaism; Arberry translates "oratories"). "Mosques" is the rendering of *masājid,* which may rather mean any place where people prostrate (Ar. *s.j.d.*) to God. This verse hardly fits with the traditional picture of Muḥammad's Mecca—which featured pagans but not Jews or Christians—or with Muḥammad's Medina—where (according to the traditional biography) he attacked and ultimately exiled, enslaved, or killed the Jewish population. It suggests that the Qurʾān's original context was quite different, that it was interreligious, marked by a significant Christian presence, including not only churches but also monasteries.

⁴¹Those who, if We granted them power in the land, will maintain the prayer, give the *zakāt,* bid what is right and forbid what is wrong, and with God rests the outcome of all matters.

⁴²If they impugn *you,* the people of Noah and ʿĀd and Thamūd have impugned before them, ⁴³[as well as] the people of Abraham, the people of Lot, ⁴⁴and the inhabitants of Midian, and Moses was also impugned. But I gave the faithless a respite, then I seized them, and how was My rebuttal! ⁴⁵How many towns We have destroyed when they had been wrongdoers! So they lie fallen on their trellises, their wells neglected and their palaces in ruins!

⁴⁶Have they not traveled through the land so that they may have hearts with which they may exercise their reason, or ears by which they may hear? Indeed, it is not the eyes that turn blind, but it is the hearts in the breasts that turn blind!

22:45–46 Here the Qurʾān suggests that its audience is close to the ruins of towns God has destroyed. One might compare the allusion in Q 37 to the ruins of Lot's people (Sodom and Gomorrah). See commentary on 37:133–38. Cf. also 14:14.

On the description of unbelievers as blind or blinded (v. 46), see commentary on 7:179 (with further references).

---

⁴⁷They ask *you* to hasten the punishment, though God will never break His promise. Indeed, a day with *your* Lord is like a thousand years by your reckoning.

22:47 On the use of a "thousand years," see commentary on 70:4 (with further references).

---

⁴⁸To how many a town did I give respite while it was doing wrong! Then I seized it, and toward Me is the destination.
⁴⁹*Say*, 'O mankind! I am only a manifest warner to you!' ⁵⁰As for those who have faith and do righteous deeds, for them will be forgiveness and a noble provision. ⁵¹But as for those who contend with Our signs, seeking to frustrate [their purpose], they shall be the inmates of hell.
⁵²We did not send any apostle or prophet before *you* but that when he recited [the scripture] Satan interjected [something] in his

recitation. Thereat God nullifies whatever Satan has interjected, and then God confirms His signs, and God is All-knowing, All-wise.

22:52 What Qarai translates as "when he recited [the scripture]" in fact means simply "when he wished" (*idhā tamannā*). Qarai's translation reflects the traditional explanation of this verse with the story of the Satanic verses, according to which Satan interjected words into the mind of Muḥammad after he recited Qur'ān 53:19-20. According to this story God "nullified" the words of Satan when the angel Gabriel informed Muḥammad that these words had come from Satan.

The notion that God protects believers from Satan's guile is common in the Qur'ān (cf. 4:117–19; 7:16–18; 15:39; 17:62–65; 38:82). Here it is applied specifically to prophets.

---

⁵³That He may make what Satan has thrown in a test for those in whose hearts is a sickness and those whose hearts have hardened. The wrongdoers are indeed steeped in extreme defiance. ⁵⁴And so that those who have been given knowledge may know that it is the truth from *your* Lord, and so that they may have faith in it, and their hearts may be humbled before Him. God indeed guides those who have faith to a straight path.

⁵⁵Those who are faithless will persist in their doubt about it until the Hour will overtake them suddenly, or they are overtaken by the punishment of an inauspicious day. ⁵⁶On that day all sovereignty will belong to God: He will judge between them. Then those who have faith and do righteous deeds will be in gardens of bliss, ⁵⁷and those who are faithless and deny Our signs—for such there will be a humiliating punishment.

⁵⁸Those who migrate in the way of God and then are slain, or die, God will surely provide them with a good provision. God is

indeed the best of providers. ⁵⁹He will admit them into an abode they are pleased with. God is indeed all-knowing, all-forbearing.

⁶⁰So will it be; and whoever retaliates with the like of what he has been made to suffer, and is aggressed against again thereafter, God will surely help him. God is indeed all-excusing, all-forgiving.

⁶¹So will it be, because God makes the night pass into the day and makes the day pass into the night, and because God is all-hearing, all-seeing.

⁶²So will it be, because God is the Reality, and what they invoke besides Him is nullity, and because God is the All-exalted, the All-great.

⁶³Have *you* not regarded that God sends down water from the sky, whereupon the earth turns green? God is indeed all-attentive, all-aware. ⁶⁴To Him belongs whatever is in the heavens and whatever is in the earth. Indeed, God is the All-sufficient, the All-laudable.

⁶⁵Have *you* not regarded that God has disposed for you[r benefit] whatever there is in the earth, and [that] the ships sail at sea by His command, and He sustains the heaven lest it should fall on the earth, excepting [when it does so] by His leave? God is indeed most kind and merciful to mankind. ⁶⁶It is He who gave you life, then He makes you die, then He brings you to life. Man is indeed very ungrateful.

⁶⁷For every nation We have appointed rites [of worship] which they observe; so let them not dispute with *you* about *your* religion. And *invite* to *your* Lord. *You* are indeed on a straight guidance. ⁶⁸But if they dispute with *you, say,* 'God knows best what you are doing. ⁶⁹God will judge between you on the Day of Resurrection concerning that about which you used to differ. ⁷⁰Do you not know that God knows whatever there is in the heaven

and the earth? All that is indeed in a Book. That is indeed easy for God.'

⁷¹They worship besides God that for which He has not sent down any authority, and of which they have no knowledge. The wrongdoers will have no helper. ⁷²When Our manifest signs are recited to them, *you* perceive denial on the faces of the faithless: they would almost pounce upon those who recite Our signs to them. *Say,* 'Shall I inform you about something worse than that? The Fire which God has promised the faithless, and it is an evil destination.'

⁷³O people! Listen to a parable that is being drawn: Indeed, those whom you invoke besides God will never create [even] a fly even if they all rallied to do so! And if a fly should take away something from them, they can not recover that from it. Feeble is the pursuer and the pursued!

⁷⁴They do not regard God with the regard due to Him. God is indeed all-strong, all-mighty. ⁷⁵God chooses messengers from angels and from mankind. God is indeed all-hearing, all-seeing.

22:75 On the idea that divine messages would be brought by an angel, see commentary on 6:50 (with further references).

---

⁷⁶He knows that which is before them and that which is behind them, and to God all matters are returned.

⁷⁷O you who have faith! Bow down and prostrate yourselves and worship your Lord, and do good, so that you may be felicitous. ⁷⁸And wage *jihād* for the sake of God, a *jihād* which is worthy of Him. He has chosen you and has not placed for you any obstacle in the religion, the faith of your father, Abraham. He

named you '*muslims*' before, and in this, so that the Apostle may be a witness to you, and that you may be witnesses to mankind. So maintain the prayer, give the *zakāt,* and hold fast to God. He is your Master—an excellent master and an excellent helper.

23. *AL-MU'MINŪN*, THE FAITHFUL

In the Name of God, the All-beneficent, the All-merciful.

¹Certainly the faithful have attained salvation ²—those who are humble in their prayers, ³avoid vain talk, ⁴carry out their [duty of] *zakāt,* ⁵guard their private parts ⁶(except from their spouses or their slave women, for then they are not blameworthy; ⁷but whoever seeks [anything] beyond that—it is they who are transgressors), ⁸and those who keep their trusts and covenants ⁹and are watchful of their prayers. ¹⁰It is they who will be the inheritors, ¹¹who shall inherit paradise and will remain in it [forever].

23:11 The word *firdaws* ("paradise," from Gr. *paradeisos,* perhaps originally from Persian *pairidaēza*) appears only here and at 18:107.

---

¹²Certainly We created man from an extract of clay.

23:12 On the creation of Adam from clay, see commentary on 6:2 (with further references).

---

¹³Then We made him a drop of [seminal] fluid [lodged] in a secure abode. ¹⁴Then We created the drop of fluid as a clinging mass. Then We created the clinging mass as a fleshy tissue. Then We created the fleshy tissue as bones. Then We clothed the bones with flesh. Then We produced him as [yet] another creature. So blessed is God, the best of creators!

¹⁵Then, of course, you die after that. ¹⁶Then you will indeed be raised up on the Day of Resurrection.

¹⁷Certainly We created above you the seven levels and We have not been oblivious of creation. ¹⁸We sent down water from the sky in a measured manner, and We lodged it within the ground, and We are indeed able to take it away. ¹⁹Then with it We produced for you gardens of date palms and vines. There are abundant fruits in them for you, and you eat from them. ²⁰And a tree that grows on Mount Sinai which produces oil and a seasoning for those who eat.

23:20 The reference to a tree on Mt. Sinai that produces oil can be compared with 24:35 (the "Light Verse"; cf. also 95:1–2, which mentions fig, olive, and Mt. Sinai). That latter verse, however, is set in heaven, whereas the Qurʾān here seems to mean a sort of tree which really does grow on Mt. Sinai and is useful to people for its oil and "seasoning." Since Mt. Sinai is not known for olive trees, however, Horovitz (*KU,* 124) wonders whether Muḥammad may have been thinking here of the Mount of Olives. Cf. commentary on 52:1 and 95:1–3.

---

²¹There is indeed a moral for you in the cattle: We give you to drink of that which is in their bellies, and you have many uses in them, and you eat some of them, ²²and you are carried on them and on ships.

²³Certainly We sent Noah to his people, and he said, 'O my people! Worship God! You have no other god besides Him. Will you not then be wary [of Him]?'

²⁴But the elite of the faithless from among his people said, 'This is just a human being like you, who seeks to dominate you. Had God wished, He would have sent down angels. We never heard of such a thing among our forefathers. ²⁵He is just a man possessed by madness. So bear with him for a while.'

²⁶He said, 'My Lord! Help me, for they impugn me.'

²⁷So We revealed to him: 'Build the ark before Our eyes and by Our revelation. When Our edict comes and the oven gushes [a stream of water], bring into it a pair of every kind [of animal], and your family, except those of them against whom the decree has gone beforehand, and do not plead with Me for those who are wrongdoers: they shall indeed be drowned.' ²⁸'When you, and those who are with you, are settled in the ark, say, "All praise belongs to God, who has delivered us from the wrongdoing lot." ²⁹And say, "My Lord! Land me with a blessed landing, for You are the best of those who bring ashore."'

³⁰There are indeed signs in this; and indeed We have been testing.

23:23–30 On Noah in the Qur'ān, see commentaries on Q 11:40–48 and Q 71:1–28 (with further references). On the expectation of unbelievers that divine messages would be brought by an angel (see v. 24), see commentary on 6:50 (with further references).

The way the Qur'ān has God tell Noah "do not plead with Me for those who are wrongdoers: they shall indeed be drowned" (v. 27) may be a reference to his lost son, regarding which see commentary on 11:40–48.

In verse 27 (cf. 11:40) the Qur'ān also speaks of the "oven" (*tannūr*) gushing forth water. This may reflect a midrashic tradition—for example, in *Leviticus Rabbah* (which dates from around the period of the Qur'ān's origins)—

mentioned by Speyer (*BEQ,* 103) that the waters of the flood were hot: "R. Joḥanan said, "Every single drop [of rain] which the Holy One, blessed be He, brought down on the generation of the Flood, He made to boil in Gehinnom" (*Leviticus Rabbah* 7:6). Similar is a tradition in the Talmud: "With hot passion they sinned, and by hot water they were punished." (b. Sanhedrin 108b; see Geiger, *Judaism and Islam,* 86).

———

³¹Then after them We brought forth another generation, ³²and We sent them an apostle from among themselves, saying, 'Worship God! You have no other god besides Him. Will you not then be wary [of Him]?'

³³Said the elite of his people who were faithless and who denied the encounter of the Hereafter and whom We had given affluence in the life of the world: 'This is just a human being like yourselves: he eats what you eat, and drinks what you drink. ³⁴If you obey a human being like yourselves, you will indeed be losers. ³⁵Does he promise you that when you have died and become bones and dust you will indeed be raised [from the dead]? ³⁶Far-fetched, far-fetched is what you are promised! ³⁷There is nothing but the life of this world: we live and die, and we will not be resurrected. ³⁸He is just a man who has fabricated a lie against God, and we will not believe in him.'

³⁹He said, 'My Lord! Help me, for they impugn me.'

⁴⁰Said He, 'In a little while they will become regretful.'

⁴¹So the Cry seized them justly and We turned them into a scum. So away with the wrongdoing lot!

23:31–41 The account of an unnamed prophet, with no obvious connection to any Biblical character. Verses 33-34 have the prophet's opponents express surprise that a mortal (i.e., not an angel) could be a divine messenger (on this see commentary on 6:50, with further references). *Tafsīr al-Jalālayn* identifies this prophet as Hūd.

---

⁴²Then after them We brought forth other generations. ⁴³No nation can advance its time nor can it defer it.

⁴⁴Then We sent Our apostles successively. Whenever there came to a nation its apostle, they impugned him, so We made them follow one another [to extinction] and We turned them into folktales. So away with the faithless lot!

⁴⁵Then We sent Moses and Aaron, his brother, with Our signs and a manifest authority ⁴⁶to Pharaoh and his elites; but they acted arrogantly and they were a tyrannical lot. ⁴⁷They said, 'Shall we believe two humans like ourselves, while their people are our slaves?' ⁴⁸So they impugned the two of them, whereat they were among those who were destroyed.

23:45–48 On Moses's and Aaron's confrontation with Pharaoh in the Qur'ān, see commentary on 26:30–45 (with further references).

---

⁴⁹Certainly We gave Moses the Book so that they might be guided, ⁵⁰and We made the son of Mary and his mother a sign and sheltered them in a level highland with flowing water.

23:50 The Qur'ān here alludes to the miracle of the water which sprang forth at the command of the infant Jesus to succor his mother, Mary (Q 19:24; on the Arabic term [*ma'īn*] translated "flowing water" cf. 37:45; 56:18; 67:30). The Qur'ānic allusion reflects both an episode from the *Gospel of Pseudo-Matthew* (20:1–2) during the Holy Family's flight to Egypt and the traditions surrounding the Kathisma church in Jerusalem, where a nearby spring of water (brought into the church through a small channel) is associated with a site connected to Jesus' birth. In the present verse the Qurʾān may allude to the site of the Kathisma church itself, which is indeed in a "highland" (outside of Jerusalem) and contained a spring (see Dye, "Lieux saints communs," 29–30). See further (including the citation from *Pseudo-Matthew*) commentary on 19:16–26.

---

⁵¹O apostles! Eat of the good things and act righteously. I indeed know well what you do. ⁵²This community of yours is indeed one community and I am your Lord, so be wary of Me.

⁵³But they fragmented their religion among themselves, each party boasting about what it had.

23:51–53 This passage seems to be addressed to all the prophets, although God addresses them as though they were living at the same time and make up one community. Verse 53 (cf. the mention of Jesus in v. 50) is likely a reference to divisions among Christians (cf. 5:14) and between Christians and Jews. This verse should be compared to 21:92–93, which likewise follows a reference to Jesus (21:91). The word in verse 53 which Qarai translates as "religion" is *zubur* and means elsewhere "scriptures" or (in the singular *zabūr*) "Psalms" (see commentary on 17:55, with further references).

---

⁵⁴So *leave* them in their stupor for a while.

⁵⁵Do they suppose that whatever wealth and children We provide them [is because] ⁵⁶We are eager to bring them good? No, they are not aware!

⁵⁷Indeed, those who are apprehensive for the fear of their Lord, ⁵⁸and believe in the signs of their Lord, ⁵⁹and do not ascribe partners to their Lord; ⁶⁰who give whatever they give while their hearts tremble with awe, that they are going to return to their

Lord [61]—it is they who are zealous in [performing] good works and take the lead in them.

[62]We task no soul except according to its capacity, and with Us is a book that speaks the truth, and they will not be wronged. [63]Their hearts are indeed in a stupor in regard to this, and there are other deeds besides, which they perpetrate.

[64]When We seize their affluent ones with punishment, behold, they make entreaties [to Us]. [65]'Do not make entreaties today! You will not receive any help from Us. [66]Certainly My signs used to be recited to you, but you used to take to your heels, [67]being disdainful of it, talking nonsense in your nightly sessions.'

[68]Have they not contemplated this discourse, or has anything come to them [in it] that did not come to their forefathers? [69]Is it that they do not recognize their apostle, and so they deny him? [70]Do they say, 'There is madness in him'? No, he has brought them the truth, and most of them are averse to the truth.

[71]Had the Truth followed their desires, the heavens and the earth would have surely fallen apart [along] with those who are in them. We have indeed brought them their reminder, but they are disregardful of their reminder.

[72]Do *you* ask a recompense from them? Yet *your* Lord's recompense is better, and He is the best of providers. [73]*You* indeed invite them to a straight path, [74]and those who do not believe in the Hereafter surely deviate from the path. [75]Should We have mercy upon them and remove their distress, they would surely persist, bewildered in their rebellion. [76]We have already seized them with punishment, yet they did not humble themselves before their Lord, nor will they entreat [Him for mercy] [77]until We open on them the gate of a severe punishment, whereupon they will be despondent in it.

⁷⁸It is He who has created for you your hearing, sight and hearts. Little do you thank. ⁷⁹It is He who created you on the earth, and you will be mustered toward Him. ⁸⁰And it is He who gives life and brings death, and due to Him is the alternation of day and night. Do you not exercise your reason?

⁸¹Indeed, they say, just like what the former peoples said. ⁸²They said, 'What, when we are dead and become dust and bones, shall we be resurrected? ⁸³Certainly we and our fathers were promised this before. [But] these are nothing but myths of the ancients.'

23:83 On the expression "myths of the ancients," see commentary on 68:15 (with further references).

---

⁸⁴*Say,* 'To whom does the earth and whoever it contains belong, if you know?' ⁸⁵They will say, 'To God.' *Say,* 'Will you not then take admonition?'

⁸⁶*Say,* 'Who is the Lord of the seven heavens and the Lord of the Great Throne?' ⁸⁷They will say, '[They belong] to God.' *Say,* 'Will you not then be wary [of Him]?'

⁸⁸*Say,* 'In whose hand is the dominion of all things, and who gives shelter and no shelter can be provided from Him, if you know?' ⁸⁹They will say, '[They all belong] to God.' *Say,* 'Then how are you being deluded?'

⁹⁰We have indeed brought them the truth, and they are surely liars. ⁹¹God has not taken any offspring, neither is there any god besides Him, for then each god would take away what he created, and some of them would surely rise up against others. Clear is God of what they allege! ⁹²The Knower of the sensible and the Unseen, He is above having any partners that they ascribe [to Him].

⁹³*Say,* 'My Lord! If You should show me what they are promised, ⁹⁴then do not put me, my Lord, among the wrongdoing lot.' ⁹⁵We are indeed able to show *you* what We promise them.

⁹⁶*Repel* ill [conduct] with that which is the best. We know best whatever they allege.

23:96 "Do not be mastered by evil, but master evil with good" (Rom 12:21). Cf. Q 13:22.

----

⁹⁷*Say,* 'My Lord! I seek Your protection from the promptings of devils, ⁹⁸and I seek Your protection, my Lord, from their presence near me.'

⁹⁹When death comes to one of them, he says, 'My Lord! Take me back, ¹⁰⁰so that I may act righteously in what I have left behind.'

'By no means! These are mere words that he says.' And before them is a barrier until the day they will be resurrected.

23:99–100 The Qur'ān's reference here (v. 100) to a "barrier" (Ar. *barzakh*) that prevents the dead from returning to the world is loosely related to the eschatology of the parable of the rich man and Lazarus in Luke 16. In this parable the rich man's request that Lazarus return to the world to warn his brothers is refused, with the declaration: "they will not be convinced even if someone should rise from the dead" (Luk 16:31). Cf. commentary on 7:44–50.

Elsewhere (Q 25:53; 55:20) the Qur'ān uses *barzakh* to refer to a barrier between two bodies of water (perhaps earthly and heavenly).

----

¹⁰¹When the Trumpet is blown, there will be no ties between them on that day, nor will they ask [about] each other.

23:101 On the trumpet blast see commentary on 78:18 (with further references).

---

¹⁰²Then those whose deeds weigh heavy in the scales—it is they who are the felicitous.

¹⁰³As for those whose deeds weigh light in the scales—they will be the ones who have ruined their souls, and they will remain in hell [forever]. ¹⁰⁴The Fire will scorch their faces, while they snarl, baring their teeth. ¹⁰⁵'Was it not that My signs were recited to you but you would deny them?' ¹⁰⁶They will say, 'Our Lord! Our wretchedness overcame us, and we were an astray lot. ¹⁰⁷Our Lord! Bring us out of this! Then, if we revert [to our previous conduct], we will indeed be wrongdoers.'

¹⁰⁸He will say, 'Get lost in it, and do not speak to Me! ¹⁰⁹Indeed, there was a part of My servants who would say, "Our Lord! We have believed. So forgive us and have mercy on us, and You are the best of the merciful." ¹¹⁰But you took them by ridicule until they made you forget My remembrance, and you used to laugh at them. ¹¹¹Indeed, I have rewarded them today for their patience. They are indeed the triumphant.'

¹¹²He will say, 'How many years did you remain on earth?' ¹¹³They will say, 'We remained for a day, or part of a day; yet ask those who keep the count.' ¹¹⁴He will say, 'You only remained a little; if only you had known. ¹¹⁵Did you suppose that We created you aimlessly, and that you will not be brought back to Us?'

¹¹⁶So exalted is God, the True Sovereign, there is no god except Him, the Lord of the Noble Throne.

[117]Whoever invokes another god besides God of which he has no proof, his reckoning will indeed rest with his Lord. The faithless will indeed not prosper.

[118]*Say,* 'My Lord, forgive and have mercy, and You are the best of the merciful.'

24. *AL-NŪR*, LIGHT

In the Name of God, the All-beneficent, the All-merciful.

¹[This is] a *sūrah* which We have sent down and prescribed, and We have sent down in it manifest signs so that you may take admonition.

²As for the fornicatress and the fornicator, strike each of them a hundred lashes, and let not pity for them overcome you in God's law, if you believe in God and the Last Day, and let their punishment be witnessed by a group of the faithful.

³The fornicator will not marry anyone but a fornicatress or an idolatress, and the fornicatress will be married by none except a fornicator or an idolater, and that is forbidden to the faithful.

⁴As for those who accuse chaste women and do not bring four witnesses, strike them eighty lashes, and never accept any testimony from them after that, and they are transgressors, ⁵excepting those who repent after that and reform, for God is indeed all-forgiving, all-merciful.

⁶As for those who accuse their wives [of adultery], but have no witnesses except themselves, the testimony of such a man shall be a fourfold testimony [sworn] by God that he is indeed stating the truth ⁷and a fifth [oath] that God's wrath shall be upon him if

he were lying. ⁸The punishment shall be averted from her by her testifying with four oaths [sworn] by God that he is indeed lying, ⁹and a fifth [oath] that God's wrath shall be upon her if he were stating the truth.

¹⁰Were it not for God's grace and His mercy upon you, and that God is all-clement, all-wise. . . . ¹¹Indeed, those who initiated the calumny are a group from among yourselves. Do not suppose it is a bad thing for you. No, it is for your good. Each man among them bears [the onus for] his part in the sin, and as for him who assumed its major burden from among them, there is a great punishment for him.

¹²When you [first] heard about it, why did not the faithful, men and women, think well of their folks, and say, 'This is an obvious calumny'? ¹³Why did they not bring four witnesses to it? So when they could not bring the witnesses, they are liars in God's sight. ¹⁴Were it not for God's grace and His mercy upon you in this world and the Hereafter, there would have befallen you a great punishment for what you ventured into, ¹⁵when you were receiving it on your tongues and were mouthing something of which you had no knowledge, supposing it to be a light matter, while it was a grave [matter] with God. ¹⁶And why did you not, when you heard it, say, 'It is not for us to say such a thing. [O God!] You are immaculate! This is a monstrous calumny!'

¹⁷God advises you lest you should ever repeat the like of it, if you are faithful. ¹⁸God clarifies the signs for you, and God is all-knowing, all-wise.

¹⁹Indeed, those who want indecency to spread among the faithful—there is a painful punishment for them in the world and the Hereafter, and God knows and you do not know. ²⁰Were it not for God's grace and His mercy upon you and that God is all-kind, all-merciful . . .

²¹O you who have faith! Do not follow in Satan's steps. Whoever follows in Satan's steps [should know that] he indeed prompts [you to commit] indecent and wrongful acts. Were it not for God's grace and His mercy upon you, not one of you would ever become pure. But God purifies whomever He wishes, and God is all-hearing, all-knowing.

²²The well-off and opulent among you should not vow that they will give no more to the relatives, the needy, and those who have migrated in the way of God; let them excuse and forbear. Do you not love that God should forgive you? God is all-forgiving, all-merciful.

²³Indeed, those who accuse chaste and unwary faithful women shall be cursed in this world and the Hereafter, and there shall be a great punishment for them ²⁴on the day when witness shall be given against them by their tongues, their hands and their feet concerning what they used to do.

24:24 The idea that one's body will testify against oneself is found in the Talmud (as pointed out already by Geiger, *Judaism and Islam,* 55):

> But the Sages say: A man's limbs testify against him, for it is said: Therefore ye are My witnesses, saith the Lord, and I am God. (b. Hagigah 16a)

The website Corpus Coranicum indicates on this verse a parallel passage in a poem by Jacob of Serugh "On the End of the World and the Day of Judgment" (1:719) in which Jacob declares "the bodies of men will be like scrolls" on which their acts will be written (cr. Joseph Witztum).

---

²⁵On that day, God will pay them in full their due recompense, and they shall know that God is the Manifest Reality.

²⁶Vicious women are for vicious men, and vicious men for vicious women. Good women are for good men, and good men for

good women. These are absolved of what they say [about them]. For them is forgiveness and a noble provision.

[27]O you who have faith! Do not enter houses other than your own until you have announced [your arrival] and greeted their occupants. That is better for you. Maybe you will take admonition. [28]But if you do not find anyone in them, do not enter them until you are given permission. And if you are told: 'Turn back,' then do turn back. That will be more decent on your part. God knows best what you do. [29]There will be no sin upon you in entering [without announcing] uninhabited houses wherein you have goods belonging to you. God knows whatever you disclose and whatever you conceal.

[30]*Tell* the faithful men to cast down their looks and to guard their private parts. That is more decent for them. God is indeed well aware of what they do. [31]And *tell* the faithful women to cast down their looks and to guard their private parts, and not to display their charms, beyond what is [acceptably] visible, and let them draw their scarfs over their bosoms, and not display their charms except to their husbands, or their fathers, or their husband's fathers, or their sons, or their husband's sons, or their brothers, or their brothers' sons, or their sisters' sons, or their women, or their slave girls, or male dependants lacking [sexual] desire, or children uninitiated to women's intimate parts. And let them not thump their feet to make known their hidden ornaments. Rally to God in repentance, O faithful, so that you may be felicitous.

24:31 As pointed out by Holger Zellentin (*Qur'ān's Legal Culture*, 35–41), the Qur'ān's instructions here (cf. 33:59) on the proper conduct and appearance of faithful women reflect the instructions of the third century Syriac Christian text the *Didascalia:*

If you want to become a faithful woman, please your husband only. And when you walk in the street, hide your head with your garment, that because of your veil your great beauty may be hidden. And adorn not the countenance of your face but have downcast looks and walk being veiled. (*Didascalia*, chap. 3, 26).

---

³²Marry off those who are single among you, and the upright among your male and female slaves. If they are poor, God will enrich them out of His bounty, and God is all-bounteous, all-knowing. ³³Those who cannot afford marriage should be continent until God enriches them out of His bounty.

As for those who seek an emancipation deal from among your slaves, make such a deal with them if you know any good in them, and give them out of the wealth of God which He has given you. Do not compel your female slaves to prostitution when they desire to be chaste, seeking the transitory wares of the life of this world. Should anyone compel them, God will indeed be forgiving and merciful to them following their compulsion.

³⁴Certainly We have sent down to you manifest signs and a description of those who passed before you, and an advice for the Godwary.

³⁵God is the Light of the heavens and the earth. The parable of His Light is a niche wherein is a lamp—the lamp is in a glass, the glass as it were a glittering star—lit from a blessed olive tree, neither eastern nor western, whose oil almost lights up, though fire should not touch it. Light upon light. God guides to His Light whomever He wishes. God draws parables for mankind, and God has knowledge of all things.

24:35 Verse 35, known to Islamic tradition as the "Light Verse," is related to the theophany of God on Mt. Sinai (see 23:20 and 95:1–2, both of which allude to an olive tree and Mt. Sinai). At the same time this verse (perhaps because the Qurʾān's author thinks of Mt. Sinai as a cosmic mountain, a meeting place of heaven and earth) also presents a vision of heaven, and the divine presence. In this it incorporates the language of vision passages such as Ezekiel 1:26–27 and Zechariah 4:

> ¹The angel who was talking to me came back and roused me as though rousing someone who was asleep.
> ²And he asked me, 'What do you see?' I replied, 'As I look, there is a lampstand entirely of gold with a bowl at the top of it; it holds seven lamps, with seven openings for the lamps on it.
> ³By it are two olive trees, one to the right and the other to the left.' (Zec 4:1–3)

The light verse (as suggested by Speyer, *BEQ,* 455) also seems to share language with 2 Peter 1:19, which alludes to a lamp in the darkness and a star: "So we have confirmation of the words of the prophets; and you will be right to pay attention to it as to a lamp for lighting a way through the dark, until the dawn comes and the morning star rises in your minds" (2Pe 1:19). From the New Testament one might also compare 1 John 1:5, which speaks of God as light.

Scholars have also speculated that the references to a lamp and a niche reflect a vision of Christian house of worship (perhaps a lighted altar). Bell, who inclines to this interpretation, argues that the following verses (36–38) allude to Christian monasteries and the monks who pray in them.

---

³⁶In houses God has allowed to be raised and wherein His Name is celebrated, He is glorified therein, morning and evening, ³⁷by men whom neither trade nor bargaining distracts from the remembrance of God and the maintenance of prayer and the giving of *zakāt.* They are fearful of a day wherein the hearts and the sights will be transformed, ³⁸so that God may reward them by the best of what they have done and enhance them out of His grace, and God provides for whomever He wishes without any reckoning.

³⁹As for the faithless, their works are like a mirage in a plain, which the thirsty man supposes to be water. When he comes to

it, he finds it to be nothing; but there he finds God, who will pay him his full account, and God is swift at reckoning. ⁴⁰Or like the manifold darkness in a deep sea, covered by billow upon billow, overcast by clouds; manifold [layers of] darkness, one on top of another: when he brings out his hand, he can hardly see it. One whom God has not granted any light has no light.

24:39–40 Speyer (*BEQ*, 455–56) compares these two verses with 2 Peter 2:17, which (although concerned with faithless people, not their works) uses much of the same imagery: "People like this are dried-up springs, fogs swirling in the wind, and the gloom of darkness is stored up for them" (2Pe 2:17). Notably 24:35 also seems to have a relationship with 2 Peter (see commentary on that verse).

----

⁴¹Have you not regarded that God is glorified by everyone in the heavens and the earth, and the birds spreading their wings. Each knows his prayer and glorification, and God knows best what they do. ⁴²To God belongs the kingdom of the heavens and the earth, and toward God is the destination.

⁴³Have you not regarded that God drives the clouds, then He composes them, then He piles them up, whereat you see the rain issuing from their midst? And He sends down hail from the sky, out of the mountains that are in it, and He strikes with it whomever He wishes and turns it away from whomever He wishes. The brilliance of its flashes almost takes away the sight.

⁴⁴God alternates the night and the day. There is indeed a lesson in that for those who have insight.

⁴⁵God created every animal from water. Among them are some that creep upon their bellies, and among them are some that walk on two feet, and among them are some that walk on four. God

creates whatever He wishes. Indeed, God has power over all things.

24:41–45 The reference to birds' glorifying God in verse 41 might be compared with references elsewhere (Q 21:79; 34:10; 38:17–19) to birds' praising God along with David.

The reference in 24:45 to God's creating animals out of water (cf. 21:30; 25:54; 32:8; 77:20; 86:6) reflects the creation story of Genesis 1, which begins with the world in a watery chaos; the implications of Genesis 1 are explicit in 2 Peter 3:5 (see commentary on 21:30) and Ephrem, who explains that God created everything through water: "Thus, through light and water the earth brought forth everything" (Ephrem, *Commentary on Genesis,* 1:10).

---

⁴⁶Certainly We have sent down illuminating signs, and God guides whomever He wishes to a straight path.

⁴⁷They say, 'We have faith in God and His Apostle and we obey.' Then, after that, a part of them refuse to comply, and they do not have faith. ⁴⁸When they are summoned to God and His Apostle that He may judge between them, behold, a part of them turn aside. ⁴⁹But if justice be on their side, they come compliantly to him. ⁵⁰Is there a sickness in their hearts? Do they have doubts, or fear that God and His Apostle will be unjust to them? Rather, it is they who are the wrongdoers.

⁵¹All the response of the faithful, when they are summoned to God and His Apostle that He may judge between them, is to say, 'We hear and obey.' It is they who will be felicitous.

24:51 The declaration attributed to the believers here (cf. 2:285 and 5:7), "We hear and obey" (*sami 'nā wa-aṭa 'nā*) matches the words of the Israelites to Moses in Deuteronomy 5:27: "Go nearer yourself and listen to everything that the Lord our God may say, and then tell us everything that the Lord our God has told you; we shall listen and put it into practice" (*we-shāma'nū we-'āsīnū*)! This declaration might be contrasted with that attributed to the Jews in 2:93 and 4:46, where they are made to say, "We hear and disobey." See further commentary on 2:93.

---

⁵²Whoever obeys God and His Apostle and fears God and is wary of Him—it is they who will be triumphant.

⁵³They swear by God with solemn oaths that if *you* order them they will surely march out. *Say,* 'Do not swear! Honourable obedience [is all that is expected of you]. God is indeed well aware of what you do.'

⁵⁴*Say,* 'Obey God and obey the Apostle.' But if you turn your backs, [you should know that] *he* is only responsible for *his* burden and you are responsible for your own burden, and if you obey *him,* you will be guided, and the Apostle's duty is only to communicate in clear terms.

⁵⁵God has promised those of you who have faith and do righteous deeds that He will surely make them successors in the earth, just as He made those who were before them successors, and He will surely establish for them their religion which He has approved for them, and that He will surely change their state to security after their fear, while they worship Me, not ascribing any partners to Me. Whoever is ungrateful after that—it is they who are the transgressors.

⁵⁶Maintain the prayer and give the *zakāt,* and obey the Apostle so that you may receive [God's] mercy.

⁵⁷Do not suppose that those who are faithless can frustrate [God] on the earth. Their refuge shall be the Fire, and it is surely an evil destination.

⁵⁸O you who have faith! Your slaves and those of you who have not yet reached puberty should seek your permission at three

times: before the dawn prayer, and when you put off your garments at noon, and after the night prayer. These are three times of privacy for you. Apart from these, it is not sinful of you or them to frequent one another [freely]. Thus does God clarify the signs for you, and God is all-knowing, all-wise. [59]When your children reach puberty, let them ask for your permission [at all times] just as those [who matured] before them asked for permission. Thus does God clarify His signs for you, and God is all-knowing, all-wise.

[60]As for women advanced in years who do not expect to marry, there will be no sin upon them if they put off their cloaks, without displaying their adornment. But it is better for them to be modest, and God is all-hearing, all-knowing.

[61]There is no blame upon the blind, nor any blame upon the lame, nor any blame upon the sick, nor upon yourselves if you eat from your own houses, or your fathers' houses, or your mothers' houses, or your brothers' houses, or your sisters' houses, or the houses of your paternal uncles, or the houses of your paternal aunts, or the houses of your maternal uncles, or the houses of your maternal aunts, or those whose keys are in your possession, or those of your friends. There will be no blame on you whether you eat together or separately. So when you enter houses, greet yourselves with a salutation from God, blessed and good. Thus does God clarify His signs for you so that you may exercise your reason.

24:61 "As you enter his house, salute it." (Mat 10:12)

---

[62]Indeed, the faithful are those who have faith in God and His Apostle, and when they are with him in a collective undertaking,

they do not leave until they have sought his permission. They who seek *your* permission are those who have faith in God and His Apostle. So when they seek *your* permission for some of their [private] work, give permission to whomever of them *you* wish and *plead* with God to forgive them. God is indeed all-forgiving, all-merciful.

⁶³Do not consider the Apostle's summons amongst you to be like your summoning one another. God certainly knows those of you who slip away shielding one another [from being noticed]. Those who disobey his orders should beware lest an affliction should visit them or a painful punishment should befall them.

⁶⁴Behold! To God indeed belongs whatever is in the heavens and the earth. He certainly knows your state of affairs. The day they are brought back to Him, He will inform them about what they have done, and God has knowledge of all things.

25. *AL-FURQĀN*, THE CRITERION

In the Name of God, the All-beneficent, the All-merciful.

¹Blessed is He who sent down the Criterion to His servant that he may be a warner to all the nations.

25:1 The Arabic behind "Criterion" is *furqān,* a term related most closely to Aramaic or Syriac *purqānā,* meaning "redemption," although here it seems to refer to some type of revelation. See further commentary on 2:53 (with further references).

---

²He, to whom belongs the sovereignty of the heavens and the earth, and who did not take up any offspring, nor has He any partner in sovereignty, and He created everything and determined it in a precise measure.

³Yet they have taken gods besides Him who create nothing and have themselves been created, and who have no control over their own harm or benefit, and have neither control over [their own] death, nor life, nor resurrection.

25:3 On the description of anything unbelievers worship other than God as powerless, see commentary on 10:18 (with further references).

⁴The faithless say, 'This is nothing but a lie that he has fabricated and other people have abetted him in it.' Thus they have certainly come out with wrongdoing and falsehood. ⁵They say, 'He has taken down myths of the ancients and they are dictated to him morning and evening.'

25:5 On the expression "myths of the ancients," see commentary on 68:15 (with further references).

⁶*Say,* 'It has been sent down by Him who knows the hidden in the heavens and the earth. Indeed, He is all-forgiving, all-merciful.'

⁷And they say, 'What sort of apostle is this who eats food and walks in the marketplaces? Why has not an angel been sent down to him so as to be a warner along with him?' ⁸Or, '[Why is not] a treasure thrown to him, or [why does] he [not] have a garden from which he may eat?' And the wrongdoers say, 'You are just following a bewitched man.'

⁹*Look,* how they coin epithets for *you;* so they go astray and cannot find the way.

¹⁰Blessed is He, who will grant *you* better than that if He wishes—gardens with streams running in them, and He will make for *you* palaces.

25:10 On the streams of paradise, see commentary on 2:25 (with further references).

¹¹Indeed, they deny the Hour, and We have prepared a Blaze for those who deny the Hour. ¹²When it sights them from a dis-

tant place, they will hear it raging and roaring. ¹³And when they are cast into a narrow place in it, bound together [in chains], they will pray for [their own] annihilation. ¹⁴[They will be told:] 'Do not pray for a single annihilation today, but pray for many annihilations!'

¹⁵*Say,* 'Is that better, or the everlasting paradise promised to the Godwary, which will be their reward and destination?' ¹⁶There they will have whatever they wish, abiding [forever]—a promise [much] besought, [binding] on *your* Lord.

¹⁷On the day that He will muster them and those whom they worship besides God, He will say, 'Was it you who led astray these servants of Mine, or did they themselves stray from the way?' ¹⁸They will say, 'Immaculate are You! It does not behoove us to take any master in Your stead! But You provided for them and their fathers until they forgot the Reminder, and they were a ruined lot.'

¹⁹So they will certainly impugn you in what you say, and you will neither be able to circumvent [punishment] nor find help, and whoever of you does wrong, We shall make him taste a terrible punishment.

²⁰We did not send any apostles before *you* but that they ate food and walked in marketplaces. We have made you a [means of] test for one another, [to see] if you will be patient [and steadfast], and *your* Lord is all-seeing.

²¹Those who do not expect to encounter Us say, 'Why have angels not been sent down to us, or why do we not see our Lord?' Certainly they are full of arrogance within their souls and have become terribly defiant. ²²The day they will see the angels, there will be no good news for the guilty on that day, and they will say, 'Keep off!' ²³Then We shall attend to the works they have done and turn them into scattered dust.

²⁴On that day the inhabitants of paradise will be in the best abode and an excellent resting place. ²⁵The day when the sky with

its clouds will be split open and the angels will be sent down [in a majestic] descent, ²⁶on that day true sovereignty will belong to the All-beneficent, and it will be a hard day for the faithless.

²⁷It will be a day when the wrongdoer will bite his hands, saying, 'I wish I had followed the Apostle's way! ²⁸Woe to me! I wish I had not taken so and so as a friend! ²⁹Certainly he led me astray from the Reminder after it had come to me, and Satan is a deserter of man.'

³⁰And the Apostle will say, 'O my Lord! Indeed, my people consigned this Qur'ān to oblivion.' ³¹That is how for every prophet We assigned an enemy from among the guilty, and *your* Lord suffices as helper and guide.

³²The faithless say, 'Why has not the Qur'ān been sent down to him all at once?' So it was, that We may strengthen *your* heart with it, and We have recited it [to *you*] in a measured tone. ³³They do not bring *you* any representation but that We bring *you* the truth [in reply to them] and the best exposition.

³⁴Those who will be gathered [scrambling] on their faces toward hell, they are the worse situated and further astray from the [right] way.

³⁵Certainly We gave Moses the Book and We made Aaron, his brother, accompany him as a minister. ³⁶Then We said, 'Let the two of you go to the people who have impugned Our signs.' Then We destroyed them utterly.

³⁷And Noah's people, We drowned them when they impugned the apostles, and We made them a sign for mankind, and We have prepared for the wrongdoers a painful punishment.

25:37 Here the Qur'ān has the people of Noah reject not only Noah but more than one prophet or messenger, a departure from the Biblical story and the other Qur'ānic references to the story of Noah (see commentary on 11:25–39, with further references).

---

³⁸And 'Ād and Thamūd, and the people of Rass, and many generations between them. ³⁹For each of them We drew examples, and each We destroyed utterly.

⁴⁰Certainly they must have passed the town on which an evil shower was rained. Have they not seen it? Rather, they did not expect resurrection [to happen].

⁴¹When they see *you,* they just take *you* in derision: 'Is this the one whom God has sent as an apostle!? ⁴²He was indeed about to lead us astray from our gods, had we not stood firm by them.' Soon they will know, when they sight the punishment, who is further astray from the [right] way.

⁴³Have *you* seen him who has taken his desire to be his god? Is it *your* duty to watch over him? ⁴⁴Do *you* suppose that most of them listen or exercise their reason? They are just like cattle; no, they are further astray from the way.

⁴⁵Have *you* not regarded how *your* Lord spreads the twilight? (Had He wished He would have made it stand still.) Then We made the sun a beacon for it. ⁴⁶Then We retract it toward Ourselves, with a gentle retracting.

⁴⁷It is He who made for you the night as a covering and sleep for rest and He made the day a recall to life.

⁴⁸And it is He who sends the winds as harbingers of His mercy, and We send down from the sky purifying water, ⁴⁹with which We revive a dead country and provide water to many of the cattle and humans We have created. ⁵⁰Certainly We distribute it among them so that they may take admonition. But most people are only bent on ingratitude.

⁵¹Had We wished, We would have sent a warner to every town. ⁵²So *do not obey* the faithless, but *wage* with it a great *jihād* against them.

⁵³It is He who merged the two seas: this one sweet and agreeable, and that one briny and bitter, and between the two He set a barrier and a forbidding hindrance.

25:53 With its reference to two seas (cf. 18:60) and a barrier (*barzakh;* cf. 55:20), the Qur'ān is alluding to the cosmological vision, seen, for example, with Ephrem, by which God set a vault or firmament on the second day of creation (see Gen 1:7) that separated waters in heaven and the waters on earth. The waters on earth became salty, and those in heaven remained fresh:

> The upper waters, because they had been separated on the second day from the lower waters by the firmament set between them, were also sweet like the lower waters. (The upper waters are not those that became salty in the seas on the third day). (Ephrem, *Commentary on Genesis,* 13:1)

---

⁵⁴It is He who created the human being from water, then invested him with ties of blood and marriage, and *your* Lord is all-powerful.

25:54 On the Qur'ān's report here (cf. 32:8, 77:20, 86:6) that God created humans out of water (in 24:45 all animals are said to be created from water), see commentary on 24:41–45.

---

⁵⁵They worship besides God that which neither brings them any benefit nor causes them any harm, and the faithless one is ever an abettor against his Lord.

25:55 On the description of anything unbelievers worship other than God as being powerless, see commentary on 10:18 (with further references).

⁵⁶We did not send *you* except as a bearer of good news and warner. ⁵⁷*Say,* 'I do not ask you any reward for it, except that anyone who wishes should take the way to his Lord.'

25:57 On the idea that a true prophet does not seek a reward, see commentary on 34:47 (with further references).

⁵⁸Put *your* trust in the Living One, who does not die, and *celebrate* His praise. He suffices as one all-aware of the sins of His servants. ⁵⁹He, who created the heavens and the earth and whatever is between them in six days, and then settled on the Throne, the All-beneficent; so ask someone who is well aware about Him.

25:59 On the creation of the heavens and the earth in six days, see commentary on 41:9–12 (with further references). Here (and in 7:54; 10:3; 25:59; 32:4) God "settles" (or "sits") on his throne after creating. Regarding this sequence, see commentary on 32:4 (with further references).

⁶⁰When they are told: 'Prostrate yourselves before the All-beneficent,' they say, 'What is "the All-beneficent"? Shall we prostrate ourselves before whatever *you* bid us?' And it increases their aversion.
⁶¹Blessed is He who appointed houses in the heavens and set in it a lamp and a shining moon. ⁶²It is He who made the night and the day alternate for someone who desires to take admonition, or desires to give thanks.

⁶³The servants of the All-beneficent are those who walk humbly on the earth, and when the ignorant address them, say, 'Peace!' ⁶⁴Those who spend the night for their Lord, prostrating and standing [in worship]. ⁶⁵Those who say, 'Our Lord! Turn away from us the punishment of hell. Its punishment is indeed enduring. ⁶⁶It is indeed an evil station and abode.' ⁶⁷Those who are neither wasteful nor tightfisted when spending, but balanced between these [two extremes]. ⁶⁸Those who do not invoke another deity besides God, and do not kill a soul [whose life] God has made inviolable, except with due cause, and do not commit fornication. (Whoever does that shall encounter its retribution, ⁶⁹the punishment being doubled for him on the Day of Resurrection. In it he will abide in humiliation forever, ⁷⁰except those who repent, attain faith, and act righteously. For such, God will replace their misdeeds with good deeds, and God is all-forgiving, all-merciful. ⁷¹And whoever repents and acts righteously indeed turns to God with due penitence). ⁷²Those who do not give false testimony, and when they come upon frivolity, pass by with dignity.

25:67–72 This passage, along with 6:151–53 and 17:22–39, is sometimes compared to the Ten Commandments (or Decalogue). See commentary on 17:22–39 (with further references).

---

⁷³Those who, when reminded of the signs of their Lord, do not turn a deaf ear and a blind eye to them. ⁷⁴And those who say, 'Our Lord! Give us joy and comfort in our spouses and offspring, and make us *imams* of the Godwary.' ⁷⁵Those shall be rewarded with sublime abodes for their patience and steadfastness, and they shall be met there with greetings and 'Peace,'

25:75 On the "abodes" or "rooms" (Ar. *ghurfa*) of heaven in the Qur'ān, see commentary on 39:20 (with further references).

––––––––––––––

[76]to abide in them [forever], an excellent station and abode.

[77]*Say,* 'Were it not for the sake of summoning you [to faith], what store my Lord would have set by you? But you impugned [me and my summons], and it will be inextricable [from you].'

26. *AL-SHU'ARĀ'*, POETS

In the Name of God, the All-beneficent, the All-merciful.

¹*Ṭā, Sīn, Mīm.* ²These are the signs of the Manifest Book

³*You* are liable to imperil *your* life [out of distress] that they will not have faith. ⁴If We wish, We will send down to them a sign from the heavens before which their heads will remain bowed in humility. ⁵There does not come to them any new reminder from the All-beneficent but that they disregard it. ⁶They have already impugned [the truth], but soon there will come to them the news of what they have been deriding.

⁷Have they not regarded the earth, how many of every splendid kind [of vegetation] We have caused to grow in it? ⁸There is indeed a sign in that; but most of them do not have faith. ⁹Indeed, *your* Lord is the All-mighty, the All-merciful.

¹⁰When *your* Lord called out to Moses: [saying,] 'Go to those wrongdoing people,

26:10–191 *overview* Unlike Q 7 (vv. 59–93), 11 (vv. 25–95), and 54 (vv. 9–42), which relate the account of Moses at the end of a series of "punishment stories," the Qur'ān here begins with an account of Moses (vv. 10–68) and Abraham (vv. 69–102). It then continues with five formulaic accounts which resemble each other closely: Noah (vv. 105–22), Hūd (vv. 123–40), Ṣāliḥ (vv. 141–49), Lot (vv. 160–75), and Shuʿayb (vv. 176–91); these are told in the same order as in Q 7 and 11. For the punishment stories, see also commentary on 7:59–137.

---

¹¹the people of Pharaoh. Will they not be wary [of God]?' ¹²He said, 'My Lord! I fear they will impugn me, ¹³and I will become upset and my tongue will fail me. So send for Aaron [to join me]. ¹⁴Besides, they have a charge against me, and I fear they will kill me.'

¹⁵He said, 'Certainly not! Let both of you go with Our signs: We will indeed be with you, hearing [everything]. ¹⁶So approach Pharaoh and say, "We are indeed envoys of the Lord of the worlds ¹⁷that you let the Children of Israel leave with us."'

26:10–17 On the call of Moses, see commentary on 20:9–16 (with further references). The mention of a "charge" against Moses in verse 14 relates to his killing of an Egyptian (cf. 20:40; 26:19–20; 28:15, 33):

> ¹¹It happened one day, when Moses was grown up, that he went to see his kinsmen. While he was watching their forced labour he also saw an Egyptian striking a Hebrew, one of his kinsmen.
> ¹²Looking this way and that and seeing no one in sight, he killed the Egyptian and hid him in the sand. (Exo 2:11–12)

On the appointment of Aaron as an assistant to Moses, cf. 20:25–32; 25:35; 26:12–14; 28:34. On the demand for the liberation of the Israelites, cf. 7:105.

---

¹⁸He [i.e., Pharaoh] said, 'Did we not rear you as a child among us, and did you not stay with us for years of your life? ¹⁹Then you committed that deed of yours, and you are an ingrate.'

[20]He said, 'I did that when I was astray. [21]So I fled from you, as I was afraid of you. Then my Lord gave me sound judgement and made me one of the apostles. [22]That you have enslaved the Children of Israel—is that the favour with which you reproach me?'

[23]He said, 'And what is "the Lord of all the worlds?"'

[24]He said, 'The Lord of the heavens and the earth and whatever is between them—should you have conviction.'

[25]He said to those who were around him, 'Are you not listening?!'

[26]He said, 'Your Lord and the Lord of your forefathers!'

[27]He said, 'Your messenger, who has been sent to you, is indeed crazy!'

[28]He said, 'The Lord of the east and the west and whatever is between them—should you exercise your reason.'

[29]He said, 'If you take up any god other than me, I will surely make you a prisoner!'

26:18–29 The Qurʾān makes Moses's meeting with Pharaoh here a reunion with his adopted father (in the Qurʾān Pharaoh and his wife adopt Moses [see 28:9], whereas in Exodus it is Pharaoh's daughter [see Exo 2:10] who does so). Pharaoh calls Moses an ingrate (Ar. *min al-kāfirīn*), and he refers to his killing of an Egyptian (cf. 20:40; 28:15, 33). The Qurʾān's notion that Moses returned to Egypt to face the *same* Pharaoh contrasts with Exodus, which has Moses return to Egypt only when the Pharaoh who sought his life for his killing of an Egyptian dies (cf. Exo 2:15; 4:19). Indeed the Qurʾān seems to think of "Pharaoh" (*firʿawn*) not as a title but as a proper name: it is used for only this one figure (the ruler of Egypt in the story of Joseph, Q 12, is referred to as a king).

In making this scene a "family reunion," the Qurʾān has Moses in this scene manifest his faithfulness to God above his faithfulness to his (adoptive) father. This matches the theme in the Qurʾān of holding ties of faith above ties of family (e.g., with Noah's son, 11:40–47 and Abraham's father, 6:74; 19:41–47; 21:51–56; 26:69–93; 37:83–87; 43:26–27).

Pharaoh's demand to be worshipped as a god (v. 29) may reflect the character of Ahasuerus in the Book of Esther. Haman, the Biblical vizier of Ahasuerus, appears in the Qurʾān as the vizier of Pharaoh (see commentary on 28:38, with further references). In (Greek) Esther the Persian king Ahasuerus is presented as a divine figure; Esther refers to him as "one of God's angels" and a "figure of wonder" (Esther 5:2a), and it is forbidden for ordinary people to address him.

Pharaoh's question to Moses in verse 23 might be compared to Exodus 5:2 (and therefore be considered a rhetorical question): "'Who is the Lord,' Pharaoh replied, 'for me to obey what he says and let Israel go? I know nothing of the Lord, and I will not let Israel go'" (Exo 5:2).

---

³⁰He said, 'What if I bring you something [as an] unmistakable [proof]?'

³¹He said, 'Then bring it, if you are truthful.'

³²Thereat he threw down his staff, and behold, it was a manifest python. ³³Then he drew out his hand, and behold, it was white and bright to the onlookers.

³⁴He said to the elite [who stood] around him, 'This is indeed an expert magician ³⁵who seeks to expel you from your land with his magic. So what do you advise?'

³⁶They said, 'Put him and his brother off for a while, and send heralds to the cities ³⁷to bring you every expert magician.'

³⁸So the magicians were gathered for the tryst of a known day, ³⁹and the people were told: 'Will you all gather?!' ⁴⁰'Maybe we will follow the magicians, if they are the victors!'

⁴¹So when the magicians came, they said to Pharaoh, 'Shall we have a reward if we were to be the victors?' ⁴²He said, ' Of course, and you will be among members of my inner circle.'

⁴³Moses said to them, 'Throw down whatever you have to throw!' ⁴⁴So they threw down their sticks and ropes, and said, 'By the might of Pharaoh, we shall surely be victorious!'

⁴⁵Thereat Moses threw down his staff, and behold, it was swallowing what they had faked.

26:30–45 Qarai relates that Moses's staff turned into a python (v. 32) but the Arabic word (*thuʿbān*) is a general term for snake. In the following verse the Qurʾān has Moses show his second wonder—the "white" hand—to Pharaoh, although in Exodus 7 Aaron (not Moses) shows only the wonder of the staff:

> [10]Moses and Aaron went to Pharaoh and did as the Lord had ordered. Aaron threw down his staff in front of Pharaoh and his officials, and it turned into a serpent.
> [11]Then Pharaoh in his turn called for the sages and sorcerers, and by their spells the magicians of Egypt did the same.
> [12]Each threw his staff down and these turned into serpents. But Aaron's staff swallowed up theirs. (Exo 7:10–12)

On the staff of Moses, cf. 2:60; 7:107, 117, 160; 20:17–21; 26:30–32; 27:10; 28:31. On the hand of Moses, cf. 7:108; 20:21; 28:32. See also commentary on 7:106–8 and 20:17–24.

The words of Pharaoh in verse 34 are attributed instead to his advisers in 7:109–10.

In verse 42, Pharaoh suggests that his magicians could be those "near" to him, an expression the Qurʾān uses for God's angels (cf. 28:38; 79:24). The way the Qurʾān has the magicians call out "by the might of Pharaoh" (v. 44) implies that they consider Pharaoh to be a god (cf. 26:29, 28:38, 79:22–24). On Moses's confrontation with Pharaoh and his sorcerers, cf. 7:103–27; 10:75–86; 20:56–73; 23:45–48; 27:10–13; 28:36–38.

---

[46]Thereat the magicians fell down prostrating. [47]They said, 'We believe in the Lord of all the worlds, [48]the Lord of Moses and Aaron.'

[49]He [i.e., Pharaoh] said, 'Did you believe him before I should permit you? He is indeed your chief who has taught you magic! Soon you will know! I will cut off your hands and feet from opposite sides, and I will crucify you all.'

[50]They said, '[There is] no harm [in that]! We shall indeed return to our Lord. [51]We indeed hope our Lord will forgive us our offences for being the first to believe.'

26:46–51 On the belief of Pharaoh's magicians in Moses and his God, cf. 7:120–26; 26:44–51 and commentary on 7:120–26.

---

⁵²Then We revealed to Moses, [saying], 'Set out with My servants at night, for you will be pursued.'

⁵³Then Pharaoh sent heralds to the cities, ⁵⁴[proclaiming:] 'These are indeed a small band. ⁵⁵They have aroused our wrath, ⁵⁶and we are alert [and fully prepared].'

⁵⁷So We took them out of gardens and springs, ⁵⁸and [made them leave behind] treasures and stately homes. ⁵⁹So it was, and We bequeathed them to the Children of Israel.

26:52–59 The reference to a journey "at night" (v. 52) reflects the description in Exodus of the Passover, which took place at night (Exo 12:31; cf. also Q 17:1). Pharaoh's appeal to the Egyptians against the Israelites (vv. 53–56) reflects Exodus 14:5–6:

> ⁵When Pharaoh king of Egypt was told that the people had fled, he and his officials changed their attitude towards the people. 'What have we done,' they said, 'allowing Israel to leave our service?'
> ⁶So Pharaoh had his chariot harnessed and set out with his troops. (Exo 14:5–6)

On the streams of paradise (v. 57), see commentary on 2:25 (with further references).

The Qurʾān's declaration that God "bequeathed" (v. 59) to the Israelites those things from which the Egyptians were expelled (vv. 58–59) may reflect the despoiling of the Egyptians of Exodus 12:35–36. However, Nicolai Sinai ("Inheriting Egypt," 203–8) raises another possibility, namely that the Qurʾān means to have the Israelites inherit the land of Egypt and settle there (instead, as in the Pentateuch, in Canaan). As Sinai notes, in this passage (vv. 46–59) the Qurʾān suggests that the Israeltes were bequeathed "gardens and springs" and "treasures and stately homes," that is, that they settled in the place of the Egyptians who were completely destroyed or expelled (this would fit those passages such as 7:74 and 33:27 that suggest that the God of the Qurʾān makes certain peoples inherit the land of other peoples, what Sinai calls "divine *istikhlāf*"). As Sinai points out, a similar scenario is suggested by 17:103–4 and 28:4–6.

⁶⁰Then they pursued them at sunrise. ⁶¹When the two hosts sighted each other, the companions of Moses said, 'We have indeed been caught up.' ⁶²He said, 'Certainly not! My Lord is indeed with me. He will guide me.'

⁶³Thereupon We revealed to Moses: 'Strike the sea with your staff!' Whereupon it parted, and each part was as if it were a great mountain. ⁶⁴There, We brought the others near, ⁶⁵and We delivered Moses and all those who were with him. ⁶⁶Then We drowned the rest.

26:60–66 Verse 61 might be compared to Exodus 14:10: "As Pharaoh approached, the Israelites looked up—and there were the Egyptians in pursuit of them! The Israelites were terrified and cried out to the Lord for help." Verses 63–64 (the only reference in the Qurʾān to the dividing of the sea) might be compared to Exodus 14:21–23:

> ²¹Then Moses stretched out his hand over the sea, and the Lord drove the sea back with a strong easterly wind all night and made the sea into dry land. The waters were divided
> ²²and the Israelites went on dry ground right through the sea, with walls of water to right and left of them.
> ²³The Egyptians gave chase, and all Pharaoh's horses, chariots and horsemen went into the sea after them.

The phrase, "Then we drowned the rest" (v. 66) appears verbatim in 37:82, where it applies to those who died in the flood of Noah's time. On the Israelites' departure from Egypt and crossing of the sea cf. 7:138; 10:90–92; 17:103; 20:77–78; 28:40; 43:55; 44:23–31.

⁶⁷There is indeed a sign in that, but most of them do not have faith. ⁶⁸Indeed, *your* Lord is the All-mighty, the All-merciful.

⁶⁹*Relate* to them the account of Abraham ⁷⁰when he said to his father and his people, 'What is it that you are worshiping?!'

⁷¹They said, 'We worship idols, and we keep on attending to them.'

⁷²He said, 'Do they hear you when you call them? ⁷³Or do they bring you any benefit, or cause you any harm?'

⁷⁴They said, 'Indeed, we found our fathers doing likewise.'

⁷⁵He said, 'Have you regarded what you have been worshiping, ⁷⁶you and your ancestors? ⁷⁷They are indeed enemies to me, but the Lord of all the worlds, ⁷⁸who created me, it is He who guides me ⁷⁹and provides me with food and drink, ⁸⁰and when I get sick it is He who cures me, ⁸¹who will make me die, then He will bring me to life, ⁸²and who, I hope, will forgive me my faults on the Day of Retribution.'

⁸³'My Lord! Grant me [unerring] judgement and unite me with the Righteous. ⁸⁴Confer on me a worthy repute among the posterity, ⁸⁵and make me one of the heirs to the paradise of bliss. ⁸⁶Forgive my father, for he is one of those who are astray. ⁸⁷Do not disgrace me on the day that they will be resurrected, ⁸⁸the day when neither wealth nor children will avail, ⁸⁹except him who comes to God with a sound heart,' ⁹⁰and paradise will be brought near for the Godwary, ⁹¹and hell will be brought into view for the perverse, ⁹²and they shall be told: 'Where is that which you used to worship ⁹³besides God? Do they help you, or do they help each other?'

26:69–93 Geiger (*Judaism and Islam,* 99) notes that whereas earlier Jewish legends have Abraham preach to his father only, the Qurʾān has him preach to his father and his people. He argues quite reasonably that this is because the Qurʾānic Abraham is meant to be a type of Muḥammad and therefore must also be a public preacher.

The Qurʾānic material (cf. 6:74–83; 19:41–48; 21:51–67; 26:69–82; 29:16–17, 24–25; 37:83–96; 43:26–27; 60:4) on Abraham's preaching to his father is related to the theme of faith over family, which is prominent in the Qurʾān. In this Sura it might be compared with Moses's preaching to Pharaoh (v. 16–31), his adoptive father (cf. also the episode of Noah and his lost son, 11:40–47). At the same time this material is a development of the Jewish and Christian exegetical traditions which have Abraham raised in the pagan city of Ur by a father (Terah, though he is named Āzar in 6:74) who is not only an idolater but a maker of idols. In the *Apocalypse of Abraham* Abraham comes to realize that his father's idols are powerless, and he seeks to convince his father to forsake them:

> And I declared to him and said to him, "Hear Terah, [my] father! It is the gods who are blessed by you, since you are a god to them, since you have made them; since their blessing is perdition, and their power is vain. They could not help themselves, how [then] will they help you or bless me? [In fact] I was for you a kind god of this gain, since it was through my cleverness that I brought you the money for the smashed [gods]." And when he heard my word his anger was kindled against me, since I had spoken harsh words against his gods." (*Apocalypse of Abraham* 4:3–6)

One might also compare the narrative of *Jubilees* 12 (2–3), where Abraham says to his father: "What help or advantage do we have from these idols before which you worship and bow down? Because there is not any spirit in them, for they are mute, and they are the misleading of the heart. Do not worship them."

In verse 86, Abraham prays to God that he forgive his father, regarding which see commentary on 60:4 (with further references). On Abraham's prayer for "judgment" (or better, "wisdom") in verse 83, see 26:21 and commentary on 26:18–29.

On the description of anything which unbelievers worship other than God (vv. 72–73) as being powerless, see commentary on 10:18 (with further references).

---

⁹⁴Then they will be cast into it on their faces—they and the perverse, ⁹⁵and the hosts of Iblis all together.

26:95 The reference in verse 95 to the "hosts" or "soldiers" (Ar. *junūd*) of the devil ("Iblīs") might be understood in light of the belief—seen, for example, in Ephesians 6:12—that the devil has spiritual forces who fight alongside with him:

> ¹²For it is not against human enemies that we have to struggle, but against the principalities and the ruling forces who are masters of the darkness in this world, the spirits of evil in the heavens.

According to *Tafsīr al-Jalālayn* the "hosts of Iblīs" include "those jinn and humans who were obedient to him."

---

⁹⁶They will say, as they wrangle in it [together], ⁹⁷'By God, we had indeed been in plain error ⁹⁸when we equated you with the

Lord of all the worlds! ⁹⁹No one led us astray except the guilty. ¹⁰⁰Now we have no intercessors, ¹⁰¹nor do we have any sympathetic friend. ¹⁰²Had there been another turn for us, we would be among the faithful.'

¹⁰³There is indeed a sign in that; but most of them do not have faith. ¹⁰⁴Indeed, *your* Lord is the All-mighty, the All-merciful.

¹⁰⁵The people of Noah impugned the apostles, ¹⁰⁶when Noah, their kinsman, said to them, 'Will you not be wary [of God]? ¹⁰⁷I am indeed a trusted apostle [sent] to you. ¹⁰⁸So be wary of God and obey me. ¹⁰⁹I do not ask you any reward for it; my reward lies only with the Lord of all the worlds. ¹¹⁰So be wary of God and obey me.'

¹¹¹They said, 'Shall we believe in you, when it is the riffraff who follow you?'

¹¹²He said, 'What do I know as to what they used to do? ¹¹³Their reckoning is only with my Lord, should you be aware. ¹¹⁴I will not drive away the faithful. ¹¹⁵I am just a manifest warner.'

¹¹⁶They said, 'Noah, if you do not desist, you will certainly be stoned [to death].'

26:105–16 On Noah's preaching to, and debate with, his people see commentary on Q 71:1–28 (with further references).

In verse 116 the Qur'ān has Noah's people threaten to stone him (as it elsewhere has God's messengers threatened with stoning: Q 11:91; 18:20; 19:46; 36:18; 44:20). This topos (which does not match the Biblical material on Noah) might be seen as a development of Jesus' lament over Jerusalem: "Jerusalem, Jerusalem, you that kill the prophets *and stone those* who are sent to you!" (Mat 23:37; cf. Luk 13:34); one might also note the stoning of Stephen (Act 7:55–59), and the way Peter (Act 5:26) and then Paul and Barnabas (Act 14:5) are threatened with stoning in Acts.

In verse 111 the Qur'ān has Noah's enemies describe his followers as "riffraff." *Tafsīr al-Jalālayn* explains "such as the weavers and the shoemakers."

On the idea that a true prophet does not seek a reward (v. 109), see commentary on 34:47 (with further references).

¹¹⁷He said, 'My Lord! My people have indeed impugned me. ¹¹⁸So judge conclusively between me and them, and deliver me and the faithful who are with me.'

¹¹⁹Thereupon We delivered him and those who were with him in the laden ark. ¹²⁰Then We drowned the rest.

¹²¹There is indeed a sign in that; but most of them do not have faith. ¹²²Indeed, *your* Lord is the All-mighty, the All-merciful.

¹²³[The people of] ʿĀd impugned the apostles, ¹²⁴when Hūd, their kinsman, said to them, 'Will you not be wary [of God]? ¹²⁵I am indeed a trusted apostle [sent] to you. ¹²⁶So be wary of God and obey me. ¹²⁷I do not ask you any reward for it; my reward lies only with the Lord of all the worlds.

26:127 On the idea that a true prophet does not seek a reward, see commentary on 34:47 (with further references).

¹²⁸Do you build an absurd sign on every prominence? ¹²⁹You set up structures as if you will be immortal, ¹³⁰and when you seize [someone for punishment], you seize [him] like tyrants. ¹³¹So be wary of God and obey me. ¹³²Be wary of Him who has provided you with whatever you know, ¹³³and aided you with sons and with cattle, ¹³⁴gardens and springs. ¹³⁵I indeed fear for you the punishment of a tremendous day.'

¹³⁶They said, 'It is the same to us whether you lecture us or not. ¹³⁷These are nothing but the traditions of the ancients, ¹³⁸and we will not be punished.'

¹³⁹So they impugned him, whereupon We destroyed them.

There is indeed a sign in that; but most of them do not have faith. ¹⁴⁰Indeed, *your* Lord is the All-mighty, the All-merciful.

[141][The people of] Thamūd impugned the apostles, [142]when Ṣāliḥ, their kinsman, said to them, 'Will you not be wary [of God]? [143]I am indeed a trusted apostle [sent] to you. [144]So be wary of God and obey me. [145]I do not ask you any reward for it; my reward lies only with the Lord of all the worlds.

26:145 On the idea that a true prophet does not seek a reward, see commentary on 34:47 (with further references).

---

[146]Will you be left secure in that which is here [147]—amid gardens and springs,

26:147 On the streams of paradise, see commentary on 2:25 (with further references).

---

[148]farms and date palms with dainty blossoms [149]and houses that you skillfully hew out of mountains? [150]So be wary of God and obey me, [151]and do not obey the dictates of the transgressors [152]who cause corruption in the land and do not set things right.'

[153]They said, 'You are indeed one of the bewitched. [154]You are just a human being like us. So bring us a sign, if you are truthful.'

[155]He said, 'This is a she-camel; she shall drink and you shall drink on known days. [156]Do not cause her any harm, for then you shall be seized by the punishment of a terrible day.' [157]But they hamstrung her, and consequently became regretful. [158]So the punishment seized them.

There is indeed a sign in that; but most of them do not have faith. ¹⁵⁹Indeed, *your* Lord is the All-mighty, the All-merciful.

¹⁶⁰The people of Lot impugned the apostles, ¹⁶¹when Lot, their townsman, said to them, 'Will you not be wary [of God]? ¹⁶²I am indeed a trusted apostle [sent] to you. ¹⁶³So be wary of God and obey me. ¹⁶⁴I do not ask you any reward for it; my reward lies only with the Lord of all the worlds. ¹⁶⁵What! Of all people do you come to males, ¹⁶⁶abandoning your wives your Lord has created for you? You are indeed a transgressing lot.'

¹⁶⁷They said, 'Lot, if you do not desist, you will surely be banished.'

¹⁶⁸He said, 'I indeed detest your conduct.' ¹⁶⁹'My Lord! Deliver me and my family from what they do.'

¹⁷⁰So We delivered him and all his family, ¹⁷¹except an old woman who remained behind. ¹⁷²Then We destroyed [all] the rest ¹⁷³and rained down upon them a rain [of stones]. Evil was the rain of those who were warned!

¹⁷⁴There is indeed a sign in that; but most of them do not have faith.

26:160–74 On Lot's family and the destruction of his people, see commentary on 15:57–74 (with further references). On Lot's wife, see commentary on 27:54–58 (with further references).

On the idea that a true prophet does not seek a reward (v. 164), see commentary on 34:47 (with further references).

---

¹⁷⁵Indeed, *your* Lord is the All-mighty, the All-merciful.

¹⁷⁶The inhabitants of Aykah impugned the apostles,

26:176 On the "inhabitants of Aykah," see commentary on 15:78–79 (with further references).

---

[177]when Shuʿayb said to them, 'Will you not be wary [of God]? [178]I am indeed a trusted apostle [sent] to you. [179]So be wary of God and obey me. [180]I do not ask you any reward for it; my reward lies only with the Lord of all the worlds.

26:180 On the idea that a true prophet does not seek a reward, see commentary on 34:47 (with further references).

---

[181]Observe the full measure, and do not be of those who give short measure. [182]Weigh with an even balance, [183]and do not cheat the people of their goods. Do not act wickedly on the earth, causing corruption.

26:181–83 On the use of proper "measuring" as an example of righteousness, see commentary on Q 83:1–3 (with further references).

---

[184]Be wary of Him who created you and the former generations.'

[185]They said, 'You are indeed one of the bewitched. [186]You are just a human being like us, and indeed we consider you to be a liar. [187]Make a fragment from the sky fall upon us, if you are truthful.'

[188]He said, 'My Lord knows best what you are doing.'

[189]So they impugned him, and then they were overtaken by the punishment of the day of the overshadowing cloud. It was indeed the punishment of a terrible day.

26:189 Yahuda (285–86) argues that this is an allusion to the day of the covenant at Sinai. He notes that that Arabic for "overshadowing cloud" is *ẓulla*, the same word which appears in 7:171 for the form which the mountain took on the day of the covenant (when God held it over the Israelites).

---

¹⁹⁰There is indeed a sign in that; but most of them do not have faith. ¹⁹¹Indeed, *your* Lord is the All-mighty, the All-merciful. ¹⁹²This is indeed [a Book] sent down by the Lord of all the worlds, ¹⁹³brought down by the Trustworthy Spirit ¹⁹⁴upon *your* heart (so that *you* may be one of the warners), ¹⁹⁵in a clear Arabic language. ¹⁹⁶It is indeed [foretold] in the scriptures of the ancients.

26:196 Here the Qurʾān uses a plural term (Ar. *zubur*)—which elsewhere in the singular (Ar. *zabūr*) apparently means Psalms—to refer generally to earlier scriptures (see commentary on 17:55, with further references).

---

¹⁹⁷Is it not a sign for them that the learned of the Children of Israel recognize it? ¹⁹⁸Had We sent it down upon some non-Arab ¹⁹⁹and had he recited it to them, they would not have believed in it.

²⁰⁰This is how We let it pass through the hearts of the guilty: ²⁰¹they do not believe in it until they sight the painful punishment. ²⁰²It will overtake them suddenly while they are unaware. ²⁰³Thereupon they will say, 'Shall we be granted any respite?'

²⁰⁴So do they seek to hasten on Our punishment?

²⁰⁵Tell me, should We let them enjoy for some years, ²⁰⁶then there comes to them what they have been promised, ²⁰⁷of what avail to them will be that which they were given to enjoy? ²⁰⁸We have not destroyed any town without its having warners ²⁰⁹for the sake of admonition, and We were not unjust.

²¹⁰It has not been brought down by the devils. ²¹¹Neither does it behoove them, nor are they capable [of doing that]. ²¹²They are indeed kept at bay [even] from hearing it.

²¹³So *do not invoke* any god besides God, lest *you* should be among the punished. ²¹⁴*Warn* the nearest of your kinsfolk, ²¹⁵and lower *your* wing to the faithful who follow *you.* ²¹⁶But if they disobey you, *say,* 'I am absolved of what you do.' ²¹⁷And put *your* trust in the All-mighty, the All-merciful, ²¹⁸who sees *you* when *you* stand [for prayer] ²¹⁹and *your* going about among those who prostrate. ²²⁰Indeed, He is the All-hearing, the All-knowing.

²²¹Shall I inform you on whom the devils descend? ²²²They descend on every sinful liar. ²²³They eavesdrop and most of them are liars. ²²⁴As for the poets, [only] the perverse follow them. ²²⁵Have *you* not regarded that they rove in every valley ²²⁶and that they say what they do not do? ²²⁷Barring those who have faith, do righteous deeds, and remember God much, and vindicate themselves after they have been wronged. And the wrongdoers will soon know at what goal they will end up.

27. *AL-NAML*, ANTS

In the Name of God, the All-beneficent, the All-merciful.

¹*Ṭā, Sīn.* These are the signs of the Qur'ān and a manifest Book, ²a guidance and good news for the faithful ³—those who maintain the prayer and pay the *zakāt,* and who are certain of the Hereafter. ⁴As for those who do not believe in the Hereafter, We have made their deeds seem decorous to them, and so they are bewildered. ⁵They are the ones for whom there is a terrible punishment, and they are the ones who will be the biggest losers in the Hereafter.

⁶*You* indeed receive the Qur'ān from One who is all-wise, all-knowing.

⁷When Moses said to his family, 'Indeed, I descry a fire! I will bring you some news from it, or bring you a firebrand so that you may warm yourselves.'

⁸When he came to it, he was called: 'Blessed is He who is in the fire and who is [as well] around it, and immaculate is God, the Lord of all the worlds!' ⁹'O Moses! I am indeed God, the All-mighty, the All-wise.' ¹⁰'Throw down your staff!'

When he saw it wriggling, as if it were a snake, he turned his back [to flee], without looking back. 'O Moses! 'Do not be afraid. Indeed, the apostles are not afraid before Me, ¹¹nor those who do wrong and then make up for [their] fault with goodness, for indeed I am all-forgiving, all-merciful.' ¹²'Insert your hand into your shirt. It will emerge white and bright without any fault— among nine signs meant for Pharaoh and his people. They are indeed a transgressing lot.'

27:7–12 On the call of Moses, see commentary on 20:9–16 (with further references). On the "nine signs" (perhaps two "wonders"—Moses's staff and his white hand—and seven plagues, although in 7:133 five plagues are specified), see commentary on 17:101–2.

---

¹³But when Our signs came to them, as eye-openers, they said, 'This is plain magic.' ¹⁴They impugned them wrongfully and out of arrogance, though they were convinced in their hearts [of their veracity]. So *observe* how was the fate of the agents of corruption!

¹⁵Certainly We gave knowledge to David and Solomon, and they said, 'All praise belongs to God, who granted us an advantage over many of His faithful servants.'

27:15 Whereas the Bible (1Ki 5:9 [1Ki 4:29 in the RSV]) makes wisdom (Hb. *ḥokmā*) a particular quality of Solomon, the Qurʾān here (cf. 2:251; 21:78–79; 38:20, 22–26) has both David and Solomon granted "knowledge" (Ar. *ʿilm*).

---

¹⁶Solomon inherited from David, and he said, 'O people! We have been taught the speech of the birds, and we have been given out of everything. This is indeed a clear advantage.'

¹⁷[Once] Solomon's hosts, comprising jinn, humans and birds, were marched out for him, and they were held in check.

27:16–17 The Qur'ān's declaration that Solomon was taught the "speech of the birds" (v. 16) and that his army included "jinn, humans, and birds" (v. 17) reflects the *Second Targum of Esther* (the date of which is disputed, but it may date originally from the fourth century AD; on its relationship with the Qur'ān see *BEQ,* 390–91; 393–98). In a passage that compares Solomon (favorably) to King Ahasuerus, the *Second Targum of Esther* (on 1:3) gives him the power to understand and subdue all sorts of creatures and spirits:

> Solomon sat upon the throne of his father David. All the kingdoms feared him, nations and languages were obedient to him; devils, demons, and ferocious beasts, evil spirits and accidents, were delivered into his hands. Imps brought him all kinds of fish from the sea, and the fowls of heaven, together with the cattle and wild animals, came of their own accord to his slaughter—house to be slaughtered for his banquet. He was rich and powerful in the possession of much silver and gold. He explained parables, solved hidden problems, and made known mysteries without end. His enemies and adversaries became his friends, and all the kings obeyed him. (*Second Targum of Esther,* 1:3, p. 269).

On Solomon and the jinn, cf. 34:12–13; 38:37 and commentary on 34:12–13.

———————

¹⁸When they came to the Valley of Ants, an ant said, 'O ants! Enter your dwellings, lest Solomon and his hosts should trample on you while they are unaware.' ¹⁹Whereat he smiled, amused at its words, and he said, 'My Lord! Inspire me to give thanks for Your blessing with which You have blessed me and my parents, and that I may do righteous deeds which please You, and admit me, by Your mercy, among Your righteous servants.'

27:18–19 The connection between Solomon and ants here may, as Geiger (*Judaism and Islam,* 150) suggests, ultimately be inspired by a passage in Proverbs (a text traditionally ascribed to Solomon):

> ⁶Idler, go to the ant; ponder her ways and grow wise:
> ⁷no one gives her orders, no overseer, no master,

[8]yet all through the summer she gets her food ready, and gathers her supplies at harvest time. (Pro 6:6–8)

Speyer (401–2; following Geiger, *Judaism and Islam,* 150) refers also to a passage in the Talmud (b. *Hullin* 57b) but the connection is not clear. Verse 19 here is close to 46:15.

---

[20][One day] he reviewed the birds, and said, 'Why do I not see the hoopoe? Or is he absent?' [21]'I will punish him with a severe punishment, or I will behead him, unless he brings me a credible excuse.'

[22]He did not stay for long [before he turned up] and said, 'I have alighted on something which you have not alighted on, and I have brought you from Sheba a definite report. [23]I found a woman ruling over them, and she has been given everything, and she has a great throne. [24]I found her and her people prostrating to the sun instead of God, and Satan has made their deeds seem decorous to them—thus he has barred them from the way [of God], so they are not guided—[25]so that they do not prostrate themselves to God, who brings forth what is hidden in the heavens and the earth, and He knows whatever you hide and whatever you disclose. [26]God—there is no god except Him—is the Lord of the Great Throne.'

[27]He said, 'We shall presently see whether you are truthful, or if you are one of the liars. [28]Take this letter of mine and deliver it to them. Then draw away from them and observe what [response] they return.'

27:20–28 After an interlude about ants (vv. 18–19), the Qur'ān returns to the narrative connected to the *Second Targum of Esther,* which gives Solomon great wealth and power (greater than that of Ahasuerus) and tells the story of how he discovered the realm of the Queen of Sheba (whose visit to Solomon is recounted in 1Ki 10). The Qur'ān uses this narrative to describe the conversion of the Queen of Sheba, leader of a people who once worshipped the sun (Q 27:24; in the *Second Targum of Esther*—see commentary on 27:29–44—she is found worshipping the sea). However, upon witnessing the signs brought forth by Solomon, she recognizes the true God (Q 27:44):

> And, further merry with wine, [Solomon] commanded the wild beasts, the birds, the reptiles, the devils, demons, and spirits to be brought, that they should dance before him, to show his greatness to the kings who were staying with him. The royal scribes called them all by their names, and they came together without being bound or forced, and without even a man leading them. At that time, the cock of the wood was missed among the fowls, and was not found. Then the king commanded in anger that he should appear before him, or else he would destroy him. Then the cock of the wood answered and said to King Solomon: "Lord of the earth, incline thine ears and hear my words. Are there not three months since thou hast put counsel in my heart and words of truth upon my tongue? Since then I have not eaten any food, nor drank any water, and have flown all over the world and made an inspection. I thought, is there a country or a kingdom which is not subject to my lord the king? Then I saw a certain country, the name of whose fortified town is Kitor, whose dust is more precious than gold, and where silver lies about like dung in the streets. Trees also are there standing from primeval times, and are watered from the garden of Eden. Great crowds of people are there from the garden of Eden, having crowns upon their heads, who know nothing of warfare, nor can they draw the bow. For, indeed, I have seen one woman who rules over them all, and her name is Queen of Saba. Now, if it please my lord the king, I shall gird my loins like a mighty man, and shall arise and go to the city of Kitor, in the land of Saba, and shall bind its kings and governor in chains of iron, and shall bring them to my lord the king." This speech pleased the king, and royal scribes were called, a letter was written and tied to the wings of the cock of the wood, who lifted up his wings and soared up in the air, and compelled other birds to fly with it. Then they came to the city of Kitor, in the land of Saba. (*Second Targum of Esther,* 1:3, pp. 276–78)

---

²⁹She said, 'O [members of the] elite! A noble letter has indeed been delivered to me. ³⁰It is from Solomon, and it begins in the name of God, the All-beneficent, the All-merciful. ³¹[It states,] "Do not defy me, and come to me in submission."'

³²She said, 'O [members of the] elite! Give me your opinion concerning my matter. I do not decide any matter until you are present.'

³³They said, 'We are powerful and possess great might. But it is up to you to command. So consider what orders you will give.'

³⁴She said, 'Indeed, when kings enter a town, they devastate it and make the mightiest of its people the weakest. That is how they act. ³⁵I will send them a gift, and then see what the envoys bring back.'

³⁶So when he came to Solomon, he said, 'Are you aiding me with wealth? What God has given me is better than what He has given you. You are indeed proud of your gift! ³⁷Go back to them, for we will come at them with hosts which they cannot face, and we will expel them from it, abased and degraded.'

³⁸He said, 'O [members of the] elite! Which of you will bring me her throne before they come to me in submission?' ³⁹An afreet from among the jinn said, 'I will bring it to you before you rise from your place. I have the power to do it and am trustworthy.'

⁴⁰The one who had knowledge of the Book said, 'I will bring it to you in the twinkling of an eye.'

So when he saw it set near him, he said, 'This is by the grace of my Lord, to test me if I will give thanks or be ungrateful. Whoever gives thanks, gives thanks only for his own sake. And whoever is ungrateful [should know that] my Lord is indeed all-sufficient, all-generous.'

⁴¹He said, 'Disguise her throne for her, so that we may see whether she is discerning or if she is one of the undiscerning ones.' ⁴²So when she came, it was said [to her], 'Is your throne like this one?' She said, 'It seems to be the same, and we were informed before it, and we had submitted.' ⁴³She had been barred

[from the way of God] by what she used to worship besides God, for she belonged to a faithless people.

⁴⁴It was said to her, 'Enter the palace.' So when she saw it, she supposed it to be a pool of water, and she bared her shanks. He said, 'It is a palace paved with crystal.' She said, 'My Lord! I have indeed wronged myself, and I submit with Solomon to God, the Lord of all the worlds.'

27:29–44 The Qurʾānic account of the Queen of Sheba's meeting with Solomon largely follows from the narrative of the *Second Targum of Esther* (see *BEQ,* 396–98). The Qurʾān's principal innovation of this narrative is its description of the miraculous theft of the Queen of Sheba's throne. Thereby the Qurʾān presumably means to emphasize that the throne of a human ruler is nothing compared to the throne of God (see 2:255; 7:54; 9:129; 11:7; 13:2; 17:42; 20:5; passim):

> Toward morning the queen went out to worship the sea, when the birds obscured the sunlight, so that the queen out of astonishment took hold of her clothes and tore them in pieces. The cock of the wood now came down, and she observed that a letter was tied to its wings, which she at once opened and read what was written therein, as follows: "From me. King Solomon, peace to thee and to thy princes. Thou must certainly know that the Holy One, blessed be He! made me to rule over the wild beasts, over the fowls of the air, over devils, demons, and spirits, and that all the kings of the East and of the West, of the South and of the North, come to salute me. If thou wilt come and salute me, I shall show thee greater dignity than I shall show to all the kings that are sojourning with me; but if thou wilt not come to salute me, I shall send kings, legions, and riders against thee. But if thou wilt ask. What sort of kings, legions, and riders has King Solomon? So know, that the wild beasts are the kings and the legions, and the riders are the birds in the air. My army consists of devils, demons, and spirits, who will strangle you in your beds, the wild beasts will kill you in your houses, and the fowls of the air will devour your flesh in the field."
>
> When the queen heard the words of the letter she again rent her clothes. Then she sent for the elders and prominent men, and said to them, "Do you know what King Solomon has sent to me?" They answered, "We do not know Solomon, nor do we esteem his kingdom." But she did not trust them, nor

listen to their words, but caused all the ships to be collected and loaded with presents of pearls and of precious stones. . . .

After three years, the Queen of Saba really came to King Solomon, who, when he heard of her arrival, sent Benayahu, son of Yehayada, to meet her. . . . Then Benayahu conducted her to the king, who, when he heard that she was coming, went and sat down in an apartment of glass. When the queen saw the king sitting there, she thought in her heart, and in fact said, that he was sitting in water, and she raised her dress to cross the water, when the king noticed that her foot was full of hair. He said to her, "Thy beauty is the beauty of women, and thy hair is the hair of men; hair is becoming to a man, but to a woman it is a shame." (*Second Targum of Esther,* 1:3, pp. 278–83)

Now, when the Queen of Saba saw his greatness and glory, she praised the Creator, and said: "Blessed be the Lord thy God, whom it has pleased to set thee upon the throne of the kingdom to do justice and right." (*Second Targum of Esther,* 1:3, p. 285)

The Queen of Sheba's hairy legs (not explicit in the Qurʾān, but alluded to with the detail, v. 44, that she uncovered her legs) return in Islamic commentaries. *Tafsīr al-Jalālayn* explains that Solomon's demons helped her address this issue: "He wanted to marry her but disliked the hair on her legs. So the devils made a [depilatory] lime mixture and she removed it therewith."

The meaning of "afreet" (*ʿifrīt*) in verse 39 is disputed—it may mean, based on context, "a bold one" (Asad).

---

⁴⁵Certainly We sent to Thamūd Ṣāliḥ, their kinsman, [with the summons:] 'Worship God!' But thereat they became two groups contending with each other.

⁴⁶He said, 'O My people! Why do you press for evil sooner than for good? Why do you not plead to God for forgiveness so that you may receive His mercy?'

⁴⁷They said, 'We take you and those who are with you for a bad omen.' He said, 'Your bad omens are from God. You are indeed a people being tested.'

⁴⁸There were nine persons in the city who caused corruption in the land and did not set things right. ⁴⁹They said, 'Swear by God that we will attack him and his family by night. Then we will tell his heir that we were not present at the murder of his family and that we indeed speak the truth.'

⁵⁰They devised a plot, and We [too] devised a plan, but they were not aware. ⁵¹So *observe* how was the outcome of their plotting, as We destroyed them and all their people. ⁵²So there lay their houses, fallen in ruin because of their wrongdoing. There is indeed a sign in that for a people who have knowledge. ⁵³And We delivered those who had faith and were Godwary.

⁵⁴[We also sent] Lot, when he said to his people, 'What! Do you commit this indecency while you look on? ⁵⁵Do you approach men with [sexual] desire instead of women?! You are indeed an ignorant lot!'

⁵⁶But the only answer of his people was that they said, 'Expel Lot's family from your town! They are indeed a puritanical lot.'

⁵⁷So We delivered him and his family, except his wife. We ordained her to be among those who remained behind. ⁵⁸Then We poured down upon them a rain [of stones]. Evil was that rain for those who had been warned!

27:54–58 On Lot in the Qur'ān, see commentary on 15:57–74 (with further references). The Qur'ān here and elsewhere (7:83; 11:81; 15:59–60; 26:170–71; 29:32–33; 37:134–35) alludes to the Biblical account by which Lot's wife turned back to look at the city of Sodom—despite the angelic warning—and was turned to a pillar of salt for her disobedience:

²⁴Then the Lord rained down on Sodom and Gomorrah brimstone and fire of his own sending.
²⁵He overthrew those cities and the whole plain, with all the people living in the cities and everything that grew there.

²⁶But Lot's wife looked back, and was turned into a pillar of salt. (Gen 19:24–26)

The Qur'ān (v. 57) attributes the action of Lot's wife to God.

---

⁵⁹*Say,* 'All praise belongs to God, and Peace be to His chosen servants.'

Is God better, or the partners they ascribe [to Him]? ⁶⁰Is He who created the heavens and the earth, and sends down for you water from the sky, whereby We grow delightful gardens, whose trees you could never cause to grow. . . ? What! Is there a god besides God? They are indeed a lot who equate [others with God].

⁶¹Is He who made the earth an abode [for you] and made rivers [flowing] through[it], and set firm mountains for it[s stability], and set a barrier between the two seas. . . ? What! Is there a god besides God? Indeed, most of them do not know.

⁶²Is He who answers the call of the distressed [person] when he invokes Him and removes his distress, and makes you successors on the earth. . . ? What! Is there a god besides God? Little is the admonition that you take.

⁶³Is He who guides you in the darkness of land and sea and who sends the winds as harbingers of His mercy. . . ? What! Is there a god besides God? Far is God above [having] any partners that they ascribe [to Him].

⁶⁴Is He who originates the creation, then He will bring it back, and who provides for you from the heavens and the earth . . . ? What! Is there a god besides God? *Say,* 'Produce your evidence, if you are truthful.'

⁶⁵*Say,* 'No one in the heavens or the earth knows the Unseen except God, nor are they aware when they will be resurrected.'

⁶⁶Is their knowledge complete [and conclusive] concerning the Hereafter? No, they are in doubt about it. Indeed, they are blind to it.

⁶⁷The faithless say, 'What! When we and our fathers have become dust will we be raised [from the dead]? ⁶⁸We and our fathers were certainly promised this before. [But] these are just myths of the ancients.'

27:68 On the expression "myths of the ancients," see commentary on 68:15 (with further references).

---

⁶⁹*Say,* 'Travel through the land and observe how was the fate of the guilty.' ⁷⁰*Do not grieve* for them, and *do not be upset* by their guile.

⁷¹They say, 'When will this promise be fulfilled, if you are truthful?'

⁷²*Say,* 'Perhaps there is right behind you some of what you seek to hasten.'

⁷³*Your* Lord is indeed gracious to mankind, but most of them do not give thanks. ⁷⁴*Your* Lord knows whatever their breasts conceal and whatever they disclose. ⁷⁵There is no invisible thing in the heaven and the earth but it is in a manifest Book.

27:75 "Your eyes could see my embryo. In your book all my days were inscribed, every one that was fixed is there" (Psa 139:16).

---

⁷⁶This Qur'ān recounts for the Children of Israel most of what they differ about, ⁷⁷and it is indeed a guidance and mercy for the

faithful. [78] *Your* Lord will decide between them by His judgement, and He is the All-mighty, the All-knowing. [79] So put *your* trust in God, for *you* indeed stand on the manifest truth. [80] *You* cannot make the dead hear, nor can *you* make the deaf hear *your* call when they turn their backs, [81] nor can *you* lead the blind out of their error. *You* can make only those hear *you* who believe in Our signs and have submitted.

[82] When the word [of judgement] falls upon them, We will bring out for them an Animal from the earth who will tell them that the people had no faith in Our signs.

27:82 Here Qarai renders the Arabic term *dābba* as "animal," but it is better understood as "beast," and as a reference to the beast which features in Christian eschatology (the eschatological nature of v. 82 is evident from the verses that follow). Of particular note is the way the Qur'ān speaks of this beast as coming "from the earth" much like the book of Revelation (13:11) speaks of the second beast "emerging from the ground." The Qur'ān, however, makes this beast an instrument of God who "speaks" to the unbelievers.

---

[83] On that day We will resurrect from every nation a group of those who denied Our signs, and they will be held in check. [84] When they come, He will say, 'Did you deny My signs without comprehending them in knowledge? What was it that you used to do?' [85] And the word [of judgement] shall fall upon them for their wrongdoing, and they will not speak.

[86] Do they not see that We made the night that they may rest in it, and the day to provide visibility. There are indeed signs in that for a people who have faith.

[87] The day when the trumpet is blown, whoever is in the heavens and whoever is on the earth will be terrified, except such as God wishes, and all will come to Him in utter humility.

27:87 On the trumpet blast, see commentary on 78:18 (with further references).

---

⁸⁸*You* see the mountains, which *you* suppose to be stationary, while they drift like passing clouds—the handiwork of God who has made everything faultless. He is indeed well aware of what you do.

⁸⁹Whoever brings virtue shall receive [a reward] better than it, and on that day they will be secure from terror. ⁹⁰But whoever brings vice—they shall be cast on their faces into the Fire [and told:] 'Shall you be requited with anything except what you used to do?'

⁹¹[*Say*], 'I have been commanded to worship the Lord of this city who has made it inviolable and to whom all things belong, and I have been commanded to be among those who submit [to God], ⁹²and to recite the Qur'ān.'

Whoever is guided is guided only for his own good, and as for him who goes astray, *say,* 'I am just one of the warners.' ⁹³And *say,* 'All praise belongs to God. Soon He will show you His signs, and you will recognize them.'

Your Lord is not oblivious of what you do.

28. *AL-QAṢAṢ*, THE STORIES

In the Name of God, the All-beneficent, the All-merciful.

¹*Ṭā, Sīn, Mīm.* ²These are the signs of the Manifest Book.

³We relate to *you* truly some of the account of Moses and Pharaoh for a people who have faith. ⁴Pharaoh indeed tyrannized over the land, reducing its people to factions, abasing one group of them, slaughtering their sons and sparing their women. Indeed, He was indeed one of the agents of corruption.

28:4 Note Exodus 1:15–16:

¹⁵The king of Egypt then spoke to the Hebrew midwives, one of whom was called Shiphrah, and the other Puah.
¹⁶'When you attend Hebrew women in childbirth,' he said, 'look at the two stones. If it is a boy, kill him; if a girl, let her live.' (Exo 1:15–16)

Cf. 7:127; 40:25; and commentary on 40:25.

⁵And We desired to show favour to those who were oppressed in the land, and to make them *imams* and to make them the heirs, ⁶and to establish them in the land and to show Pharaoh and Hāmān and their hosts from them that of which they were apprehensive.

28:5–6 This passage suggests that the Israelites settled not in the promised land but in Egypt, in place of the Egyptians. On this see commentary on 26:52–59 (with further references). On the mention of Haman (who in the Biblical book of Esther is in Persia) in Egypt with Pharaoh, see commentary on 28:38 (with further references).

---

⁷We revealed to Moses' mother, [saying], 'Nurse him; then, when you fear for him, cast him into the river, and do not fear or grieve, for We will restore him to you and make him one of the apostles.'

28:7–13 *overview* On this passage cf. 20:37–41 and commentary on those verses.

28:7 The special revelation (cf. 20:38–39) which Moses's mother receives here has no parallel in the Bible. Instead it seems to be due to the relationship between the account of Joseph in Q 12 and the account of Moses in Q 28. As Jacob receives a revelation from God to give him comfort (Q 12:5) so Moses's mother receives a similar revelation here. On this see Witztum, *Syriac Milieu,* 291. On the relationship of this passage to Exodus 2, see commentary on 20:37–41.

---

⁸Then Pharaoh's kinsmen picked him up that he might be an enemy and a cause of grief to them. Pharaoh and Hāmān and their hosts were indeed iniquitous.

28:8 On the appearance of Haman (who in the Biblical book of Esther appears in Persia) in Egypt with Pharaoh, see commentary on 28:38 (with further references).

---

⁹Pharaoh's wife said [to him], '[This infant will be] a [source of] comfort to me and to you. Do not kill him. Maybe he will

benefit us, or we will adopt him as a son.' But they were not aware.

28:9 In Exodus it is the daughter of Pharaoh who discovers the infant Moses and chooses to protect him and to "treat him like a son," whereas in the Qur'ān (cf. 20:39; 26:18) it is the wife of Pharaoh who suggests that she and her husband adopt Moses.

> [5]Now Pharaoh's daughter went down to bathe in the river, while her maids walked along the riverside. Among the reeds she noticed the basket, and she sent her maid to fetch it.
> [6]She opened it and saw the child: the baby was crying. Feeling sorry for it, she said, 'This is one of the little Hebrews.' (Exo 2:5–6)

The Qur'ān might be interested in establishing a father-son relationship between Pharaoh and Moses (on this see commentary on 26:18–29).

---

[10]The heart of Moses' mother became desolate, and indeed she was about to divulge it had We not fortified her heart so that she might have faith [in God's promise]. [11]She said to his sister, 'Follow him.' So she watched him from a distance, while they were not aware.

28:11 Cf. Exo 2:4: "His sister took up position some distance away to see what would happen to him."

---

[12]Since before We had forbidden him to be suckled by any nurse. So she said, 'Shall I show you a household that will take care of him for you and who will be his well-wishers?'
[13]That is how We restored him to his mother so that she might be comforted and not grieve, and that she might know that God's promise is true, but most of them do not know.

28:12–13 On this passage cf. Exodus 2:7–9. The Qur'ān's declaration (v. 12) "We had forbidden him to be suckled by any nurse" (v. 12) reflects a tradition in the Babylonian Talmud that Moses (from whose mouth would come forth the word of God) refused the impure breasts of Egyptian women:

> Then said his sister to Pharaoh's daughter, Shall I go and call thee a nurse of the Hebrew women? Why just 'of the Hebrew women'?—It teaches that they handed Moses about to all the Egyptian women but he would not suck. He said: Shall a mouth which will speak with [God] suck what is unclean! (b. *Sotah* 12b)

---

¹⁴When he came of age and became fully matured, We gave him judgement and knowledge, and thus do We reward the virtuous.

28:14 A tradition reported by Philo (*Life of Moses,* 1:21) relates that Moses was more knowledgeable than the teachers sent to him ("anticipating all their lessons by the excellent natural endowments of his own genius"), but this statement is standard Qur'ānic language for prophets and is almost identical to that used for Joseph in 12:22.

---

¹⁵[One day] he entered the city at a time when its people were not likely to take notice. He found there two men fighting, this one from among his followers and that one from his enemies. The one who was from his followers sought his help against him who was from his enemies. So Moses hit him with his fist, whereupon he expired. He said, 'This is of Satan's doing. He is indeed clearly a misleading enemy.'

¹⁶He said, 'My Lord! I have wronged myself. Forgive me!' So He forgave him. Indeed, He is the All-forgiving, the All-merciful. ¹⁷He said, 'My Lord! As You have blessed me, I will never be a supporter of the guilty.'

¹⁸He rose at dawn in the city, fearful and vigilant, when, lo, the one who had sought his help the day before, shouted for his help [once again]. Moses said to him, 'You are indeed clearly perverse!' ¹⁹But when he wanted to strike him who was an enemy of both of them, he said, 'Moses, do you want to kill me, just like the one you killed yesterday? You only want to be a tyrant in this land, and you do not desire to be one who set things right.'

28:15–19 The Qur'ān here alludes (v. 15) to the account in Exodus 2 of Moses's killing an Egyptian (cf. 20:40; 26:19–20; 28:33) with one notable exception: unlike Exodus (and unlike 26:19), Moses blames Satan (cf. the words of Jacob in 12:5) and asks God for forgiveness:

> ¹¹It happened one day, when Moses was grown up, that he went to see his kinsmen. While he was watching their forced labour he also saw an Egyptian striking a Hebrew, one of his kinsmen.
> ¹²Looking this way and that and seeing no one in sight, he killed the Egyptian and hid him in the sand.
> ¹³On the following day he came back, and there were two Hebrews, fighting. He said to the man who was in the wrong, 'What do you mean by hitting your kinsman?'
> ¹⁴'And who appointed you,' the man retorted, 'to be prince over us and judge? Do you intend to kill me as you killed the Egyptian?' Moses was frightened. 'Clearly that business has come to light,' he thought. (Exo 2:11–14)

---

²⁰There came a man from the city outskirts, hurrying. He said, 'Moses! The elite are indeed conspiring to kill you. So leave [this place]. I am indeed your well-wisher.'

28:20 The Qur'ān's report that the "elite" (actually the "council," Ar. *mala'*) conspired to kill Moses reflects a Qur'ānic topos (cf. Q 7:127, also in the story of Moses; 11:38, Noah; 12:43, Joseph; also Q 23:24 and 33, and passim). It may also reflect Philo's *Life of Moses,* according to which Pharaoh's advisers convince him to seek Moses's life:

But when the Egyptian authorities had once got an opportunity of attacking the young man, having already reason for looking upon him with suspicion (for they well knew that he would hereafter bear them ill-will for their evil practices, and would revenge himself on them when he had an opportunity) they poured in, at all times and from all quarters, thousands and thousands of calumnies into the willing ears of his grandfather, so that they even implanted in his mind an apprehension that Moses was plotting to deprive him of his kingdom. (Philo, *Life of Moses,* 1:46)

The reference to "a man from the city outskirts" (perhaps implying a poor man) appears to be a distinctly Qurʾānic element; the same description is given to an unnamed figure in the parable of the town in Q 36 (v. 20).

---

²¹So he left the city, fearful and vigilant. He said, 'My Lord! Deliver me from the wrongdoing lot.' ²²And when he turned his face toward Midian, he said, 'Maybe my Lord will show me the right way.'

28:21–22 "When Pharaoh heard of the matter, he tried to put Moses to death, but Moses fled from Pharaoh. He went into Midianite territory and sat down beside a well" (Exo 2:15).

---

²³When he arrived at the well of Midian, he found there a throng of people watering [their flocks] and he found, besides them, two women holding back [their flock]. He said, 'What is your business?' They said, 'We do not water [our flock] until the shepherds have driven out [their flocks] and our father is an aged man.' ²⁴So he watered [their flock] for them. Then he withdrew toward the shade and said, 'My Lord! I am indeed in need of any good You may send down to me!'

²⁵Then one of the two women approached him, walking bashfully. She said, 'My father invites you to pay you the wages for

watering [our flock] for us.' So when he came to him and re-counted the story to him, he said, 'Do not be afraid. You have been delivered from the wrongdoing lot.'

²⁶One of the two women said, 'Father, hire him. The best you can indeed hire is a powerful and trustworthy man.' ²⁷He said, 'Indeed, I desire to marry you to one of these two daughters of mine, on condition that you hire yourself to me for eight years. And if you complete ten, that will be up to you, and I do not want to be hard on you. God willing, you will find me to a righteous man.'

²⁸He said, 'This will be [by consent] between you and me. Whichever of the two terms I complete, there shall be no imposition upon me, and God is witness over what we say.'

28:23–28 Moses's prayer at the end of verse 24 departs from the Biblical account of Moses in Midian (Exo 2:16–21) in a way that reflects the account of the prayer of Abraham's servant Eliezer (who is seeking a wife for Isaac) at a well:

¹¹In the evening, at the time when women come out to draw water, he made the camels kneel outside the town near the well.
¹²And he said, 'The Lord, God of my master Abraham, give me success today and show faithful love to my master Abraham.' (Gen 24:11–12)

By having Moses choose between two daughters (see vv. 23, 27) and be bound to a period of labor as part of the marriage contract, the Qur'ān follows not the Biblical account of Moses and Jethro (who has seven daughters; see Exo 2:16) but the Biblical account of Jacob and Laban (who has two daughters, and who establishes a contract with Jacob):

¹⁶Now Laban had two daughters, the elder named Leah, and the younger Rachel.
¹⁷Leah had lovely eyes, but Rachel was shapely and beautiful,
¹⁸and Jacob had fallen in love with Rachel. So his answer was, 'I shall work for you for seven years in exchange for your younger daughter Rachel.'
¹⁹Laban replied, 'It is better for me to give her to you than to a stranger; stay with me.' (Gen 29:16–19)

The account of Jacob also begins with a scene at a well (see Gen 29:2). On Moses in Midian, see also commentary on 20:37–41.

---

²⁹So when Moses completed the term and set out with his family, he descried a fire on the side of the mountain. He said to his family, 'Wait! Indeed, I descry a fire! Maybe I will bring you some news from it, or a brand of fire so that you may warm yourselves.'

28:29–35 *overview* On the call of Moses, see commentary on 20:9–16 (with further references).

---

³⁰When he approached it, he was called from the right bank of the valley in that blessed spot from the tree: 'Moses! Indeed, I am God, the Lord of all the worlds!'

28:30 On God's speaking to Moses on the right side of Mt. Sinai (cf. v. 44, where Moses is on the "western" side), see commentary on 19:51–53.

---

³¹And: 'Throw down your staff!' And when he saw it wriggling as if it were a snake, he turned his back [to flee], without looking back. 'Moses! Come forward, and do not be afraid. You are indeed safe.' ³²'Insert your hand into your shirt. It will emerge white, without any fault, and keep your arms drawn in awe to your sides. These shall be two proofs from your Lord to Pharaoh and his elite. They are indeed a transgressing lot.'

³³He said, 'My Lord! I have killed one of their men, so I fear they will kill me. ³⁴Aaron, my brother—he is more eloquent than me in speech. So send him with me as a helper to confirm me, for I fear that they will impugn me.'

28:34 In the Qur'ān it is Moses who explains to God that Aaron is "more eloquent," whereas in Exodus (4:14–15) God decides that Aaron, a "good speaker,"
will speak on Moses's behalf. Cf. 20:25–32; 25:35; 26:12–14.

---

³⁵He said, 'We will strengthen your arm by means of your
brother, and invest both of you with such authority that they will
not touch you. With the help of Our signs, you two and those who
follow the two of you shall be the victors.'

³⁶When Moses brought them Our manifest signs, they said,
'This is nothing but concocted magic. We never heard of such a
thing among our forefathers.'

³⁷Moses said, 'My Lord knows best who brings guidance from
Him and in whose favour the outcome of that abode will be. The
wrongdoers do not prosper.'

28:36–37 On Moses's confrontation with Pharaoh and his magicians, see
commentary on 26:30–45 (with further references).

---

³⁸Pharaoh said, 'O [members of the] elite! I do not know of
any god that you may have besides me. Hāmān, light for me a
fire over clay, and build me a tower so that I may take a look at
Moses's god, and indeed I consider him to be a liar!'

28:38 The appearance of Haman—the villain of the Book of Esther—in a
Qur'ānic passage involving Pharaoh suggests a connection with the story of
Esther, presumably because Jews and Christians tended to tell the stories (both
of which involve the salvation of the Israelites from the murderous plots of gentile enemies) together. Haman's role as Pharaoh's assistant here matches well
his role as Ahasuerus' assistant in Esther. However, Pharaoh's demand in this

verse that Haman build for him a tower which will allow him to look at Moses's god (cf. 2:55 and 4:153, which have the Israelites impiously demand to see God)—that is, a tower that reaches into heaven—reflects the Biblical story of the building of the Tower of Babel (a tower meant to reach into heaven, as in Genesis 11:4: "'Come,' they said, 'let us build ourselves a city and a tower with its top reaching heaven. Let us make a name for ourselves, so that we do not get scattered all over the world'"). In *Targum Neofiti* the building of the Tower of Babel is an act of war against God:

> Come, let us build ourselves a city, and a tower whose top will reach to the heavens, and let us make for ourselves at its top an idol and we will put a sword in its hand, and it will make war against Him. (*Targum Neofiti,* Gen 11:4)

In both Jewish and Christian exegesis that project of building the Tower of Babel is attributed to Nimrod, who in Genesis appears as "a mighty hunter in the eyes of the Lord" (Gen 10.9; cf. 1Ch 1.10; but *Targum Neofiti* makes him "mighty in sinning before the Lord").

Still closer to the Qur'ānic tower account is the tale of the Assyrian sage Aḥīqar (on this see Silverstein, "Haman's Transition from the Jahiliyya to Islam"). This tale, which is extant in a variety of Near Eastern languages (and dates back to the fifth century BC in Aramaic), relates how the deceitful nephew (or, according to some versions, son) of Aḥīqar, named Nādān, informs Pharaoh (nemesis of the Assyrians) that Aḥīqar is dead. In response Pharaoh writes to the Assyrian ruler (Sennachrib) with a request that someone be sent to build for him a tower in the sky (knowing that only the wise Aḥīqar would be able to accomplish such a feat). When Aḥīqar arrives to build the tower (with the help of eagles who lift stones into the air), the plot of Nādān—who plays the role of the conspirator which Haman plays in Esther—is uncovered:

> When the Egyptian King Pharaoh heard that Akyrios [Aḥīqar] was killed he was greatly delighted, and sent a missive to King Sinagrip, in which he said: "From the Egyptian King Pharaoh to the Assyrian King, greeting! I desire thee to build a castle for me, which shall be neither in heaven nor upon earth; send me clever workmen, who will carry this out according to my wish."
>
> . . .
>
> The people had come together because of Pharaoh's missive, and I, Akyrios, said to the King: "Do not be anxious, O King! I will answer him. . . ." Then I, Akyrios, sent word to my own house, saying, "Seek out two eaglets and feed them; command my falconers to teach them how to soar; make a cage and seek out a bold boy amongst my domestics; put him in the cage

with the eagles and train them all to fly. The child must cry: 'Bring lime and stones; look! The workmen are ready.' And tie cords on their feet." (*The Story of Aḥiḳar* [Slavonic version], 17, 18).

On Haman, cf. 28:6, 8; 29:39–40; 40:23–24, 36–37. On Pharoah as a god, cf. 26:18–29; 79:24; and commentary on 26:18–29.

---

³⁹He and his hosts unduly acted arrogantly in that land and thought they would not be brought back to Us. ⁴⁰So We seized him and his hosts, and threw them into the sea. So *observe* how was the fate of the wrongdoers!

28:40 On the drowning of Pharaoh and his army, see commentary on 54:41–42 (with further references).

---

⁴¹We made them leaders who invite to the Fire, and on the Day of Resurrection they will not receive any help. ⁴²We made a curse pursue them in this world, and on the Day of Resurrection they will be among the disfigured.

⁴³Certainly We gave Moses the Book, after We had destroyed the former generations, as [a set of] eye-openers, guidance and mercy for mankind, so that they may take admonition.

⁴⁴*You* were not on the western side when We revealed the commandments to Moses, nor were *you* among the witnesses.

28:44 This verse may be an allusion to the giving of the law, or the Ten Commandments, to Moses (regarding which see commentary on 17:22–39, with further references). The "western" side seems to be equivalent to the "right side" of the mountain (regarding which see commentary on 19:51–53, with further references).

⁴⁵But We brought forth other generations and time took its toll on them. *You* did not dwell among the people of Midian reciting Our signs to them, but it is We who are the senders [of the apostles]. ⁴⁶And *you* were not on the side of the Mount when We called out [to Moses], but [We have sent *you* as] a mercy from *your* Lord that *you* may warn a people to whom there did not come any warner before *you,* so that they may take admonition. ⁴⁷And lest—if an affliction were to befall them because of what their hands have sent ahead—they should say, 'Our Lord! Why did You not send us an apostle so that we might have followed Your signs and been among the faithful?'

⁴⁸But when there came to them the truth from Us, they said, 'Why has he not been given the like of what Moses was given?' Did they not disbelieve what Moses was given before and said, 'Two magicians abetting each other,' and said, 'We indeed disbelieve both of them'?

28:48 Qarai here renders "Two magicians abetting each other" (presumably referring to Moses and Muḥammad), following the reading *sāḥirānī,* but the standard Cairo Qurʾān reading is "two magics" (*siḥrāni;* both are possible readings of the consonantal text); Hilali-Khan find here a reference to the Torah and the Qurʾān: "Two kinds of magic [the Taurat (Torah) and the Quran] each helping the other!" This is a possible reading in light of verse 49, but this verse might refer to the unbelievers in the time of Pharaoh who rejected the two miraculous signs given to Moses (see 28:31–36). Compare 20:63, where the Cairo text has instead *sāḥirāni* ("two magicians"), referring to Moses and Aaron.

⁴⁹*Say,* 'If you are truthful, bring some Book from God better in guidance than both of them so that I may follow it.' ⁵⁰Then, if they

do not respond to *you*[*r*] [summons], *know* that they only follow their desires, and who is more astray than him who follows his desires without any guidance from God? Indeed, God does not guide the wrongdoing lot.

⁵¹Certainly We have carried on this discourse for them so that they may take admonition. ⁵²Those to whom We gave the Book before it are the ones who believe in it, ⁵³and when it is recited to them, they say, 'We believe in it. It is indeed the truth from our Lord. Indeed, we were *muslims* [even] before it [came].' ⁵⁴Those will be given their reward two times for their patience. They repel evil [conduct] with good, and spend out of what We have provided them, ⁵⁵and when they hear vain talk they avoid it and say, 'Our deeds belong to us and your deeds belong to you. Peace be to you. We do not court the ignorant.'

⁵⁶*You* cannot guide whomever *you* wish, but [it is] God [who] guides whomever He wishes, and He knows best those who are guided.

⁵⁷They say, 'If we follow the guidance with *you,* we will be driven out of our territory.' Did We not establish a secure sanctuary for them where fruits of all kinds are brought as a provision from Us? But most of them do not know.

28:57 On the secure sanctuary to which the Qur'ān refers, and the fruitfulness of the land around it, see commentary on 14:35–41 (with further references).

⁵⁸How many a town We have destroyed that was proud of its lifestyle! There lie their dwellings, uninhabited after them except by a few, and We were the [sole] inheritors. ⁵⁹Your Lord would not destroy the towns until He had raised an apostle in their

mother city to recite Our signs to them. We would never destroy the towns except when their people were wrongdoers.

⁶⁰Whatever things you have been given are only the wares of the life of this world and its glitter, and what is with God is better and more lasting. Will you not exercise your reason?

⁶¹Is he to whom We have given a good promise, which he will receive, like him whom We have provided the wares of the life of this world, but who will be arraigned on the Day of Resurrection?

⁶²The day He will call out to them and ask, 'Where are My "partners" that you used to claim?' ⁶³Those against whom the word had become due will say, 'Our Lord! These are the ones whom we have perverted. We perverted them as we were perverse ourselves. We repudiate them in front of You: it was not us that they worshiped.' ⁶⁴It will be said, 'Invoke your partners!' So they will invoke them, but they will not respond to them, and they will sight the punishment, wishing they had followed guidance.

⁶⁵The day He will call out to them and say, 'What response did you give to the apostles?' ⁶⁶That day all news will be withheld from them, so they will not question one another.

⁶⁷As for him who repents, and develops faith and acts righteously, maybe he will be among the felicitous.

⁶⁸*Your* Lord creates whatever He wishes and chooses: they have no choice. Immaculate is God and far above having any partners that they ascribe [to Him]. ⁶⁹*Your* Lord knows whatever their breasts conceal and whatever they disclose. ⁷⁰He is God, there is no god except Him. All praise belongs to Him in this world and the Hereafter. All judgement belongs to Him and to Him you will be brought back.

⁷¹*Say,* 'Tell me, if God were to make the night perpetual for you until the Day of Resurrection, what god other than God can bring you light? Then, will you not listen?'

⁷²*Say,* 'Tell me, if God were to make the day perpetual for you until the Day of Resurrection, what god other than God can bring you night wherein you can rest? Will you not see?' ⁷³He has made for you night and day out of His mercy, so that you may rest therein and that you may seek His bounty and so that you may give thanks.

⁷⁴The day He will call out to them and say, 'Where are My "partners" that you used to claim?' ⁷⁵We shall draw a witness from every nation and say, 'Produce your evidence.' Then they will know that all reality belongs to God and what they used to fabricate will forsake them.

⁷⁶Korah indeed belonged to the people of Moses, but he bullied them. We had given him so much treasures that their chests indeed proved heavy for a band of stalwarts. When his people said to him, 'Do not boast! Indeed, God does not like the boasters. ⁷⁷Seek the abode of the Hereafter by the means that God has given you, while not forgetting your share of this world. Be good [to others] just as God has been good to you, and do not try to cause corruption in the land. Indeed, God does not like the agents of corruption.'

⁷⁸He said, 'I have been given [all] this just because of the knowledge that I have.'

Did he not know that God had already destroyed before him some of the generations who were more powerful than him and greater in amassing [wealth]? The guilty will not be questioned about their sins.

⁷⁹Then he emerged before his people in his finery. Those who desired the life of the world said, 'We wish we had like what Korah has been given! He is indeed greatly fortunate.' ⁸⁰Those who were given knowledge said [to them], 'Woe to you! God's reward is better for someone who has faith and acts righteously, and no one will receive it except the patient.'

[81]So We caused the earth to swallow him and his house, and he had no party that might protect him from God, nor could he rescue himself.

28:76–81 In the Book of Numbers, Korah treacherously rebels against Moses's authority. For this he is swallowed up by the earth, along with all of his possessions:

> [28]Moses said, 'This is how you will know that the Lord himself has sent me to perform all these tasks and that I am not doing them of my own accord.
> [29]If these people die a natural death such as people commonly die, then the Lord has not sent me.
> [30]But if the Lord does something utterly new, if the earth should open its mouth and swallow them and all their belongings, so that they go down alive to Sheol, then you will know that they held the Lord in contempt.'
> [31]The moment he finished saying all this, the ground split apart under their feet,
> [32]the earth opened its mouth and swallowed them, their families, all Korah's people and all their property.
> [33]They went down alive to Sheol with all their belongings. The earth closed over them and they disappeared in the middle of the community. (Num 16:28–33; cf. Psa 55:15)

The reference to Korah's possessions (Num 16:32–33) was taken by Jewish exegetes as a sign that he had grown rich: "The keys of Korah's treasure house were a load for three hundred white mules" (b. Sanhedrin 110a). One tradition in the Babylonian Talmud (b. Pesahim 119a) attributes Korah's riches to a treasure left by Joseph.

On Korah, cf. 29:39–40; 40:23–24. In those two cases he is associated with Pharaoh and Haman, whereas in this Sura he is mentioned only after the earlier references to those two figures.

---

[82]By dawn those who longed to be in his place the day before were saying, 'Don't you see that God expands the provision for whomever He wishes of His servants and tightens it? Had God

not shown us favour, He might have made the earth swallow us too. Don't you see that the faithless do not prosper?'

⁸³This is the abode of the Hereafter which We shall grant to those who do not desire to domineer in the earth nor to cause corruption, and the outcome will be in favour of the Godwary. ⁸⁴Whoever brings virtue shall receive [a reward] better than it, but whoever brings vice—those who commit misdeeds shall not be requited except for what they used to do.

⁸⁵Indeed, He who has revealed to *you* the Qur'ān will surely restore *you* to the place of return.

Say, 'My Lord knows best him who brings guidance and him who is in plain error.'

⁸⁶*You* did not expect that the Book would be delivered to *you,* but it was a mercy from *your* Lord. So *do not be* ever an advocate of the faithless. ⁸⁷*Do not* ever let them bar *you* from God's signs after they have been sent down to *you.* Invite to *your* Lord and never *be* one of the polytheists. ⁸⁸And *do not invoke* another god besides God; there is no god except Him. Everything is to perish except His Face. All judgement belongs to Him and to Him you will be brought back.

29. *AL-'ANKABŪT*, THE SPIDER

In the Name of God, the All-beneficent, the All-merciful.

¹*Alif, Lām, Mīm.* ²Do the people suppose that they will be let off because they say, 'We have faith,' and they will not be tested? ³Certainly We tested those who were before them. So God shall surely ascertain those who are truthful and He shall surely ascertain the liars.

⁴Do those who commit misdeeds suppose that they can outmaneuver Us? Evil is the judgement that they make.

⁵Whoever expects to encounter God [should know that] God's [appointed] time will indeed come, and He is the All-hearing, the All-knowing.

⁶Whoever strives, strives only for his own sake. God has indeed no need of the creatures. ⁷As for those who have faith and do righteous deeds, We will absolve them of their misdeeds and We will surely reward them by the best of what they used to do.

⁸We have enjoined man to be good to his parents. But if they urge you to ascribe to Me as partner that of which you have no knowledge, then do not obey them. To Me will be your return, whereat I will inform you concerning what you used to do. ⁹Those who have faith and do righteous deeds, We will surely admit them among the righteous.

¹⁰Among the people there are those who say, 'We have faith in God,' but if such a one is tormented in God's cause, he takes persecution by the people for God's punishment. Yet if there comes any help from *your* Lord, they will say, 'We were indeed with you.' Does not God know best what is in the breasts of the creatures? ¹¹God shall surely ascertain those who have faith and He shall surely ascertain the hypocrites.

¹²The faithless say to the faithful, 'Follow our way and we will bear [responsibility for] your iniquities.' They will not bear anything of their iniquities. They are indeed liars.

¹³But they will carry their own burdens and other burdens along with their own, and they will surely be questioned on the Day of Resurrection concerning that which they used to fabricate.

29:12–13 On the notion that no soul shall carry another's burden, see commentary on 82:19 (with further references).

––––––––––––

¹⁴Certainly We sent Noah to his people and he remained with them for a thousand-less-fifty years. Then the flood overtook them while they were wrongdoers.

29:14 Cf. Gen 9:29: "In all, Noah's life lasted nine hundred and fifty years; then he died."

––––––––––––

¹⁵Then We delivered him and those who were in the Ark and made it a sign for all the nations.

29:15 On the destruction of Noah's people, see commentary on 11:25–39 (with further references).

¹⁶And Abraham, when he said to his people, 'Worship God and be wary of Him. That is better for you, should you know. ¹⁷What you worship instead of God are mere idols, and you invent a lie. Indeed, those whom you worship besides God have no control over your provision. So seek all [your] provision from God and worship Him and thank Him, and to Him you shall be brought back.'

¹⁸If you impugn [the Apostle's teaching], then [other] nations have impugned [likewise] before you, and the Apostle's duty is only to communicate in clear terms.

¹⁹Have they not regarded how God originates the creation? Then He will bring it back. That is indeed easy for God. ²⁰*Say,* 'Travel through the land and observe how He has originated the creation.' Then God will bring about the genesis of the Hereafter. Indeed, God has power over all things.

²¹He will punish whomever He wishes and have mercy on whomever He wishes, and to Him you will be returned. ²²You cannot frustrate Him on the earth or in the heaven, nor do you have besides God any friend or helper. ²³Those who deny the signs of God and the encounter with Him—they have despaired of My mercy, and for such there is a painful punishment.

²⁴But the only answer of his people was that they said, 'Kill him, or burn him.' Then God delivered him from the fire. There are indeed signs in that for a people who have faith.

²⁵He said, 'You have taken idols [for worship] besides God for the sake of [mutual] affection amongst yourselves in the life of the world. Then on the Day of Resurrection you will disown one another and curse one another, and the Fire will be your abode and you will not have any helpers.'

29:16–25 On Abraham's preaching to, and confrontation with, his father and his people, see commentary on 26:69–93 (with further references). Here the Qurʾānic account of Abraham's confrontation with his people seems to be interrupted (vv. 18–23) by a general reflection on prophethood and divine punishment.

In verse 24 the Qurʾān alludes to the salvation of Abraham from the furnace into which his idolatrous opponents cast him. On this see commentary on 21:68–70 (with further references).

---

²⁶Thereupon Lot believed in him, and he said, 'I am indeed migrating toward my Lord. Indeed, He is the All-mighty, the All-wise.'

29:26 This verse (see *BEQ,* 146) may be a pious development of Genesis 13:8–12, which describes the parting of Lot and Abram.

---

²⁷And We gave him Isaac and Jacob and We ordained prophethood and the Book among his descendants and We gave him his reward in this world, and in the Hereafter he will indeed be among the Righteous.

29:27 Here and elsewhere (cf. 6:84; 11:71; 19:49; 21:72) the Qurʾān suggests that both Isaac and Jacob were sons of Abraham (on this see Paret, *Kommentar,* on 6:84); the Qurʾān never describes Jacob as Isaac's son. On the "prophethood and the Book," see commentary on 3:79–80 (with further references).

---

²⁸And Lot, when he said to his people, 'You indeed commit an indecency none in the world has ever committed before you! ²⁹What! Do you come to men and cut off the way, and commit outrages in your gatherings?'

But the only answer of his people was that they said, 'Bring down on us God's punishment, if you are truthful.'

³⁰He said, 'My Lord! Help me against this corruptive lot.'

³¹And when Our messengers came to Abraham with the good news, they said, 'We are going to destroy the people of this town. Its people are indeed wrongdoers.'

³²He said, 'Lot is in it.' They said, 'We know better those who are in it. We will surely deliver him and his family, except his wife: she shall be one of those who remain behind.'

³³And when Our messengers came to Lot, he was distressed on their account and in a predicament for their sake. But they said, 'Do not be afraid, nor grieve! We shall deliver you and your family, except your wife: she will be one of those who remain behind. ³⁴We are indeed going to bring down upon the people of this town a punishment from the sky because of the transgressions they used to commit.'

³⁵Certainly We have left of it a manifest sign for people who exercise their reason.

29:28–35 The allusion to the sinfulness of Lot's people (vv. 28–30) reflects not so much the narrative of Sodom and Gomorrah's destruction in Genesis 19, or other Old Testament references to Sodom, but rather 2 Peter 2:6–8:

> ⁶He condemned the cities of Sodom and Gomorrah by reducing them to ashes as a warning to future sinners;
> ⁷but rescued Lot, an upright man who had been sickened by the debauched way in which these vile people behaved,
> ⁸for that upright man, living among them, was outraged in his upright soul by the crimes that he saw and heard every day.

Like the Qur'ān, the author of 2 Peter points to Sodom and Gomorrah as an example of God's rescuing the righteous from the midst of a wicked people and refers to the ruins of those cities as a "warning to future sinners" (2Pe 2:6; cf. Q 29:35; see also Jud 1:7). There is only an allusion here ("Lot is in it"; v. 32) to Abraham's intercession for Sodom in Genesis 18 (cf. 11:74–76).

Asad sees the phrase "cut off the way" (v. 29) as a reference to the sexual habits of Lot's people ("thus cut across the way [of nature]"), while Hilali-Khan interpret this as a reference to highway robbery ("and rob the wayfarer" [e.g., traveler]).

On the debauchery of Lot's people, cf. 7:80–81; 11:78–80; 27:54–55. On the destruction of Lot's people, see commentary on 15:57–74 (with further references). On the ruins of Lot's city, cf. 15:76–77; 51:37. On Lot's wife, see commentary on 27:54–58 (with further references).

---

³⁶And to Midian We sent Shuʿayb, their townsman. He said, 'O my people! Worship God and expect [to encounter] the Last Day, and do not act wickedly on the earth causing corruption.'

³⁷But they impugned him, whereupon the earthquake seized them and they lay lifeless prostrate in their homes.

³⁸And ʿĀd and Thamūd, [whose fate] is evident to you from their habitations. Satan made their deeds seem decorous to them, thus he barred them from the way [of God], though they used to be perceptive.

³⁹And Korah, Pharaoh, and Hāmān. Certainly Moses brought them manifest proofs, but they acted arrogantly in the land; though they could not outmaneuver [God]. ⁴⁰So We seized each [of them] for his sin: among them were those upon whom We unleashed a rain of stones, and among them were those who were seized by the Cry, and among them were those whom We caused the earth to swallow, and among them were those whom We drowned. It was not God who wronged them, but it was they who used to wrong themselves.

29:39–40 In verse 39 the Qurʾān refers to three characters—Korah, Pharaoh, and Haman—all of whom are connected to the Qurʾānic account of Moses and the Israelites in Pharaoh's Egypt (on Korah see commentary on 28:76–81, with further references; on Haman see commentary on 28:38, with further references). In verse 40 the Qurʾān refers specifically to the disasters that overcame Korah (swallowed by the earth; cf. Num 16:31–33) and Pharaoh (drowned in the sea; cf. Exo 14:27–28). The first two disasters ("a rain of stones" and "the Cry") seem to be general references to the method of destruction God has used against other peoples ("rain of stones": 7:84; 11:82; 26:173; 27:58; "Cry": 11:67, 94; 15:73, 83; 23:41; 36:29, 49, 53; 38:15; 50:23; 54:31; 63:4).

------

[41]The parable of those who take protectors instead of God is that of the spider that makes a home, and indeed the frailest of homes is the home of a spider, had they known! [42]God indeed knows whatever thing they invoke besides Him, and He is the All-mighty, the All-wise.

[43]We draw these parables for mankind; but no one grasps them except those who have knowledge.

29:43 The Qurʾān's use of parables, and its concern with the inability of some people to grasp its parables, reflects a theme in the Gospels:

[10]Then the disciples went up to him and asked, 'Why do you talk to them in parables?'
[11]In answer, he said, 'Because to you is granted to understand the mysteries of the kingdom of Heaven, but to them it is not granted.' (Mat 13:10–11; cf. Mar 4:11; Luk 8:10; see *BEQ,* 456).

------

[44]God created the heavens and the earth with consummate wisdom. There is indeed a sign in that for the faithful.

[45]*Recite* what has been revealed to *you* of the Book and *maintain* the prayer. The prayer indeed restrains from indecent and wrongful conduct, and the remembrance of God is surely greater. And God knows whatever [deeds] you do.

[46]Do not argue with the People of the Book except in a manner which is best, except such of them as are wrongdoers, and say, 'We believe in what has been sent down to us and in what has

been sent down to you; our God and your God is one [and the same] and to Him do we submit.'

⁴⁷Thus have We sent down the Book to *you;* those to whom We have given the Book believe in it, and of these there are some who believe in it, and none contests Our signs except the faithless.

⁴⁸*You* did not use to recite any scripture before it, nor did *you* write it with *your* right hand, for then the impugners would have been skeptical. ⁴⁹Indeed, it is [present as] manifest signs in the breasts of those who have been given knowledge, and none contests Our signs except wrongdoers.

⁵⁰They say, 'Why has not some sign been sent down to him from his Lord?' *Say,* 'These signs are only from God, and I am only a manifest warner.'⁵¹Does it not suffice them that We have sent down to *you* the Book which is recited to them? There is indeed in that a mercy and admonition for a people who have faith.

⁵²*Say,* 'God suffices as witness between me and you: He knows whatever there is in the heavens and the earth. Those who put faith in falsehood and defy God—it is they who are the losers.'

⁵³They ask *you* to hasten the punishment. Yet were it not for a specified time, the punishment would have surely overtaken them. Surely, it will overtake them suddenly while they are unaware.

⁵⁴They ask *you* to hasten the punishment, and indeed hell will besiege the faithless ⁵⁵on the day when the punishment envelopes them from above them and from under their feet, and He will say, 'Taste what you used to do!'

⁵⁶O My servants who have faith! My earth is indeed vast. So worship [only] Me. ⁵⁷Every soul shall taste death. Then you shall be brought back to Us.

29:57 On "tasting" death, see commentary on 44:56 (with further references).

⁵⁸Those who have faith and do righteous deeds, We will settle them in the lofty abodes of paradise, with streams running in them, to remain in them [forever]. How excellent is the reward of the workers!

29:58 On the "abodes" or "rooms" (Ar. *ghuraf*) of heaven in the Qur'ān, see commentary on 39:20 (with further references). On the streams of paradise, see commentary on 2:25 (with further references).

⁵⁹—Those who are patient and who put their trust in their Lord. ⁶⁰How many an animal there is that does not carry its own provision. God provides them and you and He is the All-hearing, the All-knowing.

29:60 "Look at the birds in the sky. They do not sow or reap or gather into barns; yet your heavenly Father feeds them. Are you not worth much more than they are?" (Mat 6:26; cf. Luk 12:24).

⁶¹If *you* ask them, 'Who created the heavens and the earth and disposed the sun and the moon?' They will surely say, 'God.' Then where do they stray?

⁶²God expands the provision for whomever He wishes of His servants and tightens it for him. Indeed, God has knowledge of all things.

⁶³And if *you* ask them, 'Who sends down water from the sky, with which He revives the earth after its death?' They will surely say, 'God.' *Say,* 'All praise belongs to God!' But most of them do not exercise their reason.

⁶⁴The life of this world is nothing but diversion and play, but the abode of the Hereafter is indeed Life (itself), had they known!

⁶⁵When they board the ship, they invoke God putting exclusive faith in Him, but when He delivers them to land, behold, they ascribe partners [to Him], ⁶⁶being ungrateful for what We have given them! So let them enjoy. Soon they will know!

⁶⁷Have they not seen that We have appointed a safe sanctuary, while the people are despoiled all around them? Would they then believe in falsehood and be ungrateful toward the blessing of God?

⁶⁸Who is a greater wrongdoer than him who fabricates lies against God, or denies the truth when it comes to him? Is not the [final] abode of the faithless in hell?

⁶⁹As for those who strive in Us, We shall surely guide them in Our ways, and God is indeed with the virtuous.

30. *AL-RŪM*, The Byzantines

In the Name of God, the All-beneficent, the All-merciful.

¹*Alif, Lām, Mīm.* ²The Byzantines have been vanquished ³in a nearby territory, but after their defeat they will be victorious ⁴in a few years. All command belongs to God, before this and hereafter, and on that day the faithful will rejoice ⁵at God's help. He helps whomever He wishes, and He is the All-mighty, the All-merciful.

30:1–5 This passage is usually interpreted as a reference to the war between the Byzantines and the Sasanians during the lifetime of the Prophet (602–628 AD), and in particular as an expression of the Prophet's sympathy for the Christian Byzantines over the Zoroastrian Sasanians. This interpretation is found in Islamic traditions, such as that cited by Wāḥidī:

> The Persians defeated the Byzantines. The Prophet and his Companions heard this while in Mecca and felt sad about it. The Prophet disliked that the Magians, who did not have a revealed Scripture, have the upper hand over the Byzantines who were people of the Book. The disbelievers of Mecca, on the other hand, were exultant and spiteful. When they met the Companions of the Prophet they said to them: "You are people of the Book and the Christians are people of the Book. We are without a revealed Scripture and our brothers the Persians have defeated your brothers the Byzantines. If you ever fight us, we will defeat you too." Therefore, God revealed [this passage].

For their part academic scholars have often speculated that the victory over the Byzantines alluded to in verse 2 (although an alternate reading of this verse has this as a victory *of* the Byzantines) refers to the Sasanian conquest of Jeru-salem in 614 (or of Damascus in 613), and that the prediction of a Byzantine victory is connected to their decisive triumph over the Sasanians in Nineveh in 627. It would then be a later *"ex eventu* prophecy" made to seem like a predic-tion (i.e., this passage would be dated to the end of Muḥammad's career).

The Qur'ān's interest in raising this topic at all seems to be connected to the Byzantine conviction (common in seventh-century texts such as the *History of Maurice*) that the definitive victory of the Byzantines over the Sasanians would precede the return of Christ and the end of the world. The Qur'ān seems indeed here to see a Byzantine victory as a sign of the eschaton, when God will vanquish the unbelievers; this is why in verse 4 it declares that "the faith-ful will rejoice at God's help [or better, "victory"; Ar. *naṣr*]." The eschatologi-cal dimension of this passage is more evident in light of the end of this Sura, which (like its beginning) alludes to God's ultimate victory (cr. Tommaso Tesei).

In his translation Arthur Droge points out (note on 30:3) that the Qur'ān points to the Romans having conquered in a *nearby* land (Q 30:3, Qarai has "nearby territory"). This suggests that the geographical context in which this passage was proclaimed would presumably be well to the north of Mecca (something also suggested by 37:137–38; see commentary on 37:133–38).

---

⁶[This is] a promise of God: God does not break His promise, but most people do not know. ⁷They know just an outward aspect of the life of the world, but they are oblivious of the Hereafter.

⁸Have they not reflected in their own souls? God did not create the heavens and the earth and whatever is between them except with consummate wisdom and for a specified term. Indeed, many of these people disbelieve in the encounter with their Lord.

⁹Have they not traveled through the land and observed how was the fate of those who were before them? They were more powerful than them, and they plowed the earth and developed it more than they have developed it. Their apostles brought them manifest proofs. So it was not God who wronged them, but it was they who used to wrong themselves. ¹⁰Then the fate of those who

committed misdeeds was that they denied the signs of God and they used to deride them.

[11] God originates the creation, then He will bring it back, then you will be brought back to Him. [12] And when the Hour sets in, the guilty will despair. [13] None of those whom they ascribed as partners [to God] will intercede for them, and they will disavow their partners.

[14] The day the Hour sets in, they will be divided on that day [in separate groups]: [15] As for those who have faith and do righteous deeds, they shall be in a garden, rejoicing. [16] But as for those who were faithless and denied Our signs and the encounter of the Hereafter, they will be brought to the punishment.

[17] So glorify God when you enter evening and when you rise at dawn. [18] To Him belongs all praise in the heavens and the earth, at nightfall and when you enter noontime. [19] He brings forth the living from the dead and brings forth the dead from the living, and revives the earth after its death. Likewise you [too] shall be raised [from the dead].

[20] Of His signs is that He created you from dust, then, behold, you are humans scattering [all over]!

30:20 "The Lord God shaped man from the soil of the ground and blew the breath of life into his nostrils, and man became a living being" (Gen 2:7). On the creation of humanity from dust (or "dirt"; Ar. *turāb*), see commentary on 11:61 (with further references).

---

[21] And of His signs is that He created for you mates from your own selves that you may take comfort in them, and He ordained affection and mercy between you. There are indeed signs in that for a people who reflect.

²²Among His signs is the creation of the heavens and the earth and the difference of your languages and colours. There are indeed signs in that for those who know.

²³And of His signs is your sleep by night and day, and your pursuit of His bounty. There are indeed signs in that for a people who listen.

²⁴And of His signs is that He shows you the lightning, arousing fear and hope, and He sends down water from the sky and with it revives the earth after its death. There are indeed signs in that for people who exercise their reason.

²⁵And of His signs is that the heaven and the earth stand by His command, and then, when He calls you forth from the earth, behold, you will come forth.

²⁶To Him belongs whoever is in the heavens and the earth. All are obedient to Him.

²⁷It is He who originates the creation, and then He will bring it back—and that is more simple for Him. His is the loftiest description in the heavens and the earth, and He is the All-mighty, the All-wise.

²⁸He draws for you an example from yourselves: Do you have among your slaves any partners [who may share] in what We have provided you, so that you are equal in its respect, and you revere them as you revere one another? Thus do We elaborate the signs for people who exercise their reason.

²⁹The wrongdoers indeed follow their own desires without any knowledge. So who will guide those whom God has led astray? They will have no helpers.

³⁰So set *your* heart as a person of pure faith on this religion, the original nature endowed by God according to which He originated mankind (There is no altering God's creation; that is the upright religion, but most people do not know.)

30:30 On the term rendered here as "pure faith" (*ḥanīf*), see commentary on 16:120–23.

---

³¹—turning to Him in penitence, and *be* wary of Him, and *maintain* the prayer, and *do* not be one of the polytheists ³²—those who split up their religion and became sects: each faction boasting about what it possessed.

30:32 This verse seems to allude to Jews and Christians and the conflicts between them.

---

³³When distress befalls people, they supplicate their Lord, turning to Him in penitence. Then, when He lets them taste His mercy, behold, a part of them ascribe partners to their Lord, ³⁴being ungrateful toward what We have given them. So let them enjoy. Soon they will know! ³⁵Have We sent down to them any authority which might assert what they associate with Him?

³⁶When We let people taste [Our] mercy, they boast about it; but should an ill visit them because of what their hands have sent ahead, behold, they become despondent! ³⁷Do they not see that God expands the provision for whomever He wishes, and tightens it? There are indeed signs in that for people who have faith.

³⁸*Give* the relative his due, and the needy and the traveler [as well]. That is better for those who seek God's pleasure, and it is they who are the felicitous. ³⁹What [gift] you give in usury in order that it may increase people's wealth does not increase with

God. But what you pay as *zakāt* seeking God's pleasure—it is they who will be given a manifold increase.

30:39 On usury (cf. 2:276; 3:130; 4:161) in the Bible, see Exodus 22:24 [25 in the RSV]; Leviticus 25:36–37; Deuteronomy 23:20–21; Ezekiel 22:12; Psalm 15:5; Proverbs 28:8 (cf. also Luk 6:34–35).

---

⁴⁰It is God who created you and then He provided for you, then He makes you die, then He will bring you to life. Is there anyone among your 'partners' who does anything of that kind? Immaculate is He and far above [having] any partners that they ascribe [to Him]!

⁴¹Corruption has appeared in land and sea because of the doings of the people's hands, that He may make them taste something of what they have done, so that they may come back.

⁴²*Say,* 'Travel through the land and see how was the fate of those who were before [you], most of whom were polytheists.'

⁴³So set *your* heart on the upright religion, before there comes a day irrevocable from God. On that day they shall be split [into various groups]. ⁴⁴Whoever is faithless shall face the consequences of his unfaith, and those who act righteously only prepare for their own souls, ⁴⁵so that He may reward out of His grace those who have faith and do righteous deeds. Indeed, He does not like the faithless.

⁴⁶And of His signs is that He sends the winds as bearers of good news and to let you taste of His mercy, and that the ships may sail by His command, and that you may seek of His bounty, and so that you may give [Him] thanks.

⁴⁷Certainly We sent apostles to their people before *you* and they brought them manifest proofs. Then We took vengeance upon those who were guilty, and it was a must for Us to help the faithful.

⁴⁸It is God who sends the winds. Then they generate a cloud, then He spreads it as He wishes in the sky, and forms it into fragments, whereat you see the rain issuing from its midst. Then, when He strikes with it whomever of His servants that He wishes, behold, they rejoice; ⁴⁹and they had been indeed despondent earlier, before it was sent down upon them.

⁵⁰So observe the effects of God's mercy: how He revives the earth after its death! He is indeed the reviver of the dead and He has power over all things.

⁵¹And if We send a wind and they see it turn yellow, they will surely become ungrateful after that.

⁵²Indeed, *you* cannot make the dead hear, nor can *you* make the deaf hear the call when they turn their backs [upon *you*], ⁵³nor can *you* lead the blind out of their error. *You* can make only those hear who have faith in Our signs and have submitted.

⁵⁴It is God who created you from [a state of] weakness, then He gave you power after weakness. Then, after power, He ordained weakness and old age: He creates whatever He wishes and He is the All-knowing, the All-powerful.

⁵⁵On the day when the Hour sets in, the guilty will swear that they had remained only for an hour. That is how they were used to lying [in the world]. ⁵⁶But those who were given knowledge and faith will say, 'Certainly you remained in God's Book until the Day of Resurrection. This is the Day of Resurrection, but you did not know.'

⁵⁷On that day, the excuses of the wrongdoers will not benefit them, nor will they be asked to propitiate [God].

⁵⁸Certainly we have drawn for mankind in this Qur'ān every [kind of] parable. Indeed, if *you* bring them a sign, the faithless will surely say, 'You are nothing but fabricators!'

⁵⁹Thus does God seal the hearts of those who do not know.

⁶⁰So *be patient!* God's promise is indeed true. And do not let *yourself* be upset by those who have no conviction.

31. *LUQMĀN*, LUQMAN

In the Name of God, the All-beneficent, the All-merciful.

¹*Alif, Lām, Mīm.* ²These are the signs of the wise Book, ³a guidance and mercy for the virtuous, ⁴who maintain the prayer, pay the *zakāt,* and are certain of the Hereafter. ⁵Those follow their Lord's guidance, and it is they who are the felicitous.

⁶Among the people is he who buys diversionary talk that he may lead [people] astray from God's way without any knowledge, and he takes it in derision. For such there is a humiliating punishment. ⁷When Our signs are recited to him he turns away disdainfully, as if he had not heard them [at all], as if there were a deafness in his ears. So *inform* him of a painful punishment.

⁸As for those who have faith and do righteous deeds, for them will be gardens of bliss, ⁹to remain in them [forever]—a true promise of God, and He is the All-mighty, the All-wise.

¹⁰He created the heavens without any pillars that you may see, and cast firm mountains in the earth lest it should shake with you, and He has scattered in it every kind of animal. And We sent down water from the sky and caused every splendid kind [of plant] to grow in it.

31:10 The Qur'ān's declaration here that God "raised the heavens without any pillars that you see" (cf. 13:2) suggests that the sky is a firmament, a dome-like barrier between earth and the heavens. The Qur'ān thereby shares a cosmological vision with a number of Biblical texts:

> In wisdom, the Lord laid the earth's foundations, in understanding he spread out the heavens. (Pro 3:19; cf. Pro 8:27–28)

> He who sits enthroned above the circle of the earth, the inhabitants of which are like grasshoppers, stretches out the heavens like a cloth, spreads them out like a tent to live in. (Isa 40:22; cf. Isa 44:24; Psa 104:5)

---

[12]Certainly We gave Luqman wisdom, saying, 'Give thanks to God; and whoever gives thanks, gives thanks only for his own sake. And whoever is ungrateful, [let him know that] God is indeed all-sufficient, all-laudable.'

[13]When Luqman said to his son, as he advised him: 'O my son! Do not ascribe any partners to God. Polytheism is indeed a great injustice.'

31:12–13 Luqmān is generally understood to be a figure of Arabian lore, although Richard Bell (*Commentary,* 2:82–83), following Hirschfeld, argues that the name may be a modification of the Arabic "Sulaymān." That Luqmān (v. 13) is found giving advice to his son would correspond with Proverbs, which has Solomon advise his son (e.g., Pro 1:8: "Listen, my child, to your father's instruction, do not reject your mother's teaching").

---

[14]We have enjoined man concerning his parents: His mother carried him through weakness upon weakness, and his weaning takes two years. Give thanks to Me and to your parents. To Me is the return.

31:14 The idea that a woman should suckle for two years (cf. 2:233) has a basis in the Talmud (b. Ketubbot 60a).

---

¹⁵But if they urge you to ascribe to Me as partner that of which you have no knowledge, then do not obey them. Keep their company honourably in this world and follow the way of those who turn to Me penitently. Then to Me will be your return, whereat I will inform you concerning what you used to do.

¹⁶'O my son! Even if it should be the weight of a mustard seed, and [even though] it should be in a rock, or in the heavens, or in the earth, God will produce it. God is indeed all-attentive, all-aware.

31:16 The use of "mustard seed" to indicate a small amount (cf. 21:47) is derived ultimately from the synoptic Gospels (see also the similar expressions in 6:59; 10:61; 34:3):

> ³¹He put another parable before them, 'The kingdom of Heaven is like a mustard seed which a man took and sowed in his field.
> ³²It is the smallest of all the seeds, but when it has grown it is the biggest of shrubs and becomes a tree, so that the birds of the air can come and shelter in its branches.' (Mat 13:31–32; cf. Mar 4:30–32; Luk 13:18–19; see also Mat 17:20; Luk 17:6)

---

¹⁷O my son! Maintain the prayer and bid what is right and forbid what is wrong, and be patient through whatever may befall you. That is indeed the steadiest of courses. ¹⁸Do not turn your cheek away disdainfully from the people, and do not walk boastfully on the earth. Indeed, God does not like any swaggering braggart. ¹⁹Be modest in your bearing, and lower your voice. Indeed, the ungainliest of voices is the donkey's voice.'

31:19 This passage, as Conybeare, Rendel Harris, and Smith Lewis (*The Story of Aḥikar*) point out, is closely related to the Near Eastern legend of Aḥīqar the Assyrian sage (a legend also connected to the story of Haman in the Qurʾān; see commentary on 28:38):

> My son, cast down thine eyes, and lower thy voice, and look from beneath thine eyelids; for if a house could be built by a high voice, the ass would build two houses in one day. (*The Story of Aḥikar,* Syriac version, 104n8)

Indeed it may be that Luqmān the sage is entirely modeled on the figure of Aḥīqar.

---

²⁰Do you not see that God has disposed for you whatever there is in the heavens and whatever there is in the earth, and He has showered upon you His blessings, the outward and the inward? Yet among the people are those who dispute concerning God without any knowledge or guidance or an illuminating scripture. ²¹When they are told, 'Follow what God has sent down,' they say, 'No, we will follow what we found our fathers following.' What! Even if Satan be calling them to the punishment of the Blaze?

²²Whoever surrenders his heart to God and is virtuous, has certainly held fast to the firmest handle, and with God lies the outcome of all matters. ²³As for those who are faithless, let their unfaith not grieve *you*. To Us will be their return, and We will inform them about what they have done. Indeed, God knows best what is in the breasts. ²⁴We will provide for them for a short time, then We will shove them toward a harsh punishment.

²⁵If *you* ask them, 'Who created the heavens and the earth?' they will surely say, 'God.' *Say,* 'All praise belongs to God!' But most of them do not know.

²⁶To God belongs whatever is in the heavens and the earth. Indeed, God is the All-sufficient, the All-laudable.

²⁷If all the trees on the earth were pens, and the sea replenished with seven more seas [were ink], the words of God would not be spent. God is indeed all-mighty, all-wise.

31:27 Here (cf. 18:109) the Qur'ān applies in a new way a saying known to Jewish sources, including the Talmud:

> Raba b. Mehasia also said in the name of R. Hama b. Goria in Rab's name: If all seas were ink, reeds pens, the heavens parchment, and all men writers, they would not suffice to write down the intricacies of government. (b. Shabbat 11a)

It could be, as well, that the Qur'ān means to respond to the claim made of the deeds of Jesus at the end of the Gospel of John (see Joh 21:25: "There was much else that Jesus did; if it were written down in detail, I do not suppose the world itself would hold all the books that would be written").

———————

²⁸Your creation and your resurrection are not but as of a single soul. God is indeed all-hearing, all-seeing. ²⁹Have *you* not regarded that God makes the night pass into the day and makes the day pass into the night; and He has disposed the sun and the moon, each moving for a specified term, and that God is well aware of what you do? ³⁰That is because God is the Reality, and whatever they invoke besides Him is nullity, and because God is the All-exalted, the All-great. ³¹Have *you* not regarded that the ships sail at sea with God's blessing, that He may show you some of His signs? There are indeed signs in that for every patient and grateful [servant]. ³²When waves cover them like awnings, they invoke God, putting exclusive faith in Him. But when He delivers them towards land, [only] some of them remain unswerving. No one will impugn Our signs except an ungrateful traitor.

³³O mankind! Be wary of your Lord and fear the day when a father will not atone for his child, nor the child will atone for its father in any wise. God's promise is indeed true. So do not let the life of the world deceive you, nor let the Deceiver deceive you concerning God.

³⁴The knowledge of the Hour is indeed with God. He sends down the rain, and He knows what is in the wombs. No soul knows what it will earn tomorrow, and no soul knows in what land it will die. God is indeed all-knowing, all-aware.

31:34 On knowledge of the Hour being with God alone, see commentary on 79:42–44 (with further references).

32. *AL-SAJDA*, THE PROSTRATION

In the Name of God, the All-beneficent, the All-merciful.

¹*Alif, Lām, Mīm.* ²The [gradual] sending down of the Book, there is no doubt in it, is from the Lord of all the worlds. ³But they say, 'He has fabricated it.' No, it is the truth from *your* Lord, that *you* may warn a people to whom there did not come any warner before *you,* so that they may be guided [to the right path].

⁴It is God who created the heavens and the earth and whatever is between them in six days, then He settled on the Throne. You do not have besides Him any guardian or intercessor. Will you not then take admonition?

32:4 God's "settling" (cf. 7:54; 10:3; 13:2; 20:5; 25:59; 57:4) or sitting on the throne might be compared to the Biblical tradition of God's resting on the seventh day (Gen 2:1–2; cf. Exo 20:11) On five occasions (7:54; 10:3; 25:59; 32:4; 57:4) the Qurʾān has God "settle" on his throne immediately after creating the heavens and the earth in six days.

---

⁵He directs the command from the heaven to the earth; then it ascends toward Him in a day whose span is a thousand years by your reckoning.

32:5 On the word for "command" (*amr*), see commentary on 42:52 (with further references). This passage is roughly parallel to 70:4, but there it is the angels and Spirit that ascend to God. For the comparison of a day to a thousand years (cf. Psa 90:4; 2Pe 3:8) see 22:47 and 70:4. See also commentary on 70:4.

---

⁶That is the Knower of the sensible and the Unseen, the All-mighty, the All-merciful, ⁷who perfected everything that He created and commenced man's creation from clay.

32:7 "God saw all he had made, and indeed it was very good" (Gen 1:31). On the creation of man from clay, see commentary on 6:2 (with further references).

---

⁸Then He made his progeny from an extract of a base fluid. ⁹Then He proportioned him and breathed into him of His Spirit, and invested you with your hearing, sight, and hearts. Little do you thank.

32:8–9 On the creation of humans from water see commentary on 24:41–45 (with further references). On God's breathing his spirit into man or Adam (cf. 15:29; 38:72), one might compare Genesis 2:7: "The Lord God shaped man from the soil of the ground and blew the breath of life into his nostrils, and man became a living being" (cf. Wis 15:11; Psa 33:6).

---

¹⁰They say, 'When we have been lost in the dust, shall we be indeed created anew?' Indeed, they disbelieve in the encounter with their Lord.

¹¹*Say,* 'You will be taken away by the angel of death, who has been charged with you. Then you will be brought back to your Lord.'

32:11 The "angel of death," responsible for bringing souls to God's presence for judgment, appears only here in the Qur'ān (cf. 16:28, where angels are said to take away souls at death). The angel of death does not appear in the Bible but does appear frequently in the Talmud, for example in b. Bava Qamma 60b (cf. b. Avodah Zarah 5a):

> When there is an epidemic in a town, one should not walk in the middle of the road, as the Angel of Death walks then in the middle of the road, for since permission has been granted him, he stalks along openly. But when there is peace in the town, one should not walk at the sides of the road, for since [the Angel of Death] has no permission he slinks along in hiding.

---

¹²Were *you* to see when the guilty hang their heads before their Lord [confessing], 'Our Lord! We have seen and heard. Send us back so that we may act righteously. Indeed, we are [now] convinced.'

¹³Had We wished We would have given every soul its guidance, but My word became due [against the faithless]: 'Surely, I will fill hell with all the [guilty] jinn and humans.' ¹⁴So taste [the punishment] for your having forgotten the encounter of this day of yours. We [too] have forgotten you. Taste the everlasting punishment because of what you used to do.

¹⁵Only those believe in Our signs who, when they are reminded of them, fall down in prostration and celebrate the praise of their Lord, and they are not arrogant. ¹⁶Their sides vacate their beds to supplicate their Lord in fear and hope, and they spend out of what We have provided them. ¹⁷No one knows what delights have been kept hidden for them [in the Hereafter] as a reward for what they used to do.

32:17 Cf. "But it is as scripture says: What no eye has seen and no ear has heard, what the mind of man cannot visualise; all that God has prepared for those who love him" (1Co 2:9; cf. Isa 64:4).

¹⁸Is someone who is faithful like someone who is a transgressor? They are not equal. ¹⁹As for those who have faith and do righteous deeds, for them will be the gardens of the Abode—a hospitality for what they used to do. ²⁰As for those who have transgressed, their refuge will be the Fire. Whenever they seek to leave it, they will be turned back into it and told: 'Taste the punishment of this Fire which you used to deny.' ²¹We shall surely make them taste the nearer punishment prior to the greater punishment, so that they may come back.

²²Who is a greater wrongdoer than him who is reminded of his Lord's signs, whereat he disregards them? We shall indeed take vengeance upon the guilty.

²³Certainly We gave Moses the Book, [declaring], 'Do not be in doubt about the encounter with Him,' and We made it a [source of] guidance for the Children of Israel.

32:23 By "do not be in doubt about the encounter with Him" the Qur'ān may mean the encounter with God at the resurrection (cf. 7:147; 23:33; 30:16 which speaks of the "encounter of the hereafter") or specifically Moses's encounter with God on Sinai (cr. Andrew O'Connor). Bell (*Commentary*, 2:91), following Nöldeke-Schwally (see *History*, 118), suggests that this phrase is an interpolation.

²⁴When they had been patient and had conviction in Our signs, We appointed amongst them *imam*s to guide [the people] by Our command.

32:34 Qarai does not translate the Arabic term *imam*s ("leaders") here. However, the Qur'ān (cf. 21:72–73; in v. 73 Qarai translates *imam*s as "chiefs") may have Isaac and Jacob in mind.

---

²⁵*Your* Lord will indeed judge between them on the Day of Resurrection concerning that about which they used to differ.

²⁶Does it not dawn upon them how many generations We have destroyed before them, amid [the ruins of] whose dwellings they walk? There are indeed signs in that. Will they not then listen?

²⁷Do they not see that We carry water to the parched earth and with it We bring forth crops from which they themselves and their cattle eat? Will they not then see?

²⁸They say, 'When will this judgement be, if you are truthful?' ²⁹*Say,* 'On the day of judgement their [newly found] faith will not avail the faithless, nor will they be granted any respite.'

³⁰So *turn away* from them, and *wait.* They too are waiting.

33. *AL-AḤZĀB*, The Confederates

In the Name of God, the All-beneficent, the All-merciful.

¹O Prophet! *Be wary* of God and *do not obey* the faithless and the hypocrites. God is indeed all-knowing, all-wise. ²And *follow* that which is revealed to *you* from *your* Lord. God is indeed well aware of what you do. ³And put *your* trust in God; God suffices as trustee.

⁴God has not put two hearts within any man, nor has He made your wives whom you repudiate your mothers, nor has he made your adopted sons your [actual] sons. These are mere utterances of your mouths. But God speaks the truth and He guides to the [right] way. ⁵Call them after their fathers. That is more just with God. And if you do not know their fathers, then they are your brethren in the faith and your kinsmen. Excepting what your hearts may intend deliberately, there will be no sin upon you for any mistake that you may make therein. And God is all-forgiving, all-merciful.

⁶The Prophet is closer to the faithful than their own souls, and his wives are their mothers. The blood relatives are more entitled to inherit from one another in the Book of God than the [other] faithful and Emigrants, barring any favour you may do your kinsmen. This has been written in the Book.

⁷[Recall] when We took a pledge from the prophets and from *you* and from Noah and Abraham and Moses and Jesus son of Mary, and We took from them a solemn pledge,

---

33:7 According to *Tafsīr al-Jalālayn,* the Qur'ān is here referring to a "pledge" that God took at once from all the prophets at a primordial time, before the creation of the world. Cf. 3:81.

---

⁸so that He may question the truthful concerning their truthfulness. And He has prepared for the faithless a painful punishment.

⁹O you who have faith! Remember God's blessing upon you when the hosts came at you and We sent against them a gale and hosts whom you did not see. And God sees best what you do. ¹⁰When they came at you from above and below you, and when the eyes rolled [with fear] and the hearts leapt to the throats and you entertained misgivings about God, ¹¹it was there that the faithful were tested and jolted with a severe agitation.

¹²When the hypocrites as well as those in whose hearts is a sickness were saying, 'God and His Apostle did not promise us [anything] but delusion.' ¹³And when a group of them said, 'O people of Yathrib! This is not a place for you to stand [your ground], so go back!' And a group of them sought the Prophet's permission [to leave the scene of battle], saying, 'Our homes lie exposed [to the enemy],' although they were not exposed. They only sought to flee. ¹⁴Had they been invaded from its flanks and had they been asked to apostatize, they would have done so with only a mild hesitation, ¹⁵though they had already pledged to God before that they would not turn their backs [to flee], and pledges given to God are accountable.

[16]*Say,* 'Flight will not avail you, should you flee from death, or from being killed, and then you will be let to enjoy only for a little while.'

[17]*Say,* 'Who is it that can protect you from God if He desires to bring you harm or desires to grant you His mercy?' Besides God they will not find for themselves any friend or helper.

[18]God knows those of you who discourage others, and those who say to their brethren, 'Come to us!' and take little part in the battle, [19]grudging you [their help]. So when there is panic, *you* see them observing *you,* their eyes rolling like someone fainting at death. Then, when the panic is over, they scald you with [their] sharp tongues in their greed for the spoils. They never have had faith. So God has made their works fail, and that is easy for God. [20]They suppose the confederates have not left yet, and were the confederates to come [again], they would wish they were in the desert with the Bedouins asking about your news, and if they were with you they would fight but a little.

[21]There is certainly a good exemplar for you in the Apostle of God—for those who look forward to God and the Last Day and remember God much.

[22]But when the faithful saw the confederates, they said, 'This is what God and His Apostle had promised us, and God and His Apostle were true.' And it only increased them in faith and submission.

[23]Among the faithful are men who are true to their pledge with God: some of them have fulfilled their pledge and some of them still wait, and they have not changed in the least, [24]that God may reward the true for their truthfulness and punish the hypocrites, if He wishes, or accept their repentance. God is indeed all-forgiving, all-merciful.

²⁵God sent back the faithless in their rage without their attaining any advantage, and God spared the faithful of fighting, and God is all-strong, all-mighty. ²⁶And He dragged down from their strongholds those who had backed them from among the People of the Book and He cast terror into their hearts, [so that] you killed a part of them, and took captive [another] part of them. ²⁷He bequeathed you their land, their houses and their possessions and a territory you had not trodden, and God has power over all things.

²⁸O Prophet! *Say* to *your* wives, 'If you desire the life of the world and its glitter, come, I will provide for you and release you in a graceful manner. ²⁹But if you desire God and His Apostle and the abode of the Hereafter, then God has indeed prepared a great reward for the virtuous among you.' ³⁰O wives of the Prophet! Whoever of you commits a gross indecency, her punishment shall be doubled, and that is easy for God.

³¹But whoever of you is obedient to God and His Apostle and acts righteously, We will give her a twofold reward and hold for her in store a noble provision.

³²O wives of the Prophet! You are not like other women: if you are wary [of God], do not be complaisant in your speech, lest he in whose heart is a sickness should aspire; speak honourable words. ³³Stay in your houses and do not flaunt your finery like the former [days of pagan] ignorance. Maintain the prayer and pay the *zakāt,* and obey God and His Apostle.

Indeed, God desires to repel all impurity from you, O People of the Household, and purify you with a thorough purification.

33:33 The counsel not to "flaunt your finery" is close to that in 1 Timothy 2:9: "Similarly, women are to wear suitable clothes and to be dressed quietly and modestly, without braided hair or gold and jewellery or expensive clothes." On the expression "[days of pagan] ignorance" (v. 50), see commentary on 48:26 (with further references).

³⁴And remember what is recited in your homes of the signs of God and wisdom. God is indeed all-attentive, all-aware.

³⁵Indeed, the *muslim* men and the *muslim* women, the faithful men and the faithful women, the obedient men and the obedient women, the truthful men and the truthful women, the patient men and the patient women, the humble men and the humble women, the charitable men and the charitable women, the men who fast and the women who fast, the men who guard their private parts and the women who guard, the men who remember God much and the women who remember [God much]—God holds in store for them forgiveness and a great reward.

³⁶A faithful man or woman may not have any option in their matter, when God and His Apostle have decided on a matter, and whoever disobeys God and His Apostle has certainly strayed into manifest error.

³⁷When *you* said to him whom God had blessed, and whom *you* [too] had blessed, 'Retain your wife for yourself and be wary of God,' and *you* had hidden in *your* heart what God was to divulge, and *you* feared the people though God is worthier that *you* should fear Him, so when Zayd had got through with her, We wedded her to *you,* so that there may be no blame on the faithful in respect of the wives of their adopted sons, when the latter have got through with them, and God's command is bound to be fulfilled.

³⁸There is no blame on the Prophet in respect of that which God has made lawful for him: God's precedent with those who passed away earlier (and God's commands are ordained by a precise ordaining), ³⁹such as deliver the messages of God and fear Him and fear no one except God, and God suffices as reckoner.

⁴⁰Muhammad is not the father of any man among you, but he is the Apostle of God and the Seal of the Prophets, and God has knowledge of all things.

33:40 The phrase "seal of the prophets" is understood by most Muslim exegetes to mean that Muḥammad was the last prophet. It also forms the basis of the legend that Muḥammad literally had a "seal"—that is, a birthmark—between his shoulder blades. In some Islamic traditions this birthmark is said to have been a feature that earlier scriptures mentioned in their descriptions of a future prophet. The term for seal (*khātam,* or, in variant readings, *khātim*) is related to Syriac *ḥātmā,* "seal," or Christian Palestinian Aramaic *ḥātīmā,* "sealing, conclusion, ending" (see *FV,* 120–21). Fossum (151–52) notes that in a third century AD Samaritan text, Moses is named "apostle of God" and "seal of the prophets."

On the description of Muḥammad as the "seal of the prophets," *Tafsīr al-Jalālayn* anticipates the problem that Jesus will (according to Islamic belief) return to earth after Muḥammad: "God has knowledge of all things, among these is the fact that there will be no prophet after him, and even when the lord Jesus descends [at the end of days] he will rule according to his [Muḥammad's] Law."

Daniel 9:24 has the angel Gabriel speak to Daniel of the sealing of "vision and prophecy" for "seventy weeks." Tertullian (in his *Adversus Judaeos,* 8:11) argues that this verse refers prophetically to Christ, who would confirm and put an end to all "vision and prophecies":

> And so, since prophecy has been fulfilled through His advent—that is, through the nativity, which we have above commemorated, and the passion, which we have evidently explained—that is the reason withal why Daniel said, "Vision and prophet were sealed; "because *Christ is the "signet" of all prophets,* fulfilling all that had in days bygone been announced concerning Him: for, since His advent and personal passion, there is no longer "vision" or "prophet"; whence most emphatically he says that His advent "*seals* vision and prophecy."

---

⁴¹O you who have faith! Remember God with frequent remembrance ⁴²and glorify Him morning and evening. ⁴³It is He who blesses you—and so do His angels—that He may bring you out from darkness into light, and He is most merciful to the faithful. ⁴⁴The day they encounter Him, their greeting will be, 'Peace,' and He holds in store for them a noble reward.

⁴⁵O Prophet! We have indeed sent *you* as a witness, as a bearer of good news and warner ⁴⁶and as a summoner to God by His permission, and as a radiant lamp.

33:46 On the allusion to Muḥammad as a "lamp," see commentary on Q 5:15–16.

---

⁴⁷*Announce* to the faithful the good news that there will be for them a great grace from God. ⁴⁸*Do not obey* the faithless and the hypocrites and *disregard* their torments, and *put your* trust in God, and God suffices as trustee.

⁴⁹O you who have faith! When you marry faithful women and then divorce them before you touch them, there shall be no period [of waiting] for you to reckon. But provide for them and release them in a graceful manner.

⁵⁰O Prophet! Indeed, We have made lawful to *you your* wives whom *you* have given their dowries and those whom *your* right hand owns, of those whom God gave *you* as spoils of war, and the daughters of *your* paternal uncle, and the daughters of *your* paternal aunts, and the daughters of *your* maternal uncle, and the daughters of *your* maternal aunts who migrated with *you,* and a faithful woman if she offers herself to the Prophet and the Prophet desires to take her in marriage (a privilege exclusively for *you,* not for [the rest of] the faithful; We know what We have made lawful for them with respect to their wives and those whom their right hands own, so that there may be no blame on *you*), and God is all-forgiving, all-merciful.

⁵¹*You* may put off whichever of them *you* wish and consort with whichever of them *you* wish, and there is no sin upon *you* [in receiving again] any [of them] whom *you* may seek [to consort with] from among those *you* have set aside [earlier]. That makes it likelier that they will be comforted and not feel unhappy, and all of them will be pleased with what *you* give them. God knows what is in your hearts, and God is all-knowing, all-forbearing.

⁵²Beyond that, women are not lawful for *you,* nor that *you* should change them for other wives even though their beauty should impress *you,* except those whom *your* right hand owns. God is watchful over all things.

⁵³O you who have faith! Do not enter the Prophet's houses for a meal until you are granted permission, without waiting for it to be readied. But enter when you are invited, and disperse when you have taken your meal, without cozying up for chats. Such conduct on your part offends the Prophet, and he is ashamed of [asking] you [to leave]; but God is not ashamed of [expressing] the truth. When you ask [his] womenfolk for something, do ask them from behind a curtain. That is more chaste for your hearts and theirs. You should not offend the Apostle of God, nor may you ever marry his wives after him. That would indeed be a grave [sin] with God. ⁵⁴Whether you disclose anything or hide it, God indeed knows all things.

⁵⁵There is no sin on them [in socializing freely] with their fathers, or their sons, or their brothers, or their brothers' sons, or the sons of their sisters, or their own womenfolk, or what their right hands own. Be wary of God. God is indeed witness to all things.

⁵⁶Indeed, God and His angels bless the Prophet; O you who have faith! Invoke blessings on him and invoke Peace upon him in a worthy manner.

⁵⁷Indeed, those who offend God and His Apostle are cursed by God in the world and the Hereafter, and He has prepared a humiliating punishment for them. ⁵⁸Those who offend faithful men and women undeservedly, certainly bear the guilt of slander and flagrant sin.

⁵⁹O Prophet! Tell your wives and your daughters and the women of the faithful to draw closely over themselves their chadors

[when going out]. That makes it likely for them to be recognized and not be troubled, and God is all-forgiving, all-merciful.

⁶⁰If the hypocrites and those in whose hearts is a sickness, and the rumourmongers in the city do not desist, We will prompt *you* [to take action] against them; then they will not be *your* neighbours in it except briefly. ⁶¹Accursed, they will be seized wherever they are confronted and slain violently: ⁶²God's precedent with those who passed away before, and you will never find any change in God's precedent.

⁶³The people question *you* concerning the Hour. *Say,* 'Its knowledge is only with God.' What do *you* know, maybe the Hour is near.

33:63 On knowledge of the Hour being with God alone, see commentary on 79:42–44 (with further references).

⸻

⁶⁴Indeed, God has cursed the faithless and prepared for them a blaze ⁶⁵in which they will remain forever and will not find any friend or helper. ⁶⁶The day when their faces are turned about in the Fire, they will say, 'We wish we had obeyed God and obeyed the Apostle!' ⁶⁷They will say, 'Our Lord! We obeyed our leaders and elders and they led us astray from the way.' ⁶⁸Our Lord! Give them a double punishment and curse them with a mighty curse.'

⁶⁹O you who have faith! Do not be like those who offended Moses, whereat God cleared him of what they alleged, and he was distinguished in God's sight.

33:69 This verse may be an allusion to Numbers 12, which relates how Miriam and Aaron criticized Moses for his marriage to a Cushite woman:

¹Miriam, and Aaron too, criticised Moses over the Cushite woman he had married. He had indeed married a Cushite woman.
²They said, 'Is Moses the only one through whom the Lord has spoken? Has he not spoken through us too?' The Lord heard this.
³Now Moses was extremely humble, the humblest man on earth.
⁴Suddenly the Lord said to Moses, Aaron and Miriam, 'Come out, all three of you, to the Tent of Meeting.' They went, all three of them,
⁵and the Lord descended in a pillar of cloud and stood at the entrance of the Tent. He called Aaron and Miriam and they both came forward.
⁶The Lord said: Listen to my words! if there is a prophet among you, I reveal myself to him in a vision, I speak to him in a dream.
⁷Not so with my servant Moses; to him my whole household is entrusted;
⁸to him I speak face to face, plainly and not in riddles, and he sees the Lord's form. How, then, could you dare to criticise my servant Moses? (Num 12:1–8)

Tafsīr al-Jalālayn reports a hadith that gives a different story meant to explain how the Israelites teased Moses:

[The Israelites] would say, for example, "The only reason he does not wash with us is that he has an inflammation in his testicles"—whereat God absolved him of what they alleged: when Moses placed his robe on a rock to go to wash, the rock hurtled away with it until it came to a halt amid a group of men from the Children of Israel. As Moses chased it and took his robe to cover himself, they saw that he had no such inflammation.

---

⁷⁰O you who have faith! Be wary of God and speak upright words. ⁷¹He will rectify your conduct for you and forgive you your sins. Whoever obeys God and His Apostle will certainly achieve a great success.

⁷²Indeed, We presented the Trust to the heavens and the earth and the mountains, but they refused to undertake it and were apprehensive of it; but man undertook it. He is indeed most ignorant and unjust.

⁷³God will surely punish the hypocrites, men and women, and the polytheists, men and women, and God will turn clemently to the faithful, men and women, and God is all-forgiving, all-merciful.

34. *Saba'*, Sheba

In the Name of God, the All-beneficent, the All-merciful.

¹All praise belongs to God to whom belongs whatever is in the heavens and whatever is in the earth. To Him belongs all praise in the Hereafter, and He is the All-wise, the All-aware. ²He knows whatever enters into the earth and whatever emerges from it, and whatever descends from the sky and whatever ascends into it, and He is the All-merciful, the All-forgiving.

³The faithless say, 'The Hour will not overtake us.' *Say,* Yes, it will surely overtake you, by my Lord, the Knower of the Unseen; not [even] an atom's weight escapes Him in the heavens or in the earth, nor [is there] anything smaller than that nor bigger, but it is in a manifest Book, ⁴that He may reward those who have faith and do righteous deeds.' For such there will be forgiveness and a noble provision. ⁵But those who contend with Our signs seeking to frustrate [their purpose], for such is a painful punishment due to defilement.

⁶Those who have been given knowledge see that what has been sent down to *you* from *your* Lord is the truth and [that] it guides to the path of the All-mighty, the All-laudable.

⁷The faithless say, 'Shall we show you a man who will inform you [that] when you have been totally rent to pieces you will in-

deed have a new creation? ⁸Has he fabricated a lie against God, or is there a madness in him?' Indeed, those who do not believe in the Hereafter languish in punishment and extreme error.

⁹Have they not regarded that which is before them and that which is behind them of the heavens and the earth? If We like, We can make the earth swallow them, or let a fragment from the sky fall on them. There is indeed a sign in that for every penitent servant.

¹⁰Certainly We granted David a favour from Us [saying]: 'O mountains and birds, chime in with him!' And We made iron soft for him, ¹¹saying, 'Make easy coats of mail and keep the measure in arranging [the links], and act righteously. I indeed watch what you do.'

34:10–11 The command to the mountains and the birds to praise God with David (cf. 21:79; 38:17–19) reflects the traditional Jewish and Christian association of David with many of the Psalms (although the Qur'ān does not explicitly mention the Psalms here). See further commentary on 21:79.

The idea that David produced "coats of mail" is based on an interpretation of a term (*sābighāt*) in verse 11 and a reading of this verse in light of 21:80 (where the meaning of "coats of mail" is also not obvious). If this idea is correct (which is far from certain), it may reflect the way the Bible glorifies his military exploits. 1 Samuel 16:18 speaks of David as a fighter, and the Babylonian Talmud (b. Sanhedrin 93b) describes David as a "man of war." As Horovitz (*KU,* 109–11) points out, David is frequently described as a maker of armor in Jāhilī ("pre-Islamic") poetry (Solomon is also mentioned there in this regard), but those descriptions likely reflect the influence of the Qur'ān.

———

¹²And for Solomon [We subjected] the wind: its morning course was a month's journey and its evening course was a month's journey. We made a fount of [molten] copper flow for him, and [We

placed at his service] some of the jinn who would work for him
by the permission of his Lord, and if any of them swerved from
Our command, We would make him taste the punishment of the
Blaze. ¹³They built for him as many temples as he wished, and
figures, basins like cisterns, and caldrons fixed [in the ground].
'O House of David, work [for God] gratefully, and few of My
servants are grateful.'

34:12–13 The Qur'ān's description here of Solomon's control over the wind,
and his possession of a fount of copper, reflects the Solomonic legends that
developed in part by exegesis of the Book of Wisdom, regarding which see commentary on 21:81–82 (with further references).

The description of Solomon's authority over the jinn is part of this larger
image of Solomon as a figure on whom God bestowed divine authority. It is
particularly connected with the *Second Targum of Esther,* which describes how
Solomon had authority over spirits and demons:

> All the kingdoms feared him, nations and languages were obedient to him;
> devils, demons, and ferocious beasts, evil spirits and accidents, were deliv-
> ered into his hands. (*Second Targum of Esther,* 1:3, p. 269)

On this cf. 27:16–17; 38:37 and commentary on 27:16–17.

In verse 13 the Qur'ān describes how spirits helped Solomon "build temples"
(Ar. *maḥārīb*). Behind this description is the role of Solomon in building the Jerusalem temple (cf. 3:37, 39, where the word for the Jerusalem temple is *miḥrāb,*
singular of *maḥārīb*). The Talmud recounts a legend by which Solomon was
able to build the temple only through the aid of demons, the head of whom was
Ashmedai (connected to Asmodeus, described as the "worst of demons" in Tobit
3:8), through whom Solomon acquires a magical worm (the *shamir*) which has
the ability to cut stones:

> He said to the Rabbis, How shall I manage [without iron tools]?—They
> replied, There is the *shamir* which Moses brought for the stones of the
> ephod. . . . He asked them, Where is it to be found? They replied, Bring a
> male and a female demon and tie them together; perhaps they know and will
> tell you. So he brought a male and a female demon and tied them together.
> They said to him, We do not know, but perhaps Ashmedai the prince of the
> demons knows. He said to them, Where is he?—They answered, He is in

such-and-such a mountain. . . . Solomon kept [Ashmedai] with him until he had built the Temple. (b. Gittin 68a–b)

———————

¹⁴When We decreed death for him, nothing apprised them of his death except a worm which gnawed away at his staff. And when he fell down, [the humans] realized that had the jinn known the Unseen, they would not have remained in a humiliating torment.

———————

34:14 Speyer (*BEQ,* 402) wonders whether the Qurʾān's allusion to Solomon's staff may be related to a tradition (connected to Ecc 2:10, a book attributed to Solomon) that at the end of his reign Solomon ruled over nothing but his staff (b. Sanhedrin 20b). However, the Qurʾān makes no mention of the decline of Solomon's power.

Tafsīr al-Jalālayn explains this verse by paraphrasing: "And when We decreed for him, for Solomon, death, in other words, [when] he died—he remained supported against his staff an entire year, while the jinn continued to toil in hard labour as was customary, unaware of his death, until [finally] when a termite ate through his staff, he fell to the ground [and was seen to be] dead."

———————

¹⁵There was certainly a sign for Sheba in their habitation: two gardens, to the right and to the left. 'Eat of the provision of your Lord and give Him thanks: a good land and an all-forgiving Lord!' ¹⁶But they disregarded [the path of God], so We unleashed upon them a violent flood and replaced their two gardens with two gardens bearing bitter fruit, tamarisk, and sparse lote trees. ¹⁷We requited them with that for their ingratitude. Do We [thus] requite anyone but ingrates?

¹⁸We had placed between them and the towns which We had blessed hamlets prominent [from the main route], and We had ordained the route through them: 'Travel through them in safety,

night and day.' [19]But they said, 'Our Lord! Make the stages between our journeys far apart,' and they wronged themselves. So We turned them into folktales and caused them to disintegrate totally. There are indeed signs in that for every patient and grateful [servant].

34:15–19 The description of Sheba (or Saba) here (vv. 15, 18) is related to Jewish legends of the kingdom, such as that given by Josephus in *Jewish Antiquities,* which makes it a fantastic land and a land of security (something alluded to in Q 34:18):

> In the end they were all driven into Saba, the capital of the Ethiopian realm. . . . But the place offered extreme obstacles to a besieger, for the Nile enclosed it in a circle and other rivers, the Astapus and the Astabaras, added to the difficulty of the attack for any who attempted to cross the current. The city which lies within in fact resembles an island: strong walls encompass it and as a bulwark against its enemies built a city, called Hermopolis, in which he consecrated the ibis because it slays the creatures that injure men. it has the rivers, besides great dikes within the ramparts to protect it from inundation when the force of the swollen streams is unusually violent; and it is these which made the capture of the town so difficult even to those who had crossed the rivers. (*Jewish Antiquities,* II, 10:2)

This passage is also parallel to the Qur'ān's parable of the two gardens in Sura 18 (vv. 32–44). As did the people of Sheba, the owner of one of these gardens failed to give thanks to God. The people of Sheba (Q 34:16–17) and the ungrateful man of Sura 18 (see 18:42) accordingly see their gardens destroyed.

---

[20]Certainly Iblis had his conjecture come true about them. So they followed him—all except a part of the faithful. [21]He had no authority over them, but that We may ascertain those who believe in the Hereafter from those who are in doubt about it, and *your* Lord is watchful over all things.

[22]*Say,* 'Invoke those whom you claim [to be gods] besides God! They do not control [even] an atom's weight in the heavens or the

earth, nor do they have any share in [either of] them, nor is any of them His helper.'

²³Intercession is of no avail with Him, except for those whom He permits. When fear is lifted from their hearts, they say, 'What did your Lord say?' They say, 'The truth, and He is the All-exalted, the All-great.'

²⁴*Say,* 'Who provides for you from the heavens and the earth?' *Say,* 'God! Indeed, either we or you are rightly guided or in plain error.'

²⁵*Say,* 'You will not be questioned about our guilt, nor shall we be questioned about what you do.'

²⁶*Say,* 'Our Lord will bring us together, then He will judge between us with justice, and He is the All-knowing Judge.'

²⁷*Say,* 'Show me those whom you associate with Him as partners.' No! [They can never show any such partner]. Indeed, He is God, the All-mighty, the All-wise.

²⁸We did not send *you* except as a bearer of good news and warner to all mankind, but most people do not know.

²⁹They say, 'When will this promise be fulfilled, if you are truthful?' ³⁰*Say,* 'Your promised hour is a day that you shall neither defer nor advance by an hour.'

³¹The faithless say, 'We will never believe in this Qur'ān, nor in what was [revealed] before it.' But if *you* were to see when the wrongdoers will be made to stop before their Lord casting the blame on one another. Those who were abased will say to those who were arrogant, 'Had it not been for you, we would surely have been faithful.' ³²Those who were arrogant will say to those who were abased, 'Did we keep you from guidance after it had come to you? No, you were guilty [yourselves].' ³³Those who were abased will say to those who were arrogant, 'No, [it was your] night-and-day plotting, when you prompted us to forswear

God and to set up equals to Him.' They will hide their remorse when they sight the punishment, and We will put iron collars around the necks of the faithless. Shall they be requited with anything except what they used to do?

³⁴We did not send any warner to a town without its affluent ones saying, 'We indeed disbelieve in what you have been sent with.' ³⁵They say, 'We have greater wealth and more children, and we will not be punished!' ³⁶*Say,* 'Indeed, my Lord expands the provision for whomever He wishes and tightens it, but most people do not know.' ³⁷It is not your wealth, nor your children, that will bring you close to Us in nearness, excepting those who have faith and act righteously. It is they for whom there will be a twofold reward for what they did, and they will be secure in lofty abodes.

34:37 On the "abodes" or "rooms" (Ar. *ghurufāt*) of heaven in the Qur'ān, see commentary on 39:20 (with further references).

---

³⁸As for those who contend with Our signs seeking to frustrate [their purpose], they will be brought to the punishment.

³⁹*Say,* 'Indeed, my Lord expands the provision for whomever of His servants that He wishes and tightens it, and He will repay whatever you may spend, and He is the best of providers.'

⁴⁰On the day He will muster them all together, He will say to the angels, 'Was it you that these used to worship?' ⁴¹They will say, 'Immaculate are You! You are our Master, not they! No, they used to worship the jinn; most of them had faith in them.'

⁴²'Today you have no power to benefit or harm one another,' and We shall say to those who did wrong, 'Taste the punishment of the Fire which you used to deny.'

34:40–42 On the prohibition of worshipping angels, cf. 3:80; 4:172. On the worship of jinn, see commentary on 6:100 (with further references). On the description of anything unbelievers worship other than God as powerless (v. 42), see commentary on 10:18 (with further references). In Revelation 22 John considers worshipping an angel:

> [8]I, John, am the one who heard and saw these things. When I had heard and seen them all, I knelt at the feet of the angel who had shown them to me, to worship him;
> [9]but he said, 'Do no such thing: I am your fellow-servant and the fellow-servant of your brothers the prophets and those who keep the message of this book. God alone you must worship.' (Rev 22:8–9; cf. Rev 19:10)

---

[43]When Our clear signs are recited to them, they say, 'This is just a man who desires to keep you from what your fathers used to worship.' And they say, 'This is nothing but a fabricated lie.' The faithless say of the truth when it comes to them: 'This is nothing but plain magic,' [44]though We did not give them any scriptures that they might have studied, nor did We send them any warner before *you*. [45]Those who were before them had denied [likewise]—and these have not attained one-tenth of what We had given them—and they impugned My apostles; so how was My rebuttal!

[46]*Say,* 'I give you just a single advice: that you rise up for God's sake, in pairs or singly, and then reflect: there is no madness in your companion; he is just a warner to you before [the befalling of] a severe punishment.'

[47]*Say,* 'Whatever reward I may have asked you is for your own good. My [true] reward lies only with God, and He is witness to all things.'

34:47 Geiger (*Judaism and Islam,* 104) calls the refusal to seek a reward the "distinguishing mark common to all preachers." As Speyer mentions (*BEQ,*

456), the idea that a true prophet would not ask a reward (cf. 6:90; 10:72; 11:29; 12:104; 25:57; 26:109, 127, 145, 164, 180; 36:21; 38:86; 42:23; 52:40; 68:46) is suggested by Matthew 10:8 ("You received without charge, give without charge") and Mishnah Avot 1:3. It is prominent in the early Christian work *Shepherd of Hermas:* "Now can a divine Spirit receive money and prophesy? It is not possible for a prophet of God to do this, but the spirit of such prophets is earthly" (Mandate 11:12, p. 435).

---

⁴⁸*Say,* 'Indeed, my Lord hurls the truth. [He is] the knower of all that is Unseen.'

⁴⁹*Say,* 'The truth has come and falsehood neither originates [anything], nor restores [anything after its demise].'

⁵⁰*Say,* 'If I go astray, my going astray is only to my own harm, and if I am rightly guided that is because of what my Lord has revealed to me. He is indeed all-hearing and nearmost.'

⁵¹Were *you* to see them when they will be terror-stricken, [left] without any escape, and are seized from a close quarter. ⁵²They will say, 'We believe in it [now]!' But how can they attain it from a far-off place ⁵³when they denied it in the past and drew conjectures about the Unseen from a distant place? ⁵⁴A barrier will separate them from what they long for, as was done aforetime with their likes, who had remained in grave doubt.

35. *FĀṬIR*, THE ORIGINATOR

In the Name of God, the All-beneficent, the All-merciful.

[1]All praise belongs to God, originator of the heavens and the earth, maker of the angels [His] messengers, possessing wings, two, three or four [of them]. He adds to the creation whatever He wishes. Indeed, God has power over all things.

35:1 Several Biblical texts number the wings of angels: Isaiah 6:1–3 (six wings), Ezekiel 1:3–6 (four wings), Revelation 4:8 (six wings).

---

[2]Whatever mercy God unfolds for the people, no one can withhold it; and whatever He withholds, no one can release except Him, and He is the All-mighty, the All-wise.

[3]O mankind! Remember God's blessing upon you! Is there any creator other than God who provides for you from the heaven and the earth? There is no god except Him. So where do you stray?

[4]If they impugn *you,* certainly [many] apostles were impugned before *you,* and all matters are returned to God.

[5]O mankind! God's promise is indeed true. So do not let the life of the world deceive you, nor let the Deceiver deceive you

concerning God. ⁶Satan is indeed your enemy, so treat him as an enemy. He only invites his confederates so that they may be among the inmates of the Blaze.

35:6 On Satan as an enemy of man, cf. 36:60 (with further references).

---

⁷There is a severe punishment for the faithless; but for those who have faith and do righteous deeds, there will be forgiveness and a great reward.

⁸Is someone the evil of whose conduct is presented as decorous to him, so he regards it as good. . . . Indeed, God leads astray whomever He wishes and guides whomever He wishes. So do not fret *yourself* to death regretting for them. Indeed, God knows best what they do.

⁹It is God who sends the winds and they raise a cloud; then We drive it toward a dead land and with it revive the earth after its death. Likewise will be the resurrection [of the dead].

¹⁰Whoever seeks honour [should know that] honour entirely belongs to God. To Him ascends the good word, and He elevates righteous conduct; as for those who devise evil schemes, there is a severe punishment for them and their plotting shall come to naught.

¹¹God created you from dust, then from a drop of [seminal] fluid, then He made you mates. No female conceives or delivers except with His knowledge, and no elderly person advances in years, nor is anything diminished of his life, but it is [recorded] in a Book. That is indeed easy for God.

35:11 On the creation of humanity from dust, see commentary on 11:61 (with further references).

¹²Not alike are the two seas: this one sweet and agreeable, pleasant to drink, and that one briny and bitter, and from each you eat fresh meat and obtain ornaments which you wear. And you see the ships plowing through them, that you may seek of His bounty, and so that you may give thanks.

¹³He makes the night pass into the day and makes the day pass into the night, and He has disposed the sun and the moon, each moving for a specified term. That is God, your Lord; to Him belongs all sovereignty. As for those whom you invoke besides Him, they do not control so much as the husk of a date stone. ¹⁴If you invoke them they will not hear your invocation, and even if they heard they cannot respond to you, and on the Day of Resurrection they will forswear your polytheism, and none can inform you like the One who is all-aware.

¹⁵O mankind! You are the ones who stand in need of God, and God—He is the All-sufficient, the All-laudable. ¹⁶If He wishes, He will take you away and bring about a new creation, ¹⁷and that is not a hard thing for God.

¹⁸No bearer shall bear another's burden, and should one heavily burdened call [another] to carry it, nothing of it will be carried [by anyone] even if he were a near relative.

You can only warn those who fear their Lord in secret and maintain the prayer. Whoever purifies himself, purifies only for his own sake, and to God is the return.

35:18 On the notion that no soul shall carry another's burden, see commentary on 82:19 (with further references).

¹⁹The blind one and the seer are not equal, ²⁰nor darkness and light, ²¹nor shade and torrid heat, ²²nor are the living equal to the dead.

Indeed, God makes whomever He wishes to hear, and *you* cannot make those in the graves hear you. ²³*You* are just a warner. ²⁴We have indeed sent *you* with the truth as a bearer of good news and warner, and there is not a nation but a warner has passed in it. ²⁵If they impugn *you,* those before them have impugned [likewise]: their apostles brought them manifest proofs, [holy] writs, and illuminating scriptures.

35:25 On the term for "writs" (Ar. *zubur;* sing. *zabūr,* used also for "Psalms"), see commentary on 17:55 (with further references).

²⁶Then I seized the faithless. So how was My rebuttal! ²⁷Have you not regarded that God sends down water from the sky, with which We produce fruits of diverse hues, and in the mountains are stripes, white and red, of diverse hues, and [others] pitch black? ²⁸And of humans and beasts and cattle there are likewise diverse hues.

Only those of God's servants having knowledge fear Him. God is indeed all-mighty, all-forgiving.

²⁹Indeed, those who recite the Book of God and maintain the prayer, and spend secretly and openly out of what We have provided them, expect a commerce that will never go bankrupt, ³⁰so that He may pay them their full reward and enhance them out of His bounty. He is indeed all-forgiving, all-appreciative.

³¹That which We have revealed to *you* of the Book is the truth, confirming what was [revealed] before it. Indeed, God is aware and watchful of His servants.

³²Then We made those whom We chose from Our servants heirs to the Book. Yet some of them are those who wrong themselves, and some of them are average, and some of them are those

who take the lead in all the good works by God's will. That is the great grace [of God]! ³³Gardens of Eden, which they will enter, adorned therein with bracelets of gold and pearl, and their garments therein will be of silk.

35:33 On the description of the heavenly paradise as the "Garden of Eden," see commentary on 9:72 (with further references).

---

³⁴They will say, 'All praise belongs to God, who has removed all grief from us. Our Lord is indeed all-forgiving, all-appreciative, ³⁵who has settled us in the everlasting abode by His grace. In it we are untouched by toil and untouched by fatigue.'

35:34–35 The Qur'ān's description of God's taking away sorrow from the blessed in paradise might be compared to Revelation 21:4: "He will wipe away all tears from their eyes; there will be no more death, and no more mourning or sadness or pain. The world of the past has gone."

---

³⁶As for the faithless, there is for them the fire of hell: they will neither be done away with so that they may die, nor shall its punishment be lightened for them. Thus do We requite every ingrate. ³⁷They will cry therein for help: 'Our Lord! Bring us out, so that we may act righteously—differently from what we used to do!' 'Did We not give you a life long enough that one who is heedful might take admonition? And [moreover] the warner had [also] come to you. Now taste [the consequence of your deeds], for the wrongdoers have no helper.'

³⁸Indeed, God is the knower of the Unseen of the heavens and the earth. He indeed knows well what is in the breasts. ³⁹It is He

who made you successors on the earth. So whoever is faithless, his unfaith is to his own detriment. The unfaith of the faithless does not increase them with their Lord [in anything] except disfavour, and their unfaith increases the faithless in nothing except loss.

⁴⁰*Say*, 'Tell me about your 'partners' whom you invoke besides God? Show me what [part] of the earth have they created. Have they any share in the heavens?' Have We given them a scripture so that they stand on a manifest proof from it? No, the wrongdoers do not promise one another [anything] except delusion.

⁴¹Indeed, God sustains the heavens and the earth lest they should fall apart, and if they were to fall apart, there is none who can sustain them except Him. He is indeed all-forbearing, all-forgiving.

⁴²They had sworn by God with solemn oaths that if a warner were to come to them, they would be better guided than any of the nations. But when a warner came to them, it only increased their distance [from the truth], ⁴³due to their domineering [conduct] in the land and their devising of evil schemes; and evil schemes beset only their authors. So do they await anything except the precedent of the ancients? Yet you will never find any change in God's precedent, and you will never find any revision in God's precedent.

⁴⁴Have they not traveled through the land so that they may observe how was the fate of those who were before them? They were more powerful than them, and God is not to be frustrated by anything in the heavens or on the earth. He is indeed all-knowing, all-powerful.

⁴⁵Were God to take humans to task because of what they have earned, He would not leave any living being on its back. But He

respites them until a specified time, and when their time comes, [He judges them], for God has been watching His servants.

35:45 "If you kept a record of our sins, Lord, who could stand their ground?" (Psa 130:3).

36. *YĀ SĪN*, YĀ SĪN

In the Name of God, the All-beneficent, the All-merciful.

¹*Yā Sīn!* ²By the Wise Qur'ān, ³*you* are indeed one of the apostles, ⁴on a straight path. ⁵[It is a scripture] sent down gradually from the All-mighty, the All-merciful ⁶that *you* may warn a people whose fathers were not warned, so they are oblivious. ⁷The word has already become due against most of them, so they will not have faith. ⁸Indeed, We have put iron collars around their necks, which are up to the chins, so their heads are upturned. ⁹And We have put a barrier before them and a barrier behind them, then We have blind-folded them, so they do not see. ¹⁰It is the same to them whether *you* warn them or do not warn them, they will not have faith. ¹¹*You* can only warn someone who follows the Reminder and fears the All-beneficent in secret; so *give* him the good news of forgiveness and a noble reward.

¹²It is indeed We who revive the dead and write what they have sent ahead and their effects [which they left behind], and We have figured everything in a manifest *Imam.*

¹³Cite for them the example of the inhabitants of the town when the apostles came to it. ¹⁴When We sent to them two [apostles],

they impugned both of them. Then We reinforced them with a third, and they said, 'We have indeed been sent to you.'

¹⁵They said, 'You are nothing but humans like us, and the All-beneficent has not sent down anything, and you are only lying.'

¹⁶They said, 'Our Lord knows that we have indeed been sent to you, ¹⁷and our duty is only to communicate in clear terms.'

¹⁸They said, 'Indeed, we take you for a bad omen. If you do not desist we will stone you, and surely a painful punishment will visit you from us.'

¹⁹They said, 'Your bad omens attend you. What! If you are admonished. . . . You are indeed an unrestrained lot.'

²⁰There came a man hurrying from the city outskirts. He said, 'O my people! Follow the apostles! ²¹Follow them who do not ask you any reward and they are rightly guided. ²²Why should I not worship Him who has originated me, and to whom you will be brought back? ²³Shall I take gods besides Him? If the All-beneficent desired to cause me any distress, their intercession will not avail me in any way, nor will they rescue me. ²⁴Indeed, then I would be in plain error. ²⁵Indeed, I have faith in your Lord, so listen to me.'

²⁶He was told, 'Enter paradise!' He said, 'Alas! Had my people only known ²⁷for what my Lord forgave me and made me one of the honoured ones!'

²⁸After him We did not send down on his people a host from the heavens, nor We would have sent down. ²⁹It was but a single Cry, and behold, they were stilled [like burnt ashes]!

³⁰How regrettable of the servants! There did not come to them any apostle but that they used to deride him. ³¹Have they not regarded how many generations We have destroyed before them who will not come back to them?

36:13–31 This parable has some connections with Genesis 19, which relates that two visitors (cf. 36:14) arrive in Sodom and are threatened by its people but defended by Lot. A tradition in the Babylonian Talmud (b. Sanhedrin 109a) makes Lot's people "sinners before the Lord" with "no portion in the world to come."

However, the Qurʾān's parable here is still more closely related to the parable of the evil tenants in Matthew 21. Both refer to stoning (Q 36:18; Mat 21:35), and the figure who appears from the city outskirts in the Qurʾān (Q 36:20; cf. 28:20) could be compared to the figure of the "son" in Matthew (21:37):

> 33'Listen to another parable. There was a man, a landowner, who planted a vineyard; he fenced it round, dug a winepress in it and built a tower; then he leased it to tenants and went abroad.
>
> 34When vintage time drew near he sent his servants to the tenants to collect his produce.
>
> 35But the tenants seized his servants, thrashed one, killed another and stoned a third.
>
> 36Next he sent some more servants, this time a larger number, and they dealt with them in the same way.
>
> 37Finally he sent his son to them thinking, "They will respect my son."
>
> 38But when the tenants saw the son, they said to each other, "This is the heir. Come on, let us kill him and take over his inheritance."
>
> 39So they seized him and threw him out of the vineyard and killed him.
>
> 40Now when the owner of the vineyard comes, what will he do to those tenants?'
>
> 41They answered, 'He will bring those wretches to a wretched end and lease the vineyard to other tenants who will deliver the produce to him at the proper time.' (Mat 21:33–41; cf. Mar 12:1–9, Luk 20:9–16a)

The "son" in Matthew who is killed represents Christ (who ascends to heaven after his death). The Qurʾānic figure "from the city outskirts" is evidently killed as a martyr and ascends to heaven (note v. 26: "Enter paradise!"). Both texts refer to the divine punishment of those who persecute God's messengers (Q 36:28–29; Mat 21:41). This Qurʾānic passage is a good example of the way the Qurʾān shapes a Biblical text to advance its own religious teaching (in this case the worship of God alone; see vv. 22–24).

On the idea that a true prophet does not seek a reward (v. 21), see commentary on 34:47 (with further references).

32And all of them will indeed be presented before Us.

³³A sign for them is the dead earth, which We revive and bring forth grain out of it, so they eat of it. ³⁴We make in it orchards of date palms and vines, and We cause springs to gush forth in it,

36:34 On the streams of paradise, see commentary on 2:25 (with further references).

---

³⁵so that they may eat of its fruit and what their hands have cultivated. Will they not then give thanks?

³⁶Immaculate is He who has created all the kinds of what the earth grows, and of themselves, and of what they do not know.

³⁷A sign for them is the night, which We strip of daylight, and behold, they find themselves in the dark! ³⁸The sun runs on to its place of rest: That is the ordaining of the All-mighty, the All-knowing.

³⁹As for the moon, We have ordained its phases, until it becomes like an old palm leaf. ⁴⁰Neither it behooves the sun to overtake the moon, nor may the night outrun the day, and each swims in an orbit.

⁴¹A sign for them is that We carried their progeny in the laden ship, ⁴²and We have created for them what is similar to it, which they ride. ⁴³And if We like, We drown them, whereat they have no one to call for help, nor are they rescued

36:41–43 On Noah's ark see commentary on 71:1–28 (with further references).

---

⁴⁴except by a mercy from Us and for an enjoyment until some time.

⁴⁵And when they are told, 'Beware of that which is before you and that which is behind you, so that you may receive [His] mercy . . .' ⁴⁶There does not come to them any sign from among the signs of their Lord but that they have been disregarding it.

⁴⁷When they are told, 'Spend out of what God has provided you,' the faithless say to the faithful, 'Shall we feed [someone] whom God would feed, if He wished? You are only in plain error.'

⁴⁸And they say, 'When will this promise be fulfilled, if you are truthful?' ⁴⁹They do not await but a single Cry that will seize them as they wrangle. ⁵⁰Then they will not be able to make any will, nor will they return to their folks.

⁵¹And when the Trumpet is blown, behold, there they will be, scrambling towards their Lord from their graves!

36:51 On the trumpet blast, see commentary on 78:18 (with further references).

---

⁵²They will say, 'Woe to us! Who raised us from our place of sleep?' 'This is what the All-beneficent had promised and the apostles had spoken the truth!' ⁵³It will be but a single Cry, and behold, they will all be presented before Us! ⁵⁴'Today no soul will be wronged in the least, nor will you be requited except for what you used to do.'

⁵⁵Indeed, today the inhabitants of paradise rejoice in their engagements ⁵⁶—they and their mates, reclining on couches in the shades.

36:56 On shade in paradise, see commentary on 13:35 (with further references).

⁵⁷There they have fruits, and they have whatever they want. ⁵⁸'Peace!'—a watchword from the all-merciful Lord. ⁵⁹And 'Get apart today, you guilty ones!' ⁶⁰'Did I not exhort you, O children of Adam, saying, "Do not worship Satan. He is indeed your manifest enemy. ⁶¹Worship Me. That is a straight path"?

36:60–61 Cf. 1 Peter 5:8: "Keep sober and alert, because your enemy the devil is on the prowl like a roaring lion, looking for someone to devour." On Satan as an enemy of a man, cf. 2:168–69, 208; 6:142; 7:22; 12:5; 17:53; 28:15; 35:5–6; 43:62; 57:14. On the worship of Satan, see commentary on 18:50 (with further references).

⁶²He has already led astray many of your generations. Did you not exercise your reason? ⁶³This is the hell you had been promised! ⁶⁴Enter it today, because of what you used to deny. ⁶⁵Today We shall seal their mouths, and their hands will speak to Us, and their feet will bear witness concerning what they used to earn.'

⁶⁶Had We wished We would have blotted out their eyes: then, were they to advance towards the path, how would have they seen? ⁶⁷And had We wished We would have deformed them in their place; then they would neither have been able to move ahead nor to return.

⁶⁸And whomever We give a long life, We cause him to regress in creation. Then, will they not exercise their reason?

⁶⁹We did not teach *him* poetry, nor does it behoove *him*. This is just a reminder and a manifest Qur'ān, ⁷⁰so that anyone who is alive may be warned and that the word may come due against the faithless.

[71]Have they not seen that We have created for them, of what Our hands have worked, cattle, so they have become their masters? [72]And We made them tractable for them; so some of them make their mounts and some of them they eat. [73]There are other benefits for them therein, and drinks. Will they not then give thanks?

[74]They have taken gods besides God, [hoping] that they might be helped [by the fake deities]. [75][But] they cannot help them, while they [themselves]are an army mobilized for their defence.

[76]So do not let their remarks grieve *you.* We indeed know whatever they hide and whatever they disclose.

[77]Does not man see that We created him from a drop of [seminal] fluid, and behold, he is an open contender!? [78]He draws comparisons for Us, and forgets his own creation. He says, 'Who will revive the bones when they have decayed?'

[79]*Say,* 'He will revive them who produced them the first time, and He has knowledge of all creation. [80]He, who made for you fire out of the green tree, and behold, you light fire from it! [81]Is not He who created the heavens and the earth able to create the like of them? Yes indeed! He is the All-creator, the All-knowing. [82]All His command, when He wills something, is to say to it 'Be,' and it is.

36:82 The Qur'ān's declaration here (cf. 2:117; 3:47, 59; 6:73; 16:40; 19:35; 40:68) that God creates by speaking the word "Be!" (*kun*) may owe something to God's creating through speaking in Genesis 1, or to Psalm 33:9 ("For, the moment he spoke, it was so, no sooner had he commanded, than there it stood!").

---

[83]So immaculate is He in whose hand is the dominion of all things, and to whom you shall be brought back.

37. *AL-ṢĀFFĀT*, THE RANGED ONES

In the Name of God, the All-beneficent, the All-merciful.

¹By the [angels] ranged in ranks, ²by the ones who drive [the clouds] vigorously, ³by the ones who recite the reminder: ⁴indeed your God is certainly One, ⁵the Lord of the heavens and the earth and whatever is between them, and the Lord of the easts.

⁶We have indeed adorned the lowest heaven with the finery of the stars ⁷and to guard from every froward devil. ⁸They do not eavesdrop on the Supernal Elite—they are shot at from every side, ⁹to drive them away, and there is a perpetual punishment for them—¹⁰except any who snatches a snatch, whereat a piercing flame pursues him.

37:6–10 On the stars as a physical barrier which prevent the demons and jinn from penetrating into heaven, cf. 15:16–18; 41:12; 67:5; 72:8–9; see commentary on 15:16–18. "Supernal Elite" (v. 8; cf. 38:69) is Qarai's translation of the Arabic *al-mala' al-a'lā*. The phrase is perhaps better translated as "High Council" (thus Arberry; cf. Paret: "obersten Rat"). The Qur'ān thereby means the group of angels with whom God holds discussions in heaven (discussions which the demons seek to overhear). The *Testament of Solomon,* an early Greek Christian text, has a demon declare: "We demons go up to the firmament of heaven, fly around among the stars, and hear the decisions which issue from God concerning the lives of men" (20:12) (cr. Patricia Crone).

¹¹Ask them, is their creation more prodigious or [that of other creatures] that We have created? Indeed, We created them from a viscous clay.

¹²Indeed, *you* wonder, while they engage in ridicule, ¹³and [even] when admonished do not take admonition, ¹⁴and when they see a sign they make it an object of ridicule ¹⁵and say, 'This is nothing but plain magic!' ¹⁶'What! When we are dead and become dust and bones, shall we be indeed resurrected? ¹⁷And our forefathers, too?!'

¹⁸*Say,* 'Yes! And you will be utterly humble.'

37:12–18 On the Qur'ān's arguments for the resurrection of the body, see commentary on 13:5 (with further references).

¹⁹It will be only a single shout and behold, they will look on ²⁰and say, 'Woe to us! This is the Day of Retribution!'

²¹'This is the Day of Judgement that you used to deny!'

37:21 On the Arabic expression for "Day of Judgement," see commentary on 77:13–14 (with further references).

²²'Muster the wrongdoers and their mates and what they used to worship ²³besides God and show them the way to hell!

37:22–23 The Qur'ān's vision here, by which wrongdoers and their false gods or demons are condemned to hell, is close to the eschatological vision described by Jesus in Matthew (cf. *BEQ,* 456):

⁴¹The Son of man w··. send his angels and they will gather out of his kingdom all causes of falling and all who do evil,

⁴²and throw them into the blazing furnace, where there will be weeping and grinding of teeth. (Mat 13:41–42)

---

²⁴[But first] stop them! For they must be questioned.' ²⁵'Why is it that you do not support one another [today]?' ²⁶'They are indeed [meek and] submissive today!'

²⁷Some of them will turn to others, questioning each other. ²⁸They will say, 'Indeed, you used to accost us peremptorily.' ²⁹They will answer, 'No, you [yourselves] had no faith. ³⁰We had no authority over you. No, you [yourselves] were a rebellious lot. ³¹So our Lord's word became due against us that we shall indeed taste [the punishment]. ³²We perverted you, for we were perverse [ourselves].'

³³So that day they will share the punishment. ³⁴That is indeed how We deal with the guilty. ³⁵It was they who, when they were told, 'There is no god except God,' used to be disdainful, ³⁶and [they would] say, 'Shall we abandon our gods for a crazy poet?'

³⁷He has indeed brought [them] the truth, and confirmed the [earlier] apostles.

³⁸You will indeed taste the painful punishment ³⁹and you will be requited only for what you used to do ⁴⁰—[all] except God's exclusive servants. ⁴¹For such there is a known provision ⁴²—fruits—and they will be held in honour ⁴³in the gardens of bliss, ⁴⁴[reclining] on couches, facing one another, ⁴⁵served around with a cup from a clear fountain, ⁴⁶snow-white, delicious to the drinkers, ⁴⁷wherein there will be neither headache nor will it cause them stupefaction, ⁴⁸and with them will be maidens, of restrained glances with big [beautiful] eyes, ⁴⁹as if they were hidden ostrich eggs.

37:41–49 On heaven as a feast, see commentary on 56:15–21 (with further references). On the "maidens of paradise" in the Qurʾān, see commentary on 56:22–23 (with further references).

---

⁵⁰Some of them will turn to others, questioning each other. ⁵¹One of them will say, 'I had indeed a companion ⁵²who used to say, "Are you really among those who affirm ⁵³that when we have died and become dust and bones, we will indeed be brought to retribution?"'

⁵⁴He will say, 'Will you have a look?' ⁵⁵Then he will take a look and sight him in the middle of hell. ⁵⁶He will say, 'By God, you had almost ruined me! ⁵⁷Had it not been for my Lord's blessing, I too would have been among the arraigned!' ⁵⁸'Is it [true] that we will not die [anymore], ⁵⁹aside from our earlier death, and that we will not be punished?

37:58–59 On the description of hell as a "second death," see commentary on 40:11 (with further references).

---

⁶⁰This is indeed a mighty triumph!' ⁶¹Let all workers work for the like of this!

⁶²Is this a better reception, or the Zaqqūm tree? ⁶³Indeed, We have made it a punishment for the wrongdoers. ⁶⁴It is a tree that rises from the depths of hell. ⁶⁵Its blossoms are as if they were devils' heads. ⁶⁶They will eat from it and gorge with it their bellies. ⁶⁷On top of that they will take a solution of scalding water. ⁶⁸Then their retreat will be toward hell.

⁶⁹They had found their fathers astray, ⁷⁰yet they press onwards in their footsteps. ⁷¹Most of the former peoples went astray before them, ⁷²and We had certainly sent warners among them.

⁷³So observe how was the fate of those who were warned ⁷⁴— [all] except God's exclusive servants!

⁷⁵Certainly Noah called out to Us and how well did We respond! ⁷⁶We delivered him and his family from their great distress, ⁷⁷and made his descendants the survivors, ⁷⁸and left for him a good name among posterity: ⁷⁹'Peace to Noah, throughout the nations!' ⁸⁰Thus do We reward the virtuous. ⁸¹He is indeed one of Our faithful servants. ⁸²Then We drowned the rest.

37:73–82 On Noah in the Qur'ān, see commentary on 71:1–28 (with further references).

---

⁸³Abraham was indeed among his followers, ⁸⁴when he came to his Lord with a sound heart [untainted by sin], ⁸⁵when he said to his father and his people, 'What is it that you are worshiping? ⁸⁶Is it a lie, gods other than God, that you desire? ⁸⁷Then what is your idea about the Lord of all the worlds?'

37:83–87 On Abraham's confrontation with his people, see commentary on 26:69–93 (with further references).

---

⁸⁸Then he made an observation of the stars ⁸⁹and said, 'I am indeed sick!' ⁹⁰So they went away leaving him behind. ⁹¹Then he stole away to their gods and said, 'Will you not eat? ⁹²Why do you not speak?' ⁹³Then he attacked them, striking forcefully. ⁹⁴They came running towards him. ⁹⁵He said, 'Do you worship what you have carved yourselves, ⁹⁶when God has created you and whatever you make?'

37:88–96 On Abraham's destroying (his father's) idols, cf. 21:51–67 and commentary on that passage. In verses 91–92 (cf. 7:194–98; 19:42) the Qurʾān has Abraham question the speechless idols in a way that reflects Psalm 115:

> ⁴They have idols of silver and gold, made by human hands.
> ⁵These have mouths but say nothing, have eyes but see nothing,
> ⁶have ears but hear nothing, have noses but smell nothing.
> ⁷They have hands but cannot feel, have feet but cannot walk, no sound comes from their throats.
> ⁸Their makers will end up like them, and all who rely on them.
> (Psa 115:4–8; cf. Isa 44:9–20; Jer 10:1–16)

---

⁹⁷They said, 'Build a structure for him and cast him into a huge fire.' ⁹⁸So they sought to outwit him, but We made them the lowermost.

37:97–98 On the casting of Abraham into to the fiery furnace, and Abraham's salvation therefrom, see commentary on 21:68–70 (with further references).

---

⁹⁹He said, 'Indeed, I am going toward my Lord, who will guide me.'

37:99 This verse alludes to the migration of Abraham from his ancestral Mesopotamian home (where the trials of his childhood among the idolaters are set) to Canaan, the land to which God had called him. Cf. Genesis 12:5: "Abram took his wife Sarai, his nephew Lot, all the possessions they had amassed and the people they had acquired in Haran. They set off for the land of Canaan, and arrived there."

---

¹⁰⁰'My Lord! Give me [an heir], one of the righteous.' ¹⁰¹So We gave him the good news of a forbearing son.

¹⁰²When he was old enough to assist in his endeavour, he said, 'My son! I see in dreams that I am sacrificing you. See what you think.' He said, 'Father! Do whatever you have been commanded. If God wishes, you will find me to be patient.'

¹⁰³So when they had both surrendered [to God's will] and he had laid him down on his temple, ¹⁰⁴We called out to him, 'O Abraham! ¹⁰⁵You have indeed fulfilled your vision! Thus indeed do We reward the virtuous! ¹⁰⁶This was indeed a manifest test.'

¹⁰⁷Then We ransomed him with a great sacrifice, ¹⁰⁸and left for him a good name in posterity: ¹⁰⁹'Peace be to Abraham!' ¹¹⁰Thus do We reward the virtuous.

37:100–10 Muslim exegetes are divided over whether the son whom Abraham is commanded to sacrifice is Isaac or rather Ishmael. *Tafsīr al-Jalālayn* writes (regarding v. 107): "Then We ransomed him, the one whom he had been commanded to sacrifice, namely, Ishmael or Isaac." The announcement of Isaac's birth in verse 112 leads some to believe that Ishmael must be meant when the Qurʾān speaks of the giving of a son to Abraham in verse 101. However, it is possible that the Qurʾān simply announces Isaac's birth twice (vv. 101, 112). Elsewhere in the Qurʾān only Isaac's birth (and never Ishmael's birth) is mentioned. The basis of the sacrifice account is ultimately Genesis 22:

¹It happened some time later that God put Abraham to the test. 'Abraham, Abraham!' he called. 'Here I am,' he replied.

²God said, 'Take your son, your only son, your beloved Isaac, and go to the land of Moriah, where you are to offer him as a burnt offering on one of the mountains which I shall point out to you.'

. . .

⁷Isaac spoke to his father Abraham. 'Father?' he said. 'Yes, my son,' he replied. 'Look,' he said, 'here are the fire and the wood, but where is the lamb for the burnt offering?'

⁸Abraham replied, 'My son, God himself will provide the lamb for the burnt offering.' And the two of them went on together.

⁹When they arrived at the place which God had indicated to him, Abraham built an altar there, and arranged the wood. Then he bound his son and put him on the altar on top of the wood.

¹⁰Abraham stretched out his hand and took the knife to kill his son.

¹¹But the angel of the Lord called to him from heaven. 'Abraham, Abraham!' he said. 'Here I am,' he replied.

¹²'Do not raise your hand against the boy,' the angel said. 'Do not harm him, for now I know you fear God. You have not refused me your own beloved son.'

¹³Then looking up, Abraham saw a ram caught by its horns in a bush. Abraham took the ram and offered it as a burnt offering in place of his son. (Gen 22:1–2, 7–13)

The key difference with the account of Genesis 22 is the conversation between Abraham and his son (v. 102) in which the son declares his willingness to be sacrificed (cf. Gen 22:7). This follows from the sentiments expressed by both Jewish and Christian exegetes that Isaac, who, like Abraham, was a holy and obedient figure, understood what was going on and was willing to die (this depite Isaac asking, "where is the lamb for the burnt offering?" in Gen 22:7). A tradition in *Genesis Rabbah* has the devil (Samael) first speak to Abraham (to convince him not to follow God's command) and then to Isaac, who insists in reply that he is willing to be sacrificed: "Seeing that he could achieve nought with [Abraham], he approached Isaac and said: 'Son of an unhappy mother! He goes to slay thee.' 'I accept my fate,' he replied" (*Genesis Rabbah,* 46:4). Jacob of Serugh has Isaac assist his father in building the altar on which he would be killed (see *On Abraham and His Types,* 4:90, ll. 4–13). See also commentary on 2:125–28.

---

¹¹¹He is indeed one of Our faithful servants.

¹¹²We gave him the good news of [the birth of] Isaac, a prophet, one of the righteous. ¹¹³And We blessed him and Isaac. Among their descendants [some] are virtuous, and [some] who manifestly wrong themselves.

¹¹⁴Certainly We favoured Moses and Aaron ¹¹⁵and delivered them and their people from their great distress ¹¹⁶and We helped them, so they became the victors. ¹¹⁷We gave them the illuminating scripture ¹¹⁸and guided them to the straight path ¹¹⁹and left for them a good name in posterity. ¹²⁰'Peace be to Moses and Aaron!'

37:114–20 On the "victory" of Moses and Aaron over Pharaoh at the Red Sea, see commentary on 26:60–66 (with further references). On the revelation to Moses, see commentary on 11:110 (with further references).

---

¹²¹Thus indeed do We reward the virtuous. ¹²²They are indeed among Our faithful servants.

¹²³Ilyās was indeed one of the apostles. ¹²⁴When he said to his people, 'Will you not be Godwary? ¹²⁵Do you invoke Baal and abandon the best of creators, ¹²⁶God, your Lord and Lord of your forefathers?,' ¹²⁷they impugned him. So they will indeed be arraigned ¹²⁸—[all] except God's exclusive servants. ¹²⁹We left for him a good name in posterity. ¹³⁰'Peace be to Ilyās!' ¹³¹Thus indeed do We reward the virtuous. ¹³²He is indeed one of Our faithful servants.

37:123–32 Ilyās (v. 123; from Greek Ēlias, perhaps through Syriac, see *FV*, 68) is Elijah (cf. 6:85). In v. 130 the Arabic for his name (again rendered simply as "Ilyās" by Qarai) is different (for the sake of the rhyme): *il yāsīn.* In this passage the Qurʾān refers to Elijah's rebuke of Israel—and in particular of Ahab, king of Israel—for worshipping the Canaanite god Baal, and to Israel's refusal to listen to Elijah and forsake this worship:

> ¹⁷When he saw Elijah, Ahab said, 'So there you are, you scourge of Israel!'
> ¹⁸'Not I,' he replied, 'I am not the scourge of Israel, you and your family are; because you have deserted the Lord and followed Baal. (1Ki 18:17–18; see also 1Ki 19:9–10)

---

¹³³Lot was indeed one of the apostles. ¹³⁴When We delivered him and all his family, ¹³⁵excepting an old woman among those who remained behind, ¹³⁶Then We destroyed the rest. ¹³⁷Indeed,

you pass by them morning [138]and evening [on the Syrian route of your trade caravans]. So do you not exercise your reason?

37:133–38 On the destruction of Lot's people, see commentary on 15:57–74 (with further references). Here the Qur'ān implies (v. 137) that its listeners pass by the ruins of Sodom twice a day, which might suggest that the geographical context of this passage was somewhere much closer to the Dead Sea (the traditional site of Sodom) than to Mecca. On this see also commentary on 30:1–5. Qarai (following a traditional view found already with *Tafsīr Muqātil*) offers an alternative explanation in parentheses (v. 138), namely, that it was the trade caravans of the Quraysh that passed by these ruins. However, this passage suggests that the audience regularly, indeed daily, passed by the ruins, not only when on a journey to a distant land. On the ruins of Lot's city, cf. 15:76–77; 29:35; 51:37. On Lot's wife, see commentary on 27:54–58 (with further references).

———

[139]Jonah was indeed one of the apostles. [140]When he absconded toward the laden ship, [141]he drew lots with them and was the one to be refuted [and thrown overboard]. [142]Then the fish swallowed him while he was blameworthy. [143]Had he not been one of those who celebrate God's glory, [144]he would have surely remained in its belly till the day they will be resurrected. [145]Then We cast him on a bare shore, and he was sick. [146]So We made a gourd plant grow above him. [147]We sent him to a [community of] hundred thousand or more, [148]and they believed [in him]. So We provided for them for a while.

37:139–48 The Qur'ān follows here the Biblical story of Jonah, even in its reference to the (more than) one hundred thousand people to whom Jonah was sent (v. 147):

[3]Jonah set about running away from the Lord, and going to Tarshish. He went down to Jaffa and found a ship bound for Tarshish; he paid his fare and boarded it, to go with them to Tarshish, to get away from the Lord.
[4]But the Lord threw a hurricane at the sea, and there was such a great storm at sea that the ship threatened to break up.

⁵The sailors took fright, and each of them called on his own god, and to lighten the ship they threw the cargo overboard. Jonah, however, had gone below, had lain down in the hold and was fast asleep,

⁶when the boatswain went up to him and said, 'What do you mean by sleeping? Get up! Call on your god! Perhaps he will spare us a thought and not leave us to die.'

⁷Then they said to each other, 'Come on, let us draw lots to find out who is to blame for bringing us this bad luck.' So they cast lots, and the lot pointed to Jonah. (Jon 1:3–7)

¹Now the Lord ordained that a great fish should swallow Jonah; and Jonah remained in the belly of the fish for three days and three nights.

²From the belly of the fish, Jonah prayed to the Lord, his God

. . .

¹¹The Lord spoke to the fish, which then vomited Jonah onto the dry land. (Jon 2:1–2, 11)

⁶The Lord God then ordained that a castor-oil plant should grow up over Jonah to give shade for his head and soothe his ill-humour; Jonah was delighted with the castor-oil plant.

. . .

¹¹So why should I not be concerned for Nineveh, the great city, in which there are more than a hundred and twenty thousand people who cannot tell their right hand from their left, to say nothing of all the animals?' (Jon 4:6, 11)

Tafsīr al-Jalālayn reports that Jonah "absconded to a laden ship" only after his preaching was rejected, but in fact this phrase refers to Jonah's initial refusal to preach to Assyria (Nineveh), Israel's enemy (Jon 1:2). The Qur'ān's reference (v. 143) to Jonah's praise of God reflects Jonah's psalm of praise (Jon 2:3–10) in the fish. On Jonah, cf. 10:98; 21:87–88; 68:48–50.

The concluding note of the Jonah account here ("So We provided for them *for a while*") suggests that the people were spared from divine destruction only for a time. In fact Jewish traditions, picking up from the Books of Nahum (1:1; 3:1–4) and Tobit (14:4), explain that eventually the Ninevites sinned against God again and were destroyed. This is mentioned by Josephus (*Jewish Antiquities* IX, 11:3) and in later rabbinic works including the *Pirqe de-Rabbi Eliezer* (43).

---

¹⁴⁹Ask them, are daughters to be for your Lord while sons are to be for them? ¹⁵⁰Did We create the angels females while they

were present? ¹⁵¹Be aware that it is out of their mendacity that they say, ¹⁵²'God has begotten [offspring],' and they indeed speak a falsehood. ¹⁵³Has He preferred daughters to sons? ¹⁵⁴What is the matter with you? How do you judge? ¹⁵⁵Will you not then take admonition? ¹⁵⁶Do you have a manifest authority? ¹⁵⁷Then produce your scripture, should you be truthful.

¹⁵⁸And they have set up a kinship between Him and the jinn, while the jinn certainly know that they will be presented [before Him].

37:158 On the worship of jinn, see commentary on 6:100 (with further references). Note also that in 18:50 the Qurʾān makes the devil one of the jinn and suggests that unbelievers call on him as a god.

---

¹⁵⁹Clear is God of whatever they allege [about Him] ¹⁶⁰—[all] except God's exclusive servants.

¹⁶¹Indeed, you and what you worship ¹⁶²cannot mislead [anyone] about Him, ¹⁶³except someone who is bound for hell.

¹⁶⁴'There is none among us but has a known place. ¹⁶⁵We are indeed the ranged ones. ¹⁶⁶Indeed, we celebrate God's glory.'

¹⁶⁷Indeed, they used to say, ¹⁶⁸'Had we possessed a reminder from our predecessors, ¹⁶⁹we would have surely been God's exclusive servants.' ¹⁷⁰But they denied it [when it came to them]. Soon they will know!

¹⁷¹Certainly Our decree has gone beforehand in favour of Our servants, the apostles, ¹⁷²that they will indeed receive [God's] help, ¹⁷³and indeed Our hosts will be the victors. ¹⁷⁴So leave them alone for a while, ¹⁷⁵and watch them; soon they will see [the truth of the matter]!

¹⁷⁶Do they seek to hasten Our punishment? ¹⁷⁷But when it descends in their courtyard it will be a dismal dawn for those who had been warned. ¹⁷⁸So leave them alone for a while, ¹⁷⁹and watch; soon they will see!

¹⁸⁰Clear is *your* Lord, the Lord of Might, of whatever they allege [concerning Him]. ¹⁸¹Peace be to the apostles! ¹⁸²All praise belongs to God, Lord of all the worlds.

38. ṢĀD, ṢĀD

In the Name of God, the All-beneficent, the All-merciful.

¹*Ṣād.* By the Qur'ān bearing the Reminder. ²The faithless indeed dwell in conceit and defiance. ³How many a generation We have destroyed before them! They cried out [for help], but gone was the time for escape.

⁴They consider it odd that there should come to them a warner from among themselves, and the faithless say, 'This is a magician, a mendacious liar.' ⁵'Has he reduced the gods to one god? This is indeed an odd thing!' ⁶Their elite go about [urging others]: 'Go and stand by your gods! This is indeed the desirable thing [to do]. ⁷We did not hear of this in the latter-day creed. This is nothing but a fabrication. ⁸Has the Reminder been sent down to him out of [all of] us?'

They are indeed in doubt concerning My Reminder. Rather, they have not yet tasted My punishment. ⁹Do they possess the treasuries of the mercy of *your* Lord, the All-mighty, the All-munificent? ¹⁰Do they own the kingdom of the heavens and the earth and whatever is between them? [If so,] let them ascend [to the higher spheres] by the means [of ascension]. ¹¹[They are but] a host routed out there of the factions.

¹²Before them Noah's people impugned [their apostle] and [so did the people of] 'Ād, and Pharaoh, the Impaler [of his victims],

38:12 On the description of Pharaoh as "the Impaler," see commentary on 89:10.

---

[13]and Thamūd, and the people of Lot, and the inhabitants of Aykah: those were the factions.

38:13 On the inhabitants of "Aykah," see commentary on 15:78–79 (with further references).

---

[14]Each of them did not but impugn the apostles; so My retribution became due [against them]. [15]These [too] do not await but a single Cry which will not grant [them] any respite. [16]They say, 'Our Lord! Hasten on for us our share before the Day of Reckoning.'

[17]*Be patient* over what they say and *remember* Our servant, David, [the man] of strength. He was indeed a penitent [soul]. [18]We disposed the mountains to glorify [God] with him at evening and dawn, [19]and the birds [as well], mustered [in flocks]; all echoing him [in a chorus].

38:17–19 The reference in verse 17 to David as "penitent" (cf. v. 24), is likely an allusion to his repentance for the cuckolding and murder of Uriah (see 2Sa 12:13; cf. Psa 51). Yusuf Ali translates (instead of "penitent") as "he ever turned (to God)" (Muhammad Asad translates similarly), presumably to suggest that (being a prophet) he never sinned. On David, the mountains, and the birds, cf. 21:79; 34:10; and commentary on 21:79.

---

[20]We consolidated his kingdom and gave him wisdom and conclusive speech.

38:20 On David's "kingdom" and "wisdom," see commentary on 2:250–51 (with further references).

²¹Has there not come to you the account of the contenders when they scaled the wall into the sanctuary? ²²When they entered into the presence of David, he was alarmed by them. They said, 'Do not be afraid. [We are only] two contenders: one of us has bullied the other. So judge justly between us and do not exceed [the bounds of justice], and show us the right path.' ²³'This brother of mine has ninety-nine ewes, while I have only a single ewe, and [yet] he says, 'Commit it to my care,' and he browbeats me in speech.'

²⁴He said, 'He has certainly wronged you by asking your ewe in addition to his own ewes and indeed many partners bully one another, except such as have faith and do righteous deeds, and few are they.'

Then David knew that We had tested him, whereat he pleaded with his Lord for forgiveness, and fell down in prostration and repented. ²⁵So We forgave him that, and he has indeed [a station of] nearness with Us and a good destination.

²⁶'O David! We have indeed made you a vicegerent on the earth. So judge between people with justice, and do not follow your desire, or it will lead you astray from the way of God. There is a indeed severe punishment for those who stray from the way of God, because of their forgetting the Day of Reckoning.'

38:21–26 The Qurʾān here develops an account of 2 Samuel 11 (although the motif of *one hundred* sheep seems to come from the Gospels, notably Mat 18:12–14) by which David, after sleeping with Bathsheeba, has her husband Uriah killed, is confronted by the prophet Nathan, and repents:

> ¹The Lord sent the prophet Nathan to David. He came to him and said: In the same town were two men, one rich, the other poor.
>   ²The rich man had flocks and herds in great abundance;
> ³the poor man had nothing but a ewe lamb, only a single little one which he had bought. He fostered it and it grew up with him and his children, eating his bread, drinking from his cup, sleeping in his arms; it was like a daughter to him.

⁴When a traveller came to stay, the rich man would not take anything from his own flock or herd to provide for the wayfarer who had come to him. Instead, he stole the poor man's lamb and prepared that for his guest.

⁵David flew into a great rage with the man. 'As the Lord lives,' he said to Nathan 'the man who did this deserves to die.

⁶For doing such a thing and for having shown no pity, he shall make fourfold restitution for the lamb.'

⁷Nathan then said to David, 'You are the man!

. . .

¹³David said to Nathan, 'I have sinned against the Lord.' Nathan then said to David, 'The Lord, for his part, forgives your sin; you are not to die. (2Sa 12:1–7, 13)

Whereas in 2 Samuel, Nathan uses a parable of a poor man whose single ewe lamb is stolen to impress upon David the gravity of his sin, in the Qurʾān David actually meets this poor man and his nemesis and judges between them. In other words, the Qurʾān has turned Nathan's parable into a "real" incident involving David as a judge (presumably because the Qurʾān means to emphasize David as a just judge: see v. 26 and cf. 2:251; 21:79; 38:20—all of which emphasize David's wisdom). At the same time, however, the Qurʾān also has David repent (v. 24). The way in which hypothetical characters become real characters in a Qurʾānic narrative here might by compared to the way the hypothetical son of Noah mentioned by Ezekiel becomes a "real" character elsewhere in the Qurʾān (see commentary on 11:40–48).

In verse 26 David is described as a "vicegerent" (Ar. *khalīfa;* cf. Q 2:30), something which may reflect the later Jewish and Christian conception of David as the ideal ruler and prototype of the messiah (see, e.g., Luk 1:32).

Tafsīr al-Jalālayn relates that the two "disputants" were actually angels sent by God: "These two were angels who had come in the form of two disputants, between whom there [was supposed to have] occurred the situation mentioned— [but] only hypothetically—in order to alert David to what he had done: he had ninety nine women but desired the woman of a man who had only her and no other. He [David] had married her and consummated the marriage."

---

²⁷We did not create the heaven and the earth and whatever is between them in vain. That is a conjecture of the faithless. So woe to the faithless for the Fire!

²⁸Shall We treat those who have faith and do righteous deeds like those who cause corruption on the earth? Shall We treat the Godwary like the vicious?

²⁹[This is] a blessed Book that We have sent down to you, so that they may contemplate its signs and that those who possess intellect may take admonition.

³⁰And to David We gave Solomon—what an excellent servant he was! He was indeed a penitent [soul]. ³¹One evening when there were displayed before him prancing steeds, ³²he said, 'I have indeed preferred the love of [worldly] niceties to the re-membrance of my Lord until [the sun] disappeared behind the [night's] veil.' ³³'Bring it back for me!' Then he [and others] be-gan to wipe [their] legs and necks.

38:31–33 As discussed by Speyer (*BEQ*, 399), Solomon's penitence upon seeing horses (v. 32; cf. 3:14) might be understood in light of Deuteronomy 17:16, which explains that a righteous king should not have excessive amounts of horses and 1 Kings 5:6 (4:26 in the RSV) and 10:26, which mention the many horses of Solomon (cr. Mourad Takawi; cf. 2Ch 9:28). Speyer (*BEQ*, 399) also compares this passage with 2 Kings 23:11, which has Solomon destroy statues of horses that had been dedicated to the sun. This passage (like 34:14) is also reminiscent of Ecclesiastes, a book traditionally attributed to Solomon. Notably Ecclesiastes 1:5 points to the rising and setting of the sun as an example of the unchanging—and futile—nature of the world.

---

³⁴Certainly We tried Solomon and cast a [lifeless] body on his throne. Thereupon he was penitent. ³⁵He said, 'My Lord! Forgive me and grant me a kingdom that will not befit anyone except me. Indeed, You are the All-munificent.'

38:34–35 Behind this passage is a midrashic tale found in the Babylonian Talmud according to which the demon Ashmedai, who had been subdued by

Solomon, tricks Solomon into removing his chains and handing over his ring. Ashmedai swallows Solomon, casts him far away, takes on Solomon's likeness, and takes his place on the throne (eventually Ashmedai is recognized because of the stockings he wore to cover his roosterlike feet). Solomon returns to Jerusalem in the guise of a beggar, which may explain the humility ascribed to him in these two Qur'ānic verses:

> Solomon kept [Ashmedai] with him until he had built the Temple. One day when he was alone with him, he said . . . , "What is your superiority over us?" He said to him, "Take the chain off me and give me your ring, and I will show you." So he took the chain off him and gave him the ring. He then swallowed [Solomon] and placing one wing on the earth and one on the sky and he hurled him four hundred parasangs. . . .
>
> He used to go round begging, saying wherever he went, "I Koheleth was king over Israel in Jerusalem." When he came to the Sanhedrin, the Rabbis said: "Let us see, a madman does not stick to one thing only. What is the meaning of this?" They asked Benaiahu, "Does the king send for you?" He replied, "No." They sent to the queen saying, "Does the king visit you?" They sent back word, "Yes, he does." They then sent to them to say, "Examine his leg." They sent back to say, "He comes in stockings, and he visits them in the time of their separation and he also calls for Bathsheba his mother." They then sent for Solomon and gave him the chain and the ring on which the Name was engraved. When he went in, Ashmedai on catching sight of him flew away. (b. Gittin 68a)

------

³⁶So We disposed the wind for him, blowing softly wherever he intended by his command,

38:36 On Solomon and the winds, cf. 21:81–82 and 34:12–13, and commentary on those passages.

------

³⁷and every builder and diver from the demons, ³⁸and others [too] bound together in chains.

38:37–38 On Solomon and the jinn, cf. 27:16–17; 34:12–13; see commentary on 34:12–13.

---

³⁹'This is Our bounty: so withhold from it or bestow without any reckoning.'

⁴⁰He has indeed [a station of] nearness with Us and a good destination.

⁴¹And *mention* Our servant Job [in the Qur'ān]. When he called out to his Lord, 'The devil has visited on me hardship and torment,' ⁴²[We told him:] 'Stamp your foot on the ground; this [ensuing spring] will be a cooling bath and drink.' ⁴³We gave him [back] his family, along with others like them, as a mercy from Us and an admonition for those who possess intellect. ⁴⁴[We told him:] 'Take a faggot in your hand and then strike [your wife] with it, but do not break [your] oath.' Indeed, We found him to be patient. What an excellent servant! He was indeed a penitent [soul].

38:41–44 The way the Qur'ān has Job blame Satan reflects a larger tendency with its protagonists (with Jacob see 12:5; with Moses, see 28:15). It also reflects a tradition in the Babylonian Talmud (b. *Bava Batra* 16a) that makes Job aware that Satan is behind his troubles.

In verses 42–44 the Qur'ān seems to have taken an episode from the Biblical account of Hagar and Ishmael (Gen 21:16–19) and applied it to Job. Hagar was in great distress, to the point of death, when the Lord provided her with water. The Qur'ān seems to have attributed something similar to Job because of the Biblical account of his great distress. Cf. also the account of Mary in Q 19:23–24.

The reference in verse 43 to Job's receiving children (the Qur'ān suggests that he received his own children, back from the dead) follows the epilogue of the Biblical account (Job 42:12–13; on this see commentary on 21:83–84).

The Qur'ān also has God command (v. 44) Job to beat his wife, presumably for her insolence (cf. Job 2:9–10). However, for "faggot" (Qarai), Asad has "a small bunch of grass" (cf. Hilali-Khan, "a bundle of thin grass") and explains in a note that Job found a way to fulfill the oath to hit his wife in a way that would do her no harm. On Job, cf. 4:163; 6:83–87; 21:83–84; 38:41.

⁴⁵And *mention* Our servants, Abraham, Isaac and Jacob, men of strength and insight. ⁴⁶We indeed purified them with exclusive remembrance of the abode [of the Hereafter]. ⁴⁷With Us, they are indeed among the elect of the best.

⁴⁸And *mention* Ishmael, Elisha and Dhu'l-Kifl—each [of whom was] among the elect.

38:48 On Dhū l-Kifl, see commentary on 21:85–86.

⁴⁹This is a Reminder, and indeed the Godwary have a good destination: ⁵⁰the Gardens of Eden, whose gates will be flung open for them. ⁵¹Reclining therein [on couches], they will call for abundant fruits and drinks, ⁵²and there will be with them maidens of restrained glances, of a like age. ⁵³This is what you are promised on the Day of Reckoning. ⁵⁴This is Our provision, which will never be exhausted.

38:49–54 On the identification of the eschatological paradise in the Qurʾān with the Garden of Eden, see commentary on 9:72 (with further references).

On the maidens of paradise in the Qurʾān (v. 52), see commentary on 56:22–23 (with further references).

⁵⁵This [will be for the righteous], and as for the rebellious there will surely be a bad destination: ⁵⁶hell, which they shall enter, an evil resting place. ⁵⁷[They will be told], 'This is scalding water and pus; let them taste it ⁵⁸and other kinds [of torments] resembling it.'

⁵⁹[The leaders of the faithless will be told,] 'This is a group [of your followers] plunging [into hell] along with you.' [They will respond,] 'May wretchedness be their lot! For they will enter the Fire.' ⁶⁰They will say, 'No, may wretchedness be your lot! You prepared this [hell] for us. What an evil abode!' ⁶¹They will say, 'Our Lord! Whoever has prepared this for us, double his punishment in the Fire!' ⁶²And they will say, 'Why is it that we do not see [here] men whom we used to count among the bad ones, ⁶³ridiculing them, or do our eyes miss them [here]?'

⁶⁴That is indeed a true account of the contentions of the inmates of the Fire.

⁶⁵*Say*, 'I am just a warner, and there is no god except God, the One, the All-paramount, ⁶⁶the Lord of the heavens and the earth and whatever is between them, the All-mighty, the All-forgiving.'

⁶⁷*Say*, 'It is a great prophesy ⁶⁸of which you are disregardful. ⁶⁹I have no knowledge of the Supernal Elite when they contend. ⁷⁰All that is revealed to me is that I am just a manifest warner.'

⁷¹When *your* Lord said to the angels, 'Indeed, I am about to create a human being out of clay. ⁷²So when I have proportioned him and breathed into him of My spirit, fall down in prostration before him.'

⁷³Thereat the angels prostrated, all of them together, ⁷⁴but not Iblis; he acted arrogantly and he was one of the faithless.

⁷⁵He said, 'O Iblis! What kept you from prostrating before what I have created with My [own] two hands? Are you arrogant, or are you one of the exalted ones?' ⁷⁶'I am better than him,' he said. 'You created me from fire and You created him from clay.'

⁷⁷He said, 'Begone hence, for you are indeed an outcast, ⁷⁸and indeed My curse will be on you till the Day of Retribution.'

38:71–78 On God's breathing his Spirit into Adam, see commentary on 32:8–9 (with further references). On the refusal of the devil to prostrate himself before Adam, and his subsequent banishment from the presence of God, see commentary on 7:11–12 (with further references).

On the term in verse 78 that Qarai renders as "Retribution" (Ar. *dīn*), see commentary on 83:11 (with further references).

---

⁷⁹He said, 'My Lord! Respite me till the day they will be resurrected.'

⁸⁰Said He, 'You are indeed among the reprieved ⁸¹until the day of the known time.'

⁸²He said, 'By Your might, I will surely pervert them all, ⁸³except Your exclusive servants among them.'

⁸⁴Said He, 'The truth is that—and I speak the truth—⁸⁵I will surely fill hell with you and all of those who follow you.'

38:79–85 Here God grants to the devil, upon request, a respite from his punishment, allowing the devil to do his best to lead humans away from God (and thereby to have revenge upon the race of Adam, who caused his downfall). On this see commentary on 7:14–18 (with further references).

---

⁸⁶*Say,* 'I do not ask you any reward for it, and I am no impostor.

38:86 On the idea that a true prophet does not seek a reward, see commentary on 34:47 (with further references).

---

⁸⁷It is just a reminder for all the nations, ⁸⁸and you will surely learn its tidings in due time.'

39. *AL-ZUMAR,* THRONGS

In the Name of God, the All-beneficent, the All-merciful.

[1]The [gradual] sending down of the Book is from God, the All-mighty, the All-wise. [2]We have indeed sent down the Book to *you* with the truth; so worship God, putting exclusive faith in Him.

[3]Indeed, only exclusive faith is worthy of God, and those who take others as masters besides Him [claiming,] 'We only worship them so that they may bring us near to God,' God will judge between them concerning that about which they differ. Indeed, God does not guide someone who is a liar and an ingrate. [4]Had God intended to take an offspring, He could have chosen from those He has created whatever He wished. Immaculate is He! He is God, the One, the All-paramount.

[5]He created the heavens and the earth with consummate wisdom. He winds the night over the day, and winds the day over the night, and He has disposed the sun and the moon, each moving for a specified term. Indeed, He is the All-mighty, the All-forgiving!

[6]He created you from a single soul, then made from it its mate, and He has sent down for you eight mates of the cattle. He creates you in the wombs of your mothers, creation after creation, in a threefold darkness. That is God, your Lord! To Him belongs

all sovereignty. There is no god except Him. Then where are you being led away?

39:6 "The Lord God fashioned the rib he had taken from the man into a woman, and brought her to the man" (Gen 2:22).

---

⁷If you are ungrateful, God has indeed no need of you, though He does not approve ingratitude for His servants; and if you give thanks, He approves that for you. No bearer shall bear another's burden; then your return will be to your Lord, whereat He will inform you concerning what you used to do. Indeed, He knows best what is in the breasts.

39:7 On the notion that no soul shall carry another's burden, see commentary on 82:19 (with further references).

---

⁸When distress befalls man, he supplicates his Lord, turning to Him penitently. Then, when He grants him a blessing from Himself, he forgets that for which he had supplicated Him earlier and sets up equals to God, that he may lead [people] astray from His way. *Say,* 'Revel in your ingratitude for a while. You are indeed among the inmates of the Fire.'

⁹Is he who supplicates in the watches of the night, prostrating and standing, being apprehensive of the Hereafter and expecting the mercy of his Lord . . . ? *Say,* 'Are those who know equal to those who do not know?' Only those who possess intellect take admonition.

¹⁰*Say,* '[God declares:] "O My servants who have faith! Be wary of your Lord. For those who do good in this world there will

be a good [reward], and God's earth is vast. Indeed, the patient will be paid in full their reward without any reckoning.'"

¹¹*Say,* 'I have been commanded to worship God with exclusive faith in Him ¹²and I have been commanded to be the foremost of those who submit [to Him].'

¹³*Say,* 'Indeed, should I disobey my Lord, I fear the punishment of a tremendous day.'

¹⁴*Say,* 'I worship [only] God, putting my exclusive faith in Him. ¹⁵You worship whatever you wish besides Him.'

Say, 'The losers are those who ruin themselves and their families on the Day of Resurrection.' That is indeed a manifest loss! ¹⁶There will be canopies of fire above them, and [similar] canopies beneath them. With that God deters His servants. So, My servants, be wary of Me!

¹⁷As for those who stay clear of the worship of satanic entities and turn penitently to God, there is good news for them. So *give* good news to My servants

---

39:17 "Satanic entities" (Ar. *ṭāghūt;* Asad translates "powers of evil") here is best understood (cf. 36:60: "Do not worship Satan") as an allusion to the devil (although *Tafsīr al-Jalālayn* explains this term as a reference to "graven images"). See commentary on 4:51–52 (with further references).

---

¹⁸who listen to the word [of God] and follow the best [interpretation] of it. They are the ones whom God has guided and it is they who possess intellect.

¹⁹Can he against whom the word of punishment has become due . . . ? Can *you* rescue someone who is in the Fire? ²⁰But as for those who are wary of their Lord, for them there will be lofty abodes with [other] lofty abodes built above them, with streams

running beneath them—a promise of God. God does not break His promise.

39:20 The Qur'ān's description of paradise as a place with "rooms" or "abodes" (Ar. *ghuraf*) is close to the description of heaven in John 14:2: "In my Father's house are many rooms" (Joh 14:2 RSV; cf. Joh 14:23). Cf. Q 25:75; 29:58; 34:37. On the streams of paradise, see commentary on 2:25 (with further references).

———

²¹Have you not seen that God sends down water from the sky, then He conducts it through the ground as springs. Then He brings forth with it crops of diverse hues. Then they wither and you see them turn yellow. Then He turns them into chaff. There is indeed a lesson in that for those who possess intellect.

²²Is someone whose breast God has opened to Islam so that he walks in a light from His Lord . . . ? So woe to those whose hearts have been hardened to the remembrance of God! They are in plain error.

²³God has sent down the best of discourses, a scripture [composed] of similar motifs, whereat shiver the skins of those who fear their Lord, then their skins and hearts relax at God's remembrance. That is God's guidance, by which He guides whomever He wishes; and whomever God leads astray has no guide.

39:23 On the Qur'ān's use of *mathānī*, which Qarai renders as "similar motifs," see commentary on 15:87.

———

²⁴What! Is someone who fends off with his face the terrible punishment [meted out to him] on the Day of Resurrection . . . ? And the wrongdoers will be told, 'Taste what you used to earn.'

²⁵Those who were before them impugned [the apostles], whereat the punishment overtook them whence they were not aware. ²⁶So God made them taste disgrace in the life of the world, and the punishment of the Hereafter will surely be greater, if they knew.

²⁷We have drawn for mankind in this Qur'ān every [kind of] example so that they may take admonition: ²⁸an Arabic Qur'ān, without any deviousness, so that they may be Godwary.

²⁹God draws an example: a man jointly owned by several contending masters, and a man belonging entirely to one man: are the two equal in comparison? All praise belongs to God! But most of them do not know.

³⁰*You* will die and they [too] will die. ³¹Then on the Day of Resurrection you will contend before your Lord.

³²So who is a greater wrongdoer than him who attributes falsehoods to God and denies the truth when it reaches him? Is not the [final] abode of the faithless in hell?

³³He who brings the truth and he who confirms it—it is they who are the Godwary. ³⁴They will have what they wish near their Lord—that is the reward of the virtuous—³⁵that God may absolve them of the worst of what they did and pay them their reward by the best of what they used to do.

³⁶Does not God suffice [to defend] His servant? They would frighten *you* of others than Him. Yet whomever God leads astray has no guide, ³⁷and whomever God guides, there is no one who can lead him astray. Is not God an all-mighty avenger?

³⁸If *you* ask them, 'Who created the heavens and the earth?' they will surely say, 'God.'

Say, 'Have you considered what you invoke besides God? Should God desire some distress for me, can they remove the distress visited by Him? Or should He desire some mercy for me, can they withhold His mercy?'

Say, 'God is sufficient for me. In Him alone let all the trusting put their trust.'

³⁹*Say,* 'O my people! Act according to your ability. I too am acting. Soon you will know ⁴⁰who will be overtaken by a punishment that will disgrace him, and on whom a lasting punishment will descend.'

⁴¹Indeed, We have sent down to *you* the Book with the truth for [the deliverance of] mankind. So whoever is guided is guided for his own sake, and whoever goes astray, goes astray to his own detriment, and it is not *your* duty to watch over them.

⁴²God takes the souls at the time of their death, and those who have not died, in their sleep. Then He retains those for whom He has ordained death and releases the others until a specified time. There are indeed signs in that for people who reflect.

⁴³Have they taken intercessors besides God? *Say,* 'What! Even though they do not control anything and cannot reason?!'

⁴⁴*Say,* 'All intercession rests with God. To Him belongs the kingdom of the heavens and the earth; then you will be brought back to Him.'

⁴⁵When God is mentioned alone, [thereat] shrink away the hearts of those who do not believe in the Hereafter, but when others are mentioned besides Him, behold, they rejoice!

⁴⁶*Say,* 'O God! Originator of the heavens and the earth, Knower of the sensible and the Unseen, You will judge between Your servants concerning that about which they used to differ.'

⁴⁷Even if the wrongdoers possessed all that is on the earth and as much of it besides, they would offer it on the Day of Resurrection to redeem themselves with it from a terrible punishment, and there will appear to them from God what they had never reckoned. ⁴⁸The evils of what they had earned will appear to them, and they will be besieged by what they used to deride.

⁴⁹When distress befalls man, he supplicates Us. Then, when We grant him a blessing from Us, he says, 'I was given it by virtue of [my] knowledge.' It is indeed a test, but most of them do not know. ⁵⁰Those who were before them [also] said that, but what they used to earn did not avail them. ⁵¹So the evils of what they had earned visited them, and as for the wrongdoers among these, the evils of what they earn shall be visited on them and they will not frustrate [God].

⁵²Do they not know that God expands the provision for whomever He wishes and tightens it [for whomever He wishes]? There are indeed signs in that for a people who have faith.

⁵³*Say* [that God declares,] 'O My servants who have committed excesses against their own souls, do not despair of the mercy of God. God will indeed forgive all sins. Indeed, He is the All-forgiving, the All-merciful. ⁵⁴Turn penitently to Him and submit to Him before the punishment overtakes you, whereupon you will not be helped. ⁵⁵And follow the best of what has been sent down to you from your Lord, before the punishment overtakes you suddenly while you are unaware.'

⁵⁶Lest anyone should say, 'Alas for my negligence in the vicinage of God! I was indeed among those who ridiculed.' ⁵⁷Or say, 'Had God guided me I would have surely been among the Godwary!' ⁵⁸Or say, when he sights the punishment, 'If only there were a second chance for me, I would be among the virtuous!'

⁵⁹[They will be told,] 'Yes, My signs did come to you, but you denied them and acted arrogantly and you were among the faithless.'

⁶⁰On the Day of Resurrection *you* will see those who attributed lies to God with their faces blackened. Is not the [final] abode of the arrogant in hell?

⁶¹God will deliver those who were Godwary with their salvation. No ill shall touch them, nor will they grieve.

⁶²God is creator of all things and He watches over all things. ⁶³To Him belong the keys of the heavens and the earth, and those who disbelieve in the signs of God—it is they who are the losers.

39:63 *Tafsīr al-Jalālayn* explains "keys" here as "the keys to . . . storehouses of rain and vegetation and other things." Muhammad Asad writes that God has keys to the "mysteries" of heaven and earth. In any case, this phrase (cf. 6:59; 42:12) might be seen as the Qur'ān's response to Matthew 16:19 (see Rudolph, *Abhängigkeit,* 14):

> ¹⁸So I now say to you: You are Peter and on this rock I will build my community. And the gates of the underworld can never overpower it.
> ¹⁹I will give you the keys of the kingdom of Heaven: whatever you bind on earth will be bound in heaven; whatever you loose on earth will be loosed in heaven.' (Mat 16:18–19)

---

⁶⁴*Say,* 'Will you, then, bid me to worship other than God, O you ignorant ones?!'

⁶⁵Certainly it has been revealed to *you* and to those [who have been] before *you:* 'If you ascribe a partner to God your works shall fail and you shall surely be among the losers. ⁶⁶Rather, worship God and be among the grateful!'

⁶⁷They do not regard God with the regard due to Him, yet the entire earth will be in His fist on the Day of Resurrection, and the heavens, scrolled, in His right hand. Immaculate is He and far above [having] any partners that they ascribe [to Him].

39:67 On the symbolic imagery of heaven rolled up in a scroll in the hand of God, see commentary on 21:104.

Wāḥidī identifies the "they" of this verse with the "People of the Book" and recounts the following episode: "A man from the people of the Book went to see the Prophet and said to him: 'O Abu'l-Qasim [i.e., Muḥammad], did you not hear that God carries all created being on one finger, all the earth on one finger, all trees on one finger, all the soil on one finger and then says: I am the King?'

The Messenger of God laughed so much that his molars showed. God revealed [this verse]."

---

⁶⁸And the Trumpet will be blown and whoever is in the heavens and whoever is on the earth will swoon, except whomever God wishes. Then it will be blown a second time, and behold, they will rise up, looking on!

39:68 On the trumpet blast, see commentary on 78:18 (with further references). This is the only passage that mentions two trumpet blasts.

---

⁶⁹The earth will glow with the light of her Lord and the Book will be set up, and the prophets and the martyrs will be brought, and judgment will be made between them with justice and they will not be wronged.

39:69 On the image of light in heaven, and a heavenly book, cf. Daniel 7:10: "A stream of fire poured out, issuing from his presence. A thousand thousand waited on him, ten thousand times ten thousand stood before him. The court was in session and the books lay open."

Here the Qurʾān gives a special place to the martyrs—alongside the prophets—as witnesses to the judgment which God will deliver upon the dead. On the happy fate of martyrs, see commentary on 2:154 and 3:169 (with further references). Revelation 20:3 gives a place of judgment to the martyrs who were beheaded for their faith. Regarding the opening of a (record) book on the Day of Judgment, see commentary on 17:13–14 (with further references).

---

⁷⁰Every soul will be recompensed fully for what it has done, and He is best aware of what they do.

⁷¹The faithless will be driven to hell in throngs. When they reach it and its gates are opened, its keepers will say to them, 'Did there not come to you [any] apostles from among yourselves, reciting to you the signs of your Lord and warning you of the encounter of this day of yours?' They will say, 'Yes, but the word of punishment became due against the faithless.' ⁷²It will be said, 'Enter the gates of hell to remain in it [forever]. Evil is the [ultimate] abode of the arrogant.'

⁷³Those who are wary of their Lord will be led to paradise in throngs. When they reach it and its gates are opened, its keepers will say to them, 'Peace be to you! You are welcome! Enter it to remain [forever].'

⁷⁴They will say, 'All praise belongs to God, who has fulfilled His promise to us and made us inheritors of the earth, that we may settle in paradise wherever we may wish!' How excellent is the reward of the workers [of righteousness]!

⁷⁵And *you* will see the angels surrounding the Throne, celebrating the praise of their Lord, and judgment will be made between them with justice, and it will be said, 'All praise belongs to God, the Lord of all the worlds!'

39:75 On the divine throne in the Qur'ān, see commentary on 69:17 (with further references).

40. *GHĀFIR*, The Forgiver

In the Name of God, the All-beneficent, the All-merciful.

¹*Ḥā, Mīm.* ²The [gradual] sending down of the Book is from God, the All-mighty, the All-knowing, ³forgiver of sins and acceptor of repentance, severe in retribution, [yet] all-bountiful; there is no god except Him [and] toward Him is the destination.

⁴No one disputes the signs of God except the faithless. So *do not be* misled by their bustle in the towns.

⁵The people of Noah denied before them and the [heathen] factions [who came] after them. Every nation attempted to lay hands on their apostle and disputed erroneously to refute the truth. Then I seized them; so how was My retribution?!

⁶That is how the word of *your* Lord became due concerning the faithless, that they shall be inmates of the Fire.

⁷Those who bear the Throne and those who are around it celebrate the praise of their Lord and have faith in Him, and they plead for forgiveness for the faithful: 'Our Lord! You embrace all things in Your mercy and knowledge. So forgive those who repent and follow Your way and save them from the punishment of hell.

40:7 On angels and the throne of God, see commentary on 69:17 (with further references). On the image of the angels' praising God, see commentary on 7:206 (with further references).

---

⁸Our Lord! Admit them into the Gardens of Eden, which You have promised them, along with whoever is righteous among their forebears, their spouses and their descendants. Indeed, You are the All-mighty, the All-wise.

40:8 On the Qur'ān's description of the heavenly paradise as the Garden of Eden, see commentary on 9:72 (with further references).

---

⁹Save them from the ills [of the Day of Resurrection], and whomever You save from the ills that day, You will have had mercy upon him, and that is a mighty triumph.'

¹⁰It will be proclaimed to the faithless: 'Surely God's outrage [towards you] is greater than your outrage towards yourselves, as you were invited to faith, but you disbelieved.'

¹¹They will say, 'Our Lord! Twice did You make us die and twice did You give us life. We admit our sins. Is there any way out [from this plight]?'

40:11 The reference to dying twice in this verse (cf. 37:58–59; 44:56) may be connected to the description of hell as a "second death" in Revelation:

> But the legacy for cowards, for those who break their word, or worship obscenities, for murderers and the sexually immoral, and for sorcerers, worshippers of false gods or any other sort of liars, is the second death in the burning lake of sulphur. (Rev 21:8; cf. Rev 2:11; 20:6, 14)

¹²[They will be told,] 'This [plight of yours] is because, when God was invoked alone, you would disbelieve, but if partners were ascribed to Him you would believe. So the judgment belongs to God, the All-exalted, the All-great.'

¹³It is He who shows you His signs and sends down provision for you from the sky. Yet no one takes admonition except those who return penitently [to God].

¹⁴So supplicate God putting exclusive faith in Him, though the faithless should be averse. ¹⁵Raiser of ranks, Lord of the Throne, He casts the Spirit of His command upon whomever of His servants that He wishes, that he may warn [people] of the Day of Encounter.

40:15 On the Qur'ān's references to God's *amr* (Qarai translates "command") and Spirit, see commentary on 42:52 (with further references).

¹⁶The day when they will emerge [from their graves], nothing about them will be hidden from God. 'To whom does the sovereignty belong today?' 'To God, the One, the All-paramount!' ¹⁷'Today every soul shall be requited for what it has earned. There will be no injustice today. God is indeed swift at reckoning.'

¹⁸*Warn* them of the Approaching Day when the hearts will be at the throats, choking with suppressed agony, [and] the wrongdoers will have no sympathizer, nor any intercessor who might be heard.

¹⁹He knows the treachery of the eyes and what the breasts hide. ²⁰God judges with justice, while those whom they invoke besides Him do not judge by anything. Indeed, it is God who is the All-hearing, the All-seeing.

²¹Have they not traveled through the land to see how was the fate of those who were before them? They were greater than them

in might and with respect to the effects [they left] in the land. But then God seized them for their sins, and they had no defender against God['s punishment].

²²That was because their apostles used to bring them manifest proofs, but they defied [them]. So God seized them. He is indeed all-strong, severe in retribution.

²³Certainly We sent Moses with Our signs and a clear authority ²⁴to Pharaoh, Hāmān and Korah, but they said, 'A magician and a mendacious liar.'

40:23–24 In the Bible Haman appears as the vizier of Ahasuerus, king of Persia. The Qurʾān makes him the vizier instead of Pharaoh, king of Egypt. On this, see commentary on 28:38.

The Biblical account of Korah has him rebel against Moses (for which God orders the earth to swallow him; cf. 28:76–81). On Korah, see commentary on 28:76–81 (with further references).

²⁵So when he brought them the truth from Us, they said, 'Kill the sons of the faithful who are with him, and spare their women.' But the stratagems of the faithless only go awry.

40:25 The way the Qurʾān here has Pharaoh (and, apparently, Haman and Korah) order the killing of Israelite boys but not girls is reminiscent of Exodus 1 (vv. 15–16). However, the Qurʾān here presents this as an order made during the adulthood of Moses, after he had confronted Pharaoh with signs from God. Cf. 2:49; 7:127, 141; 14:6; 28:4.

²⁶And Pharaoh said, 'Let me slay Moses, and let him invoke his Lord. Indeed, I fear that he will change your religion, or bring forth corruption in our land.'

²⁷Moses said, 'I seek the protection of my Lord and your Lord from every arrogant one who does not believe in the Day of Reckoning.'

40:26–27 On the threat to kill Moses, cf. 44:20.

---

²⁸Said a man of faith from Pharaoh's clan, who concealed his faith, 'Will you kill a man for saying, "My Lord is God," while he has already brought you clear proofs from your Lord? Should he be lying, his falsehood will be to his own detriment; but if he is truthful, there shall visit you some of what he promises you. Indeed, God does not guide someone who is a transgressor and liar. ²⁹O my people! Today sovereignty belongs to you and you are dominant in the land. But who will save us from God's punishment should it overtake us?'

Pharaoh said, 'I just point out to you what I see [to be advisable for you], and I guide you only to the way of rectitude.'

³⁰He who had faith said, 'O my people! I indeed fear for you [a day] like the day of the [heathen] factions, ³¹like the case of the people of Noah, of Ād and Thamūd, and those who came after them, and God does not desire any wrong for [His] servants. ³²O my people! I fear for you a day of mutual distress calls, ³³a day when you will turn back [to flee], not having anyone to protect you from God, and whomever God leads astray has no guide. ³⁴Certainly Joseph brought you clear proofs earlier, but you continued to remain in doubt concerning what he had brought you. When he died, you said, "God will never send any apostle after him." That is how God leads astray those who are unrestrained and skeptical. ³⁵Those who dispute the signs of God without any

authority that may have come to them—[that is] greatly outrageous to God and to those who have faith. That is how God seals the heart of every arrogant tyrant.'

40:28–35 The Qur'ān here introduces an anonymous (and secret; see v. 28) believer (*Tafsīr al-Jalālayn* makes him Pharaoh's paternal cousin) from the midst of Pharaoh's unbelieving people. The advice (see v. 28) of this character (whose story is picked up again in vv. 41–44) is like that of the Pharisee Gamaliel in the Acts 5 (vv. 34–39), who advises the Sanhedrin not to persecute the believers with the counsel that God will grant them success in any case if their belief is truly from God.

This anonymous believer later exhorts the Egyptians with a reference to the earlier prophets and the fate of those who rejected them, and recalls in particular the mission of Joseph (sent to the Egyptians before Moses). In this he reflects the Qur'ānic prophets who often exhort their people by warning them not to repeat the mistake of earlier peoples (e.g., Ṣāliḥ, who refers to Hūd's people, 7:74; and Shuʿayb, who refers to the people of Noah, Hūd, Ṣāliḥ, and Lot, 11:89). The way the anonymous believer here threatens (vv. 30–31) all the Egyptian people with destruction suggests that not only Pharoah's forces but rather all of Egypt was drowned (cf. 43:55).

---

³⁶Pharaoh said, 'O Hāmān! Build me a tower so that I may reach the routes ³⁷—the routes of the heavens—and take a look at the God of Moses, and indeed I consider him a liar.'

The evil of his conduct was thus presented as decorous to Pharaoh, and he was kept from the way [of God]. Pharaoh's stratagems only led him into ruin.

40:36–37 Here the Qur'ān has Pharaoh order Haman (a character who appears in the Biblical Book of Esther, where he is in Persia, not Egypt) to build a tower to heaven. The idea of a tower to heaven is found in the Biblical account of the tower of Babel (Gen 11). A closer antecedent to the Qur'ān, however, is the tale of the Assyrian sage Aḥīqar, in which Pharaoh makes a request to the Assyrian ruler (Sennacherib) that someone be sent to build for him a tower. On this tradition, see commentary on 28:38 (with further references).

The term that the Qur'ān here uses for "routes" is *asbāb,* regarding which see commentary on 15:14–15 (with further references).

---

³⁸And he who had faith said, 'O my people! Follow me, I will guide you to the way of rectitude. ³⁹O my people! This life of the world is only a [passing] enjoyment, and indeed the Hereafter is the abiding home. ⁴⁰Whoever commits a misdeed shall not be requited except with its like, but whoever acts righteously, whether male or female, should he be faithful—such will enter paradise and will be provided therein without any reckoning. ⁴¹O my people! [Think,] what makes me invite you to deliverance, while you invite me toward the Fire? ⁴²You invite me to defy God and to ascribe to Him partners of which I have no knowledge, while I call you to the All-mighty, the All-forgiving. ⁴³Undoubtedly, that to which you invite me has no invitation in the world nor in the Hereafter, and indeed our return will be to God, and indeed it is the transgressors who will be inmates of the Fire. ⁴⁴Soon you will remember what I tell you, and I entrust my affair to God. God indeed watches His servants.'

40:41–44 Regarding the anonymous Egyptian believer see commentary on 40:28–35.

---

⁴⁵Then God saved him from their evil schemes, while a terrible punishment besieged Pharaoh's clan: ⁴⁶the Fire, to which they are exposed morning and evening. On the day when the Hour sets in, Pharaoh's clan will enter the severest punishment.

⁴⁷When they argue in the Fire, the oppressed will say to the oppressors, 'We used to follow you; will you avail us against any portion of the Fire?'

⁴⁸The oppressors will say, 'We are all in it [together]. Indeed, God has judged between [His] servants.'

⁴⁹Those who are in the Fire will say to the keepers of hell, 'Invoke your Lord to lighten for us [at least] a day's punishment.'

⁵⁰They will say, 'Did not your apostles bring you clear proofs?' They will say, 'Yes.' They will say, 'Then invoke [Him] yourselves.' But the invocations of the faithless only go awry.

⁵¹We shall indeed help Our apostles and those who have faith in the life of the world and on the day when the witnesses rise up, ⁵²the day when the excuses of the wrongdoers will not benefit them, the curse will lie on them, and for them will be the ills of the [ultimate] abode.

⁵³Certainly We gave guidance to Moses and gave the Book as a legacy to the Children of Israel, ⁵⁴as guidance and admonition for those who possess intellect.

⁵⁵So *be patient!* God's promise is indeed true. *Plead* [to God] for forgiveness of *your* sin, and *celebrate* the praise of *your* Lord, morning and evening.

⁵⁶Indeed, those who dispute the signs of God without any authority that may have come to them—there is only vanity in their breasts which they will never satisfy. So *seek* the protection of God; indeed He is the All-hearing, the All-seeing.

⁵⁷The creation of the heavens and the earth is surely more prodigious than the creation of mankind, but most people do not know.

⁵⁸The blind one and the seer are not equal, neither are those who work evil and those who have faith and do righteous deeds. Little is the admonition that you take!

⁵⁹The Hour is indeed bound to come; there is no doubt in it. But most people do not believe.

⁶⁰Your Lord has said, 'Call Me and I will hear you!' Indeed, those who are disdainful of My worship will enter hell in utter humiliation.

⁶¹It is God who made the night for you, that you may rest in it, and the day to provide visibility. God is indeed gracious to mankind, but most people do not give thanks.

⁶²That is God, your Lord, the creator of all things, there is no god except Him. Then where do you stray? ⁶³Those who were used to impugning the signs of God are thus made to go astray.

⁶⁴It is God who made for you the earth an abode and the sky a canopy. He formed you and perfected your forms, and provided you with all the good things. That is God, your Lord! Blessed is God, Lord of all the worlds!

40:64 The verb used for "forming" in this verse (cf. 3:6; 7:11; 59:24; 64:3)— Ar. *ṣawwara*—is related to the Hebrew *yāṣar* as it is used in Gen 2:7: "The Lord God shaped [*wayyīṣer*] man from the soil of the ground and blew the breath of life into his nostrils, and man became a living being."

———————

⁶⁵He is the Living One, there is no god except Him. So supplicate Him, putting exclusive faith in Him. All praise belongs to God, Lord of all the worlds.

⁶⁶*Say,* 'I have been forbidden to worship those whom you invoke besides God, as clear proofs have come to me from my Lord, and I have been commanded to submit to the Lord of all the worlds.'

⁶⁷It is He who created you from dust, then from a drop of [seminal] fluid, then from a clinging mass, then He brings you forth as infants, then [He nurtures you] so that you may come of age, and

then that you may become aged—though there are some of you who die earlier—and complete a specified term, and so that you may exercise your reason.

40:67 On the creation of humanity from dust (or "dirt," Ar. *turāb*), see commentary on 11:61 (with further references).

---

⁶⁸It is He who gives life and brings death. When He decides on a matter, He just says to it, 'Be!' and it is. ⁶⁹Have you not regarded those who dispute the signs of God, where they are being led away [from God's way]? ⁷⁰—Those who deny the Book and what we have sent with Our apostles. Soon they will know ⁷¹when they are dragged [with] iron collars and chains around their necks ⁷²into scalding waters and then set aflame in the Fire. ⁷³Then they will be told, 'Where are those whom you used to take as 'partners' ⁷⁴besides God?' They will say, 'They have forsaken us. Indeed, we did not invoke anything before.' That is how God leads the faithless astray.

40:68–74 On God's command "Be!" (v. 68), see commentary on 36:82 (with further references). Verses 73-74 can be compared to Deuteronomy 32:

³⁷'Where are their gods then?' he will ask, 'the rock where they sought refuge, ³⁸who ate the fat of their sacrifices and drank the wine of their libations?' Let these arise and help you, let these be the shelter above you!
³⁹See now that I, I am he, and beside me there is no other god. It is I who deal death and life; when I have struck, it is I who heal (no one can rescue anyone from me). (Deu 32:37–39)

---

⁷⁵'That [punishment] is because you used to boast unduly on the earth and because you used to strut. ⁷⁶Enter the gates of hell, to remain in it [forever].' Evil is the [final] abode of the arrogant.

⁷⁷So *be patient*! God's promise is indeed true. Whether We show *you* a part of what We promise them, or take *you* away [before that], [in any case] they will be brought back to Us.

⁷⁸Certainly We have sent apostles before *you*. Of them are those We have recounted to *you,* and of them are those We have not recounted to *you*. An apostle may not bring any sign except by God's permission. Hence, when God's edict comes, judgment is made with justice, and it is thence that the falsifiers become losers.

⁷⁹It is God who created the cattle for you that you may ride some of them, and some of them you eat; ⁸⁰and there are [numerous] uses in them for you, and that over them you may satisfy any need that is in your breasts, and you are carried on them and on ships. ⁸¹He shows you His signs. So which of the signs of God do you deny?

⁸²Have they not traveled through the land so that they may observe how was the fate of those who were before them? They were more numerous than them and were greater [than them] in power and with respect to the effects [they left] in the land. But what they used to earn did not avail them.

⁸³When their apostles brought them clear proofs, they boasted about the knowledge they possessed, and they were besieged by what they used to deride. ⁸⁴Then, when they sighted Our punishment, they said, 'We believe in God alone and disavow what we used to take as His partners.'

⁸⁵But their faith was of no benefit to them when they sighted Our punishment—God's precedent, which has passed among His servants, and it is thence that the faithless will be losers.

41. *FUṢṢILAT,* ELABORATED

In the Name of God, the All-beneficent, the All-merciful.

¹*Ḥā, Mīm.* ²A [gradually] sent down [revelation] from the All-beneficent, the All-merciful, ³[this is] a Book whose signs have been elaborated for a people who have knowledge, an Arabic Qur'ān, ⁴a bearer of good news and warner. But most of them turn away [from it], and so they do not listen.

⁵They say, 'Our hearts are in veils [which shut them off] from what you invite us to, and there is a deafness in our ears, and there is a curtain between us and you. So act [as your faith requires]; we too are acting [according to our own].'

41:5 Here the Qur'ān has unbelievers insist that their hearts are in veils (or "containers," Ar. *akinna;* cf. 6:25, 17:45–46; 18:57), and thus they do not recognize the message of the Prophet. On this see commentary on 17:45–46.

---

⁶*Say,* 'I am just a human being like you. It has been revealed to me that your God is the One God. So worship Him single-mindedly and plead to Him for forgiveness.' And woe to the polytheists ⁷—those who do not pay the *zakāt* and disbelieve in the Hereafter.

⁸As for those who have faith and do righteous deeds, there will be an everlasting reward for them.

⁹*Say,* 'Do you really disbelieve in Him who created the earth in two days, and ascribe partners to Him? That is the Lord of all the worlds!' ¹⁰He set in it firm mountains, [rising] above it, blessed it and ordained in it, in four days, [various] means of sustenance, equally for all the seekers. ¹¹Then He turned to the heaven, and it was smoke, and He said to it and to the earth, 'Come! Willingly or unwillingly!' They said, 'We come obediently.'

¹²Then He set them up as seven heavens in two days, and revealed [to the angels] in each heaven its ordinance. We have adorned the lowest heaven with lamps and guarded them. That is the ordaining of the All-mighty, the All-knowing.

41:9–12 The Qur'ān refers first to two days (v. 9), and then to four days (v. 10) of the creation of the earth, thus reflecting Genesis 1 and the Qur'ān's own report elsewhere (7:54; 10:3; 11:7; 25:59; 32:4; 50:38; 57:4) that God created the heavens and the earth in six days. However, thereafter the Qur'ān refers (v. 12) to God then creating the heavens in two days, which would seem to make eight days in all.

Asad translates the Arabic word for "days" as "aeons" to avoid the idea that creation took place in twenty-four-hour periods (in an attempt to harmonize the Qur'ān and modern science).

On the stars as lights in the firmament, the barrier which divides this world from the divine realm, see commentary on 37:6–10 (with further references). On the seven heavens (v. 12), see commentary on 67:3 (with further references).

---

¹³But if they turn away, *say,* 'I warn you of a thunderbolt, like the thunderbolt of 'Ād and Thamūd.' ¹⁴When the apostles came to them, before them and in their own time, saying, 'Worship no one except God!' They said, 'Had our Lord wished, He would have

sent down angels [to us]. We indeed disbelieve in what you have been sent with.'

¹⁵As for [the people of] 'Ād, they acted arrogantly in the land unduly, and they said, 'Who is more powerful than us?' Did they not see that God, who created them, is more powerful than them? They used to impugn Our signs; ¹⁶so We unleashed upon them an icy gale during ill-fated days, in order that We might make them taste a humiliating punishment in the life of the world. Yet the punishment of the Hereafter will surely be more disgraceful, and they will not be helped.

¹⁷As for [the people of] Thamūd, We guided them, but they preferred blindness to guidance. So the bolt of a humiliating punishment seized them because of what they used to earn.

41:17 On the blindness of unbelievers, see commentary on 2:7.

---

¹⁸And We delivered those who had faith and were Godwary.

¹⁹The day the enemies of God are gathered toward the Fire, while they are held in check, ²⁰when they come to it, their hearing, their eyes and skins will bear witness against them concerning what they used to do. ²¹They will say to their skins, 'Why did you bear witness against us?' They will say, 'We were given speech by God, who gave speech to all things. He created you the first time and you are being brought back to Him. ²²You could not hide [while perpetrating sinful acts] lest your hearing, your eyes, or your skins should bear witness against you, but you thought that God did not know most of what you did. ²³That misconception which you entertained about your Lord ruined you. So you became losers.'

²⁴Should they be patient, the Fire is their abode; and should they seek to propitiate [God], they will not be redeemed. ²⁵We have assigned them companions who make their present and their past [conduct] seem decorous to them, and the word became due against them along with the nations of jinn and humans that passed away before them. They were indeed losers.

²⁶The faithless say, 'Do not listen to this Qur'ān and hoot it down so that you may prevail [over the Apostle].'

²⁷We will surely make the faithless taste a severe punishment, and We will surely requite them by the worst of what they used to do. ²⁸That is the requital of the enemies of God—the Fire! In it they will have an everlasting abode, as a requital for their impugning Our signs.

²⁹The faithless will say, 'Our Lord! Show us those who led us astray from among jinn and humans so that we may trample them under our feet, so that they may be among the lowermost!'

³⁰Indeed, those who say, 'Our Lord is God!' and then remain steadfast, the angels descend upon them, [saying,] 'Do not fear, nor be grieved! Receive the good news of the paradise which you have been promised.

³¹We are your friends in the life of this world and in the Hereafter, and you will have in it whatever your souls desire, and you will have in it whatever you ask for, ³²as a hospitality from One all-forgiving, all-merciful.'

³³Who has a better call than him who summons to God and acts righteously and says, 'I am indeed one of the *muslims*'?

³⁴Good and evil [conduct] are not equal. Repel [evil] with what is best. [If you do so,] he between whom and you was enmity, will be as though he were a sympathetic friend. ³⁵But none is granted it except those who are patient, and none is granted it except the greatly endowed. ³⁶Should an incitement from Satan prompt *you*

[to ill feeling], seek the protection of God. Indeed, He is the All-hearing, the All-knowing.

³⁷Among His signs are night and day and the sun and the moon. Do not prostrate to the sun, nor to the moon, but prostrate to God who created them, if it is Him that you worship.

³⁸But if they disdain [the worship of God], those who are near *your* Lord glorify Him night and day and they are not wearied.

41:38 On the angels' praising God, see commentary on 7:206 (with further references).

---

³⁹Among His signs is that you see the earth desolate; but when We send down water upon it, it stirs and swells. Indeed, He who revives it will also revive the dead. Indeed, He has power over all things.

⁴⁰Those who abuse Our signs are not hidden from Us. Is someone who is cast in the Fire better off, or someone who arrives safely on the Day of Resurrection? Act as you wish; indeed He watches what you do. ⁴¹Those who deny the Reminder when it comes to them. . .

It is indeed an august Book: ⁴²falsehood cannot approach it, at present or in future, [a revelation gradually] sent down from One all-wise, all-laudable.

⁴³Nothing is said to *you* except what has already been said to the apostles before *you*. Indeed, *your* Lord is One who forgives and One who metes out a painful retribution.

⁴⁴Had We made it a non-Arabic Qur'ān, they would have said, 'Why have not its signs been articulated?' 'What! A non-Arabian [scripture] and an Arabian [prophet]!?'

Say, 'It is guidance and healing for those who have faith. As for those who are faithless, there is deafness in their ears and it is lost to their sight: [to them it is as if] they were called from a distant place.'

⁴⁵Certainly We gave Moses the Book, but differences arose about it; and were it not for a prior decree of *your* Lord, judgement would have been made between them, for they are in grave doubt concerning it.

41:45 The Qurʾān alludes here (cf. 11:110) to the disagreements among Jews and Christians over the proper interpretation of the Hebrew Bible/Old Testament (indeed it seems to threaten them with divine punishment for their confusion over this book). One might compare the way Syriac fathers such as Ephrem accuse the Jews of misreading their scriptures:

> [The Jews] rejected the trumpet of Isaiah that sounded the pure conception; they stilled the lyre of the psalms that sang about [Christ's] priesthood; they silenced the kithara that sung of his kingship. . . . Behold the fool reads in his Scriptures the promises that were distributed to us! As he boasts in his Scriptures, he reads to us his [own] accusation, and he witnesses our inheritance to us. (Ephrem, *Hymns on the Nativity,* 24:14:22)

---

⁴⁶Whoever acts righteously, it is for [the benefit of] his own soul, and whoever does evil, it is to its detriment, and *your* Lord is not tyrannical to His servants.

⁴⁷On Him devolves the knowledge of the Hour, and no fruit emerges from its covering and no female conceives or delivers except with His knowledge.

On the day when He will call out to them, 'Where are My "partners"?' They will say, 'We have informed You that there is no witness amongst us.'

41:47 On knowledge of the Hour being with God alone, see commentary on 79:42–44 (with further references).

---

⁴⁸What they used to invoke before has forsaken them, and they know there is no escape for them.

⁴⁹Man is never wearied of supplicating for good, and should any ill befall him, he becomes hopeless and despondent. ⁵⁰If, after distress has befallen him, We let him have a taste of Our mercy, he will surely say, 'This is my due! I do not think the Hour will ever come, and in case I am returned to my Lord, I will indeed have the best [reward] with Him.' So We will surely inform the faithless about what they have done, and will surely make them taste a harsh punishment.

⁵¹When We bless man, he is disregardful and turns aside; but when an ill befalls him, he makes protracted supplications.

⁵²*Say,* 'Tell me, if it is from God and you disbelieve it, who will be more astray than those who are in extreme defiance.'

⁵³Soon We will show them Our signs in the horizons and in their own souls until it becomes clear to them that He is the Real. Is it not sufficient that *your* Lord is witness to all things?

⁵⁴Behold, they are indeed in doubt about the encounter with their Lord! Indeed, He embraces all things!

42. *AL-SHŪRĀ*, THE COUNSEL

In the Name of God, the All-beneficent, the All-merciful.

¹*Ḥā, Mīm,* ²*'Ayn, Sīn, Qāf.* ³God, the All-mighty and the All-wise, thus reveals to *you* and to those who were before *you:* ⁴whatever is in the heavens and whatever is in the earth belongs to Him, and He is the All-exalted, the All-supreme.

⁵The heavens are about to be rent apart from above them, while the angels celebrate the praise of their Lord and plead for forgiveness for those [faithful] who are on the earth. Indeed, God is the All-forgiving, the All-merciful!

42:5 On the angels' praising God, see commentary on 7:206 (with further references).

---

⁶As for those who have taken masters besides Him, God is watchful over them and *you* are not their keeper.

⁷Thus have We revealed to *you* an Arabic Qur'ān that *you* may warn [the people of] the Mother of the Towns and those around it, and warn [them] of the Day of Gathering, in which there is no

doubt, [whereupon] a part [of mankind] will be in paradise and a part will be in the Blaze.

42:7 On the reference to "Mother of the Towns," cf. 6:92.

———————

⁸Had God wished, He would have surely made them one community; but He admits whomever He wishes into His mercy, and the wrongdoers do not have any friend or helper.

42:8 Regarding the Qur'ān's statements on the division of humanity into different communities, see commentary on 10:19 (with further references).

———————

⁹Have they taken masters besides Him? [*Say,*] 'It is God who is the [true] Master, and He revives the dead, and He has power over all things. ¹⁰Whatever thing you may differ about, its judgement is with God. That is God, my Lord. In Him alone I have put my trust, and to Him alone do I turn penitently. ¹¹The originator of the heavens and the earth, He made for you mates from your own selves, and mates of the cattle, by which means He multiplies you. Nothing is like Him and He is the All-hearing, the All-seeing. ¹²To Him belong the keys of the heavens and the earth: He expands the provision for whomever He wishes and tightens it [for whomever He wishes]. Indeed, He has knowledge of all things.'

42:12 On the reference to "the keys of the heavens and the earth" in this verse see commentary on 39:63 (with further references).

¹³He has prescribed for you the religion which He had enjoined upon Noah and which We have [also] revealed to *you,* and which We had enjoined upon Abraham, Moses and Jesus, declaring, 'Maintain the religion, and do not be divided in it.' Hard on the polytheists is that to which *you* summon them. God chooses for it whomever He wishes, and He guides to it whomever returns penitently [to Him].

¹⁴They did not divide [into sects] except after the knowledge had come to them, out of envy among themselves; and were it not for a prior decree of *your* Lord [granting them reprieve] until a specified time, decision would have been made between them. Indeed, those who were made heirs to the Book after them are in grave doubt concerning it.

¹⁵So *summon* to this [unity of religion], and *be* steadfast, just as *you* have been commanded, and *do not follow* their desires, and *say,* 'I believe in whatever Book God has sent down. I have been commanded to do justice among you. God is our Lord and your Lord. Our deeds belong to us and your deeds belong to you. There is no quarrel between us and you. God will bring us together and toward Him is the destination.'

¹⁶Those who argue concerning God, after His call has been answered, their argument stands refuted with their Lord, and upon them shall be [His] wrath, and there is a severe punishment for them.

¹⁷It is God who has sent down the Book with the truth and [He has sent down] the Balance. What do you know—maybe the Hour is near! ¹⁸Those who do not believe in it ask [*you*] to hasten it, but those who have faith are apprehensive of it, and know that it is true. Indeed, those who are in doubt about the Hour are in extreme error!

¹⁹God is all-attentive to His servants. He provides for whom-ever He wishes and He is the All-strong, the All-mighty.

²⁰Whoever desires the tillage of the Hereafter, We will enhance for him his tillage, and whoever desires the tillage of the world, We will give it to him, but he will have no share in the Hereafter.

42:20 The Qurʾān's use of the term "tillage" (or "harvest"; Ar. *ḥarth*) to sig-nify heaven (elsewhere the Qurʾān uses a similar expression but has "reward" instead of "tillage"; see 3:145; 4:134) is close to a common New Testament met-aphor for heaven (e.g., Gal 6:8: "If his sowing is in the field of self-indulgence, then his harvest from it will be corruption; if his sowing is in the Spirit, then his harvest from the Spirit will be eternal life; cf. Luk 8:15; Mat 13:23; Mar 13:20; 2Co 9:10).

---

²¹Do they have 'partners' [besides God] who have ordained for them a religion which has not been permitted by God? Were it not for a [prior] conclusive word, judgement would have been made between them, and a painful punishment awaits the wrongdoers. ²²When it is about to befall them, *You* will see the wrongdoers fearful because of what they have earned; but those who have faith and do righteous deeds will be in the gardens of paradise: they will have whatever they wish near their Lord. That is the great grace. ²³That is the good news that God gives to His ser-vants who have faith and do righteous deeds!

Say, 'I do not ask you any reward for it except the love of [my] relatives.' Whoever performs a good deed, We shall enhance its goodness for him. God is indeed all-forgiving, all-appreciative.

42:23 On the idea that a true prophet does not seek a reward, see commentary on 34:47 (with further references).

²⁴Do they say, 'He has fabricated a lie against God'? If so, should God wish He would set a seal on *your* heart, and God will efface the falsehood and confirm the truth with His words. He knows indeed well what is in the breasts.

²⁵It is He who accepts the repentance of His servants and excuses their misdeeds and knows what you do. ²⁶He answers [the supplications of] those who have faith and do righteous deeds and enhances them out of His grace. But as for the faithless, there is a severe punishment for them.

²⁷Were God to expand the provision for [all] His servants, they would surely create havoc on the earth. But He sends down in a [precise] measure whatever He wishes. He is indeed aware and watchful of His servants. ²⁸It is He who sends down the rain after they have been despondent and unfolds His mercy, and He is the Guardian, the All-laudable.

²⁹Among His signs is the creation of the heavens and the earth and whatever creatures He has scattered in them, and He is able to gather them whenever He wishes.

³⁰Whatever affliction that may visit you is because of what your hands have earned, and He excuses many [an offense of yours]. ³¹You cannot frustrate [God] on the earth, and you do not have besides God any friend or helper.

³²Among His signs are the ships [that run] on the sea [appearing] like landmarks. ³³If He wishes He stills the wind, whereat they remain standstill on its surface. There are indeed signs in that for every patient and grateful [servant]. ³⁴Or He wrecks them because of what they have earned, and He excuses many [an offense].

³⁵Let those who dispute Our signs know that there is no escape for them.

³⁶Whatever you have been given are the wares of the life of this world, but what is with God is better and more lasting for those

who have faith and who put their trust in their Lord ³⁷—those who avoid major sins and indecencies and forgive when angered; ³⁸those who answer their Lord, maintain the prayer, and [conduct] their affairs by counsel among themselves, and they spend out of what We have provided them; ³⁹those who, when afflicted by aggression, defend themselves.

⁴⁰The requital of evil is an evil like it, so whoever excuses and conciliates, his reward lies with God. Indeed, He does not like the wrongdoers. ⁴¹As for those who retaliate after being wronged, there is no ground for action against them. ⁴²The ground for action is only against those who oppress the people and commit tyranny in the land in violation of justice. For such there shall be a painful punishment. ⁴³As for those who endure patiently and forgive—that is indeed the steadiest of courses.

⁴⁴Those whom God leads astray have no friend apart from Him. *You* will see the wrongdoers, when they sight the punishment, saying, 'Is there any way for a retreat?' ⁴⁵*You* will see them being exposed to it, humbled by abasement, furtively looking askance. The faithful will say, 'The losers are indeed those who have ruined themselves and their families on the Day of Resurrection. Behold, the wrongdoers will indeed abide in lasting punishment. ⁴⁶They have no protectors to help them besides God. There is not way out for those whom God leads astray.'

⁴⁷Respond to your Lord before there comes a day for which there will be no revoking from God. On that day you will have no refuge, nor will you have [any chance of] denial [of your sins]. ⁴⁸But if they disregard [*your* warnings], [remember that] We have not sent *you* as their keeper. *Your* duty is only to communicate.

Indeed, when We let man taste Our mercy, he boasts about it; but should an ill visit them because of what their hands have sent ahead, then man is very ungrateful.

⁴⁹To God belongs the kingdom of the heavens and the earth. He creates whatever He wishes; He gives females to whomever He wishes and males to whomever He wishes, ⁵⁰or He combines them males and females, and makes sterile whomever He wishes. Indeed, He is all-knowing, all-powerful.

⁵¹It is not [possible] for any human that God should speak to him, except through revelation or from behind a veil, or send a messenger who reveals by His permission whatever He wishes. He is indeed all-exalted, all-wise. ⁵²Thus have We imbued *you* with a Spirit of Our command. *You* did not know what the Book is, nor what is faith; but We made it a light that We may guide by its means whomever We wish of Our servants. *You* indeed guide to a straight path,

42:52 The Arabic term rendered here as "command," *amr,* is related to Aramaic *mēmrā,* meaning "word." This locution (cf. 16:2; 17:85; 40:15; 97:4) suggests that the Qur'ān has an idea of revelation that involves the divine word and spirit. Jeffery writes: "The whole conception seems to have been strongly influenced by the Christian Logos ["Word"] doctrine" (*FV,* 69). On *amr* and spirit, see 2:87, 253; 5:110; 16:2; 40:15 65:12; 97:4.

---

⁵³the path of God, to whom belongs whatever is in the heavens and whatever is in the earth. Behold, all matters return to God!

42:53 The Qur'ān frequently (cf., 2:116, 255, 284; passim) declares that heaven and earth belong to God. Cf. Deuteronomy 10:14: "Look, to the Lord your God belong heaven and the heaven of heavens, the earth and everything on it" (cf. 1Ch 29:11; Psa 89:11).

43. *AL-ZUKHRUF*, ORNAMENTS

In the Name of God, the All-beneficent, the All-merciful.

¹*Ḥā, Mīm.* ²By the Manifest Book, ³We have made it an Arabic Qur'ān so that you may exercise your reason, ⁴and it is sublime and wise with Us in the Mother Book. ⁵Shall We keep back the Reminder from you and disregard you because you are an unrestrained lot? ⁶How many a prophet We have sent to the former peoples! ⁷There did not come to them any prophet but that they used to deride him. ⁸So We destroyed those who were stronger than these, and the example of the former peoples has come to pass.

⁹If you ask them, 'Who created the heavens and the earth?' they will surely say, 'The All-mighty and the All-knowing created them.' ¹⁰He, who made the earth a cradle for you and made for you in it ways so that you may be guided [to your destinations], ¹¹and who sent down water from the sky in a measured manner, and We revived with it a dead country. Likewise you shall be raised [from the dead]. ¹²He, who created all the kinds and made for you the ships and the cattle which you ride, ¹³that you may sit on their backs, then remember the blessing of your Lord when you are settled on them, and say, 'Immaculate is He who has dis-

posed this for us, and we [by ourselves] were no match for it. ¹⁴Indeed, we shall return to our Lord.'

¹⁵They ascribe to Him offspring from among His servants! Man is indeed a manifest ingrate. ¹⁶Did He adopt daughters from what He creates while He preferred you with sons? ¹⁷When one of them is brought the news of what he ascribes to the All-beneficent, his face becomes darkened and he chokes with suppressed rage, [and says,] ¹⁸'What! One who is brought up amid ornaments and is inconspicuous in contests?' ¹⁹They have made the angels—who are servants of the All-beneficent—females. Were they witness to their creation? Their testimony will be written down and they shall be questioned.

43:16–19 In addition to its refutation of Christians for their doctrine of Christ's divinity (see, e.g., 5:17, 72, 75) the Qurʾān also refutes those who consider certain angels to be "daughters of god" who have the power to intercede with him (cf. 4:117; 6:100; 16:57, 62; 17:40; 37:149–53; 53:21–22, 27). The Qurʾān's theological concern in both cases is the affirmation that Allāh alone is worthy of worship. Christian Robin ("Matériaux pour une typologie," 72-73) notes the presence of a pre-Islamic monument in Yemen with a representation of four female figures described as "daughters of [the god] (*[b]hnt ʾ(l)*)." The monument, however, dates to the eighth century BC. It is also possible that in this sort of passage the Qurʾān is alluding to the belief of certain Jewish groups in angels as mediators with the divine. See commentary on 17:40.

²⁰They say, 'Had the All-beneficent wished, we would not have worshiped them.' They do not have any knowledge of that and they do nothing but surmise. ²¹Did We give them a Book before this, so that they are holding fast to it? ²²No, they said, 'We found our fathers following a creed, and we are indeed guided in their footsteps.'

²³So it has been that We did not send any warner to a town before *you,* without its affluent ones saying, 'We found our fathers following a creed and we are indeed following in their footsteps.' ²⁴He would say, 'What! Even if I bring you a better guidance than what you found your fathers following?!' They would say, 'We indeed disbelieve in what you are sent with.' ²⁵Thereupon We took vengeance on them; so *observe* how was the fate of the deniers.

²⁶When Abraham said to his father and his people, 'I repudiate what you worship,

43:26 Abraham's confrontation with his unbelieving father is not found in the Bible but becomes an important theme in Jewish and Christian literature. See commentary on 26:69–93 (with further references).

²⁷excepting Him who originated me; indeed He will guide me.' ²⁸He made it a lasting word among his posterity so that they may come back [to the right path]. ²⁹Indeed, I provided for these and their fathers until the truth and a manifest apostle came to them. ³⁰But when the truth came to them, they said, 'This is magic, and we indeed disbelieve in it.' ³¹And they said, 'Why was not this Qur'ān sent down to some great man from the two cities?' ³²Is it they who dispense the mercy of *your* Lord? It is We who have dispensed among them their livelihood in the present life and raised some of them above others in rank, so that some may take others into service, and *your* Lord's mercy is better than what they amass.

³³Were it not [for the danger] that mankind would be one community, We would have made for those who defy the All-beneficent

silver roofs for their houses and [silver] stairways by which they ascend,

---

43:33 Regarding the Qur'ān's statements on the division of humanity into different communities, see commentary on 10:19 (with further references).

---

³⁴and [silver] doors for their houses and [silver] couches on which they recline, ³⁵and ornaments of gold; yet all that would be nothing but the wares of the life of this world, and the Hereafter is for the Godwary near *your* Lord.

³⁶We assign a devil to be the companion of him who turns a blind eye to the remembrance of the All-beneficent. ³⁷They indeed bar them from the way [of God], while they suppose that they are [rightly] guided. ³⁸When he comes to Us, he will say, 'I wish there had been between me and you the distance between the east and the west! What an evil companion [you are]!' ³⁹'That will be of no avail to you today. As you did wrong, so will you share in the punishment.'

⁴⁰Can *you,* then, make the deaf hear or guide the blind and those who are in plain error? ⁴¹We will indeed take vengeance on them, whether We take *you* away ⁴²or show *you* what We have promised them, for indeed We hold them in Our power. ⁴³So *hold fast* to what has been revealed to *you. You* are indeed on a straight path. ⁴⁴It is indeed a reminder for *you* and *your* people, and soon you will be questioned.

⁴⁵*Ask* those of Our apostles We have sent before *you:* Did We set up any gods to be worshiped besides the All-beneficent?

⁴⁶Certainly We sent Moses with Our signs to Pharaoh and his elite. He said, 'I am indeed an apostle of the Lord of all the worlds.' ⁴⁷But when he brought them Our signs, they indeed laughed at

them. ⁴⁸We did not show them any sign but it was greater than the other, and We visited on them punishment so that they might come back.

⁴⁹They would say, 'O magician! Invoke your Lord for us by the covenant He has made with you [to remove this scourge]. We will indeed be guided [when it is removed].' ⁵⁰But when We lifted the punishment from them, behold, they would break their pledge.

⁵¹And Pharaoh proclaimed to his people, saying, 'O my people! Do not the kingdom of Egypt and these rivers that run at my feet belong to me? Do you not see? ⁵²Am I not better than this wretch who cannot even speak clearly?

43:50–52 The Qurʾān's insistence that the Egyptians would cease believing in God whenever the punishment ceased (v. 50; cf. 7:134–35) may be related to the way Pharaoh, in Exodus, first insists that he will let the Israelites go if only a plague will be lifted and then refuses to fulfill his word when it is:

⁴Pharaoh then summoned Moses and Aaron and said, 'Entreat the Lord to take the frogs away from me and my subjects, and I promise to let the people go and sacrifice to the Lord.'

. . .

⁹The Lord did as Moses asked, and in house and courtyard and field the frogs died.

¹⁰They piled them up in heaps and the country stank.

¹¹But once Pharaoh saw that there had been a respite, he became obstinate and, as the Lord had foretold, refused to listen to them. (Exo 8:4, 9–11; cf. Exo 8:28; 9:34–35)

In this passage (v. 52) Pharaoh refers to Moses as a "wretch [Ar. *mahīn*] who cannot even speak clearly." This reflects Exodus 4:10 in which Moses complains that he is "slow and hesitant of speech."

––––––––––

⁵³Why no bracelets of gold have been cast upon him, nor any angels accompany him as escorts?' ⁵⁴Thus did he mislead his people and they obeyed him. They were indeed a transgressing lot.

⁵⁵So when they roused Our wrath, We took vengeance on them and drowned them all.

43:55 Here the Qur'ān, unlike the Bible, reports that God killed all of the Egyptians (and not only Pharaoh and his army). This reflects not Exodus but rather the Qur'ānic topos by which entire peoples were often destroyed by God (see, e.g., 7:59–137). Cf. 40:30–31; 54:41.

---

⁵⁶Thus We made them the vanguard and an example for posterity.

⁵⁷When the Son of Mary was cited as an example, behold, *your* people raise an outcry. ⁵⁸They say, 'Are our gods better or he?' They cite him to *you* only for the sake of contention. They are indeed a contentious lot. ⁵⁹He was just a servant whom We had blessed and made an exemplar for the Children of Israel. ⁶⁰Had We wished We would have set angels in your stead to be [your] successors on the earth. ⁶¹[*Say,*] 'He is indeed a portent of the Hour; so do not doubt it and follow me. This is a straight path.

43:57–61 On Jesus as servant (v. 59) cf. 4:172; 7:194; 19:30, 90–93; 21:26. The reference to Jesus as a "portent [or perhaps "knowledge"; Ar. *'ilm*] of the [apocalyptic] Hour" (v. 61) suggests that the Qur'ān agrees with the Christian tradition which makes Jesus the central figure of the end times (e.g., Luk 12:40: "You too must stand ready, because the Son of man is coming at an hour you do not expect" [cf. Mat 24:44]). In later Islamic apocalyptic traditions the role of Jesus in the end times is developed extensively. Not only is Jesus a "portent" of the Hour in such traditions, he also kills the anti-Christ (*al-Dajjāl*), breaks crosses, kills pigs, and unites the world under the banner of Islam.

---

⁶²Do not let Satan bar you [from the way of God]. He is indeed your manifest enemy.'

[63]When Jesus brought those clear proofs, he said, 'I have certainly brought you wisdom, and [I have come] to make clear to you some of the things that you differ about. So be wary of God and obey me. [64]God is indeed my Lord and your Lord; so worship Him. This is a straight path.' [65]But the factions differed among themselves. So woe to the wrongdoers for the punishment of a painful day.

43:63–65 The Qur'ān presents Jesus as a prophet sent particularly to the Israelites (Q 5:72; 61:6) and describes how one group of the Israelites believed in him (the Christians) and another rejected him (Q 61:14). The reference here to "factions" (Ar. *aḥzāb*) differing "among themselves" thus seems to suggest the division of Jews and Christians over Jesus (cf. also 3:55–57; 23:49–53).

The declaration "Indeed God is my Lord and your Lord; so worship him" (cf. 3:51; 5:72, 117; 19:36) attributed to Jesus in verse 64 may be a transformation of John 20:17, in which the resurrected Jesus declares to Mary Magdelene, "Do not cling to me, because I have not yet ascended to the Father. But go to the brothers, and tell them: I am ascending to my Father and your Father, to my God and your God."

———————

[66]Do they await anything but that the Hour should overtake them suddenly while they are unaware? [67]On that day, friends will be one another's enemies, except for the Godwary. [68][They will be told,] 'O My servants! Today you will have no fear, nor will you grieve [69]—those who believed in Our signs and had been *muslims*. [70]Enter paradise, you and your spouses, rejoicing.' [71]They will be served around with golden dishes and goblets, and therein will be whatever the souls desire and eyes delight in. 'You will remain in it [forever]. [72]That is the paradise you have been given to inherit for what you used to do. [73]There are abundant fruits for you in it from which you will eat.'

[74]The guilty will indeed remain [forever] in the punishment of hell. [75]It will not be lightened for them and they will be despondent

in it. ⁷⁶We did not wrong them, but they themselves were wrong-doers. ⁷⁷They will call out, 'O Mālik! Let your Lord finish us off!' He will say, 'You will indeed stay on.' ⁷⁸'We certainly brought you the truth, but most of you were averse to the truth.'

⁷⁹Have they settled on some [devious] plan? Indeed, We, too, are settling [on Our plans]. ⁸⁰Do they suppose that We do not hear their secret thoughts and their secret talks? Yes indeed [We do]! And with them are Our messengers, writing down [everything].

43:80 On the angels who record deeds of humans, see commentary on 82:10–12 (with further references).

———————

⁸¹*Say,* 'If the All-beneficent had offspring, I would have been the first to worship [him].'

43:81 Here the Qur'ān seems to accept the logical possibility of a divine son or offspring (cf. 19:92; 21:26; and for the opposite view, cf. 17:42; 21:22; 23:91). *Tafsīr al-Jalālayn* comments: "But it is established that He does not have a child and thus there can be no worshipping of such [a child]."

———————

⁸²Clear is the Lord of the heavens and the earth, the Lord of the Throne, of whatever they allege [concerning Him]! ⁸³So leave them to gossip and play until they encounter the day they are promised.

⁸⁴It is He who is God in the heaven and God on the earth, and He is the All-Wise, the All-Knowing. ⁸⁵Blessed is He to whom belongs the kingdom of the heavens and the earth and whatever is between them, and with Him is the knowledge of the Hour, and to Him you will be brought back.

43:85 On knowledge of the Hour being with God alone, see commentary on 79:42–44 (with further references).

---

⁸⁶Those whom they invoke besides Him have no power of intercession, except those who are witness to the truth and who know [for whom to intercede].

⁸⁷If you ask them, 'Who created them?' they will surely say, 'God.' Then where do they stray?

⁸⁸And his plaint: 'My Lord! These are indeed a people who will not have faith!'

⁸⁹So *disregard* them, and *say,* 'Peace!' Soon they will know.

44. *AL-DUKHĀN,* SMOKE

In the Name of God, the All-beneficent, the All-merciful.

¹*Ḥā, Mīm.* ²By the Manifest Book! ³We sent it down on a blessed night and We have indeed been warning [mankind]. ⁴Every definitive matter is resolved on it, ⁵as an ordinance from Us. We have been sending [apostles] ⁶as a mercy from *your* Lord—indeed He is the All-hearing, the All-knowing—⁷the Lord of the heavens and the earth, and whatever is between them, should you have conviction. ⁸There is no god except Him: He gives life and brings death, your Lord and the Lord of your forefathers.

⁹But they play around in doubt. ¹⁰So *watch out* for the day when the sky brings on a manifest smoke ¹¹enveloping the people. [They will cry out:] 'This is a painful punishment. ¹²Our Lord! Remove this punishment from us. We have indeed believed!' ¹³What will the admonition avail them, when a manifest apostle had already come to them, ¹⁴but they turned away from him and said, 'A tutored madman?'

¹⁵Indeed, We will withdraw the punishment a little; but you will revert [to your earlier ways]. ¹⁶The day We shall strike with the most terrible striking, We will indeed take vengeance [on them].

¹⁷Certainly We tried the people of Pharaoh before them, when a noble apostle came to them, ¹⁸[saying,] 'Give over the servants

of God to me; indeed I am a trusted apostle [sent] to you. ¹⁹Do not defy God. I indeed bring you a clear authority. ²⁰I seek the protection of my Lord and your Lord, lest you should stone me. ²¹And if you do not believe me, keep out of my way.'

²²Then he invoked his Lord, [saying,] 'These are indeed a guilty lot.'

²³[God told him,] 'Set out with My servants by night, for you will be pursued. ²⁴Leave behind the sea unmoved [and parted], for they will be a drowned host.'

²⁵How many gardens and springs did they leave behind! ²⁶Fields and splendid places ²⁷and the affluence wherein they rejoiced! ²⁸So it was; and We bequeathed them to another people. ²⁹So neither the heaven wept for them, nor the earth, nor were they granted any respite. ³⁰Certainly We delivered the Children of Israel from the humiliating torment ³¹of Pharaoh. He was indeed a tyrant among the transgressors.

44:17–31 On Moses's confrontation with Pharaoh, see commentary on 26:30–45 (with further references). On the Israelites' crossing the sea, see commentary on 26:52–59 (with further references).

In verse 20 Moses expresses a concern that he will be stoned. The idea of stoning never comes up in the Biblical Moses story. Instead it is a topos of Qurʾānic accounts: 11:91 (Shuʿayb); 18:20 (Companions of the Cave); 19:46 (Abraham); 26:116 (Noah); 36:18 (two anonymous prophets). It could be that the Qurʾān is influenced here by New Testament passages (e.g., Mat 21:33, 23:37; Mar 2:3; Luk 13:34, 20:10) that suggest that the prophets were stoned (while the Hebrew Bible/Old Testament describes only the stoning of a minor prophet named Zechariah son of Jehoida; 2Ch 24:20–21). See further commentary on 26:105–16.

³²Certainly We chose them knowingly above all the nations,

44:32 Here the Qur'ān reflects the perspective of the Pentateuchal narrative of God's election of Israel, e.g., Deuteronomy 7:6: "For you are a people consecrated to the Lord your God; of all the peoples on earth, you have been chosen by the Lord your God to be his own people" (cf. Exo 19:5–6; Deu 14:2). See also 2:47, 122; 7:140; 45:16.

---

^{33}and We gave them some signs in which there was a manifest test.

^{34}These ones say, ^{35}'It will be only our first death and we will not be resurrected. ^{36}Bring our fathers back [to life], if you are truthful.'

^{37}Are they better, or the people of Tubba', and those who were before them? We destroyed them; indeed they were guilty.

44:37 Perhaps the title of a South Arabian king. Cf. 50:14.

---

^{38}We did not create the heavens and the earth and whatever is between them for play. ^{39}We did not create them except with consummate wisdom; but most of them do not know.

^{40}The Day of Judgement is indeed the tryst for them all, ^{41}the day when a friend will not avail a friend in any way, nor will they be helped, ^{42}except for him on whom God has mercy. Indeed, He is the All-mighty, the All-merciful.

^{43}Indeed, the tree of Zaqqūm ^{44}will be the food of the sinful. ^{45}Like molten copper it will boil in their bellies, ^{46}seething like boiling water. ^{47}[The keepers of hell will be told,] 'Seize him and drag him to the middle of hell, ^{48}then pour over his head boiling water as punishment, ^{49}[and tell him,] "Taste this! You are indeed the [self-styled] mighty and noble! ^{50}This is what you used to doubt!"'

⁵¹The Godwary will indeed be in a safe place, ⁵²amid gardens and springs,

44:52 On the streams of paradise, see commentary on 2:25 (with further references).

———

⁵³dressed in [garments of] fine and heavy silk, sitting face to face. ⁵⁴So shall it be, and We shall wed them to black-eyed houris.

44:54 On the maidens of paradise in the Qurʾān, see commentary on 56:22–23 (with further references).

———

⁵⁵Secure [from any kind of harm,] there they will call for every kind of fruit [they wish]. ⁵⁶Other than the first death, they will not taste death therein, and He will save them from the punishment of hell

44:56 The expression "taste death" (cf. 3:185; 21:35; 29:57) is Biblical: "In truth I tell you, there are some standing here who will not taste death before they see the Son of man coming with his kingdom" (Mat 16:28; cf. Joh 8:52).

On the description of hell as a "second death," see commentary on 40:11 (with further references). Cf. *BEQ,* 456.

———

⁵⁷—a grace from *your* Lord. That is a great success.
⁵⁸We have indeed made it simple in *your* language, so that they may take admonition. ⁵⁹So *wait!* They [too] are waiting.

45. *AL-JĀTHIYA*, KNEELING

In the Name of God, the All-beneficent, the All-merciful.

¹*Ḥā, Mīm.* ²The [gradual] sending down of the Book is from God, the All-mighty, the All-wise.

³In the heavens and the earth there are indeed signs for the faithful, ⁴For people who have certainty there are signs in your own creation and in whatever animals He scatters abroad. ⁵There are signs for people who exercise their reason in the alternation of night and day, in the provision that God sends down from the sky, with which He revives the earth after its death, and in the changing of the winds. ⁶These are the signs of God that We recite for *you* in truth. So what discourse will they believe after God and His signs?

⁷Woe to every sinful liar, ⁸who hears the signs of God being recited to him, yet persists arrogantly as if he had not heard them. So *inform* him of a painful punishment. ⁹When he learns anything about Our signs, he takes them in derision. For such there is a humiliating punishment. ¹⁰Ahead of them is hell; neither what they have earned, nor what they had taken as protectors besides God will avail them in any way, and there is a great punishment for them.

¹¹This is [true] guidance, and there is a painful punishment due to defilement for those who deny the signs of their Lord.

¹²It is God who disposed the sea for you[r benefit] so that the ships may sail in it by His command, that you may seek of His bounty and that you may give thanks.

45:3–12 The Qurʾānic discourse on signs here is close to 2:164; for its relation to Biblical materials, see commentary on that verse.

---

¹³He has disposed for you[r benefit] whatever is in the heavens and whatever is on the earth; all is from Him. There are indeed signs in that for a people who reflect.

¹⁴*Say* to the faithful to forgive those who do not expect God's days, that He may [Himself] requite every people for what they used to earn.

45:14 On the expression "God's days" see commentary on 14:5–8.

---

¹⁵Whoever acts righteously, it is for his own soul, and whoever does evil, it is to its own detriment, then you will be brought back to your Lord.

¹⁶Certainly We gave the Children of Israel the Book, judgement and prophethood, and We provided them with all the good things, and We gave them an advantage over all the nations, ¹⁷and We gave them clear precepts. But they did not differ except after knowledge had come to them, out of envy among themselves. *Your* Lord will indeed judge between them on the Day of Resurrection concerning that about which they used to differ.

45:16–17 The "knowledge" (Ar. *'ilm*) which came to the Israelites (v. 17) and caused a dispute among them may be the revelation which Jesus brought; cf. 3:48, which explains that Jesus gave knowledge (*yuʿallim*); and 43:61 which makes Jesus "knowledge [*'ilm;* Qarai renders "portent"] of the Hour." The dispute alluded to in v. 17 would then be that between Jews and Christians (cf. 61:14, which makes the Christians a sect of the Israelites). The reference to "Book," "judgment," and "prophethood" (v. 16; these three are found together in cf. 3:79 and 6:89; the pair "prophethood" and "Book" are found in 29:27 and 57:26) is sometimes (probably falsely) thought to reflect the three parts of the Hebrew Bible: Torah, Writings, and Prophets (on this see J. Horovitz, *KU,* 72ff.).

Tafsīr al-Jalālayn sees this passage as a reference to a disagreement among Jews over the validity of Muḥammad's prophethood.

---

¹⁸Then We set *you* upon a clear course of the Law; so *follow* it, and *do not follow* the desires of those who do not know. ¹⁹They will indeed not avail *you* in any way against God. Indeed, the wrongdoers are friends of one another, but God is the friend of the Godwary.

²⁰These are eye-openers for mankind, and guidance and mercy for a people who have certainty.

²¹Do those who have perpetrated misdeeds suppose that We shall treat them like those who have faith and do righteous deeds, their life and death being equal? Evil is the judgement that they make!

²²God created the heavens and the earth with consummate wisdom, so that every soul may be requited for what it has earned and they will not be wronged.

²³Have *you* seen him who has taken his desire to be his god and whom God has led astray knowingly, set a seal upon his hearing and his heart, and put a blindfold on his sight? So who will guide him after God [has given him up]? Will you not then take admonition?

²⁴They say, 'There is nothing but the life of this world: we live and we die and nothing destroys us but time.' But they do not have any knowledge of that and they only make conjectures.

²⁵When Our clear signs are recited to them, their only argument is to say, 'Bring our fathers back [to life], if you are truthful.' ²⁶*Say,* 'It is God who gives you life, then He makes you die. Then He will gather you on the Day of Resurrection, in which there is no doubt. But most people do not know.'

²⁷To God belongs the kingdom of the heavens and the earth, and when the Hour sets in, the falsifiers will be losers on that day. ²⁸And *you* will see every nation fallen on its knees. Every nation will be summoned to its book: 'Today you will be requited for what you used to do. ²⁹This is Our book which speaks truly against you. Indeed, We used to record what you used to do.'

³⁰As for those who have faith and do righteous deeds, their Lord will admit them into His mercy. That is a manifest triumph! ³¹But as for the faithless, [they will be asked,] 'Were not My signs recited to you? But you were disdainful and you were a guilty lot. ³²When it was said, "God's promise is indeed true and there is no doubt about the Hour," you said, "We do not know what the Hour is. We know nothing beyond conjectures and we do not possess any certainty."'

³³The evils of what they had done will appear to them, and they will be besieged by what they used to deride. ³⁴And it will be said, 'Today We will forget you, just as you forgot the encounter of this day of yours. The Fire will be your abode, and you will not have any helpers. ³⁵That is because you took the signs of God in derision, and the life of the world had deceived you.' So today they will not be brought out of it, nor will they be asked to propitiate [God].

³⁶So all praise belongs to God, the Lord of the heavens and the Lord of the earth, the Lord of all the worlds. ³⁷To Him belongs all supremacy in the heavens and the earth, and He is the All-mighty, the All-wise.

46. *AL-AḤQĀF*, THE SAND HILLS

In the Name of God, the All-beneficent, the All-merciful.

¹*Ḥā, Mīm.* ²The [gradual] sending down of the Book is from God, the All-mighty, the All-wise.

³We did not create the heavens and the earth and whatever is between them except with consummate wisdom and for a specified term. Yet the faithless are disregardful of what they are warned.

⁴*Say,* 'Tell me about those you invoke besides God. Show me what [part] of the earth have they created. Or do they have any share in the heavens? Bring me a scripture [revealed] before this, or some vestige of [divine] knowledge, if you are truthful.'

⁵Who is more astray than him who invokes besides God such [entities] as would not respond to him until the Day of Resurrection and who are oblivious of their invocation? ⁶When mankind are gathered [on Judgement's Day] they will be their enemies and they will disavow their worship.

⁷When Our clear signs are recited to them, the faithless say of the truth when it comes to them: 'This is plain magic.' ⁸Or they say, 'He has fabricated it.' *Say,* 'Should I have fabricated it, you would not avail me anything against God. He best knows what you gossip concerning it. He suffices as witness between me and you, and He is the All-forgiving, the All-merciful.'

⁹*Say,* 'I am not a novelty among the apostles, nor do I know what will be done with me or with you. I just follow whatever is revealed to me, and I am just a manifest warner.'

¹⁰*Say,* 'Tell me, if it is from God and you disbelieve in it, and a witness from the Children of Israel has testified to its like and believed [in it], while you are disdainful [of it]?' Indeed, God does not guide the wrongdoing lot.

¹¹The faithless say about the faithful, 'Had it been [something] good, they would not have taken the lead over us toward [accepting] it.' And since they could not find the way to it, they will say, 'It is an ancient lie.' ¹²Yet before it the Book of Moses was a guide and mercy, and this is a Book in the Arabic language which confirms it, [sent] to warn the wrongdoers, and it is [a bearer of] good news for the virtuous.

46:10–12 Here (v. 10) the Qur'ān seems to affirm that a Jew has testified to something like this proclamation, perhaps another portion of the Prophet's proclamations (*Tafsīr al-Jalālayn* identifies this Jew as ʿAbdallāh b. Salām, who appears in the *sīra* as a Medinan Jew who converts to Islam).

¹³Those who say, 'Our Lord is God,' and then remain steadfast, they will have no fear, nor will they grieve. ¹⁴They shall be the inhabitants of paradise, remaining in it [forever]—a reward for what they used to do.

¹⁵We have enjoined man to be kind to his parents. His mother has carried him in travail and bore him in travail, and his gestation and weaning take thirty months. When he comes of age and reaches forty years, he says, 'My Lord! Inspire me to give thanks for Your blessing with which You have blessed me and my parents, and that I may do righteous deeds which please You, and

invest my descendants with righteousness. I have indeed turned to you in penitence, and I am one of the *muslims.*'

46:15 The pious and dutiful man presented in the first part of this verse uses language close to that of Solomon elsewhere in the Qurʾān (Q 27:19). Geiger (*Judaism and Islam,* 71) and Speyer (*BEQ,* 459) both refer to a tradition in the Mishnah (m. Avot, 5:24) by which man reaches the age of discernment at the age of forty.

---

¹⁶Such are the ones from whom We accept the best of what they do and overlook their misdeeds, [who will be] among the inhabitants of paradise—a true promise which they had been given.

¹⁷As for him who says to his parents, 'Fie on you! Do you promise me that I shall be raised [from the dead] when generations have passed away before me?' And they invoke God's help [and say]: 'Woe to you! Believe! God's promise is indeed true.' But he says, 'These are nothing but myths of the ancients.'

46:17 On the expression "myths of the ancients," see commentary on 68:15 (with further references).

---

¹⁸Such are the ones against whom the word has become due, along with the nations of jinn and humans that have passed away before them. They were the losers.

¹⁹For everyone there are degrees [of merit] pertaining to what they have done, so that He may recompense them fully for their works and they are be wronged.

²⁰The day when the faithless are exposed to the Fire, [they will be told,] 'You have exhausted your good things in the life of the

world and enjoyed them. So today you will be requited with a humiliating punishment for your acting arrogantly on the earth unduly, and for the transgressions you used to commit.'

46:20 "Abraham said, 'My son, remember that during your life you had your fill of good things, just as Lazarus his fill of bad. Now he is being comforted here while you are in agony'" (Luk 16:25).

---

²¹And mention [Hūd] the brother of ʿĀd, when he warned his people at Aḥqāf—and warners have passed away before and after him—saying, 'Do not worship anyone but God. I indeed fear for you the punishment of a tremendous day.'

²²They said, 'Have you come to turn us away from our gods? Then bring us what you threaten us with, if you are truthful.

²³He said, 'Its knowledge is with God alone, and I communicate to you what I have been sent with. But I see that you are an ignorant lot.'

²⁴When they saw it as a cloud advancing toward their valleys, they said, 'This cloud brings us rain.' 'No, it is what you sought to hasten: a hurricane carrying a painful punishment, ²⁵destroying everything by its Lord's command.' So they became such that nothing could be seen except their dwellings. Thus do We requite the guilty lot.

²⁶Certainly We had granted them power in respects that We have not granted you, and We had vested them with hearing and sight and hearts. But neither their hearing availed them in any way nor did their sight, nor their hearts when they had been impugning the signs of God. So they were besieged by what they used to deride.

²⁷Certainly We have destroyed the towns that were around you, and We have paraphrased the signs variously so that they may come back. ²⁸So why did not those [fake deities] help them whom they had taken as gods besides God, as a means of nearness [to Him]? Indeed, they forsook them; that was their lie and what they used to fabricate.

²⁹When We dispatched toward *you* a team of jinn listening to the Qur'ān, when they were in its presence, they said, 'Listen quietly!' When it was finished, they went back to their people as warners.

³⁰They said, 'O our people! We have indeed heard a Book which has been sent down after Moses, confirming what was before it. It guides to the truth and to a straight path. ³¹O our people! Respond to God's summoner and have faith in Him. He will forgive you some of your sins and deliver you from a painful punishment.'

³²Those who do not respond to God's summoner cannot frustrate [God] on the earth, and they will not find any friends besides Him. They are in manifest error.

46:29–32 On the belief of the jinn in divine revelation (in this case the message given to the Prophet, which the faithful jinn compare to the book of Moses), see commentary on 72:1–14. On knowledge of the Hour being with God alone (v. 32), see commentary on 79:42–44 (with further references).

———————

³³Do they not see that God, who created the heavens and the earth and [who] was not exhausted by their creation, is able to revive the dead? Yes, indeed He has power over all things.

³⁴The day when the faithless are exposed to the Fire, [He will say,] 'Is this not a fact?' They will say, 'Yes, by our Lord!' He

will say, 'So taste the punishment because of what you used to disbelieve.'

[35]So *be patient* just as the resolute among the apostles were patient, and *do not seek* to hasten [the punishment] for them. The day when they see what they are promised, [it will be] as though they had remained [in the world] just an hour of a day.

This is a proclamation. Will anyone be destroyed except the transgressing lot?

47. *MUḤAMMAD,* MUHAMMAD

In the Name of God, the All-beneficent, the All-merciful.

¹Those who are [themselves] faithless and bar [others] from the way of God—He will make their works go to waste. ²But those who have faith and do righteous deeds and believe in what has been sent down to Muḥammad—and it is the truth from their Lord—He shall absolve them of their misdeeds and set right their affairs. ³That is because the faithless follow falsehood and those who have faith follow the truth from their Lord. That is how God draws comparisons for mankind.

⁴When you meet the faithless in battle, strike their necks. When you have thoroughly decimated them, bind the captives firmly. Thereafter either oblige them [by setting them free] or take ransom, until the war lays down its burdens. That [is God's ordinance]. Had God wished He could have taken vengeance on them, but that He may test some of you by means of others.

As for those who were slain in the way of God, He will not let their works go to waste. ⁵He will guide them and set right their affairs ⁶and admit them into paradise with which He has acquainted them.

⁷O you who have faith! If you help God, He will help you and make your feet steady.

⁸As for the faithless, their lot will be to fall [into ruin], and He will make their works go to waste. ⁹That is because they loathed what God has sent down, so He made their works fail.

¹⁰Have they not traveled through the land to observe how was the fate of those who were before them? God destroyed them and a similar [fate] awaits these faithless. ¹¹That is because God is the Master of the faithful, and because the faithless have no master.

¹²God will indeed admit those who have faith and do righteous deeds into gardens with streams running in them. As for the faithless, they enjoy and eat like the cattle do and the Fire will be their [final] abode.

47:12 On the streams of paradise, see commentary on 2:25 (with further references).

---

¹³How many a town We have destroyed which was more powerful than *your* town which expelled *you,* and they had no helper.

¹⁴Is he who stands on a clear proof from his Lord like those to whom the evil of their conduct is made to seem decorous and who follow their desires?

¹⁵A description of the paradise promised to the Godwary: therein are streams of unstaling water and streams of milk unchanging in flavour, and streams of wine delicious to the drinkers, and streams of purified honey; there will be every kind of fruit for them in it, and forgiveness from their Lord. [Are such ones] like those who abide in the Fire and are given to drink boiling water which cuts up their bowels?

47:15 The Qur'ān imagines here that paradise includes various rivers (water, milk, wine, and honey), perhaps an extrapolation of the Biblical idea of the promised land flowing with milk and honey (see Exo 3:8, 17; 13:5; 33:3; passim).

---

¹⁶There are some among them who prick up their ears at *you*. But when they go out from *your* presence, they say to those who have been given knowledge, 'What did he say just now?' They are the ones on whose hearts God has set a seal and they follow their own desires.

¹⁷As for those who are [rightly] guided, He enhances their guidance and invests them with their Godwariness.

¹⁸Do they await anything except that the Hour should overtake them suddenly? Its portents have already come. When it overtakes them of what avail will the admonitions they were given?

¹⁹*Know* that there is no god except God, and *plead* [to God] for forgiveness of *your* sin and for the faithful, men and women. God knows your itinerary and your [final] abode.

²⁰The faithful say, 'If only a *sūrah* were sent down!' But when a conclusive *sūrah* is sent down and war is mentioned in it, *you* see those in whose hearts is sickness looking upon *you* with the look of someone fainting at death. So woe to them!

²¹Obedience and upright speech. . . . So when the matter has been resolved upon [concerning going to war], if they remain true to God, that will surely be better for them.

²²May it not be that if you were to wield authority you would cause corruption in the land and ill-treat your blood relations? ²³They are the ones whom God has cursed, so He made them deaf and blinded their sight. ²⁴Do they not contemplate the Qur'ān, or are there locks on their hearts?

47:23–24 "Their hearts, and their eyes and ears are closed" (Jacob of Serugh, *On the Flood,* 24). See also commentary on 2:7.

---

²⁵Indeed, those who turned their backs after the guidance had become clear to them, it was Satan who had seduced them and he had given them [far-flung] hopes. ²⁶That is because they said to those who loathed what God had sent down: 'We will obey you in some matters,' and God knows their secret dealings.

²⁷But how will it be [with them] when the angels take them away, striking their faces and their backs?! ²⁸That, because they pursued what displeased God and loathed His pleasure. So He has made their works fail.

²⁹Do those in whose hearts is sickness suppose that God will not expose their spite? ³⁰If We wish, We will show them to *you* so that *you* recognize them by their mark. Yet *you* will recognize them by their tone of speech, and God knows your deeds.

³¹We will surely test you until We ascertain those of you who wage *jihād* and those who are steadfast, and We shall appraise your record.

³²Indeed, those who are faithless and bar from the way of God and defy the Apostle after guidance has become clear to them, they will not hurt God in the least and He shall make their works fail.

³³O you who have faith! Obey God and obey the Apostle, and do not render your works void.

³⁴Indeed, those who are faithless and bar from the way of God and then die faithless, God will never forgive them.

³⁵So do not slacken and [do not] call for peace when you have the upper hand and God is with you, and He will not stint [the reward of] your works.

³⁶The life of the world is just play and diversion, but if you are faithful and Godwary He will give you your rewards, and will not ask your wealth [in return] from you. ³⁷Should He ask it from you and press you, you will be stingy, and He will expose your spite.

[38]Ah! There you are, being invited to spend in the way of God; yet among you there are those who are stingy; and whoever is stingy is stingy only to himself. God is the All-sufficient and you are all-needy, and if you turn away He will replace you with another people and they will not be like you.

48. *AL-FATḤ*, THE CONQUEST

In the Name of God, the All-beneficent, the All-merciful.

¹We have indeed inaugurated for *you* a clear victory, ²that God may forgive *you* what is past of *your* sin and what is to come, and that He may perfect His blessing upon *you* and guide *you* on a straight path, ³and God will help *you* with a mighty help.

⁴It is He who sent down composure into the hearts of the faithful that they might enhance in their faith. To God belong the hosts of the heavens and the earth, and God is all-knowing, all-wise.

48:4 Regarding the term translated here as "composure" (Ar. *sakīna*), which appears three times in this Sura (vv. 4, 18, 26), see commentary on 2:248 (with further references). On the expression "hosts of heaven," see commentary on 48:7.

---

⁵That He may admit the faithful, men and women, into gardens with streams running in them, to remain in them [forever], and that He may absolve them of their misdeeds. That is a great triumph with God.

48:5 On the streams of paradise, see commentary on 2:25 (with further references).

⁶That He may punish the hypocrites, men and women, and the polytheists, men and women, who entertain a bad opinion of God. For them shall be an adverse turn of fortune: God is wrathful with them and He has cursed them and prepared hell for them and it is an evil destination.

⁷To God belong the hosts of the heavens and the earth, and God is all-mighty, all-wise.

48:7 Yahuda (302) argues that the expression "hosts of heaven" (*junūd al-samāwāt;* cf. 48:4) is a calque on Hebrew *ṣebā' ha-shāmayim* ("hosts" or "array of heaven"; see, e.g., Deu 4:19).

⁸We have indeed sent *you* as a witness and as a bearer of good news and warner, ⁹that you may have faith in God and His Apostle, and that you may support him and revere him, and that you may glorify Him morning and evening.

¹⁰Indeed, those who swear allegiance to *you,* swear allegiance only to God: the hand of God is above their hands. Then whosoever breaks his oath, breaks it only to his own detriment, and whoever fulfills the covenant he has made with God, He will give him a great reward.

¹¹The Bedouins who had stayed back [from joining the Prophet in his *'umrah* journey to Makkah] will tell *you,* 'Our possessions and families kept us occupied. So plead [to God] for our forgiveness!' They will say with their tongues what is not in their hearts. *Say,* 'Whether He desires to cause you harm, or desires to bring you benefit, who can be of any avail to you against God['s will]? God is indeed well aware of what you do.'

¹²Rather, you thought that the Apostle and the faithful will not ever return to their folks and that was made to seem decorous to

your hearts; you entertained evil thoughts and you were a ruined lot. ¹³Those who have no faith in God and His Apostle [should know that] We have prepared a blaze for the faithless.

¹⁴To God belongs the kingdom of the heavens and the earth: He forgives whomever He wishes and punishes whomever He wishes, and God is all-forgiving, all-merciful.

¹⁵[In the near future] when you will set out to capture booty, those who stayed behind [in this journey] will say: 'Let us follow you.' They desire to change the word of God. *Say,* 'You will not follow us! God has said this beforehand.' Then they will say, 'You are envious of us.' Indeed, they do not understand but a little!

¹⁶*Say* to the Bedouins who stayed behind, '[Later on] you will be called against a people of great might: they will either embrace Islam, or you will fight them. So if you obey, God will give you a good reward; but if you turn away like you turned away before, He will punish you with a painful punishment.'

¹⁷There is no blame on the blind, nor is there any blame on the lame, nor is there blame on the sick [if they are unable to go out with the troops to face the enemies]; and whoever obeys God and His Apostle, He will admit him into gardens with streams running in them, and whoever refuses to comply, He will punish him with a painful punishment.

¹⁸God was certainly pleased with the faithful when they swore allegiance to *you* under the tree. He knew what was in their hearts, so He sent down composure on them and requited them with a victory near at hand

---

48:18 Regarding the term translated here as "composure" (Ar. *sakīna*), which appears three times in this Sura (vv. 4, 18, 26), see commentary on 2:248 (with further references).

¹⁹and abundant spoils that they will capture, and God is all-mighty, all-wise.

²⁰God has promised you abundant spoils which you will capture. He has expedited this one for you and withheld men's hands from you, so that it may be a sign for the faithful and that He may guide you to a straight path. ²¹And other [spoils as well] which you have not yet captured: God has comprehended them and God has power over all things.

²²If the faithless fight you, they will turn their backs [to flee]. Then they will not find any friend or helper. ²³[It is] God's precedent that has passed before and you will never find any change in God's precedents.

²⁴It is He who withheld their hands from you and your hands from them in the valley of Makkah after He had given you victory over them, and God sees best what you do. ²⁵They are the ones who disbelieved and barred you from the Sacred Mosque, and kept the offering from reaching its destination. And were it not for [certain] faithful men and faithful women, whom you did not know—lest you should trample them and thus the blame for [killing] them should fall on you unawares—. . .; [He held you back] so that God may admit into His mercy whomever He wishes. Had they been separate, We would have surely punished the faithless among them with a painful punishment.

²⁶When the faithless nourished bigotry in their hearts, the bigotry of pagan ignorance, God sent down His composure upon His Apostle and the faithful, and made them abide by the word of Godwariness, for they were the worthiest of it and deserved it, and God has knowledge of all things.

48:26 The expression "pagan ignorance" (Ar. *jāhiliyya;* cf. 3:154; 5:50; 33:33) may be connected to a passage of Paul's address to the Athenians in Acts:

²⁹'Since we are the children of God, we have no excuse for thinking that the deity looks like anything in gold, silver or stone that has been carved and designed by a man.

³⁰'But now, overlooking the *times of ignorance* (*agnoias*), God is telling everyone everywhere that they must repent. (Act 17:29–30)

On the Arabic word Qarai translates as "composure" (*sakīna*), see commentary on 2:248 (with further references).

---

²⁷Certainly God has fulfilled His Apostle's vision in all truth: You will surely enter the Sacred Mosque, God willing, in safety and without any fear, with your heads shaven or hair cropped. So He knew what you did not know, and He assigned [you] besides that a victory near at hand.

²⁸It is He who has sent His Apostle with guidance and the true religion that He may make it prevail over all religions, and God suffices as witness.

²⁹Muḥammad, the Apostle of God, and those who are with him are hard against the faithless and merciful amongst themselves. You see them bowing and prostrating [in worship], seeking God's grace and [His] pleasure. Their mark is [visible] on their faces, from the effect of prostration. Such is their description in the Torah and their description in the Evangel. Like a tillage that sends out its shoots and builds them up, and they grow stout and settle on their stalks, impressing the sowers, so that He may enrage the faithless by them. God has promised those of them who have faith and do righteous deeds forgiveness and a great reward.

48:29 Qarai punctuates this sentence (putting a period after "Evangel") to suggest that the "description" of the believers in the Torah and the Evangel (i.e., in Jewish and Christian scriptures) involves the first part of this verse, namely "bowing and prostrating [in worship], seeking God's grace and [His] pleasure.

Their mark is [visible] on their faces." However, it is the latter part of this verse, regarding the "tillage," which is in fact connected to something in the Bible, namely, the parable of Mark 4:26–32:

> [26]He also said, 'This is what the kingdom of God is like. A man scatters seed on the land.
>
> [27]Night and day, while he sleeps, when he is awake, the seed is sprouting and growing; how, he does not know.
>
> [28]Of its own accord the land produces first the shoot, then the ear, then the full grain in the ear.
>
> [29]And when the crop is ready, at once he starts to reap because the harvest has come.' (Mar 4:26–29)

On the other hand, the Qur'ān's declaration that God seeks to "enrage the faithless" has no precedent in the Markan parable.

49. *AL-ḤUJURĀT,* THE CHAMBERS

In the Name of God, the All-beneficent, the All-merciful.

¹O you who have faith! Do not venture ahead of God and His Apostle and be wary of God. God is indeed all-hearing, all-knowing. ²O you who have faith! Do not raise your voices above the voice of the Prophet, and do not speak aloud to him like you shout to one another, lest your works should fail without your being aware. ³Indeed, those who lower their voices in the presence of the Apostle of God—they are the ones whose hearts God has tested for Godwariness. For them will be forgiveness and a great reward.

⁴Indeed, those who call *you* from behind the apartments, most of them do not use their reason. ⁵Had they been patient until *you* came out for them, it would have been better for them, and God is all-forgiving, all-merciful.

⁶O you who have faith! If a vicious character brings you some news, verify it, lest you should visit [harm] on some people out of ignorance, and then become regretful for what you have done.

⁷Know that the Apostle of God is among you. Should he comply with you in many matters, you would surely suffer. But God

has endeared faith to you and made it appealing in your hearts, and He has made hateful to you faithlessness, transgression and disobedience. It is such who are the right-minded—[8]a grace and blessing from God, and God is all-knowing, all-wise.

[9]If two groups of the faithful fight one another, make peace between them. But if one party of them aggresses against the other, fight the one which aggresses until it returns to God's ordinance. Then, if it returns, make peace between them fairly, and do justice. God indeed loves the just.

[10]The faithful are indeed brothers. Therefore, make peace between your brothers and be wary of God, so that you may receive [His] mercy.

[11]O you who have faith! Let not any people ridicule another people: it may be that they are better than they are; nor let women [ridicule] women: it may be that they are better than they are. And do not defame one another, nor insult one another by [calling] nicknames. How evil are profane names subsequent to faith! As for those who are not penitent [of their past conduct]—they are the wrongdoers.

49:11 "But I say this to you, anyone who is angry with a brother will answer for it before the court; anyone who calls a brother 'Fool' will answer for it before the Sanhedrin; and anyone who calls him 'Traitor' will answer for it in hell fire" (Mat 5:22).

[12]O you who have faith! Avoid much suspicion; some suspicions are indeed sins. And do not spy on one another or backbite. Will any of you love to eat the flesh of his dead brother? You would hate it. Be wary of God; God is indeed all-clement, all-merciful.

49:12 This verse should be compared to Gal 5:13–15, which—while it does not speak of eating "the flesh of a dead brother"—speaks of those who cause discord in the Christian community as "biting" and "devouring" one another (cr. Matthew Kuiper).

----

¹³O mankind! Indeed, We created you from a male and a female and made you nations and tribes that you may be well acquainted with one another. The noblest of you in the sight of God is indeed the most Godwary among you. God is indeed all-knowing, all-aware.

49:13 This verse alludes to the creation of humans from Adam and Eve. Cf. Genesis 3:20, which speaks of Eve as "mother of all those who live."

----

¹⁴The Bedouins say, 'We have faith.' *Say,* 'You do not have faith yet; rather say, "We have embraced Islam," for faith has not yet entered into your hearts. Yet if you obey God and His Apostle, He will not stint anything of [the reward of] your works. God is indeed all-forgiving, all-merciful.'
¹⁵The faithful are only those who have attained faith in God and His Apostle and then have never doubted, and who wage *jihād* with their possessions and their persons in the way of God. It is they who are the truthful. ¹⁶*Say,* 'Will you inform God about your faith while God knows whatever there is in the heavens and whatever there is in the earth, and God has knowledge of all things?'
¹⁷They count it as a favour to *you* that they have embraced Islam. *Say,* 'Do not count your embracing of Islam as a favour to

me. Rather, it is God who has done you a favour in that He has guided you to faith, if you are truthful [in your claim]. [18]God indeed knows the Unseen of the heavens and the earth, and God watches what you do.'

50. *QĀF*, QĀF

In the Name of God, the All-beneficent, the All-merciful.

¹*Qāf.* By the glorious Qur'ān. ²They consider it indeed odd that a warner from among themselves should have come to them. So the faithless say, 'This is an odd thing.' ³'What! When we are dead and have become dust [shall we be raised again]? That is a far-fetched return!'

⁴We know what the earth diminishes from them, and with Us is a preserving Book. ⁵They indeed impugned the truth when it came to them; so they are now in a perplexed state of affairs.

⁶Have they not, then, observed the heaven above them, how We have built it and adorned it, and that there are no cracks in it? ⁷And We spread out the earth and cast in it firm mountains, and caused every delightful kind [of plant] to grow in it. ⁸[In this there is] an insight and admonition for every penitent servant.

⁹We send down from the sky salubrious water, with which We grow gardens and the grain which is harvested, ¹⁰and tall date palms with [clusters of] regularly arranged blossoms, ¹¹as a provision for Our servants, and with it We revive a dead country. Likewise will be the rising [from the dead].

¹²The people of Noah denied before them, and [so did] the people of Rass and Thamūd, ¹³and 'Ād, Pharaoh and the brethren

of Lot, ¹⁴and the inhabitants of Aykah and the people of Tubbaʿ. Each [of them] impugned the apostles and so My threat became due [against them].

50:14 On the inhabitants of "Aykah," see commentary on 15:78–79 (with further references). Tubbaʿ is perhaps the title of a South Arabian king. Cf. 44:37.

---

¹⁵Have We been exhausted by the first creation? No, they are in doubt about a new creation.

50:15 The idea of a new creation (cf. 10:4; 30:27; 36:79; 53:47) is like that found in Revelation 21: "Then the One sitting on the throne spoke. 'Look, I am making the whole of creation new. Write this, 'What I am saying is trustworthy and will come true'" (Rev 21:5–6; cf. 2Co 5:17).

---

¹⁶Certainly We have created man and We know to what his soul tempts him, and We are nearer to him than his jugular vein. ¹⁷When the twin recorders record [his deeds], seated on the right hand and on the left: ¹⁸he says no word but that there is a ready observer beside him.

50:17–18 On the angels who record deeds of humans, see commentary on 82:10–12 (with further references).

---

¹⁹The throes of death bring the truth: 'This is what you used to shun!'
²⁰And the Trumpet will be blown: 'This is the promised day.'

50:20 On the trumpet blast, see commentary on 78:18 (with further references).

---

²¹Every soul will come accompanied by [two angels], a driver and a witness: ²²[it will be told] 'You were certainly oblivious of this! We have removed your veil from you, so today your eyesight is acute.'

²³Then his companion [angel] will say, 'This is what is ready with me [of his record of deeds].'

²⁴[The two accompanying angels will be told,] 'Cast every stubborn ingrate into hell, ²⁵[every] hinderer of good, transgressor and sceptic, ²⁶who had set up another god along with God and cast him into the severe punishment.'

²⁷His companion [devil] will say, 'Our Lord! I did not incite him to rebel [against You], but he was [himself] in extreme error.'

²⁸He will say, 'Do not wrangle in My presence, for I had already warned you in advance. ²⁹The word [of judgement] is unalterable with Me, and I am not tyrannical to My servants.'

³⁰The day when We shall say to hell, 'Are you full?' It will say, 'Is there any more?'

50:30: "Sheol, the barren womb, earth which can never have its fill of water, fire which never says, 'Enough!'" (Pro 30:16).

---

³¹And paradise will be brought near for the Godwary, it will not be distant [any more]: ³²'This is what you were promised. [It is] for every penitent and dutiful [servant] ³³who fears the All-beneficent in secret and comes with a penitent heart. ³⁴Enter it

in peace! This is the day of immortality.' ³⁵There they will have whatever they wish, and with Us there is yet more.

³⁶How many generations We have destroyed before them who were stronger than these, insomuch that they ransacked the towns?! So, is there any escape [from God's punishment]?

³⁷There is indeed an admonition in that for one who has a heart, or gives ear, being attentive.

³⁸Certainly We created the heavens and the earth and whatever is between them in six days, and any fatigue did not touch Us.

50:38 Here the Qur'ān follows the Biblical tradition of creation in six days (on this see commentary on 41:9–12, with further references), but also distinguishes its god from the god of the Bible, who rests on the seventh day (Gen 2:2; cf. Q 35:35).

---

³⁹So *be patient* at what they say and *celebrate* the praise of *your* Lord before the rising of the sun and before the sunset, ⁴⁰and *glorify* Him through part of the night and after the prostrations.

⁴¹And *be on the alert* for the day when the caller calls from a close quarter, ⁴²the day when they hear the Cry in all truth. That is the day of rising [from the dead].

⁴³It is indeed We who give life and bring death, and toward Us is the [final] destination. ⁴⁴The day the earth is split open for [disentombing] them, [they will come out] hastening. That mustering is easy for Us [to carry out].

⁴⁵We know well what they say, and *you* are not there to compel them. So *admonish* by the Qur'ān those who fear My threat.

51. *AL-DHĀRIYĀT*, The Scatterers

In the Name of God, the All-beneficent, the All-merciful.

¹By the scattering [winds] that scatter [the clouds]; ²by the [rain] bearing [clouds] laden [with water]; ³by [the ships] which move gently [on the sea]; ⁴by [the angels] who dispense [livelihood] by [His] command: ⁵what you are promised is indeed true, ⁶and indeed, the retribution will surely come to pass!

⁷By the heaven full of adornment [with stars], ⁸you are indeed of different opinions! ⁹He who has been turned away [from the truth] is turned away from it.

¹⁰Perish the liars, ¹¹who are heedless in a stupor! ¹²They ask, 'When will be the Day of Retribution?'

51:12 On knowledge of the Hour being with God alone, see commentary on 79:42–44 (with further references).

¹³It is the day when they will be tormented in the Fire, ¹⁴[and told]: 'Taste your torment. This is what you used to hasten.'

¹⁵Indeed, the Godwary will be amid gardens and springs,

51:15 On the streams of paradise, see commentary on 2:25 (with further references).

---

¹⁶receiving what their Lord has given them, for they had been virtuous aforetime. ¹⁷They used to sleep a little during the night, ¹⁸and at dawns they would plead for forgiveness, ¹⁹and there was a share in their wealth for the beggar and the deprived.

²⁰In the earth are signs for those who have conviction ²¹and in your souls [as well]. Will you not then perceive? ²²And in the heaven is your provision and what you are promised.

²³By the Lord of the heaven and the earth, it is indeed the truth, just as [it is a fact that] you speak.

²⁴Did *you* receive the story of Abraham's honoured guests? ²⁵When they entered into his presence, they said, 'Peace!' 'Peace!' He answered, '[You are] an unfamiliar folk.' ²⁶Then he retired to his family and brought a fat [roasted] calf ²⁷and put it near them. He said, 'Will you not eat?' ²⁸Then he felt a fear of them. They said, 'Do not be afraid!' and they gave him the good news of a wise son. ²⁹Then his wife came forward crying [with joy]. She beat her face and said, 'A barren old woman!' ³⁰They said, 'So has your Lord said. Indeed, He is the All-wise, the All-knowing.'

51:24–30 Regarding the Qurʾānic account of Abraham's guests, see commentary on 11:69–73 (with further references). Abraham's description (v. 25) of the guests as "unusual folk" (cf. 15:62) reflects the common conviction in Jewish and Christian exegesis that the three "men" of Genesis 18:2 (called "messengers"—Ar. *rusul*—in 11:69) who visited him were in fact angels:

> Who were the three men?—Michael, Gabriel, and Raphael. Michael came to bring the tidings to Sarah [of Isaac's birth]; Raphael, to heal Abraham; and Gabriel, to overturn Sodom. (b. Bava Metziʾa 86b)

Verse 27 reflects a midrashic tradition that the guests—being angels—did not eat (pace Gen 18:8):

> Did they then eat? They pretended to eat, removing each course in turn. (*Genesis Rabbah,* 48:14).

The church fathers, who often read Genesis 18 in a Trinitarian manner (as God speaks, v. 13, from the midst of the three men), also describe the visitors as angels (see Justin Martyr, *Dialogue with Trypho,* chap. 57; Tertullian, *Against Marcion,* 3:9).

---

³¹He said, 'O messengers, what is now your errand?'

³²They said, 'We have been sent toward a guilty people ³³that We may rain upon them stones of clay, ³⁴sent for the transgressors from *your* Lord. ³⁵So We picked out those who were in it of the faithful, ³⁶but We did not find there other than one house of *muslims,* ³⁷and We have left therein a sign for those who fear a painful punishment.'

51:31–37 On the Qur'ān's references to the destruction of Lot's people, and the rescue of Lot and his family (with the exception of his wife), see 15:57–74 (with further references). Qarai renders Arabic *muslimīn* (v. 36) "*muslims*" ("We did not find there other than one house of *muslims*"). Muhammad Asad translates the Arabic and renders as "for apart from one [single] house We did not find there any who had surrendered themselves to Us."

The declaration (v. 37) that God has left a "sign" reflects the Qur'ān's convictions that the remains of Lot's city were visible to its audience (see commentary on 37:133–38, with further references). Hilali-Khan explain that this sign is "the place of the Dead Sea, well-known in Palestine."

---

³⁸And in Moses, [too, there is a sign] when We sent him to Pharaoh with a manifest authority. ³⁹But he turned away assured

of his might, and said, 'A magician or a crazy man!' ⁴⁰So We seized him and his hosts and cast them into the sea, while he was blameworthy.

51:38–40 On Moses's confrontation with Pharaoh, see commentary on 26:30–45 (with further references).

---

⁴¹And in ʿĀd when We unleashed upon them a barren wind. ⁴²It left nothing that it came upon without making it like decayed bones.

⁴³And in Thamūd, when they were told, 'Enjoy for a while.' ⁴⁴Then they defied the command of their Lord, so the thunderbolt seized them as they looked on. ⁴⁵So they were neither able to rise up, nor to come to one another's aid.

⁴⁶And the people of Noah aforetime. They were indeed a transgressing lot.

51:46 On the Qurʾānic Noah account, see commentary on 11:25–39 and 71:1–28 (with further references).

---

⁴⁷We have built the heaven with might, and We are indeed its expanders. ⁴⁸We have spread out the earth and how excellent spreaders We have been! ⁴⁹In all things We have created pairs so that you may take admonition.

⁵⁰[*Say,*] 'So flee toward God. I am indeed a manifest warner from Him to you. ⁵¹Do not set up another god besides God. I am indeed a manifest warner from Him to you.'

⁵²So it was that there did not come any apostle to those who were before them but they said, 'A magician,' or 'A crazy man!' ⁵³Did they enjoin this upon one another?! Rather, they were a rebellious lot.

⁵⁴So *turn away* from them, as *you* will not be blameworthy. ⁵⁵And *admonish,* for admonition indeed benefits the faithful.

⁵⁶I did not create the jinn and the humans except that they may worship Me. ⁵⁷I desire no provision from them, nor do I desire that they should feed Me.

51:56–57 "To which, Samuel said: Is the Lord pleased by burnt offerings and sacrifices or by obedience to the Lord's voice? Truly, obedience is better than sacrifice, submissiveness than the fat of rams" (1Sa 15:22; cf. Mic 6:8; Amo 5:21–25; Hos 6:6; Psa 50:8–13; Mat 9:13, 21:7).

⁵⁸It is God who is indeed the All-provider, Powerful and All-strong.

⁵⁹The lot of those who do wrong [now] will indeed be like the lot of their [earlier] counterparts. So let them not ask Me to hasten on [that fate]. ⁶⁰Woe to the faithless for the day they are promised!

52. *AL-ṬŪR*, THE MOUNT

In the Name of God, the All-beneficent, the All-merciful.

¹By the Mount [Sinai],

52:1 Qarai identifies the "Mount" (Ar. *ṭūr*) as Sinai, the mountain on which God gave his revelation to Moses (cf. 19:52; 20:80; 28:29, 46). He is undoubtedly right, as Aramaic *ṭūrā* was used to refer to Mt. Sinai by both Jews and Christians (on this see Horovitz, *KU*, 124). See also commentary on 23:20 and 95:1–3.

---

²by the Book inscribed ³on an unrolled parchment, ⁴by the House greatly frequented, ⁵by the vault raised high, ⁶by the surging sea:⁷indeed *your* Lord's punishment will surely befall. ⁸There is none who can avert it. ⁹On the day when the heaven whirls violently ¹⁰and the mountains move with an awful motion: ¹¹woe to the deniers on that day ¹²—those who play around in vain talk, ¹³the day when they will be shoved forcibly toward the fire of hell [and told:] ¹⁴'This is the Fire which you used to deny! ¹⁵Is this, then, [also] magic, or is it you who do not perceive? ¹⁶Enter it, and it will be the same for you whether you are patient or impatient. You are only being requited for what you used to do.'

¹⁷The Godwary will indeed be amid gardens and bliss, ¹⁸rejoicing because of what their Lord has given them and that their Lord has saved them from the punishment of hell. ¹⁹[They will be told:] 'Enjoy your food and drink [as a reward] for what you used to do.' ²⁰They will be reclining on arrayed couches, and We will wed them to big-eyed houris.

52:20 On the maidens of paradise in the Qurʾān, see commentary on 56:22–23 (with further references).

---

²¹The faithful and their descendants who followed them in faith—We will make their descendants join them and We will not stint anything from [the reward of] their deeds. Every person is hostage to what he has earned. ²²We will provide them with fruits and meat, such as they desire. ²³There they will pass from hand to hand a cup wherein there will be neither any vain talk nor sinful speech. ²⁴They will be waited upon by their youths, as if they were guarded pearls.

52:22–24 On heaven as a feast, see commentary on 56:15–21 (with further references).

---

²⁵They will turn to one another, questioning each other. ²⁶They will say, 'Indeed, aforetime, we used to be apprehensive about our families. ²⁷But God showed us favour and He saved us from the punishment of the [infernal] miasma. ²⁸We used to supplicate Him aforetime. Indeed, He is the All-benign, the All-merciful.'

²⁹So *admonish.* By *your* Lord's blessing, *you* are not a sooth-sayer, nor mad.

³⁰Do they say, '[He is] a poet, for whom we await a fatal acci-dent'? ³¹*Say,* 'Wait! I too am waiting along with you.' ³²Is it their intellect which prompts them to [say] this, or are they a rebellious lot?

³³Do they say, 'He has improvised it [himself]?' Rather, they have no faith! ³⁴Let them bring a discourse like it, if they are truthful.

³⁵Were they created from nothing? Or are they [their own] cre-ators? ³⁶Did they create the heavens and the earth? Rather, they have no certainty! ³⁷Do they possess the treasuries of *your* Lord? Or do they control them? ³⁸Do they have a ladder [leading up to the heaven] whereby they eavesdrop? If so let their eavesdropper produce a manifest authority.

52:38 The notion of a ladder to heaven (cf. 6:35) reflects a cosmology (known from Genesis) according to which heaven, where divine secrets are discussed, lies behind a dome or firmament which blocks the way to it for most creatures; it is accessible only by certain pathways (Qur'ānic *asbāb:* 2:166, 22:15, 38:10, 40:36–37; see further van Bladel, "Heavenly Cords"). This same cosmology explains the presence of a ladder in the dream of Jacob in Genesis 28:

¹⁰Jacob left Beersheba and set out for Haran.
¹¹When he had reached a certain place, he stopped there for the night, since the sun had set. Taking one of the stones of that place, he made it his pillow and lay down where he was.
¹²He had a dream: there was a ladder, planted on the ground with its top reaching to heaven; and God's angels were going up and down on it. (Gen 28:10–12)

---

³⁹Does He have daughters while you have sons?

⁴⁰Do *you* ask them for a reward, so that they are [wary of] being weighed down with debt?

52:40 On the idea that a true prophet does not seek a reward, see commentary on 34:47 (with further references).

———————

⁴¹Do they have [access to] the Unseen, which they write down? ⁴²Do they seek to outmaneuver [God]? But it is the faithless who are the outmaneuvered ones! ⁴³Do they have any god other than God? Clear is God of any partners that they may ascribe [to Him]!

⁴⁴Were they to see a fragment falling from the sky, they would say, 'A cumulous cloud.' ⁴⁵So leave them until they encounter the day when they drop down dead, ⁴⁶the day when their guile will not avail them in any way, nor will they be helped. ⁴⁷For those who do wrong, there is indeed a punishment besides that, but most of them do not know.

⁴⁸So *submit patiently* to the judgement of *your* Lord, for indeed *you* fare before Our eyes. And *celebrate* the praise of *your* Lord when *you* rise [at dawn], ⁴⁹and also *glorify* Him during the night and at the receding of the stars.

53. *AL-NAJM*, THE STAR

In the Name of God, the All-beneficent, the All-merciful.

¹By the star when it sets: ²your companion has neither gone astray, nor amiss. ³Nor does he speak out of [his own] desire: ⁴it is just a revelation that is revealed [to him], ⁵taught him by one of great powers,

---

53:5–18 *overview* This passage is closely related to early Jewish and Christian apocalyptic texts which describe a divine vision. See also commentary on the other principal "divine vision" passage in the Qurʾān: 81:18–25.

---

⁶possessed of sound judgement. He settled, ⁷while he was on the highest horizon. ⁸Then he drew nearer and nearer ⁹until he was within two bows' length or even nearer, ¹⁰whereat He revealed to His servant whatever He revealed.

53:10 The reference to Muḥammad as "His servant" here suggests that the previous passage speaks of a vision of God, although most Muslim scholars (including *Tafsīr al-Jalālayn*) generally argue that it describes a vision only of Gabriel. Muḥammad's claim to have seen God (notice vv. 19–20, where he literally asks whether his opponents have *seen* [Qarai translates "considered"] their gods) is likely based on the model of Moses (see Exo 33:11).

---

¹¹The heart did not deny what it saw. ¹²Will you then dispute with him about what he saw?!

¹³Certainly he saw it yet another time, ¹⁴by the Lote Tree of the Ultimate Boundary, ¹⁵near which is the Garden of the Abode, ¹⁶when there covered the Lote Tree what covered it. ¹⁷His gaze did not swerve, nor did it overstep the bounds. ¹⁸Certainly he saw some of the greatest signs of his Lord.

53:13–18 The Qur'ān here describes a second vision experienced by the Prophet (the first vision is described in vv. 5–12; cf. 81:18–25), which *Tafsīr al-Jalālayn* connects to his night journey and ascension to heaven. The reference to a tree in verse 14 may be connected to a conception of paradise found with Ephrem in his *Hymns on Paradise:*

> In the midst of Paradise God had planted the Tree of Knowledge / to separate off, above and below, sanctuary from Holy of Holies. (*Hymns on Paradise,* 3:14)

Ephrem places the tree of knowledge at the boundary of two levels of heaven, and relates that the tree hides "the glory of the inner Tabernacle" and acts "as a sanctuary curtain, veiling the Holy of Holies from sight" (cr. Tommaso Tesei).

Tafsīr al-Jalālayn insists that Muḥammad was blocked from seeing God, that instead he "saw from among the marvels of the Realm a green drape that obscured the [entire] horizon of the heaven and Gabriel with his six hundred wings."

---

¹⁹Have you considered Lāt and 'Uzzā? ²⁰and Manāt, the third one? ²¹Are you to have males and He females? ²²That, then, will be an unfair division! ²³These are but names which you have

coined—you and your fathers—for which God has not sent down any authority. They follow nothing but conjectures and the desires of the [lower] soul, while there has already come to them the guidance from their Lord.

53:19–23 Verse 21 suggests that Lāt, ʿUzzā, and Manāt were thought of as female offspring of God. In light of 21:26–27, which denies that angels should be considered offspring (see commentary on 21:21–29), it seems likely that they are the names of angels that the Prophet's opponents considered "daughters" of God. On the traditional interpretation of these verses, see commentary on Q 22:52.

---

²⁴Shall man have whatever he yearns for? ²⁵Yet to God belong this world and the Hereafter. ²⁶How many an angel there is in the heavens whose intercession is not of any avail, except after God permits whomever He wishes and approves of! ²⁷Indeed, those who do not believe in the Hereafter give female names to the angels. ²⁸They do not have any knowledge of that. They follow nothing but conjectures, and conjecture is no substitute for the truth.

²⁹So *disregard* those who turn away from Our remembrance and desire nothing but the life of the world. ³⁰That is the ultimate reach of their knowledge. Indeed, your Lord knows best those who stray from His way, and He knows best those who are [rightly] guided.

³¹To God belongs whatever is in the heavens and whatever is in the earth, that He may requite those who do evil for what they have done and reward those who do good with the best [of rewards]. ³²Those who avoid major sins and indecencies, apart from [minor and occasional] lapses. *Your* Lord is indeed expansive in

[His] forgiveness. He knows you best since [the time] He produced you from the earth and since you were fetuses in the bellies
of your mothers. So do not flaunt your piety: He knows best those
who are Godwary.

³³Did *you* see him who turned away, ³⁴gave a little and held
off? ³⁵Does he have the knowledge of the Unseen so that he sees?
³⁶Has he not been informed of what is in the scriptures of Moses,
³⁷and of Abraham, who fulfilled [his summons]:

53:36–37 Cf. 87:19. With "the scriptures (*ṣuḥuf*) of Moses" the Qurʾān is evidently alluding to the Torah. Regarding the "scriptures of Abraham," Yusuf Ali
writes, "No original Book of Abraham is now extant." Epiphanius of Salamis
(d. 403) refers to an apocalypse ascribed to Abraham (*Panarion*, bk. 1, 39.5.1).
An originally Jewish text known as the *Apocalypse of Abraham* (the origins of
which predate the Qurʾān) is extant (although it is unlikely that this text is the
work to which Epiphanius refers). See Kulik, *Retroverting Slavonic Pseudepigrapha*, 2–3. It is perhaps most likely that the Qurʾān's author simply imagined
that Abraham must have had a scripture like that of Moses. On the term *ṣuḥuf*,
see further commentary on 80:13–15 (with further references).

The description of Abraham as the one "who fulfilled [his summons]" may be an
allusion to his obedient willingness to sacrifice his own son (cf. 37:102–11). This
description reflects the frequent New Testament allusions to Genesis 15:6, which
speaks of Abraham's trust in God (Rom 4:1–3; Gal 3:6–9; Heb 11:17; Jam 2:23).

---

³⁸that no bearer shall bear another's burden,

53:38 The Qurʾān is here referring to a teaching in the scriptures of Moses
and Abraham, but the sentiment expressed is found elsewhere in the Qurʾān as
well. See commentary on 82:19 (with further references).

---

³⁹that nothing belongs to man except what he strives for, ⁴⁰and
that he will soon be shown his endeavour, ⁴¹then he will be re-

quited for it with the fullest requital; [42]that the terminus is toward *your* Lord, [43]that it is He who makes [men] laugh and weep, [44]that it is He who brings death and gives life,

53:44 "The Lord gives death and life, brings down to Sheol and draws up" (1Sa 2:6; cf. Deu 32:39). Speyer (*BEQ*, 460), noting the reference to the scriptures of Moses in verse 36, refers here also to the (likely mishnaic) *Shmoneh Esreh* (Amidah) prayer, which includes the line: "And who can be compared to You, King, who brings death and restores life, and causes deliverance to spring forth!"

[45]that it is He who created the mates, the male and the female, [46]from a drop of [seminal] fluid when emitted; [47]that with Him lies the second genesis,

53:47 On the allusion to the resurrection as a "new creation," or "second genesis," see commentary on 50:15.

[48]that it is He who enriches and grants possessions, [49]that it is He who is the Lord of Sirius; [50]that it is He who destroyed the former 'Ād, [51]and Thamud, sparing none [of them], [52]and the people of Noah before that; indeed they were more unjust and rebellious; [53]and He overthrew the town that was overturned,

53:53 "The town that was overturned" (Ar. *al-mu'tafika*) is an allusion to Sodom; cf. 9:70; 69:9, where the plural *al-mu'tafikāt* appears; and 11:82, which describes how God turned the city of Lot "upside down." The Arabic term for "overturned" (*al-mu'tafika*) is related to the Hebrew verb used in Genesis 19:25: "He overthrew [Hb. *wayyahapōk*] those cities and the whole plain, with all the people living in the cities and everything that grew there."

---

⁵⁴covering it with what covered it.

⁵⁵Then which of the bounties of your Lord will you dispute?

⁵⁶This is a warner, [in the tradition] of the warners of old. ⁵⁷The Imminent [Hour] is near at hand. ⁵⁸There is none who may unveil it besides God. ⁵⁹Will you then wonder at this discourse, ⁶⁰and laugh and not weep, ⁶¹while you remain heedless?!

⁶²So prostrate yourselves to God and worship Him!

54. *AL-QAMAR*, THE MOON

In the Name of God, the All-beneficent, the All-merciful.

¹The Hour has drawn near and the moon is split.

²If they see a sign, they turn away and say, 'An incessant magic!' ³They denied and followed their own desires, and every matter has its denouement [appropriate to it].

⁴There have already come to them reports containing admonishment ⁵[and representing] far-reaching wisdom; but warnings are of no avail!

⁶So *turn away* from them! The day when the Caller calls to a dire thing, ⁷with a humbled look [in their eyes], they will emerge from the graves as if they were scattered locusts, ⁸scrambling toward the summoner. The faithless will say, 'This is a hard day!'

⁹The people of Noah impugned before them. So they impugned Our servant and said, 'A crazy man,' and he was reviled.

54:9–42 *overview* On this and the other punishment story sequences in the Qur'ān, see commentary on 7:59–137 (with further references).

---

¹⁰Thereat he invoked his Lord, [saying,] 'I have been overcome, so help [me].'

54:10 Here Noah calls on God but in Genesis Noah says nothing at all before the flood. On Noah and the flood, see commentary on 71:1–28 (with further references).

---

¹¹Then We opened the gates of the sky with pouring waters ¹²and We made the earth burst forth with springs, and the waters met for a preordained purpose. ¹³We bore him on a vessel made of planks and nails, ¹⁴which sailed [over the flood waters] in Our sight, as a retribution for him who was met with disbelief. ¹⁵Certainly We have left it as a sign; so is there anyone who will be admonished?

54:15 Yusuf Ali (with reference to 29:15) suggests that the "sign" which has been left is Noah's ark (which implies that the remains of the ark are still visible).

---

¹⁶So how were My punishment and warnings?

¹⁷Certainly We have made the Qur'ān simple for the sake of admonishment. So is there anyone who will be admonished?

¹⁸[The people of] 'Ād impugned [their apostle]. So how were My punishment and warnings? ¹⁹Indeed, We unleashed upon them an icy gale on an incessantly ill-fated day, ²⁰knocking down people as if they were trunks of uprooted palm trees. ²¹So how were My punishment and warnings?!

²²Certainly We have made the Qur'ān simple for the sake of admonishment. So is there anyone who will be admonished?

²³[The people of] Thamūd denied the warnings, ²⁴and they said, 'Are we to follow a lone human from ourselves?! Then we would indeed be in error and madness.' ²⁵'Has the Reminder been cast upon him from among us? No, he is a self-conceited liar.'

²⁶'Tomorrow they will know who is a self-conceited liar. ²⁷We are sending the She-camel as a test for them; so watch them and be steadfast. ²⁸Inform them that the water is to be shared between them; each of them showing up at his turn.'

²⁹But they called their companion, and he took [a knife] and hamstrung [her]. ³⁰So how were My punishment and warnings?! ³¹We sent against them a single Cry, and they became like the dry sticks of a corral builder.

³²Certainly We have made the Qur'ān simple for the sake of admonishment. So is there anyone who will be admonished?

³³And the people of Lot denied the warnings. ³⁴We unleashed upon them a rain of stones, excepting the family of Lot, whom We delivered at dawn

³⁵as a blessing from Us. Thus do We reward those who give thanks.

³⁶He had already warned them of Our punishment, but they disputed the warnings. ³⁷They even solicited of him his guests, whereat We blotted out their eyes, [saying,] 'Taste My punishment and warnings!' ³⁸Early at dawn there visited them an abiding punishment: ³⁹'Taste My punishment and warnings!'

54:33–39 In the Qur'ān the account of Lot becomes one element of a cycle of "punishment stories." Compare, in the present Sura, the accounts of Noah (vv. 9–15); ʿĀd (to whom Hūd was sent; vv. 18–20); Thamūd (to whom Ṣāliḥ was sent; vv. 23–29); and Moses (vv. 41–42). On Lot, see commentary on 15:57–74 and 29:28–35 (with further references). Regarding verse 37, *Tafsīr al-Jalālayn* comments that God blinded Lot's enemies "by having Gabriel smack them with his wing." The detail that the Sodomites were destroyed at dawn (vv. 34, 38) follows Genesis 19:15: "When dawn broke the angels urged Lot on, 'To your feet! Take your wife and your two daughters who are here, or you will be swept away in the punishment of the city.'"

⁴⁰Certainly We have made the Qur'ān simple for the sake of admonishment. So is there anyone who will be admonished?

⁴¹Certainly Our warnings did come to Pharaoh's clan ⁴²who denied all of Our signs. So We seized them with the seizing of One [who is] all-mighty, Omnipotent.

54:41–42 The Qur'ān refers to the destruction of Pharaoh's people and not only his army (see commentary on 43:55, with further references). The way the Qur'ān celebrates God's vanquishing of Pharaoh (cf. 2:50; 10:90–92; 20:77–79; 25:36; 28:40) is reminiscent of Psalm 136:

> ¹³He split the Sea of Reeds in two, for his faithful love endures for ever.
> ¹⁴Let Israel pass through the middle, for his faithful love endures for ever.
> ¹⁵And drowned Pharaoh and all his army, for his faithful love endures for ever. (Psa 136:13–15; cf. Exo 14:21–22, 27, 30; cf. also Jos 24:6–7; Psa 77:16–20, 106:7–11; 1Co 10:1; Heb 11:29)

The following Sura also seems to have a connection with Psalm 136 (see commentary on 55 *overview*).

⁴³Are your faithless better than those? Have you [been granted] some sort of immunity in the scriptures?

54:43 Here (cf. 26:196; 54:52) the Qur'ān uses a term (Ar. *zubur*, sing. *zabūr*) that in certain places (4:163; 17:55; 21:105) seems to mean simply Psalms. Here it refers generally to earlier scriptures. On this see commentary on 17:55 (with further references).

⁴⁴Do they say, 'We are a confederate league'? ⁴⁵The league will be routed and turn its back [to flee]. ⁴⁶Indeed, the Hour is their tryst, and the Hour will be most calamitous and bitter.

⁴⁷The guilty are indeed steeped in error and madness. ⁴⁸The day when they are dragged on their faces into the Fire, [it will be said to them,] 'Taste the touch of hell!'

⁴⁹Indeed, We have created everything in a measure ⁵⁰and Our command is but a single [word], like the twinkling of an eye.

⁵¹Certainly We have destroyed your likes. So is there anyone who will be admonished?

⁵²Everything they have done is in the books,

54:52 Regarding "books" (Ar. *zubur;* sing. *zabūr*), see commentary on 17:55 (with further references).

---

⁵³and everything big and small is committed to writing.

⁵⁴The Godwary will indeed be amid gardens and streams, ⁵⁵in the abode of truthfulness with an omnipotent King.

54:54 On the streams of paradise see commentary on 2:25 (with further references).

55. *AL-RAḤMĀN,* THE ALL-BENEFICENT

In the Name of God, the All-beneficent, the All-merciful.

55 *overview* As has been suggested by Angelika Neuwirth ("Glimpses of Paradise in the World," 86–95), and before her Speyer (*BEQ,* 449), Qur'ān 55 seems to have a particularly close relationship with Psalm 136, notably with the Sura's use of a refrain (e.g., vv. 13, 16, 18, 21, 23, 25, 28, 30, 32) and in its references to the signs of God's power and mercy:

> [5] In wisdom he made the heavens, for his faithful love endures for ever.
> [6] He set the earth firm on the waters, for his faithful love endures for ever.
> [7] He made the great lights, for his faithful love endures for ever.
> [8] The sun to rule the day, for his faithful love endures for ever.
> [9] Moon and stars to rule the night, for his faithful love endures for ever.
> . . .
> [25] He provides food for all living creatures, for his faithful love endures for ever.
> [26] Give thanks to the God of heaven, for his faithful love endures for ever.
> (Psa 136:5–9, 25–26)

[1] The All-beneficent [2] has taught the Qur'ān. [3] He created man, [4] [and] taught him articulate speech.

[5] The sun and the moon are [disposed] calculatedly, [6] and the herb and the tree prostrate [to God]. [7] He raised the heaven high and set

up the balance, ⁸declaring, 'Do not infringe the balance! ⁹Maintain the weights with justice, and do not shorten the balance!'

55:7–9 On the use of proper "measuring" as an example of righteousness, see commentary on Q 83:1–3 (with further references).

---

¹⁰And the earth—He laid it out for mankind. ¹¹In it are fruits and date-palms with sheaths, ¹²grain with husk, and fragrant herbs.

¹³So which of your Lord's bounties will you both deny?

¹⁴He created man out of dry clay, like the potter's, ¹⁵and created the jinn out of a flame of a fire.

¹⁶So which of your Lord's bounties will you both deny?

¹⁷Lord of the two easts and Lord of the two wests!

¹⁸So which of your Lord's bounties will you both deny?

¹⁹He merged the two seas, meeting each other. ²⁰There is a barrier between them which they do not overstep.

55:19–20 The allusions here to two seas which are separated by a boundary (Ar. *barzakh*) reflects a cosmology based on Genesis 1:7: "God made the vault, and it divided the waters under the vault from the waters above the vault." See commentary on 23:99–100 and 25:53.

---

²¹So which of your Lord's bounties will you both deny?

²²From them emerge the pearl and the coral.

²³So which of your Lord's bounties will you both deny?

²⁴His are the sailing ships on the sea [appearing] like landmarks.

²⁵So which of your Lord's bounties will you both deny?

²⁶Everyone on it is ephemeral, ²⁷yet lasting is the majestic and munificent Face of *your* Lord.

²⁸So which of your Lord's bounties will you both deny?

²⁹Everyone in the heavens and the earth asks Him. Every day He is engaged in some work.

³⁰So which of your Lord's bounties will you both deny?

³¹Soon We shall make Ourselves unoccupied for you, O you notable two!

³²So which of your Lord's bounties will you both deny?

³³O company of jinn and humans! If you can pass through the confines of the heavens and the earth, then do pass through. But you will not pass through except by an authority [from God].

³⁴So which of your Lord's bounties will you both deny?

³⁵There will be unleashed upon you a flash of fire and a smoke; then you will not be able to help one another.

³⁶So which of your Lord's bounties will you both deny?

³⁷When the sky is split open and turns crimson like tanned leather.

³⁸So which of your Lord's bounties will you both deny?

³⁹On that day neither humans will be questioned about their sins nor jinn.

⁴⁰So which of your Lord's bounties will you both deny?

⁴¹The guilty will be recognized by their mark; so they will be seized by their forelocks and feet.

⁴²So which of your Lord's bounties will you both deny?

⁴³'This is the hell which the guilty would deny!' ⁴⁴They shall circuit between it and boiling hot water.

⁴⁵So which of your Lord's bounties will you both deny?

⁴⁶For him who stands in awe of his Lord will be two gardens.

⁴⁷So which of your Lord's bounties will you both deny?

⁴⁸Both abounding in branches.

⁴⁹So which of your Lord's bounties will you both deny?

⁵⁰In both of them will be two flowing springs.

⁵¹So which of your Lord's bounties will you both deny?

⁵²In both of them will be two kinds of every fruit.

⁵³So which of your Lord's bounties will you both deny?

⁵⁴[They will be] reclining on beds lined with heavy silk. And the fruit of the two gardens will be near at hand.

⁵⁵So which of your Lord's bounties will you both deny?

⁵⁶In them are maidens of restrained glances, whom no human has touched before, nor jinn.

⁵⁷So which of your Lord's bounties will you both deny?

⁵⁸As though they were rubies and corals.

⁵⁹So which of your Lord's bounties will you both deny?

⁶⁰Is the requital of goodness anything but goodness?

⁶¹So which of your Lord's bounties will you both deny?

⁶²Beside these two, there will be two [other] gardens.

⁶³So which of your Lord's bounties will you both deny?

⁶⁴Dark green.

⁶⁵So which of your Lord's bounties will you both deny?

⁶⁶In both of them will be two gushing springs.

⁶⁷So which of your Lord's bounties will you both deny?

⁶⁸In both of them will be fruits, date-palms and pomegranates.

⁶⁹So which of your Lord's bounties will you both deny?

⁷⁰In them are maidens good and lovely.

⁷¹So which of your Lord's bounties will you both deny?

⁷²Houris secluded in pavilions.

⁷³So which of your Lord's bounties will you both deny?

⁷⁴Whom no human has touched before, nor jinn.

55:70–74 On the maidens of paradise in the Qurʾān, see commentary on 56:22–23 (with further references).

---

[75]So which of your Lord's bounties will you both deny?

[76]Reclining on green cushions and lovely carpets.

[77]So which of your Lord's bounties will you both deny?

[78]Blessed is the Name of *your* Lord, the Majestic and the Munificent!

56. *AL-WĀQIʿA,* THE IMMINENT

In the Name of God, the All-beneficent, the All-merciful.

¹When the Imminent [Hour] befalls ²—there is no denying that it will befall—³[it will be] lowering and exalting. ⁴When the earth is shaken violently, ⁵and the mountains are shattered into bits ⁶and become scattered dust, ⁷you will be three groups:

⁸The People of the Right Hand—and what are the People of the Right Hand?!

⁹And the People of the Left Hand—and what are the People of the Left Hand?!

¹⁰And the Foremost Ones are the foremost ones: ¹¹they are the ones brought near [to God],

---

56:8–11 The division between those on the right (v. 8; cf. 74:39; 90:7–20) and left (v. 9; cf. 90:19) sides recalls the coming of the Son of Man in Matthew 25 (31–46). Similar language is also used in the *Apocalypse of Abraham* (21:7, 22:3–5), as described by Carlos Segovia in an unpublished paper ("Those on the Right' and 'Those on the Left'"). See also commentary on 90:7–20.

---

¹²[who will reside] in the gardens of bliss. ¹³A multitude from the former [generations] ¹⁴and a few from the latter ones. ¹⁵On

brocaded couches, [16]reclining on them, face to face. [17]They will be waited upon by immortal youths, [18]with goblets and ewers and a cup of a clear wine, [19]which causes them neither headache nor stupefaction, [20]and such fruits as they prefer [21]and such flesh of fowls as they desire,

56:15–21 The image of paradise as a feast might be compared to the New Testament descriptions of heaven or the kingdom of God as a feast (Mat 8:11; Mat 22:2; Luk 13:29; Rev 19:9, 17). Matthew 26:29 alludes to drinking wine in heaven.

---

[22]and big-eyed houris [23]like guarded pearls,

56:22–23 The Qurʾān presents an image of the heavenly paradise complete with women ("houris") who welcome the believers and are paired with them (Q 44:54; 52:20). This image might be inspired in part by the Syriac Christian vision of paradise as a garden. Notably, in his *Hymns on Paradise* Ephrem speaks of the vines of the garden of paradise welcoming (as though they were brides), chaste monks:

> The man who abstained / with understanding from wine, / will the vines
> of Paradise / rush out to meet, all the more joyfully, / as each one stretches
> out and proffers him / its clusters; / or if any has lived a life of virginity, /
> him too they welcome into their bosom, / for the solitary such as he / has
> never lain in any bosom / nor upon any marriage bed. (Ephrem, *Hymns on
> Paradise,* 7:18)

The Qurʾān may have turned these metaphorical brides into real brides of paradise (this idea is suggested already by Andrae in *Mohammed: The Man and His Faith,* 88). Walid Saleh suggest an alternative possibility, that the Qurʾān is in conversation with pagan Hellenistic ideas of the celestial realm. See Saleh, "Etymological Fallacy," 689–91.

   On the maidens of paradise, cf. 2:25; 3:15; 4:57; 37:48–49; 38:52; 44:54; 52:20; 55:70, 72, 74; 56:34–37; 78:33.

²⁴a reward for what they used to do. ²⁵They will not hear therein any vain talk or sinful speech, ²⁶but only the watchword, 'Peace!' 'Peace!'

²⁷And the People of the Right Hand—what are the People of the Right Hand?! ²⁸Amid thornless lote trees ²⁹and bananas in regularly set clusters, ³⁰and extended shade,

56:30 On shade in paradise, see commentary on 13:35 (with further references).

³¹and ever-flowing water ³²and abundant fruits, ³³neither inaccessible, nor forbidden, ³⁴and noble spouses. ³⁵We have created them with a special creation, ³⁶and made them virgins, ³⁷loving, of a like age,

56:34–37 On the maidens of paradise in the Qurʾān see commentary on 56:22–23 (with further references). *Tafsīr al-Jalālayn* explains verse 36 by commenting, "Every time their spouses enter them they find them virgins."

³⁸for the People of the Right Hand. ³⁹A multitude from the former [generations] ⁴⁰and a multitude from the latter [ones].

⁴¹And the People of the Left Hand—what are the People of the Left Hand?! ⁴²Amid infernal miasma and boiling water ⁴³and the shadow of a dense black smoke, ⁴⁴neither cool nor beneficial. ⁴⁵Indeed, they had been affluent before this, ⁴⁶and they used to persist in the great sin. ⁴⁷And they used to say, 'What! When we are dead and become dust and bones, shall we be resurrected?! ⁴⁸And our forefathers, too?!'

⁴⁹*Say*, 'The former and latter generations ⁵⁰will indeed be gathered for the tryst of a known day. ⁵¹Then indeed, you, astray deniers, ⁵²will surely eat from the Zaqqūm tree ⁵³and stuff your bellies with it, ⁵⁴and drink boiling water on top of it, ⁵⁵drinking like thirsty camels.' ⁵⁶Such will be the hospitality they receive on the Day of Retribution.

⁵⁷We created you. Then why do you not acknowledge it? ⁵⁸Have you considered the sperm that you emit? ⁵⁹Is it you who create it, or are We the creator?

⁶⁰We have ordained death among you, and We are not to be outmaneuvered ⁶¹from replacing you with your likes and recreating you in [a realm] you do not know. ⁶²Certainly you have known the first genesis, then why do you not take admonition?

⁶³Have you considered what you sow? ⁶⁴Is it you who make it grow, or are We the grower? ⁶⁵If We wish, We turn it into chaff, whereat you are left stunned [saying to yourselves,] ⁶⁶'We have indeed suffered loss! ⁶⁷Rather, we are [totally] deprived!'

⁶⁸Have you considered the water that you drink? ⁶⁹Is it you who bring it down from the rain cloud, or is it We who bring [it] down? ⁷⁰If We wish We can make it bitter. Then why do you not give thanks?

⁷¹Have you considered the fire that you kindle? ⁷²Was it you who caused its tree to grow, or were We the grower? ⁷³It was We who made it a reminder and a boon for the desert-dwellers.

⁷⁴So *celebrate* the Name of *your* Lord, the All-supreme.

⁷⁵I swear by the places where the stars set! ⁷⁶And indeed it is a great oath, should you know. ⁷⁷This is indeed a noble Qurʼān, ⁷⁸in a guarded Book ⁷⁹—no one touches it except the pure ones—⁸⁰sent down gradually from the Lord of all the worlds.

⁸¹What! Do you take lightly this discourse? ⁸²And make your denial of it your vocation? ⁸³So when it reaches the throat [of the

dying person], ⁸⁴and at that moment you are looking on [at his bedside] ⁸⁵—and We are nearer to him than you are, though you do not perceive—⁸⁶then why do you not restore it, if you are not subject ⁸⁷[to Divine dispensation], if you are truthful?

⁸⁸Then, if he be of those brought near,⁸⁹then ease, abundance, and a garden of bliss. ⁹⁰And if he be of the People of the Right Hand, ⁹¹[he will be told,] 'Peace be to you, from the People of the Right Hand!' ⁹²But if he be of the impugners, the astray ones, ⁹³then a treat of boiling water ⁹⁴and entry into hell. ⁹⁵This is indeed certain truth.

⁹⁶So *celebrate* the Name of *your* Lord, the All-supreme!

57. AL-ḤADĪD, IRON

In the Name of God, the All-beneficent, the All-merciful.

¹Whatever there is in the heavens and the earth glorifies God and He is the All-mighty, the All-wise. ²To Him belongs the kingdom of the heavens and the earth: He gives life and brings death, and He has power over all things.

³He is the First and the Last, the Manifest and the Hidden, and He has knowledge of all things.

57:3 "Thus says the Lord, Israel's king, the Lord Sabaoth, his redeemer: I am the first and I am the last; there is no God except me" (Isa 44:6; cf. Isa 48:12); "I am the Alpha and the Omega, the First and the Last, the Beginning and the End" (Rev 22:13; cf. Rev 1:17).

---

⁴It is He who created the heavens and the earth in six days; then settled on the Throne. He knows whatever enters the earth and whatever emerges from it and whatever descends from the heaven and whatever ascends to it, and He is with you wherever you may be, and God watches what you do.

⁵To Him belongs the kingdom of the heavens and the earth, and to God all matters are returned.

⁶He makes the night pass into the day and makes the day pass into the night, and He knows best what is in the breasts.

57:4–6 On the creation of the heavens and the earth in six days (Q 57:4), see commentary on 41:9–12 (with further references). Here (and in 7:54; 10:3; 25:59; 32:4) God "settles" (i.e., sits) on his throne after creating. Regarding this sequence, see commentary on 32:4 (with further references).

---

⁷Have faith in God and His Apostle, and spend out of that to which He has made you heirs. There is a great reward for those of you who have faith and spend [in God's way].

⁸Why should you not have faith in God when the Apostle invites you to have faith in your Lord and He has certainly made a covenant with you, if you are [genuinely] faithful?

⁹It is He who sends down manifest signs to His servant that He may bring you out of darkness into light, and indeed God is most kind and merciful to you.

¹⁰Why should you not spend in the way of God, when to God belongs the heritage of the heavens and the earth? Those of you who spent [their means] and fought before the victory are not equal [to others]. They are greater in rank than those who have spent and fought afterwards. Yet God has promised the best reward to each and God is well aware of what you do.

¹¹Who is it that will lend God a good loan, that He may multiply it for him and [that] there may be a noble reward for him?

57:10–11 The Qurʾān's discussion here (cf. 2:245; 5:12; 57:18; 64:17–18; 73:20) of giving a loan to God is close to Proverbs 19:17: "Whoever is kind to the poor is lending to the Lord who will repay him the kindness done." The notion of almsgiving as a loan given to God that will be repaid with a heavenly reward is also found with Ephrem (cr. Andrew Geist):

Your alms and prayers / are everywhere given as loans / which enrich those
who received them / while you possess the capital and the gain. / What you
have loaned out will be returned to you. / The alms of the giver / are like the
loan which a righteous one gives. / For it is entirely possessed by the one who
borrows / and by the one who lends / for it is returned to him with its gain.
(Ephrem, *Hymns to Abraham Kidunaya,* 1:7–8)

----

[12]The day *you* will see the faithful, men and women, with their
light moving swiftly in front of them and on their right, [being
greeted with the words:] 'There is good news for you today! Gardens with streams running in them, to remain in them [forever].
That is a mighty triumph.'

[13]The day the hypocrites, men and women, will say to the faithful, 'Please wait, so that we may glean something from your light!'
They will be told: 'Go back and grope for light!' Then there will
be set up between them a wall with a gate, with mercy within and
punishment without. [14]They will call out to them, 'Did we not
use to be with you?' They will say, 'Yes! But you cast yourselves
into perdition. You awaited and were skeptical, and [false] hopes
deceived you until the edict of God came, and the Deceiver deceived you concerning God. [15]Today no ransom shall be accepted
from you or the faithless. The Fire will be your abode: it is your
[ultimate] refuge and an evil destination it is.'

57:12–15 The Qurʾān here describes those who are rewarded with heaven as
those who have light. This passage might be compared to the Gospel parable of
the wise and foolish virgins (See *BEQ,* 457–58), although that parable is about
readiness for the Day of Judgment:

[1]'Then the kingdom of Heaven will be like this: Ten wedding attendants took
their lamps and went to meet the bridegroom.
[2]Five of them were foolish and five were sensible:

³the foolish ones, though they took their lamps, took no oil with them,
⁴whereas the sensible ones took flasks of oil as well as their lamps.
⁵The bridegroom was late, and they all grew drowsy and fell asleep.
⁶But at midnight there was a cry, "Look! The bridegroom! Go out and meet him."
⁷Then all those wedding attendants woke up and trimmed their lamps,
⁸and the foolish ones said to the sensible ones, "Give us some of your oil: our lamps are going out."
⁹But they replied, "There may not be enough for us and for you; you had better go to those who sell it and buy some for yourselves." (Mat 25:1–9)

On the streams of paradise (v. 12), see commentary on 2:25 (with further references).

---

¹⁶Is it not time yet for those who have faith that their hearts should be humbled for God's remembrance and toward the truth which has come down [to them], not being like those who were given the Book before? Time took its toll on them and so their hearts were hardened, and many of them are transgressors.

¹⁷Know that God revives the earth after its death. We have certainly made the signs clear for you, so that you may exercise your reason.

¹⁸Indeed, the charitable men and women and those who lend God a good loan—it shall be multiplied for them, and there will be a noble reward for them.

57:18 On the metaphor of lending to God (for a heavenly reward), see commentary on 57:10–11.

---

¹⁹Those who have faith in God and His apostles—it is they who are the truthful and the witnesses with their Lord; they shall have

their reward and their light. But as for those who are faithless and deny Our signs, they shall be the inmates of hell.

²⁰Know that the life of this world is mere diversion and play, glamour and mutual vainglory among you and rivalry for wealth and children—like rain, whose growth impresses the farmer. Then it withers and you see it turn yellow, then it becomes chaff. Whereas in the Hereafter there is forgiveness from God and His approval and a severe punishment. The life of this world is nothing but the wares of delusion.

²¹Take the lead towards forgiveness from your Lord and a paradise as vast as the heavens and the earth, prepared for those who have faith in God and His apostles. That is God's grace, which He grants to whomever He wishes, and God is dispenser of a mighty grace.

²²No affliction visits the land or yourselves but it is in a Book before We bring it about—that is indeed easy for God—²³so that you may not grieve for what escapes you, nor boast for what comes your way, and God does not like any arrogant braggart. ²⁴Such as are [themselves] stingy and bid [other] people to be stingy. And whoever refuses to comply [should know that] indeed God is the All-sufficient, the All-laudable.

²⁵Certainly We sent Our apostles with clear proofs, and We sent down with them the Book and the Balance, so that mankind may maintain justice; and We sent down iron, in which there is great might and uses for mankind, and so that God may know those who help Him and His apostles [with faith] in the Unseen. God is indeed all-strong, all-mighty.

²⁶Certainly We sent Noah and Abraham and We ordained among their descendants prophethood and the Book. Some of them are [rightly] guided, and many of them are transgressors.

57:26 On "the prophethood and the Book," see commentary on 3:79–80 (with further references).

---

²⁷Then We followed them up with Our apostles and We followed [them] with Jesus son of Mary and We gave him the Evangel, and We put kindness and mercy into the hearts of those who followed him. But as for monasticism, they innovated it—We had not prescribed it for them—only seeking God's pleasure. Yet they did not observe it with due observance. So We gave to the faithful among them their [due] reward, but many of them are transgressors.

57:27 The idea here that later followers of a prophet departed from the right path is found in two earlier verses in this Sura: 57:16, 26 (cf. 7:168). In its declaration that God placed kindness and mercy into the hearts of those who follow Jesus, the Qurʾān seems to reflect something of the spirit of the Gospels, in particular passages such as Matthew 5:7–9:

⁷Blessed are the merciful: they shall have mercy shown them.
⁸Blessed are the pure in heart: they shall see God.
⁹Blessed are the peacemakers: they shall be recognised as children of God. (Mat 5:7–9)

In this verse the Qurʾān also denies that monasticism was ordained by God. Cf. 9:34, which insists that many monks (and rabbis) are unrighteous (pace 5:82).

Tafsīr al-Jalālayn comments here that the "faithful" Christians are those who held to the Islamic teaching of Jesus and eventually believed "in our Prophet [when he came]."

---

²⁸O you who have faith! Be wary of God and have faith in His Apostle. He will grant you a double share of His mercy and

give you a light to walk by and He will forgive you, and God is all-forgiving, all-merciful; [29]so that the People of the Book may know that they do not control God's grace in any wise and that all grace is in God's hand, which He grants to whomever He wishes and God is dispenser of a mighty grace.

58. *AL-MUJĀDILA*, THE PLEADER

In the Name of God, the All-beneficent, the All-merciful.

¹God has certainly heard the speech of her who pleads with *you* about her husband and complains to God. God hears the conversation between the two of you. God is indeed all-hearing, all-seeing.

²As for those of you who repudiate their wives by *ẓihār,* they are not their mothers; their mothers are only those who bore them, and indeed they utter an outrage and lie. God is indeed all-excusing, all-forgiving.

³Those who repudiate their wives by *ẓihār* and then retract what they have said, shall set free a slave before they may touch each other. This you are advised [to carry out], and God is well aware of what you do. ⁴He who can not afford [to free a slave] shall fast for two successive months before they may touch each other. If he cannot [do so], he shall feed sixty needy persons. This, that you may have faith in God and His Apostle. These are God's bounds, and there is a painful punishment for the faithless.

58:4 The phrase which Qarai renders here as "Allah's bounds" is *ḥudūd Allāh* (cf. 2:187, 229–30; 4:13; 65:1). Here *ḥudūd* has the sense both of "limits" and "laws." It reflects the Hebrew term *ḥuqqōt* ("boundaries, statutes of God"). "You must observe my customs and keep my laws (*ḥuqqōt*), following them. 'I, the Lord, am your God.'" (Lev 18:4).

---

⁵Those who oppose God and His Apostle will indeed be subdued, just as those who passed before them were subdued. We have certainly sent down manifest signs, and there is a humiliating punishment for the faithless.

⁶The day when God will raise them all together, He will inform them about what they have done. God has kept account of it, while they have forgotten, and God is witness to all things.

⁷Have you not regarded that God knows whatever there is in the heavens and whatever there is in the earth? There does not takes place any secret talk among three, but He is their fourth [companion], nor among five but He is their sixth, nor when they are less than that or more but He is with them wherever they may be. Then He will inform them about what they have done on the Day of Resurrection. Indeed, God has knowledge of all things.

58:7 On the notion that God is present among a certain number of people one might compare Matthew 18:20: "For where two or three meet in my name, I am there among them."

---

⁸Have *you* not regarded those who were forbidden from secret talks but again resumed what they had been forbidden from, and hold secret talks [imbued] with sin and transgression and disobedience to the Apostle? And when they come to *you* they greet *you* with words with which God never greeted you and they say to themselves, 'Why does not God punish us for what we say?!' Let hell suffice them: they shall enter it, and it is an evil destination!

⁹O you who have faith! When you converse privately, do not hold private conversations [imbued] with sin and aggression [towards others' rights] and disobedience to the Apostle, but converse in [a spirit of] piety and Godfearing, and be wary of God toward whom you will be gathered.

¹⁰[Malicious] secret talks are indeed from Satan, that he may upset the faithful, but he cannot harm them in any way except by God's leave, and in God alone let all the faithful put their trust.

¹¹O you who have faith! When you are told, 'Make room,' in sittings, then do make room; God will make room for you. And when you are told, 'Rise up!' Do rise up. God will raise in rank those of you who have faith and those who have been given knowledge, and God is well aware of what you do.

58:11 "For everyone who raises himself up will be humbled, and the one who humbles himself will be raised up" (Luk 14:11).

———————

¹²O you who have faith! When you converse privately with the Apostle, offer a charity before your private talk. That is better for you and purer. But if you cannot afford [to make the offering], then God is indeed all-forgiving, all-merciful.

¹³Were you dismayed at having to offer charity before your private talks? Since you did not do it, and God has excused you [for your failure to comply], now maintain the prayer and pay the *zakāt,* and obey God and His Apostle. God is well aware of what you do.

¹⁴Have *you* not regarded those who befriend a people at whom God is wrathful? They neither belong to you, nor to them, and they swear false oaths [that they are with you] and they know.

58:14 The Qur'ān here alludes to the Jews with the phrase "a people at whom God is wrathful" (cf. 5:60; 60:13). In this the Qur'ān is following the tradition of Syriac Christian anti-Jewish polemic, found for example with Jacob of Serugh, which emphasizes the anger of God with the Jews for their rejection of Christ:

> The avenger of Jesus whom you crucified is the Lord. / He placed His hand upon you and humiliated you in all the earth. / You went up against the Son and His anger rose like smoke. / He prevented the Spirit from ever resting on your tribes. (Jacob of Serugh, *Homélies contre les juifs,* 146, homily 5, ll. 159–62)

———————

¹⁵God has prepared a severe punishment for them. Evil indeed is what they used to do.

¹⁶They make a shield of their oaths and bar [people] from the way of God; so there is a humiliating punishment for them.

¹⁷Their possessions and children will not avail them in any way against God. They shall be the inmates of the Fire and they shall remain in it [forever].

¹⁸The day when God will raise them all together, they will swear to Him just like they swear to you [now], supposing that they stand on something. Behold, they are indeed liars!

¹⁹Satan has prevailed upon them, so he has caused them to forget the remembrance of God. They are Satan's confederates. Behold, it is Satan's confederates who are indeed the losers!

²⁰Indeed, those who oppose God and His Apostle—they will be among the most abased.

²¹God has ordained: 'I shall surely prevail, I and My apostles.' God is indeed all-strong, all-mighty.

²²You will not find a people believing in God and the Last Day endearing those who oppose God and His Apostle even though they be their own parents, or children, or brothers, or kinsfolk.

[For] such, He has written faith into their hearts and strengthened them with a spirit from Him. He will admit them into gardens with streams running in them, to remain in them [forever]: God is pleased with them, and they are pleased with Him. They are God's confederates. Behold, the confederates of God are indeed felicitous!

58:22 The divine command here to have no friendship with unbelievers, even unbelieving relatives, might be compared to Matthew 10:34–37 (cf. Luk 12:49–53), which speaks of divisions within a family. However, the Gospel passage is concerned with devotion to Christ, whereas this Qur'ānic passage is concerned with solidarity among the community of believers. See also 5:51; 48:29; 64:14.

On the streams of paradise, see commentary on 2:25 (with further references).

59. *AL-ḤASHR,* THE BANISHMENT

In the Name of God, the All-beneficent, the All-merciful.

[1]Whatever there is in the heavens and whatever there is in the earth glorifies God, and He is the All-mighty, the All-wise. [2]It is He who expelled the faithless belonging to the People of the Book from their homes at the outset of [their] en masse banishment. You did not think that they would go out, and they thought their fortresses would protect them from God. But God came at them from whence they did not suppose and He cast terror into their hearts. They demolish their houses with their own hands and the hands of the faithful. So take lesson, O you who have insight!

[3]If God had not ordained banishment for them, He would have surely punished them in this world, and there is the punishment of the Fire for them in the Hereafter. [4]That is because they defied God and His Apostle; and whoever defies God, God is indeed severe in retribution. [5]Whatever palm trees you cut down or left standing on their roots, it was by God's will and in order that He may disgrace the transgressors.

[6]The spoils that God gave to His Apostle from them, you did not spur any horse for its sake nor any riding camel, but God makes His apostles prevail over whomever He wishes, and God has power over all things.

⁷The spoils that God gave to His Apostle from the people of the townships, are for God and the Apostle, the relatives and the orphans, the needy and the traveler, so that they do not circulate among the rich among you.

Take whatever the Apostle gives you, and refrain from whatever he forbids you, and be wary of God. God is indeed severe in retribution.

⁸[They are also] for the poor Emigrants who have been expelled from their homes and [wrested of] their possessions, who seek grace from God and [His] pleasure and help God and His Apostle. It is they who are the truthful.

⁹[They are as well] for those who were settled in the land and [abided] in faith before them, who love those who migrate toward them, and do not find in their breasts any need for that which is given to them, but prefer [the Immigrants] to themselves, though poverty be their own lot. Those who are saved from their own greed—it is they who are the felicitous.

¹⁰And [also for] those who came in after them, who say, 'Our Lord, forgive us and our brethren who were our forerunners in the faith, and do not put any rancour in our hearts toward the faithful. Our Lord, You are indeed most kind and merciful.'

¹¹Have *you* not regarded the hypocrites who say to their brethren, the faithless from among the People of the Book, 'If you are expelled, we will surely go out with you, and we will never obey anyone against you, and if you are fought against we will surely help you,' and God bears witness that they are indeed liars.

¹²Surely, if they are expelled they will not go out with them, and if they were fought against they will not help them, and [even if] they were to help them they will turn their backs [to flee] and eventually they will not be helped. ¹³They have indeed a greater awe of you in their hearts than of God. That is because they are a lot who do not understand.

¹⁴They will not fight against you even when united, except in fortified townships or from behind walls. Their strength is great only amongst themselves. You suppose them to be united, but their hearts are divided. That is because they are a lot who do not exercise their reason—¹⁵just like those who tasted the evil consequence of their conduct recently before them, and there is a painful punishment for them.

¹⁶[The hypocrites are] like Satan when he tells man to disbelieve, but when he disbelieves, he says, 'I am absolved of you. Indeed, I fear God, the Lord of all the worlds.'

¹⁷So the fate of both is that they will be in the Fire, to remain in it [forever]. Such is the requital of the wrongdoers.

¹⁸O you who have faith! Be wary of God and let every soul consider what it sends ahead for Tomorrow, and be wary of God. God is indeed well aware of what you do ¹⁹Do not be like those who forget God, so He makes them forget their own souls. It is they who are the transgressors.

²⁰Not equal are the inmates of the Fire and the inhabitants of paradise. It is the inhabitants of paradise who are the successful ones.

²¹Had We sent down this Qur'ān upon a mountain, *you* would have seen it humbled [and] go to pieces with the fear of God. We draw such comparisons for mankind so that they may reflect.

59:21 This verse seems to have echoes of the Gospel passages which speak of the power of prayer to move mountains:

> He answered, 'Because you have so little faith. In truth I tell you, if your faith is the size of a mustard seed you will say to this mountain, "Move from here to there," and it will move; nothing will be impossible for you.' (Mat 17:20; cf. Mat 21:21; Mar 11:23)

The Qur'ān regularly speaks of "mountains moving" as a way to illustrate the power of God. See, e.g., 13:31; 18:46; 52:10; 78:20; 81:3. This verse, however, seems to contrast with 13:31, which suggests that the *qur'ān* is unable to move mountains.

---

²²He is God—there is no god except Him—Knower of the sensible and the Unseen, He is the All-beneficent, the All-merciful.

²³He is God—there is no god except Him—the Sovereign, the All-holy, the All-benign, the Securer, the All-conserver, the All-mighty, the All-compeller and the All-magnanimous. Clear is God of any partners that they may ascribe [to Him]!

²⁴He is God, the Creator, the Maker and the Former. To Him belong the Best Names. Whatever there is in the heavens and the earth glorifies Him and He is the All-mighty, the All-wise.

59:23–24 Speyer (*BEQ,* 460) notes that the Arabic vocabulary in this list of divine praises (cf. 62:1) is close to the Hebrew turns of phrase in the *Shmoneh Esreh* (Amidah) prayer. On the Arabic word for "Former" (v. 24; i.e., "the one who shapes"), see commentary on 40:64 (with further references).

60. *AL-MUMTAḤANA*, THE WOMAN TESTED

In the Name of God, the All-beneficent, the All-merciful.

¹O you who have faith! Do not take My enemy and your enemy for allies, [secretly] offering them affection, if you have set out for *jihād* in My way and to seek My pleasure, for they have certainly denied whatever has come to you of the truth, expelling the Apostle and you because you have faith in God, your Lord. You secretly nourish affection for them, while I know well whatever you hide and whatever you disclose, and whoever among you does that has certainly strayed from the right way.

²If they were to confront you they would be your enemies, and would stretch out against you their hands and [unleash] their tongues with evil [intentions], and they are eager that you [too] should be faithless.

³Your relatives and children will not avail you on the Day of Resurrection: He will separate you [from one another], and God watches what you do.

⁴There is certainly a good exemplar for you in Abraham and those who were with him, when they said to their own people, 'We indeed repudiate you and whatever you worship besides God. We disown you, and enmity and hate have appeared between you

and us for ever, unless you come to have faith in God alone,' apart from Abraham's saying to his father, 'I will surely plead forgiveness for you, though I cannot avail you anything against God.'

[They prayed,] 'Our Lord! In You do we put our trust, to You do we turn penitently, and toward You is the destination.

60:4 Here and in other passages (Q 9:113–14; 19:47; and 26:86, where the prayer is quoted) the Qur'ān both reports that Abraham prays for his unbelieving father (named Āzar in Q 6:74, but Terah in the Bible) and qualifies that he did so only because he had promised to do so. Elsewhere (Q 9:113; cf. 11:45–46, regarding Noah) the Qur'ān instructs the believers *not* to pray for unbelievers in their family. On Abraham's confrontation with his people, see commentary on 26:69–93 (with further references).

----

⁵Our Lord! Do not make us a test for the faithless, and forgive us. Our Lord! Indeed, You are the All-mighty, the All-wise.'

⁶There is certainly a good exemplar for you in them—for those who look forward to God and the Last Day—and anyone who refuses to comply [should know that] God is indeed the All-sufficient, the All-laudable.

⁷It may be that God will bring about comity between you and those with whom you are at enmity, and God is all-powerful, and God is all-forgiving, all-merciful.

⁸God does not forbid you from dealing with kindness and justice with those [polytheists] who did not make war against you on account of religion and did not expel you from your homes. God indeed loves the just. ⁹God forbids you only in regard to those who made war against you on account of religion and expelled you from your homes and supported [the Makkans] in your expulsion, that you make friends with them, and whoever makes friends with them—it is they who are the wrongdoers.

¹⁰O you who have faith! When faithful women come to you as immigrants, test them. God knows best [the state of] their faith. Then, if you ascertain them to be [genuinely] faithful, do not send them back to the faithless. They are not lawful for them, nor are they lawful for them, but give them what they have spent [for dowry]. There is no sin upon you in marrying them when you have given them their dowries. Do not hold on to [conjugal] ties with faithless women. Demand [from the infidels] what you have spent [for dowry], and let the faithless demand [from you] what they have spent [as dowries]. That is God's judgment; He judges between you, and God is all-knowing, all-wise.

¹¹If anything [of the dowries] pertaining to your wives is not reclaimed from the faithless and then you have your turn, then give to those whose wives have left the like of what they have spent, and be wary of God in whom you have faith.

¹²O Prophet! If faithful women come to *you* to take the oath of allegiance to *you,* [pledging] that they shall not ascribe any partners to God, that they shall not steal, nor commit adultery, nor kill their children, nor produce a lie that they may have hatched between their hands and feet, nor disobey *you* in what is right, then *accept* their allegiance and *plead* for them to God for forgiveness. God is indeed all-forgiving, all-merciful

¹³O you who have faith! Do not befriend a people at whom God is wrathful: they have despaired of the Hereafter just as the faithless have despaired of the occupants of the graves.

60:13 The "people at whom God is wrathful" seems to be an allusion to the Jews. On this see commentary on 58:14.

61. *AL-ṢAFF*, RANKS

In the Name of God, the All-beneficent, the All-merciful.

[1]Whatever there is in the heavens and the earth glorifies God, and He is the All-mighty, the All-wise.

[2]O you who have faith! Why do you say what you do not do? [3]It is greatly outrageous to God that you should say what you do not do.

[4]God indeed loves those who fight in His way in ranks, as if they were a compact structure.

[5]When Moses said to his people, 'O my people! Why do you torment me, when you certainly know that I am God's apostle to you?' So when they swerved [from the right path], God made their hearts swerve, and God does not guide the transgressing lot.

61:5 The Qur'ān may be alluding here to the infidelity of the Israelites who forged the golden calf (see Exo 32, Deu 9).

---

[6]And when Jesus son of Mary said, 'O Children of Israel! I am indeed the apostle of God to you, to confirm what is before me of the Torah and to give good news of an apostle who will come

after me, whose name is Aḥmad.' But when he brought them clear proofs, they said, 'This is plain magic.'

61:6 Inasmuch as this verse seems to have Jesus predict the coming of Muḥammad (Aḥmad might be another form of Muḥammad, or perhaps a second epithet for the Prophet, whose proper name is never given), it is close to 2:129, which has Abraham pray for a prophet to be raised up, and 7:157, which insists that the Qur'ān's Prophet is found in the books of the Jews and the Christians. Some Muslim scholars (e.g., Yusuf Ali in his Qur'ān translation) connect the prediction in this verse with the promise of Jesus in the Gospel of John to send the Paraclete (Joh 14:16; cf. Joh 14:26; 15:26; 16:7), although John has Jesus explicitly (Joh 14:26) identify the Paraclete as the Holy Spirit.

The attribution of Jesus' miracles to magic (cf. 5:110) is perhaps connected to reports in the Babylonian Talmud (*Sanhedrin* 107b; *Sotah* 47a; certain manuscripts of *Sanhedrin* 107b include a report that: "Jesus the Nazarene practiced magic and led Israel astray"). Note, however, that other prophets in the Qur'ān, including Moses (and in some cases Aaron too: 10:76–81; 20:57–71; 26:35; 27:13; 28:36, 48; cf. 34:43) and perhaps Muḥammad (46:7; 74:24) are accused of magic.

---

⁷Who is a greater wrongdoer than him who fabricates lies against God while he is being summoned to Islam? And God does not guide the wrongdoing lot. ⁸They desire to put out the light of God with their mouths, but God will perfect His light, though the faithless should be averse. ⁹It is He who has sent His Apostle with guidance and the true religion that He may make it prevail over all religions though the polytheists should be averse.

¹⁰O you who have faith! Shall I show you a deal that will deliver you from a painful punishment? ¹¹Have faith in God and His Apostle and wage *jihād* in the way of God with your persons and possessions. That is better for you, should you know.

¹²He will forgive your sins and admit you into gardens with streams running in them, and into good dwellings in the Gardens of Eden. That is the great success.

61:10–12 On the Qur'ān's description of fighting the holy war as a "deal" (Ar. *tijāra;* v. 10) to be made with God, see commentary on 9:111 (with further references).

On the streams of paradise see commentary on 2:25 (with further references). On the Qur'ān's identification of paradise as the "Garden of Eden" see commentary on 9:72 (with further references).

---

¹³And other [blessings] besides which you cherish: help from God and a victory near at hand, and *give* good news to the faithful.

¹⁴O you who have faith! Be God's helpers, just as Jesus son of Mary said to his disciples, 'Who will be my helpers for God's sake?' The Disciples said, 'We will be God's helpers!' So a group of the Children of Israel believed, and a group disbelieved. Then We strengthened the faithful against their enemies and they came to prevail [over them].

61:14 This verse (cf. Exo 32:26), which is closely related to 3:52–54, reflects not so much anything in the Gospels but the perspective of later Christians, according to which Christians enjoyed good fortune (with the Christianization of the Roman Empire) because they accepted Jesus as the Christ, while Jews suffered misfortunes because they rejected him. This can be seen, for example, with Jacob of Serugh:

> The Cross, O Jew, is the cause of all of your humiliation; / the more that you refuse [it], the more as well you will be humiliated in all of the Earth. / Before the Cross what other people were like you on the face of the earth? / And since it what people are despised like you? (Jacob of Serugh, *Homélies contre les juifs,* 142, homily 5, ll. 105–8)

On the division of the Israelites into "groups" (Ar. *ṭā'ifa*), see commentary on 3:105.

62. *AL-JUMUʿA*, THE DAY OF CONGREGATION

In the Name of God, the All-beneficent, the All-merciful.

¹Whatever there is in the heavens and whatever there is in the earth glorifies God, the Sovereign, the All-holy, the All-mighty, the All-wise.

62:1 See commentary on 59:23–24.

---

²It is He who sent to the unlettered [people] an apostle from among themselves, to recite to them His signs, to purify them, and to teach them the Book and wisdom, and earlier they had indeed been in manifest error.

62:2 On the "book and wisdom," see commentary on 3:48 (with further references). *Tafsīr al-Jalālayn* describes the "unlettered" [people] as "the Arabs"; the relevant term here (Ar. *ummiyyīn*) means "gentiles," that is, any people who have not yet received divine revelation. See commentary on 2:78–79 (with further references).

As Mehdy Shaddel argues ("Qurʾānic Ummī"), this verse is closely related to 2:129, where Abraham and Ishmael pray for a messenger to be raised up from their descendants (and 2:128, where they ask God to make their descendants into a community, *umma*).

---

³And to others from among them [as well] who have not yet joined them, and He is the All-mighty, the All-wise. ⁴That is God's grace which He grants to whomever He wishes, and God is dispenser of a mighty grace.

⁵The example of those who were charged with the Torah, then failed to carry it, is that of an ass carrying books. Evil is the example of the people who deny God's signs, and God does not guide the wrongdoing lot.

62:5 Both Speyer (*BEQ,* 461) and Geiger (*Judaism and Islam,* 71) connect this metaphor to a Hebrew saying: "a donkey carrying books." Horovitz ("Jewish Proper Names," 209) thinks the expression originates with the Qurʾān and was borrowed by Jewish sources. El-Badawi (*Aramaic Gospel Traditions,* 128), argues that the polemic here is directed against Jewish scribes. He connects the expression "a donkey carrying books (Ar. *asfār*)" with the condemnation of scribes (Sy. *sāfrē*) in Matthew 23:13ff.

Tafsīr al-Jalālayn and Muhammad Asad insist that the failure of the Israelites referred to here involves their failure to recognize the predictions of Muḥammad in the Torah.

---

⁶*Say,* 'O Jews! If you claim that you are God's favourites to the exclusion of other people, then long for death if you are truthful.' ⁷Yet they will never long for it, because of what their hands have sent ahead, and God knows best the wrongdoers.

⁸*Say,* 'The death that you flee will indeed encounter you. Then you will be returned to the Knower of the sensible and the Unseen and He will inform you about what you used to do.'

62:6–8 The Qurʾān here criticizes the Jews for their self-identification as a chosen people (cf. Exo 19:5–6; Deu 7:6; 14:2; see commentary on 44:32, with further references). It also insists that the Jews should long for death (cf. 22:15; since people chosen by God would go to paradise after death). That they do not do so is a sign that they are conscious of their own wrongdoing and fear that they will be condemned to hell.

---

⁹O you who have faith! When the call is made for prayer on Friday, hurry toward the remembrance of God and leave all business. That is better for you, should you know. ¹⁰And when the prayer is finished disperse through the land and seek God's grace, and remember God much so that you may be felicitous.

¹¹When they sight a deal or a diversion, they scatter off towards it and leave *you* standing! *Say,* 'What is with God is better than diversion and dealing, and God is the best of providers.'

63. *AL-MUNĀFIQŪN*, THE HYPOCRITES

In the Name of God, the All-beneficent, the All-merciful.

¹When the hypocrites come to *you* they say, 'We bear witness that *you* are indeed the apostle of God.' God knows that *you* are indeed His Apostle, and God bears witness that the hypocrites are indeed liars.

63:1 The Qur'ān refers frequently to "hypocrites" (Ar. *munāfiqūn* and *alladhīna nāfaqū;* see index under "hypocrites"). According to Islamic tradition the hypocrites were a coherent, organized group of pseudo-Muslims in Medina. In some cases, however, the Qur'ān seems to refer more generally to anyone who feigns belief in its Prophet as a "hypocrite." The Qur'ān's interest in the category of "hypocrites" might be compared to Jesus' polemic against "hypocrites" in the Synoptic Gospels (Mat 6:2, 5, 16; Mat 22:18; 23:13, 15, 23, 25, 27, 28; 24:51; Luk 12:56; 13:15). Of particular note is Mark 7:6 (cf. Mat 15:7–8), "How rightly Isaiah prophesied about you hypocrites in the passage of scripture: 'This people honours me only with lip-service, while their hearts are far from me'" (quoting Isa 29:13).

---

²They make a shield of their oaths and bar from the way of God. Evil indeed is what they have been doing.

³That is because they believed and then disbelieved, so their hearts were sealed. Hence they do not understand.

⁴When you see them, their bodies impress you, and if they speak, *you* listen to their speech. Yet they are like dry logs set reclining [against a wall]. They suppose every cry is directed against them. They are the enemy, so beware of them. May God assail them, where do they stray?!

⁵When they are told, 'Come, that God's Apostle may plead for forgiveness for you,' they twist their heads and *you* see them turn away disdainfully. ⁶It is the same for them whether *you* plead for forgiveness for them, or do not plead for forgiveness for them: God will never forgive them. Indeed, God does not guide the transgressing lot.

⁷They are the ones who say, 'Do not spend on those who are with the Apostle of God until they scatter off [from around him].' Yet to God belong the treasuries of the heavens and the earth, but the hypocrites do not understand.

⁸They say, 'When we return to the city, the mighty will surely expel the weak from it.' Yet all might belongs to God and His Apostle and the faithful, but the hypocrites do not know.

⁹O you who have faith! Do not let your possessions and children distract you from the remembrance of God, and whoever does that—it is they who are the losers.

¹⁰Spend out of what We have provided you before death comes to any of you, whereat he might say, 'My Lord, why did You not respite me for a short time so that I could have given charity and become one of the righteous!' ¹¹But God will never respite anyone when his time has come, and God is well aware of what you do.

64. *AL-TAGHĀBUN*, DISPOSSESSION

In the Name of God, the All-beneficent, the All-merciful.

¹Whatever there is in the heavens and whatever there is in the earth glorifies God. To Him belongs all sovereignty and to Him belongs all praise, and He has power over all things. ²It is He who created you. Then some of you are faithless and some of you are faithful, and God watches what you do.

³He created the heavens and the earth with consummate wisdom, and He formed you and perfected your forms, and toward Him is your destination.

64:3 On the Arabic word for "formed" (*ṣawwara*), see commentary on 40:64 (with further references).

---

⁴He knows whatever there is in the heavens and the earth, and He knows whatever you hide and whatever you disclose, and God knows best what is in your breasts.

⁵Has there not come to you the account of those who were faithless before? They tasted the evil consequence of their conduct,

and there is a painful punishment for them. ⁶That was because their apostles would bring them clear proofs, but they said, 'Will humans be our guides?!' So they disbelieved and turned away, and God had no need [of their faith] and God is all-sufficient, all-laudable.

⁷The faithless claim that they will not be resurrected. *Say*, 'Yes, by my Lord, you will surely be resurrected; then you will surely be informed of what you did, and that is easy for God.'

⁸So have faith in God and His Apostle and the light which We have sent down, and God is well aware of what you do.

⁹When He will bring you together for the Day of Gathering, it will be a day of privation [and regret]. As for those who have faith in God and act righteously, He will absolve them of their misdeeds and admit them into gardens with streams running in them, to remain in them forever. That is a mighty triumph.

64:9 Our the streams of paradise, see commentary on 2:25 (with further references).

---

¹⁰But as for those who are faithless and deny Our signs, they will be the inmates of the Fire, to remain in it [forever], and it is an evil destination.

¹¹No affliction visits [anyone] except by God's leave. Whoever has faith in God, He guides his heart, and God has knowledge of all things.

¹²Obey God and obey the Apostle; but if you turn away, Our Apostle's duty is only to communicate in clear terms.

¹³God—there is no god except Him—in God alone let all the faithful put their trust.

¹⁴O you who have faith! You have indeed enemies among your spouses and children, so beware of them. Yet if you excuse, forbear and forgive, then God is indeed all-forgiving, all-merciful. ¹⁵Your possessions and children are only a test, and God—with Him is a great reward! ¹⁶So be wary of God as much as you can, and listen and obey, and spend [in the way of God]; that is better for yourselves. Those who are saved from their own greed—it is they who are the felicitous. ¹⁷If you lend God a good loan, He shall multiply it for you and forgive you, and God is all-appreciative, all-forbearing,

64:16–17 The Qur'ān here describes the money which one spends in a religious cause (v. 16) as a loan one gives to God (v. 17). This description reflects both Jewish and Christian language on almsgiving. See further commentary on 57:10–11 (with further references).

---

¹⁸Knower of the sensible and the Unseen, the All-mighty, the All-wise.

65. *AL-ṬALĀQ,* DIVORCE

In the Name of God, the All-beneficent, the All-merciful.

¹O Prophet! When you divorce women, divorce them at [the conclusion of] their term and calculate the term, and be wary of God, your Lord. Do not turn them out from their homes, nor shall they go out, unless they commit a gross indecency. These are God's bounds, and whoever transgresses the bounds of God certainly wrongs himself. You never know, maybe God will bring off something new later on.

65:1 On the Biblical connection with the expression "God's bounds" (*ḥudūd Allāh*), see commentary on 58:4 (with further references).

---

²Then, when they have completed their term, either retain them honourably or separate from them honourably, and take the witness of two honest men from among yourselves, and bear witness for the sake of God. Whoever believes in God and the Last Day is advised to [comply with] this. Whoever is wary of God, He shall make for him a way out [of the adversities of the world and the Hereafter] ³and provide for him from whence he does not count

upon. Whoever puts his trust in God, He will suffice him. Indeed, God carries through His commands. Certainly God has ordained a measure [and extent] for everything.

⁴As for those of your wives who have ceased having menses—[or] if you have any doubts [concerning its cause, whether it is age or something else]—their term [of waiting] and of those who have not yet had menses, shall be three months. As for those who are pregnant, their term shall be until they deliver. And whoever is wary of God, He shall grant him ease in his affairs.

65:4 As Geiger notes (*Judaism and Islam,* 69), the notion of waiting three months (cf. 2:228) before a woman might remarry has a basis in the Talmud (m. Yevamot 4:10).

---

⁵That is God's ordinance which He has sent down to you, and whoever is wary of God, He shall absolve him of his misdeeds and give him a great reward.

⁶House them where you live, in accordance with your means, and do not harass them to put them in straits, and should they be pregnant, maintain them until they deliver. If they suckle [the baby] for you, give them their wages and consult together honourably. But if you make things difficult for each other, then another woman will suckle [the baby] for him.

⁷Let the affluent man spend out of his affluence, and let he whose provision has been tightened spend out of what God has given him. God does not task any soul except [according to] what He has given it. God will bring about ease after hardship.

⁸How many a town defied the command of its Lord and His apostles, then We called it to a severe account and punished it with a dire punishment. ⁹So it tasted the evil consequences of its

conduct, and the outcome of its conduct was ruin. ¹⁰God has prepared for them a severe punishment.

So be wary of God, O you who possess intellect and have faith!
God has already sent down to you a reminder, ¹¹an apostle reciting to you the manifest signs of God, that He may bring out
those who have faith and do righteous deeds from darkness into
light. And whoever has faith in God and does righteous deeds,
He shall admit him into gardens with streams running in them, to
remain in them forever. God has certainly granted him an excellent provision.

65:11 On the streams of paradise, see commentary on 2:25 (with further
references).

———————

¹²It is God who has created seven heavens, and of the earth
[a number] similar to them. The command gradually descends
through them, that you may know that God has power over all
things, and that God comprehends all things in knowledge.

65:12 On the Arabic term Qarai renders as "command" (*amr*), see commentary on 42:52 (with further references). On the creation of seven heavens, see
commentary on 67:3 (with further references).

66. *AL-TAHRĪM*, THE FORBIDDING

In the Name of God, the All-beneficent, the All-merciful.

¹O Prophet! Why do *you* disallow [yourself] what God has made lawful for *you,* seeking to please *your* wives? And God is all-forgiving, all-merciful. ²God has certainly made lawful for you the dissolution of your oaths, and God is your Master and He is the All-knowing, the All-wise.

³When the Prophet confided a matter to one of his wives, but when she divulged it [instead of keeping the secret] and God disclosed that to him, he apprised [her] of part of the matter and ignored part of it. So when he told her about it, she said, 'Who informed you about it?' He said, 'The All-knowing and the All-aware has informed me.'

⁴If the two of you repent to God . . . for your hearts have certainly swerved, and if you back each other against him, then [know that] God is indeed his protector, and his supporters are Gabriel, the righteous among the faithful and, thereafter, the angels.

⁵It may be that if he divorces you his Lord will give him, in [your] stead, wives better than you: [such as are] *muslim,* faithful, obedient, penitent, devout and given to fasting, virgins and non-virgins.

⁶O you who have faith! Save yourselves and your families from a Fire whose fuel will be people and stones, over which are [assigned] severe and mighty angels, who do not disobey whatever God commands them and carry out what they are commanded. ⁷[They will call out to the faithless:] 'O faithless ones! Do not make any excuses today. You are being requited only for what you used to do.'

⁸O you who have faith! Repent to God with sincere repentance! Maybe your Lord will absolve you of your misdeeds and admit you into gardens with streams running in them, on the day when God will not let down the Prophet and the faithful who are with him. Their light will move swiftly before them and on their right. They will say, 'Our Lord! Perfect our light for us and forgive us! Indeed, You have power over all things.'

66:8 On the streams of paradise, see commentary on 2:25 (with further references).

———————

⁹O Prophet! Wage *jihād* against the faithless and the hypocrites and be severe with them. Their refuge will be hell, and it is an evil destination.

¹⁰God cites an example of the faithless: the wife of Noah and the wife of Lot. They were under two of our righteous servants, yet they betrayed them. So they did not avail them in any way against God, and it was said [to them], 'Enter the Fire, along with those who enter [it].'

66:10 Here the Qurʾān presents the wives of Noah and Lot as examples of unfaithful women. *Tafsīr al-Jalālayn* explains: "Noah's wife, called Wāhila, used to say to his people that he was a madman, while Lot's wife, called Wāʿila, used to tell his people the whereabouts of his guests when they stayed with him, at night by lighting a fire, and during the day by making smoke."

Noah and Lot are presented in parallel in 2 Peter 2 (see commentary on 29:28–35). It could be that the Qur'ān has extended this parallelism by making Noah's wife unfaithful in a way similar to Lot's wife, who is destroyed for disobeying the command of an angel (cf. Q 7:83; 11:81; 15:59–60; 26:170–71; 27:57; 29:32–33; 37:134–135):

> [17]When they had brought him outside, he was told, 'Flee for your life. Do not look behind you or stop anywhere on the plain. Flee to the hills or you will be swept away.'
>
> . . .
>
> [26]But Lot's wife looked back, and was turned into a pillar of salt. (Gen 19:17, 26)

However, it is important to note that already in the pre-Islamic period certain groups had developed hostile legends regarding Noah's wife. In his *Panarion* (2:26), Epiphanius (d. 403) relates how the Gnostics held that the wife of Noah (whom they named Nuria) was not allowed to join Noah in the ark after she burned it down on three occasions (the name Nuria is a play on the Syriac word *nūrā*, for "fire"—Epiphanius relates that the Greek version of her name is Pyrrha). See *The Panarion of Epiphanius*, 90–91. See also Speyer, *BEQ,* 109, n. 2. On Noah and his family (including his unfaithful son), see further commentary on 11:40–48.

———————

[11]God cites an example for the faithful: the wife of Pharaoh, when she said, 'My Lord! Build me a home near You in paradise and deliver me from Pharaoh and his conduct, and deliver me from the wrongdoing lot.' [12]And Mary, daughter of Imran, who guarded the chastity of her womb, so We breathed into it of Our spirit. She confirmed the words of her Lord and His Books, and she was one of the obedient.

66:11–12 Verse 11 should be compared to 28:9, in which Pharaoh's wife (unlike Exo 2:5–10, which has the daughter of Pharaoh adopt Moses) suggests to her husband that they adopt Moses. The juxtaposition of Pharaoh's wife (adopted mother of Moses) and Mary (mother of Jesus) in these two verses presumably reflects an interest in finding two righteous women to match the two unrighteous women of verse 10. It also seems to follow from the parallelism between the mother of Moses and the mother of Jesus seen in the writings, for example, of the Syriac father Jacob of Serugh:

> What prophet is like Moses, if not our Lord / the one whom Moses prefigured in each step of his journey. / Moses chose an adopted mother and made her his mother / and in the same way Christ chose as his mother a daughter of the poor. / When Moses was born and his birth completed / he acquired a mother to be like Mary, mother of the Son. (Jacob of Serugh, *Homélies contre les juifs*, 57, homily 1, ll. 179–84)

The declaration that Mary "confirmed [*ṣaddaqat*] the words of her Lord" might follow from her response to the annunciation in Luke 1 (e.g., Luk 1:38: "Mary said, 'You see before you the Lord's servant, let it happen to me as you have said'"). Note also 5:75, where Mary is named *ṣiddīqa* (see commentary on that verse). On Mary as "daughter of ʿImrān," see commentary on 3:33. On Mary's guarding her chastity, and conceiving Jesus through the spirit of God, note the (almost) parallel passage 21:91. In 21:91 the Qurʾān has God breathe his spirit into "her" (*fīhā*), but here into "him" or "it" (*fīhi*). Note also that in 4:171 the Qurʾān refers to Jesus as a spirit from God.

On the wife of Pharaoh *Tafsīr al-Jalālayn* relates the following tradition: "She believed in Moses, her name was Āsiya; Pharaoh chastised her by tying her hands and feet to pegs and placing a huge millstone on her chest, and having her laid out in the sun; but when those in charge of her would leave her, the angels would [come to] shade her."

67. *AL-MULK*, SOVEREIGNTY

In the Name of God, the All-beneficent, the All-merciful.

¹Blessed is He in whose hands is all sovereignty and He has power over all things. ²He, who created death and life that He may test you [to see] which of you is best in conduct. And He is the All-mighty, the All-forgiving. ³He created seven heavens in layers. You do not see any discordance in the creation of the All-beneficent. Look again! Do you see any flaw?

67:3 The notion of seven heavens (v. 12) is found in both Jewish (e.g., *BT, Ḥagīgā,* 12b) and Christian traditions. A reflection of this notion may be found in 2 Corinthians 12:2; among the church fathers, Irenaeus (*Proof of the Apostolic Preaching* 9) teaches this explicitly. The Qurʾānic imagery of seven heavens is connected to a cosmology with seven planetary spheres (see 78:12). In the *Ascension of Isaiah,* a composite text extant in Ethiopic with Jewish origins but redacted by Christians, Isaiah travels to the seventh heaven, where he sees Enoch:

> And he took me up into the seventh heaven, and there I saw a wonderful light, and also angels without number. And there I saw all the righteous from the time of Adam onwards. And there I saw the holy Abel and all the righteous. And there I saw Enoch and all who were with him. (*Ascension of Isaiah,* 9:6–9a)

On the seven heavens, cf. 2:29; 17:44; 41:12; 65:12; 71:15; 78:12.

⁴Look again once more. Your look will return to you humbled and weary.

⁵We have certainly adorned the lowest heaven with lamps and made them [the means of pelting] missiles against the devils, and We have prepared for them punishment of the Blaze.

67:5 On the stars as barriers to heaven, and on Qurʾānic cosmology generally, see commentary on 15:16–18 (with further references).

⁶For those who defy their Lord is the punishment of hell, and it is an evil destination. ⁷When they are thrown in it they hear it blaring, as it seethes, ⁸almost exploding with rage. Whenever a group is thrown in it, its keepers will ask them, 'Did not any warner come to you?' ⁹They will say, 'Yes, a warner did come to us, but we impugned [him] and said, 'God did not send down anything; you are only in great error.' ¹⁰They will say, 'Had we listened or exercised our reason, we would not have been among inmates of the Blaze.' ¹¹Thus they will admit their sin. So away with the inmates of the Blaze!

¹²Indeed, for those who fear their Lord in secret there will be forgiveness and a great reward.

¹³Speak secretly, or do so openly, indeed He knows well what is in the breasts. ¹⁴Would He who has created not know? And He is the All-attentive, the All-aware.

¹⁵It is He who made the earth tractable for you; so walk on its flanks and eat of His provision, and towards Him is the resurrection.

¹⁶Are you secure that He who is in the heaven will not make the earth swallow you while it quakes?

¹⁷Are you secure that He who is in the heaven will not unleash upon you a rain of stones? Soon you will know how My warning has been!

¹⁸Certainly those who were before them had impugned [My apostles]; but then how was My rebuttal!

¹⁹Have they not regarded the birds above them, spreading and closing their wings? No one sustains them except the All-beneficent. He indeed watches all things.

²⁰Who is it that is your host who may help you, besides the All-beneficent? The faithless only dwell in delusion.

²¹Who is it that may provide for you if He withholds His provision? Indeed, they persist in defiance and aversion.

²²Is he who walks prone on his face better guided, or he who walks upright on a straight path?

²³*Say,* 'It is He who created you and invested you with hearing, sight, and the hearts. Little do you thank.'

²⁴*Say,* 'It is He who created you on the earth, and toward Him you will be mustered.'

²⁵They say, 'When will this promise be fulfilled, if you are truthful?'

²⁶*Say,* 'Its knowledge is only with God; I am only a manifest warner.'

²⁷When they see it brought near, the countenances of the faithless will be contorted, and [they will be] told, 'This is what you had been asking for!'

²⁸*Say,* 'Tell me, [irrespective of] whether God destroys me and those who are with me, or He has mercy on us, who will shelter the faithless from a painful punishment?'

^{29}*Say,* 'He is the All-beneficent; we have faith in Him, and in Him do we trust. Soon you will know who is in plain error.'

^{30}*Say,* 'Tell me, should your water sink down [into the ground], who will bring you running water?'

68. *AL-QALAM,* THE PEN

In the Name of God, the All-beneficent, the All-merciful.

¹*Nūn.* By the Pen and what they write: ²by *your* Lord's blessing *you* are not crazy, ³and *yours* indeed will be an everlasting reward, ⁴and indeed *you* possess a great character. ⁵*You* will see and they will see, ⁶which one of you is crazy. ⁷Indeed, *your* Lord knows best those who stray from His way, and He knows best those who are guided.

⁸So *do not obey* the deniers, ⁹who are eager that *you* should be flexible, so that they [too] may be flexible [towards *you*]. ¹⁰And *do not obey* any vile swearer, ¹¹scandal-monger, talebearer, ¹²hinderer of all good, sinful transgressor, ¹³callous and, on top of that, baseborn ¹⁴—[who behaves thus only] because he has wealth and children. ¹⁵When Our signs are recited to him, he says, 'Myths of the ancients!'

68:15 The expression "myths of the ancients" is a translation of Arabic *asāṭīr al-awwalīn* (cf. 6:25; 8:31; 16:24; 23:83; 25:5; 27:68; 46:17; 83:13). *Asāṭir* is likely derived from Syriac *ashṭārā,* "deed, document." The way the Qurʾān has its opponents refer to the monotheistic preaching of its Prophet as ancient myths seems to belie the traditional image of the Meccans as pagans, children of pagans. It suggests that the ideas of monotheism and resurrection of the body had long been discussed in the Qur'ān's context.

---

¹⁶Soon We shall brand him on his snout.

¹⁷We have indeed tested them just as We tested the People of the Garden when they vowed they would gather its fruit at dawn,

---

68:17–33 *overview* This passage might be compared to the parables in Q 3:117, 18:32–44, and 36:13–29. As Neuwirth notes (*Der Koran: Band 1,* 576), it also seems to have a close relationship with Luke:

¹⁶Then he told them a parable, 'There was once a rich man who, having had a good harvest from his land,

¹⁷thought to himself, "What am I to do? I have not enough room to store my crops."

¹⁸Then he said, "This is what I will do: I will pull down my barns and build bigger ones, and store all my grain and my goods in them,

¹⁹and I will say to my soul: My soul, you have plenty of good things laid by for many years to come; take things easy, eat, drink, have a good time."

²⁰But God said to him, "Fool! This very night the demand will be made for your soul; and this hoard of yours, whose will it be then?"

²¹So it is when someone stores up treasure for himself instead of becoming rich in the sight of God.' (Luk 12:16–21)

---

¹⁸and they did not make any exception. ¹⁹Then a visitation from *your* Lord visited it while they were asleep. ²⁰So by dawn it was like a harvested field.

²¹At dawn they called out to one another, ²²'Get off early to your field if you have to gather [the fruits].'

²³So off they went, whispering to one another: ²⁴'Today no needy man shall come to you in it.' ²⁵They set out early morning [considering themselves] able to deprive [the poor of its fruit].

²⁶But when they saw it, they said, 'We have indeed lost our way!' ²⁷'No, it is we who have been deprived!'

²⁸The most upright among them said, 'Did I not tell you, "Why do you not glorify [God]?"' ²⁹They said, 'Immaculate is our Lord! We have indeed been wrongdoers!' ³⁰Then they turned to one another, blaming each other. ³¹They said, 'Woe to us! Indeed, we have been rebellious. ³²Maybe our Lord will give us a better one in its place. Indeed, we earnestly beseech our Lord.'

³³Such was their punishment, and the punishment of the Hereafter is surely greater, had they known.

³⁴For the Godwary there will indeed be gardens of bliss near their Lord.

³⁵Shall We treat those who submit [to Us] like [We treat] the guilty? ³⁶What is the matter with you? How do you judge! ³⁷Do you possess a scripture in which you read ³⁸that you shall have in it whatever you choose? ³⁹Do you have a pledge binding on Us until the Day of Resurrection that you shall indeed have whatever you decide? ⁴⁰*Ask* them, which of them will aver [any of] that! ⁴¹Do they have any 'partners' [that they claim for God]? Then let them produce their partners, if they are truthful.

⁴²The day when the catastrophe occurs and they are called to prostrate themselves, they will not be able [to do it]. ⁴³With a humbled look [in their eyes], they will be overcast by abasement. Certainly they were called to prostrate themselves while they were yet sound.

⁴⁴So *leave* Me with those who deny this discourse. We will draw them imperceptibly [into ruin] whence they do not know. ⁴⁵I will grant them respite, for My devising is indeed sure.

⁴⁶Do *you* ask them for a reward, so that they are weighed down with debt?

68:46 On the idea that a true prophet does not seek a reward, see commentary on 34:47 (with further references).

---

⁴⁷Do they possess [access to] the Unseen, so that they write it down?

⁴⁸So *submit patiently* to the judgement of *your* Lord, and do not be like the Man of the Fish who called out as he choked with grief. ⁴⁹Had it not been for a blessing that came to his rescue from his Lord, he would surely have been cast on the bare shore, being blameworthy. ⁵⁰So his Lord chose him and made him one of the righteous.

68:48–50 The phrase "Man of the Fish" is recognizable as an allusion to Jonah, who calls out to God from the belly of the great fish, repenting of his previous disobedience (cf. Jonah 2:3). Because of his repentance God rescues him from the fish. The way the Qur'ān emphasizes God's role in rescuing Jonah and using him as an instrument might be compared to Ephrem:

> The High One answered the sunken ship / for the sunken ship was all of the penitents. / He answered at sea; He answers on land. / He rescued on land as at sea. / Jonah's voice became a medicine of life. / He sowed death with it, but life sprouted. (Ephrem, *Hymns,* hymn 49, ll. 19–21)

On Jonah, see also commentary on 37:139–48 (with further references).

---

⁵¹Indeed, the faithless almost devour *you* with their eyes when they hear this Reminder, and they say, 'He is indeed crazy.' ⁵²Yet it is just a reminder for all the nations.

69. AL-ḤĀQQA, THE BESIEGER

In the Name of God, the All-beneficent, the All-merciful.

¹The Besieger! ²What is the Besieger?! ³What will show you what is the Besieger?! ⁴Thamūd and ʿĀd denied the Cataclysm. ⁵As for Thamūd, they were destroyed by the Cry. ⁶And as for ʿĀd, they were destroyed by a fierce icy gale, ⁷which He clamped upon them for seven gruelling nights and eight days, so that you could see the people there lying about prostrate, as if they were hollow trunks of palm trees.

⁸So do you see any remaining trace of them?

⁹Then Pharaoh and those who were before him, and the towns that were overturned, brought about iniquity.

69:9 On the account of Moses and Pharaoh in the Qur'ān, see commentary on 20:9–16 (with further references). The phrase "towns that were overturned" is an allusion to the cities, including Sodom and Gomorrah, which God destroyed in the time of Lot. See commentary on 53:53 (with further references).

¹⁰They disobeyed the apostle of their Lord, so He seized them with a terrible seizing.

¹¹Indeed, when the Flood rose high, We carried you in a floating ark, ¹²that We might make it a reminder for you and that receptive ears might remember it.

69:11–12 On Noah in the Qur'ān, see 71:1–28 (with further references).

———————

¹³When the Trumpet is blown with a single blast

69:13 On the trumpet blast, see commentary on 78:18 (with further references).

———————

¹⁴and the earth and the mountains are lifted and levelled with a single leveling, ¹⁵then, on that day, will the Imminent [Hour] befall ¹⁶and the heaven will be split open—for it will be frail on that day—¹⁷with the angels all over it, and the Throne of *your* Lord will be borne that day by eight [angels].

69:17 The imagery of angels who surround the throne of God (Q 39:75; 40:7) is common in the Book of Revelation (e.g., Rev 5:11), yet here (and 40:7) the Qur'ān speaks of angels who *carry* the throne, an idea alluded to by Ezekiel (e.g., Eze 10:1: "Then, in vision I saw that above the solid surface over the heads of the winged creatures there was above them something like sapphire, which seemed to be like a throne"). On the throne of God generally, cf. 7:54; 10:3; 11:7; 13:2; 17:42; 20:5; 23:86, 116; 25:59; 32:4; 57:4. On angels' surrounding the throne of God, cf. 39:75; on angels' carrying the throne of God, cf. 40:7.

The Qur'ān likely chooses eight as the number of angels who bear the throne because the Arabic (*thamāniya*) rhymes with the verses that precede and follow it (although it is possible that there is some connection with the eight days of punishment mentioned in v. 7).

[18]That day you will be presented [before your Lord]: none of your secrets will remain hidden. [19]As for him who is given his book in his right hand, he will say, 'Here, take and read my book! [20]I indeed knew that I will encounter my account [of deeds].'

[21]So he will have a pleasant life, [22]in an elevated garden, [23]whose clusters [of fruits] will be within easy reach. [24][He will be told]: 'Enjoy your food and drink, for what you had sent in advance in past days [for your future life].'

[25]But as for him who is given his book in his left hand, he will say, 'I wish I had not been given my book,

69:19–25 The Qur'ān here speaks of the righteous receiving a book in their right hand (v. 19, cf. also 17:71; 84:7) and (v. 25) the unrighteous receiving a book in their left hand. This differs from 56:8 (also 56:27–40, 90–91) and 90:18, which refer to the "People of the Right Hand," and from 56:9 (also 56:41–56, 92–94) and 90:19, which refer to the "People of the Left Hand." This latter image is closer to Matthew 25:31–46. See further commentary on 90:7–20.

[26]nor had I ever known what my account is! [27]I wish death had been the end of it all! [28]My wealth did not avail me. [29]My authority has left me.'

[30][The angels will be told:] 'Seize him and fetter him! [31]Then put him into hell. [32]Then bind him in a chain, seventy cubits in length. [33]Indeed, he had no faith in God, the All-supreme, [34]and he did not urge the feeding of the needy, [35]so he has no friend here today, [36]nor any food except pus, [37]which no one shall eat except the iniquitous.'

69:28–37 The condemnation of a rich man here whose "wealth did not avail" (v. 28) him is reminiscent of the parable of Lazarus and the rich man in Luke 16 in which Abraham tells the rich man: "My son, remember that during your life you had your fill of good things, just as Lazarus his fill of bad. Now he is being comforted here while you are in agony." (Luk 16:25). See further commentary on 90:7–20.

38I swear by what you see 39and what you do not see: 40it is indeed the speech of a noble apostle 41and it is not the speech of a poet. Little is the faith that you have!

42Nor is it the speech of a soothsayer—little is the admonition that you take 43—gradually sent down from the Lord of all the worlds.

44Had he faked any sayings in Our name, 45We would have surely seized him by the right hand 46and then cut off his aorta, 47and none of you could have held Us off from him.

48It is indeed a reminder for the Godwary. 49We indeed know that there are some among you who deny [it]. 50And it will indeed be a [matter of] regret for the faithless.

51It is indeed certain truth.

52So *celebrate* the Name of *your* Lord, the All-supreme.

70. *AL-MA ʿĀRIJ,* LOFTY STATIONS

In the Name of God, the All-beneficent, the All-merciful.

¹An asker asked for a punishment sure to befall ²—which none can avert from the faithless—³from God, Lord of the lofty stations. ⁴The angels and the Spirit ascend to Him in a day whose span is fifty thousand years.

70:4 The context around this verse (cf. 32:5; for the comparison of a day and a thousand years, see also 22:47) suggests that its sense is close to that of 2 Peter 3:7–9 (which follows Psa 90:4). Both texts teach that the believers—although they have been promised that the apocalypse will arrive soon—should not despair that it has not yet arrived, since God's perspective of time is not their own:

> ⁸But there is one thing, my dear friends, that you must never forget: that with the Lord, a day is like a thousand years, and a thousand years are like a day. ⁹The Lord is not being slow in carrying out his promises, as some people think he is; rather is he being patient with you, wanting nobody to be lost and everybody to be brought to repentance. (2Pe 3:8–9)

Tafsīr al-Jalālayn argues that this verse reflects instead the perspective of a disbeliever for whom the Day of Judgment will seem to last fifty thousand years: "on account of the calamities he will encounter in it." Here it is the Spirit and the angels which ascend to God, whereas in 32:5 it is the *amr* (on which see commentary on 42:52) which ascends to God.

⁵So *be patient,* with a patience that is graceful. ⁶They indeed see it to be far off, ⁷and We see it to be near.

⁸The day when the sky will be like molten copper, ⁹and the mountains like [tufts of] dyed wool, ¹⁰and no friend will inquire about [the welfare of his] friend, ¹¹[though] they will be placed within each other's sight. The guilty one will wish he could ransom himself from the punishment of that day at the price of his children, ¹²his spouse and his brother, ¹³his kin which had sheltered him ¹⁴and all those who are upon the earth, if that might deliver him.

¹⁵Never! It is indeed a blazing fire, ¹⁶which strips away the scalp. ¹⁷It invites him who has turned back [from the truth] and forsaken [it], ¹⁸amassing [wealth] and hoarding [it].

¹⁹Man has indeed been created covetous: ²⁰anxious when an ill befalls him ²¹and grudging [charity] when good comes his way ²²—[all are such] except the prayerful, ²³those who persevere in their prayers ²⁴and there is a known share in whose wealth ²⁵for the beggar and the deprived, ²⁶and who affirm the Day of Retribution,

70:26 On the term Qarai renders "Retribution" (Ar. *dīn*), see commentary on 83:11 (with further references).

²⁷and those who are apprehensive of the punishment of their Lord ²⁸(there is indeed no security from the punishment of their Lord) ²⁹and those who guard their private parts ³⁰(except from their spouses and their slave women, for then they are not blameworthy; ³¹but whoever seeks beyond that—it is they who are the transgressors) ³²and those who keep their trusts and covenants,

³³and those who are conscientious in their testimonies, ³⁴and those who are watchful of their prayers. ³⁵They will be in gardens, held in honour.

³⁶What is the matter with the faithless that they scramble toward *you* ³⁷from left and right in groups? ³⁸Does each man among them hope to enter the garden of bliss? ³⁹Never! Indeed, We created them from what they know.

⁴⁰So I swear by the Lord of the easts and the wests that We are able ⁴¹to replace them with [others] better than them and We are not to be outmaneuvered. ⁴²So leave them to gossip and play till they encounter the day they are promised: ⁴³the day when they emerge from the graves, hastening, as if racing toward a target, ⁴⁴with a humbled look [in their eyes], overcast by abasement. That is the day they had been promised.

71. *NŪḤ*, NOAH

In the Name of God, the All-beneficent, the All-merciful.

¹Indeed, We sent Noah to his people, [saying,] 'Warn your people before a painful punishment overtakes them.'

71:1–28 *overview* The Qur'ān relates seven substantial accounts of Noah (7:59–64; 10:71–74; 11:25–49; 23:23–30; 26:105–22; 54:9–17; 71:1–28) along with many passing references to him, or to the flood. The Qur'ānic character of Noah is quite unlike that of the Noah in Genesis, who does not speak a word until after the flood. In contrast the Noah of the Qur'ān is above all a preacher, a warner (v. 2), who seeks (like other Qur'ānic prophets of the punishment stories) to convince his people to believe in God and obey him lest they suffer divine wrath. This perspective on Noah is suggested by the way the author of 2 Peter 2 refers to him as a "preacher of uprightness" (a development of the description of Noah as a "righteous" man in Gen 6:9). It is also suggested by a passage in the Talmud:

> The righteous Noah rebuked them, urging, "Repent; for if not, the Holy One, blessed be He, will bring a deluge upon you and cause your bodies to float upon the water like gourds, as it is written, He is light [i.e., floats] upon the waters. Moreover, ye shall be taken as a curse for all future generations." (b. Sanhedrin 108a)

It is also prominent with the Syriac fathers, several of whom report that Noah preached to his people for a hundred years before God finally sent the flood:

One hundred years long Grace cried out as a herald / Sinners turn from iniquity before justice goes forth. (Narsai, "On the Flood," 33, ll. 227–30)

Noah the just, saved only by his righteousness / before God, had not even heard the proclamation of circumcision. / Five hundred years he remained in the beauty of his virginity; / One hundred years he preached to, and admonished, the children of his race. (Jacob of Serugh, *Homélies contre les juifs,* 70, homily 2, ll. 37–40; see also ibid., *On the Flood,* 23–24)

On Noah, see also commentary on 11:25–39.

———————

²He said, 'O my people! I am indeed a manifest warner to you. ³Worship God and be wary of Him, and obey me, ⁴that He may forgive you some of your sins and respite you until a specified time. When God's [appointed] time indeed comes, it cannot be deferred, if you know.'

⁵He said, 'My Lord! I have indeed summoned my people night and day ⁶but my summons only increases their evasion. ⁷Indeed, whenever I have summoned them so that You might forgive them, they would put their fingers into their ears and draw their cloaks over their heads, and they were persistent [in their unfaith] and disdainful in [their] arrogance. ⁸Again I summoned them aloud, ⁹and again appealed to them publicly and confided with them privately, ¹⁰telling [them]: "Plead to your Lord for forgiveness. He is indeed all-forgiving. ¹¹He will send for you abundant rains from the sky ¹²and aid you with wealth and sons, and provide you with gardens and provide you with streams. ¹³What is the matter with you that you do not look upon God with veneration, ¹⁴though He has created you in [various] stages? ¹⁵Have you not seen how God has created the seven heavens in layers

71:15 On the seven heavens, see commentary on 67:3 (with further references).

---

¹⁶and made therein the moon for a light and the sun for a lamp? ¹⁷God made you grow from the earth, with a [vegetable] growth. ¹⁸Then He makes you return to it, and He will bring you forth [without fail]. ¹⁹God has made the earth a vast expanse for you ²⁰so that you may travel over its spacious ways.''

²¹Noah said, 'My Lord! They have disobeyed me, following those whose wealth and children only add to their loss, ²²and they have devised an outrageous plot. ²³They say, "Do not abandon your gods. Do not abandon Wadd, nor Suwā, nor Yaghūth, Yaʿūq and Nasr,"

71:23 *Tafsīr al-Jalālayn* describes Wadd, Suwā, Yaghūth, Yaʿūq, and Nasr as names of idols worshipped by Noah's people. Some scholars argue that these are rather the names of idols worshipped by the Arabs of Muḥammad's time. A tradition in the Talmud speaks of five temples of idol worship, one of which, located in "Arabia" (but here the term applies to a broad area), is named (in Am.) *nishrā* and is likely connected to the reference in this verse to "Nasr" (meaning "eagle"):

> Said R. Hanan b. Hisda in the name of Rab . . . : There are five appointed Temples of idol-worship: they are: The Temple of Bel in Babel; the Temple of Nebo in Kursi, Tarʾata which is in Mapug. Zerifa which is in Askelon, and Nishra which is in Arabia. (b. Avodah Zarah 11b)

Hawting (*Idea of Idolatry*, 115) refers to a remark in the the fourth-or fifth-century Syriac *Doctrine of Addai* that the "Arabs" worship *neshrā* ("eagle"). See the *Doctrine of Addai*, 24.

---

²⁴and already they have led many astray. Do not increase the wrongdoers in anything but error.'

²⁵They were drowned because of their iniquities, then made to enter a Fire, and they did not find any helpers for themselves besides God.

²⁶And Noah said, 'My Lord! Do not leave on the earth any inhabitant from among the faithless. ²⁷If You leave them, they will lead astray Your servants, and will beget none except vicious ingrates. ²⁸My Lord! Forgive me and my parents, and whoever enters my house in faith, and the faithful men and women, and do not increase the wrongdoers in anything but ruin.'

72. *AL-JINN,* THE JINN

In the Name of God, the All-beneficent, the All-merciful.

¹*Say,* 'It has been revealed to me that a team of the jinn listened [to the Qurʾān] and they said, "We have indeed heard a wonderful *Qurʾān,*

72:1–14 *overview* The jinn are generally understood by Islamic tradition to be a class of beings, created from fire (see 15:27; 55:15) separate from humans (created from dirt; 3:59; 6:2; 7:12; 18:37; 22:5; 23:12; 30:20; 32:7; 35:11; 40:67), and angels (created from light, an idea not attested in the Qurʾān).

This tradition rests in part on this passage (and 46:29–32), which suggests (vv. 1–3, 11, 13–14) that the jinn may come to believe in God, whereas (according to traditional thought) demons (fallen angels) do not. It is possible, however, that jinn is simply another term for demons. This passage illustrates that the jinn, like other demons (Q 15:16–18; 37:6–10; 41:12; 67:5), seek to enter into heaven to overhear God's conversations with the angels (vv. 8–9). Moreover, Satan himself is named "one of the *jinn*" (Q 18:50). As Jacqueline Chabbi points out ("Jinn," *EQ,* 3:44), the terms *jinn* (27:17, 39; 34:12, 14) and *shayāṭīn* (21:82; 38:37) are used interchangeably to describe the beings that serve Solomon.

The belief of the jinn in this Sura should be seen in light of the way the Qurʾān refers to the belief of Satan in God (see 8:48; 59:16). One might also compare this idea to James 2:19: "You believe in the one God—that is creditable enough, but even the demons have the same belief, and they tremble with fear."

For the Qur'ān, the jinn's creation from fire is a mark of their heavenly origins; it is for this reason that Satan boasts of his creation from fire (Q 7:12; 38:76). In pre-Islamic Jewish and Christian texts angels are regularly associated with fire. The *Pseudo-Clementines* describe how one class of angels (those of the lowest heaven) mixed with humans and, learning the sinful ways of man, were transformed from fire into flesh:

> Having become in all respects men, [these angels] also partook of human lust and being brought under its subjection, they fell into cohabitation with women; and being involved with them, and sunk in defilement and altogether emptied of their first power, were unable to turn back to the first purity of their proper nature, their members turned way from their fiery substance: for the fire itself, being extinguished by the weight of lust, and changed into flesh, they trode the impious path downward. (*Pseudo-Clementines,* 8:13)

The Qur'ān does not imagine that the jinn were changed into flesh, but it has a clear vision of how the jinn, along with other demons, fell from heaven and were unable to return.

---

²which guides to rectitude. Hence we have believed in it and we will never ascribe any partner to our Lord. ³Exalted be the majesty of our Lord; He has taken neither any spouse nor offspring.

72:3 On God's "taking" a spouse and offspring (Ar. *walad*), see commentary on 6:101.

---

⁴The foolish ones among us used to speak atrocious lies concerning God. ⁵We thought that humans and jinn would never utter any falsehood concerning God. ⁶Indeed, some persons from the humans would seek the protection of some persons from the jinn, thus only adding to their rebellion.

72:6 On the worship of jinn, see commentary on 6:100 (with further references).

⁷They thought, just as you think, that God will not raise anyone from the dead. ⁸Indeed, we made for the heaven and found it full of mighty sentries and flames. ⁹We used to sit in its positions to eavesdrop, but anyone listening now finds a flame waiting for him. ¹⁰We do not know whether ill is intended for those who are on the earth, or whether their Lord intends good for them. ¹¹Among us some are righteous and some are otherwise: we are various sects. ¹²We know that we cannot frustrate God on the earth, nor can we frustrate Him by fleeing. ¹³When we heard the [message of] guidance, we believed in it. Whoever that has faith in his Lord will fear neither privation nor oppression. ¹⁴Among us some are *muslims* and some of us are perverse.'"

Those who submit [to God]—it is they who pursue rectitude. ¹⁵As for the perverse, they will be firewood for hell. ¹⁶If they are steadfast on the path [of God], We shall provide them with abundant water, ¹⁷so that We may test them therein, and whoever turns away from the remembrance of his Lord, He will let him into an escalating punishment.

¹⁸The places of worship belong to God, so do not invoke anyone along with God.

¹⁹When the servant of God rose to pray to Him, they almost crowded around him. ²⁰*Say,* 'I pray only to my Lord and I do not ascribe any partner to Him.'

²¹*Say,* 'I have no power to bring you any harm or good [of my own accord].'

²²*Say,* 'Neither can anyone shelter me from God, nor can I find any refuge besides Him. ²³[I have no duty] except to transmit from God, and [to communicate] His messages; and whoever disobeys God and His apostle, there will indeed be for him the fire of hell, to remain in it forever.'

[24]When they see what they are promised, they will know who is weaker in supporters and fewer in numbers.

[25]*Say,* 'I do not know if what you are promised is near, or if my Lord has set a [long] term for it.' [26]Knower of the Unseen, He does not disclose His [knowledge of the] Unseen to anyone [27]except an apostle that He approves of. Then He dispatches a sentinel before and behind him [28]so that He may ascertain that they have delivered the messages of their Lord, and He encompasses all that is with them, and He keeps a count of all things.

73. *al-Muzzammil*, Enwrapped

In the Name of God, the All-beneficent, the All-merciful.

¹O *you* wrapped up in *your* mantle! ²*Stand vigil* through the night, except for a little [of it], ³a half, or *reduce* a little from that ⁴or *add* to it, and *recite* the Qur'ān in a measured tone. ⁵Indeed, soon We will cast on *you* a weighty discourse. ⁶The watch of the night is indeed firmer in tread and more upright in respect to speech, ⁷for during the day *you* have drawn-out engagements. ⁸So *celebrate* the Name of *your* Lord and dedicate yourself to Him with total dedication.

⁹Lord of the east and the west, there is no god except Him; so take Him for *your* trustee, ¹⁰and *be patient* over what they say, and *distance yourself* from them in a graceful manner. ¹¹Leave Me [to deal] with the deniers, the opulent, and *give* them a little respite.

¹²With Us indeed are heavy fetters and a fierce fire, ¹³and a food that chokes [those who eat it], and a painful punishment [prepared for] ¹⁴the day when the earth and the mountains will quake, and the mountains will be like dunes of shifting sand.

¹⁵We have indeed sent to you an apostle to be a witness to you, just as We sent an apostle to Pharaoh. ¹⁶But Pharaoh disobeyed the apostle, so We seized him with a terrible seizing.

73:15–16 Whereas the Bible presents Moses as the divinely appointed leader of the Israelites who delivers them from servitude under Pharaoh, the Qurʾān presents Moses also as an apostle to Pharaoh (and the Egyptians). On this theme, see commentary on 26:18–29 (with further references); on the Qurʾānic presentation of Moses as one of the prophets of the "punishment stories," see 7:103–37; cf. also 11:102; 54:42; 69:10.

---

¹⁷So if you disbelieve, how will you avoid the day which will make children white-headed, ¹⁸and wherein the heaven will be rent apart? His promise is bound to be fulfilled.

¹⁹This is indeed a reminder. So let anyone who wishes take the way toward his Lord.

²⁰*Your* Lord indeed knows that *you* stand vigil for nearly two thirds of the night—or [at times] a half or a third of it—along with a group of those who are with *you*. God measures the night and the day. He knows that you cannot calculate it [exactly] and so He was lenient toward you. So recite as much of the Qurʾān as is feasible.

He knows that some of you will be sick, while others will travel in the land seeking God's bounty, and yet others will fight in the way of God. So recite as much of it as is feasible, and maintain the prayer and pay the *zakāt* and lend God a good loan. Whatever good you send ahead for your souls you will find it with God [in a form] that is better and greater with respect to reward.

And plead to God for forgiveness; indeed God is all-forgiving, all-merciful.

74. *AL-MUDDATHTHIR,* SHROUDED

In the Name of God, the All-beneficent, the All-merciful.

¹O *you* wrapped up in *your* mantle! ²Rise up and warn! ³Magnify *your* Lord, ⁴purify *your* clothes ⁵and *keep away* from all impurity! ⁶*Do not grant* a favour seeking a greater gain, ⁷and *be patient* for the sake of your Lord.

⁸When the Trumpet will be sounded,

74:8 On the trumpet blast, see commentary on 78:18 (with further references). Here a different word for "trumpet" (*nāqūr*) is used.

---

⁹that day will be a day of hardship, ¹⁰not at all easy for the faithless.

¹¹Leave Me [to deal] with him whom I created alone ¹²and furnished him with extensive means, ¹³and [gave him] sons to be at his side, ¹⁴and facilitated [all matters] for him. ¹⁵Still he is eager that I should give him more. ¹⁶No indeed! He is an obstinate opponent of Our signs. ¹⁷Soon I will overwhelm him with hardship.

¹⁸Indeed, he reflected and decided. ¹⁹Perish he, how he decided! ²⁰Again, perish he, how he decided! ²¹Then he looked; ²²then he frowned and scowled, ²³and turned away disdainfully, ²⁴saying, 'It is nothing but traditional sorcery. ²⁵It is nothing but the speech of a human.'

²⁶Soon I will cast him into *Saqar.* ²⁷And what will show *you* what is *Saqar*? ²⁸It neither spares, nor leaves [anything]. ²⁹It burns the skin. ³⁰There are nineteen [keepers] over it.

³¹We have assigned only angels as keepers of the Fire, and We have made their number merely a stumbling block for the faithless, so that those who were given the Book may be reassured and the faithful may increase in [their] faith, and so that those who were given the Book and the faithful may not be in doubt, and so that the faithless and those in whose hearts is sickness may say, 'What did God mean by this description?' Thus does God lead astray whomever He wishes and guides whomever He wishes. No one knows the hosts of *your* Lord except Him, and it is just an admonition for all humans.

74:30–31 The Qur'ān's declaration that there are nineteen angels (v. 30) who watch over hell has confused both traditional Islamic and academic scholars. Paret wonders (*Kommentar,* 494) if the number nineteen might come from the addition of the seven planets (known in the classical period) with the twelve signs of the zodiac. The first Book of Enoch speaks of 200 angels which descend to earth (on Mt. Hermon) and gives the names of their leaders, which in some manuscripts are numbered at nineteen (see 1 Enoch 6:7).

---

³²No indeed! By the Moon! ³³By the night when it recedes! ³⁴By the dawn when it brightens! ³⁵They are indeed one of the greatest [signs of God] ³⁶—a warner to all humans, ³⁷[alike] for

those of you who like to advance ahead and those who would remain behind.

³⁸Every soul is hostage to what it has earned, ³⁹except the People of the Right Hand.

74:39 Regarding "People of the Right Hand," see commentary on 56:8–11 and 90:7–20 (with further references).

---

⁴⁰[They will be] in gardens, questioning ⁴¹the guilty: ⁴²'What drew you into Hell?' ⁴³They will answer, 'We were not among those who prayed. ⁴⁴Nor did we feed the poor. ⁴⁵We used to indulge in [profane] gossip along with the gossipers, ⁴⁶and we used to deny the Day of Retribution

74:46 On the term in verse 46 that Qarai renders as "Retribution" (Ar. *dīn*), see commentary on 83:11 (with further references).

---

⁴⁷until death came to us.'

⁴⁸So the intercession of the intercessors will not avail them.

⁴⁹What is the matter with them that they evade the Reminder ⁵⁰as if they were terrified asses ⁵¹fleeing from a lion? ⁵²But everyone of them desires to be given unrolled scriptures [from God]!

74:52 On the Arabic term behind "scriptures" here, *ṣuḥuf,* see commentary on 80:13–15 (with further references).

53No! They do not indeed fear the Hereafter. 54No! It is indeed a reminder. 55So let anyone who wishes be mindful of it. 56And they will not be mindful unless God wishes. He is worthy of [your] being wary [of Him] and He is worthy to forgive.

75. *AL-QIYĀMA,* RESURRECTION

In the Name of God, the All-beneficent, the All-merciful.

¹I swear by the Day of Resurrection! ²And I swear by the self-critical soul! ³Does man suppose that We will not put together his bones [at resurrection]? ⁴Of course, We are able to [re]shape [even] his fingertips!

⁵Man indeed desires to go on living viciously. ⁶He asks, 'When will this "day of resurrection" be?!' ⁷But when the eyes are dazzled, ⁸the moon is eclipsed, ⁹and the sun and the moon are brought together, ¹⁰that day man will say, 'Where is the escape [from this day]?'

75:7–10 These verses are reminiscent of several passages from the Gospels: "Immediately after the distress of those days the sun will be darkened, the moon will not give its light, the stars will fall from the sky and the powers of the heavens will be shaken" (Mat 24:29; cf. Mar 13:24–25; Luk 21:25–26).

---

¹¹No indeed! There will be no refuge!

¹²That day the [final] goal will be toward *your* Lord. ¹³That day man will be informed about what [works] he had sent ahead [to

the scene of judgement] and [the legacy that he had] left behind. ¹⁴Rather, man is witness to his own self, ¹⁵though he should offer excuses [to justify his faults].

¹⁶*Do not move your* tongue with it to hasten it. ¹⁷It is indeed up to Us to put it together and to recite it. ¹⁸And when We have recited it, *follow* its recitation. ¹⁹Then, its exposition [also] lies with Us.

²⁰No! Indeed, you love this transitory life ²¹and forsake the Hereafter. ²²Some faces will be fresh on that day, ²³looking to their Lord, ²⁴and some faces will be scowling on that day, ²⁵knowing that they will be dealt out a punishment breaking the spine.

²⁶No indeed! When it reaches the collar bones, ²⁷and it is said, 'Who will take him up?' ²⁸and he knows that it is the [time of] parting, ²⁹and each shank clasps the other shank, ³⁰that day he shall be driven toward *your* Lord. ³¹He neither confirmed [God's messages], nor did he pray, ³²but denied [them] and turned away, ³³and went back swaggering to his family.

³⁴So woe to you! Woe to you! ³⁵Again, woe to you! Woe to you!

³⁶Does man suppose that he has been abandoned to futility? ³⁷Was he not a drop of emitted semen, ³⁸and then a clinging mass? Whereat He created and proportioned [him] ³⁹and made of him the two sexes, male and female. ⁴⁰Is not someone like that able to revive the dead?

76. AL-INSĀN, THE PERSON

In the Name of God, the All-beneficent, the All-merciful.

¹Has there been a period of time for man when he was not anything worthy of mention? ²We indeed created man from the drop of a mixed fluid so that We may put him to test, so We endowed him with hearing and sight. ³We have indeed guided him to the way, be he grateful or ungrateful.

⁴We have indeed prepared for the faithless chains, iron collars and a blaze.

⁵Indeed, the pious will drink from a cup seasoned with *Kāfūr,* ⁶a spring where God's servants will drink, making it gush forth as they please. ⁷They fulfill their vows and fear a day whose ill will be widespread. ⁸For the love of Him they feed the needy, the orphan and the prisoner, ⁹[saying,] 'We feed you only for the sake of God. We desire no reward from you, nor thanks.

76:8–9 In verse 9 Qarai renders a phrase that literally means "for the *face* of God" (cf. 92:20) instead as "for the sake of God." The Qur'ān's use of this expression may reflect Psalm 17:15, or more likely the Talmudic commentary on this verse which connects it to almsgiving: "If a man gives but a farthing to a beggar, he is deemed worthy to receive the Divine Presence, as it is written,

'I shall behold thy face in righteousness' (Psa 17:15)" (b. Bava Batra 10a). See Goitein, "Muhammad's Inspiration," 156.

On kindness to orphans (v. 8), see commentary on 107:2 (with further references). On this verse Wāḥidī relates the following anecdote about ʿAlī b. Abī Ṭālib's generosity: "It happened that ʿAli ibn Abi Talib hired himself one night to water some palm-trees in exchange for some barley. The following morning, he collected his barley and grinded a third of it out of which they made something to eat, called al-Khazirah. When it was cooked, a poor man came begging from them, and so they gave him the food they had prepared. They then prepared a third of the remaining barley and when it was cooked, an orphan came begging from them, and they gave him the food. They then went and prepared what was left of that barley, but when the food was cooked, a prisoner from among the idolaters came to them and they fed him that food and spent the rest of the day without eating anything."

---

¹⁰We indeed fear a frowning and fateful day from our Lord.'
¹¹So God saved them from that day's ills and graced them with freshness [on their faces] and joy [in their hearts]. ¹²He rewarded them for their patience with a garden and [garments of] silk, ¹³reclining therein on couches, without facing therein any [scorching] sun, or [biting] cold. ¹⁴Its shades will be close over them and its clusters [of fruits] will be hanging low.

76:13–14 On shade in paradise, see commentary on 13:35 (with further references).

---

¹⁵They will be served around with vessels of silver and goblets of crystal ¹⁶—crystal of silver—[from] which they will dispense in a precise measure. ¹⁷They will be served therein with a cup of a drink seasoned with *Zanjabīl*, ¹⁸from a spring in it named *Salsabīl*.

¹⁹They will be waited upon by immortal youths, whom, were you to see them, you will suppose them to be scattered pearls. ²⁰As you look on, you will see there bliss and a great kingdom. ²¹Upon them will be green garments of fine and heavy silk, and they will be adorned with bracelets of silver. Their Lord will give them to drink a pure drink. ²²[They will be told]: 'This is your reward, and your efforts have been well-appreciated.'

²³We have indeed sent down the Qur'ān to *you* in a gradual descent. ²⁴So *submit patiently* to the judgement of *your* Lord and *do not obey* any sinner or ingrate from among them, ²⁵and *celebrate* the Name of *your* Lord morning and evening, ²⁶and *worship* Him for a watch of the night and *glorify* Him the night long.

²⁷They indeed love this transitory life and disregard a heavy day that is ahead of them.

²⁸We created them and strengthened their joints, and We will replace them with others like them whenever We like. ²⁹This is indeed a reminder. So let anyone who wishes take the way toward his Lord. ³⁰But you will not wish unless it is willed by God. God is indeed all-knowing, all-wise. ³¹He admits whomever He wishes into His mercy, and He has prepared a painful punishment for the wrongdoers.

77. *AL-MURSALĀT*, THE EMISSARIES

In the Name of God, the All-beneficent, the All-merciful.

¹By the [angelic] emissaries sent successively, ²by those who sweep along like a gale, ³by those who publish [the Divine messages] far and wide, ⁴by those who separate [the truth from falsehood] distinctly, ⁵by those who inspire [God's] remembrance, ⁶as exemption or warning: ⁷what you are promised will surely befall.

⁸When the stars are blotted out ⁹and the heaven is cleft, ¹⁰when the mountains are scattered [like dust] ¹¹and the time is set for the apostles [to bear witness] ¹²—for what day has [all] that been set [to occur]? ¹³For the Day of Judgement! ¹⁴And what will show you what is the Day of Judgement!?

77:13–14 The Arabic rendered here as "Day of Judgement" is *yawm al-faṣl*, literally "the Day of Division" (cf. 37:21; 77:38; Yusuf Ali: the "Day of Sorting out"; Pickthall: the "Day of Decision"). Cf. Mat 25:32: "All nations will be assembled before him and he will separate people one from another as the shepherd separates sheep from goats."

---

¹⁵Woe to the deniers on that day!

¹⁶Did We not destroy the former peoples, ¹⁷[and] then made the latter ones follow them? ¹⁸That is how We deal with the guilty.

¹⁹Woe to the deniers on that day!

²⁰Have We not created you from a base fluid,

77:20 On the creation of humans from water, see commentary on 24:41–45 (with further references).

---

²¹[and] then lodged it in a secure abode ²²until a known span [of time]? ²³Then We determined; and how excellent determiners We are!

²⁴Woe to the deniers on that day!

²⁵Have We not made the earth a receptacle ²⁶for the living and the dead, ²⁷and set in it lofty [and] firm mountains, and given you agreeable water to drink?

²⁸Woe to the deniers on that day!

²⁹[The faithless will be told:] 'Proceed toward what you used to deny! ³⁰Proceed toward the triple-forked shadow, ³¹neither shady nor of any avail against the flames. ³²Indeed, it throws up [giant] sparks like castles, ³³[bright] like yellow camels.

³⁴Woe to the deniers on that day!

³⁵This is a day wherein they will not speak, ³⁶nor will they be permitted to offer excuses.

³⁷Woe to the deniers on that day!

³⁸'This is the Day of Judgement. We have brought you together with the former peoples. ³⁹If you have any stratagems [left], now try them out against Me!'

77:41 On the Arabic expression for "Day of Judgement," see commentary on 77:13–14 (with further references).

⁴⁰Woe to the deniers on that day!

⁴¹Indeed, the Godwary will be amid shades and springs

77:41 On shade in paradise, see commentary on 13:35 (with further references).

⁴²and [enjoying] such fruits as they desire. ⁴³[They will be told:] 'Enjoy your food and drink, [a reward] for what you used to do. ⁴⁴Thus indeed do We reward the virtuous.'

⁴⁵Woe to the deniers on that day!

⁴⁶[Let them be told:] 'Eat and enjoy a little! You are indeed guilty.'

⁴⁷Woe to the deniers on that day!

⁴⁸When they are told, 'Bow down [in prayer],' they do not bow down!

⁴⁹Woe to the deniers on that day!

⁵⁰So what discourse will they believe after this?

78. *AL-NABA'*, THE TIDING

In the Name of God, the All-beneficent, the All-merciful.

^{1}What is it about which they are questioning each other?! ^{2}[Is it] about the Great Tiding, ^{3}the one about which they differ?

^{4}Once again, no indeed! Soon they will know! ^{5}No indeed! Soon they will know for once again!

^{6}Did We not make the earth a resting place? ^{7}and the mountains stakes? ^{8}and create you in pairs? ^{9}and make your sleep for rest? ^{10}and make the night a covering? ^{11}and make the day for livelihood? ^{12}and build above you the seven mighty heavens? ^{13}and make [the sun for] a radiant lamp? ^{14}and send down water pouring from the rain-clouds, ^{15}that We may bring forth with it grains and plants, ^{16}and luxuriant gardens?

^{17}The Day of Judgement is indeed the tryst, ^{18}the day the Trumpet will be blown, and you will come in groups,

---

78:18 The Qur'ān's reference to a trumpet blast to precede the resurrection (cf. 6:73; 18:99; 20:102; 23:101; 27:87; 36:51; 39:68, where there are two trumpet blasts; 50:20; 69:13; 74:8) follows from New Testament descriptions of the Last Day:

> And he will send his angels with a loud trumpet to gather his elect from the four winds, from one end of heaven to the other. (Mat 24:31)

⁵¹Now I am going to tell you a mystery: we are not all going to fall asleep, ⁵²but we are all going to be changed, instantly, in the twinkling of an eye, when the last trumpet sounds. The trumpet is going to sound, and then the dead will be raised imperishable, and we shall be changed (1Co 15:51–52; cf. 1Th 4:16).

---

¹⁹and the heaven will be opened and become gates, ²⁰and the mountains will be set moving, becoming a mirage.

²¹Hell is indeed in ambush, ²²a resort for the rebels, ²³to reside therein for ages, ²⁴tasting in it neither any coolness nor drink, ²⁵except boiling water and pus, ²⁶a fitting requital. ²⁷Indeed, they did not expect any reckoning, ²⁸and they denied Our signs mendaciously, ²⁹and We have figured everything in a Book. ³⁰Now taste! We shall increase you in nothing but punishment!

³¹Deliverance and triumph indeed await the Godwary: ³²gardens and vineyards, ³³and buxom maidens of a like age, ³⁴and brimming cups. ³⁵Therein they will hear neither vain talk nor lies ³⁶—a reward and sufficing bounty from *your* Lord, ³⁷the All-beneficent, the Lord of the heavens and the earth and whatever is between them, whom they will not be able to address ³⁸on the day when the Spirit and the angels stand in an array. None shall speak except whom the All-beneficent permits and who says what is right.

³⁹That day is true for certain. So let anyone who wishes take resort with his Lord.

⁴⁰We have indeed warned you of a punishment near at hand—the day when a person will observe what his hands have sent ahead, and the faithless one will say, 'I wish I were dust!'

79. *AL-NĀZIʿĀT,* THE WRESTERS

In the Name of God, the All-beneficent, the All-merciful.

¹By those [angels] who wrest [the soul] violently, ²by those who draw [it] out gently, ³by those who swim smoothly, ⁴by those who, racing, take the lead, ⁵by those who direct the affairs [of creatures]: ⁶the day when the Quaker quakes ⁷and is followed by its Successor, ⁸hearts will be trembling on that day, ⁹bearing a humbled look.

¹⁰They will say, 'Are we being returned to our earlier state? ¹¹What, even after we have been decayed bones?!' ¹²They will say, 'This is, then, a ruinous return!'

¹³Yet it will be only a single shout, ¹⁴and behold, they will be awake.

¹⁵Did *you* receive the story of Moses,

79:15–20 *overview* On the call of Moses, see commentary on 20:9–16 (with further references).

---

¹⁶when his Lord called out to him in the holy valley of Ṭuwā?

882

79:16 The term *Ṭuwā* (cf. 20:12) is a puzzle to interpreters because it seems to have no parallel in Biblical tradition. Its position at the end of the verse (also in 20:12) suggests that the ending was shaped to rhyme with the end words of the verses that precede and follow it. It is possible that *Ṭuwā* is related to Syriac *ṭūrā* and Arabic *ṭūr* ("mountain" and an allusion to Mt. Sinai in particular). See Stewart, "Notes on Medieval and Modern Emendations of the Qurʾān," 236–37.

Many scholars take Ṭuwā as the proper name of the valley in which Moses encountered God, although some argue (on the basis of the Arabic root from which it is formed) that it means "folded" and thus "double" (hence Asad's translation: "the twice-hallowed valley"). Uri Rubin ("Moses and the Holy Valley Ṭuwan") translates "valley of Ṭuwā" as "the valley of the folded up holiness."

---

¹⁷[And said,] 'Go to Pharaoh, for he has indeed rebelled,

79:17 The rebellion of Pharaoh alluded to in this verse might be read in light of verse 24, where Pharaoh declares his divinity (cf. 26:29; 28:38). One might also compare Pharaoh's defiance expressed in Exodus 5:2: "'Who is the Lord,' Pharaoh replied, 'for me to obey what he says and let Israel go? I know nothing of the Lord, and I will not let Israel go.'"

---

¹⁸and say, "Would you purify yourself? ¹⁹I will guide you to your Lord, that you may fear [Him]?"' ²⁰Then he showed him the greatest sign.

79:20 *Tafsīr al-Jalālayn* explains that the "greatest sign" of Moses was either "the hand or the staff." The ambiguity is based on the connection of this verse with 20:17–23 (note the turn of phrase in 20:23).

---

²¹But he denied and disobeyed. ²²Then he turned back, walking swiftly, ²³and gathered [the people] and proclaimed, ²⁴saying, 'I am your exalted lord!'

79:22–24 On Pharaoh's declaration of his own divinity, cf. 26:29; 28:38. The Qurʾān develops here the scenario of Exodus, which has Pharaoh refuse to acknowledge the God of Israel (e.g., Exo 5:2) by having Pharaoh declare his divinity (thus "rebelling," as mentioned in v. 17; cf. v. 37).

---

²⁵So God seized him with the punishment of this life and the Hereafter. ²⁶There is indeed a moral in that for those who fear!

²⁷Is your creation more prodigious or that of the heaven He has built? ²⁸He raised its vault and fashioned it, ²⁹and darkened its night, and brought forth its daylight. ³⁰Thereafter He spread out the earth, ³¹bringing forth from it its water and pastures, ³²and setting firmly its mountains, ³³as a [place of] sustenance for you and your livestock.

³⁴When the Greatest Catastrophe befalls ³⁵—the day when man will remember his endeavours ³⁶and hell is brought into view for those who can see—³⁷as for him who has been rebellious ³⁸and who preferred the life of this world, ³⁹his refuge will indeed be hell.

⁴⁰But as for him who is awed to stand before his Lord and restrains his soul from [following] desires, ⁴¹his refuge will indeed be paradise.

⁴²They ask *you* concerning the Hour, "When will it set in, ⁴³considering *your* frequent mention of it?" ⁴⁴Its outcome is with *your* Lord.

79:42–44 The Qurʾān's declaration that knowledge of the Hour of Judgment is with God alone is close to the statement of Jesus in Mat 24:36: "But as for that day and hour, nobody knows it, neither the angels of heaven, nor the Son, no one but the Father alone" (Mat 24:36; cf. Mar 13:32; Act 1:7). Cf. Q 7:187; 31:34; 33:63; 41:47; 43:85; 45:32; 51:12–13.

⁴⁵*You* are only a warner for those who are afraid of it. ⁴⁶The day they see it, it shall be as if they had not stayed [in the world] except for an evening or forenoon.

80. 'ABASA, HE FROWNED

In the Name of God, the All-beneficent, the All-merciful.

[1]He frowned and turned away [2]when the blind man approached him. [3]And how do you know, maybe he would purify himself, [4]or take admonition and the admonition would benefit him!

[5]But as for someone who is wealthy, [6]you attend to him, [7]though you are not liable if he does not purify himself. [8]But as for someone who comes hurrying to you, [9]while he fears [God], [10]you are neglectful of him.

[11]No indeed! These [verses of the Qur'ān] are a reminder [12]—so let anyone who wishes remember it—[13]in honoured scriptures, [14]exalted and purified, [15]in the hands of envoys,

80:13–15 The term that Qarai translates in verse 13 as "scriptures" is *ṣuḥuf* (a term that probably originates from Ethiopic). In two places (Q 53:36–37; 87:18–19) the Qur'ān refers to the *ṣuḥuf* of "Moses and Abraham." According to Ben Shammai ("*Ṣuḥuf* in the Qur'ān"), the Qur'ān means thereby "apocalypses." Cf. also 20:133; 74:52; 81:10; 98:1–3.

[16]noble and pious.

¹⁷Perish man! How ungrateful is he! ¹⁸From what did He create him? ¹⁹He created him from a drop of [seminal] fluid; then proportioned him. ²⁰Then He made the way easy for him; ²¹then He made him die and buried him; ²²and then, when He wished, resurrected him. ²³No indeed! He has not yet carried out what He has commanded him.

²⁴Let man consider his food: ²⁵We pour down plenteous water [from the sky], ²⁶then We split the earth making fissures in it ²⁷and make the grain grow in it, ²⁸as well as vines and vegetables, ²⁹olives and date palms, ³⁰and densely-planted gardens, ³¹fruits and pastures, ³²as a sustenance for you and your livestock.

³³So when the deafening Cry comes—³⁴the day when a man will evade his brother, ³⁵his mother and his father, ³⁶his spouse and his sons—³⁷each of them will have a task to keep him preoccupied on that day.

³⁸Some faces will be bright on that day, ³⁹laughing and joyous, ⁴⁰and some faces on that day will be covered with dust, ⁴¹overcast with gloom. ⁴²It is they who are the faithless, the vicious.

81. *AL-TAKWĪR*, THE WINDING UP

In the Name of God, the All-beneficent, the All-merciful.

¹When the sun is wound up, ²when the stars scatter,

81:1–2 "And the stars of the sky fell onto the earth like figs dropping from a fig tree when a high wind shakes it" (Rev 6:13; cf. Isa 34:4).

³when the mountains are set moving, ⁴when the pregnant camels are neglected, ⁵when the wild beasts are mustered, ⁶when the seas are set afire, ⁷when the souls are assorted, ⁸when the girl buried-alive will be asked ⁹for what sin she was killed.

81:8–9 As Neuwirth (*Frühmekkanische Suren*, 296–97) has pointed out, the reference here (cf. 16:58–59) to an infant girl who has been buried (it is not clear from the Arabic that she has been "buried alive") is not far from a passage in a homily attributed (probably falsely) to Ephrem. In this passage the child killed in the womb and then buried in the earth is pictured as exacting revenge upon his (or her) sinful mother:

> The one who fornicates, becomes pregnant and kills / so that [the child] does not see this world, / her child will keep her / from seeing the new world. /

Since she has taken the life of the child / and the light of this world / the child will take her life / and the light of the next world. / Because the mother of the child has brought death within her womb / so that [the child] will be buried in the darkness of the earth, / so too the child will bring death to the mother / so that she will go in the outer darkness. (Ephrem, *Sermones III*, 1:537–48)

---

¹⁰When the records [of deeds] are unfolded,

81:10 On the Arabic term behind "records" here, *ṣuḥuf,* see commentary on 80:13–15 (with further references).

---

¹¹when the sky is stripped off, ¹²when hell is set ablaze, ¹³when paradise is brought near, ¹⁴then a soul shall know what it has readied [for itself].

¹⁵So I swear by the stars that return, ¹⁶the comets, ¹⁷by the night as it approaches, ¹⁸by the dawn as it breathes: ¹⁹it is indeed the speech of a noble apostle, ²⁰powerful and eminent with the Lord of the Throne, ²¹one who is obeyed and is trustworthy as well.

²²Your companion is not crazy: ²³certainly *he* saw him on the manifest horizon, ²⁴and *he* is not miserly concerning the Unseen. ²⁵And it is not the speech of an outcast Satan.

81:18–25 This passage, along with 53:5–18, is one of two passages in the Qurʾān that describe a heavenly vision. In Q 53 the vision is of God (see commentary on 53:10), whereas here the vision is only of an angel (see v. 19 and the parallel verse 69:40, where the "apostle" seems to be Muḥammad). *Tafsīr al-Jalālayn* relates that the angel is Gabriel. This passage (like 53:5–18) is related to early Jewish and Christian apocalyptic texts which describe a vision of an angel. As Paul Neuenkirchen ("Visions et Ascensions") has described, it seems to have a special relationship to the Ethiopic *Ascension of Isaiah,* a text originally compiled in the third century AD. In the *Ascension,* Isaiah sees a "glorious angel," while this passage (vv. 19–20), speaks of a "noble apostle, powerful and eminent":

> When I prophesied in accordance with the message which you have heard, I saw a glorious angel; his glory was not like the glory of the angels which I always used to see, but he had great glory, and an office, such that I cannot describe the glory of this angel. And I saw when he took hold of me by my hand, and I said to him, "Who are you? And what is your name? And where are you taking me up?" For strength had been given to me that I might speak with him. And he said to me, "When I have taken you up through (all) the stages and have shown you the vision on account of which I was sent, then you will understand who I am; but my name you will not know. (*Ascension of Isaiah,* 7:2–4)

The Qur'ān's declaration in verse 25 that it is "not the speech of an outcast Satan" has a cosmological aspect: whereas the demons have been cast down from heaven (and can only guess at God's words), the Prophet (v. 23) advanced up to the very threshold of God.

―――――――――

²⁶So where are you going?

²⁷It is just a reminder for all the nations, ²⁸for those of you who wish to walk straight; ²⁹but you will not wish unless it is wished by God, the Lord of all the worlds.

82. *AL-INFIṬĀR*, THE RENDING

In the Name of God, the All-beneficent, the All-merciful.

[1]When the sky is rent apart, [2]when the stars are scattered, [3]when the seas are merged, [4]when the graves are overturned, [5]then a soul shall know what it has sent ahead and left behind.

[6]O man! What has deceived you about your generous Lord, [7]who created you and proportioned you, and gave you an upright nature, [8]and composed you in any form that He wished?

[9]No indeed! You rather deny the Retribution.

[10]There are indeed watchers over you, [11]noble writers [12]who know whatever you do.

82:10–12 Here (cf. Q; 43:80; 50:17–18; 86:4) the Qurʾān refers to angels who record the deeds of humans. One might compare this to the role of angels in 2 Enoch (cf. also 1 Enoch 98:8; Mal 3:16):

[4]And there are angels over seasons and years, and there are also angels over rivers and oceans, angels over fruit and grass, and of everything that breeds;
[5]and angels of all people, and all their life they organize and write it down before the face of the Lord. (2 Enoch 19:4–5)

---

¹³The pious shall indeed be amid bliss, ¹⁴and the vicious shall indeed be in hell, ¹⁵entering it on the Day of Retribution, ¹⁶and they shall not be absent from it.

¹⁷And what will show you what is the Day of Retribution?

¹⁸Again, what will show you what is the Day of Retribution?

¹⁹It is a day when no soul will be of any avail to another soul and all command that day will belong to God.

82:19 The Qur'ān's insistence that on the Day of Resurrection no soul shall bear the burdens of another (cf. 2:286; 4:111; 6:164; 17:13–15; 29:12; 35:18; 39:7; 53:38–42; but pace 5:29; 6:31, 119; 16:25; 29:13) is loosely related to Biblical affirmations that all people are responsible for their own sin, such as Ezekiel 18:20: "He one who has sinned is the one who must die; a son is not to bear his father's guilt, nor a father his son's guilt. The upright will be credited with his uprightness, and the wicked with his wickedness" (cf. Deu 24:16; 2Ki 14:6; Jer 31:30; Mat 16:27; Rom 2:6).

On a related Qur'ānic passage (53:38), Speyer (*BEQ,* 457) refers to Galatians 2:5: "Each one has his own load to carry." Yet note also Galatians 2:2, where Paul recommends, "Carry each other's burdens."

However, in passages such as 82:19 the Qur'ān is concerned with the Day of Judgement. It is on that day when "when no soul will be of any avail to another soul." Tor Andrae (*Les origines de l'islam,* 149-50) notes that this is a prominent theme in the works (both Syriac and Greek) attributed to the Syriac father Ephrem. Andrae writes, "One will note in particular the expression 'everyone will carry his own burden' which appears so frequently in the works of Ephrem." He adds that—in distinction to other Syriac fathers—"The possibility of intercession is categorically combatted by Ephrem" (p. 150). At one point Ephrem writes, "The saints will not dare to address a prayer [to God] because the burning breath of His anger will rise up. They will tremble with fear." (see Andrae, 150, quoting Ephrem Syrus, *Op. Syr.* 3:635).

83. *AL-MUṬAFFIFĪN*, THE DEFRAUDERS

In the Name of God, the All-beneficent, the All-merciful.

¹Woe to the defrauders who use short measures, ²who, when they measure [a commodity bought] from the people, take the full measure, ³but diminish when they measure or weigh for them.

83:1–3 Here and on several other occasions (cf. 6:152; 7:85; 11:84–85; 17:35; 26:181–183; 55:7–9) the Qur'ān uses the case of just dealing in trade to teach a lesson on righteousness. This passage might be compared to Deuteronomy 25:13–16:

> ¹³You must not keep two different weights in your bag, one heavy, one light.
> ¹⁴You must not keep two different measures in your house, one large, one small.
> ¹⁵You must keep one weight, full and accurate, so that you may have long life in the country given you by the Lord your God.
> ¹⁶For anyone who does things of this kind and acts dishonestly is detestable to the Lord your God. (Deu 25:13–16; cf. Lev 19:35)

---

⁴Do they not know that they will be resurrected ⁵on a tremendous day, ⁶a day when mankind will stand before the Lord of all the worlds?

⁷Indeed, the record of the vicious is in *Sijjīn*. ⁸And what will show you what is *Sijjīn*? ⁹It is a written record.

83:7–9 See commentary on 83:18–21.

---

¹⁰Woe to the deniers on that day, ¹¹who deny the Day of Retribution;

83:11 Qarai (correctly) translates here the Arabic *yawm al-dīn* as "Day of Retribution"; cf. 1:4; 12:76; 15:34; 38:78; 70:26; 74:46; 82:15–17. This sense of the word seems to be confirmed by 12:76, where the expression *dīn al-malik* is appropriately translated by Qarai as "the king's justice" (cf. Syr. *dīnā,* "judgment"). Elsewhere (e.g., 2:132, 193, 256; 3:19; passim) *dīn* means something closer to "religion," "faith," or "practice."

---

¹²and none denies it except every sinful transgressor. ¹³When Our signs are recited to him, he says, 'Myths of the ancients!'

83:13 On the expression "myths of the ancients," see commentary on 68:15 (with further references).

---

¹⁴No! Rather, their hearts have been sullied by what they have been earning.

¹⁵They will indeed be alienated from their Lord on that day. ¹⁶Then they will enter hell ¹⁷and be told, 'This is what you used to deny!'

¹⁸Indeed, the record of the pious is in *Illiyūn.* ¹⁹And what will show you what is *Illiyūn?* ²⁰It is a written record, ²¹witnessed by those brought near [to God].

83:18–21 The Qur'ān here refers to a heavenly book which is the register of the good deeds of humans and is located in *'illiyūn* (although v. 20 suggests that *'illiyūn* is the record itself) in contrast to the book mentioned in verses 7–9 which contains their evil deeds and is located *in sijjīn* (although v. 9 suggests that *sijjīn* is the register itself). The term *'illiyūn* derives ultimately from Hebrew *'elyōn,* "the highest," and implies that the book of good deeds is in the highest heaven. *Tafsīr al-Jalālayn* notes a tradition that *'illiyūn* is in fact "a place below the Throne in the seventh heaven." The derivation of *sijjīn* is unclear, but one imagines that it should mean the lowest level of the underworld. (On *sijjīn Tafsīr al-Jalālayn* comments: "It is also said to be a location in the lowermost part of the seventh earth, the place of Satan and his hosts.")

The topos of a heavenly register of human deeds is found in Daniel 7:10; Malachi 3:16; Revelation 20:12; Mishnah Avot (2:1); and 2 Enoch (see commentary on 82:10–12). In 84:7–16 the Qur'ān contrasts the giving of a heavenly register to the blessed with the giving of a heavenly register to the damned. Otherwise for references to the heavenly register, see 3:181; 4:81; 9:120–21; 10:21; 17:13–14; 18:49; 19:79; 21:94; 36:12; 39:69; 43:80; 45:29; 50:17; 54:52–53; 78:29; 83:7–9, 18–21; 84:7, 10.

---

²²The pious will be amid bliss, ²³observing [as they recline] on couches. ²⁴You will perceive in their faces the freshness of bliss. ²⁵They will be served with a sealed pure wine, ²⁶whose seal is musk—for such let the viers vie—²⁷and whose seasoning is from *Tasnīm,* a spring where those brought near [to God] drink.

²⁹Indeed, the guilty used to laugh at the faithful, ³⁰and when they passed them by they would wink at each other, ³¹and when they returned to their folks they would return amused, ³²and

when they saw them they would say, 'Those are indeed astray!'
[33]Though they were not sent to watch over them.

[34]So today the faithful will laugh at the faithless, [35]observing
from their couches: [36]Have the faithless been requited for what
they used to do?

84. *AL-INSHIQĀQ,* The Splitting

In the Name of God, the All-beneficent, the All-merciful.

¹When the heaven is split open ²and gives ear to its Lord as it should. ³When the earth is spread out ⁴and throws out what is in it, emptying itself, ⁵and gives ear to its Lord as it should.

⁶O man! You are labouring toward your Lord laboriously, and you will encounter Him.

⁷As for him who is given his record [of deeds] in his right hand, ⁸he will receive an easy reckoning, ⁹and he will return to his folks joyfully.

¹⁰But as for him who is given his record from behind his back, ¹¹he will pray for annihilation ¹²and enter the Blaze. ¹³Indeed, he used to be joyful among his folk, ¹⁴and he thought that he would never return. ¹⁵Yes, his Lord had been watching him.

¹⁶I swear by the evening glow,

84:7–16 On the heavenly register of good and evil deeds in the Qur'ān, see commentary on 82:10–12 and 83:18–21 (with further references).

---

¹⁷by the night and what it is fraught with, ¹⁸by the moon when it blooms full: ¹⁹you will surely fare from stage to stage.

²⁰What is the matter with them that they will not believe, ²¹and will not prostrate when the Qur'ān is recited to them?

²²The faithless indeed impugn [the Apostle], ²³and God knows best what they keep to themselves. ²⁴So *inform* them of a painful punishment, ²⁵excepting such as are faithful and do righteous deeds: for them there will be an everlasting reward.

85. *AL-BURŪJ*, THE CONSTELLATIONS

In the Name of God, the All-beneficent, the All-merciful.

¹By the heaven with its houses, ²by the Promised Day, ³by the Witness and the Witnessed: ⁴perish the People of the Ditch! ⁵The fire abounding in fuel, ⁶above which they sat ⁷as they were themselves witness to what they did to the faithful.

85:4–7 The "Men of the Ditch" are traditionally identified with Christians who were martyred (in a ditch) by the Jewish Yemeni ruler Dhū Nuwās (see Ibn Hishām, 24; English trans.: p. 17). In fact (and as Blachère points out in his translation: 644–45n4), with "Men of the Ditch" the Qurʾān likely means the persecutors, and not to the ones persecuted (see v. 7). The Qurʾān may be alluding to the story of the three Israelites cast into a fiery furnace in Daniel 3 (which has those who cast the Israelites into the furnace killed by its flames). In contrast, Rudi Paret (505–6) argues that this passage alludes instead to those cast into the "ditch" of hell. His view is shaped in part by Marc Philonenko ("Une expression qoumrânienne dans le Coran," 555), who argues that the Arabic phrase that Qarai renders as "Men of the Ditch" (*aṣḥāb al-ukhdūd*) is a calque on a Hebrew idiom (*benē* or *aneshē ha-shaḥat*, "sons" or "people of the ditch") found in the Dead Sea Scroll texts for the impious.

---

⁸They were vindictive towards them only because they had faith in God, the All-mighty and the All-laudable, ⁹to whom

belongs the kingdom of the heavens and the earth, and God is witness to all things.

[10]Indeed, those who persecute the faithful men and women, and do not repent thereafter, there is for them the punishment of hell and the punishment of burning.

[11]Indeed, those who have faith and do righteous deeds—for them will be gardens with streams running in them. That is the supreme triumph.

85:11 On the streams of paradise, see commentary on 2:25 (with further references).

---

[12]Your Lord's seizing is indeed severe. [13]It is He who initiates [the creation] and brings it back, [14]and He is the All-forgiving, the All-affectionate, [15]Lord of the Throne, the All-glorious, [16]doer of what He desires.

[17]Did *you* receive the story of the hosts [18]of Pharaoh and Thamūd?

85:18 On Pharaoh in the Qur'ān, see commentary on 26:18–29, 30–45 (with further references).

---

[19]The faithless indeed dwell in denial [20]and God besieges them from all around.

[21]It is indeed a glorious Qur'ān, [22]in a preserved tablet.

86. *AL-ṬĀRIQ*, THE NIGHTLY VISITOR

In the Name of God, the All-beneficent, the All-merciful.

¹By the heaven and the nightly visitor ²(and what will show *you* what is the nightly visitor? ³It is the brilliant star): ⁴there is a guard over every soul.

86:4 Qarai renders the Arabic *ḥāfiẓ* as "guard." It more likely means "record keeper," that is, an angel who records the deeds of each human. Cf. the plural *ḥāfiẓūn* in 82:10, who are described as "writers" in the following verse (Q 82:11). See commentary on 82:10–12 (with further references).

---

⁵So let man consider from what he was created. ⁶He was created from an effusing fluid

86:6 On the creation of humans from water, see commentary on 24:41–45 (with further references).

---

⁷which issues from between the loins and the breast-bones.

⁸He is indeed able to bring him back [after death], ⁹on the day when the secrets are examined ¹⁰and he shall have neither power nor helper.

¹¹By the resurgent heaven, ¹²and by the furrowed earth: ¹³it is indeed a conclusive discourse ¹⁴and not a jest.

¹⁵They are indeed devising a stratagem, ¹⁶and I [too] am devising a plan. ¹⁷So *respite* the faithless; *give* them a gentle respite.

87. *AL-A'LĀ,* The Most Exalted

In the Name of God, the All-beneficent, the All-merciful.

¹*Celebrate* the Name of *your* Lord, the Most Exalted, ²who created and proportioned, ³who determined and guided, ⁴who brought forth the pasture, ⁵and then turned it into a black scum.

⁶We shall have *you* recite [the Qurʾān], then *you* will not forget [any of it] ⁷except what God may wish. He knows indeed what is open to view and hidden.

⁸We shall smooth *your* way to [preach] the easiest [canon]. ⁹So *admonish,* for admonition is indeed beneficial: ¹⁰he who fears [God] will take admonition, ¹¹and the most wretched will shun it ¹²—he who will enter the Great Fire, ¹³then he will neither live in it, nor die.

¹⁴'Felicitous is he who purifies himself, ¹⁵celebrates the Name of his Lord, and prays.

¹⁶Rather, you prefer the life of this world, ¹⁷while the Hereafter is better and more lasting.' ¹⁸This is indeed in the former scriptures, ¹⁹the scriptures of Abraham and Moses.

87:18–19 On the scriptures (*ṣuḥuf*) of Moses and Abraham, see commentary on 53:36–37. See also commentary on 80:13–15 (with further references).

88. AL-GHĀSHIYA, THE ENVELOPER

In the Name of God, the All-beneficent, the All-merciful.

¹Did *you* receive the account of the Enveloper? ²Some faces on that day will be humbled, ³wrought-up and weary: ⁴they will enter a scorching fire ⁵and made to drink from a boiling spring. ⁶They will have no food except cactus, ⁷neither nourishing, nor of avail against hunger.

⁸Some faces on that day will be joyous, ⁹pleased with their endeavour, ¹⁰in a lofty garden,

88:10 The garden of paradise is lofty in the Qur'ān because it is connected to the Garden of Eden (see commentary on 9:72, with further references) which, in line with Syriac Christian tradition, is imagined to be at the top of a cosmic mountain that reaches into heaven. See further the commentary on 2:25.

¹¹where they will not hear any vain talk. ¹²In it there is a flowing spring ¹³and raised couches, ¹⁴with goblets set, ¹⁵and cushions laid out in an array, ¹⁶and carpets spread out.

¹⁷Do they not consider the camel, [to see] how it has been created? ¹⁸and the heaven, how it has been raised? ¹⁹and the moun-

tains, how they have been set? ²⁰and the earth, how it has been surfaced?

88:17–20 The divine voice of the Qur'ān points to these elements of nature (camel, the sky or heaven, mountains, earth) as signs that point to God's power. In Job 28 God speaks, "from the heart of the tempest" and begins to describe similar elements of nature in order to show the limitations of human knowledge and the extent of God's power:

> ⁴Where were you when I laid the earth's foundations? Tell me, since you are so well-informed!
> ⁵Who decided its dimensions, do you know? Or who stretched the measuring line across it?
> ⁶What supports its pillars at their bases? Who laid its cornerstone
> ⁷to the joyful concert of the morning stars and unanimous acclaim of the sons of God? (Job 38:4–7)

> ¹Do you know when mountain goats give birth? Have you ever watched deer in labour?
> ²Have you ever counted the months that they carry their young? Do you know when they give birth? (Job 39:1–2)

Note that Muhammad Asad argues (based on a variant reading) that the term in verse 17 rendered by Qarai as camel (*ibil;* Asad reads *ibill*) means instead clouds "pregnant with water" (cr. Joseph Witztum).

———————

²¹So *admonish*—for *you* are only an admonisher, ²²and not a taskmaster over them—²³except him who turns back and disbelieves. ²⁴Him God will punish with the greatest punishment.

²⁵To Us indeed will be their return. ²⁶Then, indeed, their reckoning will lie with Us.

89. *AL-FAJR,* THE DAWN

In the Name of God, the All-beneficent, the All-merciful.

¹By the Dawn, ²by the ten nights, ³by the Even and the Odd, ⁴by the night when it departs! ⁵Is there an oath in that for one possessing intellect?

⁶Have *you* not regarded how *your* Lord dealt with [the people of] ʿĀd, ⁷[and] Iram, [the city] of the pillars, ⁸the like of which was not created among cities, ⁹and [the people of] Thamūd, who hollowed out the rocks in the valley, ¹⁰and Pharaoh, the impaler

---

89:10 Qarai renders here (and in 38:12) the Arabic *dhū l-awtād* (lit. "the possessor of stakes") as "impaler" (explaining that Pharaoh used to execute his opponents by impaling them with stakes), but there is no little confusion over this term among interpreters. Yusuf Ali translates "lord of stakes," and Asad, "Pharaoh of the [many] tent-poles" (which, he explains, is a symbolic allusion to power). Hilali-Khan (following a medieval tradition found with *Tafsīr al-Jalālayn*) renders as "he who had pegs (who used to torture men by binding them to pegs)." Speyer (*BEQ,* 283) suggests that there is a connection here to the story of the Tower of Babel. The possibility that the Qurʾān is alluding to Pharaoh as a builder is suggested by the tower to heaven which the Qurʾān has Pharaoh demand that Haman build him (28:38) and the reference to God's destroying what Pharaoh built (7:137).

---

[11]—those who rebelled [against God] in their cities [12]and caused much corruption in them, [13]so *your* Lord poured on them lashes of punishment.

[14]*Your* Lord is indeed in ambush.

[15]As for man, whenever his Lord tests him and grants him honour and blesses him, he says, 'My Lord has honoured me.' [16]But when He tests him and tightens for him his provision, he says, 'My Lord has humiliated me.'

[17]No indeed! No, you do not honour the orphan

89:17 On the importance of kindness to orphans, see commentary on 107:2 (with further references).

---

[18]and do not urge the feeding of the needy. [19]You eat your inheritance rapaciously, [20]and love wealth with much fondness.

[21]No indeed! When the earth is levelled to a plain, [22]and *your* Lord['s edict] arrives with the angels in ranks, [23]the day when hell is brought [near], man will take admonition on that day, but what will the admonition avail him?

[24]He will say, 'Alas, had I sent ahead for my life [in the Hereafter]!' [25]On that day none shall punish as He punishes, [26]and none shall bind as He binds.

[27]'O soul at peace! [28]Return to your Lord, pleased [with Him] and pleasing [to Him]! [29]Then enter among My servants [30]and enter My paradise!'

90. *AL-BALAD,* THE TOWN

In the Name of God, the All-beneficent, the All-merciful.

¹I swear by this town, ²as *you* reside in this town, ³and by the father and him whom he begot: ⁴certainly We created man in travail. ⁵Does he suppose that no one will ever have power over him?

⁶He says, 'I have squandered immense wealth.'

⁷Does he suppose that no one sees him?

⁸Have We not made for him two eyes, ⁹a tongue, and two lips, ¹⁰and shown him the two paths [of good and evil]?

¹¹Yet he has not embarked upon the uphill task.

¹²And what will show *you* what is the uphill task?

¹³[It is] the freeing of a slave, ¹⁴or feeding during days of [general] starvation ¹⁵an orphan among relatives ¹⁶or a needy person in desolation, ¹⁷while being one of those who have faith and enjoin one another to patience and enjoin one another to compassion. ¹⁸They are the People of the Right Hand.

¹⁹But those who deny Our signs, they are the People of the Left Hand. ²⁰A closed Fire will be [imposed] upon them.

90:7–20 The Qur'ān here puts the blessed on the right hand (cf. 56:8, 27–40, 90; 74:39) and the condemned on the left hand (cf. 56:9, 41–56, 92–94). Elsewhere the Qur'ān refers to those who receive a book with their right (17:71; 69:19; 84:7) or left (69:25) hand (or behind their back, 84:10). This division, and the way the Qur'ān here makes good works the standard with which humans are sent to one side or another, reflects the judgment scene of Matthew 25:

> ³⁴Then the King will say to those on his right hand, "Come, you whom my Father has blessed, take as your heritage the kingdom prepared for you since the foundation of the world.
>
> ³⁵For I was hungry and you gave me food, I was thirsty and you gave me drink, I was a stranger and you made me welcome,
>
> ³⁶lacking clothes and you clothed me, sick and you visited me, in prison and you came to see me."
>
> ³⁷Then the upright will say to him in reply, "Lord, when did we see you hungry and feed you, or thirsty and give you drink?
>
> ³⁸When did we see you a stranger and make you welcome, lacking clothes and clothe you?
>
> ³⁹When did we find you sick or in prison and go to see you?"
>
> ⁴⁰And the King will answer, "In truth I tell you, in so far as you did this to one of the least of these brothers of mine, you did it to me."
>
> ⁴¹Then he will say to those on his left hand, "Go away from me, with your curse upon you, to the eternal fire prepared for the devil and his angels. (Mat 25:34–41)

Neuwirth (*Der Koran: Band 1,* 244; cf. Rudolph, *Abhängigkeit,* 10) also sees a direct connection with Isaiah 58:6–7 (which informs Matthew 25). See also commentary on 56:8–11.

On the Qur'ānic allusions to eye, tongue, and lips (vv. 8–9), Neuwirth (*Der Koran: Band 1,* 242) refers to a number of passages in the Psalms which mention the sense organs: Psalm 12:3–4; 15:3; 40:6; 94:9. Rudolph (*Abhängigkeit,* 13) connects verse 10 to Matthew 7:13: "Enter by the narrow gate, since the road that leads to destruction is wide and spacious, and many take it." On kindness to orphans (v. 15), see commentary on 107:2 (with further references).

91. *AL-SHAMS*, THE SUN

In the Name of God, the All-beneficent, the All-merciful.
[1]By the sun and her forenoon splendour, [2]by the moon when he follows her, [3]by the day when it reveals her, [4]by the night when it covers her, [5]by the heaven and Him who built it, [6]by the earth and Him who spread it, [7]by the soul and Him who fashioned it, [8]and inspired it with [discernment between] its virtues and vices: [9]one who purifies it is felicitous [10]and one who betrays it fails.

[11]The [people of] Thamūd denied [God's signs] out of their rebellion, [12]when the most wretched of them rose up. [13]The apostle of God had told them, 'This is God's she-camel, let her drink!' [14]But they impugned him and hamstrung her. So their Lord took them unawares by night because of their sin, and levelled it, [15]and He does not fear its outcome.

92. *AL-LAYL,* THE NIGHT

In the Name of God, the All-beneficent, the All-merciful.

¹By the night when it envelops, ²and by the day when it brightens, ³by Him who created the male and the female: ⁴your endeavours are indeed diverse.

⁵As for him who gives and is Godwary and confirms the best promise, ⁷We will ease him toward facility.

⁸But as for him who is stingy and self-complacent, ⁹and denies the best promise, ¹⁰We will ease him toward hardship. ¹¹His wealth shall not avail him when he perishes.

¹²Guidance indeed rests with Us ¹³and to Us belong the world and the Hereafter. ¹⁴So I warn you of a blazing fire, ¹⁵which none shall enter except the most wretched [of persons], ¹⁶he who impugns [God's prophets] and turns his back.

¹⁷The Godwary will be spared of that ¹⁸—those who give their wealth to purify themselves ¹⁹and do not expect any reward from anyone, ²⁰but seek only the pleasure of their Lord, the Most Exalted, ²¹and soon they will be well-pleased.

92:17–21 The idea that almsgiving is a path to purity (v. 18; cf. 76:9; 87:14; 91:9) is a prominent Biblical theme, and reflects in particular the notion of interior purity emphasized in Luke:

³⁹But the Lord said to him, 'You Pharisees! You clean the outside of cup and plate, while inside yourselves you are filled with extortion and wickedness. ⁴⁰Fools! Did not he who made the outside make the inside too? ⁴¹Instead, give alms from what you have and, look, everything will be clean for you. (Luk 11:39–41)

For his part Wāḥidī explains verses 19–21 with a story about the well-known companion of the Prophet (and onetime slave) Bilāl:

Upon embracing Islam, Bilal—who was a slave of 'Abd Allah ibn Jud'an—proceeded to the idols [of the Ka'bah] and defecated on them. . . . The idolaters took Bilal and tortured him in the scorchedness of the desert. . . . The Messenger of God then informed Abu Bakr, saying: 'Bilal is being tortured for the sake of God!' Abu Bakr took with him a pound of gold and went and bought Bilal. The idolaters said: 'Abu Bakr did what he did only because he is obliged to Bilal for a favour,' and so God revealed [Q 92:19–21].

93. *AL-ḌUḤĀ*, MORNING BRIGHTNESS

In the Name of God, the All-beneficent, the All-merciful.

¹By the morning brightness, ²and by the night when it is calm! ³*Your* Lord has neither forsaken *you,* nor is He displeased with *you,* ⁴and the Hereafter shall be better for *you* than the world. ⁵Soon *your* Lord will give *you* [that with which] *you* will be pleased.

⁶Did He not find *you* an orphan and shelter *you*? ⁷Did He not find *you* astray and guide *you*? ⁸Did He not find *you* needy and enrich *you*?

⁹So, as for the orphan, do not oppress him; ¹⁰and as for the beggar, do not chide him; ¹¹and as for *your* Lord's blessing, proclaim it!

93:1–11 This Sura has often been read by Western scholars as proof that Muḥammad was an orphan (v. 6) and that he went through a period when he was deprived of revelations or went unheeded (vv. 3–5). Such ideas are likely derived from this Sura itself (it is then circular to rely on them to explain the Sura). The website Corpus Coranicum notes the liturgical quality of this Sura and points out a number of parallels with the Psalms, including: verse 3 and Psalm 22:24: "For he has not despised nor disregarded the poverty of the poor, has not turned away his face, but has listened to the cry for help," and verse 5 and Psalm 20:4"May he grant you your heart's desire and crown all your plans with success!" On the appeal to kindness to orphans (v. 9), see commentary on 107:2.

The way the Qur'ān uses a reflection on God's goodness to make an ethical appeal to its audience in this Sura is similar to New Testament passages such as Luke 6:36: "Be compassionate just as your Father is compassionate" (cf. Eph 5:1–2).

94. *AL-SHARḤ,* OPENING

In the Name of God, the All-beneficent, the All-merciful.

94 *overview* The biography of the Prophet spins from this Sura a tale of an-gels who physically open Muḥammad's body and remove an impurity from it: "I was suckled among the B. Sa'd b. Bakr, and while I was with a brother of mine behind our tents shepherding the lambs, two men in white raiment came to me with a gold basin full of snow. Then they seized me and opened up my belly, extracted my heart and split it; then they extracted a black drop from it and threw it away; then they washed my heart and my belly with that snow until they had thoroughly cleansed them" (Ibn Hishām 106; English trans.: 72). However, the "opening" (or better "expansion") of one's breast is a metaphor in the Qur'ān (cf. 6:125; 16:106; 20:25, in the mouth of Moses; 39:22) for guidance or enlight-enment. Generally this Sura should be taken (like 93:6–11) as an exhortation to worship God in thanksgiving for his compassion (cf. Heb 12:28).

---

¹Did We not open *your* breast for *you* ²and relieve *you* of *your* burden ³which [almost] broke *your* back? ⁴Did We not exalt *your* name?

⁵Ease indeed accompanies hardship. ⁶Ease indeed accompanies hardship. ⁷So when *you* are done, *appoint,* ⁸and *supplicate your* Lord.

95. *AL-TĪN,* The Fig

In the Name of God, the All-beneficent, the All-merciful.

¹By the fig and the olive, ²by Mount Sinai, ³and by this secure town:

95:1–3 It is not clear why the Qur'ān connects an oath on figs (only here in the Qur'ān) and olives (v. 1) with Mt. Sinai, a location which is not known for either (cf. 23:20, which also seems to connect Mt. Sinai with an olive tree). It could be, as Horovitz proposes (*KU,* 124) that the Qur'ān means here to portray a vision of heaven, symbolized by Mt. Sinai, since it is the location of the divine theophany.

Tafsīr al-Jalālayn suggests that by "fig and olive" the Qur'ān might mean "the two mountains in greater Syria" (probably one of these mountains is meant to be the Mount of Olives in Jerusalem; cr. Joseph Witztum). On Mount Sinai (v. 2), cf. 23:20; 52:1.

---

⁴We certainly created man in the best of forms; ⁵then We relegated him to the lowest of the low, ⁶except those who have faith and do righteous deeds. There will be an everlasting reward for them.

⁷So what makes you deny the Retribution? ⁸Is not God the fairest of all judges?

96. AL-'ALAQ, THE CLINGING MASS

In the Name of God, the All-beneficent, the All-merciful.

¹*Read* in the Name of *your* Lord who created;

96:1 Islamic tradition generally makes this verse the first revelation spoken by the angel Gabriel to Muḥammad. One well-known tradition explains that Gabriel showed Muḥammad a sort of cloth with words on it and commanded him to "read": "When it was the night on which God honoured him with his mission and showed mercy on His servants thereby, Gabriel brought him the command of God. 'He came to me,' said the apostle of God, 'while I was asleep, with a coverlet of brocade whereon was some writing, and said, "Read!" (Ibn Hishām 152; English trans.: 106). Yet the opening command of this Sura (Ar. *iqra' bi-smi rabbika*) reflects the Hebrew phrase *wa-yiqra' bi-shem YHWH*, which appears several times in the Pentateuch (e.g., Gen 12:8: "There he built an altar to the Lord and *invoked the name of the Lord* [*wa-yiqra' bi-shem YHWH*] (cf. Gen 26:25; Exo 34:5; Isa 12:4; Psa 116:13; 17). This might suggest that the meaning of the verse is not "Read" in the name of God (as Qarai has it) but rather "Invoke" (cf. the similar Qur'ānic locution with *sabbiḥ:* 56:74; 69:52; see also 73:8; 76:25; 87:1). Rubin ("*Iqra' bi-smi rabbika*") sees this is as a command to perform a "devotional act" (216).

---

²created man from a clinging mass.

917

³*Read,* and *your* Lord is the most generous, ⁴who taught by the pen, ⁵taught man what he did not know.

⁶Man indeed becomes rebellious ⁷when he considers himself without need.

⁸To *your* Lord is indeed the return.

⁹Tell me, he who forbids ¹⁰a servant when he prays, ¹¹tell me, should he be on [true] guidance, ¹²or bid [others] to Godwariness, ¹³tell me, should he call him a liar and turn away ¹⁴—does he not know that God sees [him]?

¹⁵No indeed! If he does not stop, We shall seize him by the forelock,

96:15 As Andrew Rippin has commented (*QSC,* 423), the reference to the forelock here is close to Ezekiel 8:3, where Ezekiel is dragged to Jerusalem: "Something like a hand was stretched out and it took me by a lock of my hair; and the spirit lifted me between heaven and earth and, in visions from God, took me to Jerusalem."

¹⁶a lying, sinful forelock! ¹⁷Then let him call out his gang! ¹⁸We [too] shall call the keepers of hell.

¹⁹No indeed! *Do not obey* him, but prostrate and draw near [to God]!

97. *AL-QADR,* THE ORDAINMENT

In the Name of God, the All-beneficent, the All-merciful.

97 *overview* Muslim scholars identify the "it" of verse 1 (sometimes with reference to 44:2–5) with the Qur'ān itself. *Tafsīr al-Jalālayn* comments: "Lo! We revealed it, that is, the Qur'ān, in its entirety, [sending it down] from the Preserved Tablet to the heaven of this world, on the Night of Ordainment, that is, [the Night] of great eminence." However, instead of imagining that the Qur'ān has an image of itself as a preexisting book in heaven, one could see 97:1 as a reference to an earlier revelation (i.e., a *qur'ān* but not *the* Qur'ān).

Another possibility, which has been raised by Christoph Luxenberg ("Nöel dans le Coran") and Guillaume Dye ("La nuit du Destin") is that the Qur'ān is referring here instead to the descent of Jesus—whom the Qur'ān describes as a "word from God" (Q 3:45; cf. 4:171; 19:34)—from heaven to earth. The language of this Sura, with its reference to angels (v. 4) and a peaceful night (v. 5) indeed seems to bear some similarity to Luke's account of the birth of Christ:

> [13]And all at once with the angel there was a great throng of the hosts of heaven, praising God with the words:
> [14]Glory to God in the highest heaven, and on earth peace for those he favours.
> (Luk 2:13–14)

However, it is perhaps more likely that the Qur'ān is reapplying "Christmas" imagery for its own purposes. On this see Sinai, "Weihnachten im Koran?" (esp. p. 30).

On the reference to a "thousand" months, one might compare Psalm 84:10: "Better one day in your courts than a thousand at my own devices, to stand on the threshold of God's house than to live in the tents of the wicked" (see Rudolph, *Abhängigkeit,* 10).

---

¹Indeed, We sent it down on the Night of Ordainment. ²And what will show you what is the Night of Ordainment?

³The Night of Ordainment is better than a thousand months. ⁴In it, the angels and the Spirit descend by the leave of their Lord with every command.

⁵It is peaceful until the rising of the dawn.

98. *AL-BAYYINA,* THE PROOF

In the Name of God, the All-beneficent, the All-merciful.

¹The faithless from among the People of the Book and the polytheists were not set apart [from the community of the faithful] until the proof had come to them: ²an apostle from God reciting impeccable scriptures, ³wherein are upright writings.

⁴Those who were given the Book did not divide except after the proof had come to them, ⁵though all they were told was to worship God, dedicating their faith to Him as men of pure faith, and to maintain the prayer and pay the *zakāt,* and that is the upright religion.

98:1–5 Here the Qur'ān suggests that the revelations recited by its Prophet divided the Jews and Christians (the People of the Book), as some of them respected these revelations while others did not. In verse 5 the Qur'ān declares that the People of the Book should strive to worship God as "men of pure faith" (Ar. *ḥunafā'*; sing. *ḥanīf*). The term *ḥanīf* is frequently associated in the Qur'ān with Abraham (see 2:135; 3:67, 95, 4:125; 6:79, 161; 10:105; 16:120–23; cf. 30:30). It is derived from Syriac *ḥanpā,* meaning "pagan" or "gentile." See further commentary on 16:120–23.

On the Arabic term behind "scriptures" in verse 2, *ṣuḥuf,* see commentary on 80:13–15 (with further references).

⁶Indeed, the faithless from among the People of the Book and the polytheists will be in the fire of hell, to remain in it [forever]. It is they who are the worst of creatures.

⁷Indeed, those who have faith and do righteous deeds—it is they who are the best of creatures. ⁸Their reward, near their Lord, is the Gardens of Eden, with streams running in them, to remain in them forever. God is pleased with them, and they are pleased with Him. That is for those who fear their Lord.

98:8 On the Qurʾān's association of heaven with the Garden of Eden, see commentary on 9:72 (with further references). On the streams of paradise, see commentary on 2:25 (with further references).

99. *AL-ZALZALA,* THE QUAKE

In the Name of God, the All-beneficent, the All-merciful.

¹When the earth is rocked with a terrible quake ²and discharges her burdens, ³and man says, 'What is the matter with her?' ⁴On that day she will relate her chronicles ⁵for her Lord will have inspired her.

⁶On that day, mankind will issue forth in various groups to be shown their deeds. ⁷So whoever does an atom's weight of good will see it, ⁸and whoever does an atom's weight of evil will see it.

100. *AL-ʿĀDIYĀT*, THE CHARGERS

In the Name of God, the All-beneficent, the All-merciful.

100 *overview* Both Qarai and Neuwirth (*Der Koran: Band 1,* 169) follow Islamic tradition in identifying the "chargers" of verse 1 with "horses" (note the addition to Qarai's translation in v. 2) who make a loud noise when their hoofs strike the ground. Neuwirth wonders whether the subtext here could be the prophecy that warns of an Assyrian invasion in Isaiah 5. For his part Muhammad Asad (*Message,* 1105n2) argues that "the chargers' symbolize the erring human soul or self—a soul devoid of all spiritual direction."

---

[1]By the snorting chargers, [2]by the strikers of sparks [with their hoofs], [3]by the raiders at dawn, [4]raising therein a trail of dust, [5]and cleaving therein a host!

[6]Man is indeed ungrateful to his Lord, [7]and indeed he is [himself] witness to that! [8]And indeed he is an avid lover of wealth.

[9]Does he not know that when what is [buried] in the graves is turned over, [10]and what is [concealed] in the breasts is divulged,[11]their Lord will be well-informed about them [and their deeds] on that day ?

101. *AL-QĀRIʿA,* THE CATASTROPHE

In the Name of God, the All-beneficent, the All-merciful.

¹The Catastrophe! ²What is the Catastrophe? ³What will show you what is the Catastrophe?

⁴It is the day when mankind will be like scattered moths ⁵and the mountains will be like carded [tufts of] dyed wool.

⁶As for him whose deeds weigh heavy in the scales, ⁷he will have a pleasing life. ⁸But as for him whose deeds weigh light in the scales, ⁹his home will be the Abyss.

¹⁰And what will show you what it is? ¹¹It is a scorching fire!

102. *AL-TAKĀTHUR,* RIVALRY

In the Name of God, the All-beneficent, the All-merciful.

¹Rivalry [and vainglory] distracted you ²until you visited [even] the graves.

³Once again, no indeed! Soon you will know! ⁴No indeed, soon you will know for once again!

⁵No indeed, were you to know with certain knowledge, ⁶you would have surely seen hell [in this very life]. ⁷Afterwards you will surely see it with the eye of certainty. ⁸Then, on that day, you will surely be questioned concerning the Blessing.

103. AL-ʿAṢR, TIME

In the Name of God, the All-beneficent, the All-merciful.

[1]By Time! [2]Man is indeed in loss, [3]except those who have faith and do righteous deeds, and enjoin one another to [follow] the truth, and enjoin one another to patience [and fortitude].

104. *AL-HUMAZA,* THE SCANDAL-MONGER

In the Name of God, the All-beneficent, the All-merciful.

[1]Woe to every scandal-monger and slanderer, [2]who amasses wealth and counts it over. [3]He supposes his wealth will make him immortal!

[4]No indeed! He will surely be cast into the Crusher. [5]And what will show you what is the Crusher? [6][It is] the fire of God, set ablaze, [7]which will overspread the hearts. [8]Indeed, it will close in upon them [9]in outstretched columns.

105. *AL-FĪL*, THE ELEPHANT

In the Name of God, the All-beneficent, the All-merciful.

[1]Have *you* not regarded how *your* Lord dealt with the army of the elephants? [2]Did He not make their stratagems go awry, [3]and send against them flocks of birds [4]pelting them with stones of shale, [5]thus making them like chewed-up straw?

105:1–5 This Sura is traditionally understood to refer to a campaign led by an Ethiopian king (ruling in Yemen at the time) named Abraha in the year of the Prophet's birth. According to the traditional story Abraha attacked Mecca with (African) elephants but was repulsed when God sent flocks of birds which dropped stones on his army. It is probably better to understand this Sura as a development of the traditions in the Deuterocanonical books 2 and 3 Maccabees which tell stories of pagan armies (a Seleucid army in 2 Maccabees and a Ptolemaic army in 3 Maccabees), each accompanied by elephants, which attacked different communities of Jews. Particularly notable is the way 3 Maccabees 6:18–21 describes how angels descend from heaven to defeat the invaders and their beasts (compare Q 105:3, where Qarai renders Ar. *ṭayr,* "birds" in light of the traditional story; this term however, could refer to any flying creature). The argument is presented in detail by D. A. Beck in his article "Maccabees not Mecca." Beck also points out that African elephants are difficult to train and are not known to have been used in warfare after the first century BC.

106. *AL-QURAYSH,* QURAYSH

In the Name of God, the All-beneficent, the All-merciful.

¹[In gratitude] for solidarity among the Quraysh, ²their solidarity during winter and summer journeys, ³let them worship the Lord of this House, ⁴who has fed them [and saved them] from hunger, and secured them from fear.

106:4 The Arabic behind "secured them" (*āmanahum*) might be connected to the way Abraham prays elsewhere (14:35), "My Lord make this city a sanctuary (*āminan*)." This suggests that the locus of Q 106 is the same as the "city" which Abraham founds. Islamic tradition, of course, identifies this city with Mecca, but see commentary on 14:35–41 (with further references).

107. *AL-MĀ'ŪN,* AID

In the Name of God, the All-beneficent, the All-merciful.

¹Did you see him who denies the Retribution? ²That is the one who drives away the orphan,

107:2 The Qur'ān here (cf. the parallel passage 89:17ff.) suggests that believers should be aware of a responsibility toward orphans, a prominent theme in both the Old and New Testaments (which often join care for orphans with care for widows):

> Learn to do good, search for justice, discipline the violent, be just to the orphan, plead for the widow. (Isa 1:17; cf. Exo 22:22–24; Deu 26:12–13; Isa 1:17; 61:1–2; Jer 7:5–6; Zec 7:10)

> Pure, unspoilt religion, in the eyes of God our Father, is this: coming to the help of orphans and widows in their hardships, and keeping oneself uncontaminated by the world. (Jam 1:27)

On this theme in the Qur'ān, see 2:83, 177, 215; 4:1–10, 36; 6:152; 17:34; 76:8; 89:17; 90:15; 93:9.

---

³and does not urge the feeding of the needy.

[4]Woe to those who pray [5]but are heedless of their prayers [6]— who show off [7]but deny aid.

107:4–7 Neuwirth (*Der Koran: Band 1,* 137; cf. Rudolph *Abhängigkeit,* 13) compares the Qurʾān's condemnation of religious hypocrisy here to Matthew 6:5 (cf. Luke 11:43): "And when you pray, do not imitate the hypocrites: they love to say their prayers standing up in the synagogues and at the street corners for people to see them. In truth I tell you, they have had their reward."

108. *AL-KAWTHAR,* ABUNDANCE

In the Name of God, the All-beneficent, the All-merciful.

[1]We have indeed given *you* abundance. [2]So pray to *your* Lord, and sacrifice [the sacrificial camel]. [3]Indeed, it is *your* enemy who is without posterity.

108:3 As Christoph Luxenberg argues (*Syro-aramaic,* 297), the mention of an enemy (lit. "hater") here might in fact be an allusion to the devil. 1 Peter 5:8 refers to the devil as an enemy (but note the Qur'ān's reference to the devil's "offspring" in 18:50, which does not seem to match v. 3 here).

109. AL-KĀFIRŪN, THE FAITHLESS

In the Name of God, the All-beneficent, the All-merciful.

¹*Say,* 'O faithless ones! ²I do not worship what you worship, ³nor do you worship what I worship; ⁴nor will I worship what you have worshiped, ⁵nor will you worship what I worship. ⁶To you your religion, and to me my religion.'

110. *AL-NAṢR,* HELP

In the Name of God, the All-beneficent, the All-merciful.

[1]When God's help comes with victory [2]and *you* see the people entering God's religion in throngs, [3]*celebrate* the praise of *your* Lord, and *plead* to Him for forgiveness. He is indeed all-clement.

111. *AL-MASAD,* PALM FIBER

In the Name of God, the All-beneficent, the All-merciful.
¹Perish the hands of Abu Lahab and perish he!

111:1 Islamic tradition identifies Abū Lahab as the uncle of the Prophet (or more specifically, half brother of Muḥammad's father). More likely, however, Abū Lahab ("father of flame") is an epithet for enemies of the Prophet (and this Sura is meant to discourage opposition). Neuwirth (*Der Koran: Band 1,* 142) compares the way the Qur'ān curses "Abū Lahab" in this Sura with Psalm 137. Note in particular Psalm 137:5: "If I forget you, Jerusalem, may my right hand wither!"

---

²Neither his wealth availed him, nor what he had earned. ³Soon he will enter the blazing fire, ⁴and his wife, [too], the firewood carrier, ⁵with a rope of palm fibre around her neck.

112. *AL-IKHLĀṢ,* PURITY

In the Name of God, the All-beneficent, the All-merciful.

¹*Say,* 'He is God, the One. ²God is the All-embracing. ³He neither begat, nor was begotten, ⁴nor has He any equal.'

112:1–4 Islamic tradition puts the proclamation of this Sura in pagan Mecca but the Qurʾān's insistence that God neither begets nor is begotten (v. 3) leads some scholars (see esp. Kropp, "Tripartite, but Anti-Trinitarian Formulas") to see it as a response to Christian doctrine, and perhaps in particular to the Nicene Creed (according to which Christ is the "only begotten" [Gk. *monogenēs*] son of God). This Sura would then match those Qurʾānic passages (see 5:17, 72) which deny that "God is Christ." However, the Qurʾān's rhetoric against God's begetting is not always clearly directed against Christians. In some places (e.g., 21:26; see commentary on 21:21–29) where the Qurʾān denies that God has "taken" offspring (Ar. *walad,* which can have a singular or plural meaning) it is concerned with angels. The Qurʾān's rhetoric in this Sura might also be compared with the Jewish declaration of God's oneness, known as the *Shema* prayer (taken from Deu 6:4) which describes God as "one," in Hebrew, *eḥād* (compare the Arabic *aḥad,* for "one" in v. 1 of the present Sura). On this see Neuwirth, *Zur Komposition,* 26.

113. *AL-Falaq,* Daybreak

In the Name of God, the All-beneficent, the All-merciful.

[1]Say, 'I seek the protection of the Lord of the daybreak [2]from the evil of what He has created, [3]and from the evil of the dark night when it falls, [4]and from the evil of the witches who blow on knots, [5]and from the evil of the envious one when he envies.'

114. *AL-NĀS*, HUMANS

In the Name of God, the All-beneficent, the All-merciful.

[1]Say, 'I seek the protection of the Lord of humans, [2]Sovereign of humans, [3]God of humans, [4]from the evil of the sneaky tempter [5]who puts temptations into the breasts of humans, [6]from among the jinn and humans.'

A Note on Sources

I have benefited from a number of earlier works that involve a comparison of Bible and Qur'ān. These include, most notably, Abraham Geiger's 1833 *Was hat Mohammed aus dem Judenthume aufgenommen* (Bonn: Baaden, 1833; reprint, Leipzig: Kaufmann, 1902) and Heinrich Speyer's 1937 *Die biblischen Erzählungen im Qoran,* a work that remains the standard source for understanding the Qur'ān's references to Jewish (especially) and Christian traditions and narratives. The publication details of Speyer's work are given as Gräfenhainichen: Schulze, 1931 (reprint, Hildesheim: Olms, 1961); however, as F. Rosenthal notes in his "The History of Heinrich Speyer's *Die biblischen Erzählungen im Qoran,*" the printing was in fact done in 1937 in Breslau. See F. Rosenthal in D. Hartwig, W. Homolka, M. Marx, and A. Neuwirth (eds.), *Im vollen Licht der Geschichte: Die Wissenschaft des Judentums und die Anfänge der kritischen Koranforschung* (Würzburg: Ergon, 2008, 113–16), which is the transcript of an address that Prof. Rosenthal delivered in Berkeley, California, in 1993.

Also of note is the work of Denise Masson: *Le Coran et la révélation judéo-chrétienne* (Paris: Adrien-Maisonneuve, 1958), updated as *Monothéisme coranique et monothéisme biblique* (Paris: Desclée de Brouwer, 1976). In their method the works of Speyer and Masson differ substantially from the present work. Speyer's chapters proceed according to a Biblical chronology (beginning with creation, then Adam, and so on); he analyzes together all the Qur'ānic material connected to the particular Biblical topic at hand. Masson's work proceeds according to themes ("God," "creation," "revelation and prophetology," "duties of the believer," and "eschatology"). In addition, Masson refrains from a discussion of the Qur'ān's historical relationship with Jewish and Christian literature, and instead restricts herself to a literary and theological comparison of the Bible and the Qur'ān.

As regards Qurʾān and Bible, special mention must be made of the Corpus Coranicum web database (http://koran.bbaw.de/mitarbeiter/ehemalige-mitarbeiter) developed by the team led by Prof. Neuwirth (but involving also, at various stages, David Kiltz, Yousef Kouriyhe, Michael Marx, Veronika Roth, Nora Schmid, Nicolai Sinai, and others). The database, published online with open access, includes a section on *Umwelttexte* (http://www.corpuscoranicum.de/kontexte) that presents excerpts of pre-Qurʾānic Late Antique texts related to particular Qurʾānic passages (the main commentary section of the database also includes discussion of Biblical subtexts to Qurʾānic passages). Thus, for example, by selecting Qurʾān 2:4, one will find the Arabic text, an excerpt from the Babylonian Talmud (b. Sanhedrin 90a–b) in the original, a German translation, and a detailed discussion of the relationship between the two texts (by Veronika Roth and Nicolai Sinai).

Mention must also be made of the insightful studies of Guillaume Dye, Nicolai Sinai, and others who show the complexities of the Qurʾān's relationship with earlier Jewish and Christian literature. For the present work I have benefited in particular from Dye's "La nuit du Destin et la nuit de la Nativité," in G. Dye and Fabien Nobilio (eds.), *Figures bibliques en islam* (Brussels and Fernelmont: EME, 2011), 107–69; "Lieux saints communs, partagés ou confisqués: Aux sources de quelques péricopes coraniques (Q 19: 16-33)," in I. Dépret and G. Dye (eds.), *Partage du sacré: Transferts, dévotions mixtes, rivalités interconfessionnelles* (Brussels: EME and Intercommunications, 2012), 55–122; and from Sinai: "An Interpretation of Sūrat al-Najm (Q. 53)," *JQS* 13, no. 2 (2011): 1–28; "Weihnachten im Koran' oder 'Nacht der Bestimmung'? Eine Deutung von Sure 97," *Der Islam* 88 (2012): 11–32.

Other works have appeared since those of Speyer and Masson that also involve a comparison of Bible and Qurʾān. These include Ugo Bonanate's *Bibbia e Corano: I testi sacri confrontati* (Turin: Bollati Boringhieri, 1995); Johann-Dietrich Thyen's *Bibel und Koran: Eine Synopse gemeinsamer Überlieferungen* (Cologne: Böhlan, 2003); Stefan Jakob Wimmer and Stephan Leimgruber, *Von Adam bis Muhammad: Bibel und Koran im Vergleich* (Stuttgart: Katholisches Bibelwerk, 2005); and Marlies ter Borg (ed.), *Qurʾan and Bible Side by Side* (Charleston: CreateSpace, 2011). Compare the Dutch version: *Koran en Bijbel in verhalen.* Houten: Unieboek, 2007, 2013). More recently a former American politician, Mark Siljander, in the hope of promoting Muslim-Christian understanding, has sponsored a Qurʾān translation with copious quotations of Biblical verses (but no substantial explanations) in the notes: *The Qurʾān—with References to the Bible: A Contemporary Understanding,* trans. S. Kaskas with D. Hungerford (N.p.: New Diaspora Books, 2016).

All these works principally involve a comparison of the Qur'ān with the canonical Bible (although Thyen's work adds some of the Christian traditions surrounding the Sleepers of Ephesus and Alexander for the sake of comparison with Qur'ān 18 [*al-Kahf*]). The present work, in contrast, is an exploration of the Qur'ān's relationship with Jewish and Christian traditions generally, whether or not those traditions are found in the canonical Bible (and indeed it should be remembered that the precise nature of the Biblical canon varied in Late Antiquity). Put otherwise, this work is not a literary or theological comparison of Qur'ān and Bible but an attempt to better understand the Qur'ān through an investigation of its relationship with earlier literature.

Inasmuch as the present work proceeds according to the order of the Qur'ān, it has something in common with academic commentaries on the Qur'ān. Of these the two most notable works, and the most useful to me as I muddled through my research for this volume, were *A Commentary on the Qur'ān* of Richard Bell (C. E. Bosworth and M. E. J. Richardson, eds.) (Manchester: University of Manchester, 1991), and especially Rudi Paret's *Kommentar und Konkordanz* (Stuttgart: Kohlhammer, 1971). One might refer also to the lesser known, and earlier, commentary of E. M. Wherry (in four volumes): *A Comprehensive Commentary on the Qurán* (London: K. Paul, Trench, Trübner, 1896). I should also mention here the usefulness of the Qur'ān dictionary of A. Ambros, which offers etymologies for many Qur'ānic terms: A. A. Ambros and S. Procházka, *A Concise Dictionary of Koranic Arabic* (Wiesbaden: Reichert Verlag, 2004).

The works of Bell and Paret are different from the present work as they are interested in the Qur'ān generally and not in its relationship to Biblical literature particularly. In his *Commentary* Bell focuses on the question of the edition and collection process that led to the canonical text of the Qur'ān and less on the Qur'ān's relationship to earlier literature. This often leads him to imagine possible ways the Qur'ān could be understood in light of the *sīra;* indeed, his efforts to do so are on occasion so creative that they seem to prove the point that the method itself is flawed. Paret is less speculative in this regard. In addition he includes a useful system of cross-references. Paret also includes frequent references to earlier literature on the Qur'ān, especially the works of Josef Horovitz (*Koranische Untersuchungen;* Berlin: de Gruyter, 1926), the aforementioned Heinrich Speyer, Arthur Jeffery (*The Foreign Vocabulary of the Qur'ān;* Baroda: Oriental Institute, 1938; reprint, Leiden: Brill, 2007), and *Die Geschichte des Qorans* of Theodor Nöldeke et al. (Hildesheim: Olms, 1970; *History of the Qur'ān,* ed. and trans. Wolfgang H. Behn [Leiden: Brill, 2013]).

While Bell and Paret both include their commentaries on the Qur'ān in separate volumes from their translations, others have published translations accompanied by annotations meant to explain the text. Of these, however, most are religious works that offer commentary informed by a confessional Islamic perspective (there are, of course, many and diverse Islamic perspectives). Among English translations with annotations those of the progressive Pakistani Ahmed Ali (*Al-Qur'ān: A Contemporary Translation;* 1984, Princeton, NJ: Princeton University Press, 2001); the hadith-minded team of Muhsin Khan, Pakistani, and Taqi-ud-Din al-Hilali, Moroccan (*The Noble Qur'an;* Medina: King Fahd Complex, 1417/1996); and the idiosyncratic Austrian convert Muhammad Asad (*The Message of the Qur'ān;* Gibraltar: Al-Andalus, 1984) stand out (the latter two in particular feature relatively frequently in my commentary as examples of different Islamic perspectives).

There are only a few translations with academic annotations. Among these are the German translation of Hartmut Bobzin (with notes at the end of the volume: *Der Koran;* Munich: Beck, 2010) and, most notably, the recent (and excellent) translation of Arthur Droge: *The Qur'ān: A New Annotated Translation* (Sheffield: Equinox, 2013). One might also note here two partial translations of the Qur'ān accompanied by annotations. The first includes only the second Sura: Bertram Schmitz, *Der Koran: Sure 2 "Die Kuh"* (Stuttgart: Kohlhammer, 2009). The second involves highly eccentric and speculative revisionist readings (often based on Hebrew) of the first five Suras of the Qur'ān: Bruno Bonnet-Eymard, *Le Coran: Traduction et commentaire systématique,* 3 vols. (Saint-Parres-lès-Vaudes: La Contre-Réforme Catholique, 1988–1997).

Three other works that inspired the present work are not commentaries. The first of these is Max Grünbaum's 1893 *Neue Beiträge zur semitischen Sagenkunde* (Leiden: Brill, 1893). Many early scholars look at Qur'ānic material through the lens of later *tafsīr* traditions which explain that material in light of medieval reports (*akhbār*) on the life of Muḥammad. To give one of many possible examples, Richard Bell explains the story of Noah's lost son (Q 11:42–47) by imagining that Muḥammad sought to deliver a message to *muhājirūn* in Medina who had left relatives behind in Mecca, namely, that they should consider such unbelieving relatives to be lost: "There were no doubt, regrets for their relatives in the minds of the Muhājirīn and perhaps even in the Prophet's own mind, but such feelings could not be encouraged" (*Commentary,* 1:359). Grünbaum avoids such speculation. Unlike Bell he includes the Qur'ān as one work to be considered in a larger discussion of narratives shared among various Semitic literary traditions. Thereby the Qur'ān's relationship to its literary context emerges.

A second work which helped formed my vision for this book is Reuven Firestone's *Journeys in Holy Lands* (Albany: SUNY Press, 1990). Although Firestone is particularly interested in the development of the Abraham-Ishmael narrative in later Islamic exegesis, he discusses insightfully the ways both the Qur'ān and *tafsīr* relate to pre-Islamic versions of that narrative.

The third work in this category is James Kugel's *Traditions of the Bible: A Guide to the Bible as It Was at the Start of the Common Era* (Cambridge, MA: Harvard University Press, 1998; one might note also his *How to Read the Bible: A Guide to Scripture, Then and Now;* New York: Free Press, 2007). In *Traditions of the Bible* Kugel demonstrates the manner in which the Bible was read in the first century AD through a discussion of the midrashic and other traditions (both Jewish and Christian) which expand and develop the narratives of the Hebrew Bible. Kugel shows that the Bible was not experienced by most Jewish and Christian believers simply according to its contents alone but according to the way those contents had been explained and expanded on by later readers. While Kugel focuses on a period well before the composition of the Qur'ān this insight is nonetheless relevant, mutatis mutandis. In thinking of the Qur'ān's relationship with the Bible, we should not think simply of the canonical Bible but rather of "the Bible as it was in the Late Antique Near East." Many apparent cases of conflict between the Bible and the Qur'ān disappear when we remember to contextualize the way the author(s) of the Qur'ān would have experienced the Bible. Thus, in some ways the present work applies the insights of Kugel in a different context. The Qur'ān, which is of course of immense interest in its own right, also shows us something of how the Bible was understood in the Late Antique Near East.

Selected Bibliography

QUR'ĀN TRANSLATIONS

Aldeeb Abu-Sahlieh, Sami Awad. *Le Coran: Version bilingue arabe-francaise*. Paris: L'Aire, 2008.

Ali, Ahmed. *Al-Qur'an: A Contemporary Translation*. 1984; Princeton, NJ: Princeton University Press, 2001.

Arberry, Arthur. *The Koran Interpreted*. London: Allen and Unwin, 1955. Reprint, New York: Simon and Schuster, 1996.

Asad, Muhammad. *The Message of the Qur'ān*. Gibraltar: Al-Andalus, 1984.

Bell, Richard. *The Qur'ān: Translated with a Critical Re-arrangement of the Suras*. Edinburgh: T. and T. Clark, 1937.

Blachère, Régis. *Le Coran*. Paris: Maisonneuve, 1949.

Bobzin, Hartmut. *Der Koran*. Munich: Beck, 2010.

Bonnet-Eymard, Bruno. *Le Coran: Traduction et commentaire systématique. Tome 1 (Sourates I-II). Tome 2 (Sourate III). Tome 3 (Sourates IV-V)*. Saint-Parres-lès-Vaudes: La Contre-Réforme Catholique, 1988, 1990, 1997.

Droge, Arthur. *The Qur'ān: A New Annotated Translation*. Sheffield: Equinox, 2013.

Hilali, Taqi-ud-Din, and Muhammad Muhsin Khan. *The Noble Qur'an*. Medina: King Fahd Complex, 1417/1996.

Khalidi, Tarif. *The Qur'ān: A New Translation*. London: Penguin Classics, 2008.

Nasr, Seyyed Hossein, C. K. Dagli, M. M. Dakake, J. E. B. Lumbard, and M. Rustom. *The Study Qur'an*. San Francisco: HarperOne, 2015.

Paret, Rudi. *Der Koran: Übersetzung*. Stuttgart: Kohlhammer, 1962.

Pickthall, Muhammad. *The Meaning of the Glorious Qur'ān*. London: Knopf, 1930. Reprint, Kuala Lumpur: Islamic Book Trust, 1422/2001 (incorporating 248 "corrections" by Iqbal Husain Ansari of Karachi).

Qarai, Ali Quli. *The Qur'an: With a Phrase-by-Phrase English Translation*. 2nd ed. Elmhurst, NY: Tahrike Tarsile Qur'an, 2011.

Yusuf Ali, Abdullah. *The Holy Quran: Text, Translation and Commentary.* Lahore: Muḥammad Ashraf, 1938.

PRIMARY SOURCES (ISLAMIC)

Ibn Hishām. *Sīrat Rasūl Allāh.* Ed. F. Wüstenfeld. Göttingen: Dieterich, 1858–1860. English trans.: Ibn Isḥāq, *The Life of Muḥammad.* Trans. A. Guillaume. Oxford: Oxford University Press, 1955.

Ibn Kathīr. *Tafsīr.* Ed. Muḥammad Bayḍūn. Beirut: Dār al-Kutub al-ʿIlmiyya, 1424/2004.

al-Maḥallī, Jalāl al-Dīn, and Jalāl al-Dīn al-Suyūṭī. *Tafsīr al-Jalālayn.* Ed. Marwān Siwār. Beirut: Dār al-Jīl, 1410/1995. English trans.: *Tafsīr al-Jalālayn.* Trans. F. Hamza. Louisville, KY: Fons Vitae, 2008.

Ibn Manẓūr. *Lisān al-ʿarab.* Beirut: Dār Iḥyāʾ al-Turāth al-ʿArabī, 1418/1997.

Ibn Muğāhid. *Kitāb al-sabʿa fī al-qirāʾāt.* Ed. Shawqī Ḍayf. Cairo: Dār al-Maʿārif, 1972.

Muqātil b. Sulaymān, *Tafsīr.* Ed. ʿAbdallāh Muḥammad al-Shiḥāta. Beirut: Dār al-Turāth al-ʿArabī, 2002 (Reprint, Cairo: Muʾassasat al-Ḥalabī, n.d.).

Al-Rāzī, Fakhr al-Dīn. *Mafātīḥ al-ghayb.* Ed. Muḥammad Bayḍūn. Beirut: Dār al-Kutub al-ʿIlmiyya, 1421/2000.

al-Ṭabarī, Abū Jaʿfar Muḥammad b. Jarīr. *Jāmiʿ al-bayān ʿan taʾwīl āy al-Qurʾān.* Ed. Maḥmūd Shākir and ʿAlī ʿĀshūr. Beirut: Dār Iḥyāʾ al-Turāth al-ʿArabī, 2001.

al-Thaʿlabī, Abū Isḥāq. *ʿArāʾis al-majālis fī qiṣaṣ al-anbiyāʾ.* Ed. Ḥasan ʿAbd al-Raḥmān. Beirut: Dār al-Kutub al-ʿIlmiyya, 1425/2004.

al-Wāḥidī, Abū l-Ḥasan. *Asbāb nuzūl al-Qurʾān.* Ed. Kamāl Zaghlūl. Beirut: Dār al-Kutub al-ʿIlmiyya, 1411/1991. English trans.: M. Guezzou, *Al-Wāḥidī's Asbāb al-Nuzūl.* Louisville, KY: Fons Vitae, 2008.

PRIMARY SOURCES (NON-ISLAMIC)

Aphrahat (d. ca. 345 AD). "Demonstratio XX De Sustentatione egenorum." Ed. R. Graffin. In *Patrologia Syriaca I,* ed. I. Parisot, cols. 893–930. Paris: Firmin-Didot, 1897.

———. *Demonstrations.* Ed. William Wright. London: Williams and Norgate, 1869.

———. *Homilies.* In W. Wright (ed. and trans.), *The Homilies of Aphraates, the Persian Sage.* London: Williams and Norgate, 1869; later English trans. in J. Neusner, *Aphrahat and Judaism: The Christian-Jewish Argument in Fourth-Century Iran.* Leiden: Brill, 1971; French trans.: *Les exposés. Sources chrétiennes* 359. Trans. M.-J. Pierre. Paris: Cerf, 1988–1989.

Apocalypse of Abraham (2nd cen. AD). English trans.: A. Kulik, *Retroverting Slavonic Pseudepigrapha: Toward the Original of the Apocalypse of Abraham,* ed. J. R. Adair, 9–35. Leiden: Brill, 2004.

Aramaic Bowl Spells: Jewish Babylonian Aramaic Bowls. Ed. S. Shaked, J. N. Ford, and S. Bhayro. Leiden: Brill, 2013.

Ascension of Isaiah (2nd cen. BC-4th cen. AD). Ethiopic text in E. Norelli, *Ascensio Isaiae Corpus Scriptorum Series Apocryphorum.* Turnhout: Brepols, 1995. English trans. M.

A. Knibb in *The Old Testament Pseudepigrapha*. Ed. J. H. Charlesworth. Garden City, NY: Doubleday, 1985, 2:156–76.

Babai the Great (d. 628 AD). *Liber de unione. CSCO* 79 (Syriac text) and 80 (Latin trans.). Ed. and trans. A. Vaschalde. Louvain: Imprimerie Orientaliste, 1953.

Balai (early 5th cen.). In P. Bedjan (who attributes the work to Ephrem), *Histoire complète de Joseph par Saint Ephrem: Poème en douze livres*. Paris: Harrassowitz, 1891.

Cave of Treasures (4th–early 7th cen. AD). *CSCO* 486 (Syriac text) and 487 (French trans.). Ed. and trans. S.-M. Ri. Louvain: Peeters, 1987 (includes Occidental [Oc.] and Oriental [Or.] versions of the text).

Didache (1st–2nd cen. AD). In *The Apostolic Fathers: Greek Texts and English Translations of their Writings,* ed. and trans. J. B. Lightfoot, 2nd ed. Grand Rapids, MI: Baker Book House, 1989, 145–58.

The Didascalia Apostolorum in Syriac (3rd cen. AD). *CSCO* 401/407 (Syriac text) and 402/408 (English trans.). Ed. and trans. Arthur Vööbus. Louvain: Secrétariat du CorpusSCO, 1979.

The Doctrine of Addai (ca. AD 400). Trans. G. Phillips. London: Trübner, 1876.

I Enoch (2nd century BC–1st cen. AD). Trans. E. Isaac in *The Old Testament Pseudepigrapha*. Ed. J. H. Charlesworth. Garden City, NY: Doubleday, 1985, 1:5–89.

II Enoch (1st cen. AD). Trans. F. I. Anderson in *The Old Testament Pseudepigrapha*. Ed. J. H. Charlesworth. Garden City, NY: Doubleday, 1985, 1:91–221.

Ephrem the Syrian (d. ca. AD 373). *Histoire complète de Joseph par Saint Ephrem: Poème en douze livres*. Ed. P. Bedjan. Paris: Harrassowitz, 1891.

———. *Hymns*. Trans. K. E. McVey. New York: Paulist Press, 1989.

———. *Hymns on Paradise*. Trans. S. Brock. Crestwood, NY: St. Vladimir's Seminary Press, 1998.

———. *Hymns on the Nativity. CSCO* 186 (Syriac text) and 187 (German trans.). Ed. and trans. E. Beck. Louvain: Peeters, 1959.

———. *Hymns to Abraham Kidunaya: Des Heiligen Ephraem des Syrers Hymnen auf Abraham Kidunaya und Julianos Saba. CSCO* 322 (Syriac text) and 323 (German trans.). Ed. and trans. E. Beck. Louvain: Secrétariat du CorpusSCO, 1972.

———. *Letter to the Mountain Dwellers*. In *Des Heiligen Ephraem des Syrers Sermones IV. CSCO* 334 (Syriac text) and 335 (German trans.), ed. and trans. E. Beck. Louvain: Secrétariat du CorpusSCO, 1973.

———. *On the Mother of God. CSCO* 363 (Syriac text) and 364 (German trans.), ed. and trans. E. Beck. Louvain: Peeters, 1975.

———. "Rhythm against the Jews, Delivered upon Palm Sunday." In *A Library of Fathers of the Holy Catholic Church, Anterior to the Division of the East and West* 41, ed. and trans. J. B. Morris. Oxford: John Henry Parker, 1847, 61–83.

———. *Sancti Ephraem Syri in Genesim et in Exodum Commentarii*. Ed. and trans. R. M. Tonneau. Louvain: Durbecq, 1955.

———. *Sermones III (Sermons). CSCO* 320 (Syriac text) and 321 (German trans.). Ed. and trans. E. Beck. Louvain: Secrétariat du CorpusSCO, 1972.

———. *Sermones de fide (Sermons on Faith). CSCO* 212 (Syriac text) and 213 (German trans.). Ed. and trans. E. Beck. Louvain: Secrétariat du CorpusSCO, 1961.

————. *St. Ephrem the Syrian. Selected Prose Works: Commentary on Genesis, Commentary on Exodus, Homily on Our Lord, Letter to Publius.* Trans. E. G. Mathews, and J. P. Amar. Washington, DC: Catholic University of America Press, 1994.

Eusebius (d. ca. AD 340). *Ecclesiastical History.* Trans. K. Lake, J. E. L. Oulton, and H. J. Lawlor. Cambridge, MA: Harvard University Press, 1949.

4 Ezra (1st cen. AD). Trans. B. Metzger in *The Old Testament Pseudepigrapha.* Ed. J. H. Charlesworth. Garden City, NY: Doubleday, 1985, 1:517–59.

Genesis Rabbah, in *Midrash Rabbah.* Ed. H. Freedman and M. Simon and trans. H. Freedman, 3rd ed., vols. 1–2. London: Soncino Press, 1983.

Gospel of Philip (ca. 3rd cen. AD). In H. Lundhaug, *Images of Rebirth: Cognitive Poetics and Transformational Soteriology in the* Gospel of Philip *and the Exegesis on the Soul.* Leiden: Brill, 2010.

Gospel of Pseudo-Matthew (late 6th or 7th cen. AD). In *New Testament Apocrypha,* ed. W. Schneemelcher and trans. R. Wilson. Cambridge: J. Clarke and Co., 1991, 1:462–65.

Infancy Gospel of Thomas (2nd century AD). Trans. T. Burke. 2009. http://www.tonyburke .ca/infancy-gospel-of-thomas/the-childhood-of-the-saviour-infancy-gospel-of-thomas-a -new-translation/.

Irenaeus (d. AD 202). *Proof of the Apostolic Preaching.* Trans. J. P. Smith. Westminster, MD: Newman, 1952.

Isaac of Antioch (d. late 5th cen. AD). *Homily against the Jews.* In S. Kazan, "Isaac of Antioch's Homily against the Jews [part 1]." *Oriens Christianus* 45 (1961), 30–78. For an introduction to Isaac and his anti-Jewish writing, see Kazan, "Isaac of Antioch's Homily against the Jews [part 2]." *Oriens Christianus* 47 (1963): 93–97.

Jacob of Serugh (d. 521 AD). *Homélies contre les juifs. PO* 174. Ed. and trans. M. Albert. Turnhout: Brepols, 1976.

————. *Homily on the Departure of Adam from Paradise.* In *Quatre homélies métriques sur la création. CSCO* 508 (Syriac text) and 509 (French trans.), ed. and trans. K. Alwan. Louvain: Peeters, 1989.

————. "Jacob of Serūgh on the Veil of Moses." Trans. S. Brock. In *Sobornost* 3 (1981): 1, 70–85.

————. *Mēmrā on the Sleepers of Ephesus.* Trans. S. Brock in "Jacob of Serugh's Poem on the Sleepers of Ephesus." In P. Allen, M. Franzmann, and R. Strelan (eds.), *"I Sowed Fruits into Hearts" (Odes Sol. 17:13): Festschrift for Professor Michael Lattke.* Strathfield: St. Paul's Publications, 2007, 13–30.

————. *On Abraham and His Types.* In *Homiliae Selectae Mar-Jacobi Sarugensis.* Ed. P. Bedjan. Paris: Harrassowitz, 1905–10, 4:61–103.

————. *On the End of the World and the Day of Judgment.* In *Homiliae Selectae Mar-Jacobi Sarugensis.* Ed. P. Bedjan. Paris: Harrassowitz, 1905–10, 1:713–20.

————. *On the Flood.* In *Homiliae Selectae Mar-Jacobi Sarugensis.* Ed. P. Bedjan. Paris: Harrassowitz, 1905–10, 4:1–60.

James of Edessa (d. ca. 708). *The Hymns of Severus of Antioch and Others. PO* 6:1 (Syriac text with English trans.). Ed. and trans. E. W. Brooks. Turnhout: Brepols, 1971.

Jesse of Edessa (Mar Isaï; d. late 6th cen.). *Traités sur les martyrs. PO* 7:1. Trans. A. Scher. Paris: Firmin-Didot, 1911.

Josephus, Flavius (d. ca. AD 100). *Jewish Antiquities I–III.* English trans. H. St. J. Thackeray et al. Cambridge, MA: Harvard University Press, 1998; *Jewish Antiquities IX–XI.* English trans. R. Marcus. Cambridge, MA: Harvard University Press, 1998.

Jubilees (2nd cen. BC). Trans. O. S. Wintermute in *The Old Testament Pseudepigrapha.* Ed. J. H. Charlesworth. Garden City, NY: Doubleday, 1985, 2:35–142.

Justin Martyr (d. 165 AD). *Dialogue with Trypho.* Ed. M. Slusser. Washington, DC: Catholic University of America Press, 2003.

The Life of Adam and Eve (3rd–5th cen. AD). In *Die Apokryphen und Pseudepigraphen des Alten Testaments.* Ed. E. Kautzch. Tübingen: Mohr, 1900, 2:506–28. English trans. G. A. Anderson and M. E. Stone in *A Synopsis of the Books of Adam and Eve.* Atlanta: Scholars Press, 1999, 1–96.

Lives of the Prophets (5th–6th cen. AD). In David Satran, *Biblical Prophets in Byzantine Palestine: Reassessing the* Lives of the Prophets. *Studia in Veteris Testamenti Pseudepigrapha* 11. Leiden: E. J. Brill, 1995.

Mar Isaï (ca. 6th cen. AD). *Traités sur les martyrs. PO* 7:1 (Syriac text with French trans.). Trans. A. Scher. Turnhout: Brepols, 1971.

Mekilta de-Rabbi Ishmael (ca. late 4th cen. AD). Trans. J. Z. Lauterbach. Philadelphia: Jewish Publication Society of America, 1976.

Midrash Rabbah: Genesis, Exodus, Leviticus, Numbers, Deuteronomy, Lamentations, Ruth, Ecclesiastes, Esther, Song of Songs, 10 vols., 3rd ed. Ed. H. Freedman and M. Simon and trans. H. Freedman. London: Soncino Press, 1983.

[*Midrash*] *Tanhuma-Yelammedunu* (A late addition to *Genesis Rabbah*). Trans. S. A. Berman. Hoboken, NJ: KTAV, 1996.

The Mishnah. Trans. Herbert Danby. London: Oxford University Press, 1967.

Narsai (d. 503 AD). *Homilies on Creation.* In *Homélies de Narsaï sur la création.* Ed. P. Gignoux. *PO* 34:3 (Syriac text) and 34:4 (French trans.). Turnhout: Brepols, 1968.

———. *Homily on Joseph.* In *Narsai Doctoris Syri Homiliae et Carmina.* Ed. A. Mingana. Mosul: Typis Fratrum Praedicatorum, 1905, 2:265–88.

———. *Narsai's Metrical Homilies on the Nativity, Epiphany, Passion, Resurrection and Ascension. PO* 40.1. Trans. F. G. McLeod. Turnhout: Brepols, 1979.

———. "On the Flood." Ed. and trans. in J. Frishman, *The Ways and Means of the Divine Economy.* PhD dissertation. Leiden, 1992.

———. *On the Revelations to Abraham.* In *Narsai Doctoris Syri Homiliae et Carmina.* Ed. A. Mingana. Mosul: Typis Fratrum Praedicatorum, 1905, 1:57–68.

Origen (d. ca. 254 AD). *Contra Celsum.* Trans. H. Chadwick. Cambridge: Cambridge University Press, 1953.

The Panarion of Epiphanius of Salamis: Book 1. Trans. F. Williams. Leiden: Brill, 2009.

Paraleipomena of Jeremiah (1st–2nd cen. AD). Trans. E. Robinson ("4 Baruch") in *The Old Testament Pseudepigrapha: Apocalyptic Literature and Testaments.* Ed. J. H. Charlesworth. Garden City, NY: Doubleday, 1985, 2:413–14.

Philo (d. ca. AD 50). *The Life of Moses*. Trans. C. D. Yonge in *The Works of Philo: Complete and Unabridged*. London: H. G. Bohn, 1854–55; reprint, Peabody, MA: Hendrickson Publishers, 1993.

Pirke de-Rabbi Elieser (*Pirqe de-Rabbi Eliezer;* final version 9th cen. AD). Ed. and Trans. D. Börner-Klein. Berlin: de Gruyter, 2004.

The Protoevangelium of James (2nd cen. AD). Trans. O. Cullman in *New Testament Apocrypha*. Ed. W. Schneemelcher and trans. R. Wilson. Cambridge: J. Clarke and Co., 1991, 1:426–39.

Pseudo-Basil of Caesarea (ca. 5th cen. AD). *The Syriac History of Joseph*. English trans. K. Heal, "The Syriac History of Joseph." In *Old Testament Pseudepigrapha: More Noncanonical Scriptures*. Ed. R. Bauckham et al. Grand Rapids, MI: Eerdmans, 2013, 85–102.

Pseudo-Callisthenes. *The Legend of Alexander* (*Neṣḥānā d-leh d-Aleksandrōs*) (ca. AD 200). Ed. and trans. E. A. Wallis Budge in *The History of Alexander the Great, Being the Syriac Version of the Pseudo-Callisthenes*. Cambridge: Cambridge University Press, 1889, 144–58.

The Pseudo-Clementines (3rd–4th cen. AD). Trans. A. Roberts and J. Donaldson in *Ante-Nicene Fathers* 8. Grand Rapids, MI: Eerdmans Publishing Co., 1978. (Citations according to homily: chapter.)

Pseudo-Narsai (ca. 5th cen. AD). *Homilies on Joseph*. In *Homiliae Mar-Narsetis in Joseph*. In P. Bedjan (ed. and trans.), *Liber Superiorum*. Paris: Harrassowitz, 1901, 521–629. German trans. of first two homilies in H. Näf, *Syrische Josef-Gedichte*. Zurich: Buchdruckerei A. Schwarzenbach, 1923; English trans. of last two homilies in A. S. Rodrigues Pereira, "Two Syriac Verse Homilies on Joseph." *Jaarbericht Ex Oriente Lux* 31 (1989–90), 95–120.

Romanus Melodus (d. ca. AD 560). "De Joseph" and "Tentation de Joseph." In J. Grosdidier de Matons, *Romanos le Mélode: Hymns* I. Paris: Éditions du Cerf, 1964, 1:202–45; 1:260–93.

Shepherd of Hermas (late 1st cen. AD). Trans. J. B. Lightfoot in *Apostolic Fathers*. London: MacMillan, 1912, 289–483.

Sibylline Oracles (2nd cen. BC-7th cen. AD). Greek text in *Die Apokryphen und Pseudepigraphen des Alten Testaments*. Ed. E. Kautzsch. Tübingen: J. C. B. Mohr, 1900, 2:177–217. English trans. in *The Old Testament Pseudepigrapha*. Ed. J. H. Charlesworth. Garden City, NY: Doubleday, 1983, 1:317–472.

The Soncino Talmud. 1952; London: Soncino, 1961.

Song of Alexander. Das Syrische Alexanderlied: Die drei Rezensionen (ca. AD 630–35). *CSCO* 454 (Syriac text) and 455 (German trans.). Ed. and trans. G. J. Reinink. Louvain: Peeters, 1983.

Sozomen (d. ca. AD 450). *The Ecclesiastical History*. Trans. C. D. Hartranft in *The Nicene and Post-Nicene Fathers,* series 2. Ed. P. Schaff and H. Wace. Grand Rapids, MI: Eerdmans Publishing Co., 1978.

The Story of Aḥiḳar (ca. 4th–2nd cen. BC). Ed. and trans. F. C. Conybeare, J. R. Harris, and A. S. Lewis. 2nd ed. Cambridge: Cambridge University Press, 1913.

Symmachus (late 5th–early 6th cen. AD). *Life of Abel.* Ed. And trans. S. Brock in "A Syriac Life of Abel." *Le Muséon* 87 (1974) 467–92.

Syriac Dialogue Poem on Abel and Cain (5th cen. AD). In S. Brock, "Two Syriac Dialogue Poems on Abel and Cain." *Le Muséon* 113 (2000), 333–75 (see 335–63).

Targum Neofiti 1, Deuteronomy (ca. 4th–5th cen. AD). Ed. and trans. M. McNamara. Collegeville, MN: Liturgical Press, 1997.

Targum Neofiti 1, Genesis (ca. 4th–5th cen. AD). Ed. and trans. M. McNamara. Collegeville, MN: Liturgical Press, 1992.

Targum Onqelos to Exodus (ca. 3rd cen. AD). Trans. B. Grossfeld. Collegeville, MN: M. Glazier, 1988.

Targum Onqelos to Leviticus and Numbers (ca. 3rd cen. AD). Trans. B. Grossfeld. Collegeville, MN: M. Glazier, 1988.

Targum Sheni of Esther (date disputed, 4th–11th cen. AD). Trans. A. D. Bernstein in P. S. Cassel, *An Explanatory Commentary on Esther.* Edinburgh: T. and T. Clark, 1888, 263–344.

Tertullian (d. ca. AD 220). *Adversus Judaeos* (*An Answer to the Jews*). Trans. S. Thelwall in *The Writings of Tertullian* 3. *Translations of the Writings of the Fathers* 18. Ed. A. Roberts and J. Donaldson. Edinburgh: T. and T. Clark, 1870, 201–258.

Testament of Solomon: a New Translation and Introduction (1st–3rd cen. AD). Trans. D. C. Duling in James H. Charlesworth (ed.), *The Old Testament Pseudepigrapha. Vol. I: Apocalyptic Literature and Testaments.* New York: Doubleday, 1983, 1:935–95.

Theodosius (d. ca. AD 530). *The Pilgrimage of Theodosius.* Trans. J. H. Bernard. London: Palestine Pilgrims Text Society, 1893.

SECONDARY SOURCES

Ahrens, Karl. "Christliches im Qoran." *ZDMG* 84 (1930): 15–68, 148–90.

Albin, Michael. "Printing of the Qurʾan." *EQ*, 4:264–76.

Altmann, Alexander, "The Gnostic Background of the Rabbinic Adam Legends." *Jewish Quarterly Review* 35 (1945): 371–91.

Ambros, Arne A., and Stephan Procházka. *A Concise Dictionary of Koranic Arabic.* Wiesbaden: Reichert Verlag, 2004.

Andrae, Tor. *Mohammed, sein Leben und sein Glaube.* Göttingen: Vandenhoeck and Ruprecht, 1932. Trans.: *Mohammed: The Man and His Faith.* Trans. T. Menzel. New York: Charles Scribner's Sons, 1936.

———. *Les origines de l'islam et le christianisme.* Trans. J. Roche. Paris: Adrien-Maisonneuve, 1955. Originally published in German as "Der Ursprung des Islams und das Christentum." *Kyrkshistorisk årsskrift* 23 (1923): 149–206; 24 (1924): 213–25; 25 (1925): 45–112.

Anthony, Sean W. "Further Notes on the Word Ṣibgha in Qurʾan 2:138." *JSS* 59 (2014): 117–29.

Azaiez, Mehdi. *Le contre-discours coranique.* Berlin: de Gruyter, 2015.

Azmeh, Aziz. *The Emergence of Islam in Late Antiquity.* Cambridge: Cambridge University Press, 2014.

Badawi, Elsaid M., and Muhammad Abdel Haleem. *Arabic-English Dictionary of Qur'anic Usage.* Leiden: Brill, 2008.

Bannister, Andrew. *An Oral-Formulaic Study of the Qur'ān.* Lanham, MD: Lexington, 2014.

Beck, Daniel. "Maccabees not Mecca: The Biblical Subtext of *Sūrat al-Fīl.*" https://www .academia.edu/11493284/Maccabees_Not_Mecca_The_Biblical_Subtext_of_S%C5% ABrat_al-F%C4%ABl_Q_105_.

Beck, Edmund. *Das christliche Mönchtum im Koran.* Helsinki: Societas Orientalis Fennica, 1946.

———. "Iblis und Mensch, Satan und Adam: Der Werdegang einer koranischen Erzählung." *Le Muséon* 89 (1976): 195–244.

Bell, Richard. *A Commentary on the Qur'an.* Ed. C. E. Bosworth and M. E. J. Richardson. Manchester: University of Manchester, 1991.

———. *The Origin of Islam in Its Christian Environment.* London: MacMillan, 1926.

Benin, Stephen. "Commandments, Covenants, and the Jews in Aphrahat, Ephrem, and Jacob of Sarug." In D. R. Blumenthal (ed.), *Approaches to Judaism in Medieval Times.* Chico, CA: Scholars Press, 1984, 135–56.

Ben-Shammai, Haggai. "*Ṣuḥuf* in the Qur'ān: A Loan Translation for 'Apocalypses.'" In H. Ben-Shammai, S. Shaked, and S. Stroumsa (eds.), *Exchange and Transmission across Cultural Boundaries: Philosophy, Mysticism and Science in the Mediterranean World.* Jerusalem: Israel Academy of Sciences and Humanities, 2013, 1–15.

Bergsträsser, Gotthelf. "Koranlesung in Kairo." *Der Islam* 20 (1932): 1–42.

Birkeland, Harris. *The Lord Guideth: Studies in Primitive Islam.* Oslo: Aschehoug, 1956.

Boisliveau, Anne-Sylvie. *Le Coran par lui-même: Vocabulaire et argumentation du discours coranique autoréférentiel.* Leiden: Brill, 2015.

Bonnet-Eymard, Bruno. *Le Coran. Traduction et commentaire systématique. Tome 1 (Sourates I-II). Tome 2 (Sourate III). Tome 3 (Sourates IV-V).* Saint-Parres-lès-Vaudes: La Contre-Réforme Catholique, 1988, 1990, 1997.

Brady, David. "The Book of Revelation and the Qur'an: Is There a Possible Literary Relationship?" *JSS* 23 (1978): 216–25.

Brinner, William M. "An Islamic Decalogue." In W. M. Brinner and S. D. Ricks (eds.), *Studies in Islamic and Judaic Traditions.* Atlanta: Scholars Press, 1986, 67–84.

Brock, Sebastian. "Syriac Dispute Poems: The Various Types." In G. J. Reinink and H. L. J. Vanstiphout (eds.), *Dispute Poems and Dialogues in the Ancient and Mediaeval Near East.* Leuven: Peeters, 1991, 109–19.

Casanova, Paul. *Mohammed et la fin du monde.* Paris: Geuthner, 1911–24.

Chabbi, Jacqueline. *Le Coran décrypté. Figures bibliques en Arabie.* Paris: Fayard, 2008.

———. "Jinn." *EQ,* 3:43–50.

———. *Le Seigneur des tribus. L'islam de Mahomet.* Paris: CNRS Éditions, 2010.

———. *Les trois piliers de l'Islam: Une lecture anthropologique du Coran.* Paris: Éditions du Seuil, 2016.

Cragg, Kenneth. *Readings in the Qurʾān: Selected and Translated with an Introductory Essay.* London: HarperCollins: 1988.

Crone, Patricia. "Angels versus Humans as Messengers of God." In P. Townsend and M. Vidas (eds.), *Revelation, Literature, and Community in Late Antiquity.* Texts and Studies in Ancient Judaism 146. Tübingen: Mohr Siebeck, 2011, 315–36.

———. *"The Book of Watchers* in the Qurʾan." In H. Ben-Shammai, S. Shaked, and S. Stroumsa (eds.), *Exchange and Transmission across Cultural Boundaries: Philosophy, Mysticism and Science in the Mediterranean World.* Jerusalem: Israel Academy of Sciences and Humanities, 2013, 16–51.

———. "Jewish Christianity and the Qurʾān (Part Two)." *JNES* 75 (2016): 1–21.

———. "The Qurʾanic *Mushrikūn* and the Resurrection: Part I." *BSOAS* 75 (2012): 445–72.

———. "The Religion of the Qurʾanic Pagans." *Arabica* 57 (2010): 151–200.

Cuypers, Michel. "Une analyse rhétorique du début et de la fin du Coran." *Al-Kitāb. La sacralité du texte dans le monde de l'Islam. Acta Orientalia Belgica Subsidia* 3. Brussels: Société belge d'études orientales, 2004, 233–72.

———. *L'apocalypse du Coran: Lecture des trente-trois dernières sourates du Coran.* Paris: Gabalda, 2014.

———. *La composition du Coran.* Rhétorique sémitique IX. Paris: Librairie Gabalda, 2012. English trans.: J. Ryan, *The Composition of the Qurʾan.* London: Bloomsbury, 2015.

———. *Le festin: une lecture de la sourate al-Mâʾida.* Paris: Lethielleux, 2007. English trans.: P. Kelly, *The Banquet: A Reading of the Fifth Sura of the Qurʾan.* Miami: Convivium, 2009.

———. "Une lecture rhétorique et intertextuelle de la sourate *al-Ikhlâs.*" *MIDEO* 25–26 (2004): 141–75.

Czeglédy, K. "The Syriac Legend Concerning Alexander the Great." *Acta Orientalia* 7 (1957): 231–49.

de Blois, François. "Naṣrānī (Ναζωραῖος) and Ḥanīf (ἐθνικός): Studies in the Religious Vocabulary of Christianity and Islam." *BSOAS* 65 (2002): 1–30.

Dejmiri, Lejla. *Muslim Exegesis of the Bible in Medieval Cairo.* Leiden: Brill, 2013.

de Prémare, Alfred-Louis. *Joseph et Muhammad. Le chapitre 12 du Coran: étude textuelle.* Aix-en-Provence: Publications de l'Université de Provence, 1989.

Donner, Fred. "Qurʾanic *Furqān.*" *JSS* 52 (2007): 279–300.

Dye, Guillaume. "Lieux saints communs, partagés ou confisqués: aux sources de quelques péricopes coraniques (Q 19: 16–33)." In I. Dépret and G. Dye (eds.), *Partage du sacré: Transferts, dévotions mixtes, rivalités interconfessionnelles.* Brussels: E. M. E. and Intercommunications, 2012, 55–122.

———. "La nuit du Destin et la nuit de la Nativité." In G. Dye and F. Nobilio (eds.), *Figures bibliques en islam.* Bruxelles-Fernelmont: EME, 2011, 107–69.

———. "Réflexions méthodologiques sur la 'rhétorique coranique.'" In D. de Smet and M. A. Amir-Moezzi (eds.), *Controverses sur les écritures canoniques de l'islam.* Paris: Éditions du Cerf, 2014, 147–76.

Eichler, Paul Arno. *Die Dschinn, Teufel und Engel im Qur'ān.* Leipzig: Klein, 1928.

El-Badawi, Emran. *The Qur'an and the Aramaic Gospel Traditions.* London: Routledge Press, 2013.

Farahi, Hamiduddin. *Exordium to the Coherence in the Qur'an. An English Translation of Muqaddamah Niẓām al-Qur'an.* Trans. T. M. Hashmi. Lahore: Al-Mawrid, 2008.

Firestone, Reuven. *Jihad: The Origin of Holy War in Islam.* Oxford: Oxford University Press, 1999.

———. *Journeys in Holy Lands: The Evolution of the Abraham-Ishmael Legends in Islamic Exegesis.* Albany: SUNY Press, 1990.

Fossum, Jarl E. "The Apostle Concept in the Qur'ān and Pre-Islamic Near Eastern Literature." In M. Mir (ed.), *Literary Heritage of Classical Islam: Arabic and Islamic Studies in Honor of James A. Bellamy.* Princeton, NJ: Darwin Press, 1993, 149–67.

Gallez, Edouard-Marie. *Le Messie et son prophète. Aux origines de l'Islam.* Versailles: Éditions de Paris, 2005.

Geiger, Abraham. *Was hat Mohammed aus dem Judenthume aufgenommen.* Bonn: Baaden, 1833. Reprint, Leipzig: Kaufmann, 1902. English trans.: F. M. Young, *Judaism and Islam.* Madras: Delhi Mission, 1896.

Ginzberg, Louis. *Legends of the Jews.* Philadelphia: Jewish Publication Society, 1947.

Gobillot, Geneviève. "Histoire et géographie sacrées dans le Coran. L'exemple de Sodome." *MIDEO* 31 (2015): 1–54.

———. "Des textes Pseudo Clementins à la mystique juive des premiers siècles et du Sinaï à Ma'rib." In C. A. Segovia and Basil B. Lourié (eds.), *The Coming of the Comforter: When, Where, and to Whom? Studies on the Rise of Islam and Various Other Topics in Memory of John Wansbrough.* Piscataway, NJ: Gorgias Press, 2012, 3–90.

Goitein, Shlomo D. "Muhammad's Inspiration by Judaism." *Journal of Jewish Studies* 9 (1958): 149–62.

Griffith, Sidney. *The Bible in Arabic—The Scriptures of the "People of the Book" in the Language of Islam.* Princeton, NJ: Princeton University Press, 2013.

———. "Christian Lore and the Arabic Qur'an: The 'Companions of the Cave' in *Sūrat al-Kahf* and in Syriac Christian tradition." *QHC,* 109–38.

———. "Al-Naṣārā in the Qur'an: A Hermeneutical Reflection." *QHC2,* 301–22.

———. "Syriacisms in the Arabic Qur'ān: Who Were Those Who Said 'Allah Is Third of Three?" In M. Bar-Asher et al. (eds.), *A Word Fitly Spoken: Studies in Medieval Exegeses of the Hebrew Bible and the Qur'ān.* Jerusalem: Ben-Zvi Institute, 2007, 83–110.

Hawting, Gerald. "Eavesdropping on the Heavenly Assembly and the Protection of the Revelation from Demonic Corruption." In Stefan Wild (ed.), *Self-Referentiality in the Qur'an.* Wiesbaden: Harrassowitz, 2006, 25–37.

———. *The Idea of Idolatry and the Emergence of Islam.* Cambridge: Cambridge University Press, 1999.

Heal, Kristian. *Tradition and Transformation: Genesis 37 and 39 in Early Syriac Sources.* PhD dissertation. Birmingham: University of Birmingham, 2008.

Hilali, Asma. *The Sanaa Palimpsest: The Transmission of the Qur'an in the First Centuries AH.* Oxford: Oxford University Press, 2017.

Himmelfarb, Martha. *Ascent to Heaven in Jewish and Christian Apocalypses.* Oxford: Oxford University Press, 1993.

Hirschfeld, Hartwig. *New Researches into the Composition and Exegesis of the Qoran.* London: Royal Asiatic Society, 1902.

Horovitz, Josef. "Jewish Proper Names and Derivatives in the Koran." *Hebrew Union College Annual* 2 (1925): 145–227. Reprint, Hildesheim: Georg Olms, 1964.

———. "Das Koranische Paradies." In I. Velikovsky and H. Loewe (eds.), *Scripta Universitatis Atque Bibliothecae Hierosolymitanarum. Orientalia et Judaica, Volumen I.* Frankfurt am Main: Hierosolymis, 1923, 6:1–16.

———. *Koranische Untersuchungen.* Berlin: de Gruyter, 1926.

Hoyland, Robert. *Arabia and the Arabs: From the Bronze Age to the Coming of Islam.* London: Routledge, 2001.

Huart, Clément. "Une nouvelle source du Qoran." *Journal Asiatique* 10 (1904): 125–67.

Jandora, John. *The Latent Trace of Islamic Origins.* Piscataway, NJ: Gorgias Press, 2012.

Jeffery, Arthur. *The Foreign Vocabulary of the Qur'an.* Baroda: Oriental Institute, 1938. Reprint, Leiden: Brill, 2007.

Johns, Anthony H. "The Qur'anic Presentation of the Joseph Story: Naturalistic or Formulaic Language?" In G. R. Hawting and A. A. Shareef (eds.), *Approaches to the Qur'an.* London: Routledge, 1993, 37–70.

Khalfallah, Nejmeddine. "*Asāṭīr al-awwalīn:* Une expression coranique ambigüe." *Arabica* 59 (2012): 145–56.

Kister, Meir J. "*'An yadin* (Qur'an, IX/29): An Attempt at Interpretation." *Arabica* 11 (1964): 272–78.

Kropp, Manfred. "Der äthiopische Satan = *šayṭān* und seine koranischen Ausläufer; mit einer Bemerkung über verbales Steinigen." *Oriens Christianus* 89 (2005): 93–102.

———. "Beyond Single Words: *Mā'ida—Shayṭān—Jibt* and *Ṭāghūt:* Mechanisms of Transmission into the Ethiopic (Ge'ez) Bible and the Qur'anic text," *QHC,* 204–16.

———. "Braucht das heilige Tal einen Namen, oder ist es einfach bekannt? Erwägungen zu dem Namen Ṭuwā in Koran 20 Ṭahā, 12 und 79 an-Nāzi'āt, 15 mit einer Alternativdeutung. " In M. Groß and K.-H. Ohlig (eds.): *Die Enstehung einer Weltreligion III.* Berlin: Schiler, 2014, 443–46.

———. "Tripartite, but anti-Trinitarian Formulas in the Qur'ānic Corpus, Possibly pre-Qur'ānic." *QHC2,* 247–64.

Kugel, James. *In Potiphar's House: The Interpretive Life of Biblical Texts.* San Francisco: Harper, 1990.

———. *Traditions of the Bible: A Guide to the Bible as It Was at the Start of the Common Era.* Cambridge, MA: Harvard University Press, 1998.

Lassner, Jacob. *Demonizing the Queen of Sheba: Boundaries of Gender and Culture in Postbiblical Judaism and Medieval Islam.* Chicago: University of Chicago Press, 1993.

Lee, Samuel. *Controversial Tracts on Christianity and Mohammedanism.* Cambridge: J. Smith, 1824.

Lüling, Günter. *Über den Ur-Qur'an: Ansätze zur Rekonstruktion vorislamischer christlicher Strophenlieder im Qur'an.* Erlangen: Lüling, 1974; 2nd ed., Erlangen: Lüling,

1993. Translated and expanded as *A Challenge to Islam for Reformation.* Delhi: Molital Banarsidass, 2003.

Luxenberg, Christoph. *Die syro-aramäische Lesart des Koran.* 3rd ed. Berlin: Schiler, 2007. English trans.: *The Syro-Aramaic Reading of the Koran.* Berlin, Schiler, 2007.

———. "Neudeutung der arabischen Inschrift im Felsendom zu Jerusalem." In K.-H. Ohlig and G.-R. Puin (eds.), *Die dunklen Anfänge. Neue Forschungen zur Enstehung und frühen Geschichte des Islam.* Berlin: Hans Schiler, 2005, 124–47.

———. "Nöel dans le Coran." In A.-M. Delcambre et al. (eds.), *Enquêtes sur l'Islam.* Paris: Éditions Desclée de Brouwer, 2004, 117–38. Expanded French version of "Weihnachten im Koran," in C. Burgmer (ed.), *Streit um den Koran.* Berlin: Schiler, 2004, 35–41.

———. "Zur Morphologie und Etymologie von syro-aramäisch *sāṭānā*=Satan und koranisch-arabisch *šayṭān.*" In C. Burgmer (ed.), *Streit um den Koran.* Berlin: Schiler, 2004, 46–66.

Madigan, Daniel. *The Qur'an's Self-Image: Writing and Authority in Islam's Scripture.* Princeton, NJ: Princeton University Press, 2001.

Marshall, David. *God, Muhammad and the Unbelievers: A Qur'anic Study.* Richmond, VA: Curzon, 1999.

Masson, Denise. *Monothéisme coranique et monothéisme biblique.* Paris: Desclée de Brouwer, 1976.

Mingana, Alphonse. "Syriac Influence on the Style of the Kur'ān." *Bulletin of the John Rylands Library* 11, January 1928, 77–98. Reprint, *What the Koran Really Says: Language, Text and Commentary.* Ed. Ibn Warraq. Amherst, NY: Prometheus, 2002, 171–92.

Minov, Sergey. "Date and Provenance of the Syriac *Cave of Treasures:* A Reappraisal." *Hugoye* 20 (2017): 129–229.

Mir, Mustansir. *Dictionary of Qur'ānic Terms and Concepts.* New York: Garland, 1987.

———. "The Qur'anic Story of Joseph: Plot, Themes, and Characters." *MW* 76 (1986): 1–15.

———. *Verbal Idioms of the Qur'ān.* Ann Arbor: University of Michigan Press, 1989.

Muth, Franz-Christoph. "Reflections on the Relationship of Early Arabic Poetry and the Qur'ān: Meaning and Origin of the Qur'ānic Term *ṭayran abābīla* according to Early Arabic Poetry and Other Sources." In M. Kropp (ed.), *Results of Contemporary Research on the Qur'ān: The Question of a Historio-Critical Text of the Qur'ān.* Beirut: Ergon, 2007, 147–56.

Näf, Heinrich. *Syrische Josef-Gedichte mit Uebersetzung des Gedichts von Narsai und Proben aus Balai und Jaqob von Sarug.* Zürich: Schwärzenbad, 1923.

Nagel, Tilman. *Medinensische Einschübe in mekkanischen Suren.* Göttingen: Vandenhoeck and Ruprecht, 1995.

Neuenkirchen, Paul. "Visions et ascensions. Deux péricopes coraniques à la lumière d'un apocryphe chrétien." *Journal Asiatique* 302 (2014): 303–47.

Neuwirth, Angelika. "A Discovery of Evil in the Qur'an? Revisiting Qur'anic Versions of the Decalogue in the Context of Pagan Arab Late Antiquity." In *Scripture, Poetry, and the Making of a Community: Reading the Qur'an as a Literary Text.* Oxford: Oxford University Press, 2014, 253–75.

———. "From the Sacred Mosque to the Remote Temple: *Sūrat al-Isrāʾ* (Q. 17): between Text and Commentary." In *Scripture, Poetry, and the Making of a Community: Reading the Qurʾan as a Literary Text.* Oxford: Oxford University Press, 2014, 216–52. Originally printed in J. D. McAuliffe, B. Walfish, and J. Goering (eds.), *With Reverence for the Word.* Oxford: Oxford University Press, 2003, 376–407.

———. "Glimpses of Paradise in the World and Lost Aspects of the World in the Hereafter: Two Qurʾanic Re-readings of Biblical Psalms." In *Scripture, Poetry, and the Making of a Community: Reading the Qurʾan as a Literary Text.* Oxford: Oxford University Press, 2014, 76–101.

———. "The House of Abraham and House of Amram." *QC,* 499–531.

———. *Der Koran als Text der Spätantike. Ein europäischer Zugang.* Berlin: Verlag der Weltreligionen, 2010.

———. *Der Koran: Band 1 Frühmekkanische Suren, poetische Prophetie.* Berlin: Verlag der Weltreligionen, 2011.

———. "Meccan Texts—Medinan Additions? Politics and the Re-Reading of Liturgical Communications." In R. Arnzen and J. Thielmann (eds.), *Words, Texts and Concepts Cruising the Mediterranean Sea.* Leuven: Peeters, 2004, 73–93.

———. "Qurʾanic Reading of the Psalms." *QC,* 733–78.

———. *Studien zur Komposition der mekkanischen Suren.* 2nd ed. Berlin: de Gruyter, 2007.

Newby, Gordon D. "The Drowned Son: Midrash and Midrash Making in the Qurʾān and Tafsīr." In S. D. Ricks (ed.), *Studies in Islamic and Judaic Traditions: Papers Presented at the Institute for Islamic-Judaic Studies, Center for Judaic Studies, University of Denver.* Atlanta: Scholars Press, 1986, 19–32.

Nissen, Theodor. "Unbekannte Erzählungen aus dem *Pratum Spirituale.*" *Byzantinische Zeitschrift* 38 (1938): 351–76.

Nöldeke, Theodor. "Hatte Muḥammad christliche Lehrer?" *ZDMG* 12 (1858): 699–708.

———. *Neue Beiträge zur semitischen Sprachwissenschaft.* Strassburg: Trübner, 1910.

Nöldeke, Theodor, et al. *Geschichte des Qorāns.* Göttingen: Verlag der Dieterichschen Buchhandlung, 1860; 2nd ed. in two parts: Nöldeke's revised work, titled "Über den Ursprung des Qorāns" [*GdQ1*], and F. Schwally, *Die Sammlung des Qorāns* [*GdQ2*], ed. and revised by F. Schwally, Leipzig: T. Weicher, 1909, 1919; 2nd ed. including G. Bergsträsser and O. Pretzl, "Die Geschichte des Koran-texts" [*GdQ3*], Leipzig: T. Weicher, 1938; reprint, 3 vols. in 1, Hildesheim: Olms, 1970. English trans.: *The History of the Qurʾān,* ed. and trans. W. H. Behn, Leiden: Brill, 2013.

O'Shaughnessy, Thomas J. *The Development of the Meaning of Spirit in the Koran.* Rome: Pontificium Institutum Orientalium Studiorum, 1953.

———. "God's Throne and the Biblical Symbolism of the Qurʾān." *Numen* 20 (1973): 202–21.

———. *The Koranic Concept of the Word of God.* Biblica et Orientalia 11. Rome: Pontificio Istituto Biblico, 1948.

———. *Muḥammad's Thoughts on Death. A Thematic Study of the Qurʾānic Data.* Leiden: Brill, 1969.

Paret, Roger. "Un parallèle Byzantin à Coran XVIII, 59–81." *Revue des études byzantines* 26 (1968): 137–59.

Paret, Rudi. *Der Koran. Kommentar und Konkordanz.* Stuttgart: Kohlhammer, 1971.

Pennacchietti, Fabrizio A. "La reine de Saba, le pavé de cristal et le tronc flottant." *Arabica* 49 (2002): 1–26.

Pennachio, Catherine. *Les emprunts à l'hébreu et au judéo-araméen dans le Coran.* Paris: Maisonneuve, 2014.

Penrice, John. *A Dictionary and Glossary of the Ḳor-ân with Copious Grammatical References and Explanation of the Text.* London: King and Co., 1873.

Philonenko, Marc. "Une expression qoumrânienne dans le Coran." *Atti del Terzo Congresso di Studi Arabi e Islamici, Ravello 1–6 settembre 1966.* Naples: Istituto universitario orientale, 1967, 553–56.

Pines, Shlomo. "Notes on Islam and on Arabic Christianity and Judaeo-Christianity." *JSAI* 4 (1984): 135–52.

Pohlmann, Karl-Friedrich. *Die Entstehung des Korans. Neue Erkenntnisse aus Sicht der historisch-kritischen Bibelwissenschaft.* Darmstadt: Wissenschaftliche Buchgesellschaft, 2012–13.

Powers, David S. *Muḥammad Is Not the Father of Any of Your Men: The Making of the Last Prophet.* Philadelphia: University of Pennsylvania Press, 2009.

Pregill, Michael E. "Ahab, Bar Kokhba, Muḥammad, and the Lying Spirit: Prophetic Discourse before and after the Rise of Islam." In P. Townsend and M. Vidas (eds.), *Revelation, Literature, and Community in Late Antiquity.* Tübingen: Mohr Sieback, 2011, 271–313.

Puin, Gerd. "Leuke Kome = Laykah, the Arsians—'Aṣḥāb 'al-Rass, and Other Pre-Islamic Names in the Qur'ān: A Way out of the 'Tanglewood'?" In K.-H. Ohlig and G.-R. Puin (eds.), *The Hidden Origins of Islam: New Research into Its Early History.* Amherst, NY: Prometheus, 2010 (trans. of *Die dunklen Anfänge,* 2005), 335–60.

The Qur'ān Seminar Commentary: A Collaborative Study of 50 Qur'anic Passages/Le Qur'an Seminar: Commentaire collaboratif de 50 passages coraniques. Ed. M. Azaiez, G. S. Reynolds, et al. Berlin: de Gruyter, 2016.

Radscheit, Mattias. "Der Höllenbaum." In T. Nagel (ed.), *Der Koran und sein religiöses und kulturelles Umfeld.* Munich: Oldenbourg 2010, 97–134.

Reynolds, Gabriel Said. "The Muslim Jesus: Dead or Alive?" *BSOAS* 72 (2009): 237–58.

———. "On the Presentation of Christianity in the Qur'ān and the Many Aspects of Qur'anic Rhetoric." *Al-Bayan—Journal of Qur'an and Hadith Studies* 12 (2014): 42–54.

———. "On the Qur'an and the Theme of Jews as "Killers of the Prophets." *Al-Bayān* 10 (2012): 9–32.

———. "On the Qur'an's *Mā'ida* Passage and the Wanderings of the Israelites." In C. A. Segovia and Basil B. Lourié (eds.), *The Coming of the Comforter: When, Where, and to Whom? Studies on the Rise of Islam and Various Other Topics in Memory of John Wansbrough.* Piscataway, NJ: Gorgias, 2012, 91–108.

———. "On the Qur'ānic Accusation of Scriptural Falsification (*taḥrīf*) and Christian Anti-Jewish Polemic." *JAOS* 130 (2010): 1–14.

———. "Le problème de la chronologie du Coran." *Arabica* 58 (2011): 477–502.

———. *The Qur'an and Its Biblical Subtext.* London: Routledge, 2010.

Rippin, Andrew. "The Commerce of Eschatology." In S. Wild (ed.), *The Qur'ān as Text.* Leiden: Brill, 1996, 125–35.

———. "The Function of *Asbāb Al-Nuzūl*' in Qur'ānic Exegesis." *BSOAS* 51 (1988): 1–20.

———. "Muḥammad in the Qur'ān: Reading Scripture in the 21st Century." In H. Motzki (ed.), *The Biography of Muḥammad: The Issue of the Sources.* Leiden: Brill, 2000, 298–309.

———. "RḤMNN and the Ḥanīfs." In W. B. Hallaq and D. P. Little (eds.), *Islamic Studies Presented to Charles J. Adams.* Leiden: Brill, 1991, 153–68.

Robin, Christian. "Du paganisme au monothéisme." *Revue des mondes musulmans et de la Méditerranée* 61 (1991): 139–55.

———. "Le judaïsme de Ḥimyar." *Arabia* 1 (2003): 71–172.

———. "Matériaux pour une typologie des divinités arabiques et de leurs représentations." In I. Sachet and C. Robin (eds.), *Dieux et déesses d'Arabie. Images et représentations. Actes de la table ronde tenue au Collège de France (Paris) les 1er et 2 octobre 2007.* Paris: De Boccard, 2012, 7–118.

Rosenthal, Franz. "Some Minor Problems in the Qur'an." In *The Joshua Starr Memorial Volume.* New York: n.p., 1953, 68–72. Reprint, Ibn Warraq (ed.), *What the Qur'an Really Says.* Amherst, NY: Prometheus, 2002, 322–42.

Rubin, Uri. *"Iqra' bi-smi rabbika . . .* : Some Notes on the Interpretation of Surat al-'Alaq." *Israel Oriental Studies* 13 (1993): 213–30.

———. "Moses and the Holy Valley Ṭuwan: On the Biblical and Midrashic Background of a Qur'anic Scene." *JNES* 73 (2014): 73–81.

———. "On the Arabian Origins of the Qur'an: The Case of *al-Furqān*." *JSS* 54 (2009): 421–33.

———. "Quraysh and Their Winter and Summer Journey: On the Interpretation of Sura 106." *Muhammad the Prophet and Arabia.* Variorum Collected Studies Series. Aldershot: Ashgate, 2011, xiii.

Rudolph, Wilhelm. *Die Abhängigkeit des Qorans von Judentum und Christentum.* Stuttgart: Kohlhammer, 1922.

Sadeghi, Behnam and M. Goudarzi. "San'ā' 1 and the Origins of the Qur'ān." *Der Islam* 87 (2010): 1–129.

Saleh, Walid. "The Etymological Fallacy and Qur'ānic Studies: Muhammad, Paradise, and Late Antiquity." In *QC,* 469–98.

———. *In Defense of the Bible: A Critical Edition and an Introduction to al-Biqā'īs Bible Treatise.* Leiden: Brill, 2008.

———. "What If You Refuse, When Ordered to Fight? King Saul (Ṭālūt) in the Qur'ān and Post-Quranic Literature." In C. S. Ehrlich (ed.), *Saul in Story and Tradition.* Forschungen zum Alten Testament 47. Tübingen: Mohr Siebeck, 2006, 261–83.

Schäfer, Peter. *Jesus in the Talmud.* Princeton, NJ: Princeton University Press, 2007.

Schedl, Claus. *Muhammad und Jesus: Die christologisch relevanten Texte des Koran.* Freiburg: Herder, 1978.

Schmitz, Bertram. *Der Koran: Sure 2 "Die Kuh."* Stuttgart: Kohlhammer, 2009.

Schoeler, Gregor. "Oral Poetry Theory and Arabic Literature." Trans. W. Vagelpohl in J. E. Montgomery (ed.), *The Oral and Written in Early Islam.* London: Routledge, 2006, 87–110. Originally published as "Die Anwendung der oral-poetry-Theorie auf die arabische Literatur." *Der Islam* 58 (1981): 205–36.

Schulthess, Friedrich. *Lexicon Syropalaestinum.* Berlin: Reimer, 1903.

Seale, Morris. "How the Qur'an Interprets the Bible." In *Qur'an and Bible: Studies in Interpretation and Dialogue.* London: Croom Helm, 1978, 51–66.

Segovia, Carlos A. *The Quranic Noah and the Making of the Islamic Prophet: A Study of Intertextuality and Religious Identity Formation in Late Antiquity.* Berlin: de Gruyter, 2015.

———. "Thematic and Structural Affinities between 1 Enoch and the Qur'an: A Contribution to the Study of the Judaeo-Christian Apocalyptic Setting of the Early Islamic Faith." In C. A. Segovia and Basil B. Lourié (eds.), *The Coming of the Comforter: When, Where, and to Whom? Studies on the Rise of Islam and Various Other Topics in Memory of John Wansbrough.* Piscataway, NJ: Gorgias Press, 2012, 231–67.

———. "'Those on the Right' and 'Those on the Left': Rereading Qur'ân 56:1–6 (and the Founding Myth of Islam) in Light of Apocalypse of Abraham 21–2." *Oriens Christianus.* Forthcoming.

Shaddel, Mehdy. "Qur'ānic Ummī: Genealogy, 'Ethnicity,' and the Foundation of a New Community." *JSAI* 43 (2016): 1–60.

Shahid, Irfan. "Two Qur'anic Sūras: al-Fīl and Qurayš." In Wadād al-Qāḍī (ed.), *Studia Arabica et Islamica: Festschrift for Iḥsān ʿAbbās on His Sixtieth Birthday.* Beirut: American University, 1981, 429–36.

Sherif, Faruq. *A Guide to the Contents of the Qur'an.* London: Ithaca, 1985.

Shoemaker, Stephen. "Christmas in the Qur'an: The Qur'anic Account of Jesus' Nativity and Palestinian Local Tradition." *JSAI* 28 (2003): 11–39.

———. *The Death of a Prophet: The End of Muḥammad's Life and the Beginnings of Islam.* Philadelphia: University of Pennsylvania Press, 2011.

Sidersky, Daniel. *Les origines des légendes musulmanes dans le Coran et dans les vies des prophètes.* Paris: Geuthner, 1933.

Silverstein, Adam. "Haman's Transition from the Jahiliyya to Islam." *JSAI* 34 (2008): 285–308.

———. "The Qur'ānic Pharaoh." *QHC2,* 467–77.

Sinai, Nicolai. *Fortschreibung und Auslegung: Studien zur frühen Koraninterpretation.* Wiesbaden: Harrassowitz, 2009.

———. "Inheriting Egypt: The Israelites and the Exodus in the Meccan Qur'ān." In M. Daneshgar and W. Saleh (eds.), *Islamic Studies Today: Essays in Honor of Andrew Rippin.* Leiden: Brill, 2016, 198–214.

———. "Inner-Qur'anic Chronology." In M. A. Haleem and M. Shah (eds.), *The Oxford Handbook of Qur'anic Studies.* Oxford: Oxford University Press, forthcoming.

———. "An Interpretation of Sūrat al-Najm (Q. 53)." *JQS* 13 (2011): 1–28.

———. "The Qur'an as Process." *QC,* 407–39.

———. "Religious Poetry from the Quranic Milieu: Umayya b. Abī l-Ṣalt on the Fate of the Thamūd." *BSOAS* 74 (2011): 397–416.

———. "The Unknown Known: Some Groundwork for Interpreting the Medinan Qur'an." *Mélanges de l'Université Saint-Joseph* 66 (2015–16): 47–96.

———. "Weihnachten im Koran' oder 'Nacht der Bestimmung'? Eine Deutung von Sure 97." *Der Islam* 88 (2012): 11–32.

Speyer, Heinrich. *Die biblischen Erzählungen im Qoran.* Gräfenhainichen: Schulze, 1931. Reprint, Hildesheim: Olms, 1961.

Stefanidis, Emmanuelle. "The Qur'ān Made Linear: A Study of the *Geschichte des Qorâns*' Chronological Reordering." *JQS* 10 (2008): 1–22.

Stewart, Devin. "Divine Epithets and the *Dibacchius: Clausulae* and Qur'ānic Rhythm." *JQS* 15 (2013): 22–64.

———. "Notes on Medieval and Modern Emendations of the Qur'ān." *QHC*, 225–48.

———. "Poetic License in the Qur'an: Ibn al-Sa'igh al-Ḥanafi's *Iḥkām al-rāy fī aḥkām al-āy.*" *JQS* 11 (2009): 1–54.

———. "*Sajʿ* in the Qur'ān: Prosody and Structure." *Journal of Arabic Literature* 21 (1990): 101–39.

———. "Understanding the Koran in English: Notes on Translation, Form, and Prophetic Typology." In Z. Ibrahim, N. Kasabgy, and S. Aydelott (eds.), *Diversity in Language: Contrastive Studies in English and Arabic Theoretical and Applied Linguistics.* Cairo: American University in Cairo Press, 2000, 31–48.

Su-Min Ri, Andreas. *Commentaire de la Caverne des trésors. Étude sur l'histoire du texte et des sources.* CSCO 581. Louvain: Peeters, 2000.

Tardieu, Michel. "Les Septs Dormants: magie, facétie, temps infini." In G. Dye and F. Nobilio (eds.), *Figures bibliques en islam.* Bruxelles-Fernelmont: EME, 2011, 37–58.

Tengour, Esma Hind. *L'Arabie des jinns. Fragments d'un imaginaire.* Bruxelles-Fernelmont: E. M. E. and InterCommunications, 2013.

Tesei, Tommaso. "The Chronological Problems of the Qur'an: The Case of the Story of Ḏū l-Qarnayn (Q 18:83–102)." *Rivista degli Studi Orientali* 84 (2011): 457–66.

———. "The Notion of Barzakh and the Question of the Intermediate State of the Dead in the Qur'an." In C. Lange (ed.), *Locating Hell in Islamic Traditions.* Leiden: Brill, 2015, 29–55.

———. "Some Cosmological Notions from Late Antiquity in Q 18:60–65: The Qur'an in Light of Its Cultural Context." *JAOS* 135 (2015): 19–32.

Three Testaments. Ed. B. A. Brown and A. Hussain. Lanham: Rowman and Littlefield, 2012.

Toelle, Heidi. *Le Coran revisité. Le feu, l'eau, l'air et la terre.* Damas: IFEAD, 1999.

Toorawa, Shawkat M. "Hapaxes in the Qur'an: Identifying and Cataloguing Lone Words (and Loanwords)." *QHC2*, 193–246.

———. "*Sūrat Maryam* (Q. 19) in the Qur'an: Lexicon, Lexical Echoes, Translation." *JQS* 13 (2011): 25–78.

Torrey, Charles C. *The Jewish Foundation of Islam.* New York: Jewish Institute of Religion, 1933.

Tottoli, Roberto. "Origin and Use of the Term Isrāʾīliyyāt in Muslim Literature." *Arabica* 46 (1999): 193–210.

van Bladel, Kevin. "Heavenly Cords and Prophetic Authority in the Quran and Its Late Antique Context." *BSOAS* 70 (2007): 223–46.

———. "The Legend of Alexander the Great in the Qurʾān 18:83–102." *QHC,* 175–203.

van der Velden, Frank. "Kotexte im Konvergenzstrang—die Bedeutung textkritischer Varianten und christlicher Bezugstexte für die Redaktion von Sure 61 und Sure 5, 110–119." *Oriens Christianus* 92 (2008): 130–73.

van Donzel, Emeri and Schmidt, Andrea. *Gog and Magog in Early Syriac and Islamic Sources.* Leiden: Brill, 2009.

Waldman, Marilyn R. "New Approaches to 'Biblical' Material in the Qurʾān." In W. M. Brinner and S. D. Ricks (eds.), *Studies in Islamic and Judaic Traditions.* Atlanta: Scholars Press, 1986, 47–64.

Wansbrough, John. *Quranic Studies: Sources and Methods of Scriptural Interpretation.* Oxford: Oxford University Press, 1977; Amherst, NY: Prometheus, 2004.

Wherry, Elwood M. *A Comprehensive Commentary on the Qurán.* London: K. Paul, Trench, Trübner, 1896.

Witztum, Joseph. "The Foundations of the House." *BSOAS* 72 (2009): 25–40.

———. "Ibn Isḥāq and the Pentateuch in Arabic." *JSAI* 40 (2013): 1–71.

———. "Joseph among the Ishmaelites: Q 12 in Light of Syriac Sources." *QHC2,* 425–48.

———. *The Syriac Milieu of the Qurʾan: the Recasting of Biblical Narratives.* PhD dissertation. Princeton, NJ: Princeton University, 2011.

———. "Variant Traditions, Relative Chronology, and the Study of Intra Quranic Parallels." In B. Sadeghi et al. (eds.), *Islamic Cultures, Islamic Contexts: Essays in Honor of Professor Patricia Crone.* Leiden: Brill, 2015, 1–50.

Yahuda, Abraham. "A Contribution to Qurʾān and Ḥadīth Interpretation." In S. Löwinger and J. Somogyi (eds.), *Ignace Goldziher Memorial Volume.* Budapest: Globus, 1948, 280–308.

Zammit, Martin. *A Comparative Lexical Study of Qurʾānic Arabic.* Leiden: Brill, 2002.

Zellentin, Holger. "*Aḥbār* and *Ruhbān:* Religious Leaders in the Qurʾān in Dialogue with Christian and Rabbinic Literature." In A. Neuwirth and M. Sells (eds.), *Qurʾānic Studies Today.* London: Routledge, 2016, 262–93.

———. *The Qurʾān's Legal Culture: The Didascalia Apostolorum as a Point of Departure.* Tübingen: Mohr Siebeck, 2013.

INDEX TO THE QUR'ĀN

References are to Sura:Verse of the Qur'ānic text.

Opposition to creation of Adam, 2:30
Prostration before human, 2:34,
    7:11–12, 15:28–33, 17:61–62, 18:50,
    20:115–16, 38:71–78
Take souls at death, 4:97, 6:61

Anṣār ("helpers")
    2:270, 3:52, 3:192, 8:72–75, 8:109,
    59:9, 61:14

Apocalypse
    Beast of the Apocalypse, 27:82
    Day of Retribution (*yawm al-dīn*), 1:4,
        15:34, 38:78, 70:26, 74:46, 82:15–17,
        83:11
    Knowledge of the Hour, 7:187, 31:34,
        33:63, 41:47, 43:85, 45:32, 51:12–13,
        79:42–44
    Trumpet will be sounded, 6:73, 18:99,
        20:102, 23:101, 27:87, 36:51, 39:68,
        50:20, 69:13, 74:8, 78:18

Apostle/Prophet (*see also* Prophets)
    2:87, 2:101, 3:81, 3:183, 4:42, 4:64,
        5:70, 5:75, 5:99, 7:61, 7:67, 7:104,
        10:47, 12:50, 14:14, 17:93–95, 19:51,
        20:96, 20:134, 23:32, 26:107, 26:125,
        26:143, 26:163, 26:178, 40:34, 40:78,
        42:51, 43:46, 44:13, 44:18, 51:52,
        72:27, 73:15

Apostles, of Jesus (*see also* Disciples)
    3:52–53, 5:111–15, 61:14

Arabs/Bedouins
    9:90, 9:97–99, 9:101, 9:120, 33:20,
        48:11, 48:16, 49:14

Ark (*see also* Ark of the Covenant; Flood;
    Noah)
    54:13, 69:11

Ark of the Covenant
    2:248

al-Ayka
    15:78–79, 26:176–89, 38:13, 50:14

Āzar (or Terah, father of Abraham)
    6:74

Babylon
    2:102

Barzakh
    Boundary between waters, 25:53, 55:20
    Heavenly division, 23:99–100

Battle of Badr
    3:123–29

Bedouins
    9:90, 9:97, 9:99–103, 9:120, 33:20,
        49:14, 49:17

Beggars (*see also* Poor/Needy)
    22:36, 51:19, 70:25, 93:10

Benjamin (*see also* Joseph)
    12:8, 12:59, 12:63, 12:69, 12:76–83,
        12:87–90

Birds
    Glorifying God, 24:41
    Praising God with David, 21:79, 34:10,
        38:17–19
    Signs of God, 16:79, 67:19

Blessings
    1:7, 2:40, 2:44, 2:47, 2:122, 2:158,
        2:211, 2:231, 2:271, 3:103, 3:171,
        3:174, 4:69, 4:72, 5:3, 5:6–7, 5:11,
        5:23, 5:110, 6:141–44, 7:9, 7:25,
        8:26, 8:53, 8:63, 9:88, 11:10, 12:6,
        14:6, 14:28, 14:34, 16:18, 16:53,
        16:71–72, 16:81, 16:83, 16:112,
        16:114, 16:121, 17:66, 17:70, 17:83,
        19:58, 21:42, 21:73, 21:80, 21:90,
        26:22, 27:19, 27:73, 28:17, 29:67,

Hand(s)

2:79, 2:95, 2:149, 2:195, 2:255, 3:73, 3:182, 4:43, 4:62, 4:77, 4:91, 5:6, 5:11, 5:28, 5:33, 5:38, 5:64, 5:94, 7:7, 7:17, 7:93, 7:124, 7:149, 8:51, 8:70, 9:29, 9:52, 11:71, 12:31, 14:9, 17:29, 24:40, 30:36, 30:41, 51:47, 57:12, 59:2, 60:2, 60:12, 62:7, 66:8, 80:15

Left hand, 7:17, 16:48, 34:15, 50:18, 69:25, 70:37

People of the left hand, 56:9, 56:41–56, 90:19

People of the right hand, 56:8, 56:27–40, 56:90–91, 74:39–41, 90:18

People on the right hand and left hand of God, 56:8–9

Receiving the book in one's left hand, 69:25

Receiving the book in one's right hand, 17:71, 69:19, 84:7

Right hand, 7:17, 16:48, 17:71, 18:17–18, 20:17, 34:15, 37:28, 37:93, 50:18, 69:19, 70:37

Ḥanīf

2:135, 3:67, 3:95, 4:125, 6:79, 6:161, 10:105, 16:120–23, 22:31, 30:30, 98:5

Hear/Hearing

Exhortation to, 30:23, 36:25

God creates, 16:78, 23:78, 32:9, 46:26, 67:23

God removes/seals, 2:7, 2:20, 6:46, 16:108

Those who cannot, 7:179, 7:195, 8:21–22, 11:20, 18:101, 19:38, 41:4

Hearts

God places a stamp on them, 4:155, 5:13, 47:23–24

Hardhearted, 3:159, 22:53, 39:22, 57:16

Sealed, 2:7, 4:155, 6:46, 7:100–1, 9:87, 9:93, 10:74, 16:108, 30:59, 40:35, 45:23, 47:16, 63:3

Uncircumcised, 2:88, 4:155

Veiled, 6:25, 17:45–46, 18:57, 41:5

Heaven/Heavens (*see also* Cosmology; Garden; Paradise)

Barriers between dead and living/ between heaven and hell, 6:111, 7:44–50, 23:99–100

Created without pillars, 13:2, 31:10

Gates of, 7:40, 15:14–15, 54:11, 87:19

Glorification of inhabitants, 57:1, 59:1, 59:24, 61:1, 62:1, 64:1

Ladder to heaven, 6:35, 52:38

Paths (*sabab/asbāb*) to heaven, 2:166, 15:14–15, 18:84, 18:85, 18:89, 18:92, 22:15, 38:10, 40:36–37

Rolled up like a scroll, 21:104, 39:67

Seven heavens, 2:29, 17:44, 41:12, 65:12, 67:3, 71:15, 78:12

Sky as a barrier (firmament) between heaven and earth/waters, 13:2, 25:53, 31:10, 55:20

Heavenly Register (of good and evil deeds)

3:181, 4:81, 9:120–21, 19:79, 21:94, 36:12, 45:29, 54:52–53, 83:7–9, 83:18–21, 84:7–16

Angels record, 10:21, 43:80, 50:17, 82:10–2

Opened on the Day of Judgment, 17:13–14, 17:71, 18:49, 39:69, 78:29

Hell

2:24, 2:206, 3:197, 4:93, 4:115, 4:122, 4:140, 5:72, 7:179, 8:16, 8:37, 9:35, 9:81, 9:95, 9:109, 11:98, 14:16–17, 15:43, 17:63, 17:97, 18:106, 19:68, 29:68, 35:36, 36:63, 45:10, 48:6, 52:13, 52:16, 55:43, 57:13

Worship (*continued*)
10:106, 11:101, 12:40, 13:16, 14:30,
16:20, 16:35, 16:73, 19:48–49, 19:81,
21:66–67, 22:71, 25:55, 26:70,
26:92–93, 27:24, 27:43, 28:63–64,
29:17, 37:85–86, 37:95, 39:15, 43:26,
43:45, 46:6, 60:4

Zabūr/Zubur (*see also* Psalms)
3:184, 4:163, 16:44, 17:55, 21:105,
23:53, 26:196, 35:25, 54:43, 54:52

Zakāt (*see also* Alms/Almsgiving)
2:43, 2:83, 2:110, 2:177, 2:277, 4:77,
4:162, 5:12, 5:55, 6:141, 7:155–56,
9:5, 9:11, 9:18, 9:71, 9:103, 19:31,
19:55, 22:41, 22:78, 23:4, 24:37,
24:56, 27:3, 30:39, 33:33, 41:7,
73:20, 98:5

Zechariah
3:37–44, 6:85, 19:2–15, 21:89–90

INDEX TO CITATIONS OF BIBLICAL VERSES

Micah
  5:5   512
  6:6–7   528
  6:8   780

Nahum
  1:1   685
  3:1–4   685

Zechariah
  4   551
  4:1–3   551
  7:10   931
  13:9   56

Tobit
  3:8   654
  12:9   320
  14:4   685

Malachi
  3:16   891, 895

Wisdom
  7:17–20   516
  15:11   637
  17:11   38

NEW TESTAMENT

Matthew
  3:1   117
  3:16   98, 427
  3:16–17   57
  4:1   57
  4:8–9   254
  4:16   194
  5   81
  5:4   24, 521
  5:7–9   811
  5:22   769
  5:29–30   86
  5:38–39   81, 203, 431

  5:45   22
  6:1–4   105, 159
  6:2   831
  6:5   831, 932
  6:9–13   29
  6:16   831
  6:26   424, 620
  7   321
  7:13   909
  7:17–19   400
  7:24–27   321
  8:2–3   122
  8:11   802
  8:23–27   330
  8:28–34   205
  9   528
  9:3–8   139
  9:13   528, 780
  9:27–30   122
  10:8   660
  10:12   555
  10:28   75, 86
  10:29   28, 424
  10:34–37   323, 817
  10:37   306
  10:39   46
  11   301
  11:23–24   296
  11:28–30   157
  11:30   281
  12   430
  12:5–8   431
  12:22   122
  12:31–32   173
  12:38   66
  12:38–39   329
  12:39–41   341
  13:1–9   104
  13:3–9   263
  13:10–11   618
  13:10–17   288
  13:13–15   440
  13:14   32, 162
  13:15–16   193